# THE
# CANADIAN
# WRITER'S
# GUIDE

## TWELFTH EDITION

# THE
# CANADIAN
# WRITER'S
# GUIDE

## TWELFTH EDITION

Managing Editor
**Murphy O. Shewchuk**

Editor
**Anne Osborne**

Researchers
Contests and Awards: **Gill Foss**
Grants: **Karleen Bradford**
Literary Agents: **Deidre Hill**
Organizations: **Murphy O. Shewchuk**
Book Publishers: **Bryan Roscoe**
Periodical Publishers: **Sandra Weatherby & Albert Fowler**

Designer
**Darrell McCalla**

Official Handbook of the
Canadian Authors Association

**Fitzhenry & Whiteside**

**The Canadian Writers Guide**
**Twelfth Edition**
© 1997 Fitzhenry & Whiteside

**Canadian Cataloguing in Publication Data**
Main entry under title:
The Canadian writer's guide: official handbook of the
Canadian Authors Association

12th ed.
Includes bibliographical references and index.
ISBN 1-55041-191-8

1. Authorship. 2. Canadian periodicals (English) -Directories.
3. Publishers and publishing - Canada - Directories.
I Shewchuck, Murphy, II Canadian Authors Association

PN161.C33 1997          808'.02          C97-931478-X

Printed and bound in the United States

Fitzhenry & Whiteside
195 Allstate Parkway
Markham, Ontario
L3R 4T8

*Cover design:* Darrell McCalla
*Cover photo:* Weinberg/Clark/Image Bank

# Contents

## Develop Your Style

# Techniques of Fiction

# Theatre, Screen and Radio

# Children and Young Adults

# Poetry

# Newspapers and Periodicals

# People and Places Past

# New and Non-Traditional Markets

# The Writer's Reference Shelf

x

# Foreword

The Twelfth Edition of *The Canadian Writer's Guide* is an international effort. It is the result of the hard work and dedication of a diverse group of contributors, researchers and editors from coast to coast in Canada and extending into the United States. Within this geographic range, locating contributors to previous editions and new specialists was a challenging and often rewarding undertaking. It helped me appreciate the skills of a private investigator. The broad base of expertise assembled for this edition is the result of hundreds of hours of modern Internet research and many more hours of plain old-fashioned networking.

The Contributor's Notes at the end of the book lists the participants. However, there are many that deserve more recognition than can be successfully presented in a brief biographical note. Thanks must go to Fred Kerner, editor of numerous earlier editions of *The Canadian Writer's Guide*. Without his dedication and hard work, we would not have had a firm foundation. Gordon Symons' efforts, as the previous markets editor and a past editor of *Canadian Author* magazine, also served as important building blocks. Welwyn Wilton Katz and Doug Bale, more recent editors of *Canadian Author*, helped nurture contributors to the magazine and locate those writers whose material fit into the appropriate niches in this book.

In addition to the people listed on the title page, there are many others who made the project possible. When I put out a call for volunteers for the "CWG Team", Nancy Smith of Montreal was one of the first to respond. She helped coordinate the efforts of the Montreal contributors, providing an important "ethnic" perspective to the book. Cathy Payne of Hamilton and Perry and Rosemary Bauchman of Victoria spent uncounted hours reviewing the material from the Eleventh Edition. As the project grew, many more people came forward to help. If there are any I have inadvertently missed, my apologies – your work has been much appreciated.

The result, I feel, is a book that will help carry readers and their writing toward the new millennium with confidence. It is a blend of advice from experts in various genres and the related fields of business, computers, law, research, and publishing. In addition to valuable advice, this book contains an extensive reference section. Where available, we have included Internet e-mail and web site addresses (a risky step, considering the rapidly changing face of the Internet).

I thank all those who made this Twelfth Edition possible and I look forward to receiving suggestions for future editions.

– Murphy O. Shewchuk
Merritt, British Columbia. June, 1997.

# Inspiration and Action

# Courage and Creativity: The Psychology of Writing

*by Margaret Springer*

The best writing is like jumping out of a plane. I know that the parachute will open, though nothing in life is 100 per cent certain. I just have to get out there, count to three, and pull the rip cord.

That's when it happens.

A wonderful rush of exhilaration and excitement. Billowing colours unfolding above. Patchwork fields spread out below. I'm moving fast and I'm getting there, but not by my own power.

All I have to do is jump.

Is that how it feels to you?

The more writing I do, the more mysterious the creative process becomes.

There's something going on just beyond the reach of my conscious mind, and I have to let go of control. That's scary.

Will my writing be any good? Will anyone want to read it? What should I do with it? Will anyone care? And, if I've sold good stuff before, can I do it again? Where did that come from? What if I go dry?

It takes courage to deal with failure, and equal courage to deal with success. (Falling on my face is harder when I know the editor!) It also takes courage to deal with other people's reactions to my success and failure.

I've found that courage is as important as talent, technique, and marketing strategies, because without it, my writing cannot blossom. The trick, I've discovered, is to know enough about the creative process to let it work for me as a writer, rather than against me. A prerequisite is occasional solitude. Not necessarily alone-ness, though that is helpful, but at least an inner solitude now and then. My friend Eva Tucker, a novelist living in England, tells of her frustration whenever her family interrupts her while she's staring out of the window. "Can't they see I'm working?" she exclaims.

Dorothea Brande, in her classic *Becoming a Writer* (Los Angeles, J.P. Tarcher, 1981) refers to this state as "the artistic coma": time to dream, to sit idle, to be detached. For me, it's that misty time between sleep and waking in the early morning, where dreams and creativity meet. (That's when the first images for this article took shape.) My writing friend Don Gordon doodles on a restaurant placemat. Perhaps your daydreams take other forms. A lot more than nothing is happening here. Ideas arrive. Thoughts crystallize.

Psychologists use varying terminology, but they all agree on the process.

Once a project presents itself and demands expression, the brain works best if it's allowed to go through four distinct stages of activity.

The first stage is total immersion. This is the hard slogging: research and more research, making notes, laying the groundwork, thinking out plot, playing with approach, homing in on focus, soaking up information like a sponge.

Successful writing, whatever the genre, depends on good preparation. I feel comfortable with this, because that's what I learned in school, and I suspect most writers do, also.

At the saturation point, the natural urge is to begin writing. But this is the second stage, where it's important to do the opposite. Forget about the project. Leave the brain alone. Let the ideas cook, or jell, or grow.

Learning this, for me, has been like learning to steer into a skid on an icy road. It doesn't come naturally. I'm busy, and I want to keep going. But pieces of the puzzle are being fitted together behind the scenes, "harnessing the unconscious", as Dorothea Brande puts it.

This is when writer Henry Wiebe heaves rocks and mixes cement for his garden wall. Edna Staebler relaxes with her knitting. Maybe you go for long walks in the evening rain. I head to the gym for an exercise class.

In good time, out of the blue, an approach becomes obvious. An angle is clear. Words suggest themselves. The enthusiasm is overwhelming. Now I must write.

This is my jump out of the plane. Time to take a deep breath, let go of control, and let it flow. Time to write fast, grabbing a sentence or a scene or a phrase which excites and pulling at it however it presents itself. Most of all, time to hang on, white-knuckled, beyond where I think I can go.

Leonard Bishop calls this "the alchemy of writing", the place where lead is turned into gold. "Now you are into the dark, almost arcane dimension of the writing process that no one can explain," he writes in *Dare to be a Great Writer: 329 Keys to Powerful Fiction* (Cincinnati, Writer's Digest Books, 1988).

"Before you can grow as a writer, you must touch this unexplainable dimension."

For me, and for writer friends I've spoken to, this is the exciting, exhilarating, scary and exhausting stage. It's easy to lose track of time and place, of here and now. Just for a moment, we're on another world.

And don't stop too soon. "Sometimes when you think you are done, it is just the edge of the beginning," suggests Natalie Goldberg in her wonderful book *Writing Down the Bones: Freeing the Writer Within* (Boston, Shambhala, 1986). "It is beyond the point when you think you are done that often something strong comes out."

Finally, the fourth stage. The shape is there; time to polish and buff and shine. Time for controlled, careful, finicky attention to detail. Time to check facts, spelling, and mechanics, to verify sources and compile a bibliography. Time to be transformed, as Peter Elbow puts it in *Writing with Power: Techniques for Mastering the Writing Process* (NY, Oxford UP, 1981), "from a fast-and-loose-thinking person who is open to every whim and feeling, into a ruthless, toughminded, rigorously logical editor."

Often, especially in larger projects, we need to shift back and forth between these gears of creativity. Ray Bradbury labels them "Work, Relaxation, Don't Think, More Relaxation" (*Zen in the Art of Writing: Essays on Creativity*, Santa Barbara, CA, Capra, 1990). The important thing is to fight the impulse to be in control from beginning to end.

My first published story for children almost didn't get finished. I was stumped for several days at the climax because I had an elephant who insisted on standing on his head, and I had no idea how to get him down. Sitting at my desk for hours, grimly determined to hammer out the end of my plot, got me nowhere.

(Being funny doesn't fit with being grim!) Finally I gave up. But doing the laundry later, thinking other things, the solution suddenly came to me unbidden.

[He sneezed a gigantic elephant sneeze, which turned him right-side-up again.]

So we ebb and flow in our levels of achievement, self-confidence, commitment. Mediocre writers may earn strings of publishing credits.

Winners of prestigious awards may get discouraged and quit. And all of us use only a small percentage of our potential.

Which brings us back to courage. It takes courage to write, whether we are neurotic loners full of angst and insecurity, or happy optimists feeling loved and self-confident. It takes courage to deal with failure and rejection, part of every writer's life.

As Ted Solotaroff, in *Writing in the Cold*, points out, the decisive element in eventual success is durability: "how one deals with uncertainty, rejection, and disappointment, from within as well as without, and how effectively one incorporates them into the creative process itself, particularly in the prolonged first stage of a career."

So inside every successful writer is a fragile flicker of stubborn determination. It lives deep within, where no-one else sees, fueled by an abiding love—a passion—for the process of writing. You and I know it when we see it, in ourselves and in others.

A skydiver's goal is a successful landing. But skydivers don't jump for the thrill of arriving on the ground. They jump for the thrill of the journey, for the thrill of the leap out of that plane.

As writers, our goal is a finished piece. Preparation is essential.

Talent is important. But the thrill is in the journey, in that leap into the unknown.

And every journey is different.

So I stand on the edge, looking down, scared. It never gets easier. All I have to do is jump.

And would I ever, really, want to do anything else?

Margaret Springer is an award-winning author of dozens of published stories, articles and poems for children. Her book credits include *A Royal Ball* (Boyds Mills Press) and *Move Over, Einstein* (Penguin UK, 1997). She also teaches writing and gives workshops.

# Precision, Organization and Discipline: A Schedule for Success

*by Bryan M. Knight* _____

A successful creation to a writer is like a splendid meal to a chef: tasty enough to please the palate of its creator and good enough to be sold to a gourmet.

Superior chefs are **P**recise, **O**rganized and **D**isciplined. Take a pea from their **POD** to create your success schedule.

## Precision.

Be precise about the ingredients: what you will write, how much, when and where. Is your goal to write a book of inspirational non-fiction? A spy novel? Your life story? A fable for children? Decide on the end product. Then cut the task into easy-to-digest bites, for example, a chapter a month, or a page a day. Establish goals and sub-goals that make you reach, but not overextend yourself.

Be specific. Aim to spend a certain amount of time or create a certain number of words or pages each session. Will you write for three hours on Sunday afternoons, or ten pages a week or three hundred words every day beginning at seven a.m.? Match your formula to your personality. Time frames allow you the flexibility to produce a lot or a little. Word or page objectives must challenge yet not overwhelm. Experiment.

Also be precise about when you will write. Some writers may write only when they feel like it, but most of us need to fix a regular time and place. A routine stint at writing is what separates the professional from the dilettante ("someday I'll write a book").

Find out through self-observation when you feel most alert. Arrange your writing periods around those peaks. Aspiring writers are often advised to rise at four or five a.m. to write when they are freshest. I don't know about you, but I can hardly pry my eyes open at eight a.m., let alone five a.m. If you peak at ten p.m., that's when you should write. But if the only time you can possibly salvage is lunch hour at the office, or a half-hour at the end of the factory day, so be it. You'll be amazed at how much you can churn out in an empty office or silent factory.

Never write on a full stomach: it's the cells in your brain, not your tummy, that need replenishing. Similarly, when you know you're going to write, be sure to eat foods that invigorate. Tofu rather than spaghetti, for example. Discover your body's unique response to various foods. And don't be deceived by drugs; there are few writers who can truly write well in an alcoholic or other chemical haze.

Make it a practice to write in the same surroundings. Self-conditioning works, so develop helpful, rather than harmful, habits. Prepare beforehand all the equipment you'll need. Prime your writing capacity: immerse yourself in the stimuli of familiar desk, comforting rituals, and accustomed writing tools. Explore different musical backgrounds—or even white noise.

The pleasure and pain of pushing pen, pencil or processor will gradually inculcate professional skills. Along the way you will probably whet your appetite by reading great literature, seek writing recipes in the pages of *Canadian Author* magazine or the *Canadian Writer's Journal*, feast on books about writing, and dip into formal studies on how to write. The more organized your approach, the more you'll learn, the more you'll write, and the more your skills and self-confidence will flourish.

### Organization.

The second ingredient of POD simply means to rank your priorities and to simplify your chores to maximize time for what is most important: writing. This involves the eight Rs: reward, reverie, reading, research, rewriting, recreation, resubmission and rest.

Reward yourself. The final banquet will be the completed book. But as you cook, take delight in delicious nibbles. For instance, if you work best in the morning, your bonus for achieving your quota could be that you give yourself the rest of the day off. If your writing is squeezed into available minutes and hours away from a nine-to-five job, choose less drastic rewards: a ten-minute nap, a warm bath, a cup of coffee, a quick game on the video, a plunge into a favorite novel. The bigger the accomplishment, the more you should reward yourself. Ten chapters merits new apparel; meeting your self-imposed deadlines six months in a row deserves a night on the town, etc.

Reverie—daydreaming—is essential to the creative process. Fantasize about the content of your book (worthwhile for both fiction and non-fiction), but also visualize yourself having written: the joy of achievement and the subsequent sale to publisher and public. Images influence. Flood your mind with pictures of yourself as a successful writer. Used while you sit comfortably, muscles untensed, such imaging is akin to self-hypnosis. It won't in itself make you a fine writer, but it will deliver a powerful boost of encouragement from your subconscious to your conscious mind.

Breathes there a writer who does not love to read? Whether for escape, pleasure or instruction, to read is to expand your repertoire of recipes, and thereby enrich what you write.

Writing requires research, even if that means merely to check a date or locate a publisher. Some writers research voluminously before committing a word to paper. Others write first, research later. Your preference for cooking-by-the-book or the "pinch and taste" school will be reflected in your success schedule. Provide enough hours for research that your work will be accurate, but not so much that you spend more time researching than writing.

Rewriting, unless you're an Isaac Asimov, is a necessity. Again, whether you rewrite as you go, or in two or twenty-two sessions, depends on your temperament and your skills. A master chef knows a pinch of which herb to add to enhance the flavor of a lobster bisque; the novice has to begin all over again. Create first, critique later.

Recreation is part of the rhythm of a healthy life. As the word implies, recreation encompasses anything that refreshes you, including exercise. Don't be misled by the current mania for strenuous activity. Choose what suits you. If you like to swim, fine. If a walk around the block is more your style, then stick with that. An excellent "exercise" can be to write standing up. At a minimum, your success schedule should include internal jogging: laugh breaks. A hearty laugh does wonders for your heart, your blood pressure and your digestion, not to mention your enthusiasm. Stir up your creative juices with laughs at comedy records or TV sitcoms or audio tapes of your children's giggles or anything else that momentarily derails your train of thought.

Writers who schedule success are like chefs who use all four burners on the stove top: something's always cooking.

Resubmission—sending your query letters or book proposals out again and again—maintains your stove's heat. It's the only way you can be sure one of your bubbling pots will eventually yield a satisfying result. To make resubmission easier, draw up a reverse menu: luscious desserts first. Thus your preferred publisher will head your list of potential buyers. Multiple-submit to your top four or five choices. Tell them it's a multiple submission. When a rejection arrives, immediately send a new query to that publisher and the "rejected" query or proposal to the next company on your list.

Rest cannot be ignored. But it cannot be overindulged. Too much sleep and you'll be groggy at the typewriter. Too many breaks and you'll be drinking tea or walking the dog more than you'll be writing. Sleep the minimum amount necessary for you to feel great during the day. Arrange your breaks according to your natural cycle. One and a half hours of mental exertion is a common rhythm. "Three hours a day will produce as much as a man ought to write," said Trollope.

### Discipline.

Once your goals are precise, your work habits organized, then discipline—the remaining element of POD—is the yeast you need to raise your success schedule out of the ordinary.

Discipline includes ruthlessness with friends and family. First you and then others must view your writing time as sacred. To permit interruptions is to demean your craft. When you sit down (or stand) to write, write. Freewrite on the topic; write whatever you feel at that moment; write your objectives for that session. "The important thing is that at the moment, on the dot of the moment, you are to be writing, and that you teach yourself that no excuse of any nature can be offered when the moment comes," says Dorothea Brande (*Becoming A Writer*). She claims such practice—even for fifteen minutes a day—will ultimately enable you to write any time you put your mind to it.

Use a kitchen timer to jolt you to begin to write or to end a break. Unless you delight in disaster, or write horror stories, avoid newscasts and newspapers. Slot them where they'll do you the least harm.

Regard deadlines as lifelines: promises to yourself to achieve a specific piece of writing by a definite date. Editors prize a reliable writer. It's well worth training yourself to reach (and surpass) deadlines.

Persevere. Like John Creasey: rejected 744 times, he nevertheless wrote steadily and eventually saw 560 of his novels published. Such prolificity amazes; such perseverance inspires. Although I've relished the joy of book proposals being accepted on their initial submissions several times, one manuscript of mine visited thirty-one houses before finally finding a home. Then many months of disciplined effort went into molding that manuscript according to the editors' suggestions. I carved, spiced, reshaped until every paragraph smacked of exactly the right flavor.

Precision. Organization. Discipline. POD. It's not surprising these are the makings of your success schedule; the same ingredients constitute the stock for good writing.

Bryan M. Knight, MSW. PhD., is the author of several books, including *Love, Sex & Hypnosis: Secrets of Psychotherapy and Health and Happiness with Hypnosis.* More of his material can be read on his web site at <http://www.odyssee.net/~drknight/>.

# Pan For Gold: Find Success in a Writing Workshop

*by W. D. Valgardson*  _____

We teach terrible things to people in our society. How do I know that? I see the results every year in my writing workshops. Year after year I've had students say "I'm in your workshop this year and I want you to tear me apart. Don't worry, I can handle it."

An image of savage conflict appears when I hear that. I see them dressed as gladiators fighting desperately for their lives, neither giving nor expecting quarter. Writing is filled with pain, not pleasure. There are only winners and losers.

I explain to them that my job is to help people set and achieve writing goals, not to tear them or their creative work apart. When the workshop first meets, I emphasize and re-emphasize that the reason we have gathered together is to help each individual be successful. That success can be quite easily defined. It is to help each person write more and write better. If we can find ways to help someone write more than when he came to the workshop, then we've been successful. If we can help someone write better than she did when she came to the workshop, then we've been successful. After thirty years of teaching writing workshops in fiction, poetry and drama both in Canada and abroad, I've never seen an instance where turning a workshop into a combative arena has helped a writer be more productive or increase the quality of his writing.

With these goals in mind, I suggest that the members of the group, as they prepare their remarks, ask themselves this question, "How will what I'm going to say help the writer write more or write better?" Generally, everyone is pretty good about following this rule with one exception. That exception? When they apply it to themselves.

I first realized this many years ago while leading a fiction workshop. We were discussing a story while the author was listening and making notes. The longer we discussed her story, the more unhappy she looked.

Because she was an older student, a nurse, and emotionally mature, I risked stopping the discussion to say to her, "Quick, now, no second thoughts. Just tell us what you're feeling."

To her credit, she did just that. She said, "I don't know why I thought I could write. I'm too old. Everyone knows more than me. I can't write. I don't have any talent. I shouldn't be here."

There was surprised silence. I waited a moment then asked, "We've discussed the plot of your story. We've talked about the characterization of our protagonist. We've touched on theme. But has anyone said you can't write or that you shouldn't be here?"

She admitted no one had and, when I asked her who had said these terrible things to her, she admitted, "Me."

I then asked the class if any of them talked to themselves. There were a few giggles but eventually they all admitted they talked to themselves. They also admitted that they, too, had been saying negative things to themselves.

That's when I laid down the law. "No negative self-talk."

I see my creative self as a small, rather shy child who likes to make up stories. Sort of like my five-year-old grandson. If, when my grandson brings me the artistic things he makes, I said, "Look at this. It's not very good. It's not professional. If you can't do it perfectly, don't do it at all. What kind of picture is this? The perspective is all wrong.", how many times would it be before he quit bringing anything to show me?

And if I say the same kind of nasty things to my creative self, how long before that part of me quits bringing me creative gifts?

That's why I'm not interested in tearing apart first drafts. First drafts are acts of inspiration, gifts from our creative self. I want my writers to write first drafts without any concern that they will be criticized. When we discuss first drafts, we'll discuss not what is wrong with them but what is right with them. We'll look at them to find what works, what can be developed. We won't discuss language. That's for later drafts. We won't copy edit. That's for final drafts. We'll raise possibilities. We'll brainstorm.

We'll give thought to the wildest ideas inspired by the first draft because we know that the writer has the right to accept or reject anything we say.

Our goal is to send the writer home with a head full of ideas. Later, as the story develops we'll start to concentrate on technical matters. How much narrative should there be, how much exposition, how many scenes. What would be the best dramatic structure? But even these will only be possibilities.

And even here, although we'll identify problems and try to find solutions, we'll concentrate on what works, not on what doesn't work.

Sometimes, even in the best workshops, with people dedicated to the success of everyone in the group, we stray. After all, we live in a society that is quick to criticize and punish but slow to reward. We'll spend a million dollars to prosecute a criminal case but refuse to spend a thousand dollars to reward someone who's stopped a crime. When we start to focus on what's wrong, rather than what's right, I stop the class. I ask everyone to participate in a small exercise in visualization.

I ask the workshop to imagine all of us getting onto a bus. Imagine that we're driving north on the Island Highway, I say. We turn off and drive until we come to a stream. As you all get off the bus, I hand each person a gold pan. You all go to the stream and begin to pan for gold. Now, as you pan for gold do you think that you, or anyone else in the group, is going to keep running up to me to say "Look, Bill. Look, I found gravel."? We all know there's gravel. Everywhere we look, we can see it. Don't you think that automatically, without even thinking about it, you'd wait until you found some gold and then you'd rush up and say, "Look, look, everyone. I've found some colour." Or better yet, "I've found a nugget."

It is more valuable for a writer to be able to identify one word that has been well chosen, one sentence that has been well written, one paragraph that has been well constructed, than it is to be shown five pages of what doesn't work. Find the best sentence in a story and you have discovered how well you can write. No one else wrote that sentence. You wrote it. It's yours. It was created by your talent, your intelligence, your experience.

Now, like an athlete that has just set a new personal record, you have to practice until you can write at that level consistently.

Negative self-talk is incredibly destructive. It undermines success. It blocks people from being productive. It sabotages goals. However, the good news is that it is a behavior that is learned and, so, it can be unlearned.

If you want to be a successful writer, unlearn it. Replace it with positive self-talk. Say I can, instead of I can't. Say I will, instead of I won't.

Say I know what to do next, instead of I don't know what to do next.

Keep your goal of being a successful writer clearly in focus. Remind yourself each day that you want to write more and write better. When you're tempted to spend all your time concentrating on what doesn't work, what you haven't learned yet, what you haven't accomplished yet, remember that it's gravel. Swirl it out of your pan. Pay attention to the gold.

W. D. Valgardson is the author of numerous books and plays. He has recently written two children's picture books: *Thor* (Mr. Christie Award Winner) and *Sarah and the People of Sand River*. He is a member of the Department of Writing at the University of Victoria.

# Get Your Money's W Invest in a Creative Writing Course

*by Linda Jeays*

To get the best out of a writing class, take a soapy washcloth and clean off the kitchen calendar. Your private life must be put on hold for the duration of the course. You will not have time to divorce your spouse, direct the Scout pantomime, take in washing, knit a plant hanger, or take evening classes in micro-technology. You need the chance between classes to write, write, read–and then write again. This is also no time to let the kids get the chicken pox.

If the attendance column under your name looks like the diagram for a needlepoint design, your learning will be equally patchy. A good teacher has new material for every session. Each part of the curriculum builds on what went before. Without the keystones in the course you may be left with a heap of unrelated building materials.

If you have conflicting engagements on writing night, reschedule the cat's appointment at the vet's, ask your mother-in-law to dinner another night, and send out for a hamburger instead of cooking Cordon Bleu. Do not take a writing course unless you are prepared for a serious investment of time.

If your canary gets malaria and your Ferrari blows a gasket, do not ask the teacher for a Xerox copy of the notes for the missed class. These notes are her bread-and-butter ticket. If everything she had to say could be written down on four sheets of paper, she would be running a correspondence course.

Many teachers offer individual help throughout the program. If you missed a class because of a blizzard or boils, ask the instructor to give you the main points of the missed session in one of the individual periods. Use, but don't abuse, your teacher.

Educators place their spare time, their writing time, and their expertise on the altar of your creativity for the duration of the writing course.

teachers will read, correct, encourage, and make constructive suggestions throughout the classes.

One of the most frustrating situations an educator has to face is the student who brings a 60,000-word novel, which has brilliant possibilities, to the class in the ninth week of a ten-week course. Strut your stuff during the first class and every class after that.

Don't procrastinate. Get your writing, however rudimentary, onto paper. No good teacher is ever dismayed by honest work. The first step on the road to improvement is rewarding for both instructor and student. If the written work is presented, help can be given. A teacher can do nothing with good intentions.

Remember that you are taking the course to acquire new skills. No one expects your first poem to win the Better Beer Golden Award for Best Cinquain. The teacher should see both prose and poetry early on in the course. Practicing word choice in poetry, experimenting with form, shape, and pattern is a valuable exercise for a wordsmith. As Tom Lehrer says, the important thing is not to get the right answer, but to understand the method. To learn to write, sit down regularly and tap those kettle-drum keys or scratch the quill across the parchment.

Don't just write what you know you *can* write—follow up on every assignment suggestion the teacher makes. With luck you will receive positive advice on strengthening and compensating for weak areas in your writing.

An encounter with an editor's hieroglyphics is the hardest way to learn that your words, lovingly selected, are not sacrosanct. Why not learn this lesson less painfully from your teacher?

If she says your poetry is shapeless, erratic, and that the form detracts from the sense, believe her. Are you the student who believes that the way he first wrote the poem (in the bare patches of a Playboy centre-fold with coffee stains covering most of the sins) is the final untouchable version, the sacred cow?

Learn to take advice. A poet with an original viewpoint, economical word use, and a grasp of poetic phrasing, may still be unsure of form and punctuation. A teacher can show him how to slip a poem past an editor by denuding his work of punctuation, justifying his left-hand margin, and using a capital letter for the beginning of each new thought. While the result may not be *great* poetry, it may fit into a leftover bit of column space and earn money enough to buy a textbook on poetic techniques.

It is the middle of summer and the instructor asks you to write a letter to Santa Claus from Rudolph the Red-Nosed Reindeer. Do it. For the duration of the course, you are exposed to new ideas, new methods, new ways of thinking. Keep an open mind. The occasional student does his own thing throughout the course, convinced his originality will be tarnished by contact with others. He finishes the program with his identity intact and his mind no richer. Don't waste your teacher's creativity and your chance to experiment.

Few teachers limit the amount of work they mark during a writing course. If you are asked for a description of a fat, juicy ant from the point of view of a mosquito, write it. Attach your own epic poem to the back page.

Do not give your teacher a ninety-minute tape of your poetic offerings. The spoken word is different than the written word. Speech rhythms make their own patterns. While the oral version may sound plausible, the written version may be ill-spelled, badly punctuated, and lacking in valid poetic shape and style. If you like making tapes, take a multi-media course.

"Do you mind if Shirley sits in on this session?"

An innocent-sounding request such as that drives adult educators to drink. Shirley is always a delicious 23-year-old blonde in a tight-fitting wool dress. Everyone is instantly less interested in the statistics used to establish credibility in an article and more interested in the three-dimensional ones on display.

Every group of students quickly establishes a working relationship with the teacher. Whether you bring in a good friend, your mother, or someone who wants to take the course next time, you change the dynamics of the group.

The instructor may be distracted by the new member. The newcomer may be disinterested in the class or ask a lot of questions already covered. Park your out-of-town visitor beside a coffee machine or in a bar.

For the same reasons, never miss classes and then ask to sit in on the missed topics during the second section of the class. Any new presence in a class, unless it is to be permanent, is an imposition on the teacher and the students.

In the course of a year, an educator sees many first-class writing students who are working on novels or full-length non-fiction. Do not turn up on your instructor's doorstep with a bag of doughnuts, a spaniel with pleading eyes, a copy of *Inspirational Poems for Terminal Cancer Patients* by Eliza Doomuch, and this request: "I took your class in 1989 so will you read my book? There are ten pages at the end for your detailed written comments. Will you decide where I need chapters? The dog ate the dictionary and so a few words are misspelled. I'll come back on Monday and we can spend the day going over it."

Even for a teacher who is afraid of cancer, spaniels and doughnuts, it is not easy to say, "My reading fee is $40.00 an hour and I've forgotten your name."

An instructor's time is worth money. In favor of your heroic tome, the teacher/writer will have to shelve her own slim volume of verse. Offer her dough instead of doughnuts.

An alternative approach is to slip a chapter of your book in with each batch of work submitted during the course. The teacher will comment on many chapters and may even ask to see your finished book.

Adult education classes are available in Basic English, Business English, Technical Writing and Calligraphy. Should you be taking one of these options instead?

Here are some quotations from notes written to a creative writing teacher on the first day.

"I am taking this course because my mother had beautiful handwriting and I want to have it too."

"I want to learn to write better personnel evaluation reports so I can get a promotion at work."

"I have never been able to spel and I think I could learn alot from this Coarse."

These students dropped out of Creative Writing after the first class when they were bombarded with free verse, concrete poetry and the word "imagery."

Before taking a writing course, read the outline carefully and speak to the instructor. Know whether your expectations of the course are likely to be fulfilled. If you are truly a beginner, almost any class is a step in the right direction. If you have some experience, look for university or community college courses, writers' conferences and workshops that bring you the stimulation of your peers in the writing world.

Remember that most writing instructors are sitting uncomfortably on the horns of a dilemma: do they teach, or do they write? Be kind to your instructor to ensure he or she stays in Education and does not add to the competition in the freelance writing field!

Linda Jeays often uses her experience as a High School teacher, workshop leader, post graduate student and adult educator in her freelance articles. She is also a poet with almost 100 published poems. She writes regularly for a wide variety of magazines and newspapers from her home in Nepean, Ontario.

# Your Journal and Your Ears

*by Anne Rockwell Fairley* _____

Today, computer technology offers a memory bank of information and publishable material at the editor's fingertips. Syndicate and staff writers are able to produce a publishable piece at almost a moment's notice. Therefore, even more than in previous decades, a free-lance writer must unearth material that is unusual or unique, then prepare a manuscript an editor wants.

Your *ears* combined with a *journal* will help you create marketable products.

I use the public transportation system a great deal. As a result, I hear the most intriguing conversations. Sometimes the language in a direct quote would be "off limits" to most publications, especially newspapers, but often a casual remark means instant inspiration.

The question, "How's your mother doing these days?" might have been ignored by me if it hadn't been for the reply. When I heard, "We take her every third Sunday," I was hooked. The idea those six words spawned, resulted in a short story that just rolled onto the page and became my first fiction sale. The protagonist, Margaret, still surfaces from time to time.

Your ears capture those special nuances that can never be gleaned from looking or reading. Whether you are a creator of fiction or non-fiction, listening is a prerequisite. To write dialogue, it's necessary to be aware of the way people speak, so that what you write really sounds authentic. The same is true in article writing; it is important to record what you hear when the emotions the words evoke are fresh.

Everywhere you travel—by plane, taxi, bus, motor coach or cruise ship—to the Far East, Southern U.S., Caribbean, South America, or downtown to work or shop, be a listener and a journalist in the truest sense of the word. When you are waiting—in a restaurant, theatre or dentist office—keep ears tuned and journal ready, but be discreet and sincere and, if possible, invisible.

William Faulkner once said, "Everything goes by the board—honor, pride, decency, security, happiness, all—to get the book written." Remember his words when you undertake this eavesdropping work. Don't sacrifice your principles.

Most of the examples I will share with you have happened to me while travelling, but whether travelling or not, a journal should be part of a writer's lifestyle. It should be used to record ideas, thoughts, happenings, phrases, and tidbits of information you happen to hear anytime and anywhere. In a foreign country, record other languages spoken in addition to that country's native ones. If you discover, for instance, that Kyoto, Japan, is filled with Australians, this could make an interesting article. Why are they there?

In Moscow and Kiev, I heard so many locals trying out English proverbs and expressions, I made a list. It became the basis for a newspaper article "Erase the Language Barrier." Travel books and brochures rarely provide that colour.

On a tour, I watched several people videotape the entire city excursion, while their companions snapped away at every tour guide highlight. Not once did I see the photographers write down specific information about a particular building or monument. I assumed (incorrectly, as it turned out) that the people using video cameras were recording the sound. Later, when I asked how they managed to remember all the details and whether they showed their videos and slides "back home," they smiled. One said, "Well, the people I show it to have never been here, so it doesn't matter."

The gist of that conversation went into my journal along with my immediate reaction. The result was an article I have sold many times about how to present an evening of holiday pictures to friends back home.

While visiting Greece, Delphi and the Oracle, legends interested me so much that I kept a chronicle of my feelings as I walked the ruins. That material has spawned not only travel material but poems.

Single words spoken by others on the trip have reinforced my impressions.

"Magnificent!" "Spiritual." "Conceptual." "Wow, that was a climb," said one exhausted tourist. All of these images recorded as they happened are useful to me now, months after the experience.

In the Acropolis in Athens, our guide used the word "rape" when she announced the fact that Lord Elgin helped himself to many unearthed

Parthenon artifacts and one of six Caryatids of the Erechtheum. (Caryatids are draped female figures used in place of columns as architectural supports.) The missing one remains housed in the British Museum. The guide's use of this single word creates invaluable impressions to a writer. Think of the feelings and images it formulates.

Years before the horrendous problems in Yugoslavia, I explored its Dalmatian Coast. Quickly, I realized that every second person in hotel dining rooms had British accents. In conversation, I discovered they had chosen to visit at that time of year mainly because the resorts offered special rates to compete with the popular vacation areas of Portugal and Spain. With this information in my journal, I began to dig. I learned that all sorts of things contributed to the tourist mosaic including summer— plant shutdowns, school and university mid-term breaks, and religious celebrations. Digging further, I discovered that the resort owners knew exactly when to expect Italian, German, British and North American tourists. This information resulted in a different slant for a travel piece.

Stephen Leacock once remarked that "people when they travel really see nothing at all except the reflection of their own ideas." Leacock was referring to people in general—but this is especially hazardous for writers. Accepting everything by sight and not really investigating and listening can result in misleading conclusions. Yet even those misconceptions, when corrected, can provide material for saleable work.

In Istanbul, I heard much laughing and chuckling between a guide and a person who happened to be walking by the tour buses parked at a mosque. They were both looking at the "Lunch On Board" sign in a bus window. What the sign was meant to convey was that the people using that particular bus were returning to the cruise ship for lunch "on board." What the person thought it meant was that the passengers were having lunch served on the bus. When I read through my journal notes from that period, it induced myriad memories from that afternoon.

Recording what you hear, and your immediate reaction to it, will be invaluable as you sit in front of the screen. It is not easy, as I said in the opening, to be a free-lancer today. The more special your manuscript's slant, the more you will sell. Use your ears and your journal to keep you one stride ahead.

Anne Rockwell Fairley is a Winnipeg-based writer who uses travel and research experiences to publish articles in periodicals across Canada. She teaches writing and has edited four books. With a collection of 5,000 herbal and old-time cure-alls in her database, she also entices editors to accept manuscripts on such eclectic topics as contraception, whooping cough and warts!

# The Writer and the Diary

*by John Melady*

Aside from a pen and a scrap of paper, a diary may be a writer's most overlooked aid.

It's cheap, readily available and easy to use. It may be highly personal, completely public or anywhere in between. The writing may be florid, the tone reflective, the organization an idiosyncratic disaster—yet the end result is as unique as a fingerprint.

Consider the work of some of the diarists in literature: Somerset Maugham, Charles Ritchie, Samuel Pepys, Anaïs Nin among them. Even though their writings were vastly different, think of how much poorer we would be had they not written.

Then there are the well-known diaries of two individuals who wrote about events of the same era, though from markedly opposing perspectives. One was Albert Speer, Adolf Hitler's architect and the man who designed some of the most notorious monuments of the Third Reich. It was he who was responsible for the grandstand at Nuremberg's Zeppelin Field, where the Fuhrer ranted in the glory days of the Nazi regime. I remember climbing around on what remains of the structure and wondering how one madman needed something so obscene. Then, when I read Speer's diary entries about designing the place, I understood why, although the explanation did not make the creation more palatable.

Speer also agonized about his slavish adulation of Hitler. After the war, and during his twenty-year prison term for crimes against humanity, the architect wrote thousands of words in an attempt to come to terms with what he had done, but also to justify his place in history. However, those diary entries as read today are often little more than the superficial piffle of a master dissembler, their sincerity as chimerical as a dream.

In direct contrast to the writings of Speer are those innocent, bittersweet diary jottings of Anne Frank, who with seven others hid for her life from the lawlessness wrought on the world by Speer and his cohorts. Anne wrote to preserve her sanity, to keep her hopes alive, to endure. And while she occasionally became depressed, she never despaired, although at times she admitted being unable to deny her own soul. For example, on Christmas Eve, 1943, after being confined for a year and a half, she lamented: "Cycling, dancing, whistling, looking out into the world, feeling young, to know that I'm free—that's what I long for."

I defy anyone to read Anne's diary and not be moved by what she wrote. Even more, a visit to Prinsengracht 263 in Amsterdam can reduce the most jaded to tears. I recall looking around those pathetically cramped quarters, touching the walls Anne touched, climbing the stairs she climbed, as the echo of her story burned into my brain. Such was the worth of her words—the words of her diary.

But even while most of us who write will never be historical figures, we can all keep diaries. I have for many years and intend to continue doing so. Here are a few reasons why you, as a writer, might consider doing the same thing:

### Making regular entries in a diary helps to keep you organized.

If you keep an ongoing record of the steps you follow in researching and writing, you can often pick out inconsistencies in the way you are doing things, periods of time that were wasted, possible areas of research that were overlooked, short cuts, or even the hours during which you do your best writing. Of course, you must first pick a convenient time to complete the diary itself. Then, note your peak performance times in it. Note also when most interruptions occur. In other words, try to isolate the good times from the bad and act on that knowledge. Your production and the quality of your work should improve.

### Keeping a diary helps you to express, record and recall your feelings and impressions.

Suppose you are making your first visit to a famous landmark in a foreign country. As soon as convenient after you leave the place, describe not only *what* you saw, but your *impressions* of what you saw. Later on, you may be able to use the diary material in something you write. For example, I made my first visit to the Tower of London many years ago. While taking a tour of the place, I listened as a guide told the story of the two little sons of Edward IV who were imprisoned there. The tale chilled me to the point that I never forgot it. Sometime later, as I wrote my book *The Little Princes*, I referred constantly to what I had recorded that day. Still later, as the novel took shape, I returned to the Tower several times, but those first impressions were always intact. Had it not been for a diary entry, the book itself likely would not have been done.

### Doing a diary provides a personal forum for commenting on private events, public events, even imaginary events.

While the first two of these are fairly self-explanatory, the third can be a gold mine for a future book. In essence, you keep a diary of an imaginary person, doing imaginary things, in whatever situation you alone envision. Write an entry each day for your protagonist. Have him or her do things, say things, interact with others—anything you wish. At the end of several weeks or months, the "diary", which need not have been at all difficult to do, may well become the nucleus of a novel.

### A diary is a good place to vent one's spleen.

When rejection slips, ignored queries, editor incompetence and poor reviews grow frustrating, instead of taking it out on those closest to you, leave your anger for your diary. Your loved ones will rejoice. So will anyone reading your journal after your demise. By that time, of course, your fury will probably be funny.

### A diary can help you remember people.

Record information on editors, publicists, interview subjects who might be helpful contacts for later writing. As well, your diary is a good place to record and keep track of suggestions editors may make. This is particularly true if the suggestion was offered during a phone call. Recording the advice as soon as possible after hanging up will help you not only to understand what it was you were told, but it will help you fashion the piece in question into the masterpiece the editor expects.

### Use your diary to help you keep track of housekeeping items.

Here, include such things as deadlines, interview times, book signing appointments, speeches to be made, queries to be followed up on, calls to be made, letters to be answered and so on. Then as each of these is done, it may simply be checked off and put behind you. Then you can actually write with fewer distractions.

### Don't forget that a diary can be very helpful around tax time.

Because your writing is a business, Revenue Canada expects you to conduct your literary endeavors in a businesslike way. Any accountant will tell you to keep receipts for any writing materials, of course, but in case of an audit, just how do you prove that all those post office receipts involved writing? Daily diary entries can support your contention that you did mail these queries, that manuscript, and those letters of reply to readers. Diary entries regarding phone calls or faxes can be just as relevant. Even though the phone company includes numbers called with your monthly statement, only you know which of perhaps many were actually concerned with writing. Your diary records can tell you.

### Your diary may even have a dollar value.

If it is extensive enough, and unique enough, you might be able to donate it for tax purposes to a public or university archive. When you do, you would be expected to declare how soon, and by whom, it might be used. More likely however, your heirs may have a greater chance of unloading it. A hundred years from now, your writings about today might be of great worth to a researcher attempting to understand how an ordinary person lived and thought in the period leading up to the year 2000. For this reason, your comments about current events, day-to-day struggles, times of happiness and the like could be invaluable.

### Last, a diary can be what you write when you can't write.

Most of us have gone through days, or even weeks when we seem to be unable to compose anything worthwhile. We stare at the blank paper or empty screen, and nothing comes. All the desk-straightening, coffee-brewing, file-arranging, pencil-sharpening and so on do nothing for us. We can go for a walk, clean the house, mow the grass or wash the car, but none of these becomes saleable words. At such times, however, all of us can do a diary entry. It may not be much, but it is writing, and it's as permanent as we want to make it.

Then there are those other times, and hopefully these are few, when we cannot write because of personal crises in our lives, or in the lives of those closest to us. Sooner of later we will all face such things, and while our writing production may virtually dry up, our hopes, even our prayers reflected in the pages of our diary may be the only lifeline we have. That's when our diary is an invaluable support, a friend that is there, a writer's confidant that does not talk back.

John Melady is the author of seven books and numerous magazine and newspaper articles. Among his books are: *Korea: Canada's Forgotten War* and *Pilots, Canadian Stories from the Cockpit*. He was a secondary school vice-principal for many years, but now writes full time.

# Research and Love it

*by John Melady* _____

**D**oing research for an article or book need never be boring. Tracking down leads, meeting new people, hearing fascinating stories, and visiting unfamiliar places can make research an exhilarating experience. Here are a few suggestions for making it so.

## *Make a flow chart and block out the necessary parts of whatever you are writing.*

The blocks will keep you organized and on track and enable you to complete the whole in an orderly fashion. As well, completing each block can be both satisfying and fun.

One of my books was about the Canadian involvement in the Korean war. In order to ensure that all pertinent aspects of that conflict were addressed, I literally drew a series of squares on a large sheet of paper, and filled each in as I completed the research required in that area. The men who did the fighting had their own square, as did the generals who commanded them, the women who tended the wounded, the journalists who covered the war, the widows whose husbands never returned, and many more.

Filling in the squares is like playing a board game. In a game, one letter can make a word complete. In a book, one anecdote can shape an entire chapter, or make organizational links within or between chapters. When the entire sheet of squares is filled in, careful study will tell you a great deal about the organization of your book.

## *Set matters in context.*

Suppose you are doing research for a biography of a famous politician. You will probably go to a reference library and go over the newspapers on microfilm for the coverage of her speeches. As you are doing so, read about the other events that were happening at the same time. Look at the clothing styles. Check the prices in the advertisements. Note the movies that were playing. All of these things can be helpful when you are at your desk, attempting to set the scene. They may result in new squares being added to your flowchart of areas to research.

### Develop a positive attitude toward your research.

Decide beforehand that no matter who you are interviewing, or what you are seeking, you will learn something you never knew before. As long as you feel this, your research time will be neither wasted nor dull. Indeed, something that at first seems a waste can become the basis for a future story.

Several years ago, I was asked to do a piece about a nurse who had just retired. I assumed the assignment would be routine, and it was—initially. This modest, self-effacing woman spoke at first rather predictably about her career. However, when she began talking about her love for newborn infants, the interview took on a different slant entirely. She had worked in many hospitals, and was present for the arrival of hundreds of children, all of whom were listed by name and birth date in a journal she kept. I will never forget the moment when we stumbled onto the realization that I was one of them! Both of us actually wept at the discovery. Needless to say, I have never forgotten that "routine" interview.

### Cultivate your sources.

Try to develop a comfortable and trusting rapport with whomever is vital to the subject you are researching. If you are writing about cats, for instance, a knowledgeable pet shop owner could be helpful. He would be able to answer many of your questions, but could likely direct you to others in the field such as exhibitors, veterinarians, or breeders.

### Do your homework first.

Learn as much as possible about the person you wish to interview before you talk to her. If you know she dislikes journalists, get right to the point and don't waste her time. On the other hand, if you know she loves good art, for example, ask about the watercolour on the wall by her desk. Doing so will help break the ice and make your research more pleasant. (And don't be surprised if the conversation about art leads to another story.)

I once wrote a book called *Escape From Canada!* about the 40,000 German prisoners of war who were incarcerated here during World War II. One man I wanted to interview was a doctor who had steadfastly refused to talk to the media about his experiences behind barbed wire. I knew about his reticence, and so I posed as a patient, confronted the man in his examining room, and confessed my duplicity. "Well, I'll be god-damned," he roared—and then burst into laughter. He did not call the police, as I had feared, but agreed to talk to me after office hours. It was only then that he told me he admired my initiative. The resulting interview was invaluable.

### Whenever possible, interview subjects on their own turf.

It doesn't matter whether it is in someone's home, work place, or club—they will be more relaxed there. If you are talking to them about their occupation, for instance, actually seeing them on the job will make describing what they do easier for you.

My most recent book was called *Pilots*. It covered the story of flying, from the bush pilots to the jet age. But, because I am not a pilot, I found it necessary—and fun—to interview fliers while they were at work. Doing so enabled me to understand what they actually meant when they talked of turbulence, G forces, grey-out and afterburner takeoff. Being there helped me to write about the experience.

### Whenever possible, tape-record your interviews.

Because the tape recorder is so commonplace today, few request that it not be used. Do ask permission, however! As soon as possible after the interview, play back the tape. Doing so not only fixes in your mind what was said, it enables you to check on something you may have forgotten to ask. In situations where a follow-up session is needed, you may find it helpful to listen to the tape of the first interview in your car on the way to the second. Then you will know exactly what was covered and what will need attention.

Reviewing the tape can be helpful in another way as well. The person you have interviewed may have mentioned particular names or places. Hearing your discussion played back will remind you to double-check exact spellings and factual inferences. After all, neither of you wants to see errors in the published story.

### Use the phone.

While a telephone interview may not be as satisfying as a personal one, it is generally cheaper than travel, often easier, and certainly less time-consuming. If you don't trust your memory, or if you feel you can't jot down all that the person is saying, then tape the call. (Most electronics outlets can provide you with inexpensive equipment for doing this.) Always ask your subject's permission before taping.

Many agencies and companies have free long-distance 800 numbers. These may be obtained through the Directory Assistance listing in your telephone book.

## Buy a map.

If you are doing research about something in a distant town, have a map of the place handy, not just for orienting yourself on site, but for reference when you begin to write your story. You can then say, with confidence, that something or other is ten blocks from a local landmark.

In a children's novel I had the lead character being taken from the Westminster area of London, England, to prison in the Tower. Even though I had walked between the two points, I had never really paid much attention to how far apart they were. At the last minute I found a good map and was able to check the distance before submitting the manuscript to a publisher. Don't make the mistake I did, waiting too long to get the map you need.

## Take pictures.

Buy and learn to use the best camera you can afford. Photos help sell an article. In addition, shots taken at the time of an interview or during related research can be invaluable. A single photograph of the area where an occurrence took place can jog your memory when you are preparing your story.

For example, when I was writing a hockey book, I had to describe the dense bush where former Toronto Maple Leaf defenceman Bill Barilko died in a plane crash. It was only after seeing several wide-angle Search-and-Rescue photographs of the location that I was able to paint the proper word-pictures of the crash site. Ever since that experience, I take pictures as a matter of course during research.

## Know when the research is over.

Sooner or later, you will come to the realization that you have sufficient material to do your story. At this point, you have to stop procrastinating and begin to actually write the thing. That is when you realize that the research, for all its surface tedium, was fun. It's the writing that's hard.

John Melady is the author of seven books and numerous magazine and newspaper articles. Among his books are: *Korea: Canada's Forgotten War* and *Pilots, Canadian Stories from the Cockpit*. He was a secondary school vice-principal for many years, but now writes full time.

# Your Own Clipping Service

*by Betty Dyck*_____

Have you ever seated yourself enthusiastically in front of your typewriter or word processor to compose an article or begin a story and then remembered you had seen just the thing you needed for a "hook," or for rounding out an argument, in a recent paper? But which paper? What day?

Then the frantic search begins, sometimes involving more than merely minutes, often ending in frustration. Even if you finally locate the material, the inspiration to write may be gone—or the time.

Several years ago I found the answer to this kind of problem; I began my own clipping service. Ideas for articles or stories are all round in newspapers, magazines, and periodicals. To make them easily accessible for future use, I invented a filing system. Here are some of the ideas I found useful:

• If no filing cabinet is available, a sturdy cardboard carton big enough to hold file folders will do.

• Establish subject files and arrange them alphabetically.

• As you are reading a publication, tick off with a pencil pertinent articles for clipping later. In the case of daily papers, do not let yourself get behind in your clipping or it can become a tedious chore. (Or you may find someone has already used the paper for other purposes, accidentally destroying your clipping.) Make a habit of collecting all pertinent articles as soon as your paper has been read.

• Always date and document the article. You need the publication's name and the date, as well as the author's name, in order to give appropriate credit when you quote them in your own writing. It also helps keep you aware of the age of your information—an important factor if you write topical articles.

Betty Dyck is the Winnipeg-based author of three non-fiction books, editor of two church histories, and freelance writer who conducts workshops for the CAA Manitoba Branch.

# Conducting Interviews

*by Robert H. Jones*

When the editor of an art magazine asked me if a particular artist used the "dry brush" technique when he painted, I answered truthfully, "How should I know?"

"Because you write about art," she said.

"No," I replied, "I write about artists. *They* know about art; *I* know how to push buttons on my tape recorder and keys on my computer."

That pretty well sums up an interview. It is simply a means of gathering information. For example: while researching Saltwater Destination articles for *BC Outdoors* magazine, a two-day trip to an area will not make me an expert on important topics like the fish species present, feeding patterns, spawning migrations, weather variables, best fishing periods, and myriad other questions readers want answered. However, there are usually a few locals around who are experts, and when properly approached most are willing to share their knowledge and expertise. However, "willing" is a key word. I have found the most willing people are those involved with the tourism industry, wildlife and fishery biologists and technicians, artists, fishing guides and resort operators. Least willing have been politicians, senior and mid-level bureaucrats, and representatives from industries which have a poor track record in the realm of natural resource harvesting.

There are basically two types of interviews: personal—face-to-face—and via the telephone. Whichever method is used, it is important for the interviewer to appear reasonably knowledgeable about the topic, and well prepared. This means having some basic questions available beforehand, and having your equipment ready to set up quickly: tape recorder, microphone, extension cord, batteries (if required), and spare tapes ready to replace those which fill up. In the case of telephone interviews, it means having everything prepared ahead of time, so the interviewee does not have to wait while you fumble around.

First, let's examine the machinery: Some writers swear by tiny tape recorders which fit in their shirt pocket or purse.

I have a Realistic Micro-26 that has proved reliable and amazingly easy on batteries. However, I use it only when I can't use its big brother, a fairly hefty Realistic CTR68 with six piano-type keys. I like this large machine because it is sturdy, easy to use, economical, and it doesn't move around on the desk while I am transcribing. Its price, $105 plus tax at Radio Shack, did not include a microphone, but I had one from a previous machine. I prefer the external over the internal microphone because it can be positioned in front of the person being interviewed, while I sit across the table, or to one side, monitoring the tape and voice level. When it comes to playing back the tape, there is less extraneous noise, and the person's voice is loud and clear.

My old "mike" did not have a stand, so I jury-rigged one that has since served well. It is fashioned from a Bilora Model 1600 swivel-head camera C-clamp, which has two L-shaped legs that slide out from the body to form a small bipod. A metal wall clamp used for hanging brooms and mops is secured to the adjustable head with a 1/4-inch nut. The mike fits tightly in the broom clamp, and the adjustable head allows it to be swiveled up or down so it directly faces the person being interviewed. In addition, the C-clamp can be clamped to the side or top of an easel, which allows an artist to sketch or paint as the interview progresses.

I conduct telephone interviews with the help of an Archer Telephone Recording Control (Radio Shack, about $30). This device remains plugged in at all times, so hooking up or removing the CTR68 tape recorder takes less than a minute. A word of warning: if you have a weak or noisy telephone connection, when it comes time to transcribe the interview the sound quality will have you crawling the wall in frustration.

Whenever possible, insist on conducting interviews one on one. Having two or more persons involved usually confuses matters, especially when everyone starts talking at once or an argument ensues. If possible, select a room with no telephone, TV, radio or piped-in music, no window open to noisy traffic, and no loudly-droning air conditioner.

Let's now cover the basic steps by conducting a personal interview with mythical fishing guide Merton Mayers. First, prepare a list of logical questions which relate to the topic you wish discussed. If possible, do some research on Merton prior to the interview. Has he guided somebody famous? Did he guide someone to a record fish? Is he involved with a conservation group? Some good information sources might be his relatives, friends, co-workers, or even Merton himself.

Before switching on the machine, explain how you intend to use the recorded material, then give him a quick rundown of what you wish to cover. Ask if there are any topics or areas he might wish to avoid. This will help you bypass questions that might cause tension or embarrassment. If he asks that something be kept off the record, honour his request. After all, you might want to interview him again at some later date.

Artists like Robert Bateman, Ron Parker and Fenwick Lansdowne were easy interviews. No strangers to newspaper reporters, magazine writers and TV correspondents, they are living proof that practice makes perfect. It was just a case of switching on the machine, asking a leading question to get the interview started, then sitting back to listen. However, some folks are nervous or uneasy about speaking into a microphone, while others are downright taciturn. In either case, switch on your recorder, then hit the "pause" button while you chat them up. Eventually they will relax, especially if you get on a topic in which they have an intent interest or opinion. Once the flow of words begins, start the tape rolling.

Be a good listener, but don't sit there like the proverbial bump on a log. Above all, pay attention to what is being said. If Merton finishes expounding on a topic and asks for your opinion, it helps if you can respond with a reasonably intelligent answer or comment. If you have an opinion or something to add to whatever Merton is talking about, do so—but not at great length. This lets him know you are interested, and may jog his memory about something that might otherwise be overlooked. If something he says alerts you to another question, jot it down and cover it later. Occasional interruptions on your part will also help steer Merton onto or away from a specific topic, and will give him a short breather. Key word: occasional.

If you don't understand what is being said during the interview, you probably still won't when you transcribe it. Ask for clarification or descriptions to help you relate to what he is saying. If he mentions fishing with Bjornar Svenderhaaven on the Zymagotitz River, ask him to spell out the names while you write them down on a note pad. If you have a map of the area, ask him to point out the location (a tributary of the Skeena River, it's near Terrace, B.C.). Later, while transcribing the tape onto your computer, check the spelling of place names against a gazetteer, an atlas or a road map. Merton might be a great guide, but he's a lousy speller.

Finally, you picked Merton's brain in order to write a travel destination piece on the Zymagotitz River. While writing your article, give him credit wherever it is due: "According to veteran fishing guide Merton Mayoro..." or "Few people know the Zymagotitz River as well as..."

One last point: Experience will teach you that the most important control on your tape recorder is the "pause" button. Other than short questions or comments pertaining to the topic, whenever you feel the urge to talk—hit the pause button. Otherwise, while transcribing a lengthy interview from tape to disk or paper, you will discover the sound you least want to hear is that of your own voice.

Robert H. (Bob) Jones is the author of *Tangled Lines and Patched Waders* (1995) and *Dull Hooks and Squeaky Reels* (1997), both published by Horsdal & Schubart. He has won numerous awards for his book and magazine writing. He is a past president and life member of the Outdoor Writers of Canada, and an active member of the Outdoor Writers Association of America. He resides in Courtenay, B.C., with Vera, his wife of 40 years, who is also a writer.

# Write In Freefall

*by Mark Zuehlke* _____

For the past fifteen or more years I have been living and writing in freefall—an exhilarating existence on the edge of the danger zone of creativity. In freefall there are no warning markers, no limits, no constraints. You are on your own and the feeling is one of ultimate freedom. This freedom first came as a realization of how a writing method gave me creative liberty and eventually evolved into a life approach.

Freefall is living and writing with something akin to wild abandon. I like to think of it as anarchistic or living by your instincts.

Instincts. Not reason. That's the key to freefalling, both in creativity and in life. The abandonment of reason? Anarchy? All sounds utterly unwriterly, at least in this day of scientific rationalism, doesn't it? Yes, and you're right.

Freefallers burn outlines and refuse to draft others. They scorn thinking before writing. They run wildly wherever their thoughts take them and never look back until the writing is done. Self-imposed censors on creativity are driven off at gunpoint.

Freefall is a writing method that frees a writer's creativity. The phrase was probably first coined by W.O. Mitchell, author of *Who Has Seen The Wind* and other Prairie stories. Freefall gained academic grace when it became the writing method used at the Banff School of Fine Arts. But a true freefaller, doesn't give whit (not a typo) whether the method is accepted at academic institutions or extolled by English instructors. Better that it should seem slightly rebellious and outside the accepted horizons of academia.

The amazing thing about freefall is it is so easy to practice and so hard to explain. Here goes. Freefall is sitting down and writing. Not thinking about writing, not sharpening pencils, learning a word processing package, or making detailed outlines to guide writerly thoughts. A freefaller sits down and, if well practiced at the technique, says today I write that article on franchising for *Canadian*, or today I write the first chapter of the novel I've been thinking about.

Research of the franchising article is in the bag already. The basic plot that will drive the novel's hero forward is already roughed out. There is no need to spend time beyond that initial research or plot roughing-out phase preparing to write. No need for an outline meticulously sketching each point the article will cover.

With the research in hand the freefaller sits down at a computer, typewriter, or, God forbid, a piece of paper with pen in hand and starts writing the article or story. You just start. Maybe it's not the right place (usually it will be) but what does it matter? What the freefaller is searching for by just writing down the material that comes to mind is a flow, a consistency and depth of storytelling that comes from linking with the subconscious rather than the conscious mind. The ultimate creative power a writer can tap is the subconscious and freefall is the path to that power.

This is not far out Shirley MacLaine metaphysical gibberish I'm talking here. You have all probably put a writing problem on the shelf overnight by saying, "I'll sleep on it." And in the morning, many times the answer was there just waiting. During the night while your conscious mind was dreaming about the boy or girl next door and other interesting happenings, your subconscious was busily jotting down the story that had log-jammed you the day before.

When you become an adept freefaller you don't have to spend all this time in dreamland to solve writing problems. You learn to let the subconscious have its voice during the waking hours.

And the only way to learn how to do that is to spend time freefalling. Sit down and write. If you can't do that and focus on a writing topic at the same time don't bother. Just write what comes into your mind, no matter what gibberish it may be. Don't worry about punctuation, spelling, grammatical correctness or any other linguistic niceties. Worry about images. Relax your writing pace, slow down to a crawl. Expand every image you create. Add in material from all five of your senses, so the reader can see, smell, feel, hear, and taste the image created. Don't leave one image until it is as complete as your subconscious can make it. Then move on to the next image or detail and repeat the procedure.

Eventually, and probably more quickly than you expected, you will find that you can sit down and decide what you are going to write about and the subconscious will start kicking the material you need out into your conscious mind for transposing onto paper. It's kind of eerie when this first happens. The feeling is like being a medium through which this material comes. But it is your creation. It's just that not many of us know our subconscious selves that well, so it's kind of like taking candy from a stranger when the writing comes this way.

Too many people shy away from freefall writing because it seems too easy. Writing should be harder work, they reason. It makes them feel guilty to freefall and find that writing can be (sorry William Zinsser and friends) FUN! Yes. This is true. You can write and have fun doing it.

The downside of freefalling is that when you have jumbled all these great subconscious images and details out on the paper, you are not done. At this stage you have to bully your subconscious back into that cage in the recesses of your mind and bring out the conscious mind all dressed up in its black leather tiger training outfit. Now armed with dictionaries, grammar books, assigned word counts and a long black whip, you allow the conscious trainer to rewrite and edit the material until it is as readable as it can be.

New freefallers usually find that initially the conscious has a lot of whip cracking to do to get the article pared down and structured into a workable piece. It is not uncommon for a freefall first draft to run twice the word length of that assigned. Getting the word count back under control is the conscious trainer's job; along with ensuring consistent transitions, coverage of all assigned points, good grammar and exactingly correct spelling.

With practice the subconscious and conscious tend to work together like a team, though, and the amount of reworking needed lessens until often there is virtually nothing for the trainer to do, except keep a watchful eye. At this stage the writer has become a seasoned freefaller. There is no time limit on this. For some it will happen after a few hours or weeks, others may never be able to trust their instincts sufficiently to freefall.

It all has to do with instinct. Instinct is not a conscious thing, it is something you feel and do without thinking. The freefaller instinctively trusts the mind to provide the right material to make the writing work at whatever level it is supposed to work. Once that trust is there the subconscious will provide the rest.

And this is where freefalling ceases to be simply a writing method and becomes a life approach. Many seasoned freefallers find they start living at an instinctual level. They make snap decisions. If it feels good they do it. They look to their inner selves for guidance rather than to outward authorities. They seek freedom above all else. They tend toward hedonism.

It's a wonderful way to live and write.

Mark Zuehlke has been freefalling since 1975 and still hasn't hit the ground. He is co-author of the critically acclaimed how-to-book *Magazine Writing From The Boonies* (Carleton University Press, 1992).

# Write From Life

*by Lois J. Peterson*

**A**s a teenager I spent hours writing in my journal while Bob Dylan droned on in the background. Ignoring my heavy eyelids and the gray dawn sloping through the window, I plundered my soul, exposed my nerve endings, wrung anguished words from my mind. I would have nothing of the world. I needed only solitude and isolation from which to conjure my poems, stories and long, tortured essays.

I re-read some of it lately, and it's all self-indulgent drivel. Just what you'd expect from an angst-ridden teenager.

What I didn't know then was that in order to write I had to be part of the world, not apart from it. I had to witness its follies, its idiosyncrasies. I needed to note the colour of its days and the shape of those who populated them.

What I didn't know then was that the life I had already lived was worth writing about. As a small child I had lived in the Middle East and I still carried its smells, sounds and colours inside me; I'd spent six years in boarding school, which had yielded experiences and sensations that were part of the person I had become; and through these two lives was threaded the stability of my grandmother's home in a small English village, memories of which I still use in my work.

As a teenager I didn't know that both my past and my present could provide material for my writing. Later I would be told to write what I knew, but no one told me what that might be, or how to write about it.

So I had to discover ways to access my past and my present, and only then was I able to put it in writing. Now I teach adults how to ask these same questions of themselves, and what to do with the answers. I try to show them that writers can't work in isolation from the world if they want to write convincingly about it.

I call this process "writing from life." This is not the same as writing your life story. The latter involves taking a chronological slant, a systematic view of events, experiences and relationships. Rather, you decide what material you want, then file it carefully in memory for when you need it.

In 1989 I travelled by camel in the Sinai. A camel's gait is hardly conducive to on-board note-taking and I was frustrated at not being able to record my impressions of that "great and terrible wilderness". One of my companions suggested that each night I note just six things in my journal—something I had seen, felt, touched, tasted, smelled and heard.

That evening I very briefly noted the sounds of a camel chewing an acacia bush; the light on a Bedouin's face as he crouched over his fire preparing the evening meal; the taste of the ice cream flavoured with rosewater that I had eaten at the day's rest stop; the roughness of the saddle chafing my legs at each lurch of the camel's stride; the feeling of lying under the dark desert sky, willing myself to stay awake; the smell of the fires that burned all night around me. That's all I wrote, but now, years later, these notes are enough to stimulate a hundred other sensations of that day.

This checklist works well for anyone who wants to write from life. It works well in recording details of place. See what you capture if you employ all your senses at the ball game or the bus station, the staff room or the soccer field, at your daughter's ballet class or your son's Boy Scout meeting.

Places from your past also yield good material. Write about your first bedroom. Now move through the house to the kitchen, the living room, then beyond to the back yard, to the neighbour's house and then along the street or across town to your best friend's house. If you use all your senses you may find that one memory leads to another, and the past opens like a book that has been closed for too long. Now put people in the picture. Describe who else was there, how they look, move, speak.

You can unearth rich materials from the past by developing a "lifeline." To do this you need to break down your life, or a block of it (this could be decades, a year, a month, a week) into chunks. Then, from each chunk extract the most resonant incident. Then, brainstorming your memories of this incident, make notes on the people and places you associate with it.

Employ all your senses. Describe what you see, feel, hear, smell, taste and touch. You may find that when you start looking at the past through the lens of your senses, new memories will spring to mind. Follow where they lead and soon you'll have a rich heap of incidents, sensations, sights and insights that you can use in your writing in any number of ways.

Graphically, your lifeline might look like this:

| TIME/PLACE | INCIDENT | SENSUAL TRIGGERS |
|---|---|---|
| 1962/move to Winnipeg | First room of my own. Sneaking out of my window, landing in the rhododendrons | Smell of the uncarpeted floor. Gravel underfoot. Sprinklers left on all night. Streetlight lighting hood of father's car. |
| 1967/cousins' farm for summer' | Riding the tractor Getting ducked; fear of drowning | Heat from engine and sun; dust and flies Wet swimsuit under clothes |

The fascinating thing about this approach is that each time you do it you come up with something new. You may already have explored the summer you stayed on your uncle's farm, but last time you remembered riding behind him on the tractor, and this time you recall going to the swimming hole with your cousins.

People in the present provide rich material too. If you write about someone you know well as if you were writing about them for someone who has never met them, you may discover elements of your subject's personality or appearance that you'd never noticed. How about describing something you dislike about someone you love, something appealing about someone you hate? Exercises like this broaden your ability to develop characters who are neither all good nor all bad—people who are believable.

Strangers can be a wonderful source for new characters. I use a caricature approach to describe people I glimpse on the street, in the library, at the bank. I imagine that with just a few concise pen strokes I have to make an accurate rendering of that person. Do they have bushy eyebrows? Bright lipstick? Are their pants too short? Do they limp, swing their arms when they walk, or hold them tight to their sides? Are they carrying a diaper bag, a briefcase, a walking stick?

Later I'll imagine what kind of toothpaste they use. Do they use skim milk or cream in their coffee? Who's their best friend? Where do they go on holiday? Do they like dogs? Before long, what began as a brief glimpse of a stranger in real life becomes a fully-rounded character in fiction.

Good listening skills are important for writers. We need to hear real conversation to write good dialogue (with some adjustments for all the repetition, unfinished sentences, etc., that we use in real life). Restaurants, movie line-ups, bus stops and grocery store check-outs are just a few places that provide great eavesdropping opportunities. People say all kinds of things that can generate ideas for fiction, poetry, even essays. Passing a group of teenagers at a bus stop, I heard one say, "I don't know shit about fascism. I just wing it." A man on a radio documentary about wild bird enthusiasts told his interviewer, "A number of my marriages have come to grief on account of my birding." And one night in his sleep my husband said, "What are you going to do with the chicken afterwards?" (I'm still wondering, after what?)

Someone who writes from life needs to keep both eyes open. A small incident can become an image that prompts a poem, a metaphor or theme for a story, a germ of an idea for a non-fiction piece. I once watched an elderly woman cross a busy intersection. Her hair was the texture and color of shredded wheat. She wore too-short cotton pants and cheap runners with no socks, and she walked with her hands jammed in her pockets, her eyes lowered to watch the road in front of her. When she reached the other side I noticed that her hands, now freed from her pockets, were shaking badly. My friend, who had also been watching the woman's progress, told me that alcoholics often keep their hands hidden to hide the shakes, and that older people like to keep their hands free in case they fall. That image, and that woman's dilemma, has haunted me for years and will, I'm sure, turn up in my writing one day.

Slighter incidents are worth noting too. Seeing a man in a wheelchair prompted me to wonder whether disabled people dream about walking, or flying. One day I witnessed a surrealistic scene in which a man wrestled what appeared to be a huge soap bubble along the street. (A little further along was his pickup truck, in the back of which was the base of one of those giant bubble gum dispensing machines.) The man-wrestling-killer-bubble image will come in handy one day, I'm sure.

Learn to pay attention to other people's stories as well as your own. Ask questions. Stay alert for the punchline. What happens to the friend of a cousin's friend, or what they've seen or heard, can be just as useful and stimulating as what's happened to you.

Every day we are surrounded by radio and TV reports, fillers in newspapers, and classified ads that, if we attend closely, can provide wonderful quotations, germs of ideas for fiction, starting points for articles and issues for discussion in essays. These too are part of your life, as much as all those things you've experienced at first hand.

So what do you do with all these sights, scenes, sounds and sensations? You need to develop a system to record them and the discipline to work with them. Don't rely on your memory. What seemed compelling one minute can easily be sent packing by what you notice next.

I always carry two notebooks. In the smallest, my "commonplace" book, I record brief snippets of conversation, sightings, thoughts, etc., for exploring later. I use a larger notebook for longer work and for developing ideas recorded in the commonplace book. I might grab a few minutes when waiting for the dentist or on a coffee break to do some descriptive writing, write a caricature, test a few lines for a poem, develop some dialogue. One writer I know keeps an index card and pen in the pocket of her jacket at all times, just in case inspiration strikes when she's out walking the dog or running to the store for a quart of milk, or on any other occasion when she has no other notebook with her.

Once you've worked out your own system for keeping track of all this rich material, you'll want to develop a way to organize and review it so you can retrieve it when you need to. You might want to keep files of material that has been generated by one of your sensory triggers—sight, sound, taste, touch, smell. You might have an idea how you will use what you've recorded and so organize your files by genre. Perhaps you'll want to keep newspaper clippings, quotations, notes on stories recounted to you by other people in a separate file.

So now you've trained your eyes and ears; you have a way to record your thoughts and impressions; you've organized them so you can retrieve them when you need to. A further discipline to develop is that of working with this material, looking at it from all sides and deciding what it is that you have growing on your compost heap and what you can do with it. I recommend to my students that, apart from their other planned work, they set aside two short periods a week (from twenty to forty minutes each) to work with the serendipitous material they've gathered.

The more you train yourself to be an observer of your own life, the more you'll find to note, record and use. And sometimes, something that you've only noted in passing will become embedded in your psyche. You'll dwell on it for days, weeks, months, then one day you'll sit down to work to find that your creative mind is ready to build upon it.

Then you know that you are truly writing from your life, and your work will ring with the authenticity of your experience and your voice.

Lois J. Peterson teaches students to write from life through Continuing Education classes in Surrey, British Columbia, and to inmates at the Corrections Canada Matsqui Institute. She also uses these methods in her own fiction, poetry and nonfiction. She has developed an on-line writing workshop on the Web at <http://mindlink.net/summit/welcome.htm>.

# Be a Truth Writer

*by Gordon E. Symons* _____

I am a fiction writer.

I am a published writer, having sold an average of one article a month. But I am not yet a published fiction writer. Yet I believe that writing fiction has made me a successful writer of non-fiction. I also believe the writing of essays and articles has increased my chance of success in the highly competitive fiction markets.

For many years I wrote fiction exclusively: three novels, one novella, one screen script, thirty-nine short stories, eleven short-shorts. My stories went off to magazines aimed at men, women, children, teens and seniors. Zilch. My novels bounced from book publisher to book publisher while I went to college to study creative writing. More zilch. I joined a writers' group. I attended writers' conferences.

At the University of Indiana Arthur Hailey said, "Gordon, the first chapter of your novel needs to go in the trash bin. No one cares what you saw or thought on a train trip to Toronto. I like the next couple of chapters, though." He gave me a letter of introduction to his publisher. I rewrote the book and submitted it but later received a standard rejection slip.

A couple of years ago I was ready to quit. Obviously, I thought, I have no talent. Only a stupid person, having diligently served a long apprenticeship without finally becoming a craftsman, would continue. I would not be the literary equivalent of a tone-deaf singer who remains in the choir, an unknowing embarrassment to all. In the middle of a harsh Canadian winter I gave up. As the howling wind blasted snow against the window of my den, I yanked the dust cover over my battered Smith-Corona for the final time.

It did not feel good. I could not get in the mood to take up macramé. I enjoyed reading, but the more I read the more I had the urge to write again. I was absolutely certain, however, that it would be impossible to once again endure the unrelieved rejection of my work . A few mornings after my surrender I was in my den at five a.m. (habits die hard). Outside it was below freezing. The shrill wind screeched still. With a cup of boiling-hot black coffee in one hand and my summer journal in the other I sank into my shabby La-Z-Boy, searching for something—anything.

My wife and I are boaters and I read my daily accounts of a journey we'd made around Lake Huron: up the Canadian side, under the bellies of Manitoulin and Mackinac Islands and down the American side. My notes described the state of the water; the harbors, good and bad; the unique features of dockside towns and the interesting people we'd met. I'd taken pains to record colors and smells; things we'd tasted and touched; our feelings. I'd also taken color slides, having found it helpful in the past to recreate a scene by seeing it again on a large screen.

I started a story with a marine setting, the only way I could think to make use of my material. Three pages later I abandoned it. Next I tried to outline a novel. I knew it would be rejected. I'm not sure why I did what I did next. I may not have even known at the time what I was doing, but I wrote an article. I used the fiction techniques I'd learned—to write the truth.

I told what happened to my wife and me, trying to lift the reader onto the boat with us: bracing against bulldozer waves, inhaling the crisp clean smell of lake water, shuddering at the sight of dark rocks ahead. I used plenty of dialogue. Then I selected a dozen transparencies, packaged them with what I'd written (I hesitate even now to call it an article) and mailed everything to the local newspaper. It appeared as a feature on the front page of the travel section and a few days later I received a cheque for $300. Finally I was a writer. I *did* possess some measure of talent.

As the thrill began to wear off, however, I began worrying that this had been too easy. Determined to discover whether I'd just been the beneficiary of a divine accident, I decided to try the process once again. I subscribe to *Canadian Yachting*. Each issue contains a "Cruise Guide." Basically, someone who has been someplace in a boat describes how he got there and what he found when he arrived. Armed with my journal, my navigation charts and the log book from our cruise, I wrote a guide— a true account of the trip my wife and I had experienced the summer before—and sent it off to the magazine. Not long afterward I received a cheque for $800.

At this point I was able to begin writing fiction again, my confidence restored. I was, after all, a twice-published writer: a paid storyteller.

Following another string of fiction rejections, I hammered out—in one sitting—a short piece on Loran-C, an electronic location-identification device we'd installed on our boat. It brought an immediate cheque for $219 from *Canadian Boating* and a phone call from the editor asking if I could possibly do another article on radar. I did—it took two sittings for this one—and received another $270.

My next fiction rejection slip from *Saturday Evening Post* included a handwritten note: "I really enjoyed the style and the plot. The crying kid was a bit much. Thanks for the story." A month later *Esquire* sent back another effort and scribbled "Thanks for the look" on the rejection. The editor of *My Weekly* returned a manuscript and enclosed a letter. "Your story is nicely written," he wrote, "However we feel the plot is rather too predictable to suit our style. I shall be pleased to consider any other material you may care to send along."

Progress. Not payment, but progress. I'd applied fiction techniques: description, characterization and dialogue, to articles. They had sold. Now I considered the reverse: what had I learned marketing non-fiction that I might be able to apply to fiction? I'd counted the words in magazine articles and produced no more or less for my submissions. I'd noted if they were long or short words in long or short paragraphs and replicated the pattern. I had not tried to sell a boating piece to a dog-lover's magazine. I wrote about subjects I knew and loved.

I'm sixty-plus. I may not exactly love being old but I know about it, so I selected *Discovery*, "The Lifestyle Magazine for Mature Canadians." I wrote a story the correct length, whose protagonist was the correct age, facing a problem I knew concerned "mature" adults. The editor replied, "I truly enjoyed 'The Other Stars' but cannot purchase it." She pleaded tight budgets and space allocations.

The day I received that letter I sat down and wrote a piece I titled, "Some Day." It was the same length, had a protagonist the same age and dealt with a similar problem. It displayed the same writing style and *Discovery* purchased it within a week, paying on acceptance. The *Ottawa Citizen* has since reprinted it. The difference: my second piece was true.

Since then I've sold essays, editorials, travel pieces, trade articles and general articles to newspapers and magazines in Canada and the United States. The interesting fact for me is that my foray into the world of non-fiction has helped, not hindered, my fiction. I write more stories now than ever before. I get notes from editors regularly, and recently won second prize in a local fiction contest. The research I do for fiction prompts dozens of article ideas, and the people I meet while digging for article facts often pop up in my stories.

There is one other thing I've learned from writing articles: editors and readers are interested in the truth. My fiction rejection-slips began garnering editor's comments only after I began generously lacing my stories with the truth: people, places, events and feelings I knew about. I no longer think of myself as a fiction writer. The term is too limiting. There is no limit, however, to writing about what is true.

I am a truth writer.

Gordon E. Symons, a former business executive, retired to write fiction and non-fiction from his home in Ailsa Craig, Ontario.

# Write on the Side

*by Mark Kearney* ────────────

I thought it would be an easy request to fill. The writing organization to which I belong, the Periodical Writers Association of Canada, had sent a letter to members asking for submissions for an anthology it wanted to produce. We were to comb our files for articles, essays or feature stories we had written that could be included in what was to be something of a *Best of PWAC* book. They were to reflect the Canadian spirit in any form possible and were to be able to stand the test of time.

I liked the idea of such an anthology and quickly sent off a first person story I had written about trying to trade hockey cards to merchants on the streets of Russia, where I had recently been on a trip.

I sent it knowing it wasn't the greatest story I'd ever written, but one that seemed to fit the bill. It was distinctively Canadian, humorous, and could probably hold up over time. I didn't think much about it until the anthology committee sent out another request saying that what they had received so far was okay, but that they really could use more samples.

Judging from some of the other stories submitted, I got the impression they were looking for the crème de la crème of non-fiction magazine and newspaper writing. The stories that make you think, that move you in some way. That don't just provide a laugh or two and/or are run-of-the-mill informative articles that are often so much junk food for the brain.

I dug out my scrapbooks again and looked through virtually every story I had written as a full-time freelance writer. I've been doing it full-time for four years and have been a journalist of one sort or another for more than 16. Surely I'd find something.

Wrong. In my years of full-time freelancing I couldn't find one article I felt worthy of submitting. The ones that did have a bit of spark were unfortunately dated. I write steadily for several different magazines and newspapers and like most full-timers support that income with government and corporate writing and some teaching. And yet because I was more concerned with deadlines and paying bills, it hit me that I had been taking on routine assignments, doing the best job I could, but ultimately churning something out and getting onto the next job.

Don't get me wrong. I like being successful enough to made a full-time living from my writing. It's one of the perks of the job that other people envy. Being able to live exclusively off your writing is the dream of thousands of would-be writers everywhere.

But now I envy the part-timers, the people who "do it on the side." It's unfortunate that in today's economy most full-time freelance writers seem to be caught in the same trap. One colleague told me ruefully that the most exciting thing she had written in the past year was a brochure for a printing company. No wonder the anthology organizers are having trouble getting enough submissions. We're all too busy going after the higher paying writing jobs instead of the magazine work that, on average, pays much less. And forget about fiction. When you're sitting in front of a computer screen most of the day to make money, the last thing you feel like doing at night is sitting there trying to write something else.

Because we're doing this to make a living, it makes writing very much a business like any other. No matter how much we might love it, we still have to do the work to pay the bills, keep up our stock of office supplies, and have complete records so we know what we can and can't deduct come tax time. And while there's no escaping these realities of the "business" of writing, it's a shame that something we all love is sometimes only done to help pay off a mortgage or allow us to maintain the lifestyle we've chosen.

Having to write something out of necessity often draws us away from the kind of writing we really want to do or the kind of commitment we want to make. For example, you want to spend weeks or months on a particular subject you feel strongly about for a magazine, but find the pay so poor that it makes no economical sense to pursue it. Out goes the impassioned idea; in its place is the quick, not-too-much-bother writing job that pays well enough and is easily completed. Is this why we got into the profession in the first place? Is this why you want to be a full-time writer?

Consider the opening of a typical article written during my years as a full-time freelancer. "A stroll in the garden can be made even more pleasant by the paths you build there. Walkways are essential to any landscape plan and should complement the look of your backyard."

Nothing wrong with that. It was a how-to article on building different kinds of walkways in your yard. I got paid about $500 and learned more than I'll probably ever use about interlocking brick, gravel and flagstone.

Interesting, maybe, factual and informative, yes. But would you read something like that in a book that's supposed to include the best of periodical writing? Is this what I would show family and friends if they asked me what I've been writing lately?

Now consider an essay on whether we as a society are becoming more easily bored than previous generations, an article I wrote a few years back when I was freelancing on the side. I interviewed several experts, quoted from *The Rolling Stones* and *Winnie the Pooh*, and most importantly, spent time reflecting on the subject.

Halfway through the article I wrote "We live in an age where social change seems to be measured in days rather than decades, where trends are passé by the time most of us realize they're trendy, where today's fashion is literally next season's bargain bin. There's an underlying restlessness that picks at people, giving them a feeling that if they stay too long in one job or one relationship, they'll miss something. That maybe the grass is greener."

You probably won't find that kind of philosophizing in an article about walkways.

I didn't just churn this story out; I thought about what I wanted to say, constructed the story so that anecdotes flowed from each other and reflections supported the main theme. I wrote it, rewrote it, rewrote it again, and polished it some more before submitting it. In short, a story that I had to work at, think about and on which I could afford to spend time.

The deadline was still there, but I had a regular salary coming in. When I worked on this story I felt I could take more time to research it because I didn't have the spectre of a mortgage payment depending on it or another two or three assignments to juggle.

I could craft the words until I was completely satisfied. So what if I spent the equivalent of a week or two on it for $400—it was more a labour of love than a pay cheque.

So what does this mean for aspiring part-timers who want to make the jump to full-time. A few years ago I would have immediately said "Jump. Follow your dream and see what happens." And there's a part of me that still believes that—after all I'm still doing it full-time. But if you're happy doing it on the side, why not stay there. In fact, in the past year I've been telling students in my "Writing for Fun and Profit" course to think seriously about doing it on the side instead of full-time. You have more flexibility in picking and choosing your topics. You're not worrying so much about where the money is coming from and how much it will be; you can give the story your full attention and handle it with loving care.

The myth of full-time freelancing is that you can do whatever you want whenever you want. "Oh, I'd love to do what you do," my non-freelance friends say. "If you don't feel like working you don't have to. You can write anything you want."

I can hear the laughter of full-time writers everywhere. But laughter sprinkled with a few tears. Sure, there's a small element of that kind of freedom, but the more likely scenario is the editor who calls up to ask if you'll do a 700-word article on franchising or a 1000-word how-to feature with a sidebar on renovating kitchens. Even if the only thing you know about franchises has been gleaned from visiting a McDonald's, or your idea of renovating is hammering in screws, you say yes to the assignment, plunge in and do whatever is "good enough" to get published and nothing more.

You'd love to spend more time and write the pants off these subjects, researching them, crafting each word. But you can't afford to. You want to get it done as quickly as you can so that the cheque will soon follow (well, that's another myth, but I digress).

The demands of full-time freelancing, the organization it takes, the planning and the scrambling all work against why we do this job in the first place—we have a passion for writing. And if you do, too, and don't mind being someone on the sidelines who joins the fray occasionally, your passion may last a lot longer.

Who knows, I just may head for the sidelines myself.

Mark Kearney has been a journalist for 20 years and has published hundreds of articles in some 40 magazines and newspapers in North America. His latest book, *The Great Canadian Trivia Book*, was published in 1996. He lives in London, Ont.

# Edit Your Own Words

*by Bruce O. Boston*

Peter Drucker, the management consultant, has a reputation for calling them the way he sees them. Writers can learn something from Drucker, who refers to his first draft as "the zero draft." His reasoning is that he is entitled to start counting only after he gets something down on paper.

Everyone who writes seriously knows that the real work begins only after there is something to work on. Beginners think to themselves, "If I come up with a great idea, it can carry me." Wrong. Even the noblest of ideas, the most absorbing of themes, can be twisted out of shape in the hands of a careless craftsman; but, in the loving hands of a master like Annie Dillard, even so prosaic a thing as the description of an anthill or a leaf can dazzle.

Good writing is mostly rewriting. Anthony Burgess said he might revise a page as many as twenty times. Short-story writer Roald Dahl states that by the time he nears the end of a story, the first part will have been reread and corrected as many as one hundred fifty times. If memory serves, Hemingway claimed to have rewritten the final chapter of *A Farewell to Arms* thirty-nine times.

There is nothing particularly praiseworthy in this; it is simply a fact of life for people who care about language, or more to the point, about getting things right. If you want to be a pianist, you practice. If you want to be a runner, you train. If you want to write, you rewrite. But editing yourself is hard to do, mostly because writers are easily seduced by their own prose. The editorial act must therefore be a deliberate infliction of pain, a conscious and vigorous assent to the proposition well expressed by magazine writer Bil Gilbert: "Writing is essentially weeding out your own stupidity."

There are tools that writers can use to improve their work. The first is the axe. It should be laid to the root of entire paragraphs—those that don't belong, that belabor the obvious, or that add just enough detail to distract the reader instead of providing essential information. I often find, on rewriting, that an entire paragraph can be distilled into a phrase, or sometimes even a word, which can be added to a preceding or following paragraph. The result is a piece that becomes more taut, and taut is better than slack.

Second is the pruning hook. This is the tool that inflicts the most pain, because the pruning hook is best applied to the turns of phrase we most admire. Disagreeable as it is, writers would do well to follow the advice of novelist Nancy Hale, who counsels excising the language you believe most clever, most apt, most apposite. Her perfectly sound reasoning is that writers wouldn't admire their own words so much if they weren't protecting them. (No mother believes her baby is ugly!)

Pruning writing is the same as pruning apple trees: the point is not so much to get rid of the dead branches (which are easy enough to spot) as it is to shape the tree to produce the best possible fruit. This can involve cutting off live limbs, which may be beautiful in themselves, but bad for the whole tree in light of its purpose. Unpruned writing, like an unpruned tree, wastes its natural energy.

Third, is the Exacto knife, a tool as essential to self-editing as it is to doing paste-up. Use it to attack the manuscript phrase by phrase and word by word: Is this verb the best possible one? Does this analogy work? Is this metaphor the right one? Isn't that phrase really too threadbare to use? As a precision instrument, the Exacto knife is well designed for the surgical removal of such minute blemishes as the misplaced comma and the superfluous adverb.

Finally, one of the tools of self-editing most often neglected by even the most careful writers is the metronome. Its job is to measure out the cadence of the writer's words. James J. Kilpatrick recommends (in *The Writer's Art*) that writers who wish to master cadence write verse. This does not mean writing free verse—which Robert Frost once likened to playing tennis with the net down—but verse with rhyme schemes and meter: sonnets, rondeaux, villanelles, haiku. The poetry doesn't have to be good; it just has to be workmanlike. Sound out the sentences. Unless writers want their words to march across the page with all the discipline of the Keystone Cops, they need to pay attention to cadence.

When does this process end, if at all? Any good piece of writing can be ruined by too much tinkering, but, as Tolstoy observed, "I scarcely ever read my published writings, but if by chance I come across a page, it always strikes me: all this must be rewritten; this is how I should have written it." The real writer is never satisfied because every piece, if it is done right, is still full of potential the moment it is finished.

So, the short answer is that the process never ends; the clock merely runs out, and the time comes to tear the paper from the typewriter or print the word-processing file and press it into the hands of the next editor. Each piece must be sent off the way the girl back home sends her young soldier off to war, with a heart that longs for just one more day, hour, minute.

Bruce O. Boston is a columnist, book author and editorial consultant. He operates Wordsmith Inc., from a base in Reston, Virginia. He is a former editor of *The Editorial Eye* newsletter and author of *Language on a Leash*.

# Understand the Editor

*by Mark Leiren-Young* ——————————————

I was an editor once. Briefly.

I'd always wondered what it would be like, and the title appealed to me, so when I was approached with the offer of becoming "associate editor" of a new entertainment magazine, I took the plunge.

To be honest, I didn't have much in the way of editorial powers and I didn't last long (believe it or not, I missed the freedom of freelancing), but I did find out some startling things during my brief walk on the red-pencil side.

The first lesson was about waiting. Much to my surprise, writers were perpetually late with stories. Tensions would build as I started to wonder if I was going to have to instantly whip up some filler to cover two pages of blank space that was being held for some freelancer's opus. At times I actually tried to convince the editor to turf good writers because no matter how sparkling their prose, it wasn't worth the weekly drama of panicky phone calls to their answering machines, asking if and when the story would arrive. I had my own work to do. I didn't need to be stuck pounding out a last-minute replacement for something that had been assigned three months earlier.

When stories did arrive, most not only needed to be edited, many of them needed to be proofread. I was stunned when work by writers I admired arrived with sloppy pages of copy and even sloppier typos. One writer insisted in submitting her material in pencil with EVERYTHING WRITTEN IN CAPITAL LETTERS. I had to decipher this stuff and input it into the computer. Her work was interesting but if the boss had let me I would have burned each submission.

Work was often loaded with typos—and a frightening amount of it usually needed tidying up in more important areas, too. Stories would be overwritten or lacking some crucial detail, such as the first name of a major interview subject.

Now, as associate editor, I wasn't the one who did most of the tidying, but I did get to see the red-pencil marks through the works of some of my favorite writers—writers I had always imagined turned in flawless prose. There were some longtime pros who desperately needed someone to get them a word processor with a "speller" program for Christmas. The real problem wasn't just spelling, though, as much as the feeling that the moment the writers had banged out the last letter on the page, they clearly figured their job was done. They'd written it—someone else could clean it up.

Before my brief stint at editorship, I had assumed it was simple professionalism to make sure you turned in clean copy on time. If I'm ever going to be late with a story I call and apologize profusely—giving as much advance warning as humanly possible. The one time that I missed a deadline (I somehow mixed up the due date of a story) I apologized, groveled, and spent the weekend contemplating *hara-kiri*. I had lost face, dishonored myself, screwed up real bad. I figure that's how a writer ought to feel if he misses a deadline.

To me, deadlines frequently mean staying up late the night before and pounding out the prose until the story is ready. And "ready" has always meant after I've read a story at least two or three times, generally aloud, so that if there is a typo or some bit of poor phrasing I'll catch it myself. If something isn't quite right I keep at it. It never occurred to me to intentionally leave in an awkward passage in the hope that an editor would know what to do with it.

I hate being edited so I try to make it as difficult for the editor as possible. If I'm asked for 750 words, I aim for 750 words—maybe a handful more for good measure. When I've typed the last line of a story I relax for a few minutes, but then I check it out as carefully as possible. If there's a typo in the published version, I want it to be the typesetter who screwed up the spelling. If there's a mistake, I want it to be the editor's fault because he cut something he shouldn't have. Although I know there are editors who won't rest until they fiddle with each story they receive, no matter how flawless it may be, I see no reason to encourage them to edit with an ax.

Now, complaints about late stories and sloppy copy are editorial clichés, but I wasn't looking at these problems as a harassed editor. I felt like a freelance writer on a reconnaissance mission inside enemy territory. So instead of moaning about the lack of quality writers and how tough an editor's lot is, I pondered these clichés-come-true from a free-lancer's perspective. My conclusion made me feel pretty cocky: if you can deliver a clean copy of the story you promised, on time, editors will love you.

See, I also made one other major discovery while I was on the other side of the fence—editors have a lot of things they'd rather do than fix writers' mistakes.

Mark Leiren-Young is a screenwriter, playwright, journalist and performer. In addition to extensive TV and stage credits, his humorous commentaries have been featured in such publications as *The Hollywood Reporter*, *The Toronto Star* and *The Vancouver Sun* and are heard on CBC radio. Mark is the writer for the new CBC TV variety series *Terminal City*.

# Block Breakers

*by Ishbel Moore* _____

t's freezing! I'm standing half-way up a hill trying to decide what to do. People, mostly children and teenagers are zooming by on snow-racers, toboggans, snow boards and garbage can lids. They're having so much fun. I get a kick out of watching them but I'm not having nearly as much fun as they are—obviously.

"Come on!" they urge as I reach them, at last, at the top. The winter wonderland below is picture perfect.

"Oh, no," I say. "I want to but I couldn't. I haven't been on a toboggan for years. I'm too afraid I'd hit someone or some tree."

"Nah! You just stick out your foot or fall off," explains one very patient acquaintance. "You've gotta try. It's no fun just standing here on the sidelines."

"Well, maybe later," I add and turn away to help my three kids align themselves on the long wooden toboggan. Inside my head and heart little voices are reprimanding me. *Coward. Boring. Wimp!*

I give the toboggan a hearty push and watch the gaily coloured hats, shaped like jester caps and dragon tails, bouncing as the kids squeal and laugh all the way to the bottom. Oh, what fun! *What are you? A spectator or a participant?*

It dawns on me—the similarity between this tobogganers block and writers block. I haven't, so far, touch wood (other than toboggans), suffered from the latter. But, if it feels anything like the former, then I sympathize. No amount of urging, fast talking or reassurance is going to get me to hurtle down that hill on a plank until I'm ready. No amount of urging, fast talking or reassurance is going to get someone with writers block to create until they are ready.

So, standing here, frowning, in the freezing wind, I figure it's ironic. I've been known to pace up and down in front of beginning or experienced writers in the darkest throes of despair and indecision and tell them in no uncertain terms that writers block simply doesn't exist unless you let it exist. On the top of this hill, people are telling me, in different words or with eloquent facial expressions, that tobogganers block doesn't exist unless I let it.

What my acquaintances and kids, and you, don't know is my toboggan history. Once, in the not-so-distant past, I chose the BIG hill less tobogganed. Against advice, I plunged downward over hillock and past bushes, screaming all the way. Over the river bank I flew only to land on a mound of frozen muck with coccyx-crunching force. Let me simply say that I crawled, (yes, on my belly) to the nearby farmhouse, and sat on cushions for the next two weeks suffering excruciating ridicule in silence.

And that sensation of pain is not so different from receiving your first rejection letter which could lead to a nasty writers block. It just hits in a different part of the anatomy and becomes ego crunching and confidence busting. It's easy to turn away, let the darkness engulf you and when someone says you've got to try again, you answer "Well, maybe later."

The jesters and dragons and parents have returned, panting, faces red with cold and exertion, grinning from ear to frozen ear. They don't bother to ask me this time if I want to join them. One hands me the rope and says, "If you're just gonna stand there, hold this till we get on. Then give us a good push."

My eyebrows shoot up as the arrow hits home. Indignantly, I snarl, "Step aside!"

Gulp! I wriggle into place behind a jester and a dragon. Should I close my eyes? Change my mind? Too late! The mighty shove on my shoulder blades forces the toboggan to fly and my scream to escape. Snow sprays my face. We're almost sideswiped by a snow racer. We topple sideways at the end. I lie at the edge of a snowdrift, staring at the blue sky. Triumph! What a weight is lifted from me. I reckon I've beaten my self-inflicted tobogganers block.

And now I'm writing about it. Do you see a connection here? Of course, you do. Sometimes, you've just got to take a deep breath and do it. Write (or go tobogganing) for the fun of it. That's how many of us started. And, if I insist on equating writing with tobogganing, I guess I should end with "See all you block breakers on the slopes!"

Ishbel Moore is the author of *The Summer of the Hand*, *The Medal*, *Branch of the Talking Teeth*, and *Dolina May*, all novels for young adults. Ishbel has also won awards for her short stories. In the non-fiction field, she researched and wrote the text for the Winnipeg Philharmonic Choir's 75th anniversary publication. An active member of the Canadian Authors Association, she facilitates writing-related workshops for teens and adults throughout Manitoba.

# Work While You Sleep

*by J. A. Davidson* —————————————————

Whon you seem to have struck a dead end in a piece of writing it is often helpful to set it aside for a day, or two, or more. The subconscious part of your mind does not sleep while the rest of you does. You will often be able to deal with your writing problem after it has had time to simmer in your subconscious.

Bertrand Russell, one of the influential thinkers of this century and one of its better writers of clear, effective prose, said this about his methods in writing:

"The unconscious can be led to do a lot of useful work. I have found, for example, that if I have to write upon some rather difficult topic the best plan is to think about it with very great intensity—the greatest intensity of which I am capable—for a few hours or days, and at the end of that time give orders, so to speak, that the work is to proceed underground. After some months I return consciously to the topic and find that the work has been done."

Yes, "some months"—or some weeks or days, or, at times, merely overnight. This suggests why many writers like to have several projects underway, in varying degrees of development, at any one time. Some articles are in the process of creation for long periods—for instance, this one.

E. M. Forster, the distinguished novelist, said that inspiration is "the subconscious stuff that comes up in the bucket." Then he commented, "In the creative state a man is taken out of himself. He lets down as it were a bucket into his subconscious, and draws up something which is normally beyond his reach. He mixes this with his normal experience, and out of the mixture he makes a work of art."

This reflects what Henry James had in mind when, in the preface to his novel *The American*, he mentioned "the deep well of unconscious cerebration." The word generally applied to this psychological phenomenon is *incubation*.

Incubation (from the latin *incubare*, to lie in or upon) pertains not only to poultry and diseases and prematurely born babies, but to a subconscious mental process. J. P. Chaplin's *Dictionary of Psychology* defines it as "a period of no activity, or apparent inactivity, in thinking during which a solution to a problem may occur." In other words, it is often better to put off until tomorrow what you are likely to botch today. Or, as one of my writing friends puts it, articles, like whiskey, should be allowed to mature.

Slowly, and after many fumbles, I learned how incubation works. After I have selected a theme and collected materials and developed a tentative outline, I quickly write a first draft which in most cases is merely a bundle of notes. Then I put the whole thing into a mental "pot" and let it simmer for a day, or two, or more—up to a month sometimes. I have found that sometimes it helps, shortly after I have quit work for the day (or the night), to read—generally aloud—the draft on which I have bogged down, along with any related notes.

Jules-Henri Poincaré, a French mathematician, physicist and philosopher of science, described how incubation worked for him, although he did not use that term. He had been working, with little success, on an important problem in mathematics. One evening he drank black coffee before going to bed. During the restless night that followed he had a strange, dreamlike experience. Ideas crowded one another in his restless mind. He said that he seemed to be a spectator seeing several "hooked atoms" combining and recombining in one pattern after another.

In the morning, despite little deliberate effort by him, the solution to his problem emerged. Then, after two hours of hard work, he was able to set down the proof he had been seeking.

Out of this and similar experiences Poincaré set down his pattern for creative thinking:

First, a period of conscious and conscientious work is undertaken—assembly of data, definition of the problem, a few attempts at solution.

Second, the unconscious is allowed to take over. The problem is neglected for a time, left to simmer below the level of conscious concern. Eventually a hypothesis emerges into the consciousness. Poincaré held that this hypothesis has esthetic properties of a kind, which he saw as a clue to its soundness. The psychology of this is not quite clear, but a period of incubation does seem essential in the creative process.

Last, the hypothesis is carefully formulated. This provides merely a hint or a direction to be followed, not a final result.

Poincaré gave this warning: "The unconscious work is not possible or in any case fruitful, unless it is first preceded and then followed by a period of conscious work."

A final example of incubation is from the diaries of the English diplomat and writer Harold Nicolson: "I wake up at six to find the plan of my book has suddenly become quite clear during the night. This is unconscious cerebration. All yesterday I was feeling so stupid and inert."

I must confess that, in my retirement, I have been known to use the term incubation to dignify my laziness and justify my procrastination. But when I am truly bogged down, it is to the incubation technique that I turn for real help.

J. A. Davidson, a retired minister of The United Church of Canada, lives in Victoria, B.C.

# Hypnosis for Writers

*by Bryan M. Knight* ⎯⎯⎯⎯⎯⎯⎯⎯⎯⎯⎯⎯⎯

I f you're looking for a way to stop dreaming about writing and actually write, here's a simple technique: hypnosis. Since hypnotic capacity is biologically built in, you have already experienced hypnosis. It's like daydreaming: concentrated use of your imagination. Why not harness that talent to produce?

You can develop your hypnotic talent on your own or with the guidance of a competent hypnotherapist. Hypnosis can help writers to fight writer's block, generate ideas, improve concentration, end procrastination, increase motivation, enrich characterization, or deal with rejection.

### Writer's Block.

The writer stares helplessly at a blank sheet of paper, or at the empty eye of a computer. Writer's Block is about fear. Fear of failure or fear of success. Either is paralyzing. Neither is necessarily conscious. But both failure and success are excused if the writer refrains from committing words to paper or screen. (The writer has not really "failed" because the work is not finished; he or she has postponed success because there's nothing to judge).

Hypnosis can be used either in advance of a Block or during one. Hypnosis can conquer the Block in several ways:

• by getting to the root cause
• by post-hypnotic suggestion
• by imaginative destruction.

In hypnosis, the writer can delve into his or her subconscious to uncover the underlying reason(s) for the Block. These are legion. Typical would be a fear of failing as the writer's father failed, or conversely, fear of succeeding because this would signify outstripping the father. Another deep cause could be the fear of rejection. There might even have been a long-forgotten traumatic incident of a teacher scoffing at the writer when he or she was a child, and saying something like, "You're hopeless, Jimmy, you'll never learn how to write properly." Yet another cause could be the fear of being judged.

Getting to the cause via hypnosis is best done with the aid of a competent hypnotherapist. The therapist will then help the writer deal with that cause in a constructive way.

With or without delving into the cause, post-hypnotic suggestions are an ideal way to program oneself to write. These are simply positive suggestions the writer gives to herself while in hypnosis.

Conceiving of the Block as an object or symbol of some kind, and then destroying it while the writer is relaxed in hypnosis, is yet another way to overcome Writer's Block.

### Generate Ideas.

The well-worn advice to "sleep on it", when you are confronted with a tough problem, really means "prime your subconscious." And so it is with hypnosis. Instead of drifting off to sleep, you drift into hypnosis. You could have asked your subconscious for ideas, or just let yourself flow with whatever it pops into your conscious mind.

Ideas for nonfiction books or articles or for fictional plots and sub-plots—in fact, for anything to do with writing—can also be discovered by using the House of Ideas or the Wise Author in the Forest imagery.

The House of Ideas is an imaginary house which you explore while in hypnosis. You may do this on your own, or with the guidance of a hypnotherapist. What's inside the House is up to you. For instance, you could begin with a series of doors on which appear the names of characters in your novel, or you might imagine meeting a historian who is going to guide you into various epochs of the House, for that new history text you're writing. Or perhaps there are key documents hidden in the House which you uncover so as to make your mystery novel more complex. The possibilities are endless.

The Wise Author in the Forest is an adaptation of a popular hypnotherapy technique. Briefly, you imagine yourself in a safe, friendly forest where, in a beautiful clearing, you meet up with The Wise Author. You then ask whatever questions you wish, including a request for ideas.

Post-hypnotic suggestion can also be used to generate ideas. The most straight-forward way to do this would be to give your subconscious instruction and permission to allow ideas to pop up into your conscious mind as needed. You could also add a suggestion that ideas will come to you from a more acute awareness of your environment.

### Improve concentration.

Most of us enter a hypnotic state when we write. This applies to non-fiction writers but especially to authors of fiction. We want our readers to suspend disbelief, to enter our make-believe worlds and experience them as real as they were to us when we created them. And when we wrote, it was with concentration. Our attention was focused, our critical mind was on hold, our imagination engaged. This is hypnosis. So the more we formally practice going into such a trance, the more we develop our capacity to concentrate. Post-hypnotic suggestions and imagining ourselves (while in hypnosis) relaxed in concentration, can also be helpful.

### End procrastination.

The hypnotic approach to ending procrastination is similar to that for conquering Writer's Block: a combination of rooting out the cause and positive post-hypnotic suggestions. Just as the knowledgeable hypnotherapist talks about "discomfort" rather than "pain", you would feed yourself images and words about "doing it now", "writing immediately", "enjoying the process of writing". You would not give yourself suggestions which include the actual word "procrastination." The point is to avoid negative reinforcement.

### Increase Motivation.

Writers need motivation to write, and to sell their writing. Hypnosis can build your motivation through similar ways to those mentioned above in answer to other challenges.

Visualization in hypnosis is one of the most powerful ways to build motivation. You enter hypnosis (either with direction from a hypnotherapist, or on your own) and visualize your goal. For one writer this would be her finished book so she imagines the cover, complete with title and her name emblazoned thereon. Another writer's goal may be fame. Thus he might visualize himself on a book tour, being interviewed on television. Yet another writer's goal might be to become rich, so she would use her session of hypnosis to imagine a stack of royalties.

### Enrich Characterization.

Fiction writers go into trance when entering into their characters. This is the common experience often described as "the story wrote itself", or that "the characters say and do things which I hadn't thought of."

Relaxing into hypnosis enables you to imagine details of your character's appearance, speech and actions.

One way to use hypnosis for character development is to let yourself drift into hypnosis while becoming "absorbed" in the fictional mind of your creation. You could write the experience immediately after the hypnotic session or, if you choose to talk during the hypnosis, you could tape-record the character's activities for later transcription.

### Deal with Rejection.

Almost every writer has to face rejection. That marvelous memoir is returned with a curt refusal, or no note at all; that book outline you slaved over is turned down by a score of publishers; that novel in which you bared your soul sells only 20 copies. How can hypnosis help you deal with such hurt? By enabling you to *continue writing*.

As long as you are churning out more articles, more books, more essays, any single rejection has less power to hurt. And hypnosis helps you to generate ideas, improve concentration, end procrastination, increase motivation, and enrich characterization. It creates all those positive ions!

Incidentally, this article was written through the use of several of the hypnotic techniques mentioned within it. Additionally, I made use of the hypnagogic state just before falling asleep to prime myself with positive suggestions and images about writing worthwhile content.

Bryan M. Knight, MSW. PhD., is the author of several books, including *Love, Sex & Hypnosis: Secrets of Psychotherapy* and *Health and Happiness with Hypnosis*. More of his material can be read on his web site at <http://www.odyssee.net/~drknight/>.

# Your Social Responsibilities

*by Raymond Hull* ⎯⎯⎯⎯⎯⎯⎯⎯⎯

For the purposes of this article, I define "responsibility" as "accountability for the good or bad results of one's actions."

Responsibility also presupposes, first, the ability to discriminate between good and bad and between right and wrong and, second, the will to act, to do what is right and to avoid what is wrong.

I believe that the writer carries weighty responsibilities with his art, and for the language he uses; but here I am concerned mainly with his responsibilities toward other people.

The writer should be honest in negotiating with publishers. Whatever samples are shown should fairly represent what you will deliver in the finished work. In discussing lengths and deadlines, propose and agree to only what you know you can and will do.

"That sounds obvious," you say?

I once heard an author deliver this opening to a lecture: "I guess I *should* feel guilty! At the other side of the platform I see my publisher. Twelve months ago, I signed a contract with him to write a book. I've spent the advance; the deadline has passed by several months; and I haven't yet written the first word!"

Most of the audience—writers themselves—roared with laughter. The publisher on the platform looked somewhat embarrassed. We can imagine what he thought of the author-speaker, and of writers in general.

Another author told me she had signed a contract for a 70,000-word book on a specific subject. She delivered her typescript on schedule, but it was 60,000 words on an entirely different subject. She was quite annoyed because the publisher did not accept it!

The writer is responsible for delivering a technically sound, workmanlike product: a clean manuscript, accurate as to spelling, punctuation and grammar.

A writer once said to me, "I don't bother with all those details: the editor can put them right." True, the editor can put them right but "all those details" will lower the editor's opinion of that writer—and perhaps of writers in general.

The writer should be businesslike in dealing with publishers: that involves such things as answering correspondence promptly, putting correct postage on letters and manuscripts, and promptly correcting proofs of works that require proofreading. It also involves cheerful, active cooperation with the publisher in promoting sales of a work. Some writers won't give that cooperation, thinking it is not worth their time or that it is beneath their dignity.

Most people agree that it is wrong for a food-store to sell a product—coffee, sugar or bacon—that is short on weight. It is also wrong for a fake mail-order firm to take a customer's money and not deliver any merchandise. I suggest that it is equally wrong—indeed, it is irresponsible—for a writer to be dishonest, sloppy and un-businesslike in his dealings with publishers.

Writers—from a reader's standpoint—have two main roles: to entertain and to educate. Sometimes an author plays both roles at the same time; yet in any work, one or the other of them will predominate. So let me discuss each separately.

The fiction writer should remember that he is writing for the entertainment of the readers to whom his publisher will be offering the work. Some writers shrug off that responsibility and write instead to entertain themselves, their friends, and a little clique of critics. That is undoubtedly one reason for the present shrunken state of the short-story market.

The non-fiction writer's main purpose is to impart information. He should, of course, be honest—should tell the truth as far as he can discover it.

One author, describing her work on a British newspaper, wrote, "We used to be kind of wild... I remember interviews with people who wouldn't see me." In my judgment, "kind of wild" is a very mild description of such writing.

A few years ago I looked in on a political demonstration in Vancouver. By my count, about three thousand people were present. One newspaper reported that attendance was less than one thousand; the other said more than ten thousand!

I have heard it said that any time you have personal knowledge of a reported event, you will find the report to be wrong. This, perhaps, is an exaggeration; yet the fact that such an observation can be seriously made suggests that some of the people involved in reporting are not particularly responsible.

A writer also has an obligation not to corrupt his readers. I have heard of published books describing such things as *How to Commit Perfect Murders* or *How To Cheat On Your Tax Return.*

Such things may be true, may be interesting; yet in my judgment they should not be written. They have a poisonous influence on readers. Macaulay said of the readers of an earlier day, "From the poetry of Lord Byron they drew a system of ethics in which the two great commandments were to hate your neighbour and to love your neighbour's wife."

What if too many of us shirk these responsibilities? These results will follow:

• Publishers will increasingly turn away from dealing with freelance writers and move toward the use of staff writers.

• Readers will turn away from the printed page and drift toward the visual and sound media.

• Governments will certainly abandon the shaky tradition of a free press and will impose some kind of censorship on us and our works.

None of these things do I want to see.

Raymond Hull was the author of over a dozen books. One of his best-known works was *The Peter Principle: Why Things Go Wrong,* (New York: Morrow, 1969) co-authored with Laurence J. Peter. To quote *The Peter Principle,* "In a hierarchy every employee tends to rise to his level of incompetence."

# Libel and Slander

*by Renato M. Gasparotto* ————

The mutual trust and reliance necessary for any society to function requires that the reputations of its members be safe-guarded. Throughout history, virtually all societies have developed laws to do this.

In pre-Christian Rome, the law of the Twelve Tables mandated a beating for anyone who slandered another. Early Anglo-Saxon and Germanic laws, paralleling the Old Testament's "an eye for an eye", punished slander by cutting out the offender's tongue. Ultimately, however, the laws of defamation developed as a less violent means of settling matters of honour.

Except for Québec, Canada's legal system has its roots in English common law, that body of judge-made law developed by the courts over centuries, based on precedent rather than government statutes. (Québec's legal system has its genesis in the French civil code, based on Roman law.)

Uniquely among the world's legal systems, English common law divides defamation into two categories: libel, which covers publication in a form with some permanence, such as books or newspapers, and slander, which deals with the more transitory publication by spoken word.

The distinction arises from an accident of history, the sixteenth-century competition for power and jurisdiction between the Ecclesiastical Courts and the Star Chamber. The Ecclesiastical Courts dealt with defamation, both written and oral, as sin, imposing penance on the wrongdoer. The Star Chamber punished "libel", both written and oral, as a crime.

When the Star Chamber was abolished in 1641, the civil Courts of King's Bench inherited its jurisdiction over libel as a crime, and in 1855 the Ecclesiastical Courts lost their power to prosecute defamation as sin.

For the first time, one court had jurisdiction over all written and oral defamation. Rather than merging the two, however, the Court of King's Bench separated written and oral publications into libel and slander, respectively.

The common law's rather artificial distinction between libel and slander does not readily lend itself to an easy classification of defamation published by twentieth-century technology. For instance, are defamatory words broadcast by radio a slander or a libel? Similarly, how are words and images communicated by television to be categorized?

Under Canada's federal system, jurisdiction over property and civil rights, which includes the law of defamation, falls to the provinces, and each province and territory, except Québec, has enacted its own Libel and Slander Act, Defamation Act or territorial ordinance, incorporating the old common law with minor modifications to take account of such modern issues. Ontario's Libel and Slander Act, for instance, deems the broadcast of defamatory words, pictures, visual images, gestures and other methods of signifying meaning to constitute libel. Legislation hasn't yet caught up to the fax machine or the Internet but I would anticipate that publication of defamatory material by such means would also be seen as libel rather than slander.

Since this article is aimed principally at authors, it will concentrate on the written word.

Blasphemous libel, seditious libel and defamatory libel are, in theory at least, still considered crimes, prosecutable under the Criminal Code. Prosecutions for seditious libel were popular during World War I and the Winnipeg general strike of 1919, but have otherwise lost their appeal. Blasphemous libel, should such a prosecution be ventured today, would likely fall afoul of the Charter of Rights. Defamatory libel, however, is still very much with us.

Theoretically, defamatory libel could be prosecuted either as a crime or a civil wrong or both—the legal principles of criminal and civil libel are virtually the same. Prosecutions for criminal libel, however, are virtually unheard-of today, so this discussion will deal with libel as a civil wrong, or tort.

Unlike criminal proceedings, in which it is the state that prosecutes the accused, a civil action is essentially a private dispute between two or more individuals which is resolved publicly through the courts.

There is no all-encompassing definition of defamation. *Gatley on Libel and Slander*, the recognized bible on the subject, says that "a defamatory imputation is one to a man's discredit or which tends to lower him in the estimation of others, or to expose him to hatred, contempt or ridicule, or to injure his reputation in his office, trade or profession or to injure his financial credit."

Jeremy Williams in *The Law of Defamation in Canada* describes defamation more simply as "an invasion of the plaintiffs interest in his reputation and good name."

The reputation to be protected is not the one that the plaintiff believes he or she has, wishes he or she had or even deserves, but rather the one actually held of him or her by the community in general. Reputation is what others think of you, not what you think of yourself.

For this reason, the defamatory words, to be actionable, must be communicated (published) to at least one other person. Such publication is an essential element that must be proven by the plaintiff, unless the communication occurs in the mass media, in which case the Libel and Slander Act deems publication to have occurred, without further proof. Defamation is virtually the only cause of action where it takes more than two to tango.

Defamation is a strict liability tort. The intention of the writer or publisher has no bearing on the outcome. If the words at issue are capable of bearing defamatory imputation, liability will attach whether or not those words were intended innocently. Once published, particularly in the mass media, words take on a life of their own and their author can no longer control the meaning or meanings that may be attached to them by the reader. Unlike the tort of negligence, fault on the part of the defendant is not necessary to establish liability (except in Quebec), although fault, if found, will certainly exacerbate the damages that may be awarded.

Defamation as a cause of action is personal to the person aggrieved and may only be maintained and prosecuted by that person. The cause of action dies with the complainant, even should such death occur in mid-trial, so long as a verdict has not been rendered. It is not a cause of action that can be maintained by the deceased's heirs or executors. The corollary is that the dead cannot be defamed—but writers must take care not to convey any defamatory imputation against the deceased's family or associates.

### Elements of a libel action.

The law of defamation seeks to balance two often opposing societal interests: freedom of speech and of the press on the one hand and the importance of reputation on the other. In an action for libel, the plaintiff is required to prove:

(a) that the libelous statement has been communicated to some person other than the person of whom it is written (when published through the mass media this is presumed);

(b) that the libel refers to him or her (or it, because a corporation too has a reputation to protect); and

(c) that the statement is defamatory.

In libel law, there are essentially three types of defamatory statements:

The first is a statement that is defamatory on its face and which is obviously defamatory;

The second is a statement which contains false innuendo—words carrying an inference that possibly may be seen as defamatory only by persons possessing the necessary contextual knowledge. The particular juxtaposition of words, phrases, sentences or even paragraphs may give rise to additional meanings never intended by the author but inferred from the particular construction of the writing at issue.

The third category is the legal or true innuendo. A legal innuendo is not defamatory on its face but becomes defamatory when it is conjoined with facts or circumstances extrinsic to the article in question but known to at least some members of the audience. The innuendo may arise from the use of special language—technical terminology or slang or terms of art—which, to people who know that language, carries local meaning and conveys a defamatory imputation, although the words would not ordinarily bear that meaning.

**REVERSE ONUS:** Once the plaintiff has proven these three elements, (a), (b) and (c), the law presumes that:

(a) The statement is false;

(b) It was published with malice, that is, without an honest belief in its truth or recklessly as to its truth, or was published for some ulterior purpose; and

(c) The plaintiff has suffered damage.

These legal presumptions are often referred to as a reverse onus. Unlike virtually every other form of civil litigation, which requires the plaintiff to prove his or her case on a balance of probabilities and requires the defendant to do nothing until such proof occurs, the law of defamation deems the plaintiffs case to be proved once evidence of the three elements referred to above has been produced. Unless the defendant displaces the presumptions, the plaintiff will succeed.

This shift in onus places a heavy burden on the defendant, often requiring them to prove a negative, which may be difficult, if not impossible, to do.

## Defences.

Despite the reverse onus, a defendant in a libel action does have a number of defences available that provide a fair degree of protection. They include:

**TRUTH:** Also known as justification, truth is a complete defence to an action for libel. Malice does not negate this defence. For the defence to succeed, however, the words must be true in substance and in fact and according to their natural and ordinary meaning. The court will determine the natural and ordinary meaning to be attributed to the words in question.

**FAIR COMMENT:** This defence is available when the alleged defamatory words are expressions of opinion on matters of public interest. This defence may be lost if malice is shown. In order for such a defence to succeed, the facts being commented upon must be correctly stated or, under Libel and Slander Act modifications, substantially correct, so long as the comment is applicable to the correct facts actually proven.

The words at issue must clearly be an expression of opinion and not a statement of fact. If there is any doubt whether the statement is an expression of opinion or a statement of fact, the law will deem it to be a statement of fact. In such a case, the fair comment defence will not be available.

If, for example, one writes that a politician was seen taking money in exchange for political favours, that is a statement of fact. If it is further suggested that such is improper or dishonourable, that is a statement of opinion based on those facts. The statement of fact is libellous on its face unless it is proved in court to be true or to fall within one of the privilege defences. If the facts are true, the opinion expressed, which may also be defamatory, would be protected by fair comment. If the words that were intended as opinion referred to the conduct as "illegal" then, short of an actual charge and conviction pursuant to criminal law, such could be seen as either a statement of fact or an expression of opinion, in which case the law would presume it to be a statement of fact for which only the defence of truth or perhaps privilege would be available. Should the plaintiff not be prosecuted or not prosecuted successfully pursuant to criminal law, it would be extremely difficult for the defendant to prove that such conduct was in fact illegal.

When in doubt as to whether words are capable of being viewed as statements of fact or expressions of opinion, so-called "weasel words" may help tip the balance in favour of a finding that such is an expression of opinion. Words such as "I believe" or "it appears" or "in my view" may be sufficient to remove any such doubt.

**PRIVILEGE:** Privilege is either absolute or qualified. Absolute privilege is a creature of the common law, while qualified privilege has been largely codified and circumscribed by statute. It is the occasion upon which the communication is made that is privileged, rather than the communication itself. A privilege defence will protect the writer/publisher even when the words at issue are defamatory. The occasions when such a defence applies are those in which public policy dictates that the protection of private reputation must give way to the greater societal good.

There are only a few circumstances where absolute privilege attaches. It extends to the publication of words used in the course of traditional or legislative proceedings, statements made between executive officers of government and communications between lawyers and clients. Malice will not defeat the privilege inherent in these cases. All other forms of privilege are qualified in that they may be defeated by malice.

Qualified privilege at common law attaches to those statements made in the protection of an interest or the performance of a duty, and requires a reciprocity of duty and interest between the person publishing the statement and the person or persons receiving the statement. If published too widely, the defence is lost. As such, this defence, in its common law form, is of little or no use to authors who communicate with the public at large, except where proceedings of Parliament, the legislatures or quasi-legislative bodies are involved.

For the most part, the qualified privilege protection afforded to writers and authors is embodied in the various provincial and territorial libel and slander acts, rather than in common law. Under the Ontario Libel and Slander Act, for instance, statutory qualified privilege applies in the following circumstances:

(1) a fair and accurate report in a newspaper or broadcast of the publicly open proceedings of, or a synopsis of any report or other document issued for the information of the public by or on behalf of:

(i) any legislative body or part or committee thereof;

(ii) any administrative body constituted by any public authority;

(iii) a commission of inquiry constituted by any public authority;

(iv) any organization whose members in whole or in part represent any public authority in Canada;

(2) a fair and accurate report in a newspaper or broadcast of the proceedings of a bona fide and lawful meeting for the discussion of any matter of public concern, including a synopsis of any report, bulletin or

notice issued for the information of the public emanating from such meeting;

(3) a fair and accurate report in a newspaper or broadcast of the findings or decision of any of the following Canadian associations or any part or committee thereof relating to a member of the association or a person subject to its control:

(i) an association for promoting or encouraging the exercise of or interest in any art, science, religion or learning;

(ii) an association for promoting or safeguarding the interest of any trade, business, industry or profession;

(iii) an association for promoting or safeguarding the interest of any game, sport or pastime to which the public are invited or admitted;

(4) a fair and accurate report without comment in a newspaper or broadcast of proceedings publicly heard before a court of justice, if published contemporaneously with such proceedings. This is an absolute privilege unless the publisher refuses to publish a reasonable statement of explanation or contradiction by or on behalf of the complainant.

The statutory privileges referred to above apply only if the words written by you are published by broadcast or in a newspaper or periodical appearing "at least twelve times a year." They don't extend to other forms of writing such as books. Newspapers and broadcasters enjoy additional protections in that, in Ontario at least, any complainant wishing to sue for libel must notify the prospective defendants in writing within six weeks of discovering the libel, and must start an action within three months of discovering it. Otherwise, the limitation period for libel is six years and for slander two years, and no notice is required for either.

Additionally, a newspaper, once notice of libel is received, has the option of publishing a retraction either in the next regular issue or within three days after receipt of the notice. Should it do so, the plaintiff can then seek only actual real damages or losses, which in most cases are non-existent. This, in most cases, effectively removes the cause of action.

**CONSENT:** If it can be shown that the plaintiff consented to the publication, even generally, such a defence may succeed. A defence of consent would apply in the case of letters to the editor where a plaintiff has submitted a letter for publication and by doing so has attracted perhaps harsh replies. In such a case, the courts would likely find that having gone into the arena of public opinion the plaintiff could not then withdraw with impunity when it was no longer to his or her liking.

If a subject is interviewed either for an article or a book, and so long as full disclosure is made as to the identity of the interviewer, the purpose of the interview and the general thrust of the writing to be published, any comments or information given by the interviewee, assuming them to be accurately described, would likely give rise to a valid defence of consent should the interviewee object to what is ultimately published.

**INNOCENT DISSEMINATION:** This defence does not apply to the author or writer but is meant to apply to any person in the chain of publication who innocently and without knowledge as to the contents was involved in distributing the offending words. This defence would apply to the newspaper carrier and others who have no editorial or decision-making function in the distribution process.

## Québec.

Should your writing be distributed in Québec you should be familiar, at least in general, with the significantly different approach taken there. In Québec, defamation is treated much like any other civil wrong in that fault is required for there to be liability.

"Every person capable of discerning right from wrong is responsible for the damage caused by his fault to another," the Québec Civil Code states, "whether by positive act, imprudence, neglect or want of skill."

The plaintiff, therefore, must prove fault on the part of the defendant, prejudice to the plaintiff, and causal connection between one and the other.

Truth is not necessarily an absolute defence under Québec law, unless the defendant can also show that the defamatory publication was made with respect to a matter of public interest and without intention to cause damage.

If you are threatened with a libel action, whether in Québec or anywhere else, these standard responses are prudent:

Once the word "libel" has been uttered, listen to any further threats or demands politely, without getting angry. Don't try to defend what's been written but don't admit any fault or error on your part or anyone else's. If the complainant becomes insistent, say that in raising the issue of libel he or she has made it a legal matter on which you must consult your lawyer before taking any further action. Then do that.

Better still, don't wait until a mistake has been made. If you think that something you're writing, recording or photographing may involve a potential libel problem, consult your lawyer first. It can be a lot less expensive.

Renato M. Gasparotto is a lawyer in London, Ontario, whose practice includes advising several newspapers and radio stations on libel issues. He has lectured occasionally in media law at the School of Journalism, Ryerson Polytechnic University, Toronto, Ontario.

# Look After the Business

# Mechanics, Marketing and Morale

*by Kevin Longfield*

very writer receives one of those "Unfortunately we can't use..." letters at some time. No one enjoys them. They hurt. In some cases, they are a fatal blow to an author's aspirations. The truth is, no matter how well you write, some rejections are inevitable. After all, even editors aren't perfect. Many rejections are avoidable, however, and even the unavoidable rejections can be dealt with in a way that won't bring your writing to a halt. Three strategies will help you to bypass the rejection slip blues: mechanics, marketing and morale.

## Think about mechanics.

If you were an editor, what manuscripts would you want to receive? Every editor would agree to the following list:

- Neatly typed or machine printed, double spaced.
- Good quality white bond paper.
- Standard size paper (8.5 by 11 inches or, in metric, 21.5 by 28 cm).
- Correct spelling, including English spelling to markets using English spelling, and American spelling to markets using American. ("Canadian" spelling is another matter entirely.)
- Correct grammar.
- No onion skin, erasable or coloured paper.

Will an editor still accept a manuscript if you violate one of these rules? Possibly. But why reduce your chances? A professional-looking manuscript gets you off to a good start.

Many editors are now asking that, in addition to clean copy, you submit assigned articles on computer disk in a text or recognized word-processing format. With the enormous number of manuscripts editors receive, you need every advantage.

## Market your work intelligently.

Once you have a professional product, you must send it to the editor who at that very moment leans back in his chair and says, "If only I had an article (or story or poem) about..." and yours is it. For that reason, I never send anything to a publication I have never read. There's no point in sending a beef stew recipe to *Modern Vegetarian*. Furthermore, you must know that your idea has not been covered by the publication recently, and that your style suits the publication.

You must also consider the editor's plans for future issues. Seasonal stories should be sent to magazines at least six months in advance. That wonderful Christmas dinner Uncle Ed just prepared is next year's story. Newspapers work on less lead time, but no one is interested in cold news.

The same story must be written differently if you wish to sell it to different markets. Some publications are scholarly, and expect documentation; others are trendy and expect breezy writing. To avoid guesswork, ask for a copy of writers' guidelines, if the publication provides them. Offer to pay for a sample copy, especially if you are approaching a magazine that does not carry much advertising, since it probably is on a tight budget and cannot afford to send free samples.

To avoid disappointment, and to save time, I usually query first. When I have a hot idea, I ask myself what markets are likely to be interested. If I can't think of any, I consult marketing aids such as this guide, or the market column in such magazines as *Canadian Author*, *Canadian Writer's Journal* and *Writer's Digest*. (These aids will also tell you whether or not a publication accepts freelance work.) Once I have a potential market, I write a brief letter to the editor outlining the story, telling why I think the readers would be interested in it, and summarizing my writing credits.

I naturally jot down some notes while the idea is still fresh so that if I get a go-ahead, I won't be starting over again cold.

Most important, once you agree with an editor to send a story of a certain length by a certain time, stick to it. You have a professional obligation to do so. If an editor asks for six hundred words, a two thousand-word story will probably be rejected, no matter how well written.

## Maintain high morale.

Even if you do everything right, and send only your best work out, occasionally you will get manuscripts back. As I said before, no editor is perfect. How do you stop mere disappointment from turning into despair?

You'll get by with a little help from your friends. Workshops, courses, and other writers' events can help you improve your work to the point where it sells. Joining a writers' group will provide you with a source of professional opinions on your work.

More important, however, a supportive group can keep you going when a devastating rejection makes you feel like quitting.

After sending out one of my favorite stories, I had it returned with the most stunning negative criticism I have ever received. It could have been a crushing blow, but for one thing: the workshop I belong to loved the story.

I sent it out again, after removing two clichés and correcting the spelling. A local CBC literary program bought it. It has since been used as course material in writing classes. Without the support of my workshop, however, the story might never have reached the public. I can't be too upset at the editor who turned it down, either. She did make suggestions I could use.

That's the next point: read every non-form letter rejection for useful advice. If the editor invites you to resubmit, do so. An editor who will work with beginning writers is a treasure.

You can boost your morale in other, more subtle ways. Join a national writers organization. For an example of the benefits, consider the Canadian Authors Association's annual conferences. At these gatherings you get to meet living breathing writers, editors and publishers from all across Canada, and learn first-hand what makes them tick. You learn what is happening in the writing and publishing business, collect ideas for writing projects, and leads for markets that may be interested in your work. More important, you become inspired. I have yet to attend a conference that didn't provoke me to write and sell something.

If you live close enough to a Canadian Authors Association Branch to attend its monthly meetings, you will meet writers who live in your area, and become part of a literary community. Hearing of others' trials and successes gives you hope that you, too, will make it.

Finally, always keep an ace up your sleeve: never have fewer than two manuscripts out at a time. I usually have three or four. By doing this, I can transfer all my hopes to the surviving submissions when a rejection arrives.

The law of averages dictates that some manuscripts will come back. However, following these strategies will certainly improve your odds.

Kevin Longfield has a long list of publishing credits in poetry, fiction, non-fiction and drama. He was the Winnipeg correspondent for *Theatrum* magazine for five years. His play, *Going Down the River*, has won three awards and was published in the anthology, *Canadian Mosaic*.

# Change the Way You Write: Retire your Typewriter

*by Sarah Yates*

P utting words on paper is second nature to me. It's the way I express my views, inform, entertain, cajole and, finally, pay the mortgage. But when that paper first became a video display screen, it was another story. The thought of words and sentences slipping into the world of bits and bytes stopped me cold.

People raised my hackles by suggesting I would write better on a word processor. But none of those who made the claim were writers I respected. The cost of the investment provided another deterrent. Wouldn't I be inclined to accept more work and deliver less quality under duress of the debt? Finally, I had no time to take a few months to work more slowly while I learned.

All my arguments were "erased" when I signed a contract that required me to deliver on disk. It was my first lesson about the power of the word processor—the ease of erasure.

I'm not a technically adept person. I made my purchase from the shop where I had bought my electronic typewriter. I knew that the salesman, Paul, liked and respected writers and was someone from whom I could get straight answers. Continuing backup and support were essential to me.

William Zinsser's book *Writing With a Word Processor* also proved invaluable. It took me through the painful learning process with humor. Zinsser also offered some practical advice to overcome the inevitable eyestrain that makes your head ache and words begin to dance on the screen. This advice is well heeded. "Don't look at the words...any more than you need to. Look down at the keyboard or into space while you're waiting for the next sentence to form."

Following his advice gave my bleary eyes a rest; reading his book gave my mind a rest from the plethora of technical information gathered in my search for the perfect machine.

With book read and support in place, and after a few preliminary demonstrations in my office with the machine set up properly, I was ready to go. Paul set up my machine with double spacing and adequate margins so that I could sit down and write without any of the computer-ish preamble. (The manual, which accompanied my word processing program, was written for illiterate technocrats and deserved only a cursory glance.)

It is probably a good idea to start off slowly, perhaps by transcribing some interview notes. It's the old story of overcoming your fear of the blank page or, in this case, the blank screen.

My first job as a writer held similar horrors. I had begun my first article in longhand when from behind me, my editor boomed, "Sarah, there's no damned time for that amateur stuff. If you want to survive, write at the typewriter like everybody else here." That first week was one of frustration and fear. But I made that switch, and I achieved the same transition with my personal computer. I learned the basics and wrote to deadline.

As any artist who has changed her medium can tell you, things are different. You have to learn your craft with the capabilities and demands of the new technology. But it is still the words that you play with; you are still a writer.

The first rule of thumb you must learn about word processing is to save what you are writing, first on disk and later in hard copy. I've seen my words disappear on more than one occasion. But contrary to what you may believe, you can write it all again and the next time it will be better.

As your work becomes more complex, not only must you save it more often, but you should also make backup disks. Making a backup becomes second nature, like making a carbon copy or a photocopy.

Despite all precautions, that desperate afternoon arrives when you are terrorized by spewing paper, a screen that scrolls, a machine that bleeps, and none of your favorite words anywhere in sight. That's when support counts. On some occasions, a talk-through via telephone might be sufficient to solve the problem, but at least once you'll welcome the arrival of your wonderful wizard of word processing.

Since my machine seemed to have a mind of her own, I gave her a name. My Olivetti M-24 became Olive. Personalized, she became less adversarial. I cursed Olive, pitted myself against her and finally we cooperated.

I don't suggest that you get rid of your typewriter altogether, but I do suggest that you cover it during the first few weeks. While I word-processed my first story, I would retire to my typewriter whenever I needed that creative fix or simply a break. But for the story itself, I didn't allow myself near it.

After I had written my first story on the word processor—using it simply as an advanced typewriter, I spent an evening with a writer friend who uses the same word processing program as I. It was well worth the bottle of cognac it cost me. Matthew showed me how to edit, retrieve text, change the order of lines and check spelling for starters—all the things he knew I needed as a writer. Together, we played with the machine. Slowly, I became less fearful and more familiar. It can be a wonderful tool.

Will the personal computer or a dedicated word processor change the way you write? Will it improve what you write?

When writers changed from quill pen to steel nib, from pencil to typewriter, both the way they wrote physically and the kind of work they undertook changed. Virginia Woolf was profoundly affected by the physical circumstances of her work. She stood at a writing desk which she had designed specially; a new nib or pen always acted as a creative stimulant to her.

For Henry James, working with the typewriter dramatically changed his writing. After 1896, suffering from severe writer's cramp, he learned to dictate his novels directly to a typist. His biographer, Leon Edel, noted that his "sentences were to become...elaborate...filled with qualifications and parentheses."

Like Henry James, I've found that my writing has changed by becoming longer. Perhaps it is because I know I can edit more easily. Perhaps a residue of fear remains about the loss of words gone forever in the electronic void. I include a greater number of quotes in my articles, because my word-processing program splits the screen; interviews and notes can be displayed underneath the article on which I am working. I can literally pull passages into the copy to see how they read. It's the old cut-and-paste routine with a twist.

The question is not really whether you will write better. You have to write with the same commitment, finding your own approach. I have not yet overcome my feelings about the fleeting quality of the words on the screen. They seem to lack substance. At first I found it difficult to choose a word, knowing I could change it or, worse, that it might disappear. I chose words more casually and edited endlessly.

Later, I fight for the right lead, search and insert the right quote, change and rearrange. If the words are right, I save them. Writing with a word processor requires the same concentration and care as writing in longhand or on the typewriter. But editing is a dream.

The prolific mystery writer, Dick Francis, writes every book in long-hand first and then sits down at the word processor and keys in his story, editing as he goes. His method allows him to take advantage of the word processor's real strength—the editing process.

Olive hasn't destroyed any of my love of writing. I still love to see my words on the page, and on the screen. I've rearranged my office to place Olive where there is no glare. I have a comfortable chair, one that moves. But the business of writing—because I have ideas I want to disseminate to others—is still my prime goal.

I spend long hours writing and rewriting—not retyping. Olive has indeed thrown me a few blanks, swallowed some sentences and converted the logic of some of my analytical writing into garble. But as Paul tells me, "It's not the machine, Sarah, it's you. Computers are unfailingly logical. You don't always display the same characteristic."

*Authors Note:* I first wrote this story about Olive in the late 1980s and have recently retired Olive to a lesser role in my office. She provides backup and tracks my billing hours. Writing on the computer is now second nature to me and I'm now learning about e-mail, online services and the next generation of information tools.

As a writer, I'm proving myself able to cope with the challenges of change. It's a gas. I'm still technologically quite inept but I'm thoroughly convinced nothing could be better for a writer. With a poorly catalogued library at our fingertips via the Internet and an electronic page on which to work, we're still in the business of creating context, analysis and meaning to the information with which we work. With a little luck and continued work, we can also contribute style.

Sarah Yates, a member of the Periodical Writers Association of Canada, has been a professional free-lance writer, editor and researcher for more than 20 years, publishing in Canada and internationally. She's written more than nine books, has started Gemma B. Publishing to provide role models for disabled children and continues to write articles for magazines.

# The Electronic Cottage: 1. Set up Your Own Virtual Company

*by Katharine and Eric Fletcher* _____

**W**hat is an electronic cottage?

It is a home-based business that uses telecommunications technology to procure, do and deliver work.

## What is a virtual company?

It is a group of businesses or individuals that work together on an "as required" basis. There need not be an employer/employee relationship. Instead, highly skilled individuals can work together on different facets of a project. Writers, editors, proofreaders and designers who publish CD-ROMs and web pages are ideally situated to set up electronic cottages in a virtual company.

Our electronic cottage is an old farmhouse nestled beside Gatineau Park, within a 50-minute drive of Ottawa, Ontario. From this pastoral site we telecommute with writers, editors and publishers across North America. I, Katharine, am a freelance writer and editor; my husband and business partner, Eric, is a computer and electronic publications specialist. Together, we have managed the publishing process of hundreds of documents in English, French and Spanish.

Our electronic cottage is one node of a "virtual company," a team of co-workers who seldom (if ever) physically meet but who are connected, sometimes daily, via telecommunications technology. As governments downsize, as people become increasingly interested in—or pushed into—home-based businesses, starting an electronic cottage may make good business sense for you. We believe it's the wave of the future.

How, then, can you catch the wave?

### Setting up an electronic cottage.

Because it is a business, the steps to setting up an electronic cottage share many of the essential steps of establishing a new business venture.

### Develop a plan.

Your "electronic cottage" may be one node of a virtual company— but the work must be real! In fact, first make a business plan.

Ask yourself these questions:

• What are your skills? Make three columns: strong skills, skills you need to learn; skills you don't have to (or don't want to) learn—you may need to be flexible here!

• What is your business? This is not so easy to define as you might think. Take your time, assess whether what you are currently doing is what you want to be doing in 2, 5 or 10 years.

• What are your goals? Short- and long-term goals need to be defined. Also, start small: don't expect "the moon" when you start out.

• Who do you know who could help you define your business? Network! Read up on who is doing what and contact them for advice. Local newspapers are vital keys here, as may be your writers groups.

• Who do you know who might be potential clients? This assumes you have defined your business and its target market.

Now tackle your formal business plan. If you need financing from a bank, a solid business plan is a prerequisite to borrowing money. Remember: just because you'll be running your own business and be your own boss does not mean you shouldn't have a plan!

Do you have a business partner? You must share a complimentary vision. Is your spouse your partner? The latter poses additional challenges: you must clearly identify your roles and be able to communicate extremely well.

### Develop a realistic financial strategy.

This is key. People are often eager to quit their jobs and be their own bosses. But remember: while you have a job, it's easy to criticize "management." Do you possess the skills to manage a project, yourself, your spouse, your family efficiently and professionally?

Here are some tips:

• What are your current, ongoing fixed and variable requirements? Shelter, taxes and food are the basics. Transportation, insurance and retirement planning are important. Beyond these, your leisure time is also important—without it, you'll burn out.

• How much money will it take to set up your business? What do you need? Cost of materials (pencils to computers); cost of knowledge (courses, software—and how to use it), cost of marketing materials, etc. Remember that many costs may be business expenses for tax purposes.

### Accounting issues.

• Do you know an accountant who is familiar with home businesses? If not, find one. How? Network.

• Get an accountant to set up a system that works for you from the start.

• What can you depreciate and claim as business expenses? What percent of your home can you write off?

• Should you operate as a proprietorship, a partnership or incorporate?

### Legal issues.

• Do you need copyright advice or protection?

• Will you require patent information?

• Will your business raise liability issues? Leading custom bus tours or having clients in your home, for example, all include liability issues.

### Insurance issues.

• Check your household policy with your agent. Computers over a certain limit, say $4,000, may require special coverage. If you have a laptop, ensure it is covered while it is in your car or at an off-site location.

• Does your car insurance coverage permit its use for business?

• What about your personal coverage? Can you afford your own coverage in medical, dental, unemployment or disability insurance?

### Marketing and promotion.

Allow time for this because without it, you'll have no business! Many people mistakenly think that a home-based business means you can work your own hours, set your own schedule and wear what you want. Think again. Marketing is critical and entails a host of "hidden issues."

• Do you know how much time marketing takes? Plan for 20-25 per cent of your time.

• Project a professional image that suits your business. Do you lead hikes in Gatineau Park? Do you work off-site (at client's offices)? Dress appropriately!

• Your hours are not your own! Your business is comprised of paying clients. They expect you to work for them economically, efficiently and to produce work on time. Face it: most clients work from 9:00 a.m. until 5:00 p.m. Be scrupulous about being available by phone during normal business hours.

• Keep files of ongoing opportunities. Keep an electronic file of business opportunities that crop up. Keep a paper file of newspaper clippings, flyer samples that spark ideas.

• The Internet presents new marketing opportunities. Learn how you might create your own web page and link to other sites (such as catalogues) that can increase your exposure to untapped markets.

### Pricing.

Do you think you can quit your job, set up your electronic cottage— and charge top rates? Think again.

• What is your competition charging? Find out what competitive rates are. And remember: don't undersell yourself—but also do not charge top rates at the outset if you want to work. Be flexible!

• Cover your overhead as well as direct costs.

• Hourly rate? Fixed price? Clients want a fixed price, you want an hourly rate. Be realistic.

• Do you understand what your client really wants? Ensure that you do before you submit your bid.

• Do you have the terms of agreement in written form before you start work? Some clients do not want contracts. Others do. At minimum, write a letter of understanding, outlining what the job is and how you propose to achieve it.

### Be cautious about "being virtual".

Sure you're eager to be a node of a virtual company. It sounds "cool"! But what does it really entail? Can you count on your other "virtual partners" if you don't know them? Be careful: staying at your current job while you plan your new business venture is the smart way to create your new business.

• Don't just jump in to freelancing. There are peaks and valleys to freelance work. Can you budget? Can you save for a rainy day? Do you have a family or dependents to support? How will you survive the financial "valleys"?

• Have you considered part-time work or job sharing? This may actually be your comfort zone. Think it through before you jump.

• Talk to your family or "significant others." Do you have their support? Do they need your financial support?

• Do you want to ski all day and work all night? Forget it! Even a cellular phone will not save you if this is your secret goal. Clients expect you to be available.

• Can you say "no"? There's a limit to being flexible. You must establish limits upon your availability. Can you tell the persistent client who phones you to "talk shop" at 11:00 p.m. that you are unavailable until the following morning? Some jobs (like speech-writing or annual reports) make this unavoidable: but most don't.

### Operating a virtual organization.

Is your business suited to operating "virtually" without physical contact with partners on a regular basis? Operating a remote electronic cottage demands that you think this through carefully.

• Who is your partner? Is it your spouse? A friend? Do you know how they actually do business? Business is completely different than simply being friends who share leisure time. What are their ethics? What is their attitude to business and timeliness? You have lots to discuss.

• If you need a partner, where will they work? Will you need to occasionally or permanently share space? How will you do this? Remember the liability issue.

• Virtual partners are not employees. Your co-workers in a virtual company are highly-skilled professionals who come together, solely on an as-required basis, to complete a given project or portion of a project.

• Virtual partners may truly never need to meet together. Wordsmiths such as editors, writers or proofreaders are good examples of this because work can be transferred electronically, without physical contact.

• Are you in a remote location? Can you get courier service? As a writer or editor, how will you deliver hard copy to clients? Sometimes this is still unavoidable.

### Room of your own.

If you work at home, don't skimp. Purchase the best you can get for each functional requirement. What are the key items?

• "Virtual" vs. "real" office space. Can you shut the door on your work? This is a psychological if not a physical necessity. Having a "virtual" office is not ideal if you cannot put it out of mind and sight. A door is necessary to keep the puppy out, to ensure privacy for client conversations, sales calls and interviews.

• Remember that for income tax purposes, business deductions for electricity, heat, taxes, renovations and other expenses hinge on the size of your office space. Tax breaks are available for home-businesses.

• Details, details! Natural lighting is important—and don't forget the reflection of that light on computer screens. North corner of your old farmhouse is the coldest spot: take care where your office is located in your home. Having a ceiling fan is a good idea—as long as it doesn't blow your papers around.

### Combating isolation.

When Peter Gzowski interviewed me first in September 1994 and then again in '95 for his series the new world of work, he was most intrigued with this dilemma. Didn't I miss the "water cooler" and its implied casual or focused chit-chat with fellow workers? It's a key question. What professional organizations could you join? Writers have many choices, along with the Canadian Authors Association (CAA), there's the Periodical Writers Association of Canada (PWAC), The Writer's Union of Canada (TWUC) and the Editors' Association of Canada (EAC) These are all powerful networking sources for you as a self-employed freelancer. There are also a host of other specialty organizations from romance to science fiction to medical writers groups, technical editors' associations, and so on. Using the Internet, listservers connect members to one another, making such professional memberships worth their weight in gold. Find out what associations exist, which interest you, and consider the price of membership as part of your critical business expenses. Remember: this can be another tax write-off. And, if you become a conference speaker or part of the executive, often your travel expenses (at minimum) are paid.

What volunteer organizations could you join? Especially if you, like Eric and I, move into a new community simultaneously to setting up a new business, you might like to plunge into your local community's life. I scouted around and since 1989 have written my local paper's environment column; I am also a founder of the Pontiac Artists Studio Tour during which I open up my home and showcase the work of local authors. What can you do?

## Lifestyle.

There are many factors that influence people to become self-employed. Here are just a few.

• "Green lifestyle." Your decision to work at home is an environmentally sound decision. Why? For example, you may be able to substantially reduce your use (or perhaps even your need) of an automobile. You will save commuting time. These, plus a host of other "green" reasons, were significant goals for Eric and me.

• Control. You will have more control over your lifestyle—if you manage it! What you do with your normal commuting time is up to you: you may use it to sleep. You may use it to read. It will truly be your decision.

• Independence. You are your own boss. You will call the shots. You will sink or swim. Can you deal with ultimate independence? If you can, you may be ready to set up your own electronic cottage!

## Final Note.

Freelancing from your home electronic cottage is the ultimate entrepreneurial business. It is a demanding lifestyle, make no mistake. And, if you are married—and especially if you have children—you need to think about the fiscal as well as day-to-day ramifications with detailed care. Do not embark upon this lifestyle if you do not have the full support of your significant others.

Katharine Fletcher has over 23 years experience in writing, editing and publishing. She thrives on diversification: she gives seminars (e.g. *Publish Yourself!*), leads hikes of Gatineau Park—and telecommutes from her electronic cottage in West Quebec. Since 1970, Eric Fletcher has assisted clients with their computer, software training and electronic publishing needs. He leads seminars, such as *The Electronic Cottage*. Eric and Katharine can be reached via e-mail at: <fletcher@hookup.net>.

# The Electronic Cottage: 2. Essential equipment and services

*by Katharine and Eric Fletcher* _____

**N**ow that you know the basics of setting up an electronic cottage, what essential equipment and services you will need? Are you like my husband and I who wanted to completely alter our urban lifestyle? If you do what we did and move to a rural community, there are even more things to consider carefully. Read on!

• Make a budget. Decide what is a "must have" and what you "want." Then buy the best quality product in the "must have" column that you can afford. Note that this does not necessarily mean the most expensive.

• Remember, office-related investments may represent tax deductions. Talk to your accountant before you buy anything.

• You know how quickly technology changes! Keep that in mind, for this early 1997 list will soon be obsolete.

### Things that don't need plugs.

• Furniture. You'll probably need a desk, a comfortable chair, filing cabinet, etc. Check out ergonomic considerations such as the optimum height for a desk and chair combination.

• Personal space. Where is your home office? Does it have natural lighting? How can you make it personally inviting specifically as a work space? Should you invest in a fresh coat of paint on the walls? Should you put up a wall and a door?

• Mail and couriers. What are your options? Canada Post has special services such as courier, priority post and so on. Research what your specific business requirements are and then call Canada Post. If you live in the country, "RR" (rural route) addresses may be filtered out of mailing lists. Is there a municipal address with a street number that you can use? Find out what "next-day" courier service *really* means if you live in the country! It may mean "whenever." Can you utilize the Internet's e-mail facilities and by-pass a major need for mail or courier services?

• Office supplies. Can you get an account at an office-specialty shop? Professional associations such as the Periodical Writers' Association of Canada (PWAC) and the Editors' Association of Canada (EAC) offer discounts for members.

• Custom items (business cards, letterhead). You may be able to design and print these yourself at your home office depending upon what computer and peripherals you have. Otherwise, printers and copy shops can do it for you. Avoid large runs: you may decide to further customize your business cards, for example.

• Storage space. Don't get over-zealous in purchasing stuff! Where are you going to put it? Where will you put your inventory?

### Things you need to plug in.

Surge protectors help guard against power fluctuations and brown-outs which can be damaging to electronic circuits in all your office equipment. Invest in protection: get a good surge protector from a computer store. If you experience frequent power outages, you may want to consider an uninteruptable power supply (UPS).

### Telephony.

• This includes not only the telephone, but answering and fax machine.

What kind of telephone features do you need? Do you need call forwarding, for example? Which company is the best provider for your needs?

• Do you need a second line (or more)? Balance your family's needs with your business needs. If you have kids, a second line may be strategically important! Teenagers want easy (and frequent) access to a phone. The expense of a second line may be worth its weight in gold—and be an excellent "bargaining chip" when you are seeking the "buy-in" from your family to set up a business.

• Rural telephone line costs may be pricey. Check out whether there is a distance surcharge for your country phone.

• Specialized services. A business line may represent a tax deduction. But what do you get for the extra charge? Find out.

• ISDN and leased lines may be needed for direct connect and data-intensive work, but they are expensive. Do your homework.

• Answering machine. Some kind of voice message service is mandatory for any home business operator. *Do not* use "cute" messages. *Do* respond promptly to your calls.

• A fax machine or fax software and a fax modem resident on your computer? For my needs, I have a second telephone line that is a dedicated fax line. I do not use my computer for faxes. Why? Faxes take up a lot of disk space and must be on all the time; fax modems are often more sensitive to line problems; all outgoing messages must be originated on the computer. In short: it's inconvenient.

• Combination telephone/fax/copier/answering machine. Ask yourself this: what happens if this single-system fails? You're out of luck. But it could be a cost-effective solution for some specialized single-line offices.

### Computers.

• What platform should you choose? PC or Macintosh? Roughly 80 per cent of all businesses use PCs; less than 10 per cent use Mac. Who are your major clients? What do they use? What do your business colleagues use? Why? What do they like about the system? What don't they like?

• CPU: get the fastest you can afford. Beware of "version 1.0" of anything. For a PC, get a 486 processor or better; in fact, Pentium is the norm in early 1997. For Mac platforms: at least a 68040-based processor; PowerPC is now the norm.

• Memory. At least 8 megabytes (MB). The more, the better. Windows 95 "must have" 4MB but is actually almost unusable with less than 8MB; it works well at 16MB and "purrs" at 32MB! Mac System 7.5 needs 4MB for basics but at least 8MB if you want to use all its features.

• Monitors. The faster refresh rate is more important than size. A hidden cost may be the need for a video card. A 14-inch screen is typical; 15-inch is becoming standard; 17 and 19 inch are nice if you are working at the computer all of the time. Be kind to your eyes!

• Hard disk. At minimum 1.2 gigabytes (GB) for a PC; 250MB for a Mac. Hard disks are getting faster, bigger and cheaper. Remember that as your needs progress, you can add an extra drive.

• Keyboard: new ergonomic keyboards may reduce the risk of repetitive strain injury (RSI). Try them out. They can be raised and lowered. Remember that the level of your keyboard is vital for the health of your neck or shoulder muscles.

• Mouse. It must fit because you'll use it more than you think! A mouse for a PC normally has 2 buttons, some have 3. Make sure the software drivers are the latest to take advantage of features! A Mac mouse has one button and there are fewer alternatives.

• CD-ROMs are quickly becoming "must haves" for your electronic cottage. Why? There's a huge selection of CD material, from phone books to maps, from McClelland & Stewart's *Canadian Encyclopedia* to Audubon bird guides with audio so you can identify bird songs! All of these resources are sometimes the least expensive in a CD-ROM version.

• Backup. How do you intend to archive your files? This is an important consideration because many clients ask you to sign contracts stipulating that you must keep their work on-site from five to seven years. Tape backups can store vast amounts of data and have widely accepted standards. Backups can be done automatically, too. Tip: develop a workable file-naming convention (where it is, how you store it) and stick to it!

• Sound. It is essential to games, useful for increasingly more software, comes with most CD packages. Remember: get speakers and earphones so you won't blast your office mate out of your electronic cottage!

## Computer peripherals.
### Laser printers.

• Excellent quality and dropping prices make these extremely affordable and indispensable items for the electronic cottage. Colour printers are still pricey but are rapidly decreasing in cost. Assess your needs carefully because a printer of any kind can still be a luxury, depending upon your business needs. Many service providers offer good deals on printing so do your costing carefully.

• Printer resolution. 600 dots per inch (dpi) is standard and greater resolution will soon replace it.

• Speed. 6 to 8 pages per minute (ppm) is typical. But how fast do you need? Your computer's operating system may allow you to print in background while you do other work.

• Special feed options. Do you need to print envelopes, heavy stock, different colours? If so, inquire about special feeds.

• Memory in printer vs. CPU. In your business, do you print a lot of graphics? These can take a lot of processing power and therefore, time . Although it is less costly if the computer's CPU does it, don't risk slowing down your entire system.

• Consumable supplies. Toner cartridges add up. Ensure you check out the recycling market because you can take in your empty cartridges and have them recycled. Re-built cartridges save you money—always a great reason to recycle! Paper is less expensive by the box—and check out recycled newsprint for those draft copies. Tip: For your high-quality printing, get a package of specialty paper.

### Ink jet printers.

Many of the same variables listed above apply here. However, here are some things to consider for ink jet rather than laser printers.

• Small footprint. They are typically smaller and hence take up less office space.

• Resolution. Typically these are 720 dpi.

• Ink cartridges are expensive and, if pages are dense, can be used up very quickly. Some can be recycled.

• Colour. More expensive inks are used and the quality is usually better only if used with more expensive paper.

### Dot matrix printers.

Don't bother. They are noisy, costly (for what you get) and the quality just doesn't measure up, these days—even if you *could* find one!

### Modems.

Typically, modems are a hassle to retro-fit to an already-existing system. Buy a system which includes one or get the seller to set it up for you.

• How fast? The faster the better. Speed is measured in baud, basically this is characters per second, where 28,800 baud is standard; 33,600 is available for many modems; 57,600 arrived as of late 1996.

• Internal or external? Internal is often cheaper and doesn't use up a serial port. But you cannot share it—nor can you sell it if you upgrade—so watch out! Not incidentally, because it's internal to your computer, if something goes wrong you are left defenceless without a system. Think it through carefully. It may be wiser to pay a bit more for an external modem.

• Fax modems: do they make sense? Yes! Few modems don't include faxes now. This is great for outgoing but less useful for incoming. Tip: if you have both and a second telephone line, you have a scanner! (Send the item by your fax, receive it by your fax modem.)

• Communications software. Operating systems for both PC and Macs include basic software. Commercial software is easier to use and usually includes configuration files for all major modems.

### Cost of complete computer system.

Yikes! Sounds like loads of money, doesn't it? You'll note I have not itemized every cost because prices fluctuate. However, the above list and recommendations will give you a good checklist start to your own personal business analysis. Then you must start your field research. Check out all available stores. Tip: the best deal may not be the lowest price. I firmly believe the attitude of not only the sales but also the support staff is absolutely critical. Do not support techno-junkies who cannot answer your questions or "stoop" to your level of questions. Insist on your rights as a consumer and business professional to get the service you need.

This being said, *as of early 1997*, realistically expect to pay between $2,500 to $3,500 for a system. But remember, you also need to buy software!

### Other office plug-ins (photocopier, scanner, bindery...)

Do your needs analysis. What are your alternatives to these costly add-ons? Do your needs demand them? For example, your fax machine can double as a copier for small items that do not need to be preserved for a long time (typically, thermal paper fax copies are light-sensitive). If you have a laser or ink-jet printer, do you really need a photocopier? As well, many small businesses exist that specialize in photocopies, scanning, printing and binding. Analyse your true needs—ensuring that you objectively quantify how frequently you require these services. It may be far more cost-effective to use a service business.

Scanners: can you use your fax machine instead of buying a scanner? If you have a fax modem and a second telephone line, you already have the capabilities of a scanner! Do you need colour? Make sure your computer can handle the larger files and that you have the software to work with them.

## Software and resources.

### The Basics.

• Word Processor. Everyone needs one! They make writing easier and more efficient. You can do your letters and labels (ensure your printer can cope with different weights of paper stock!) You can also do your company signs, logo, flyers, "corporate profile" etc.

• Spreadsheet. For me, they make math (which I dislike!) do-able. Once you build a spreadsheet model (for tracking your inventory, distribution and sales of self-published books, for example) it does the math and you can have fun with "what if..." projections. Spreadsheets also manage conversions (metric to imperial) and many include a wide range of specialty functions (financial, scientific, mathematical, even text or data conversion).

• Accounting software. Get help from a professional to get you started. Ask your colleagues what they use, who they use as an accountant. Once set up, an accounting package will keep you organized and give you a clear picture of your business status. Tip: technology is not everything. You need to have the discipline to do your numbers *regularly*.

• Industry-specific. Such programs as Computer-Aided-Design (CAD) systems are indispensable aids for some businesses. What is your business? Research what is on the market that can help you perform work more efficiently. Tip: there's a learning curve associated with all of these items. The cost (time being money) for you to learn how to use each software package must be factored in to your assessment of what you need—and when you need to buy it. That is: is it a basic need? Or a later goal?

### "Nice to have" software.

• Database. This technology is powerful and easy to use (i.e. Microsoft Access, Lotus Approach) but you will need to invest time to customize it to your specific requirements.

• Language spelling checkers. Most word processors include a spelling checker for one language. What about French? Spanish? Depending on your business, you may need a foreign-language checker.

• Optical Character Recognition (OCR). Can you scan it instead of re-keying text? If so, perhaps you should investigate OCR packages.

• Games. Okay, okay. Yes, this is an electronic cottage, but you gotta have fun, right? Tip: Balance your urge to get your kids interested in computers against your ability to get them off your computer if you allow your office machine to be used for games!

### Using the Networks.

Should you get access to the Internet? I think so, because the Internet permits wide, instant access to markets or research sources that are otherwise prohibitively costly—or that you would simply never hear about! However, like anything else, Internet has its costs, as does having your own web page. Hidden costs, for example, are the time you will undoubtedly spend browsing (searching and reading and getting sidetracked!) on the Net. Tip: watch out for the maintenance costs to a web page. One honest specialist mentioned it's a minimum of 5-6 hours a week. Can you afford this? I suggest that if you have a website, you cannot afford not to spend this time, because an old, non-current website is worse than none at all.

### Internet.

What do you need in order to get the Internet? You need an Internet service provider (ISP)—another monthly charge for your business. As of early 1997, $20 to $30 a month is typical. (Most ISPs have plans that include a space for a WWW address as well, so you can put up a web page.)

Modem. You will need 14,400 baud for the World Wide Web (WWW) although 28,800 is often considered minimum; communications software (basic access software is usually provided as "freeware" at no cost by ISPs); you also need an access account.

What you get. E-mail is an inexpensive business and private tool that connects you to global businesses, associations, governments and individuals. And, if your computer system has graphics capability, browsers like Netscape or Internet Explorer give you a graphical interface to the Internet through the World Wide Web, complete with extensive search and linking capabilities. Newsgroups will keep you informed about topics you're keen about, from hobbies to how to figure out a word processing problem.

Commercial online services. Compuserve and America Online are online services that provide access to their own network of services and to the Internet. With local connections from cities throughout North America and major centres elsewhere, they can be a good alternative if you travel.

### How do you start?

It always seems overwhelming when you start to analyze setting up your own business. These tips may help!

• Talk to friends.

• Talk to clients. (What are your business strengths and, more importantly, your weaknesses?)

• Discover your competition.

• Be a good listener.

• Ask questions.

• Browse magazines.

• Visit local computer stores.

• Join relevant, professional associations.

Katharine Fletcher has over 23 years experience in writing, editing and publishing. She thrives on diversification: she gives seminars (e.g. *Publish Yourself!*), leads hikes of Gatineau Park—and telecommutes from her electronic cottage. Since 1970, Eric Fletcher has assisted clients with their computer, software training and electronic publishing needs. He leads seminars, such as *The Electronic Cottage*. He and Katharine freelance from their cozy electronic cottage in West Quebec. E-mail either of them at: <fletcher@hookup.net>.

# The Electronic Cottage:
# 3. Use the Internet

*by Katharine Fletcher*

Here in my cozy electronic cottage, I use the Internet on a daily basis. It's not only because I live in the relatively remote countryside of West Quebec that I use it so often. It is because it has become an indispensable part of my business of writing. As well, it is a fast, convenient and fun way for me to keep in touch with friends, family, fellow writers and editors who live across our expansive Canadian landscape.

How do I actually use "the Net"? First of all, let me step back and tell you what I do. That will give you a perspective on why I might need to use a global resource such as the Internet. I'm sure you'll find some parallels with what you do!

Reminder: What follows is a personalized window into how I use the Net. You will come across certain products that I use (for example, I use Netscape, not the also-popular Microsoft Internet Explorer, as my primary browser). My intention here is to outline how I, as a professional writer and editor, use the Internet. My hope is that perhaps you'll find some neat stuff to try out.

Questions? Contact Eric or myself by e-mail address at <fletcher@hookup.net>.

### Brief backgrounder.

My electronic cottage is where my husband and business partner, Eric, and I live and work. Ours is an old farmhouse nestled beside the wilderness sector of Gatineau Park, but which is within a 50-minute easy (and picturesque) drive from Ottawa. From this pastoral site we telecommute with writers, editors and publishers across North America. This is possible thanks to the Internet.

## What is my freelance editing business?

Electronic publishing. I am a freelance writer and editor; my husband and business partner Eric is a computer and electronic publications specialist. I am managing editor for a series of publications; Eric is the computer wizard who ensures our technology is kept up-to-date and seamlessly efficient in its operations. We have managed the publishing process of hundreds of documents in English, French and Spanish.

Eric pulls writers' work off the Internet via ftp (file transfer protocol). The writers are located throughout North America. Eric has written a customized series of macros (computer programs) which massage raw text into documents with chapter headings, paragraph styles and codes. He also creates customized spelling and grammar routines that correct particular author's typical errors.

The next step is the editing process. This can be done on hard copy, with a traditional word processing operator entering updates. Usually, however, we transfer soft copy documents via an e-mail attachment to an editor who edits on-screen, using revision marks. The document is then uploaded back to us.

The final text is transferred to designers for publishing using any of these technologies: hardcopy printing, fax-back, CD-ROM and HTML coding for the Internet. As well, many documents undergo a French and sometimes a Spanish translation/editing cycle.

## What is my freelance writing business?

I am a frequent correspondent to *The Ottawa Citizen*, for which I write destination/travel pieces. For seven years I have written the weekly "Environment Forum", a column for *The Equity*, my community newspaper. I have self-published two editions of *Historical Walks: The Gatineau Park Story*, written *Capital Walks: Walking Tours of Ottawa* (McClelland & Stewart, 1993), contributed to Reader's Digest's 1994 *Back Roads and Getaway Places in Canada*, and have written for magazines like *Harrowsmith Country Life*, *Earthkeeper* and *This Country Canada*.

How does the Internet help me sell my work to magazine, newspaper or book publishers? I use the Internet to contact potential editors. Likely as not, the publisher has a web site and you can browse their writers' guidelines online—or else ask them to e-mail them to you, along with a sample magazine! Why not? Most editors have e-mail. And, it's so much easier to upload a file using e-mail attachment than sending a fax. (Not all editors accept e-mails... but the numbers who do are growing!)

### Use the Internet.

The Internet is an integral part of my work. Every morning I check our incoming e-mail which streams in from friends and family. But it also comes in for me from listservers of two professional writers' associations (The Writer's Union of Canada [TWUC] and Periodical Writers Association of Canada [PWAC]). Eric receives mail from a number of newsgroups.

How do we do our work in electronic publishing? Both of us receive work from clients and fellow contractors, be they in Ottawa, Victoria or in the Bahamas—forming what I call a virtual company. (See my article on "The Electronic Cottage", parts 1 and 2.) Instead of sending large text and graphical files as e-mail attachments, the writers, clients and other subcontractors sometimes use the Internet's file transfer protocol (ftp) capability to transfer text. This may be in the form of a 200-page book or a four-page newsletter.

For my freelance writing, I find that exploring the world wide web (WWW) using Netscape as my browser is a great research tool. Not only can I use various search engines such as AltaVista to find sites using its Boolean advanced search capabilities, once I find appropriate sites, I can then contact them personally. As well, site links to other sites are a major benefit. Why? Because they create jumps to other associated people/places/organizations that I may never have considered.

Finally, the Internet provides a great way to "interview" people. Not only can you post questions via e-mail to contacts found on the Net, you can also verify information, or confirm analyses that as a freelancer you may have read/heard in other media. For example, an author interviewed me for her book on mid-life women. Not only did I get a synopsis of her book and understand what she wanted to ask me: I was able to focus my responses and when she sent me her final draft, I was able to comment on what she wrote. This opens up an exciting dimension to writers who strive for accuracy in their written work. All of us, in other words!

### Think laterally.

One of the exciting aspects of the Net is its ability to promote and encourage lateral thinking. By that I mean exploring unthought-of linkages to other subjects. The Net offers a great way to "brainstorm" and do research.

### User beware!

You know that old warning: "garbage in, garbage out." This phrase has been particularly useful in describing computer systems and their actual usability—and factual reliability.

In its way, the Internet is the logical extension of desktop publishing, where the art, craft and business of design and publishing was suddenly available to anyone. Similarly, the Internet is the global, computer-systems extension of self-publishing. Anyone can get his or her words out to anyone.

It is up to each one of us, writer or not, to validate what we find on the Internet. This should not be perceived as a barrier. It is the logical extension of the verification process we all perform if we are ethical writers. After all, it is possible to do extensive research and get responses in writing from interview subjects via e-mail.

### Permissions.

In my workshops and mentoring, I emphasize that writers should first get permission from the author to post (copy and send on) their e-mails to individuals, other listservers or newsgroups.

Many people trivialize this business of permissions. I suppose I am passionate about asking permission because of the whole e-rights issue (see Mark Zuehlke's article on e-rights in this book). I want to know where my words go and how they are used: don't you? That's what we all demand from our publishers, after all, so we can get fairly compensated and recognized. Think about this. My advice is always ask for permission. I have made good friends, made a positive impression with my interview subjects, just by asking permission from them. It's easy. Do it!

### Replacement to reality? NOT!

But let's not go hog-wild over the Net. Hey! Don't forget that there's nothing that replaces getting out there and interviewing real people in their physical, on-site locations. Remember the writer's old adage: write what you know. Technology won't change that truism. Your readers will discern when you are not writing from personal knowledge. Just as the fiction writer needs to experience that smoky blues bar in order to evoke its authentic atmosphere, so does the journalist need to visit, whenever possible, the actual locale.

### A useful tool.

Like any computer device, be it hardware or software, the Internet is a tool that can be used by writers to improve their craft. Use it wisely— and have fun!

### What I use.

**Web browser:** A software package, like Netscape, which allows you to surf the world wide web.

**E-mail:** An electronic message that is transmitted from one user to another. It is usually plain text but many e-mail programs enable you to attach documents (files). However, there are a number of conflicting protocols, so the file may not be accessible at the other end. Use e-mail messages first to establish connection and send a small test, not a gigantic file!

**E-mail attachments:** Files that can be added to and sent with an e-mail from one computer to another.

**File transfer protocol (ftp):** The standard protocol for transferring files over the Internet.

**Listservers:** E-mail systems that permits members of an association, for example, to use a common e-mail address to exchange information.

**Newsgroups:** Computer discussion groups that are not limited to members-only, as are listservers.

**Telecommuting:** Using the computer and Internet (the information highway) such that you don't travel the "physical highway" to an external work site. Synonym for "tele-work."

**Threads:** E-mail entries on a listserver or newsgroup that continue "conversations" about a particular theme.

**World Wide Web:** Also known as WWW, W3 or "The Web", this is a distributed information retrieval system based on the Internet's hypertext transfer protocol (http) which manages the transfer of hypertext documents amongst a wide variety of computers.

Katharine Fletcher has over 23 years experience in writing, editing and publishing. She thrives on diversification: she gives seminars (e.g. *Publish Yourself!*, leads hikes of Gatineau Park—and telecommutes from her electronic cottage. E-mail her at: <fletcher@hookup.net>.

# Electronic Rights

*by Mark Zuehlke* ⎯⎯⎯⎯⎯⎯⎯

Before the summer of 1995, most freelance writers, editors, and publishers gave little thought to matters of copyright. Why should they? Copyright was simple. The Canadian Copyright Act held that, in the absence of a jointly-signed agreement between the publisher and the writer, copyright remained the sole property of the writer. When a publisher of a magazine, for instance, purchased an article from a writer the purchase price only allowed one-time use in print form within North America or Canada (depending on the publication's distribution). Any other rights of usage had to be negotiated and acquired for an additional fee.

The clarity of the act resulted in few periodicals using written contracts and most writers were happy enough with this arrangement. Writers were more inclined to issue letters of agreement clarifying the nature of the assignment, fees paid, and expenses covered. In such letters the copyright ownership or rights being issued were seldom mentioned.

New technologies often render traditional ways obsolete. So it was when electronic media began to look profitable. Publishers realized they could not only issue print forms of articles and books, but could also sell the work in whole or in part through commercial databases, make it available on a World Wide Web (WWW) site, and issue it on a CD-ROM. And who knew what the future might bring? Suddenly acquiring only first-time print rights was insufficient to enable publishers to realize maximum revenue potential from a writer's work.

But it was all new media, so just how much revenue could be generated? What would the market pay for these privileges? In the absence of hard data, publishers made a curious decision. They decided what they should do is try to bully writers into giving them electronic rights for either nothing or next to nothing. Following the summer of 1995, a spate of what became known to writers as rights-grabbing contracts spewed from editors' desks into writers' mailboxes. The contracts almost universally required writers to sign over electronic rights in exchange for the right to continue doing business as usual. It was either tacitly stated or overtly implied that failure to sign the contract would result in the writer being refused further assignments.

No sooner did the contracts come out then writers and publishers plunged into a bitter struggle over copyright. That struggle continues. There have been victories on both sides, but the copyright war has clearly become a war of attrition with mounting casualties on both sides. Costly lawsuits, boycotts by writers of publishers, and publishers refusing to pay writers who won't sign the contracts are all aspects of this battle. Various peace initiatives have been mounted. There are indications that both sides are increasingly looking for a way to negotiate an equitable cease-fire and lasting treaty. One development showing great promise is an initiative by the Periodical Writers Association of Canada to create a transactional-based electronic rights licensing agency which will enable publishers to acquire the license to the works of writers through the agency rather than having to track down each specific writer and negotiate separate agreements.

In the interim, however, until such solutions are realized you need to protect the copyright to your work. You may be wondering how to do that and still find writing work. So here's a quick-and-dirty guide to electronic copyright.

First, electronic rights come in two parts. There are primary rights and secondary rights.

A primary right in electronic media exists when an article, poem, book, or work in any form is published first and only in electronic form. If you sell an article to an electronic magazine (e-zine) appearing only on the Internet then in the absence of any written agreement to the contrary between yourself and the publisher, the e-zine has only a first publication right similar to that publishers traditionally acquired when publishing in print form.

You will, however, want a written contract between yourself and the e-zine publisher because this is all new technology and you don't want to have to end up in court trying to sort out ownership issues. In the contract between yourself and the e-zine you should ensure that it is clearly stated the publication is only being licensed first-time rights to publish the work in its e-zine. As the Internet is a global medium you will probably grant the e-zine worldwide first-time rights. Any other rights you agree (preferably for additional payment) to license to the e-zine should be clearly stated and limited both in scope and time. A year or six months is a reasonable time, for example, to allow a publication the right to post your article on its WWW site. After that term expires a new fee for that usage should be negotiated or the rights revert to you and can be sold elsewhere.

Never sign a contract that requires you to give the publisher (whether in print, electronic, or both media) blanket electronic rights to your work. Just as is true of print-form publishing, electronic publishing takes many different forms. You will lose money and some control of your work if you sign such a carte-blanche clause. Always try to limit the right of use as narrowly as possible in any contract you sign, so any additional uses require extra fee payment.

Currently most freelance writers' work appearing in electronic form falls into the secondary right category. This simply means that it originally appeared in print form and is then being republished in some electronic form. Each of these electronic forms of republication, however, is distinct from the rest. If a publisher wants to use your work on its WWW site, a specific fee for that use should be negotiated. Should the publisher also want to include your work on its commercial database, another fee should apply, as is also the case for releasing the work on a CD-ROM version of the publication.

Publishers generally don't like this approach. It costs them money and requires their going back to the writer to negotiate each specific use. Alternatively they can pay extra fees for rights at the outset that might not end up being used.

But we're writers not publishers and our livelihoods are at stake here. It is not the job of writers to smooth the entrepreneurial waters for publishers. We want to be right in there sharing in the revenue stream generated by the use of our work. So every time a publisher makes money from our work we should get a piece of the action. It's that simple.

And it should be a significant piece, not a crumb or two. You created the work. Without it the publisher has nothing to sell. That's even more the case in electronic media than in print media.

Secondary rights in print media traditionally were licensed to the publisher for 50 per cent of the original fee paid for the work. This is a good benchmark figure to use when negotiating the licensing of electronic secondary rights to your work. In 1995-1996 most publishers would have guffawed at such a figure being proposed. But increasingly publishers are accepting such percentages. They are accepting them because writers are refusing to finance, through acceptance of token payment or no payment at all, the publishers' entry into electronic media.

This piece began by talking about publishers buying rights and you may have noticed the term licensing has now replaced buying. Traditionally everyone in the print industry thought of rights as something that were bought or sold. Truth is, however, the language was sloppy. You can't sell a right. You can only license it. Now that so many new electronic media rights exist it's important to be clear about these distinctions.

What a writer grants a publisher for any form of usage is a specific license to that part of the writer's copyrighted work. It's the difference between buying and renting a home. A publisher is a renter, the writer is the landlord. If the rent isn't paid or the publisher breaks the terms of the lease mutually agreed upon the writer can take the property back and rent it to somebody else.

Notice the shift in power that has taken place here. Landlords generally have more power than renters, but as a writer you may imagine the publisher having more power than you. Don't. After all, you own everything you write. The publisher just gets to pay the rent.

In 1996-1997, BC freelance writer Mark Zuehlke served as National President of the Periodical Writers Association of Canada and remains deeply involved in the issue of defending writer's copyright.

# Select the Right Photographic Tools

*by Murphy Shewchuk* _____

**"**❚ *f a photograph makes you laugh, if a photograph makes you cry, or if a photograph rips your heart out, then it's a great photograph."* Eddie Adams, Pulitzer Prize winning photographer and director.

Photography is an art form best described as painting with light. If your photographs are not sparking the emotional response that your talent deserves, it may be time to take a closer look at the tools you are using—and the way you are using them. Without the right tools to capture and manipulate the light, the images you visualize will be much more difficult to turn into slides or prints. And without the basic skills, tools alone will not make you a craftsman.

Here are 10 basic steps to help you produce the best possible photographs to complement your writing sales:

### 1. Determine what you want to spend.

If you have thousands of dollars to invest, a medium or large format camera may be an option. However, if your reason for taking up photography is to illustrate your writing rather than to start a new vocation, may I suggest that you stick with the 35 mm format. Forget everything you ever read about a different camera or a different lens for every situation. You can capture a great variety of scenes and activities with just a few basic pieces of equipment. Even professional photographers find that one particular camera and lens combination fits a high percentage of their requirements.

### 2. Choose your camera body.

Look for a camera body with as many of the following features as possible:

• Single-lens-reflex (SLR) optics. Composing through the same lens that takes the photo should eliminate most fuzzy images and headless bodies.

• Through-the-lens light metering. This important feature automatically compensates for different lenses, filters and adapters.

• Easy lens changing. This is a necessity when you graduate to telephoto or macro photography.

• Wide shutter speed range. Time exposure to 1/1,000 second or less.

• Manual over-rides. Be sure that you can easily over-ride the automatic features. This is especially true when you want to create special effects.

• Light weight and rugged design. Remember that you may be carrying this fine instrument for many years, so get a good protective case.

### 3. Choose your basic lens.

After you've chosen your camera body, the next item on the list is a good all-purpose lens. At one time, the basic lens had a 50 or 55 mm focal length that gave you passable snapshots just like everyone else. Today, the options (and optics) are much better. For most indoor and outdoor photography, a good start is a zoom lens with a minimum range of 35 mm to 100 mm and a close-focusing (macro) option. The 35 mm wide-angle end of the range is often best for scenes and small groups while good portraits are best shot at the 100 mm end of the range. If you intend to shoot a lot of close-ups, consider the macro option. If wildlife is your specialty, price out the longer telephoto lenses—then start saving.

### 4. Consider additional lenses.

While you are at it, consider an inexpensive set of close-up lenses. If you didn't get the close-focusing macro option on your main lens, you can add filter-like lenses to the front that will allow you to get excellent photos of that butterfly or handicraft.

### 5. Select your lens accessories.

Filters and a lens hood are next. An ultra-violet (UV) filter can be good insurance if you plan to pack your camera around on your travel adventures. Except for especially demanding shots, you can leave this filter on the camera to reduce haze and protect the lens from scratches. You may also want to purchase a polarizing filter to reduce reflections off water or glass and to add a touch of contrast to sky shots. If you choose an auto-focus camera, be sure that the filters are appropriate for the focusing system.

## 6. Purchase a tripod.

Unplanned camera movement ruins more photographs than any other error. With the newest electronics, auto-focus cameras can overcome your bad eyesight, but they can do little about your shaky hands.

## 7. Get a good flash—and use it.

The flash built in to many of the modern cameras will serve as a starting point. It will help erase the high-noon shadows that can destroy a good photo. However, when you are ready to get creative, look for a powerful, removable flash that will work with the electronic controls of your camera. It will allow you the freedom to paint with light in ways that a fixed flash cannot.

## 8. Film is next on the list.

Choose your film to suit your light conditions and your ultimate product. If the light is low or the action is hot, you will need a film with a higher ISO (formerly ASA) rating—with a corresponding trade-off in graininess. In basic terms, ISO 64 film needs more light than ISO 400 film, but ISO 400 film is likely to be grainier. If the family album is your ultimate destination, a good quality print film will be your first choice. If, however, if you have publication in mind, consider slide film. I've tried a variety of slide films in my 40 years of picture making and my basic stock is still Kodachrome 64. I have 30-year-old Kodachrome slides that are still earning money, while most of my E-6 process films such as Ektachrome and Fujichrome have deteriorated beyond usability after 15 years.

## 9. Practice your craft.

Develop a working knowledge of your photographic equipment. Don't head out on your dream assignment without knowing how to use your camera. Buy a couple of rolls of film and try a variety of techniques while making notes. Then get the films developed and compare what you got with what you expected. If they don't match, determine why. If you're a little confused, a library or camera shop has lots of books and magazines to help you better understand the art of painting with light.

## *10. Protect your investment.*

Finally, get your films processed as soon as possible. Leaving exposed film in your camera over a long period of time is a sure way to ruin otherwise good images. Heat and time can result in noticeable color shifts.

Carefully store the results of your photo safaris. If you are shooting slide film, archival grade slide sheets are a useful investment. Insurance on your equipment is also an investment worth making. Most household policies will not cover much beyond the basics, so double-check your coverage.

Paying close attention to these 10 basic steps may not guarantee perfect results every time but, with a little understanding and persistence, your images will begin to take on the look of a professional.

Murphy Shewchuk is a British Columbia freelance writer/photographer with nine illustrated books, hundreds of newspaper and magazine articles and over 1,000 photographs published. His articles, photographs and maps appear regularly in *BC Outdoors* magazine. He also offers a stock photo service and can be reached via e-mail at <mshewchu@vbcs.awinc.com>.

# Don't Play Film Roulette with Airport Security

*by Robert H. Jones*

M y trips involving flying are usually work oriented, which means up to six cameras may be included in my luggage: three 35mm single lens reflex (SLR) and three range finder (RF). The SLRs, a selection of "must have" lenses, dedicated flash and power winders go into my carryon bag, as does all of the film (usually 40 to 50 rolls of Fujichrome 100, plus a dozen or so rolls of high speed Ektachrome and B&W). The RF cameras and other photographic equipment, including specialty lenses, ring flash and spare batteries, goes into my unaccompanied luggage. The fragile equipment is first stored in a sturdy, highdensity polyethylene tackle box from which the innards have been removed to make space. Pieces of foam rubber placed between the equipment provides shock protection and prevents the contents from moving around.

Despite airline notices to the contrary, repeated X-rays at security check points will fog film. I do a fine job of destroying my own film through improper ASA and/or aperture settings which have nothing whatsoever to do with existing light conditions, therefore, I do everything within my power to thwart the airport security people from adding to my problems.

Film should *never*, ever be stored in unaccompanied luggage as it is subjected to X-ray scanning, and I'm told on good authority that the scanner settings are much higher than for carry-on.

All film—unexposed and exposed—is carried in clear plastic Fuji film containers, which in turn are placed in clear plastic bags. Loosely— so the security guards can simply roll the bags around and check the containers as they tumble about inside the bag.

Prior to entering the security check point, I remove the plastic bags from my carry-on luggage, then request they be visually inspected as the remainder of my carry-ons go through the X-ray scanner. Nicely.

Security staff endure a lot of jerks during the course of a shift, so I try to not be one. Even when I encounter the odd jerk who happens to be an airport security guard.

Prior to continuing a trip or returning home, if my cameras contain partly-shot rolls of film they are rewound and the number of frames *exposed*—plus two frames—is written on the film canister with a felt-tip pen. Prior to rewinding the partial roll, check the number in the film counter window. Whatever it reads, add two. In other words, if the counter reads 10, write 12 on the container label. Better to waste a frame or two that you can be sure of than to lose two or more possibly good shots because they overlapped.

As ink and wax crayon can be easily rubbed off the smooth plastic surface of a film container, I affix blank adhesive paper labels to at least a half dozen containers prior to departure. I don't worry about which have blank labels until such time as I am making a move that requires the removal of partially shot rolls. It then takes only a few minutes to sort through the containers and switch fresh film into unlabelled ones, thus making the labelled ones available for the partially used rolls.

If manually rewinding a film, hold the camera against your ear. Stop winding when you hear the film leader snap free of the take-up spool. To double check, activate the film advance lever a couple of times to ensure the film wind-up knob doesn't move.

When two of my RF cameras are finished rewinding film (a Nikon and a Minolta), a half inch or so of the leader is left exposed. Fine and well if the roll is only partly exposed—I usually tug the leader out another half inch or so just to make sure I don't lose it. However, if the film has been fully exposed, I wind the leader inside the container. I forgot to do this once, then later re-shot an entire roll of previously exposed film. As I said, I don't need any help from airport security staff to ruin my film, I do quite well on my own.

Robert H. (Bob) Jones is the author of *Tangled Lines and Patched Waders* (1995) and *Dull Hooks and Squeaky Reels* (1997), both published by Horsdal & Schubart. He has won numerous awards for his book and magazine writing. He is a past president and life member of the Outdoor Writers of Canada, and an active member of the Outdoor Writers Association of America. He resides in Courtenay, B.C., with Vera, his wife of 40 years, who is also a writer.

# Get Organized

*by Robert H. Jones* ──────────

A fellow writer recently asked how my work days are structured. "Other than putting your butt on a chair in front of the computer and keeping it there as long as possible," he added, thereby stealing my thunder. "I'm interested in how you organize your day in order to maximize your output."

The truth is my days are not very well organized at all, but my office is. I state this despite the fact that people entering my basement office and workshop for the first time often ask if there were any survivors after the bomb blast. There is a difference between organized and neat.

Some folks produce best by following a set schedule, but after working for other people for 31 years, when I tackled full-time freelancing my first act was to forget we own an alarm clock. Thus, for 15 years I have slept as late as I wish, except when early morning flights or meetings are scheduled, or friends in Ontario forget about the three hour time difference and telephone at eight a.m.—their time. However, likely as not I am already up having my first coffee, or pounding computer keys. It is amazing how much work can be accomplished in three uninterrupted, early morning hours before the telephone and doorbell kick in. Conversely, I might also be in my office until midnight or later (which is the case as this is being written). Obviously, there is not much structure or organization to my work days, so let's take a peek into the 11x11-foot disaster area where I work.

Three sets of shelves are filled with reference books, which equates to one shelf 35 feet long. The books are in groups relating to subject material: saltwater fishing, freshwater fishing, fly-tying, writer's guides, mammals, birds, trees and shrubs, etc. One complete wall is lined with shelves containing 35mm slide pages which are separated and identified by category (steelhead, chinook, coho, bass, etc.), backed-up computer disks, stationary, a Canadian postal code directory, and 10 business card organizer books. Each holds up to 100 cards, and is identified by category: Writers, Government, Guides & Resorts, Tackle Reps, etc. There is a small light table, two 5-drawer filing cabinets, two 4-drawer, one 3-drawer, plus four 10-drawer organizer cabinets. Full, and with everything indexed by name or category. Stored in these filing cabinets is personal and business correspondence, over 1,000 35mm slide pages, 40 B.C. marine charts, and about 200 topographic maps (about 50/50 B.C. and Ont.). Charts and maps are folded so their names and identification numbers are visible, albeit upside down in some cases, and each has a drawer index number in the upper left corner so it can be replaced in proper sequence.

One of the most important books in my reference library is a dog-eared British Columbia Gazetteer. When I am faced with an unknown place name, it reveals the proper spelling, which topographical map number to look for, and provides its latitude and longitude. As much of my output deals with saltwater fishing around Vancouver Island and the adjoining mainland coast, a 12x14-inch, hand-drawn map of this area is pinned to the wall by my computer. Blocked out with appropriate latitude and longitude lines, it shows me at a glance the general area for which I need a marine chart to pinpoint a specific location.

Also on the wall are pieces of paper with formulas for converting back and forth between metric and imperial, the province and state abbreviations for Canada and the USA, a calendar showing assignment deadlines in red, and an extremely cluttered cork board. On it are pinned written reminders that "grey" is preferred over "gray" for Canadian publications; the differences between continual/continuous, farther/further, and e.g./i.e.; that the Norwegian lady who ties magnificently intricate flies is named Torill Kolbu; and the dejected little fellow in Li'l Abner who had the perennial black cloud over his head was Joe Btfsplk. While cryptic notes like these might read like gibberish to others, they save me from having to stop writing in order to look up the spelling for stumble-words I can never remember; the proper usage of grammar or punctuation; or spending far too much time hunting for some vague snippet of information that annoys hell out of me until I pursue it long enough to discover I didn't need it after all.

A clip board holds several sheets of lined writing paper on which six vertical lines have been drawn. Three narrow rows are headed PUB (publisher's name), DUE (date), and SENT (date). A wide section in the centre is headed TOPIC (working title), followed by AMNT (amount), GST (#@+%!) and RECD (date). A red adhesive dot is placed beside each assignment when it is mailed. This is removed when payment is received, and a check mark indicates it has been published.

I often find that some of the best research material available is from articles I have written previously. For this reason, chronological lists of my published articles and fillers, categorized by magazine or newspaper title, are kept in a three-ring binder and on a computer file. Say I am writing a general article about fishing for chinook salmon during the winter. My index tells me which saltwater destinations I have written about, each of which probably makes reference to where and when winter fishing is best for chinooks.

Reading through the index also provides ideas for new articles, and reminds me of which ones might be worth recycling to other publications. If an article has been recycled, the margin is annotated with the magazine's or newspaper's name and date of publication.

All of this indexing and categorizing is not something I sat down and did overnight. It has evolved over the years, and continues to do so as I discover new or better ways to keep track of things. Some of it takes time and effort to initiate and keep up to date, but the end result is worth it. With virtually everything in my office indexed, named, or sorted into groups, less time is spent searching for information, which results in more time for writing, editing, photographing, labeling slides, and that other thing I used to do... I think it was called fishing.

Robert H. (Bob) Jones is the author of *Tangled Lines and Patched Waders* (1995) and *Dull Hooks and Squeaky Reels* (1997), both published by Horsdal & Schubart. He has won numerous awards for his book and magazine writing. He is a past president of the Outdoor Writers of Canada, and an active member of the Outdoor Writers Association of America.

# Ten Year-Round Resolutions For Writers

*by Margaret Springer*

Writing is a mental game. Ideas and talent and marketing savvy are important, but what really matters to our success or failure is the way we think about ourselves and our work.

Too often we get in our own way.

Here are ten resolutions to help overcome the negative, self-defeating myths which so often silence us. Don't save them just for New Year's:

1: I will practice regularly and write, write, write, and I will set aside time to read and study my craft.

2: I will join a new (to me) writers' group, take a course from time to time, and attend writers' conferences regularly.

3: I will listen to, learn from, and share with writers in all genres, because I know that writing is not separated into watertight compartments.

4: I will explore various methods of writing, but regardless of how others do it, I will use the approach which best fits ME.

5: I will do my best work and send it to the top appropriate markets, working down from there as necessary. (Otherwise I'll never know how good I am!)

6: I will write in the area(s) where I feel most comfortable, and where I have something to say. I will be myself.

7: I will treat editors and publishers with respect as professional friends and colleagues. I will recognize that it is in their interest to help me do the best work possible.

8: I will send out my work confident that I'll be judged on the merit of my writing only. I do not need to know anyone in the publishing business.

9: I will start all over again with every new piece of writing, regardless of success or failure. The reward is in the journey, not the destination.

10: I will not compare myself to other writers. I will give myself permission to succeed and to fail. And I will have fun along the way!

Margaret Springer is an award-winning author of dozens of published stories, articles and poems for children. Her book credits include *A Royal Ball* (Boyds Mills Press) and *Move Over, Einstein* (Penguin UK, 1997). She also teaches writing and gives workshops.

# A Christmas List for Freelancers

*by Florence M. Weekes* ———————————

S orry to interrupt your daydreaming, but it's time to brush off your Christmas list. Oh, I'm not talking about your gift shopping list. You can still wait until the last minute to decide whether to give Aunt Nellie the plaster fruit you won at the fair or just buy her another azalea. But for freelance writers, Christmas is seldom far away. Magazine editors need their copy months in advance. Newspaper editors will be planning for it about the time the Thanksgiving turkey is being turned into soup.

It's hard to envision reindeer on a snowy roof when you haven't put the sprinkler away yet, so here are a few suggestions to help get you going:

• **Humor.** Editors love it. Remember the time you dropped the salad as you got out of the car and Jack slipped in it and disappeared down the hill in a shower of lettuce and mayo? Or the time you got the gift cards mixed up between Lil's lace panties and the minister's scarf?

• **Pathos.** Has anyone you loved ever died at Christmas? Do you know of a quarrel that was patched up, a gift that changed a life?

• **Legends.** There are legends about almost everything to do with Christmas. One old Norse myth says Balder, god of light, was killed by an arrow made from the mistletoe plant. He came back to life and his mother Frigga, goddess of love, promised the mistletoe would never again be used for harmful purposes and that she would even kiss anyone who walked under it. (How well your resident teenager would enjoy being bussed by Balder's—or anybody's—mother, is hard to say, but that's the story.)

Check the mythology books at the library. There's a gold mine there.

• **Christmas in different lands.** How is it in Iceland? In Samoa? In some countries, they give gifts on different dates or children leave shoes to be filled instead of stockings.

• **Religion.** Lots of scope here. After all, Christmas is a religious holiday and took over from a pagan one. What about other religions and their celebrations?

• **Entertaining.** Remember any good Christmas dinner or parties you've been to? Know any amusing games or quizzes? Can you explain how to organize a sleigh ride, a concert or see-the-lights tour? How to cope with house guests?

• **Decorating.** Ever had people oh and ah over the way you dressed a tree, a mantel or the front lawn? Can you tell others how to do it, the cost, which parts are reusable, the low-down on live versus artificial trees?

• **Food.** How about suggesting a quick-and-easy recipe for the tired hostess or a light-meal idea for a food-weary-but-still-hungry crowd? A new way to serve punch? A dozen-variations cookie recipe?

• **Children.** How to feed them, dress them, entertain them, discipline them, teach them, travel with them—all are grist for the writing mill.

• **Toys.** Which are popular? How much to spend on them? What safety or educational features should you look for?

• **Electronic stuff.** Maybe this should go under "toys," but oh well. What computer to buy, what accessories? How to use the one the family gets for Christmas. What to give the computer user in the way of gadgets and games.

• **Gifts.** What to give to whom. The meaning of various gifts, flowers, jewels. How to organize shopping. What gifts can you make? How about catalogues and mail order? Wrapping and mailing parcels. Thank-you notes.

• **Fashion.** What to wear on the big day, Christmas Eve, for a country weekend or big city soirée. How have fashions changed?

• **Nostalgia.** Tell of Christmas long ago, for your grandparents, yourself when you were young or when your children were babies. Weird or wonderful Christmases you've known.

• **Carols and carolling.** Stories behind specific carols are popular. Groups that go carolling in unusual places make heart-warming stories.

• **Psychology and health**. Save a life, tell how to survive the whole affair, rationing time and energy, keeping down or getting rid of add-on pounds. How to get the most out of it all, for yourself and for your family.

• **Literature, art and music.** There are countless books, plays, paintings, songs and musical compositions on the Christmas theme, some secular and some religious. Check it out.

• **Your own fiction and poetry.** Christmas offers a wonderful theme for your own creative work. Even publications that don't generally use stories and poems will sometimes buy holiday ones.

Many of these ideas overlap; you can use them separately or together. Just feed them into your typewriter or word processor, mix, sort and serve. With any luck at all (and some research where necessary), you could come up with at least one saleable article, every year from now on.

Florence M. Weekes has worked as newspaper reporter and columnist, television news writer and producer, public relations writer, editor, and freelancer in non-fiction, poetry and fiction. Her work has appeared in many newspapers and magazines in Canada and the United States.

# Do Your Own Market Research

*by Brenda Gibson* ─────────────

O f course you know the basics of market research. You wouldn't be reading this book if you didn't. You undoubtedly subscribe to *Canadian Author* and *Canadian Writer's Journal*. You probably read at least one other magazine for writers, plus the newsletter of your local writers' group. All of these contain good, up-to-date market information. But there are a large number of other sources of information on markets that you may not be aware of. They range from directories to handbooks to monthly and quarterly journals to newsletters. Some are specifically aimed at the freelance writer, giving editorial requirements and payment; others are simply listings of current publications. And they are, for the most part, available at your local library; or, if not, at the library of the nearest big city.

Let us start with directories compiled with the writer in mind. Perhaps the most useful is *Writer's Market*. Published annually in the U.S. by *Writers Digest* magazine, it tells you where you can sell your short stories, books, articles, poetry, plays, scripts, fillers, and photos, in the U.S. and in Canada. It gives detailed listings of company and consumer publications, trade, technical and professional journals; also outlets for stage, screen and TV scripts. Included are names and addresses of editors, manuscript requirements, rights purchased and other significant details.

*The Writer's Handbook*, though similar in appearance, is somewhat different in scope. More oriented towards the writer of fiction (it is published by *The Writer*), it is chiefly devoted to articles by successful writers on how they approach their writing. But it has a markets section with U.S. and Canadian publications listed according to type and subject matter. Not a lot of detail is supplied, but it does give rates of pay.

For those with aspirations to appear on the publishing scene beyond North America, there is the *International Writers' and Artists' Yearbook*, also from *Writers Digest*. A world-wide directory of markets for writers, artists, publishers, photographers, designers and composers, it lists newspapers and magazines, book publishers, theatre, TV and radio outlets, and agents in the UK, Africa, Australia, New Zealand, India and Ireland, as well as North America. It also lists literary prizes and awards.

For more specialized markets, you should try the *Gebbie House Magazine Directory*, published in the U.S. by the National Research Bureau. A public relations and freelance guide to leading house magazines, it indicates which take freelance material, and what they pay.

An excellent source of markets that covers radio, television and various aspects of the print press in Canada is *Matthews Media Directory*, a three-times-a-year guide published by Canadian Corporate News in Toronto. The reference or communications section of any major public library should carry this volume.

The *Canadian Writer's Guide* lists a wide range of markets and awards. *The Canadian Writer's Market* by Adrian Waller is similar in scope. *Canadian Markets for Writers and Photographers* includes references for photojournalists.

Those of a more academic bent should take a look at the *Directory of Publishing Opportunities in Journals and Periodicals* (you may have to consult a university library for this one). Published in Chicago, it itemizes more than three thousand specialized and professional journals in the U.S. and Canada, with detailed editorial description and manuscript requirements. Most are non-paying (for some you even have to pay to be included!) but some do pay, and handsomely.

If you don't find what you want in the publications aimed at writers, it is worth turning to listings of a more general nature. The two best known are *Ayer's Directory of Publications* and *Ulrich's International Periodicals Directory*. *Ayer's* covers chiefly the U.S. and Canada, and lists daily and weekly newspapers, plus consumer, business, technical, professional, trade and farm magazines. It is indexed according to state and province, cross-referenced for type, and grouped according to subject. If that sounds complicated, it is; but it can repay the effort needed to master the system. *Ulrich's* is international, and claims to list sixty-five thousand periodicals originating throughout the world. It covers everything from company publications to literary magazines. *Ulrich's* offers a quarterly update. It lists periodicals under five hundred fifty-six subject headings, with fourteen thousand eight hundred cross-references; it also has a cessation index, for periodicals that have ceased publication since the previous edition.

A relative newcomer, the *Standard Periodical Directory*, is published by Oxbridge Communications and claims to be the largest authoritative guide to U.S. and Canadian periodicals. It covers consumer, business and trade magazines, ethnic and religious publications, scientific and technical journals, poetry and creative writing magazines—all under subject headings from Accountancy to Zoology.

Also useful is the *Magazine Industry Market Place* which, together with a lot of information on the business of magazine publishing, contains lists of publications classified by type: consumer, trade, professional, technical, farm, religious, scholarly, literary, and children's, with detailed descriptions including whether freelance material is purchased.

For publishing opportunities in the UK and beyond, take a look at *Willings Press Guide*, published by Skinner. A guide to the press of the UK and principal publications in Europe, Australia, the Far East, Middle East and the U.S., it lists newspapers and periodicals according to country, with a classified subject index.

Turning to other sources of information that can be put to good use by writers, there is *Reader's Guide to Periodical Literature*. Published quarterly, it lists fiction and non-fiction published in leading U.S. periodicals by subject and by author. Not exactly a market guide, but it tells you who is publishing what, where and, more important, who is accepting what, thus suggesting what you can get published, and where. It is also, of course, a useful source of information for researching your article. *The Canadian Periodical Index* does the same thing for Canadian periodicals and the *Canadian News Index* (formerly *Canadian Newspaper Index*) covers leading Canadian newspapers.

The Canadian Magazine Publishers' Association puts out an annual list of its members, with addresses, and, at intervals, an illustrated catalogue with much descriptive detail, aimed at the reading public. You would have to write for editorial requirements and rates of pay. Another useful source is *CARD* (Canadian Advertising Rates and Data), which details more than one thousand consumer, farm and business publications including editorial descriptions. Though aimed at advertisers, it, too, can augment your market resources. There is also a U.S. version, called *Standard Rate and Data Service*.

Never forget the importance of reading at least one copy of any magazine to which you are considering submitting your work. It can save a lot of wasted effort in inappropriate queries and submissions. You really cannot decide from its title (or even a brief description) that this is just the magazine to take your work. If you cannot find the magazine in your local store or library, it is worth writing for a copy. Many magazines will

send you a sample copy free of charge, but you should, in courtesy, suggest they bill you.

It is all too true that periodicals—especially in the literary field—rise
and fall like the flowers in spring. In the few days before this *Guide*
went to press, a half-dozen changes were required in the Periodicals
Market section. Thus it is important to have up-to-date information to
avoid the waste of time, money, and effort of sending your manuscript or
query to a defunct publication. For this you need to consult the writers
magazines with good, up-to-date market information, such as *Canadian
Author, Quill & Quire* and, from the U.S. *Writer's Digest* and *The
Writer*. There are also a number of good newsletters put out by Canadian
Authors Association Branches and writers groups in various provinces.
Those with access to the Internet may wish to use a "search engine" such
as AltaVista to seek market information.

And, finally, don't forget the importance of consulting writers working in the particular field that interests you. Find out if there is a
Canadian Authors Association Branch or writers group in your area and
join it. Writers, generally speaking, are generous with their advice and
help and it is from your fellow-writers that you may well get the best
market tips of all.

Canadian Author Magazine
Box 419, 27 Doxsee Avenue North, Campbellford, Ontario K0L 1L0
Phone: (705) 653-0323; Fax: (705) 653-0593,
E-Mail: <canauth@redden.on.ca>

Canadian Magazine Publishers Association
130 Spadina Ave., Suite 202, Toronto, ON M5V 2L4
Web listing at <http://www.cmpa.ca/>

Canadian Writer's Journal
Box 5180, New Liskeard, Ontario P0J 1P0
Toll Free: 1-800-258-5451. Phone (705) 647-5424 Fax: (705) 647-8366
E-Mail: <dranchuk@aol.com>

Gebbie House Magazine Directory, National Research Bureau,
200N 4th St. Burlington, IA 52601-5305

Matthews Media Directory
Suite 500, 25 Adelaide St. E., Toronto, ON, M5C 3A1

Quill & Quire
70 the Esplanade, Suite 210, Toronto, ON M5E 1R2

Standard Periodical Dictionary, Oxbridge Communications
150-5th Ave. New York, NY 10011-4311

The Writer
120 Boylston St. Boston, MA 02116-4611

Writer's Digest Books
1507 Dana Ave, Cincinnati, OH 45207-1056
Phone: (513) 531-2222 Fax: (513) 531-1843

Brenda Gibson is a freelance writer and photographer who teaches adult literacy.

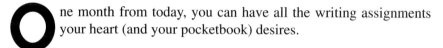

# The Ten-Day Marketing Plan

*by Ron Reichart*

One month from today, you can have all the writing assignments your heart (and your pocketbook) desires.

The catch? Only the one where it says anything worthwhile is difficult and usually involves hard work. The plan outlined here does involve hard work and I suppose it could be difficult for some. However, getting all the writing assignments you ever wanted, but were afraid to dream about, is worthy of some honest toil.

The work portion of the plan requires only ten days. Each of these days will be filled with marketing activities guaranteed to produce the promised writing assignments within the time frame mentioned in the first paragraph.

Some writers may find it impossible to follow the plan exactly as written. No matter. Since we are all blessed with varied talents, interests and ability, it is reasonable to assume that each of us will handle the work in a different way.

The important thing is to make the commitment to follow the plan as closely as possible within the boundaries of your personal likes and dislikes. If you do, you will acquire that in-basket full of writing assignments.

In today's competitive marketplace, a successful freelancer is usually a good salesperson—one who recognizes the advantages of a strong, selling query letter, one who is not afraid to roll up the sleeves and call on a few editors in person. The writer should not shirk the selling aspect of his job. It is the sale that assures your work seeing print where it can do the most good. You will note this plan of action requires plenty of selling. That's because it gets results.

Here is a day-by-day marketing plan that will produce the results you want.

• **Day One:** The best place to start is right in your own neighborhood. The project for today is to visit the editors of your local newspapers. Of course, you will telephone before your visit. It is always best to have an appointment. In your briefcase you will have several proposals for articles and/or columns that you consider to be just right for the local audience. Convince the editor, and you have an assignment (or two) and a place to make repeat sales for years to come. It was just such a visit that netted me a regular assignment with a weekly. I edit some sports copy for them and write a weekly feature on the local legislative body. Result? A regular weekly paycheque for a very few hours work. What do you have to offer this market?

• **Day Two:** You get to stay home today, but your work will be just as important as yesterday's. For today, read back copies of every magazine you can find, with these thoughts in mind: Can I slant a similar piece for this magazine? Can I do a similar piece for a competitive magazine (different theme)? If you are conscientious in doing this project, you will be bleary-eyed by day's end, but you will find enough concrete ideas to write at least five good queries to five separate publications. The queries will have the inherent advantage of being on target with respect to the type of idea the magazine is using. Remember, at least five queries today. Does this idea really work? You bet it does. I could furnish many examples, but here are two that come quickly to mind.

A young writer friend was studying back copies of old magazines. She happened across an aviation publication with a story about a man who had made a fortune, despite lack of any formal training, by inventing a small jet plane. A query to the *National Enquirer* produced an assignment and an all-expense paid trip to interview the subject who lived several hundred miles away.

A recent example from my own experience is easy since I use this idea all the time. I read a story in *Merchandising Magazine* called "Marketplace Indianapolis." It detailed why that town is a good place to do business in the retail appliance field. The resultant query was a natural. I could come up with a similar idea about my own town. I sold the story to another magazine. What variation can you offer?

• **Day Three:** Today your task is to run an ad in your local newspaper. The ad will be designed to pull in writing assignments.

Writing such an ad can be a real challenge. Here are some guidelines that should help you. First, decide what type of need exists in your community, then determine what skills you possess that meet those needs. Where the two match your ad begins.

For example, I placed an advertisement under "Business Services" in the classified section of a large metropolitan daily. Result: I was asked to write a newsletter for a school, a brochure for a non-profit organization, and a sales letter for an individual who wanted an audition with a local television show. I wrote the sales letter, my client got his audition. The fee I charged more than paid for the ad, and we both were happy. What can you offer in your ad?

• **Day Four:** Today's assignment is the flip side of yesterday's: answer all those ads that beg for writers. What ads?

The daily newspaper is the largest source. Make a trip to the library to check at least thirty days of back issues. Don't make the mistake of confining your search to only one newspaper. Check the dailies of neighboring cities and check all the weeklies.

Another good classified source is *Editor & Publisher* magazine. They have a "Freelance Wanted" section. I recently obtained a regular weekly assignment from this very source. *Editor & Publisher* is a weekly, so you have 52 shots a year.

Completion of Day Four calls for you to actually answer at least three ads. This should result in some assignments.

• **Day Five:** Today's assignment can be one of the best result-producers of all. It calls for you to search your dead file for at least one article that can be reworked and sent off to a new market. Your own files are a good source of material. Don't overlook them.

Every writer, excluding the newest tenderfoot, has done this at one time or another and has hit the mark with the rewrite.

Completion of the assignment calls for sending out the rewrite to a brand new market.

• **Day Six:** This one is pure fun. Editors get pressed occasionally for holiday material so get yourself one of those calendars that list all the holidays and special-events days—even National Ice Cream Week.

Write at least five queries today regarding ideas for holiday pieces. These queries should be sent to five different publications. Your best chance may be with lesser known holidays. Let the editor know why you are the perfect person to do this holiday piece. What can you offer this market?

• **Day Seven:** I'll issue a challenge. If you can read every listing in the Markets section of *Canadian Author* magazine the *Canadian Writer's Journal* and not have at least one good idea article come to the surface— I'll give you a free lesson in "How To Get Good Articles Ideas."

Seriously, this is one of the soundest marketing ideas open to a writer. Read what the market wants, then offer to provide the finished product.

Let your imagination soar. Today's effort should result in at least ten queries. The key is reading every listing.

• **Day Eight:** Read your daily newspaper with an eye to the story behind the story. Many writers make the newspapers their prime source of ideas. Hayes B. Jacobs, in his book, *Writing and Selling Non-Fiction*, reported that the newspaper triggers many of his memory exercises.

*The National Enquirer*, which proclaims itself to be the largest newspaper (circulation) in the world, uses stories "behind the news" all the time.

It is not too much to expect a workable idea a day from this source, each resulting in a query to an editor. Be sure and send at least one today. Then make reading the newspaper this way a daily event.

• **Days Nine and Ten:** These last two days will get you out of the house again and into some good old-fashioned street pounding. In terms of realized income, they can be your most rewarding days.

Hit the street, but not until you are properly prepared.

Here's how to prepare: Type a résumé listing all your qualifications. Stress your accomplishments as a writer. If you don't have many yet, make a point of stressing your education and/or interests. Prepare copies of published articles if you have any, taking a cross-section of your best material.

Fortified with this paper arsenal, you will make "cold calls" on the following: public relations agencies, photographers, radio stations, and advertising agencies.

Each of these businesses deals in the printed word. They all have a basic need for your services. Convince them you can fill this need and you have an assignment.

These calls are not hard to make. Simply introduce yourself as a freelance writer. Tell the receptionist you would like to see the person in charge of freelance writers. I have found this usually gets results mainly because most places do not have anyone assigned to freelance writers, thus the receptionist calls the manager for an answer to the problem.

Once you meet the person in charge, offer your services, then let the conversation be guided by what happens next. In almost every case, you will be asked to leave samples of your writing. If you have impressed at all, you have an excellent chance of obtaining a trial assignment. If you can really produce, that's all you need.

There you are. Ten days of action calculated to produce at least twenty writing assignments within a thirty-day period of time.

Do you really want solid writing assignments? Want them enough to pay the price in hard work and effort to obtain them? If so, this plan, or parts of it, may be just the push you need to get started. Only ten days. What do you have to lose?

Spend your next ten working days in selling your way to success.

*Ron Reichart is a freelance writer who understands the secrets of how to sell successfully.*

# Fish for Multiple Sales

*by Gary Thomson*

The little Welsh pub in the hill country near Pandy was a charmer measured by any standard. Old, eccentric character associations, spectacular setting. Built when Shakespeare was a budding playwright. A Victorian-era landlady with a wooden leg and a tremendous appetite for brandy. Two trout streams rushing past the patio.

Potential here for a travel article?

As a practicing freelance for 15 years, I thought maybe—but not quite. Britain boasts at least 3,000 pubs in the "charming" category; editors wouldn't bite if that was all I could offer. What this place needed was a unique angle.

When I stepped into the bar area, I saw the singularity that would guarantee not only a travel piece, but also one with profitable cross-market potential. Past the bar stools and darts area ran a sluiceway that channeled water from one of the mountain streams. Sleek trout darted along the channel, toward the exit beyond a polished oak table near the dart board.

Now I had it. The only pub in England, or maybe the world, where you can fish for your dinner while enjoying a pint.

So...an interview with the landlord and friendly drop-in locals, some interior and exterior photos, information on the history of the Woolpack Fishing Pub, relevant service details, and I had enough material for a small feature that proved fun in the writing—and one that returned healthy rates for my brief stopover.

## Compose constructively

Before we take the piece to market, consider the instructive elements in this small creation:

Plan ahead. In my preliminary research through guidebooks and British Tourist Authority publicity I had noticed a brief mention of the

Woolpack Pub and its unique bar. The sluiceway was a legacy of the building's sixteenth-century use as a fulling mill; hill folk had once brought their raw fleeces here for washing. Since the pub lay near my other planned destinations, a detour presented no problem.

Let your subject tell you its scope and limitations. Pubs are affable, communal places, so my article had to reflect active characters and genial atmosphere. Like the snatches of conversation and personal inter-action there, it had to be brief and escapist. A couple of quotes from the landlord and a few colourful historical details captured that atmosphere. The finished piece felt complete at 725 words. Editors favour 700- to 1,000-word lightweights that fill a page easily and offer their readers concise information or playful diversion.

Write to entertain, always. Tell a story that moves your readers, preferably toward humor. Begin with an active lead that sets place, sub-ject and focus: I dramatized patrons at the ready, each with a pint in one hand, fishing rod in the other. Use sensory details to let your reader hear, see and smell your subject. Use specific details: these were not just fish in the sluiceway, but eight-inch graylings. Remember the power of fic-tion techniques: setting, dialogue; create characters with a painter's light stroke; let them speak of memories and desires. Interweave historic tra-dition with current activities.

### Sell aggressively

Now, to market. Make a list of potential outlets even as you first con-sider, or later investigate, your destination. Early decisions here will focus and direct your research, interviews, photography and fact-list content. And your writing.

Because of the Woolpack's subject matter and unique angle, it was suited ideally for a fishing magazine. I sent it unsolicited (with accompa-nying photos) to a national slick. The editor bought it for $300. Later I sold it to a major newspaper travel editor for $200. Now I'm revising it for a trade magazine that manufactures fishing equipment. Again, some instructive elements here.

Always think of cross-marketing your scripts, even as early as initial research. The increased financial payoff reminds you that writing has a business side. Be mindful always, of the rights you offer with each version.

Reworking for additional markets can be easy. Visualize the reader-ship of potential outlets, then look in your subject material for a unique or unusual character, episode or fact that will help you speak to those readers. Consider places you can make minor changes: lead, emphasis, quotes, selected detail. You may change the clothing of the piece, but always keep the heart.

Learn market sources. Haunt your local library and familiarize yourself with reference volumes and magazines that provide market outlets for your work. As a travel writer I consult *Writer's Digest Yearbook* and *Gale's Directory of Publications* frequently. The best newsletter for market updates is the monthly *Travelwriter Marketletter*. For worldwide markets I refer to *Writers' and Artists' Yearbook*.

A final tip on photos. Editors prefer color slides. Never send originals. When taking your own scenery or people shots, shoot several—it's less expensive than making duplicates. Pack your slides in a plastic sleeve, and identify each with an adhesive address label.

Ideas for articles abound. The smart freelancer looks at them all with the same thought in mind: How can I shape this piece for additional markets? Keep that notion close and your sales will improve dramatically.

Gale's Directory of Publications and Broadcast Media.
Gale Research.
835 Penobscot Bldg., Detroit, MI 48226.
Phone: (800) 877-4253. Fax (800) 414-5043.
Website: http://www.thomson.com/gale/default.html

Travelwriter Marketletter
301 Park Ave, New York, NY 10022-6806
Phone: (212) 759-6744 Fax: (212) 872-7272

Writer's Digest Books
1507 Dana Ave, Cincinnati, OH 45207-1056
Phone: (513) 531-2222 Fax: (513) 531-1843

Writers' and Artists' Yearbook
A. & C. Black, 35 Bedford Row, London, WC 1R 4JH

Gary Thomson is the author of one book, *Village Life in Upper Canada*, and numerous travel and feature pieces for Canadian, U.S. and British magazines. He teaches senior secondary school English in Belleville, Ontario.

# Cycle and Recycle

*by Joan Eyolfson Cadham* ————

**M**y late husband, Jack, used to tease me about the Rideau Canal, calling it my Brooklyn Bridge—I've "sold" it so many times. However, my solar-powered calculator has verified some statistics that I had estimated easily just by watching the rise and fall of my cheque book. If I am going to survive as a freelancer in Canada, writing the sort of articles I enjoy writing for the magazines in which I want to be published, I'd better fine tune the art of recycling materials.

I write regularly for two small town Saskatchewan weeklies, producing features, profiles, editorials and columns. I also have regular columns with *Prairie Messenger*, out of Muenster, Saskatchewan. I would not trade the flexibility, the sure markets, and the complete freedom to express my ideas in print. However, small papers can't pay a living wage to a freelance reporter. Achieving a modest income as a full-time freelance writer means selling to other markets as well.

I usually write 1,500- to 3,000-word non-fiction articles for family-style Canadian magazines, features and profiles for farm magazines, and non-fiction for church-based weeklies and monthlies. One of my high-paying markets in Canadian magazines shrank a few years ago when most of the boat makers went out of business and many of the Canadian yachting magazines died. Many of my other markets aren't top cash providers. However, they are hungry for material. The trick is to produce enough copy. It didn't seem like such an impossible task until I put a little calculation into the production of all those words.

I'm congenitally incapable of doing on-the-beat reporting. I need to have ideas fester and ferment before I can begin to write the first draft. I spend hours on the phone, digging up ideas and talking to editors. There's interview time, and time for photo sessions. There are the trips back and forth to my photo-processor (who makes me look better than I really am). There are impatient daily journeys to the post office to see whether I have any happy mail. There's research time, and travel time, writing time and the times when my brain shuts down so that I might as well go sit in a patch of daisies and enjoy the sunshine. And there are the times when I want to shut down the factory and go play, or cook a meal, or take a walk, or go to a movie, or visit with my family. Besides, I spend hours looking for sources for new markets. (Filing, sorting and tidying gets done only when I am too brain-dead to write. That time doesn't count.) It's clear that I'm not going to survive if I need to rely on fresh material as my only source of income.

Recycling means I can skip all the research and interview time. I get to use up photos that would otherwise decompose in my files. And on the days when I'm only comatose, not completely brain-dead, I've got a head start on a fresh piece so that I might just get some productive work done during my self-imposed exile at the computer.

Because most of the periodicals that publish my work with any regularity are slanted to a specific audience, I can't dust off old manuscripts and sell second rights over and over. I dust off my original idea—ideas can't be copyrighted although the position of words as they fall in line, one after the other can—and I rework the story for a new audience.

I have drawn up my own ethical guidelines. I try not to sell the same story idea to competitive magazines unless I can come up with a really different slant for each of them. I write for a wide selection of inspirational magazines, and I consider using the same idea for a Catholic weekly and a Baptist monthly fair game because the readership will be different (although the editors will probably get to read both versions, since they read each other's publications). I've been honest about my philosophy and I submit that, at the rates paid by Canadian inspirational magazines, a determined freelancer must use the same idea more than once if she's at all addicted to eating anything but curried cat food.

I've sold the wall beside my computer almost as often as I've sold the Rideau Canal. Many years ago, when my kids were little, in a moment of frustration I decided to counter pornography, violence, depressing news stories and consumerism by finding an upbeat newspaper clipping that I could tack up on our old tongue-and-groove kitchen walls. The kids responded to the first clipping so I began to add others. One day, in a wild burst of enthusiasm, the kids added clippings of their own. Finally, one side of our kitchen became known as The Happy Wall or, simply, The Wall.

Developing and updating our wall was just another family tradition, I thought, until I discovered that visitors would slip out into the kitchen and work their way around The Wall, sometimes making a comment, sometimes asking for a copy of something.

I don't know why I wrote the first piece about The Wall. The response was instant. I got a happy note with my author's copies of the periodical: "Your Happy Wall happily filled a vacant spot in this issue."

By now I've slanted one piece as a "how-to" for a high school magazine. For another article, the slant was the "visiting adult" reaction to The Wall. A third gave the tradition of The Wall and talked about how the kids have grown up and moved away but still send home significant bits for it. As I highlight different types of Happy Wall materials—photos, cards, notes, cartoons, prayers, mottoes—and because The Wall itself is a growing, evolving structure, fresh possibilities continue to appear.

We cruised the Rideau Canal three times. I sold Rideau pieces a dozen times. There's the Rideau trip that I slanted to the owners of big power-cruisers although we did it in a 40-year-old wooden sailboat. There was the intellectual, philosophical, geographical, historical approach. There was "how to keep kids amused by playing games using old Rideau charts." A story on a little town with a welcoming congregation went to a religious monthly and was subsequently picked up by a local newspaper. An American small boats magazine got a piece recognizing that the Rideau is idyllic for small craft.

I've already bought all the Rideau books I'll ever need. I've got all the pamphlets, I've interviewed enough lockmasters and fellow tourists and inhabitants of the little towns along the way. There's no more money to be spent, no more time necessary for serious research. Now I spend my time considering new angles for other articles—and that's work I can do while I'm waiting to fall asleep.

I've got enough Rideau photos to see me through three or four more articles. Because I am not a professional photographer but a technically illiterate self-taught amateur with an eye for composition and a camera that does all the work, I lean towards quantity. Anyway, my photo-processor tells me that if I can get a couple of really good photos out of a roll, I've achieved the goal of most professionals.

In the same way that I won't send out the same copy to two magazines, I won't reuse photos except in the most extreme circumstances, even though some of the periodicals for which I write either don't pay extra at all for photos or pay a nominal amount that barely covers my costs. I realize that the "photos included" notation increases my sales potential.

I am a compulsive buyer of writer's market guides. I never pass a magazine rack without having a little peek to see whether there is a periodical that suits my particular style and interests.

We moved from Montreal to Foam Lake, Saskatchewan in 1992 so that I could write full-time without holding a "real job." I was determined to make it as a freelancer, however I define that goal. One major factor in any success I have achieved is that, early in my writing career, I honed the ability to extract every possible dollar out of every good story idea I have ever had, without offending editors.

And now, how do I credit this piece? Does it get filed under RIDEAU #12, or HAPPY WALL #7, or do I start a fresh new category with its own endless possibilities?

Joan Eyolfson Cadham, a past CAA regional vice-president is now a Saskatchewan Writers Guild board member. She counts two top Saskatchewan weekly newspaper editorials and two winning Canadian church press columns among her 4,000 plus writing credits. She is an occasional contributor to CBC radio, is in two editions of *Morningside Papers* and is a storyteller of Icelandic fables.

# Take off the Blinders

*by Gordon E. Symons*

'Ve met a hundred thousand writers, give or take a dozen or so, and discovered something self-defeating in more than half of them.

I've studied creative writing with these people at the University of Indiana, shared rejection-letter stories with them at conferences in California, and listened to the woes of writers from the Atlantic to the Pacific at writers' conferences across Canada. I've come to the conclusion that far too many writers wear blinders.

You know what blinders are: those leather flaps on a bridle that keep a horse from seeing to the sides. They're designed to prevent the animal from being distracted by forcing it to maintain a narrow, focused view of the road ahead.

That doesn't sound like a bad idea at first. Lord knows there are a million distractions out there. The sidelines are enticing. The action always seems to be somewhere else, not on the road to our writing goals. I once believed that if I marched single-mindedly forward, without pausing to look to the left or right, I'd eventually become a paid, published writer. Many of the dedicated but unpublished writers I meet each year have the same narrow vision I once had.

"I'm a poet and I create nothing but free verse," one woman told me after a writer's club meeting. Another said, "I'm a poet too, but I only do haiku." A man I met in Manitoba refuses to write anything but travel articles, and a woman who complained to me about how difficult it is to earn money as a writer confessed that she has never tried to do anything but essays for the op-ed pages of newspapers.

My own passion was fiction, and my specialty was the short story—specifically, the 4,000-word short story. I'm embarrassed to admit, even after all these years, that back then I sent my manuscripts only to *Esquire* and *The Atlantic*. Now that's what I call narrow!

Blinders are fine for horses. They may even be practical for some writers. I only know that I never saw my work in print or cashed a publisher's cheque while I suffered from tunnel vision. Once I discovered the many purposes of writing, however, and began trying to see how many of them I might be good at, it's not hyperbole to say that the course of my life changed.

My writing income has increased so dramatically in recent years that I submitted my resignation to the company that employed me for decades. Editors now call me to ask if I have time to take on another assignment. I've become a contributing writer for a national Canadian magazine, and recently I was asked to write a regular column for another national publication.

I've been asked to speak at universities and colleges, and encouraged to conduct writing workshops. I meet people, go places, and do things which wouldn't have been possible for me before. All this is because I finally took off my blinders, saw that I was surrounded by opportunities, and began to take advantage of many of them. I have fun, and I make money while I'm at it.

This is what I now tell new writers, and some old ones who aren't being published regularly: if you've never written a poem, try it, you'll be amazed at how much it can help you. At the very least it will teach you the importance of imagery. If you haven't been interested in non-fiction, get interested. In addition to helping you develop a sense of structure, gathering material for articles will get you out into the community, meeting new people and acquiring fresh knowledge.

If you hate experimental fiction, try your hand at it anyway. Perhaps you'll stumble across a technique that will put zing in your non-fiction efforts and make them stand out from the hundreds of submissions that cross an editor's desk each day. You don't have to stop doing what you love best; just look around and find out what else you're capable of.

The trouble with writing but not selling is that you can get terribly discouraged after a while. I did. I was ready to give up altogether a few years ago. I'd been doing the right things, I thought. I wrote for three hours every day. I took short-story courses and bought how-to-write-fiction books. Yet every story I sent out came back like a boomerang with a rejection slip attached.

There seemed no point in going on pretending I was a writer. Then one night I read in *The Writer* that there's always a market for humorous non-fiction—"Erma Bombeck" material. I sat down and wrote an essay called "Getting Old." I sent it to the local newspaper, something I'd never done before. A week later a co-worker approached me in the company cafeteria and said, "I enjoyed your piece in the paper this morning."

I hadn't even looked for it! I was so used to rejection, I had been certain it would never see print. The day the postman delivered a $100 cheque for my 700 words I suspected I was on to something. When I sold the same essay again two months later, I knew I was on the right track.

Ed Murray and his wife sailed their yacht around Lake Huron one summer. They stopped at out-of-the-way ports, anchored overnight in secluded coves, visited a lighthouse keeper and his family, battled ten-foot waves in a ferocious storm, and strolled across Mackinac Island. Before the cruise ended, Murray had filled a journal with the things he saw, touched, smelled and heard. He made notes about the way he and his wife felt when they got lost, and recorded the emotions they experienced reeling in a giant pike. His plan had been to gather background material for a novel and several short stories, and he achieved his goal.

But Murray also took a lot of photographs. He selected half a dozen of them, wrote a layman's account of the cruise, and sold it to his local newspaper. He wrote another version of the trip, this time telling other sailors how to repeat the journey, and sold it to a yachting magazine. A month later, he described the event from the perspective of a mature couple (he and his wife are in their 60s) for a seniors' magazine. Tear sheets of that article went to the Lifestyle section of a newspaper, which mailed Murray a cheque for reprint rights. A west coast magazine picked up the same piece.

Using experience gained from a portion of the cruise completed in heavy fog, Murray wrote and sold an article on the use of radar, followed by a piece describing some of his other electronic boating gear. Extracting weather observations from his journal, Murray created an essay on weather watching.

If Ed Murray had travelled with blinders on, refusing to consider any kind of writing activity but the fiction which is his first priority, he'd have passed up more than $2,000, not including the tax write-off he has been able to take on a good portion of the trip expenses.

What do you know a lot about? What are your hobbies, the things that interest you most. Have you ever written about them? What do you do for a living while you're waiting for someone to publish your first bestseller? Chances are there's a special-interest publication for your hobby or vocation. You probably have more knowledge and contacts in your areas of interest and expertise than do many of the writers already selling to these trade publications.

If your factory has found a new way to make ball bearings, someone wants to know about it and will pay—and pay well—to find out about it. If you work in a store which has tripled its business in a year, you have a great story on your hands.

That's not what you really want to do? It's your choice, but I know dozens of writers who are so encouraged by a steady flow of acceptances that they are much more prolific in their favorite field. Learning story-telling techniques won't impair your ability to write articles, and selling non-fiction won't mysteriously destroy your integrity as a novelist. Improvements in one area have a habit of spilling over into others. All it takes is the effort to get the blinders off.

Allow yourself to be distracted. Be open to new ideas, different markets, other writing disciplines. Spend an hour or two each week examining the listings in writer's magazines. There's a lot of satisfaction out there for writers who are willing to keep their eyes moving.

Ed Murray was able to pay for a unique three-week boat vacation by taking off his blinders. I plan to use my new earnings to retire early and write the Great Canadian Novel. Got a goal? Take off the blinders and go for it!

Gordon E. Symons, a former business executive, retired to write fiction and non-fiction from his home in Ailsa Craig, Ontario.

# Make Writers' Conferences Work For You

*by Audrey W. Babb*

Writing is a business with as many angles as any other business—technical details, bookkeeping, record keeping —but one thing we seldom consider is Public Relations.

Many writers are shy types, loners. Rather than join the crowd they prefer to crawl into a corner of the coffee shop and sip their drink or read or take notes. Now if, like me, you are one of these, you must strive to overcome that inclination.

I remember one morning at a Canadian Authors Association conference. I was the second person to enter the cafeteria for breakfast. The first was Duncan Pollock, then editor of *Canadian Author and Bookman*, who had given a talk to delegates the previous day. My first instinct was to take my tray to a far corner, but instead I made myself approach him, and he invited me to join him.

Over breakfast we talked of many things including typing and our wonder that anyone becoming a writer would not learn to type. I pointed out that as a former teacher of typing, I knew that a person could learn in a month of half-day instruction and attain a speed of forty words per minute with ninety percent accuracy. At that point Duncan said, "Write an article about it and I'll publish it." Which I did and he did.

That's what I mean by a writer's "public relations." In other words get in there and mix. Meet other writers, editors, and publishers. Join more than one organization to do with writing. Attend their conferences and seminars where you meet these people and you push in and talk.

Do I hear you say, "I can't do that. I like to be alone so I can think about my next piece of writing. I'm always thinking about writing!"

Of course you are. And soon that piece of writing will be finished. Surely you will want to see it published. That is your objective.

Let us say that you have written a book about the Canadian North. You have tried all the usual steps toward publication, but so far without success. Now, before you start your next writing objective why not put a few days into public relations?

Look for notices of writers meetings, conferences, readings, or festivals. They are advertised in club newsletters, newspapers, and writers magazines. There will be publishers and editors attending, some of whom will be happy to answer questions and talk to you between meetings or at dinners or social affairs.

You will come prepared with information gathered from the markets section of *The Canadian Writer's Guide* and other writers market publications. The best of these listings tells what material publishers are seeking. Some will list recent titles so you can examine the material at local bookstores.

Since you have done your marketing homework in advance, you will be prepared to network with the people who are most likely to be interested in your book project. Over several days of the conference you will mention your topic many times, and you have a good chance of having someone say, "I would like to look at your book...".

Remember, writing is your business. You need your own hard-working public relations representative—you!

Audrey W. Babb is a Victoria, BC writer with several books and numerous periodical credits. Her work has been published in *Western People*, *Modern Romance*, *Monday Magazine*, *Canadian Writer's Journal* and, of course, *Canadian Author & Bookman* (now *Canadian Author*) magazine.

# A Marriage of Minds: Ghost and Collaborative Writing

*by Douglas Waugh* _____

Two heads are better than one, goes the old saw. However, it is not very often, other than in the scientific or professional literature, that we find authors getting together to produce a book or article. Perhaps this is because journalists and other writers, in the pursuit of their solitary profession, prefer to remain, well, solitary, independent of others. While it is true that all authors must, whether they like it or not, collaborate with their editors and/or publishers, even when they are self-published, this is the only form of partnership most of us are willing to accept. Even this arrangement is often agreed to by authors only with grudging reluctance. This is a great pity, in my view, since there is much to be gained from the willing and enthusiastic linking of two minds in the production of a literary work.

My first effort in this direction was as a ghost-writer for a speech that was to be delivered by the late Dr. John Deutsch. He was then Principal at Queen's University where I was Dean of the medical faculty. Dr. Deutsch had been invited to give the keynote address at a retreat being held at the Chateau Montebello by the Medical Research Council of Canada. Presumably he had been invited because of his prominence as Canada's outstanding economist (he had been the founding chairman of the Economic Council of Canada). Furthermore, he was principal of a university that had a medical school in which there was a good deal of research, with the management of which he was well acquainted.

I don't remember the exact words I put into the Principal's mouth. I do recall that I tried to frame them in such a way as to reflect his background as an economist, and what I knew of his views on the management of the medical research enterprise. He approved of my first draft, adding a few pertinent comments of his own which I incorporated.

Since I was not among those invited to the retreat, I had to wait until it was over to ask one of my Queen's colleagues how the Principal's speech had gone over. "Not bad," he said, "of course it was just what you'd expect from an economist." I wasn't sure whether this meant I had been promoted or downgraded.

A collaborative adventure occurred when I was asked by the Hannah Institute for the History of Medicine to rewrite the biography of an outstanding Canadian physician. This biography had originally been written by one of my senior medical colleagues who had in fact undergone his training in that physician's department. This was a tricky assignment for a couple of reasons. First, the writer was himself a distinguished senior member of the medical profession and secondly, he lived in Vancouver, nearly three thousand miles away. Also, he was a rather straight-laced individual, not likely to be too receptive to the kind of irreverent commentary that is a feature of much of my writing.

After first negotiating with the Hannah Institute to the effect that I was to have a free hand and final say on the eventual text, I also agreed to pass all of my rewritten material to the original author for his comments and suggestions, though not necessarily for his approval. As things turned out, the arrangement worked remarkably well. To my surprise, most of what I wrote was accepted without demur, although there were a few objections to some historical details I had inserted, and to some inferences I had drawn from the original text. These were all resolved in the exchange of correspondence between us and the book was eventually published under the title of: *Duncan Graham: Medical Reformer and Educator.* My payment from the Institute covered my expenses, including the cost of a new computer and quite adequate compensation for my time and effort. In this case I was a true collaborator, although rather reluctantly accepted by my colleague, but nonetheless with the good grace of a well-mannered medical confrere.

My next ghost-writing assignment was a speech that was to be delivered at a medical meeting by the Hon. Jake Epp when he was Minister of National Health and Welfare. In this case my invitation came from an old friend, Dr. Peter Glynn, who was then the Deputy Minister. In this case, I was given no specific direction other than the identity of the group to be addressed and an undertaking on my part to clear what I wrote with Dr. Glynn. To the best of my knowledge this worked out well, although I never got any feedback on how the speech went over. It must have been all right, however, because a short time later I was invited to write a second speech. That may have been less successful, since I was never asked again. In any case I was well paid for both efforts, on the basis of the CV I had submitted to the Federal civil service.

On another occasion I was asked to provide the text for a coffee table book entitled, *This Is Our Work: The Legacy of Sir William Osler*. This was another transcontinental collaboration, in this case with photographer Ken Grant who had retired from the National Film Board to live in Victoria. Ken had assembled a collection of his startlingly vivid photographs of hospital scenes and physician-patient encounters under headings he had taken from Osler's writings. The book was to be published by Five Span Bridge Publishers of Packenham, Ontario, and I was asked to provide an account of Osler's life and work to accompany the pictures.

In this case, although the work was technically a collaboration, my role was so discrete and separate from Ken's contribution that there was little need for communication between us. The publisher agreed on a payment amount, with one third to be paid in advance and the remainder on acceptance of my final draft. I submitted my work to an editor with whom I had no difficulty agreeing on minor changes—all improvements, in my view. In due course a truly beautiful book was produced, of which I received two copies. As it turned out, that is all I received since, after the passage of many months my next communication was from a firm of accountants who had been named receivers in the publisher's bankruptcy. In a case like that all one can do is sit down and weep, while awaiting the letter that tells you how many cents on the dollar you are likely to get in the final liquidation. Three years later, I and my agent are still waiting, minus the $5,000 we are still owed. At least the one third advance payment was all mine, since I received it before I had engaged an agent.

With this background, perhaps I can generalize about the collaborative process. The first step in bringing this about is the acceptance by potential collaborators that there are skills, attitudes or other attributes that some individuals possess, if not uniquely, at least in special abundance or facility of use. Once that is recognized, the next step is to accept the desirability of joining forces with the possessor of those special attributes. Once that is done then, and only then, are you ready to seriously consider embarking on a collaborative writing effort. In some ways it's rather like embarking on a marriage, although literary collaborators may be rather more tolerant of each other's foibles than are marriage partners, perhaps because mutual exposure is less—I'm not sure about that.

Sometimes the choice of collaborator is made for you—an arranged marriage—as has been the case with my collaborative efforts. Here your only choice may be to take it or leave it, although you should never overlook the possibility of negotiating for a partner or terms of your own choice. Many editors are willing to dicker on this, provided they have not already made a commitment or the collaborator they have in mind has exceptional qualifications or abilities, as was the case in my work with Ken Grant.

In other situations you may be the one with the idea for a collaborative project. In such a situation all you need to do is formulate a proposal for presentation to an editor/publisher and to find a collaborator. I have no experience with this kind of collaboration, although I can see it would have the advantage of placing much of the control in your hands.

Whatever the collaborative situation, the only additional advice I can offer is to develop a "pre-nuptial agreement" between yourself and your collaborator. Such agreements can save untold amounts of heartburn and even retain valued friendships. It should go without saying that a similarly inclusive agreement should be negotiated with your publisher. If you can find a lawyer who knows the ways of writers and publishers, you should have him/her read and approve any agreements you contemplate entering.

An alternative to a formal agreement that I once used, when no agreement seemed to be forthcoming, was to write to my collaborator a letter along the lines of "Further to our discussions about collaborating on a book, it is my understanding that..." I then went on to itemize the details that a formal agreement should include. You can then invite your collaborator to suggest any changes, and/or to sign and return a copy of the letter. This is probably not as secure as a more formal agreement, but I can imagine situations where it may be the best you can do, short of abandoning the project.

Finally, collaborative writing can be a valuable experience. It can be rewarding in the exposure to another person's ways and useful in giving you access to ideas and information you might otherwise have overlooked or had difficulty in finding. Perhaps most important, you may gain access to financial rewards that might otherwise have been beyond you. Try it, you'll like it!

Douglas Waugh had a checkered career that took him from railway labourer to army medical officer to Dean of the Medical Faculty at Queens University. After his professional retirement in 1983, he was a columnist, book author and speech writer. Several of his essays have been reprinted in *Reader's Digest.*

# Translation—Art, Science, and Business

*by Roma Quapp*

## Translation: Art or Science?

Is translation a science or an art? This question occupied no small amount of our time when I was studying translation in university.

The proponents of translation as a science pointed to the use of the linguistic sciences as the foundation for their view. Language has structure, they argued, and this structure can be dissected and compared. Both the syntax (grammar) and semantics (meaning) of various languages can be scientifically analyzed. Once translators fully understand how these language structures differ, they will be better prepared to transpose the text they are working with from one into the other and to come up with a pleasing, natural-sounding translation. In fact, so the theory goes, soon we won't need translators at all—once the science is fully developed we will simply need to feed the right information and analysis into a computer and it will be able to churn out a perfect translation in a fraction of the time it takes a human translator!

Fie! cried the proponents of translation as art. Language has context, nuance, and emotion, which defy the minimizing attempts of science to limit it to a handful of easily applied rules. Many words have multiple meanings, and many meanings can be expressed through a variety of words. A sensitive, artistic touch is required to do justice to the transposition of the soul's expression from one concrete form into another. While computers may have impressive speed and analytical capabilities, they are not able to think, only to obey rules, and the rules for choosing among synonyms and contextualizing utterances are infinite and infinitely variable. The human translator will never be out of work.

The debate—minus the computers, and with a few other angles thrown in—has been raging through translation theory for over two thousand years, and this short article does not pretend to have the definitive word. But it should be evident to most thoughtful persons that both sides of the camp have some truth to them.

Language does have structure, and a good knowledge of the structures and structural tendencies of a language is of great assistance in translating.

This shows up at an elementary level in simple expressions. Someone who tries to translate, for example, "j'ai faim" literally as "I have hunger" either hasn't got a clue about the natural English form or is purposefully trying to make the English sound "foreign" for some reason. At a more advanced level, knowing that the French language has a love of noun phrases while English tends towards verbal expressions can be very helpful in creating translations that are natural-sounding in both languages.

On the other side of the coin, language does have a creative edge that is more suitable to an artistic understanding of it. Language play—puns, jokes, alliteration, and so on—easily escapes the rule-making attempts of science. Allegorical and symbolic language requires an understanding of the context outside the text itself. Even "ordinary" language that makes heavy use of description, through metaphor, simile, or plain old adjectives, requires the translator to be sensitive to how language relates to and expresses the culture out of which it arises.

Computer-assisted translation can be very helpful with texts where there is a limited, repetitive vocabulary, for example. But it is fair to say that as long as humans continue to speak and write in different languages, the translator will indeed never be out of work.

### Who can be a translator?

Since this guide is intended for writers, I will not address the question of interpretation—that is, the practice of translating spoken language, necessary for conferences, parliaments, and the like.

The practice of translation, as a minimum, requires an excellent command of two (or more) languages. Most professional translators will say, however, that it is not enough simply to know these languages, however fluently. Some scientific analysis of the languages in question is very helpful. Specialized training will help the translator-to-be to understand the different methods and styles of translation, which is useful in determining how to approach a specific text.

Specialized vocabulary study is essential for a person who wishes to translate medical, legal, or scientific documents, for example.

Knowledge of the cultures of both languages—preferably first-hand knowledge—is also essential to the production of translations that ring true. An ability to write well in the target language (the language one is translating into) is a must.

Normally one translates from a second language into one's mother tongue. Translation into a second language should only be attempted once the translator has achieved an extremely high degree of fluency in that language and is very familiar with the culture—usually only when one lives or has lived in that environment for some time. Anyone who has ever opened a user's manual for an electronic appliance made overseas and found the English almost impossible to understand will realize the truth of this. There is a vast need for good translators—translators who are well-trained professionals.

Several universities and colleges in Canada offer translation degrees. As well, most provinces have translators associations that provide certification and assistance. Translation is not a regulated profession; that is, translators are not required by law to obtain certification before hanging out their shingle. But anyone interested in working in the field would do well to contact the association in their region to find out what training is advisable, where it can be obtained, how to find work, and so on.

### The translation business: What kind of work is there?

The need for translation, particularly in a global economy, is vast and unending. Businesses wanting to buy from or sell to another country need documents translated; governments in multi-lingual countries need laws translated; parents wanting to adopt children from overseas need documents translated; and the list goes on.

Governments and large companies may have their own in-house translation departments, especially if they work in a limited number of languages. Smaller companies and those with only occasional needs for translation, or those who require translations into and from a large variety of languages, will tend to turn to translation companies or to freelancers. Translation companies themselves will often maintain a "stable" of freelancers in addition to any in-house staff.

If you can find permanent employment as an in-house translator, great. If you're among the ranks of freelancers, you need to make yourself known. One way to do this, and to gain some experience at the same time, is to contact any translation agencies and see if you can become part of their "stable". Beyond that, the usual rules apply: call the companies you would like to freelance for and speak to the person who farms out translations. Arrange to send that person your resume along with samples of your work. Ask if you can call back in a month or two to check whether they have work and to give them an update on your experience and skills, if applicable. Be sure to follow through! Be persistent, but not bothersome. Always ask if it's okay for you to call back again.

When people send you work, be thorough, be accurate, and be on time. Often companies are working to deadlines, and if they have to wait for you to finish the translation they are unlikely to give you more work. If the translation is too difficult, or is in a field that you are unfamiliar with, say so. It is better to be honest about one's limitations than to pretend to know it all. If you do so, you will probably retain a client; but if you do an unacceptable job they may withhold full or partial payment and are unlikely ever to give you more work.

Payment for translation is generally calculated on a per-word basis. More can be charged for "exotic" languages, for which qualified translators are difficult to find, than for common languages such as French. Technical translations or those with charts and graphs and other non-textual elements can also be charged at a higher rate. If you freelance for a translation company you can expect to receive a slightly lower rate than if you freelance directly, as the company will need to take its cut and still remain competitive. But that can be a small price to pay for regular work and for relief from the hassles of self-marketing. To find out what current rates are in your area, call your translation association, or call a few translation companies and ask what they charge.

### What about translating articles or books?

The market for translations of articles or books is smaller than the realm of business translations. The astute translator may be able to break into this field, but it takes a good knowledge of the magazines you are targeting.

Articles are generally written specifically for a given magazine in a given country or context. Attempting to place an article in a different country or context may be difficult. A Japanese article on gardening in a Japanese magazine is, for example, unlikely to interest the publishers of a Canadian gardening magazine—unless they happen to be doing an issue on "comparative gardening around the world"!

Even within Canada articles in French and English magazines are not necessarily that easy to transpose, depending on how localized the contents are and how perishable the article is—that is, how quickly the information goes out of date.

In the realm of books, these same variables apply. Certain non-fiction books suffer from some of the same difficulties as articles: they are too localized or too perishable to be marketable in a different language and culture. Histories, biographies, criticism, and technical books are probable exceptions.

Fiction is one area where being regional and out of date is basically irrelevant. In fact, as a tool to help us understand how people of different lands live and think and behave, fiction is unparalleled. The more regional and time-specific it is, the better. However, translations of fiction are also extremely difficult to market. While the Governor General's awards do well in acknowledging excellence in literary translation, Canadian publishers publish only a handful of translations every year. Many of those will be from French; some will not. Those publishers who do publish translations often work with the same translators repeatedly, making it difficult to break into the market.

Those translators wishing to translate fiction would do well to research which publishers in fact publish translations. Then send them a query letter along with a sample of the proposed translation.

One thing to be aware of when translating articles and books is the thorny question of rights. Unlike business translations, which are usually owned by the companies that request the translations or their associates, articles and books are owned by their original authors or publishers. Before translating and marketing an article, you must be sure to contact the original publisher and obtain the translation rights. When proposing a book translation to a publisher, you must make it clear whether you have already obtained the translation rights from the original publisher, or whether you expect them to negotiate the rights.

### Art, Science, & Business combined.

All in all, work in translation can be very rewarding. The opportunity to write creatively, the chance to learn about languages and cultures, and the possibility of earning money while doing so combine to make translation a truly enriching—and challenging—endeavour.

Roma Quapp is an award-winning author whose numerous stories and articles have appeared in magazines and newspapers as diverse as *The New Quarterly*, *Peace and Environment News* and *The Globe and Mail*. She was employed as a federal government translator for six years and edited a monthly magazine for the Conference of Mennonites in Canada for three.

# Find the Right Publisher

*by Crawford Kilian* ————————————————

T oo many people submit manuscripts to publishers.

Simply to read enough of those manuscripts to judge them unworthy would take the full-time services of several salaried editors. Most publishers simply can't afford to plow through the slush pile in hopes of someday finding a Great Novelist. So they indicate in *Writer's Market* that they will consider only "agented submissions"—work that a professional literary agent, who knows the market, thinks has some sales potential. That simply draws fire onto the agents, who now find that they too have huge slush piles. And, like the publishers, the agents can't make money reading unsaleable junk.

Where does that leave you?

In better shape than you think. If you've hammered out a credible but surprising plot about interesting people in a hell of a jam, and you're showing them in action instead of telling us what they're like, and your grammar, spelling and punctuation are first-rate—you're already ahead of 80 per cent of your competition.

Now the problem is finding the right market. Too many novice writers simply fire off their work to a publisher they've vaguely heard of, or one that's supposed to be prestigious, or even one that happens to be conveniently located right in town. (Those were precisely my three motives in submitting my first children's book to Parnassus Press. They bought it, which shows that sometimes even ignoramuses can get lucky. By rights, I should have had to send the manuscript to a couple of dozen houses before hitting the right one—if I ever did.)

Publishers tend to carve out special markets for themselves. A couple of sharp editors can dominate a genre; because they know how to reach a certain kind of reader, they attract a certain kind of writer. Or a publisher may be passionately devoted to supporting a certain kind of fiction, but is deeply uninterested in any other kind. A feminist publisher wouldn't have the faintest desire to market a men's action-adventure novel, and wouldn't care to try. A children's publisher won't care how well-crafted your murder mystery is. And so on.

So step one is almost embarrassingly obvious: Notice which houses publish the kind of story you're working on. Look carefully at the story elements in the titles they publish; Del Rey fantasy novels, for example, require magic as a major component, not just frosting or a gimmick to get the hero somewhere interesting. Out of all the publishers in North America, only a few are potentially yours.

Then consult those potential publishers' entries in *The Canadian Writer's Guide*, *Writer's Market* and other listings to see what they have to say about their own needs and who their editors are in specific genres. You may learn that your work in progress is too long, or too short, or needs some particular quality like a heroine aged over 35. You may also learn how long it takes them to respond to queries and submissions. However, don't take those statements as legally binding promises; responses almost always take far longer, especially for unagented submissions.

*Writer's Market* also lists publishers by the genres they publish. This list can lead you to houses you're not familiar with, but don't just rush your manuscript off to some publisher in Podunk. Check out the entries of these houses also, and also track down some of their recent titles in your genre. If they strike you as dreadful garbage, avoid them. Better to stay unpublished than to be trapped with a bad publisher.

Another useful source of research information is the publishing trade press. *Quill & Quire* in Canada, and *Publisher's Weekly* in the US, are much more up-to-date than any annual can be. So if the top horror editor in New York has just moved to a new publisher, or a publisher is starting a new line of romance novels aimed at Asian women, you may adjust your marketing strategy accordingly. Magazines like *Canadian Author*, *Canadian Writer's Journal*, *The Writer* and *Writer's Digest* supply similar market news.

If every possible publisher warns you off with "No unagented submissions," you then have to go through a similar process with literary agents. You should be able to find an annually updated list of agents in your local library or the reference section of a good bookstore. Some agents, like the late Scott Meredith and Richard Curtis, have themselves written books about the publishing business; these are worth reading.

As a general rule, you probably need an agent in the city where most of your publishers are. You also need an agent who knows the market for your particular genre, so your work will go as promptly as possible to the most likely markets. (Some agents may submit a work in multiple copies to all potential publishers; this can really speed up the process.)

Consider whether you want a big agent with scores or hundreds of clients, or a small outfit. The big agent may have clout but little stake in promoting you; the small agent may work hard for you, but lack entree to some editors. Talk to published writers, if possible, about their experiences with agents; sometimes a sympathetic author can suggest a good one.

No agent, however good, can sell your work to an editor who doesn't want to buy it. What the agent offers the editor is a reasonably trustworthy opinion about the marketability of a particular manuscript. It's in the agent's interest to deal only in work with serious sales potential, and to get it quickly into the hands of its most likely buyers.

You may therefore have to query a number of agents before you find one who's willing to take you on. And you may find that some highly reputable agents won't look at your stuff unless you pay them to. This is not a racket. If you agree to the agent's terms, the reading may give you a very frank response. Sometimes you'll get a detailed critique that may devastate your ego but teach you just what you need to learn. In many cases the agent will waive the reading fee if he feels you're a commercial possibility and you're willing to sign on as one of his clients. That should be an encouraging offer indeed.

Sometimes an agent will take you on but strongly suggest certain kinds of revisions, or even that you tackle a completely different kind of story. Listen carefully; you're getting advice from someone who knows the market and wants to share in your prosperity. At least one of my novels greatly profited from the advice of an agent who thought my proposed ending was a disaster.

Your agreement with an agent may take the form of a detailed contract, or a simple agreement over the phone, or something in between. Be sure you understand and accept the terms your agent requires: Ten per cent of what he makes you, or 15? Deductions for photocopying, postage and phone bills? Control over all your writing, or just your fiction output?

Once you have an agent, don't be a pest. When there's something to report, he or she will let you know. If you've got something to report, like the completion of the manuscript or an idea for turning it into a series, let the agent know. Otherwise, stay off the phone and stick to your writing.

In some cases, of course, you may find you've sold a novel on your own hook and then decide to go looking for an agent. Under these happy circumstances you should find it fairly easy to get an agent's interest. If the publisher's already offered you a contract (and you haven't signed yet), the agent may be willing to take you on and then bargain a better deal for you.

But you'll probably do all right even if you negotiate that first contract on your own. Most publishers are honorable and decent people; sometimes their integrity is positively intimidating. Even if they weren't honorable, your first book is likely to make so little money that it wouldn't be worth it to screw you out of spare change.

Crawford Kilian has published almost 20 books since 1968, including 11 science-fiction and fantasy novels, and over 500 articles in newspapers and magazines. His most recent titles include *2020 Visions: The Futures of Canadian Education* (Arsenal Pulp Press, 1995) and *The Communications Book: Writing for the Workplace* (Allyn & Bacon Canada, 1997). He teaches at Capilano College in North Vancouver, BC.

# Prepare a Convincing Book Proposal

*by Katharine Fletcher*

H*ow can you ensure that your book will be published?*

The simple answer is that there's no guarantee that it will be. But writers can immeasurably increase their chances of getting published if they first do some thorough research. Which publisher is likely to be interested in their genre and topic? Does the book have an international focus? A Canadian focus? Is it a software manual, a poetry book or a non-fiction exposé?

After researching exactly which publisher might actually be interested in publishing your book, you are ready to familiarize yourself with the dos and don'ts of the book proposal. Also, be aware that different publishers want different things in their proposals.

## How do you decide which publishers to approach?

• Network and get a mentor! Use your local and national writers networks such as the Canadian Authors Association, Periodical Writers Association of Canada, or The Writers' Union of Canada. Find out who has been published by a publisher you think might be interested in your book. Write or e-mail such authors: ask politely if they have time to help you with your book proposal. The key is to network so as to inform yourself. When I was working on my first book proposal for McClelland & Stewart, another M&S author acted as my mentor. Not only did he review my proposal, he also showed me his contract. *Tip:* Don't ever be afraid to ask for help: that's a key piece of advice to remember!

• Browse the web. That's right: many publishers have an Internet website that you can study. On it you can also find out the name of the

editor to whom you should send your proposal. This is a key preliminary step many writers neglect. Try using a search engine such as
AltaVista's Advanced Search, <http://www.altavista.digital.com/> using
keywords such as: "book proposals" OR "how to get published".

• Look at the publisher's catalogues. Has your idea already been published? Is the non-fiction publisher interested in biographies, or your
particular niche? Be informed: before you write your proposal, find out
if your unique idea has already been written.

• Review guidebooks and markets listings. Books such as this one
can be a valuable resource.

## What is a book proposal?

A book proposal is a comprehensive marketing tool that sells your
product concept (that's right: your book!) to a prospective client: the
publisher.

Many authors are unprepared to consider that their book is a product
that needs selling. Instead, many writers consider their book to be different, a labour of love, a sure-fire best seller that any publisher worth its
salt would publish in an instant.

The reality is that your oeuvre is a product, a commodity that must
find a market. That is, your book needs an audience that is clearly
defined. Whether it is to be the next Giller or Booker award-winner, or
whether it's a travel guide to Ottawa, the prospective publisher must
have an exquisitely clear idea of exactly who will read your book. How
does the publisher figure this out? Through your well-crafted, well-
researched book proposal.

## What does a book proposal contain?

Ah, here's the rub! Not all book publishers want exactly the same sort
of book proposal. Some want the entire book written (in most fiction
cases, so I am told). Others want one-to-three completed chapters and a
full TOC (Table of Contents) that will outline the structure and contents
of your entire book. This is where your preliminary research (and web
browsing) will be of special help to you, in order to ascertain exactly
what the particular publisher wants. However, based on my successful
proposal to McClelland & Stewart, here's some tips that will help you
formulate the groundwork to your proposal:

• Covering letter. This is written to the attention of the editor who is
responsible for reviewing the type of book you are proposing. In the
case of a small press, there may only be one editor. In a large publish-

ing house, such as the UK's Butterworth Heineman or Oxford University Press, or Canada's McClelland and Stewart, there may be several. It behooves you to take the time to find out which editor should receive your book proposal. Ensure you spell his or her name perfectly and be sure to use that person's correct title, along with the correct company name and full address.

The letter should succinctly describe your book project: its working title, its theme, its scope in an introductory paragraph. In another paragraph, briefly introduce yourself and mention why you are the best author for the project. (Yes: the book is a project. And, publishing your book is a process!)

Tone: Always remember that your book needs editing. The editor is your ally, with whom you will spend a considerable amount of time as your manuscript is edited and shaped into its final draft. Ensure the tone of your letter arouses the editor's interest. The editor/publisher and the writer must form a cohesive team. Your introductory letter can convey valuable information about your perception of your role as a team player in the publication venture.

• Working title/subtitle of book. What is the title of your book? Keep it short, targetted and give it a hook.

• Author(s), illustrator(s), photographer(s) names and addresses. Are you the only author? If not, list your co-author(s) and the illustrator(s), photographer(s) you intend to use. Be sure to include your full name, address, telephone and fax numbers, Internet website and e-mail addresses.

• Synopsis. This is an overview; a brief description of the book that, in paragraph form, establishes the main goals and themes of your book. Why do you want to write it? What is in it? What will be left out? Why is the book needed? What insights will readers gain from your new book? Is the title going to be required reading for a course? Does the book have a market as a course prerequisite? What are your primary and secondary markets? The primary market for my first book, *Historical Walks: the Gatineau Park Story* are active outdoors people who want to hike, mountain bike or ski in Gatineau Park. The secondary market are "armchair hikers" who want to know about the human and natural history of Gatineau Park, located 20 minutes north of Ottawa, Canada's capital city. The book is an indispensable guide to the park, and since 1988 I've led guided hikes in the park to people who buy the book as part of my course curriculum. Such details would go into a book proposal.

• Table of contents. List a full table of contents, including all sections that you want to include in your book. What are normal sections of a book? Look in *The Chicago Manual of Style* to find out. Components of a book are: Preface, Acknowledgments, Introduction, Chapters of book, Conclusion, Endnotes, Bibliographic references/other reading; Glossary, Index.

• Sample chapter(s). In the case of my second book, *Capital Walks: Walking Tours of Ottawa*, McClelland and Stewart advised me that they did not need sample chapters, because they had a good understanding of my writing capabilities from my first, self-published book. You may be in the same situation.

However, do not assume this unless you are specifically told not to submit a sample chapter or chapters. Generally speaking, publishers do want to see one to three sample chapters. This not only proves that you can write; it demonstrates that you can stay on target as well as maintain a theme and reader interest.

Continue with a detailed list of subsequent chapters and their relevant sub-headings, if applicable.

• Competing books. What is currently published in your chosen field of interest? Go to your local independent as well as large chain book stores and research current titles. Ask the bookshop managers for help. Often they know of what new releases are coming—and from which publishers. Bookstore owners are book lovers and are professionals: they know their readers and their publishers inside-out. If they don't, they're dead in the water. Get to know them: call them in advance and ask when you can drop in for a chat. Ask their advice.

Also use tools such as *Books in Print* and your library catalogue system—and don't forget the Internet, either. Thoroughly research what's both in and out of print that covers your chosen topic. Don't be discouraged if there are several books already in print: you may just have come up with the definitive work on the subject!

Now you are ready to list the competition. List them in bibliographic format, sorted alphabetically by surname of the author. (Again, refer to *The Chicago Manual of Style* for this information.) In addition to the name of the author, book title, etc., I also added a brief sentence or two describing the focus of each competing title, mentioning why my book would be different.

*Tip:* Don't denigrate the competition. Point out their good (and bad) points, highlighting where it fails to deliver—but where your won't. Some measurements are: is it too technical? Too out-of-date? Is it poorly written? Incomplete? Or, is it very popular? Be fair. Remember that your assessments speak volumes about yourself; how you assess others work—and how you think.

• The market. What is the target audience for this book? What are the demographics: "the educated lay-person", professional group(s), the health-conscious senior's market? Do your research: if it is a travel guide, find out how many tourists come to the region you are describing.

Spell all of this out for the editor/publisher. Although they should be able to grasp all of these details themselves, it is important that you demonstrate, as author, that you understand your book's intent, its market and its marketability.

• Promotion campaign. What are the sales handles? What are the sales opportunities? Is the book seasonal—if it is a hiking book, can you expand it to include skiing and canoeing, thus widening its appeal, for example. Is the book politically sensitive? Will it have a brief window of opportunity for sales, as in a political exposé to be printed in the few months leading up to an election?

• Your curriculum vitae. Who are you? Why are you the perfect author for this book? Are you a subject matter specialist? Have you been interviewed on television or radio about this topic? Are you well-known in the area, across Canada, or internationally? Have your won awards for your work? Do you give courses/workshops? What associations do you belong to? What are your hobbies?

Spell out your qualification for the role of author. Stress your particular credentials as well as your promotability. What are your relevant experiences? What are your publishing credits?

• Appendix. Here's where you include supporting material. Are you already a published author? If so, include at least a list of titles and better still, include a complimentary copy of the book that you think best represents you. Do you have book reviews, tear sheets of magazine or newspaper articles, samples of brochures, photographs that you have produced? Send copies.

### Some general pointers

Before you dash off a copy of the book proposal and submit it to the editor(s), here's a few final words of caution and also of advice:

• Use a word processing package. It will be much easier to create a neatly formatted proposal than using a typewriter. An eleven-point serif font is a good size and typeface. Try out Palatino, Bookman or possibly Times New Roman. Avoid using sans-serif fonts such as Helvetica. Do not clutter your proposal with different faces (bold, italic) nor with a variety of typefaces.

• Copyright your proposal. Insert the copyright symbol © and your name and date as part of the footer on every page. An idea cannot be copyrighted, but neither ought your proposal be "stolen". Don't be paranoid. Do be smart: protect your rights.

• Include generous margins. Use about an inch (72 points) along the top, bottom and sides so that the editor/publisher can make their notes.

• Include a header and footer on every page. The heading should contain the working title and your name and date. The footer should include the page number (page x of x).

• Do not staple your manuscript.

• Keep copies. Absolutely ensure that you keep a complete copy not only of your typed proposal, but a copy of all tearsheets, reviews etc., that you include in your Appendix.

• Be patient. Many publishers do not accept unsolicited manuscripts. It is discouraging, but a fact. Do expect a response to take up to several months. Some publishers do not return proposals, others do. Consider sending an SASE (self-addressed, stamped envelope) that is large enough to contain your complete proposal, should you wish to increase the likelihood of getting it back. Do consider asking, in your covering letter, to hear back by a specific date (say, two to three months from submitting it).

• Consider simultaneous submissions. Should you send the proposal simultaneously to more than one publisher? Many people do because getting published is so difficult these days. If you do, tell the editor in the covering letter that this is what you have done.

• Consider your alternatives. If you decide to self-publish, note that every author ought to still go through this process of writing a proposal. It helps to establish the contents, structure and market for your book.

Author Katharine Fletcher has over 23 years experience in writing, editing and publishing. She thrives on diversification: she gives seminars (e.g. *Publish Yourself!*), leads hikes of Gatineau Park—and telecommutes from her electronic cottage. E-mail her at: <fletcher@hookup.net>.

# Negotiating Book Contracts

*by Marian Dingman Hebb*

**W**hen you are offered a contract by a publisher, the temptation is to sign it without careful consideration of its contents. Contracts are not written in stone, even the ones which appear to be a standard printed form with little or no space for amendments. Editors and publishers are not surprised to be asked to make changes. In fact, most probably expect this. Many authors, and the agents and lawyers who represent some of them, ask for and very often get important changes in the contracts offered. The discussion itself with the publisher about the contract is often useful, whether or not it results in changes to the contract, as it makes clear to both author and publisher the expectations of the other and reduces the risk of later misunderstandings.

### Protect your copyright.

When looking at a contract for publication of a book, first ask yourself these two basic questions: What are you giving (and what aren't you giving) to the publisher? And when will you get it back?

Don't give copyright. In a few situations it may be appropriate to do so, but these are limited. The usual grant to the publisher is an exclusive license to publish throughout the term of copyright. It may be limited to Canada or to the English language, and it may also be limited to publication in book form. Occasionally the licence is limited to a specified number of years. Before requesting such limitations, you should endeavour to find out the publisher's track record in licensing publishers outside Canada or in selling or licensing film and other non-print rights. You should also consider whether you have alternative ways of placing these rights yourself. In other words, retaining rights to exploit them yourself may not always be a wise decision. Another possibility is to give the publisher the right to exploit certain rights for several years following publication of its own edition and, if it hasn't successfully done so, to reclaim the right to do so yourself.

It is smart to have a clause which says that "all rights not specifically granted to the publisher" are retained by you as author. Then, if there is uncertainty later over what you actually granted to the publisher, a dispute is more likely to be resolved in your favour. But, if the contract seems unclear to you at the outset, do not rely on this outcome, and specify also that you are keeping certain rights "including but not limited to all motion picture, sound recording and electronic rights" (for example).

### Don't lose control of electronic rights.

Unless the publisher is an electronic publisher and you intend to grant electronic rights, it is wise to specify that you are keeping "all electronic rights". It is reasonable, however, for the book publisher to want electronic database rights which would allow (subject to your written approval and a payment to you of a percentage of revenues received) customers of the book publisher or another publisher licensed by the book publisher to download and print out the verbatim text without adaptation or added elements (music, other sound, graphics, animation, links to other text etc.) Some book publishers ask for these verbatim electronic rights or database storage and retrieval rights because they fear that you will grant these rights to a competing publisher who might provide your text to its customers on demand and undercut sales of the original book. Alternatively, it would be reasonable for the contract to contain a prohibition against your granting such rights to another publisher or a requirement that if you are going to offer these rights to any publisher they must be offered first to your book publisher.

Interactive CD-ROM or similar electronic rights are very different and, unless you reserve all electronic rights, should be dealt with separately and differently. An electronic product has many added elements and does not usually compete with the original book. You might easily have to undertake a great deal of further work if you were to become involved in an adaptation of your book for a CD-ROM, although you might just be asked for permission to allow others to adapt your work or part of it. Or your work might be one of a large number of other works incorporated into an electronic product. No one yet knows all the possibilities for electronic publication and keeping these electronic rights yourself preserves your flexibility to dealing with them. If you do grant any electronic rights to the publisher, try to be very specific about which electronic rights you are granting ( for example, English- language CD-ROM, Macintosh platform, for North America only) and which you are retaining, and insist on approval over any use of the rights either by the publisher or someone licensed by the publisher.

### Preserve the right to regain control of your rights in certain situations.

Although you will not have assigned your copyright to the publisher in most cases, the contract will still determine the control which you and the publisher will each have over your material. The difference between "assigning" copyright and granting a licence is rather like the difference between selling and renting your house. If you license certain rights—as when you rent your house—you retain ownership. However, retaining copyright and granting a licence does not mean that you can grant permission to others to use your material in different ways unless the contract between you and the publisher permits this.

The most important reason to retain your copyright is that in certain instances you will be able to regain control of your material at a later time without having to obtain a reassignment or written transfer of the copyright back to you from the publisher. For example, you may (and should) seek to negotiate that all publishing rights revert to you automatically if the publisher becomes insolvent or bankrupt.

There are a number of other situations where all publishing rights should revert to you—not automatically, but if you so wish. You will probably want your contract to provide that rights may revert to you in the following circumstances:

• The book is not published within, say, twenty-four months of delivery of the manuscript, or within a much shorter time if the success of the book depends on its timing.

• The book is out of print and is not reprinted, following your request that the publisher do so, within a certain period, say, six or nine months. Contrary to what many authors think, you are not usually entitled to take a book away from the publisher simply because it is out of print, unless the contract makes it clear that you can.

• The publisher fails to send royalty statements and payments, if any are owing. This clause—not a common one—is worth its weight in gold on occasion! Either the publisher finds it can pay you after all—or you become free to take your book to another publisher.

### Clarify the publication date.

Another basic question to be resolved is when the book is to be published. It is surprising how many contracts are completely silent on a date of publication. An obligation to publish may be implied, and if so, publication should be within a reasonable time after delivery of the complete, final manuscript. How long is "reasonable"? Eighteen months is usual, but it would depend on the circumstances. Avoid this uncertainty by checking your contract for a publication date before signing!

### Establish a consultative process.

When you enter a contract with a publisher, you give the publisher the power to do a number of things for your mutual benefit. Usually most of the decisions other than on content become entirely the publisher's, unless you write in clauses that require it to obtain your approval or at least to consult you at certain points. Many publishers—the good ones—do consult their authors, whether or not it is in the contract. But there are oversights. People forget or make mistakes—and if there is a formal requirement to consult or obtain approval, it seems such oversights happen less often! If you ask for consultation or approval, it is clear to the publisher that you are interested and want to be involved in particular aspects of the publishing process which are sometimes considered not a legitimate concern of the author. Certainly you should have the opportunity to approve the copy-edited manuscript before it goes for typesetting. You should see the cover artwork and may wish to see the page layout and design. You should check the biographical blurb and any other text on the book jacket or paperback cover. Publishers are usually appreciative of an author's input and are always grateful when an author has saved them from making an embarrassing and sometimes costly mistake. You may also want the right of approval on foreign publishing or other sub-licenses granted, although some publishers regard this requirement as a hindrance to them.

### Negotiate a "no assignment" clause.

A wise author knows his or her own publisher. Try to ensure that a contract has a "no assignment" clause, so that it will clearly be necessary for the publisher to obtain your consent before selling or otherwise disposing of your contract—and hence, control of your book—to another publisher. If your contract is a license only (and not a copyright assignment), you can probably stop your publisher from assigning or disposing of your contract to another publisher, unless there is a clause—as there sometimes is—expressly permitting the publisher to sell off your contract as a business asset, along with the computers and desks. You made the initial choice of whom you wanted as your publisher. Take care that a subsequent publisher is not foisted on you. You may not hit it lucky, or be compatible with the publisher someone else has "chosen" for you in such a situation.

### Additional clauses to consider.

Some additional clauses to look for in your contract-and to bargain for if you don't find them-are listed below:

• When you sign a contract you should receive an advance that is not returnable. Otherwise the publisher has obtained, at no cost, the right to see and consider your manuscript when you have completed it. The publisher can then decide that your manuscript isn't "satisfactory" and reject it. The wording of many contracts is such that this may be a subjective decision by the publisher, rather than an objective assessment of the manuscript. (An advance should only be repayable if you default on delivery of a complete manuscript.)

• If your contract gives the publisher the right to reject an "unsatisfactory" manuscript, there should be safeguards to protect you from an arbitrary rejection—for example, a clause requiring the publisher to give you written reasons for its dissatisfaction and an opportunity to revise the manuscript to meet its requirements. (You may prefer to keep the advance, if the contract permits, and take your manuscript to another publisher who finds it satisfactory in its present form!)

• Royalties! This is probably the first clause you look for. Most publishers offer 10 per cent on the suggested retail price of a trade book (that is, a book which is not for the educational or technical markets) on the first five thousand copies sold, 12½ per cent on the next five thousand copies sold, and 15 per cent on all copies sold thereafter.

• Most publishers pay royalties twice a year and many will pay you your share of any revenues received from sub-licenses within thirty days of when such revenues are received by them.

• Many contracts have a clause that permits you or your accountant to inspect the publisher's financial records relating to your own particular book.

• Your contract should contain a clause that permits the Canadian Copyright Licensing Agency (CANCOPY) to authorize photocopying and similar forms of reproduction of your book. CANCOPY and its Quebec sister, Union des écrivaines et écrivains québecois, are reproduction rights organizations which license copying on behalf of writers and publishers in Canada and through similar, sister organizations outside Canada, throughout the world.

• Warranty and indemnification clauses should always be read with great care. The publisher is entitled to a warranty from you that your book is not plagiarized or copied from the work of another author. You should not have to give an unqualified warranty to a publisher that your work contains no libellous material, although as author you should be prepared to stand behind the professionalism of your research and it is clearly not fair to depict your landlady, for example, in your novel. However, if you are writing on a controversial subject and about contemporary persons, to take one example, you and the publisher should share the risks of any libel action and the publisher should not ask you to indemnify it for any financial loss in respect to an action or threat of action. If you anticipate a possible problem of this sort, you and your publisher should discuss the advisability of insurance coverage. If the publisher already has libel insurance, this can probably be extended to insure you as well. But you should be sure that any commitment from the publisher to provide you with insurance is included in your contract. If you are giving any warranty on libel, whether or not there is insurance, you should limit any promise to indemnify the publisher to costs resulting from actual breaches of your warranty, and not to all costs resulting from mere threats and claims. If an unknown glory-seeker claims to be one of the characters in your novel, your publisher should neither blame you nor collect its defence costs from you!

• Your life will be simpler if you don't give your publisher an option to publish or make an offer on your next work. A publisher is usually content to rely on your goodwill to give it the first opportunity to do so. But if the contract does contain an option clause, be sure that the publisher must make its offer or decision to publish within a specified period, say, thirty days, of receiving an outline and sample material.

• If the publisher decides that the time has come when it is no longer economic to keep your book in stock, it should first offer you an opportunity to purchase any or all remaining copies at the same low price as it is prepared to sell them to a remainder dealer or book jobber. Authors sometimes become apoplectic when they see their books selling for a dollar or two on a discount table, especially when they have a yen to go into the mail-order book business themselves.

Most of the above suggestions cost a publisher financially very little. In certain circumstances, it may cost you a lot if you do not have these protections.

Marian Dingman Hebb spent ten years as a book and magazine editor before becoming a lawyer and specializing in arts and entertainment law. She has advised authors on book contracts for close to two decades and has written self-help guides on book contracts entitled *Help Yourself to a Better Contract*, *Ghost Writing*, and *Writers' Guide to Electronic Publishing Rights*, all published by the Writers' Union of Canada.

# The Five Ws of Indexing

*by Heather Ebbs*

Indexing is a specialized form of writing in which the primary resource is the book, journal or other document being indexed. As with all written works, indexes adhere to an extensive but flexible set of standards to ensure their readability, usefulness and accuracy. There are two main types of indexing—open-system indexing, used by such things as periodicals and databases, and closed-system or book indexing. We shall focus on book indexing here.

## What is an index, and why write one?

Indexes are book maps. Like road maps, they make it easier for users to find their way to the specific place they want to go. Even documents that don't have a back-of-the-book index usually have a table of contents, which is a simple index arranged in chronological form (the linear chronology of the book). The back-of-the-book index is a more detailed map of the contents of the book, and is usually arranged alphabetically. It can be fun to explore a country, or a book, just by moving forward from the point of entry, but often a traveller (or reader) wants to know first how to get to a specific place.

Book indexes are of two primary types: subject indexes and proper noun indexes. Proper noun indexes are the easiest to create. The proper noun index is like the everyday road map, which contains the names of all the places in the map area. For a proper noun index, the indexer reads through the text looking for any relevant mention of a person, place, organization or other named thing. Relevance is the guiding principle: For example, an index to a television network history might contain relevant mentions of TV programs, stations and networks; an index to a politician's biography might include discussions of ridings and political parties; an index to a movie star's autobiography should include every juicy referral to other stars, as well as all the other people, movies and studios described.

Subject indexes can be vastly more difficult than proper noun indexes. The subject index is comparable to a topographical map, showing all the complexities of the landscape in the area. The indexer must be familiar enough with the text to have an understanding of the concepts, how they relate and which aspects the reader is likely to want to explore. The terms chosen to represent these concepts must reflect both the author's style and the anticipated reader's sensibilities. Condensing a complex text into a tidy map that readers can easily use to follow whatever trails of information interest them can be a formidable—but intensely satisfying—task.

## Who writes indexes?

People who enjoy indexing are often people who enjoy solving puzzles and crosswords. They have a love of order, but that doesn't mean they're rigid. They have to be flexible, intelligent and empathic enough to be able to understand and respect the author's ideas, emphasis and style while simultaneously imagining the readers' needs and level of knowledge. They need to be meticulous, methodical and thorough. Being well-read and having a broad vocabulary are essential, as is the ability to work well and quickly under pressure. It helps to be able to read fast.

More practically speaking, the indexer can be the author, an outside (often freelance) indexer or the editor. There are advantages to each. The author is most familiar with the material, and becoming familiar with the material is the first step of any indexer. The indexer should be able to get inside the author's head to understand fully the intent, style, tone and emphasis of the text—who can do that better than the author? An outside indexer, on the other hand, takes a totally fresh look at the material—perhaps a view more akin to that of the reader. Since the indexer's second step is to understand the potential needs of the reader, an objective eye is valuable. The editor is somewhere between these two heads—still familiar with the writing, but a bit more distant from it.

## Who buys them?

The market for indexes is huge and growing, as more and more non-traditional publishers—government departments, national and regional associations, high tech corporations—are recognizing the need for an index to their published material. These organizations realize that, in the long term, customer satisfaction (and the customer might be the general public, an association member or a product purchaser) depends on whether that customer can use the product or document easily and get quick answers to questions. In today's high-speed world, people expect to be able to find information *now*. A good index enables them to make that rapid connection between curiosity and information.

The most non-traditional publisher of all, the online world, is desperate for useable indexes to organize the mass of information available. The Net is a market just beginning to be explored. Meanwhile, traditional publishers of scholarly books and trade non-fiction, for adults and children, continue to appreciate the value of an index to the book's readers.

For corporate, government or other non-trade publications, the index writers are generally paid by the publisher. In the book trade, the indexer's payment usually comes out of the author's pocket, either directly from author to indexer, or indirectly through the publisher, with the author "repaying" the publisher out of royalties. Having the author pay for the index makes sense, as the index is an intellectual part of the created work (as opposed to a physical part, which the publisher pays for).

### How is an index created?

Anyone who hasn't prepared an index may think of indexing as a fairly mechanical task, but anyone who has indexed knows that it requires a surprising amount of knowledge, judgement and editorial skill. The indexer's job is to identify the information the reader is likely to want, label it in a way the potential readers can understand and indicate its location in the text. The key phrase is "information the reader is likely to want." Choosing what information to index is the most difficult, least mechanical part of the task. Part of the difficulty is that every book has two types of readers: porers and dippers. Porers read the book cover to cover, then later use the index to go back to information they remember. These readers know the author's intent and terminology, and they know whether a piece of information is in the book or not. Dippers haven't read the book. They use it only as a resource for the information they are interested in: The index is the tool that helps them find this information. These readers do not know what terms the author has used, and don't even know if what they want is in the book. The indexer has to be sensitive to the needs and understanding of both types of readers.

There are a variety of techniques and tools for indexing. The techniques all boil down to knowing the text, choosing information to index, labeling it, sorting it and editing and revising a number of times to prepare a final draft. It's a subject too big to cover in a few paragraphs—it needs a book: See the resources listed below. The tools include everything from pencils, highlighters and index cards to sophisticated indexing software. Most word processing packages include a capability to tag text and generate a rough, first draft index. Dedicated indexing software enables indexers to edit on-screen using an array of powerful editing aids and to customize sorting, compiling and layout rapidly and easily.

## When does the indexing start?

In most cases, book indexing does not begin until final page proofs are available, although it is helpful if the indexer can read the material before the page proof stage to become familiar with the content. Until final proofs are available, page numbers are unknown and content is indefinite. True, the indexer can still begin work, but the farther the publication is from final proofs, the longer and more arduous the indexer's task, as repeated passes must be made to ensure accuracy and completeness of content and locators.

Whether the publisher is a trade firm, a government department, a national association or a private organization, the page proof stage tends to be the "hurry-up-we-haven't-got-much-time-the-printer-is-booked-how-fast-can-you-get-this-back-to-us" stage. Presses may be booked, release promotion timed, shipping dates promised. There is intense pressure on the indexer to perform fast, accurately and comprehensively in a tight time frame. For the indexer, *when* is *now*.

## Where can I find out more?

In addition to the primary resource (the document being indexed), the indexer needs a library of useful reference texts: good dictionaries (Oxford, Webster's and appropriate subject-specific dictionaries), encyclopedias (literary, current and historical) and a biographical dictionary are the bare minimum. For further information, I recommend three sources:

• Mulvany, Nancy C. *Indexing Books*. Chicago, IL: University of Chicago Press, 1994.

• Wellisch, Hans H. *Indexing from A to Z*. New York, NY: H.W. Wilson Co., 1991.

• "Indexes." Chapter 17 in *The Chicago Manual of Style*. 14th edition. Chicago, IL: University of Chicago Press, 1993.

Finally, because knowing others you can turn to for support, advice and state-of-the-art information is vital to excellence in any field, I encourage membership in Canada's association for indexers: Indexing and Abstracting Society of Canada / Société canadienne pour l'analyse de documents, P.O. Box 744, Station F, Toronto, Ontario, M4Y 2N6.

Heather Ebbs, a book, periodical and database indexer, has indexed 100s of items in a broad range of subjects and genres. Her clients include trade publishers, national associations, high tech firms and individual authors. She is a past president of the (Freelance) Editors' Association of Canada and the winner of the 1986 Tom Fairley Award for Editorial Excellence for a book she both edited and indexed.

# Self-Publish Your Book

*by Katharine Fletcher*

For those of us who are professional writers, getting our words published—and read—is our life's work. In 1985, I recall talking to thirty publishers about my first book. What did I get for my efforts? Rejections and one tentative bite from a publisher who said she would give no advance and a royalty of only four per cent—if she published my book.

Discouraging? Totally. Fortunately, my husband Eric suggested we publish it ourselves. So began a three-year project which ended in the release of what has become a local bestseller. *Historical Walks: The Gatineau Park Story* still sells well. In the spring of 1997, I released a second edition, the first having sold over 8,200 copies in four printings.

What did self-publishing do for me? It launched my highly diversified writing career! On the strength of my first book, in 1990 I published two local histories for authors. In 1993, McClelland and Stewart published my second book, *Capital Walks: Walking Tours of Ottawa*. In 1994, Reader's Digest Canada asked me to contribute two destinations to their 1994 *Back Roads and Country Getaway Places in Canada*. Since October 1989, I've written a weekly environment column for *The Equity*, my community paper, and I am a regular contributor to *The Ottawa Citizen*. I've written for *This Country Canada*, *Earthkeeper*, *Harrowsmith Country Life*, *The New Federation*, and *Roads To... Canada's Great Drives*.

All of these opportunities, along with my seminars on self publishing, the electronic cottage and my slide shows, talks and guided hikes/bus tours of the National Capital Region, *are direct spinoffs* of my self-published book. I believe a writer must diversify in order to live: self-publishing can open many doors.

Yes, self-publishing is a definite option for authors. But it is not easy. It is a journey during which you adopt many roles: publisher, designer, marketer, distributor, literary publicist, public speaker and accountant. Multi-talented you must become. It's do-able. Here's how!

### First things first: you're in great company.

Many famous writers have self-published. Among these literary greats are Anais Nin, D. H. Lawrence and William Blake. But even today, far too many publishers and writers consider self-published authors to be somehow "lesser writers" than those who are published by "recognized trade publishers."

Why is this? Because publishers have a vested interest in making money from your writing: that's their business. Writers primarily want to write.

Even in 1997, organizations like The Writers Union of Canada (TWUC) still do not allow *solely* self-published authors to be members. I did not know this in 1988. I was astounded that TWUC would not accept me as a member after I wrote and published *Historical Walks*—especially when I sold out of my first print run of 1,500 copies in six weeks. I am a TWUC member now—but I was accepted only *after* McClelland & Stewart published my second book in 1993. And, as recently as the TWUC AGM of 1996, totally self-published authors are still excluded. To date, the suggestion that every book should be judged on its own intrinsic merit has not gained sufficient momentum. Times will change, I predict, and very soon. Technology and our depressed economy are redefining the roles of writer and publisher—as well as redefining what readers want to read.

The point is this: as a writer, educate yourself and have no illusions. Examine your publishing options carefully. Self-publishing *can* give you a superb edge over other writers. Media love a "local interest" story. You can leverage your self-publishing into excellent promotion and thus great sales. Just remember: your attitude is absolutely key. Be strong, be resilient, be smart. Add a dash of humility to the recipe, ensure you are a good listener, and self-publishing can be a superb route for a targeted, well-written and well-produced product.

### What is vanity press?

In 1996 the Globe and Mail published an article about self-publishing, equating it with vanity press. They were wrong. As self-publisher, *you* are in *total intellectual and business control of your publication*. As a writer published by a vanity press you have little control over the design of your book; you pay a lot to get the book printed and bound;

and (scrupulously check your contract with the vanity press) you are still left with the storage of inventory, the promotion and distribution of *every* book. Beware of vanity presses.

Okay, so you know what self-publishing is. What's next?

### Write a book proposal.

Why do you need to bother writing a book proposal, you ask, if you are going to publish your own book? (What's a book proposal? See my article in this book on the topic!)

Because as self-publisher, you must have a strong business sense. In your role as your own publisher, you must be sure that there is a market for your book. Publishing is a risk-venture: be absolutely clear about this. Writing a solid, well-thought-out proposal demands that you consider the structure, content and goals of your book. It means you will analyze the market, define the target audience, determine the best season to release it. It ensures you have the best chance to write a focused, readable book that is the *best of its kind* within its genre and subject matter. It's a useful exercise *all* writers should undergo *before* starting to write.

### Funding.

As self-publisher, you underwrite all costs. What grants or loans are available? For *Historical Walks*, I was unsuccessful in getting any provincial or federal funding. But I procured an interest-free loan from a historical society. The loan covered only the direct cost of printing: $6,150.00. The terms were that I had to pay it back in full in two installments over five years.

You may be even more fortunate! You could consider sponsorship from corporations or associations which have an interest in your topic. Thoroughly investigate funding from your local municipality, arts programs, and traditional sources such as the Canada Council. Don't leave any stone unturned in your quest for funding. But beware. Be careful who you agree to accept money from: especially as a self-publisher, stay completely independent of anything that smacks of influence peddling. Perception is key to how you and your book are received, and your credibility will be on the line with your book.

### Market analysis.

There are two major components to this: first, are there other books available on your subject? Second, what is the estimated potential buying readership for your book? I'll cover this second point in the next section.

Is your book concept unique? Don't despair if there are competing titles on the market. How current are they? Are they still in print? Do they have the same goals, themes, audience as your book? If so, you may need to seriously rethink your idea. But if you have a different twist on even a familiar theme, the risk may still be worthwhile.

How do you research this? Visit your local independent bookstores. Talk to the managers there, who are usually familiar with the local writers' scene—and their books. Managers and staff can tell you if your concept is likely to sell. Don't take one person's opinion as gospel: ask around and do thorough research: it's your own time and money you'll be saving. Also check out the chains: these sales managers will have a different viewpoint which is invaluable to you. Also search libraries and the Internet.

### Target audience.

How do you estimate how many people are potential buyers? This is tricky: if there was a formula, writers and publishers would really make money! How did I assess the market for *Historical Walks*? I studied the demographics of my region, the number of visitors that go to the park and the number of tourists who visit the National Capital Region. If the numbers are big enough, you may have a worthwhile book on your hands!

### Target readership.

Who will read your book? You must have a clear idea about this before you start to write. If you don't know whether the reader is a generalist or a specialist you won't know what vocabulary to use, or how in-depth to be. Identify your readers and write to them always.

I'll share a trick with you. For *Historical Walks*, I deliberately designed a "three-in-one" approach. Part I discusses the human history of Gatineau Park; Part II is an overview of ecological habitats; Part III describes the hikes including maps. Black and white photographs, both historical and my own natural history shots, pepper the text. Thus, my book appeals to hikers, bikers and skiers as well as to what I call "armchair" walkers who want to learn about the history of their region—and who may only imagine a hike along a woodland path!

### ISBN.

Every trade publication has an International Standard Book Number (ISBN) and as a self-publisher, you must get one for your book too.

The number is a unique identifier: you may share your name with another author, your book title may even be identical or close to another. But the ISBN is unique. To get one, contact the National Library of Canada at (819) 994-6872; Fax: (819) 953-8508. It's a free service.

### *CIP.*

Every book printed in Canada should be registered with Cataloguing in Publication data, also a free service. This is the information that uniquely describes your book with appropriate keywords. Contact CIP at the National Library of Canada at (819) 994-6881; Fax: (819) 997-7517.

### *Copyright.*

There are two main points to copyright for writers and publishers. First, writers should retain the rights to their work and in Canada have the legal right to be paid for use of their work. This includes copyright of the published book or manuscript in entirety, as well as any part of it (say, the photocopying of a portion of it). An associated issue in today's wired world is electronic rights. Second, if quotations are used in the author's book, it is the responsibility of the writer to obtain permission from other authors, or speakers to use their work. In all cases, it is advisable to get permissions in writing.

Copyright is a huge topic. As self-publisher, you must inform yourself about this issue. For copyright information, read Lesley Ellen Harris' comprehensive book *Canadian Copyright Law*. Or, contact the Periodical Writers Association of Canada (PWAC) or The Writers' Union of Canada (TWUC).

### *Book design.*

There are many components to the look and feel of a book that are critical. Are you familiar with paper density, book sizes, the cost of black and white vs. colour printing? Do you know the difference between perfect binding and saddle stitching? What are Bookman, New Century Schoolbook, and Helvetica? What is a gutter—and why should you care?

Each item I have mentioned above only touches the surface of what you, as self-publisher, must become familiar with. How do you find out about this stuff? I recommend that you start by talking to printers. These professionals know more than you'll ever want to know about book size, whether or not to laminate the cover, and most important, how much each of these issues will cost you.

Also, include book design in your market research. While you're at the book shops start looking at books. Determine what elements of design you like. Why are they appealing? Keep them in mind when you visit the printer.

## Computers.

Do you have a computer? Do you know how to type? If you say no to both these questions, writing and self-publishing is definitely more problematic. But it still can be achieved. You may need to include purchasing a system and learning how to use it (and how to type) in your time and cost budget. Or, you may pay someone to transcribe your work into computer memory.

Assuming you are computer literate and know how to type, you need to ensure you have the right software for your type of book. Word processing packages like Microsoft Word can handle a lot of page layout and copy fitting these days. However there are layout packages available on the market, from PageMaker to Quark and Corel Ventura. How complex is your book? Is it straight text, like a novel? Does it have illustrations, sidebars, photographs or maps? Each of these elements not only raises a design question, but also a software question.

This is where networking will greatly assist you. Contact a writer's group, talk to published authors: find out who used what—for what product. Then find a computer store whose staff don't speak "technobabble". How do you find one of those? Again, ask around.

Remember: if you have to buy software or hardware you must include this in your budget. And, keep those receipts for tax purposes!

## Writing.

Usually concurrent to all this process is the actual field research, the hiking, the travelling, the agony of sleepless nights of struggling over theme and denouement, the ecstasy of writing when the words are flowing; the interviewing and the angst of re-writes. The fun stuff!

## The editorial process.

After nine years of teaching, I *still* have writers come up to me after class and say, "Katharine: I'm not like the others here; I'm a professional writer like you and my work does not need an editor." Oh, *please*.

They are wrong. Dead wrong. Get yourself an editor. I enjoy the editorial process because I'm too close to my own work to count on detecting all structural problems or omissions. *Don't* trust your best friend, spouse, lover or Great Aunt Betty. Hire a professional editor to go through your text. Publishers do that. *Ask yourself why*.

### The production process.

After you have the technological tools, and after you have completed writing your text, you are ready to commence the production of your book. This means producing the elements of the design from the cover through the table of contents to the chapters (with their illustrations, maps etc.) up to and including the compilation of an index. What are these components and what do they look like? Refer to *The Chicago Manual of Style*.

### Printing.

Printing is the most significant direct cost you will absorb. How many books should you print?

The cost per unit (book) decreases as the volume of books printed increases. Note that there are fixed costs for the production of a book. For example, the cost of making the plates and shooting colour separations will be the same for 1 copy as for 10,000 (the printer only makes one plate, and uses it to print all the pages). Variable costs include paper and press time.

Don't be alarmed when you realize there's a Catch-22 here. For example, you'll need to know how many pages your book will have before the printer can give you a firm quote. Ask the printer for a series of quotes: x number of pages for 1,500, 2,000, 3,000 and 5,000 copies— and the cost of additional pages for each print run. You'll start to get a feel for the cost breakdown at this point.

*Tip:* As self-publisher, you will probably distribute the books. Do not print too many at first: you'll be alarmed at how many boxes (and how much space) even 1,000 books take! You have to store them safely from damp and your dog; you have to sell each and every one. Beware!

### Cost of the book.

There is a general rule of thumb that the ratio of the cost to the retail price of a book ought to 1:5. That is, the price paid at the cash register should be five times the production cost. You can only clearly identify what your unit cost will be after you procure a print estimate from the printer. This is an iterative process largely between you and the printer, to find out what you can afford. Other costs of the book are those you will incur in marketing and promoting, distribution and sales. These are all variable costs that you may not be able to factor into your retail price point. Beware: these costs will be paid by you: *you must have an ongoing budget for your project.*

*Tip:* Visit the bookstores. Look at comparable books. Ask the manager about the best price point for the subject matter and type of book you want to write. This is another aspect of market analysis: finding out what the market will bear. Don't forget: *your goal is to sell books.*

### Distribution and sales.

Now that your inventory of books is stored in your apartment, you need to start distribution. Where do you go? Start compiling a list of all the bookstores in your area. Then get a comprehensive listing of libraries, associations, corporations, societies, schools and alternative outlets such as outdoor stores, that may be interested in your book. (Of course, you will have prepared promotional material by now! Ensure each of these potential sales markets knows about the upcoming release.) As distributor, you will take (or mail) samples of your book to potential markets.

Retail outlets expect a discount of 40 per cent; libraries 10 per cent. Only your direct sales to a customer give you 100 per cent of the retail price. You can sell books on consignment, which means that you leave them at the shop for a specified length of time and you do not get paid until they sell. I don't do this. Books get looked over, and get a worn look which means the prospective buyer wants a discount. Beware of consignment.

The first four printings of *Historical Walks* were priced at $11.95. With the 40 per cent discount to a bookstore, it means they pay me $7.17 for each book they order. And, even though my income was well below $30,000, I needed to register myself with a GST number. Why? Because book stores will not place an order for books unless the publisher has a GST number. They must account for every piece of inventory (books) in their store. By the way: ask your accountant for help because Revenue Canada will want to know about your inventory, too.

### Promotional campaign.

How will you raise awareness of your book? Advanced promotional releases to newspaper and magazine editors as well as to book shops need to be prepared. What are the local radio and television stations in your area? Which shows and which hosts might be particularly interested in you and your book? Make a list. Ask all your friends and relatives for help because they might know of a favourite show that you would otherwise miss. Network with your writers and other professional associations.

Find out about local shows. There are home shows, seniors shows, craft shows: all kinds of targetted conferences and seminars that may be a sales opportunity for your book.

Sell yourself as a specialist who can speak authoritatively on the topic of your book. Send out announcements, offering to speak at luncheon engagements, or as the keynote speaker for an association's AGM.

### Packaging yourself.

What kind of a book are you writing? Ensure you package yourself appropriately. Don't wear a power suit and dress shoes to an interview if you are writing a hiking book.

Are you going on TV? Find out if the studio has a make-up department. Find out what colours to avoid (don't wear black and white, for example). Are you going on radio? Is it an in-studio interview or an on-site? Find out: the more you know, the more you can prepare yourself.

Be prepared. Remember that the interviewer wants a good show and has no intention of making it difficult for you! Relax: it's not an exam. Remember to listen to the question. Don't be afraid to pause, to reflect before just jumping in and answering in a rush what you thought was the question.

Above all, remember that you are *above all* a writer who has just produced an exciting new book! Enthusiasm combined with specialized knowledge of your subject matter is an irresistible combination. The public will catch your delight—and will want to buy your book.

### The business end.

You are now a publisher and this is your new business. You are also a writer who is excited about his or her new creation!

Are you already employed full time? How are you going to have time to design, promote, distribute, sell your book? You'll note I've not even discussed the creative time it takes to actually write! You'll have to figure all of this out, and don't forget to include your family in your timeline. You will need their support for every phase of this project.

Do you have an answering machine? A separate phone line? A fax? An e-mail address and/or a website? Do you have an office in your home where you write? Does it have an extra telephone in it? Now may be the time when you procure a second line for your home business. It must not become the teen's phone. Make it clear that the office phone is exclusively for your business use. Otherwise, you'll battle with kids or pets clamoring at your side as you do that telephone interview or try to determine if that store wants five or 50 books. Remember: you are a business professional. *Set up your home so you can behave like a professional.*

Keep a running account of all costs associated with the writing and publication of your book.

### Finances and accounting.

Establish a budget. Go through this article and highlight all items representing direct costs in one colour. Highlight indirect costs (the time it takes to write!) in another colour. Make a list of all these costs in two columns. Review the list with other writers, editors, printers, booksellers: anyone in the business who can provide professional, knowledgeable advice.

Time is one of your most significant costs. It took me three years to research, write, edit, and produce *Historical Walks*. Three years appears to be a typical gestation period for a book—even for writers who don't self-publish.

Keep a record of every book you sell, where it sold, for how much. I use a spreadsheet for this. You'll need it for your taxes. Isolate and record every single cost associated with your book because some will be valid business write-offs. In addition, it is invaluable information for your next project.

### Have fun.

My article only briefly touches on the issues involved with self-publishing. If you decide it's too much work, then you'll have made an important decision! Self-publishing is *not* for everyone. However, note that after reading this article, or attending a self-publishing workshop, you'll have learned a lot about the ins and outs of publishing. And that's valuable: it's one of the main reasons that royalties and advances are what they are. After all, publishing is a risk venture, isn't it?

Author Katharine Fletcher has over 23 years experience in writing, editing and publishing. She thrives on diversification: she gives seminars (e.g. *Publish Yourself!*), leads hikes of Gatineau Park—and telecommutes from her electronic cottage. E-mail her at: <fletcher@hookup.net>.

# What to do After Your Book is Published

*by Jeff Herman*

ongratulations! You've sold your book to a well-established publishing house, and now belong to the elite club of published authors. You'll soon discover that your personal credibility is enhanced whenever this fact is made evident to others. It may also prove to be a powerful marketing vehicle for your business or professional practice.

Unfortunately, once your book is actually published, there's a better-than-even possibility that you'll encounter several disappointments. Some of the most common are:

1. Neither you nor anyone you know can find the book anywhere.

2. The publisher doesn't appear to be doing anything to market the book.

3. You detest the title and the jacket.

4. No one at the publishing house seems to be listening to you. In fact, you may feel that you don't even exist for them.

As a literary agent, I live through these frustrations with my clients every day, and I try to explain to them at the outset what the realities of the business are. But I never advocate abdication or pessimism. There are ways in which every author can substantially remedy these endemic problems.

What follows are practical means by which each of these four most common failures can be preempted. I'm not suggesting that you can compensate entirely for the publisher's failures; that's a tall order. However, with lots of smarts and a little luck you can accomplish a great deal.

## Attacking problem No. 1:
### Neither you nor anyone you know can find the book anywhere.

This can be the most painful failure. After all, what was the point of writing the book if it's virtually invisible?

Let me digress briefly by introducing a bit of philosophy. As many of you may know from the popular material on codependency, to be a victim is to be powerless, which means you don't have the ability to improve your situation. With that in mind, avoid becoming merely an author who only complains and remains forever bitter.

No matter how badly your publisher screws up, don't fall into the victim trap. Instead, find positive ways to affect what is or is not happening for you. Your publisher is like an indispensable employee whom you are not at liberty to fire. You don't have to work with this publisher the next time; but this time it's the only one you've got.

There are a handful of writers, such as Norman Mailer, whose books pay a large part of the publisher's rent. These writers have earned the luxury of being very difficult, if they so choose. But the other 99.98 per cent of writers are not so fortunate. No matter how justified your methods may be, if you become an author to whom everyone at the publishing house dreads speaking, you've lost the game. They still have their jobs, and they see no reason to have you in their face. In other words: Always seek what's legitimately yours, but always try to do it in a way that might work for you, as opposed to making yourself persona non grata till the end of time.

Trade book distribution is a mysterious process, even for people in the business. Most bookstore sales are dominated by the large national and regional chains, such as Waldenbooks, B. Dalton, Barnes and Noble, and Crown [in Canada, Coles and SmithBooks]. No shopping mall is complete without at least one of these stores. Publishers always have the chain stores in mind when they determine what to publish. Thankfully, there are also a few thousand independently owned shops throughout the country.

Thousands of new titles are published each year, and these books are added to the seemingly infinite number that are already in print. Considering the limitations of the existing retail channels, it should be no surprise that only a small fraction of all these books achieves a significant and enduring bookstore presence. The bookstore will dedicate most of its visual space to displaying healthy quantities of the titles they feel are safe sells: books by celebrities and well-established authors, or books that are being given extra large printings and marketing budgets by their publishers, thereby promising to create demand.

The rest of the store will generally provide a liberal mix of titles, organized by subject area. This is where the backlisted titles try to stake their claims. For instance, the business section will probably offer two dozen or so sales books. Most of the displayed titles will tend to be by the biggest names in the genre, and their month-to-month sales probably remain strong even if the book was first published several years ago. In other words, there are probably hundreds of other sales books written in recent years that, as far as retail distribution is concerned, barely made it out of the womb. You see, the stores aren't out there to do you any favors. They are going to stock whatever they feel they can sell the most of. There are too many titles chasing too little space.

It's the job of the publisher's sales representative to lobby the chain and store buyers individually about the merits of her publisher's respective list. But here too the numbers can be numbing. The large houses publish many books each season, and it's not possible for the rep to do justice to each of them.

Priority will be given to the relatively few titles that get the exceptional advances. Because most advances are modest, and since the average book costs about $20,000 to produce, some publishers can afford to simply sow a large field of books and observe passively as some of them sprout. The many that don't bloom are soon forgotten as a new harvest dominates the bureaucracy's energy. Every season, many very fine books are terminated by the publishing reaper. The wisdom and magic these books may have offered is thus sealed away.

I have just covered a complicated process in a brief fashion. Nonetheless, the overall consequences for your book are in essence the same. Here, now, are a few things you may attempt in order to override such a stacked situation. However, these methods will not appeal to the shy or passive:

Make direct contact with the publisher's sales representatives.

Do to them what they do to the store buyers—sell 'em! Get them to like you and your book. Take the reps near you to lunch and ball games. If you travel, do the same for local reps wherever you go.

Make direct contact with the buyers at the national chains. If you're good enough to actually get this kind of access, you probably don't need to be told what to do next. Organize a national marketing program aimed at local bookstores throughout the country. There's no law that says only your publisher has the right to market your book to the stores. (Of course, all orders must go through your publisher.) For the usual reasons, your publisher's first reaction may be "What the hell are you doing?" But that's okay; make them happy by making your efforts work. It would be wise, however, to let the publisher in on your efforts up front. If your publisher objects—which she may—you might choose to interpret those remarks as simply the admonitions they are, and then proceed to make money for all.

## *Attacking problem No. 2:*
### *The publisher doesn't appear to be doing anything to market the book.*

If it looks as if your publisher is doing nothing to promote your book, then it's probably true. Your mistake is being surprised and unprepared.

The vast majority of titles published receive little or no marketing attention from the publisher beyond catalogue listings. The titles that get big advances are likely to get some support, since the publisher would like to justify the advance by creating a good seller. Compared to those in other Fortune 500 industries, publishers' in-house marketing departments tend to be woefully understaffed, under-trained, and underpaid. Companies like Procter & Gamble will tap the finest business schools, pay competitive salaries, and strive to nurture marketing superstars.

Book publishers don't do this. As a result, adult trade book publishing has never been especially profitable, and countless sales probably go unmade. The sales volumes and profits for large, diversified publishers are mostly due to the lucrative-and captive-textbook trade. Adult trade sales aren't the reason that companies like Random House can generate more than $1 billion in annual revenues.

Here's what you can do:

Hire your own public relations firm to promote you and your book. Your publisher is likely to be grateful and cooperative. But you must communicate carefully with your publishing house.

Once your manuscript is completed, you should request a group meeting with your editor and people from the marketing, sales, and publicity departments. You should focus on what their marketing agenda will be. If you've decided to retain your own PR firm, this is the time to impress the people at your publishing house with your commitment, and pressure them to help pay for it. At the very least, the publisher should provide plenty of free books.

Beware of this common problem: Even if you do a national TV show, your book may not be abundantly available in bookstores that day—at least not everywhere. An obvious answer is setting up 800 numbers to fill orders, and it baffles me that publishers don't make wider use of them. There are many people watching Oprah who won't ever make it to the bookstore, but who would be willing to order then and there with a credit card. Infomercials have proven this.

Not all shows will cooperate, but whenever possible you should try to have your publisher's 800 number (or yours) displayed as a purchasing method in addition to the neighborhood bookstore. If you use your own number, make sure you can handle a potential flood.

If retaining a PR firm isn't realistic for you, then do your own media promotions. There are many good books in print about how to do your own PR.

### Attacking problem No. 3:
### You detest the title and jacket.

Almost always, your publisher will have final contractual discretion over title, jacket design, and copy. But that doesn't mean you can't be actively involved. In my opinion you had better be. Once your final manuscript is submitted, make it clear to your editor that you expect to see all prospective covers and titles.

But simply trying to veto what the publisher comes up with won't be enough. You should try to counter the negatives with positive alternatives. You might even want to go as far as having your own prospective covers professionally created. If the publisher were to actually choose your version, the house might reimburse you. At any rate, don't wait until it's after the fact to decide you don't like your cover, title, and so forth. It's like voting: Participate or shut up.

### Attacking problem No. 4:
### No one at the publishing house seems to be listening to you.

This happens a lot, though I bet it happens to certain people in everything they do. The primary reasons for this situation may be:

1. That the people you're trying to access are incompetent.

2. That you're not a priority for them.

3. That they simply hate talking to you.

Here are a few things you might try to do about it:

If the contact person is incompetent, what can he or she really accomplish for you anyway? It's probably best to find a way to work around this person, even if he begins to return your calls before you place them.

The people you want access to may be just too busy to give you time. Screaming may be a temporary remedy, but eventually they'll go deaf again. Obviously their time is being spent somewhere.

Thinking logically, how can you make it worthwhile for these people to spend more time on you? If being a pain in the neck is your best card, then perhaps you should play it. But there's no leverage like being valuable.

Maybe someone just hates talking to you. That may be their problem. But, as many wise men and women have taught, allies are better than adversaries. And to convert an adversary is invaluable.

## Conclusion.

This essay may come across as cynical. But I want you to be realistic and be prepared. There are many publishing success stories out there, and many of them happened because the authors made them happen.

For every manuscript that is published, there are probably a few thousand that were rejected. To be published is a great accomplishment—and a great asset. If well tended, it can pay tremendous dividends.

Regardless of your publisher's commitment at the outset, if you can somehow generate sales momentum, the publisher will most likely join your march to success and allocate a substantial investment to ensure it. In turn, he may even assume all the credit. But so what?

Jeff Herman is a respected and well-known New York agent and author of *Insider's Guide To Book Editors, Publishers And Literary Agents*. Contact him at (212) 941-0540 or look for more information at AUTHORLINK!, an on-line information service for editors, agents and writers, located at <http://www.authorlink.com>.

# The Act of Purchasing a Book

*by Rowland Lorimer* _____

W hat makes a book purchaser pick up one book as opposed to another?

An author, as much as anyone in the book business, should be aware of the major factors that contribute to book buying. Plainly speaking, these are not the same factors that contribute to enjoyment of a book, or even perception of its long term value, although past experience certainly informs new purchases. First impressions, first encounters, and notable encounters all make a difference. A study carried out for the Association of Canadian Publishers in March and April of 1996 by Roger Barnes and Rowland Lorimer of the Canadian Centre for Studies in Publishing addressed these issues.

This national study, conducted in independent and chain bookstores in Vancouver, Calgary, Toronto, Montreal, and Halifax, had two unique elements. First, only purchasers of Canadian-published books were interviewed. Secondly it caught buyers "in the act" of buying. Just over 300 purchasers of Canadian books were interviewed as they left the store with freshly purchased books in hand. They were asked twenty questions about their purchases. Such a study yields results with statistical confidence limits +/- 6 per cent, 19 times out of 20. And, most important, it minimizes the impact of after-the-fact construction of reasons for book purchase.

The most dramatic finding of the study emphasized the importance of the retail environment. Sixty per cent of the interviewees decided what book to buy after they entered the bookstore. Moreover, 40 per cent purchased a book they had not heard of before entering the store. And what was the most significant factor affecting the choice of both groups? Two-thirds of interviewees bought books that were displayed face out.

In keeping with these findings, the strongest influence on buyers' choices was the bookstore, followed by friends' recommendations. But that did not turn out to be the case for all books. While 70 per cent of purchase decisions of new releases are made in the store (10 per cent more than all titles together), forty per cent of interviewees cited publicity—reviews and media commentary—as the source of their awareness of a title, a figure that placed publicity twice as important for these new books as older titles (those more than three months on the market). The impact of publicity is especially strong for buyers of fiction.

What about authors? Authors, too, are important, especially for fiction and children's books. Overall, 25 per cent of interviewees purchased a book written by an author they had previously read. However for fiction and children's titles, 50 per cent purchased books by authors they had previously read. When asked a direct question on the matter, 30 per cent of fiction buyers say that author is of major importance. For other genres, the identity of the author appears somewhat immaterial. For genre categories together, 40 per cent of interviewees said that subject matter—specifically Canadian subject matter—was of major importance.

The study also showed that 60 per cent of Canadian book purchases are made by women. The Canadian book buyers that the study encountered in bookstores across the nation were mostly up-scale, two-thirds having graduated from university, and more than half having a household income of more than $55,000 per annum. All age groups are well represented. Buyers spent an average of $15.90 on each book. On average, buyers bought 2.3 books in total. Women purchased more fiction than other groups.

The kinds of people who buy Canadian books in chain stores were very similar to buyers in independent stores. Differences did appear in the two populations but they were statistically insignificant. Chain store customers are younger, have slightly less education, are less exposed to book reviews and radio coverage of books, and more likely to make impulse purchases.

### Marketing Implications.

The major marketing implication of this study is as important for authors as it is for publishers. Commanding good quality in-store presence is critical for Canadian authors and publishers to maximize sales of their titles to book buyers. This in-store presence includes displays, prominence in the store and quality of presence on the shelf. Encouraging face-out shelving should be a priority where practical. Merchandising devices such as shelf-talkers may be useful approaches to improve on-shelf presence, especially for smaller titles unable to command face-out presentation. In-store marketing plans should be an integral part of the overall marketing plans. Even new books, where media attention is concentrated, require good in-store presence to capitalize on publishers' investments in generating reviews and radio interviews.

Can authors do anything to ensure they get the best possible treatment? Two good approaches are to make yourself available for signings—if bookstores are interested—and to engage in friendly discussions with booksellers to make them personally aware of you and your book. Another method is gaining media attention. This may encourage bookstores to feature your books in a display or at least to be ready should there be any inquiries following your media exposure. You may also find that your appearance in magazines stimulates book sales so making both bookstores and your publisher aware of coming appearances can also work to your benefit.

Rowland Lorimer is the director of Simon Fraser University's Master of Publishing program and Canadian Centre for Studies in Publishing. He conducts research on a wide variety of publishing and communication issues. Study co-author, Roger Barnes, is a marketing planning consultant and bookstore co-owner.

# Read Your Royalty Statement

*by Fred Kerner* _____

I f your publisher issues royalty statements that you can interpret easily, consider yourself lucky. Interpret? Yes, because when it comes to royalty statements, simple "reading" is often insufficient. If you are published by more than one publisher, the odds are high that each company's statement presents different problems of interpretation. Careful perusal of a royalty statement is called for each time you get one.

It should be said at the outset that I will give the publishers the benefit of the doubt in this discussion. That is, I am not assuming that they, in general, are out to confuse you with a royalty statement. Even so, the chances are good that your royalty statements are obscure.

### Study your original contract.

So, how do you start to read and understand that royalty statement? Before you do anything else, get out your contract and re-read the clauses that have to do with your earnings from the book in question. That must be done before you try to interpret the royalty statement.

Don't forget that you were paid an advance against royalties before publication of your book. All earnings from sale of the book, up to the amount of that advance, are deducted from your earned royalties until the entire advance is covered.

Before you check the numbers, determine whether you got your statement and cheque within the time frame called for. For example, some contracts call for the publisher to issue a royalty report, and pay you, within ninety days after the end of the sales period. If the publisher is late with payments, you are losing the use of that money until it is paid to you. Now let's proceed from there.

1. Does the time frame for earned royalties coincide with the royalty period called for in the contract? Are the sales reported ostensibly those

that took place in the appropriate royalty period? For example, if your contract says that royalties will be paid semi-annually on sales recorded between January 1 and June 30, and between July 1 and December 31, one of those two sales periods should be specified as the time frame for which royalties are being paid.

2. Does the statement indicate the total number of books sold both for the period covered by the statement and cumulatively? This is important in a contract that calls for your royalty percentage to escalate after a certain point. For example, the first 5,000 copies might bring you a 10 per cent revenue, the next 5,000 a twelve and one-half percent revenue, and all copies thereafter 15 per cent. If the publisher's statement does not give a cumulative figure, you have to dig out your previous statements and total the sales yourself to assure that when 5,000 copies have been sold, the royalty rate has increased.

3. Is the number of copies sold listed in various separate categories— such as sales directly to bookstores, sales to wholesalers, sales to overseas distributors, sales of publication rights to foreign publishers, etc.? Your contract may call for a different royalty scale in some or all of these categories. If that's the case, is the appropriate royalty rate shown for each of these categories? The earned royalty in each category should be calculated based on the specific royalty for that category.

4. Are all the mathematical calculations correct? I know that your royalty statement is probably a computer printout. You may assume that computers don't make errors. People do! Incorrect data may have been entered in the first place, causing your statement to be incorrect. Or, worse still (and it has happened) the computer program designed to calculate royalty statements can have an error built into it.

5. Check all the income from subsidiary rights. The statement should show the actual dollar income to the publisher for the sale of any rights, and then show your percentage of that income. Remember that the percentages will probably vary depending on rights sold: you may have agreed to accept 90 per cent of first serial rights, but 50 per cent of second serial rights. Check each category against your contract.

6. How does your contract treat income from subsidiary rights? If the advance given to you covers all income to the publisher, then your subsidiary rights' income counts into the calculations. If not, the royalty advance is to be earned out on the sale of copies of the publisher's edition only, not on the sale of such rights as mass market paperback, book club, TV and radio, serialization, etc.

7. Does your contract have a "reserve against returns" clause? This clause allows a publisher to withhold a portion of your royalties for a

limited period, in case sales have to be recalculated because of high levels of returns from bookstores. Your contract may, for example, call for the publisher to withhold 20 per cent until the next royalty statement. Such a clause is more common in contracts for mass market paperbacks, but it is now being incorporated into many hardcover book contracts. If there is such a clause, make sure that the percentage of royalties being withheld is correct and that the calculation of that percentage is also correct.

8. With a "reserve against returns" in operation, you must carefully check all royalty statements after the first one to assure that the sum of money that was reserved has been reversed before a newly calculated reserve was deducted from your royalty income. If, for example, $100 was withheld in the first statement, it should be added to your account before the reserve is calculated for the second royalty period. And double check your contract to see for how many royalty periods the publisher may use the reserve-against-earnings calculation. If the contract calls for three royalty periods, for example, and you're checking your fourth royalty statement, that previously withheld sum must be credited to you and no further reverses are permissible.

### Use common sense and patience.

As you can see, you need an accountant's eye to wend your way through royalty statements—but you don't necessarily need to have been trained as an accountant. Common sense (and some patience) will take you through the statement, and then a little bit of arguing with your publisher's royalty department may be necessary to prove that your interpretation of the contract and your calculations are the correct ones.

Your contract probably allows for an audit to be made at your request if you have serious doubts about the publisher's calculations. But remember, if your audit doesn't prove to uncover serious discrepancies (most contracts call for the publisher to pay for the audit if the discrepancy is five percent or greater in its favor) then you pay for the audit—and that can be expensive.

If you still can't figure out your statement, perhaps your tax accountant can help. Or contact your editor and let the publisher's accounting department explain it to you. Or is there a CPA in your family?—in which case, maybe a phone call is in order.

Fred Kerner is well acquainted with royalty statements, having been involved with them for more than 50 years: as the author of dozens of books; as an executive of publishing houses large and small; and as chairman of grievance committees for four national writers' organizations in Canada and the United States.

# Welcome to Vanity Publishing

*by Therese Goulet* _____

"**B**ook Manuscripts Invited—New Authors Welcome" reads the enticing ad placed by a New York publisher in Yellow Pages across the country. The ad might as well say: "Make your folks proud! Be a big shot in your home town! Impress the gang at the office!"

Impress them, heck, maybe I can quit my job once the book hits the bestseller lists, thinks the Margaret Atwood wannabe. So with visions of talk shows and book signings dancing in their heads, they dig out an old manuscript, or hammer out a new one, and away it goes. The next few weeks are spent in anxious anticipation of the publisher's reply.

And when the reply comes—jubilation! They loved it They're so eager to get going they sent a contract. It looks exciting. Not only does it cover the original hardcover publication, it also talks about royalties for reprints, sales to book clubs, foreign language publication, merchandising tie-ins, even motion picture rights. But what's this part that says I have to pay for it? Welcome to Vanity Publishing.

That's the term used for book publishers who prey on author's egos to generate those profits publishing companies are known for. What? You say publishing isn't profitable? Well it certainly is for the vanity presses. Unfortunately, those profits come from authors' pockets.

That's why one American firm was recently at the receiving end of a $15 million class-action suit brought against it by some 3,600 disgruntled authors who've dealt with it since 1971. The charge? Fraudulent and deceptive characterization of the company as a book publisher.

To see what all the angst is about, let's look at a typical contract offered to a novelist friend I'll call Roger. On the surface, the contract—a lengthy legal document heavily sprinkled with publishing industry jargon—looks impressive. In exchange for a payment by Roger of $9,675 (for a book of about 200 pages), the company agrees to print the book, provide him with

50 copies and keep an additional 400 copies available for sales and promotion purposes. It also promises that extra copies will be printed to fill any bona fide orders, and that Roger will receive a generous 80% royalty on all sales (the standard book publishing royalty is 10 to 15%).

But guess what? There will probably never be any sales, unless Roger makes them. This is true for most vanity publishers. Why should the company try to move your book when its already been paid for, and when you're the one who'll make most of the income anyway?

Vanity presses promise to promote the books they publish, and indeed they do—mailing out review copies to the media and sending catalogues to book stores, wholesalers and libraries. But the very fact that promotional literature comes from a vanity press is cause for it to end up lining most reviewers' garbage pails.

According to Genevieve Stuttaford, former coordinator of pre-publication reviews for *Publisher's Weekly*, their policy is simple. "We don't review vanity press books. That's pretty much the policy among most book reviewers." And indeed it is, judging from the absence of reviews of vanity press books in *Quill & Quire*, *Books in Canada*, *Canadian Author*, and other respected literary publications. Book store shelves aren't exactly groaning under the weight of such books either.

Why? Because vanity presses have a reputation for printing virtually anything that someone is willing to pay to have published, unless the manuscript is obscene or libellous, in which case the company figures it's more trouble to print than it's worth.

Unlike a conventional publishing house, which assigns an editor to refine your work before publication, a vanity press just typesets it, prints it, slaps a cover on it, and out it goes. It doesn't matter how ill-conceived, how badly written or how boring the manuscript is.

Nevertheless, vanity publishing can be seductive for those who dream of seeing their words in print. Can you think of anyone who doesn't think his autobiography would make a fascinating story? Especially when they see how even the famous have been seduced into going the way of the vanity press. One catalogue highlights a book written by actress Ellen Corby, Grandma on television's *The Waltons*, while another press includes a quote from "Leo Lanier, Poet Laureate of Louisiana," who tells the folks at that vanity press "I love you all."

### How to identify Vanity publishers.

Unless your only objective is to see your book in print, in which case it's thousands of dollars cheaper just to use a local printer, you'll probably want to avoid vanity presses. To help you do so, I've come up with a few clues to identify them:

### Don't send your manuscript to a publishing company that advertises for manuscripts.

The fact is reputable publishers don't need to advertise; they're swamped with manuscripts. HarperCollins, typical of the U.S. publishing giants, receives more than 10,000 manuscripts a year. Even the average Canadian publisher is flooded with manuscripts. British Columbia's Douglas & McIntyre, for example, receives more than 1,000 submissions annually.

These manuscripts, especially those not submitted through a literary agent or another friend of the editor, end up in the "slush pile" where they await their turn to be discovered by some overworked and underpaid editorial assistant, usually someone who's just graduated from university and will decide in one cursory glance whether or not your missive is worth publishing. For up to 99% of the manuscripts received, the decision is that it's not. (For many years the novel *Ordinary People* was the talk of the publishing world because it was that true rarity, a gem discovered in the slush pile.) It usually takes several months before you receive a reply.

Not so with the vanity presses. Of course, they don't actually read your manuscript. What they do might more accurately be described as skimming it to see if you've written anything coherent which could be considered libellous or obscene, but they do give you a prompt reply. And the nature of that reply provides another clue.

### Beware of glowing praise.

I don't mean the legitimate praise an editor may afford the true literary genius. I mean praise that seems, well, just a little unseemly. A few years ago I received such a letter from a publishing company that almost had me blushing. Here's an excerpt.

"Dear Ms. Goulet:

"It's amazing how you hit home again and again. I really hated to put this one down and kept turning the pages. What can I say about a book like this? It stopped me in my tracks. I guess all I can do is thank you for letting me have the opportunity to read it. The editors that saw it all had the same feeling as I did. Every one of the editors saw great potential with this book and it was given top priority and pushed ahead of every other book in house."

It went on in a similar vein for a couple of pages until the zinger: "I'm going to make a proposition for you to involve yourself with us."

The type of letters that are more typical of conventional publishing companies are generally less effusive. Legitimate publishers forgo the ego strokes for comments such as, "We are concerned about the tone being more academic than general." "Would it be possible to extend the ms to 250 pages? How many illustrations would there be? We like the dwarf but think his character needs to be developed a little more."

### If they ask for money, beware.

Most publishers who ask authors to pay are little more than vanity presses. Furthermore, there are alternatives to paying someone else to publish your book. Chief among these is self-publishing, where you hire a printer and produce the book yourself.

### Consider self-publishing as an alternative.

Self-publishing may appear to be essentially the same thing as vanity publishing, but it is not. Not because the books produced by self-publishers are necessarily more well-written or have more literary merit than vanity press books. Many are just as trite, boring or ill-conceived.

What distinguishes self-publishing is that some of the books actually make money. This is because the authors know from the outset they'll have to hustle if they want to make any kind of return on their printing investment. Furthermore, self-publishing does not carry the stigma attached to the vanity press. Says *Publisher's Weekly's* Stuttaford, "We do review self-published books. Of course, if they're semi-literate, we ignore them."

Although many turn in this direction because they can't convince a conventional publisher to take their book, success stories in self-publishing are legion. Robert Ringer did it with his classic business bestseller *Winning Through Intimidation*. A group of Calgary women compiled a series of cookbooks called *The Best of Bridge* and sold more than three million copies. Canadian physician Peter Hanson published *The Joy of Stress* under the name of the Hanson Stress Management Corporation in 1985 and has sold almost a million copies to date. Hanson probably received some effusive letters from legitimate publishers fighting to win the rights to his 1989 follow up, *Stress for Success*. And David Chilton's *The Wealthy Barber* is another such example which now is published under the Stoddart imprint.

### Approach the trade publishers.

You'll notice that none of these books is fiction. That's because self-published fiction has as much chance of cracking the bestseller lists as your Aunt Bertha's memoirs. Vanity presses like to tout the literary giants who, at one time or another, subsidized the cost of producing their own books. The fact is that bestselling subsidized fiction is a thing of the past, while bestselling poetry is a contradiction in terms.

So skip self-publishing if you have a novel or a collection of poems and want to reach a wider audience than your immediate family. Instead, send your manuscript off to as many publishers as you can; if your book has any literary merit you will probably find someone willing to publish it.

Don't make the mistake of sending out your queries one by one. Instead, consider doing what Vancouver's Walter Block did with his first book, a collection of essays titled *Defending the Undefendable*. Block mailed out query letters to 500 publishers (not one after the other, of course, because he'd have died of old age before he'd heard from number 75) and received one offer, from Fleet Press in the United States. But that was all he needed. His book has so far sold out five printings.

If conventional publishers turn you down and all you really want is 500 copies of a book to hand out to friends and relatives, go ahead and self-publish. It will cost you less than a vanity press, although it may not have the cachet of "a real published book."

At least you'll know you have a publisher you can trust.

Theresa Goulet has spent more than a decade as an editor and consultant in the book-publishing field.

# Get the Tax Breaks!

*by Arthur Bray* ———————————————

Freelance writers are people who write independently, whether it be full-time or part-time, and whose services are not sold exclusively to any one buyer. If you are freelancing, regardless of any other employment you may have, and meet certain criteria, you are self-employed for tax purposes and you should take advantage of all available tax breaks. You must remember that you are in business and are obligated to act in a professional manner by observing all the tax laws and regulations, and not bring discredit on the writing profession by acting unethically.

## The Profit Motive

A reasonable expectation of profit must exist before Revenue Canada will allow tax-deductible losses arising from your writing. Revenue Canada regards writers as "hobbyists" if there is no serious intent to be a profitable writer. Artistic expression in the form of writing receives no recognition for tax purposes unless the profit motive is present.

Revenue Canada realizes, however, that the nature of literature is such that a considerable period of time may elapse before a writer becomes established and profitable. It is possible that a writer may not realize a profit during his or her lifetime, but still have a reasonable expectation of profit.

Factors, among others, that will be considered by Revenue Canada in determining whether a writer has a reasonable expectation of profit, are, in summary:

1. The extent of time devoted to literary endeavours.

2. The extent to which a writer has presented his or her own works in public and private settings.

3. The extent to which a writer is represented by an agent or publisher.

4. The amount of time devoted to promoting and marketing the writer's own works.

5. The amount of revenue received that is relevant to the writer's own works.

6. The historical record over a significant number of years of annual profits or losses.

7. The variation, over a period of time, in the value or popularity of the individual's literary work.

8. The type and relevance of expenditures claimed, i.e., there would be a positive indication of business activity if a substantial portion of expenses were incurred for research.

9. The writer's qualifications as a writer.

10. Membership in a professional association of writers whose membership is limited under standards established by that association.

I recommend you obtain a copy of Revenue Canada's Interpretation Bulletin IT 504 (Visual Artists and Writers), from your nearest Revenue Canada office and read it in detail.

### Income Tax

As you are in business, you must report your profit or loss for income tax purposes, and there are two aspects to this reporting. First is the revenue and expense of your actual writing, and second is the cost of maintaining a work space in your home—your home office.

Claim your writing income and expenses on form T2124 (Statement of Business Activities) and include it with your regular tax return. A partial list of expenses deductible from your business income includes manuscript paper, other office supplies, photocopying, professional membership fees, purchase of (and repairs to) typewriters, computers and other office equipment, furniture, car expenses for business use, legal and accounting fees, postage, depreciation of your office equipment, and travel for earning business income. It is essential that you keep every piece of paper relating to your revenue and expense to ensure ease of preparation of your return and to protect yourself in the event the tax auditors decide to pay you a visit.

The next important point concerns the business aspects of your home office. Remember that the expenses you incur in writing are unrelated to the expenses of maintaining an office in your home. This is because your writing expenses have no relationship to where you write. The work space must be:

1. Your principal place of business, (there need not be more than one place, and it need not be used exclusively for business).

2. Or it must be used exclusively to earn business income and on a regular and continuous basis for meeting clients or other people in respect of earning business income.

You must use your work space for specified purposes and you may not claim related expenses exceeding your net income from the business for the taxation year. Such work space expenses could include, for example, the prorated portion of rent, property insurance, property taxes, mortgage interest, or operating costs such as heating or lighting, as well as building repairs. Do not claim depreciation on a portion of your home or you could end up paying taxes on any profit you make when you sell your house later. To determine the prorated amount of your household expenses, you must apportion your work space in a reasonable manner. This may be a percentage of the floor space of your home, or a fraction of the number of rooms, such as one sixth.

In the case of situation (1) above, you need not use the work space solely for your business, as it can also be put to personal use. However, you can claim a deduction only for the portion that you use for your business. For example, if you use your office for personal use 20 per cent of the time, you may claim only 80 per cent of your prorated work space expenses as a tax deduction. You should refer to Revenue Canada's Interpretation Bulletin IT 514 (Work Space in Home Expenses).

Note again that you may not claim your writing expenses as part of your office-in-the-home expenses. Writing expenses are claimed separately from home office expenses on form T2124. You then transfer the net amount of profit or loss to line 135 of your tax return.

### Goods and Services Tax

There is another important tax matter of concern to writers—the Goods and Services Tax (GST). Many writers feel that because their revenue from business operations is less than $30,000 annually, there is no need to register. Technically, they are correct. But if you have not registered, you cannot claim "input tax credits", which are credits claimed for the GST you paid on taxable items used in your writing activities. If your credits are greater than the GST you owe to the government, you may claim a refund for the difference.

It is also important to be registered so your GST registration number can be shown on your invoices (if you use them) or your contracts or agreements. You could even have it imprinted on your business cheques. Your GST-registered clients or publishers will then be able to claim their own tax credits. Keep in mind that if you register so you can claim these credits, you must also charge GST on all your written work. Your publishers or other clients must pay you the GST and you then remit it to the government. For authors of books, remember that the GST does not apply to payments from the Public Lending Right (PLR) for your books in libraries.

Writers do not usually send invoices, but, rather, the publishers send statements and cheques. You must collect 7 per cent GST on royalties and payments if you register. In such a case, ensure that your contracts require the publisher to pay the GST to you in addition to the royalty or other payment and to show the amount of the GST separately on the statement. Think about this: if you fail to arrange it with your publisher, you could find that in both old and new contracts, the GST becomes absorbed in royalty payments. Revenue Canada will hold you liable and you will have to pay the GST from your own pocket.

My advice to those writers who have not already registered is to consider carefully the implications of the GST. It is likely to be to your advantage to register. Why should you pay all that GST on your expenses and not get any of it back? Remember, you're in business!

If you don't register, this then tells all your clients and publishers that you earn less than $30,000 annually from your writing. Do you want them to know that? This little fact can possibly affect the image they have of you. It is also nobody's business (with the exception of the tax collector) whether your writing earnings are greater or less than this figure.

Bear in mind that tax rules are never static. Governments love to tinker with them. Even the GST has already been affected by adjustments and major changes are foreseen. If you are already registered, you must remain alert to changes as they occur. For example, there was the introduction of the Business Number (BN) which converted all business accounts you may have had with Revenue Canada to a single number. For many writers, that meant just your GST registration number, which then became the root of your new Business Number.

As well, if you are a self-employed GST registrant or a member of a partnership that is a GST registrant, you (or the partnership) can no longer claim certain input tax credits. This applies to supplies you use or consume in relation to a work space in your home and may include pro-rated portions of the operating costs, such as heating and lighting. Input tax credits will be denied for home work space unless the work space meets the same criteria as the income tax restriction for work-space-in-home expenses mentioned earlier.

A further change to the GST is its blending with Provincial Sales Taxes. The federal government and three Atlantic provinces, Nova Scotia, New Brunswick and Newfoundland, introduced a combined rate of 15 per cent effective 1 April 1997. This combined tax is called the Harmonized Sales Tax (HST). The GST part of this remains at 7 per cent. Harmonization with the Quebec Sales Tax began a phase-in during 1992 and was completed in April 1997.

All businesses across Canada were automatically registered for HST purposes and are required to collect and remit the 15 per cent tax on any taxable products shipped or mailed to recipients in participating provinces. Input tax credits can also be claimed for HST paid on purchases.

There is no lack of information available on income tax and the GST to self-employed writers. All GST-registered writers are on the mailing list for Revenue Canada's quarterly newsletter, *The Excise/GST News*, and you should read all issues carefully. Also, call Revenue Canada, both the income tax and GST offices, and ask them to send you all relevant booklets, in particular the two referred to above. You will find the numbers in the blue pages of your telephone directory. Alternatively, if you have a computer and a modem, you can connect on-line, free, to the Revenue Canada bulletin board system (BBS), called the Customs and GST Information Service, a good source of information. Dial 1-800-267-5979 on your modem. There is also a Revenue Canada Internet site at <http://www.revcan.ca/menue.html> where information is available as well as on-line copies of their guides and pamphlets which, of course, you can print. By whatever method you obtain your detailed information, be sure you get all you can, and follow it precisely. If you don't follow the rules, you may lose your tax status as a professional writer and there goes your profit.

Arthur Bray lives in Ottawa and is the author of four non-fiction books, two on Unidentified Flying Objects and two on financial planning. He is currently working on another non-fiction book on an unrelated topic.

# Bankruptcy and the Writer

*by Lesley Ellen Harris*

B ankruptcy affects writers in two ways. A writer may become a bankrupt; a debtor with a commitment to pay for a loan, goods or services. Or a writer might be creditor; someone owed money, goods or services by a person or organization that has become bankrupt.

Writers in financial difficulties have usually gotten there because of an overload of debts, an inability to collect due payments, a personal or family crisis, a continuous borrowing of money or an inability to earn enough money to pay for essential services such as rent or utilities. You can sometimes forestall harassment by collection agencies or the repossession of cars, furniture, etc. if you make an informal payment arrangement with your creditors. Alternatively, you could consolidate your debts into one loan with a bank or financial institution allowing you to make one manageable monthly payment.

At some point, you might have to approach a trustee in bankruptcy (consult Industry Canada or the Yellow Pages). Your licensed trustee will assist you in the formal procedures of declaring bankruptcy. Your assets will be assigned to the trustee, and you will be relieved of most of your debts and any related legal proceedings against you. Once you declare bankruptcy, you must give any income that exceeds the budget arranged with your trustee for distribution to your creditors until you have been discharged from bankruptcy. Your trustee will apply to the court within one year of your declaration of bankruptcy to "discharge" you, or end your bankruptcy. Once you are discharged, you can obtain credit after convincing a potential lender of your earning capacity and financial responsibility.

The trustee's fees are paid by the bankrupt or from the money received for selling your assets. Neither legal aid nor the government will pay the trustee's fees.

What can you do if you find yourself a *creditor* in a bankruptcy? Once a debtor declares bankruptcy there is a formal procedure to be followed under the Bankruptcy Act. A court-appointed trustee will collect information about the bankrupt's property and creditors, publish notices of the bankruptcy and call a meeting of creditors. The trustee will sell the bankrupt's property and distribute the proceeds to the creditors according to a hierarchy outlined in the Bankruptcy Act. As a creditor, it is important that you fill out the proof of claim the trustee sends you (possibly upon your request) and get your name on the list of creditors. The amount of money, if any, you receive will depend on the sale price of assets and your priority of claim, that is, whether it is secured, preferred or unsecured.

An example of a secured creditor is someone with a registered interest under a provincial property security act or possessing a realty mortgage. Prior to bankruptcy it is only a secured creditor who can put a defaulted debtor into receivership requiring a trustee to run the business until that creditor is paid off.

Employees are preferred creditors and are next in line in receiving proceeds from the sale of the bankrupt's assets. Writers who are employees of a bankrupt film company, for example, would be preferred creditors and may submit a claim for up to $2,000 for salaries and wages. Any wages beyond $2,000 can be claimed as an unsecured or ordinary creditor (such creditors are last to receive payment in a bankruptcy). Unfortunately, since secured creditors are paid before preferred creditors, there is often little money left for employees.

Writers who have works on consignment in a bankrupt company— for example, copies of their self-published books in a bankrupt bookstore—are not considered creditors and may be able to get their works back from a trustee. However, a trustee must return unsold works *only* if a consignment agreement was made between the writer and the bookstore ahead of time. (The consignment agreement should state that the writer's share of money from sales by the bookstore will be held in trust by the bookstore on behalf of the writer, because money held in trust is not bankruptcy property.)

What happens if your publisher goes bankrupt? Creditors whose claims are with respect to intangible property like copyright are protected by special provisions in the Bankruptcy Act. For instance, if a copyright work has not actually been published and put on the market at the time of the publisher's bankruptcy and no expenses have been incurred, any agreement between the author and publisher regarding the transfer of copyright terminates upon bankruptcy.

If at the time of bankruptcy the work was published and for sale, the author may purchase the published copies at a fair price or have the trustee sell them, with the author receiving the same royalties which would have been payable by the bankrupt. Further, the trustee cannot assign copyright without the written consent of the author except on terms that entitle the author to the same royalties the bankrupt was liable to pay. Other scenarios concerning copyright and bankruptcy can be covered by contract and should be included in your publishing agreement.

In a lean economy, people are careful to protect their interests in case of bankruptcy. However, bankruptcies occur in every economy and proper protection is always important.

*Note: This article contains general comments. It is not meant to be exhaustive and should not be considered legal advice. Should a bankruptcy matter arise, proper advice should be sought.*

Lesley Ellen Harris is a lawyer specializing in copyright and new media law, and the author of *Canadian Copyright Law* (second edition, 1995, McGraw-Hal Ryerson). She can be reached at (416) 226-6768 or at <copylaw@interlog.com>.

# Bequeath Your Literary Rights

*by Lesley Ellen Harris* ⎯⎯⎯⎯⎯⎯⎯⎯⎯⎯⎯⎯⎯⎯⎯⎯

Writers often ask what becomes of their rights to their intellectual property—their writings—when they die. Do a dead author's works fall into the public domain or can they be passed on to children or other heirs just like any other property?

In Canada, published literary works are protected by copyright until the calendar end of the fiftieth year after the deaths of their authors. If Joan Smith dies on November 2, 1997, there is copyright in all her published works, no matter when they were created, until December 31, 2047.

The same is not true for her unpublished works. For any of those, copyright lasts in perpetuity or, if they are published after her death, for fifty years from the date of their publication. In copyright, "publish" or "publication" has a slightly different meaning than what most writers are used to: It means the issuing of copies to the public. Handing out copies to students in a classroom would suffice; it needn't involve any printing and binding and marketing.

(Bill C-32 on copyright reform proposes the eventual phasing-out of perpetual copyright protection in unpublished works. This bill, if it becomes law, is unlikely to do so until at least 1998.)

Although rights in copyright works do not last forever, they last for a significant number of years and you will want to ensure that after your death, yours fall into the proper hands. Whoever has the right to these works will be able to control their print and electronic publication, translation, adaptation to stage or film and any other uses and also be entitled to royalties for those uses.

Like your tangible property—house, jewelry, financial investments—copyright can be bequeathed to others through a will. Unless your will specifies otherwise, the person(s) inheriting your tangible property will also inherit the intangible rights of copyright. Therefore, you should think carefully about who you want to control your copyright works after your death, and you should ensure that your will specifies this.

You might consider appointing a "copyright executor"—someone with special knowledge in the area of your literary works, who understands your desires with respect to them. It is important that the copyright executor be someone who's in a position to carry out your desires but who won't potentially end up in a conflict of interest. For example, a publisher might be in an awkward position to be act as executor for a writer whose works are issued by that publisher's firm.

A copyright holder is not limited to specifying one copyright executor. Two people may be executors jointly or there may be different executors for different works or with respect to different rights in the same work. You should try to ensure that your works will be in the hands of executors who are best placed to do as you would wish with them.

It is not merely your economic rights (e.g., the right to publish, translate, distribute on the Internet) which you are passing on, but also your moral rights. Moral rights, which are set out in the Canadian Copyright Act, allow you to have your name appear in association with your work, or to remain anonymous or to use a pseudonym. Moral rights also protect against any modifications to your work, or uses in association with a service, cause, product or institution, that may be prejudicial to your reputation. Choose someone who will continue to protect that reputation after your death.

An interesting provision, commonly called the reversionary interest, limits certain assignments of copyright to twenty-five years. Where an author of a work is the first owner of the copyright in it (that is, it is not a situation of employment, Crown works or a photograph or portrait), any copyright acquired by contract becomes void twenty-five years after the author's death. This means that any assignee or licensee of copyright (e.g., a publisher) loses his or her rights twenty-five years after the author's death. The copyright then becomes part of the author's estate and only the estate has the right to deal with it.

There is no reversion where the author disposes of the copyright by will for the period following the twenty-five-year limit to the assignee who is already assigned the copyright. Thus, the section may be avoided by bequeathing copyright for the period between twenty-five and fifty years after the author's death (but only if the bequest is to the assignee and not to some other person.) It also does not apply where a work has been assigned as part of a collective work or where a licence has been granted to publish a work or part of a work within a larger collective work.

Your estate lawyer can ensure that your will provides satisfactorily for protection and control of your intellectual property after your death. If unfamiliar with copyright (which is probable), he or she will consult first with a copyright lawyer. But before consulting with any lawyers, you should take the time to consider how you want your copyright works used after your death and who would be the best person or persons to ensure that your wishes are respected.

*This article is for information purposes and should not be construed as legal advice. Proper legal advice should be sought when necessary.*

Lesley Ellen Harris is a lawyer specializing in copyright and new media, and the author of *Canadian Copyright Law* (second edition, 1995, McGraw-Hal Ryerson). She can be reached at (416) 226-6768 or at <copylaw@interlog.com> or <http://www.mcgrawhill.ca/copyrightlaw>.

# Develop Your Style

# The "You" in Style

*by Fred Kerner* ⸺⸺⸺⸺⸺⸺⸺

S tyle is the *you* in writing; it is very personal. It is, as Cardinal Newman once said, "thinking-out in language," though I prefer to think of it more as self-escaping into language. It is as personal as the nose on your face, as personal as the way you walk. So let that be a warning: it is dangerous to become self-conscious about your style.

Every year thousands of runners attend running clinics. They are not there to learn *how* to run, nor are they there to learn a new style of running. They are there to learn how to use their own style more effectively and efficiently. That is the key to writing style: effective and efficient.

There is a letter, now famous in the annals of American history, that is worth reading with that dictum in mind. It was written by a near-illiterate man who, along with a friend named Sacco, was executed in the United States in 1927 for a murder they claimed they did not commit. This is what he wrote before he died:

> "If it had not been for these thing, I might have live out my life talking at street corners to scorning men. I might have die unmarked, unknown, a failure. Never in our full life could we hope to do what we do by accident. Our words, our lives, our pain, nothing. The taking of our lives—the lives of a good shoemaker and a poor fishpeddler—all. That last moment belong to us—that agony is our triumph."

There are a lot of things wrong with that letter. You can correct it, but you cannot make it more efficient or effective. And you cannot change it without changing the character of the man who wrote it.

There is one rule in writing that transcends every other rule. It was propounded by writer Margaret Kennedy who said: "You *may* do what you *can* do." The errors in Vanzetti's letter are not errors of character, they are only errors of learning.

If you wish to develop your style, then, you must first learn to love the basic tools of the writer's craft: words. Learn to love them for their colour, their texture, their weight, their sound—even their visual impact.

Some writers are more interested in the weight of a word than in its colour. Some are more interested in the sound of words than in their meaning.

That is what makes style—the writer's own style! Love words, too, for their precision. Note that I used the word *love*. I did not use like, relish, fancy, admire, cherish, esteem, regard, respect, or even dote on. All those words are sometimes interchangeable. But no woman wants to hear her true love say, "I relish you." Nor does an ardent Romeo want to hear the object of his desire say, "I respect you."

I don't mean that you should fall in love with every word you write. Long-distance phone calls are good practice, particularly if you are paying for them—and if they are to people to whom you don't particularly wish to speak. At such times, you speak directly and without preamble.

So love words, and read—widely, but eclectically. If you read one author, you are likely to be influenced by that author. If you read many authors, you will be influenced by most, if not all of them. You will certainly learn from all. "The only way in which reading can form style," said Schopenhauer, "is by teaching us the use to which we can put our own natural gifts." He meant that if you have a gift for humour you can learn to write humour by reading those who write humour. If you don't, you cannot.

So learn to love words and to read... and also to *write*. Practice writing to discover and improve your style. No one who writes an occasional letter is likely to have much of a writing style. And no one who writes every day is likely to be without one. But be warned: A bad habit does not become a good habit through practice.

A writer learns his or her craft and perfects style not so much from writing as from rewriting. And rewriting does not mean copying the same words, or copying the same form. It means rethinking what you are doing, and trying to improve.

Good writers must be good critics of their own work. But in becoming a critic of your own work you must not be critical at the wrong time. Writers who are critical too early have a tendency never to get anything on paper. They discard ideas even before they are written down. On the other hand, some writers become critical too late; they produce pages bulging with unessential words and elliptical thoughts.

If you have problems beginning a story because you can't find an idea, or you have trouble finishing a story because you fall out of love with it, then you are probably becoming too critical, too soon. If you have endless drafts of three or four stories that refuse to become one, then you are probably not critical enough, early enough.

The first thing you want to look for with your cold critical eye is precision. Writing is a precise art, no matter how many books seek to prove otherwise. Precision means that you have to use words that are distinct and use them precisely. Avoid imprecise words, or words that have taken some current—and probably temporary—meaning. A word like "nice" means little—and hasn't meant much in years. Nor do filler words, words such as "pretty" (not referring to beauty) or "very" offer any precise meaning to your writing. These words add clutter without adding substance. To write something like "He was pretty dead," might be effective in some kinds of humour. But outside of that, if you admire that kind of writing, you are admiring the sound of your own voice—and nothing more.

Where you have two words of exact meaning use the word richer in color, texture, sound, evocation; or sometimes use the one having the greater visual impact. Remember that writing is usually a visual medium. Viper has more sting than snake—but snake looks snakier!

Beware of ostentation, fashion and special vocabularies. My mind goes blank every time I see or hear "impact" or "access" used as verbs, unless they are in conjunction with technical usage.

Search and destroy the merely adequate. There is no place in a circus for a juggler who can juggle only one orange at a time. Nor is there a place in writing for a sentence that accomplishes only one purpose. "Then they were there." That sentence informs, but it evokes no memories, tells nothing of character, or setting, or atmosphere, or tone.

Avoid, shun, and eschew repetition of words—or sentences, paragraphs or chapters that begin and end in the same way, are of the same length, have the same rhythm. Repetition *can* be a valuable tool for writers when used with care and with purpose. In one of humanity's oldest stories we have the repetition of "And the evening and the morning were the first day." In the movies we have "What do you want to do, Marty?" "I don't know. What do you want to do?"

Repetition is a two-edged sword. If you use it, use it deliberately, not carelessly.

Take the time to read what you have written—aloud. Listen to the words, and the rhythms. Does the writing flow? Is it natural? Does it convey the mood you wish? The purpose of all this activity is clarity. If it isn't clear, you are not finished with it. Most failures of clarity are failures of thinking. You cannot express an idea that you do not hold clearly. Did you every try to give directions when you were not sure of how to get there yourself? Don't write to impress the reader, write to serve the reader.

I have little patience with writers who require me to re-read a sentence more times than they have rewritten it. Nor do I continue for long with paragraphs that take more time to read than they took to compose.

After clarity, strive for brevity. In the words of Mies van der Rohe, "Less is more." But brevity is not an end in itself. When the Greeks were considering war against the Persians, they consulted the Oracle. The Oracle said: "The Greeks the Persians shall subdue." That's short; but what does it mean? Brevity must be the companion of clarity. "In the eyes of its mother, every ass is a gazelle." That's short; it is also clear.

The natural result of writing is proliferation, not brevity. Brevity must be achieved. It comes through selection, through discarding thoughts. Pattern bombing destroys brevity. That's when you can't think of the exact word, so you use three nearly right words, hoping to cover the target. "He rose, soared and surged..., then you add "upwards" just to make sure the reader knows in what direction your hero is going.

Brevity can also be lost through lack of a clear goal. You don't know what the target of the piece is, so you sit at the keyboard and turn over a few words to see what crawls out. In the military that's called "reconnaissance by fire." Having nothing to aim at, you shoot in a general area until something shoots back—then you have a target. That may not be a bad way to write on those days when nothing seems to be going on in your head. But it's a disastrous way to rewrite. Such fumbling efforts should never reach the eye of the reader.

Seek a liberal style, a style that is open, generous and without mean spirit. Respect your characters enough to get to know them, to understand them and to be honest with them. Not every villain slurps instead of sips, or belches instead of burps, or shuffles instead of walks. Using such devices to turn a reader against a character is not only mean-spirited toward the character, but it's playing a trick on the reader.

Don't manipulate the reader's emotions nor play tricks at the reader's expense. You should, instead, be investigating the character's motivations. The reader will not respect the writer if the writer does not respect the reader.

Your style should also be liberal enough to encompass different styles. Hemingway so limited his style that he sometimes wrote parodies of it. Style is not determined only by who you are, but also by the information you have to convey and the audience you are addressing.

One of the greatest joys of writing is discovering your own intellectual, emotional inner self—and giving it expression.

Admit that you are peculiar. If you weren't peculiar you wouldn't be a writer. And when I say peculiar I don't mean strange, unique, eccentric, erratic, odd, quaint, outlandish, exceptional, abnormal, aberrant, irregular, fantastic, bizarre, grotesque, or off-the-wall. Think of how many writers could be saved from a *Penthouse* purgatory or a *Cosmopolitan* confessional if they had but looked in the dictionary and discovered that peculiar does not mean outlandish, but comes from the Latin *peculium*, meaning private property.

Your style is your private property. Admit it and glory in it. In writing, be yourself.

But be your *best* self.

Fred Kerner has conducted writing classes across Canada and the United States—including sessions at Stanford University and Long Island University—and has given workshops at writers conferences including Breadloaf, Cape Cod, Suncoast, American University, and Oakland College among others.

# On Being an Ethnic Writer

*by Shulamis Yelin* _____

've been asked to write a personal essay entitled "On Being An Ethnic Writer." According to the Oxford Dictionary the word ethnic means "pertaining to a particular racial historical or religious group or common culture." (Gr. *ethnos*, meaning a nation.)

I am an ethnic, born in Montreal, Quebec of Russo-Jewish parents who came to Canada in 1910. My early education, my teaching diplomas and my BA were achieved at Macdonald School for Teachers and Sir George Williams College, (now Concordia University) in the English Protestant education system of my province, my MA (*magna cum laude*), at the French Catholic University of Montreal. I taught for the Protestant School Board of Greater Montreal for over thirty years. I am a Jew and my first language was Yiddish. I'm an ethnic.

I absorbed the culture and the ancient values my scattered people had passed on through the generations. From the 18th century they had set roots in Chernobyl, a garden town in the Ukraine. the seat of a line of illustrious rabbis and scholars. With the destruction of the Jewish population by the Russians during the Hitler era, Chernobyl became the seat of atomic research. The subsequent explosion of its atomic reactor turned Chernobyl into a charnel house. Its radiation still strikes terror in the hearts of the world around it.

From my readings and studies I've learned that all Canadians are ethnic. Anthropologists tell us that even the First Nations came from elsewhere—from Asia, across the Bering Sea. All my friends are ethnic. Their roots are in Great Britain, in various countries on the European Continent, in Asia, Africa, South America, the Islands. Today we are all Canadians. Our friendship has enriched both their lives and my own as we learned of each other's religious and cultural heritage, were fascinated by their similarities and differences, enjoyed each other's festivals and festivities.

We became aware that all our cultures celebrated the solstices under other names, all our languages had idioms that were untranslatable but carried the same thought. Our proverbs spoken in other tongues with other images, embraced the same wisdom, and all our people had, at one time or another, suffered the anguish and the indignities of war.

We acknowledged that we are all vulnerable, that we all had prejudices we had learned very early in our lives, prejudices that needed to be eradicated.

What we shared most intensely was the appreciation of our mutual condition: our intense gratitude for living in Canada. What we also shared was the constant awareness of living in two cultures, knowing two allegiances: one to Canada, the other to the collective memory of our own people, an issue that often included the further difference of race or religion. As a Jew born in Canada, I very early became aware of these differences. So did my friends.

What we discovered was that despite our differences, our values and our dreams were pretty much the same.

As writers, we asked ourselves the same questions: In what language shall we write? What stories shall we tell? How much dare we reveal? The Canadian experience belongs to all of us, and yet, and yet?

My parents arrived in Canada with three languages: Yiddish, Russian and biblical Hebrew. They brought with them, together with their own culture, a love for the richness they had acquired from the cultures around them.

From my earliest years I wanted to be a writer. Books had the place of honor in our house. It was Papa's books, not Mama's fine china, which had the place of honor in the china cabinet of our new walnut dining room set. Behind the leaded glass doors with their shining brass knobs, the books stood in rows behind each other in their colored cloth bindings. The arrival of a new book was cause for celebration at our Sunday dinner table. Sunday was the one day Papa could have dinner with us since he had to work even on Saturday.

"Books are teachers," Papa said. "We have to give them a place of honor in our home."

Together with the works of our own classicists, Peretz, Sholem Aleichem and Mendele, there were works by Russian, English, French and Scandinavian writers in Yiddish translation. Thus I became acquainted with the names of famous writers of various cultures. The first name to draw my attention was that of Shakespeare, whose *Merchant of Venice*, in a bright red cloth binding, Papa laid upon the dining room table one Sunday morning. As he opened the cover to show us the poet's portrait, he spoke the title carefully, and the playwright's name with awe: "*Shylock. Der Koifman fun Venedig*, fun Villyam Shekspir."

"One of the world's greatest writers," Papa added.

I was enthralled by the high forehead, the penetrating eyes, the shoulder-length wavy hair and the dashing mustache and beard of the man.

I looked with Papa at the first printed Yiddish page and was proud.

This exhilarating enchantment, however, was soon brought to an aching debacle in my Strathearn School Grade V class, when I shared this wondrous knowledge with my Scottish teacher, explaining to her that the book was in YIDDISH about a man called Shylock and it was by a great Jewish writer called VILLYAM SHEKSPIR. She was stunned.

"In Yiddish? Really! Well, Shylock was hardly a man to be proud of! Why would your father have that book on his shelf?"

I didn't understand her words but her tone shriveled me.

I wept all the way home from school. Of course, Papa wasn't home at that hour. I couldn't bear to tell this to Mama. It was to my teacher in the afternoon Jewish school that I confided my grief. She listened to my sobbing and my hiccoughed questions. "What's wrong with Shylock? Why shouldn't my father keep that book on his shelf?"

In time I would learn the answers.

I wrote my first poem in Grade Seven. It was a ballad in English called "The Fair Sad Maid." Mama was very proud and suggested I show it to my Yiddish teacher. My Yiddish teacher thought it was wonderful, but asked, "Why don't you write in Yiddish?"

I began to write in Yiddish as well and discovered I had two separate different voices: My English voice spoke of fairies and chimneys, my Jewish voice of feelings and ideas. My English poems appeared in the Sunday English page of the *Canadian Jewish Eagle*, my Jewish poems in the *Peretz Shula Children's Magazine*. By the time I had reached my midteens, I was strangled by my ambivalence and could write in neither. The gift was lost. It would be decades before I began to write poetry again.

As a teenager at Baron Byng High School, I began to hear the name of A.M. Klein. I learned he was studying Law at McGill University, a gifted Jewish poet much involved in the life and history of his people. He was also the Executive Director of Young Judea, a Zionist organization that sought to keep the young Jews close to their roots and traditions and the editor of the *Canadian Jewish Chronicle*. He and his close friend, David Lewis, (later the leader of the national C.C.F. Party) were the brilliant debating team at McGill University.

When, as a student at Macdonald School for Teachers, I wrote him a letter asking for some material I needed for a project, he sent me a packet together with an enclosed letter. In it he wrote that he had seen my poems in the Sunday English Page of the *Jewish Daily Eagle*, adding "and I hope you will turn your talent to our cause."

A letter from A.M. Klein—a cherished gift, a treasured memory.

Abraham Moses Klein, the acknowledged foremost poet of his generation, Abraham Moses Klein, a brilliant multilingual scholar and communicator, could not get a full-time position in the English department at McGill University. His early poems had been published in the *McGill Daily*, in the *McGill Fortnightly Review* and in the *Menorah* journal. Together with A.J.M. Smith, F.R. Scott and Leo Kennedy he had founded the Montreal Group of Four which in the '40s re-energized Canadian English poetry. Abraham Moses Klein could only teach at McGill as a visiting lecturer, and then, only through the good offices of McGill's Jewish benefactor, Mr. Samuel Bronfman.

During the Second World War, when Jews were seeking refuge from the Nazi Terror, when a passport meant the difference between life and death, Canada refused them entry. In a haggling reminiscent of the Patriarch Abraham's haggling with God for the survival of 10 souls in Sodom and winning his argument, the Canadian Government's answer was NONE IS TOO MANY.

Even in the postwar era, it was not easy for a Jew to get a book published in Canada. Klein's first two books, *Hath Not A Jew* and *Poems*, and later, his *Hitleriad*, had to find a publisher in the United States. He was never elected to fellowship in the Royal Society, nor was he ever awarded any of the prizes bestowed by the Canada Council. His friend, the poet Desmond Pacey, author of *Creative Writing In Canada*, noted, that if Klein could divest himself of his "Jewish baggage", his true talent would emerge. Klein was too ethnic!

Klein's so-called "true talent" emerged in 1948, with the publication of *The Rocking & Other Poems*. He was awarded the Governor-General's Medal. The book was cheered as one of the finest interpretations of French Canada.

How could the Jew, A.M. Klein, have so deeply understood and so skillfully interpreted the French Canadian had he not himself experienced the pain and the discrimination they were experiencing? How could he have recognized "the odor of race" at their political meeting had he not known it himself?

I am indebted to A.M. Klein whose heritage, which is also my own, is clearly recognizable in my work. Both my books of prose and poetry are written in English, but they are Jewish books. My first book of poetry, *Seeded In Sinai*, (148 pages), was published in New York and sold 1500 copies. I am more fortunate than Klein in that a more open climate prevails. The book is now available in French translation, titled *Au Soleil De Ma Nuit*. My Chapbook, *Many Mirrors Many Faces*, has just about sold out its second printing. My themes are many and varied, but my Jewish experience is ever evident and several of my poems have won prizes. I am also included in a number of fine anthologies. I look forward to having another book published before long.

My volume of biographical short stories, *Shulamis: Stories From A Montreal Childhood*, came out in three successive printings within eight months. In 1993, a 10th anniversary celebratory fourth printing, a second issue, appeared and is enjoying new popularity. The book is used in many schools and colleges and is now being translated into French, to be published by Humanitas Press.

A book has a life of its own. Over the years I have received dozens of letters from various parts of the world. A Quebecois professor wrote, "I read your stories and I laughed and I cried, and for each of your Jewish stories I can tell you a parallel story of my own French Canadian childhood." A retired Welsh teacher wrote, "Thank you for your heart-warming stories. I didn't know Jews do so many things we do too!" A lady from Reykjavik, Iceland, wrote "How did you know my grandfather?!" And Nobel Laureate, Saul Bellow, who spent the early years of his childhood in Montreal, wrote, "I have forgotten nothing of those marvelous years. I read your stories in a kind of nostalgic ecstasy."

I've read my poetry and prose in coffee shops, in schools, at group readings, on radio and TV across Canada. I've also read in the U.S. and in Mexico to multicultural audiences who lovingly accepted my Jewish voice in my English stories. While critics praised "the tone", "the insight", "the style", "the sharp ear for dialogue", what readers obviously respond to is the clear sense of self, a focus which draws them into my "humorous, warm, wistful stories".

With the need for greater population in our vast multifaceted land, with the influx of hundreds of thousands of immigrants from other cultures and with the concept of multiculturalism firmly entrenched, Canada has been enriched with fine writers from different parts of the world, ethnics all. Each has brought his or her own "baggage". Each has helped us broaden our vista, to feel more at home in the world.

What then, is it to be an ethnic writer? It is to appreciate the labors of those who have gone before us, to explore and enrich our heritage and to reveal it to the rest of the world.

As Jews, we have served as catalysts through the centuries in every land that has given us shelter. We have paid allegiance to its government, have shown our appreciation for the labors of those who have gone before us, and have enriched the land both economically and culturally.

As an ethnic writer, I seek to create a better understanding of what it means to be "other", and to foster an environment where all citizens can enjoy the fragrance and fruit from each other's vineyards.

As a Jew, I look forward with hope and faith to the continued harvest of peace and creativity in this brave new land.

Shulamis Yelin is a Montreal-born poet and writer. Some of her books of poetry include: *Seeded In Sinai*, *Au Soleil de Ma Nuit*, and *Many Mirrors Many Faces*. She was the recipient of the Canadian 125 Anniversary of Confederation Medal and a winner in the 1996 Greater Montreal Prix des Aìnés Contest. Shulamis has also appeared regularly on CBC TV.

# The Trouble With Words

*by Linda Jeays*

"It's 2:00 a.m. For Chrissake, get up and *go*," snarls your bed partner.

So you do. Off to the kitchen. Put on the kettle. Grab pen and paper. Make tea. Start to write a poem beginning with the single line which obsesses you. Time passes.

The Snarler mellows: calls friendly invitations from underneath warm blankets. Ten of your toes are frozen into elongated ice cubes and the heating system has quit, but still you write. You have no alternative: a crazed mob of words holds you hostage at pen-point.

Words have their own lust for fifteen minutes of fame, and on this particular night, you are their chosen channel from the abstract to the concrete world.

And that, fellow sufferers, is the trouble with words: they have minds of their own.

Rebels. Sometimes, a word does not want to be in your article. You are galloping along at sixty words a minute when you experience a sudden tight feeling in your chest. Relax. It is a WrongWordAttack, not a heart attack. Scrutinize your line. Find the rebels and the pain will subside. Practice on this sentence: *Sally speared her foot on a sticking-up sea shell.*

Worry at words the way a dog worries at a bone: over and over again (without apparent progress), until, Crunch! you are through to the marrow of your thought. Realize the possibilities and limitations of words. Never stretch them (or analogies) to impossible lengths.

Be sensitive to different communities of words: to their common voice. Words are choosy about their friends. The Great One crammed the following good companions into the first four lines of *Titus Andronicus: noble, patricians, patrons, right, defend, justice, cause, arms, country-*

*men, followers, title, swords.* When grouped so closely together, our unconscious mind adds in other words from the same gang: *leader, might, war, struggle, issue, battle, conflict.* Prompt a reader's conscious and unconscious minds to join forces and you create a powerful text.

The WWU (Working Words Union) protects the rights of special interest word-groups. Section 4, subsection (ii) of the Current Agreement stipulates equal pay for equal work. Jobs must be offered to union members before non-professional words are considered. For example, magazine items about the garment industry must employ words such as *faux, palazzo, A-line* and *retro.* Unfortunately, this means extra work for writers, who need to research appropriate vocabulary before they can write in specialized subject areas.

Recognize non-union words by their vapid personality and tendency to tag along with other weaklings: *The weather is fine. We needed a break. Have a nice day.* Postcard language.

While clichés protrude from a manuscript, like a bandaged thumb on a concert pianist, redundant idioms seem innocuous but have a debilitating effect on prose: *in essence*; *to tell the truth*; *as previously mentioned.* Unless you are a civil servant and your livelihood depends on the mastery of such poverty-stricken phrases, follow the instincts of every fine editor and surgeon: if it doesn't need to be in there, cut it out.

Some words engage in group circumlocution every chance they get. Control their urges. Close cousins to redundant idioms, these word-groups carry a smidgen of meaning, therefore should be replaced, not merely detonated. Think simple: *on the grounds that* (because); *for the purpose of* (to); *in short supply* (scarce); *reconnaissance asset* (spy); *sex trade worker* (- - o - -).

Writers must build a dike against the growing Sea of Babblespeak: "I was able to use the information centre data to debottleneck production capacity" (James Martin, technical writer). He meant: "The system fixed itself." And from NASA, "We have a determination to scrub the launch": "Quick! Turn it off."

Many individual words are ho-hum, arthritic or dead. This happened because they were smoking for years and wore themselves out. See: *thrilling, fluffy, pleasant.* Lots of similes are past their heyday: *as smooth as silk*; *as mad as a hatter*; *as high as a kite...*though the meaning of the last expression has expanded somewhat over the years. A to Z, aim for language which pulsates with youthful zest.

In the techno-crazy nineties, words realized that motherboards offered them fresh ways of proliferating in virtually real forms. Accepted with stomach-churning by people who remember typewriters, Nerdo has successfully enriched the English language. Eyebrows raised? How else would you communicate efficiently the meaning of *software, download, WordPerfect,* and *Interface, the Verb*?

New words must have staying power and not seem outdated by the time your piece hits the newsstand. Avoid *uptight, awesome* and their ilk. People who use these words dye their hair green, or buy golf balls that have electronic beepers. Be creative, but conservative. (Not a political statement.)

Clowns. They look funny; they sound funny, and they make you smile. *Clown* is not a funny word. *Comic* tries hard to be a funny word. Here are some funny words: *giggle, titter, snigger, chortle.*

More hilarious words: *knickers, knackers, knockers; kook, kazoo, kiddie.* The letter *k* is always good for a laugh; the silent *k* even more hysterical; the *z* and *oo* co-operative. Did you notice that *kook* is a palindrome? Kinda cute, eh?

Some words do nothing except fool around. What can you expect? They mostly have silly-looking double letters. So, if your subject matter is dead serious—for example, burial versus cremation—avoid words that begin with *k* and have double letters. Jus' kiddin'. Be aware that words may go over the top if ewes misspell them.

Decades ago, English teachers whose underwear was too tight noticed that when words with common characteristics (e.g. same initial letter or same vowel sound) congregated, they had lots of spirit and were difficult to discipline. In a conspiracy to assign these alternative word-groups to a dusty closet, English teachers gave them soul-destroying names. The plot failed. Poetic devices (such as alliteration) still have a significant gut-grabbing presence in our language—and not only in humor and poetry.

In fact, in their fight against pedantry, words have simply became more artful. For instance, they employ drunks to sing "Roll me over in the clover" to propagate the use of assonance and internal rhyme.

Words stutter, hiss, ring, bellow, sizzle. From the time that Mom says "choo-choo," and the cow (and the kid) say "moo-moo," onomatopoeia is a part of everyday speech. *Plop, gulp, zoom, whizz, oink, sprinkle.* Just imagine the possibilities of a metrical verse which rhymes *sprinkle* with *tinkle.*

Think. Play. Learn.

Take a cold hard stare at the appearance of these words: *moon, geese, gaggle, Orion, skiing.* Do not make them into a haiku. See how pleasing the shapes of the letters are? See how moonlike an "o" is? How squiggly a "g"? Aren't the little dots on "ii" thoroughly inimitable?

Words like to try on masks (italics, quotation marks, capital letters; a bold face). As natural-born actors, they enjoy an audience's reaction to their costume. Experiment; but don't slip into pretension. For example: words may become too "loud" and "in your face" if they are emphasized by speech marks.

Caps can change meaning radically. If patience sits on a monument, we have Nonsense. If Patience sits on a monument, the sweet child is probably watching out for pigeons overhead. (There may be other interpretations.)

In E.M. Forster's *A Passage to India*, there is a cave which echoes "Ou-boum...Ou-boum." So do words. Echo. I recently made an enemy-for-life when I pointed out to a journalist-friend that she had used the word *cookie* nine times in a 54-word lead paragraph. Sloppy and Picky don't speak any more.

Helper words (articles, conjunctions, prepositions) may sneak into text once too often without destroying it, but if your copy is about diabetes or fruitcake (where synonyms are hard to find), beware echo words. When spotted, choose substitutes wisely. Using *jawbreaker* as a synonym for your mother-in-law's fruitcake may be hazardous to your marriage.

Echo words used for special effect are, of course, not baddies. The second messenger in *Coriolanus* (a good play) announces, "Good news, good news!" This is a good use of repetition. Go figure.

Please make a pot of soup. All done? Now, let it cool. See how the fatty scum rises to the top? Scoop off the mush to reduce the fat content of the meal.

That short story you are writing...Scrape off the first 100 words and drop them in the garbage can. Froth. The words are still arguing about who gets to be leader. Check paragraph two. The opening sentence, tone and style of your narrative is there.

Immigrants. They work hard and contribute much to the linguistic mosaic: *verandah* (Hindi), *beleaguer* (Dutch), *cantata* (Italian), *berserk* (Old Norse). Use freely. Avoid words like *wrasse* (Cornish), *zeitgeist* (German) and *heuristic* (Whocares); readers do not know their meanings either. Promote native-born sons and daughters from Canadian French, such as *voyageur*, *toque* and *toboggan*. (A political statement.)

Pity the writer who says, "I love words." The object of love should be the free choice of a sane mind; and no one with all marbles intact chooses to write a poem at two a.m. on a chilly night instead of...but enough.

Linda Jeays has almost 100 published poems, most of which began in the middle of the night. However, any similarity between her lead anecdote and her *real* life as a freelance writer in Nepean, Ontario, is purely coincidental.

# Write for the Heart

*by Dorothy M. Powell* ─────────────

The respected editor of a major American periodical, when asked what he wanted in a short story, once replied, "Touch me—and you have a good chance of a sale." What he wanted, then, was to feel emotion: love, hate, fear, a twinge of sympathy, the lilt of laughter and maybe even a tear or two. Which brings up the subject of emotion, one of the greatest omissions in the stories of beginning writers. Without emotion, characters become cardboard cut-outs with nothing beneath their glossy surface but compressed paper. No wonder editors and magazine readers—if they have the time and happen to be impressed with your writing—keep chiding, "But your characterization is poor."

The secret is simple. Not one writer has been without emotions throughout his lifetime—scared witless, trembling with anticipation, convulsed with laughter, reduced to hopeless tears or sailing high on the wings of happiness. The list is endless and from it one gives to fictional characters those same personal feelings.

Take, for example, the feeling of fear. Who has not been afraid at some time in their lives? Not only are there inner feelings but, also, outward physical signs of this more dramatic emotion. Inwardly, the muscles quiver, the blood pumps faster, sweat streams from every pore and the skin becomes clammy. Sounds like a medical textbook, doesn't it? A good idea, though, might be to glance through such a book: it is a known fact that fear can actually kill! Outwardly, the pupils dilate, color drains from the face, and according to how you have drawn your character, he will remain paralyzed or erupt into frenzied action. All of this, of course, when a protagonist comes face-to-face with a frightening situation.

Naturally, there are other fears, less obvious but just as disastrous to a character's well-being. An interesting assignment in a creative writing class never failed to have fascinating results—a paragraph written within fifteen minutes about some experienced fear.

One young student, within weeks of giving birth to her first-born, had attended a familiarization tour of the maternity wing with her husband. Rather than being reassured, her paragraph read aloud to the class admitted, with complete honesty, of that inner corrosive fear which we all harbor concerning the unknown: in this particular case, the unknown experience of giving birth. From the facial expressions of both male and female students it was not difficult to see that they were touched. And, when she returned to night school after missing just one weekly session to be delivered of a baby boy, the whole class gave her a standing ovation. What this young woman had managed was the magic of communication, she had touched a human chord, she had tingled the senses.

Emotion, though, can never be complete without the inclusion of the five senses: sight, sound, smell, taste and touch. Your reader must *see* the light in a child's eye to appreciate again the wonder of Christmas. Must *hear* the pleased laughter when a gift is unwrapped. Must *smell* the brown aroma of roasting turkey and curl his tongue around the *taste* of brandied plum pudding. Must know the warmth of a hand when it *touches* your character's own. Only then will a reader comprehend a character's joy, that added sense of inner feeling. A sixth sense, if you like. A memorable day, your character will think, a day to be cherished.

A good exercise for any writer, either beginner or recognized professional, would be to read Nobel prizewinner Sigrid Undset's book, *Kristin Lavransdatter* in which she uses the sense of smell more than any other author I know. There is no way, of course, that a short story writer could dwell on the senses at such length. One or two vibrant words will do. No matter if it takes an hour, a day or a week to find the right ones—find them!

When dealing with emotion there will be one last difficulty that every writer will have to face. Yourself! Your own point of view about life in general. We are all biased when it comes to our own feelings. So, don't turn away from something you instinctively dislike. If you do, you will miss something you ought to see, some quality your more distasteful characters should have to make them more lifelike; the twisted logic of hatred, the vulgar words shouted in anger, the unreasoning act of jealousy. I am not suggesting that you discard your beliefs, but simply, that a writer must stand back and look at a character through the window of those beliefs.

Hand-in-hand with emotion goes action. Merely to tell a reader that a man is angry is not enough. Anger is usually crude and forthright, so your character will likely feel a sinking sensation in his throat, his belly will tighten, his legs shake. Outwardly, he might curse and shout, his voice change pitch and his fists clench. The reader then *sees* how he looks as well as how he *feels*.

Down through the years, the most successful authors are the ones who have created fictional characters who live far longer than their creators. The Walter Mittys, the Simon Legrees, the Scarlett O'Haras are characters so true to life that a reader shares their confusions, their griefs, and shouts with exultation at their triumphs. To make a reader care what happens to your character, and to inject adrenalin into the arteries of your writing, you must let the reader know your protagonist from the inside out.

Don't be afraid to write from the heart. There is nothing wrong with warmth, sentiment and nostalgia—just as long as it does not become maudlin. Two helpings of Lobster Newburg along with the same of Cherries Jubilee will sicken both gourmet and reader alike. Tenderness, though, and a belief in what you are saying can start the music of words to singing. And music, it is said, is never entirely lost.

"Touch me," the editor said.

Dorothy M. Powell has sold short stories to many major magazines, has written a children's book, and has taught creative writing at the college level.

# How to Write Dialect

*by L. B. Greenwood* _____

**D**ialect is the speech used by a minority, is argot, patios, cant, even jargon, and is thus automatically socially reprehensible. Or so a dictionary compiled three or more decades ago would have informed you. More recently, linguistic scholars have realized that verbal norms are not nearly as normal as was once so thoughtlessly thought, and have accordingly become much less judgmental in their definitions.

Dialect now is considered to be merely that manner of speech which is particular to a particular person or group: therefore *you* speak in dialect, and so do I, the Queen as much as Andy Capp. And when Eliza Doolittle asks Professor Higgins to teach her to talk more genteel, she isn't asking to discard dialect (a total impossibility), but rather to learn to substitute the speech—that is, the dialect—of the drawing-room for that of the gutter.

Indeed, with this shift of understanding of what dialect is we have returned to the oldest definition of all. The ancient Greeks who first coined the word meant by it, "what is revealed *through*," not merely "*by*," speech. Your native origins, social background, education, experience, age and attitudes are all indicated by the sounds you make in order to communicate with your fellow beings.

The same principle applies to the characters whom you as a writer create. Each one will have habits of speech (and thought that is expressed in words) that belong to him alone, and that reveal more about him than is contained in the words alone. On the simplest level, dialect helps identify speakers: if Tom always says "Yeah" and Mary "Yes," the reader soon knows that a speech starting "Yeah" belongs to Tom.

But you can do much more.

Consider Dr. Percy Wellington, professor of romantic poetry, stepping out of his pristine front door on his way to his university teaching post. He notes his wife's cleaning woman trudging up the driveway and calls, "Good day, Elizabeth. Most glorious weather, is it not? As Wordsworth would say, 'Bliss was it in that morn to be alive.'"

The woman gives a mute and noncommittal nod as the sixteen-year-old son, a precocious engineering freshman, comes out on his father's gleaming heels. "Hi, Ms. Yablowski. Nice out, ain't it?" The father slams the car door, and we expect it; the boy has the triumphant grin of one who has scored a point, and we expect that, too.

What we don't yet know, and what will be of great interest, is the attitude to this little confrontation of Elizabeth Yablowski, recent immigrant, abused wife, mother of two. Does she side with the rebel son against the stuffed shirt condescension of the father, or with the father as pater familias and provider of a secure, comfortable life? Perhaps, even as she mutters, "Morn', Muz Wellin't'n. Ya, ya, nice vedder ve have," she is mentally correcting the professor's inaccurate quotation ("*dawn*, you fool, not morn!") because perhaps she has a PhD. in English literature herself, and is in temporary hiding in this menial role because she has left her alcoholic husband. Her English speech may thus be fractured by design, and inaccurate because of it.

Certainly Elizabeth Yablowski would use words differently than Professor Wellington, his son and his wife.

How can you create her dialect? By the necessary understanding being bred in your bones, learned through a schoolmate's grandmother, picked up from TV, the movies, reading, and good old-fashioned eavesdropping—all of the above and more. What is important (and this is more than important, it's vital) is that you *do* know the dialect of each of your characters, know it so well that you could hold auditions for a radio version of your story and unhesitatingly choose the actors who most sound like your characters. How you reach that point is your problem, your business, and your reward as a writer.

Just a minute, you say. I might be able to create the broken English Elizabeth Yablowski speaks (whether by cunning or not), but how about her thoughts? She'd think in Polish, wouldn't she? And even if I understand Polish, I can't expect my readers to do so.

Quite true, and not to worry: a long accepted literary convention is our salvation. A character is assumed by the reader to be speaking (and thinking) in his native tongue whenever the situation makes this appropriate. So when George Smiley goes to Berlin, Le Carré doesn't waste time telling us that—big surprise!—Berliners speak German; he only makes sure that we understand that Smiley is himself fluent in the language. The reader then accepts that while he is reading English, for these conversations he is hearing—as it were—German.

The same handy rule makes it possible for us to create extraterrestrial and other fantasy creations who yet speak correctly: that is, their speech and thoughts give an impression that fits the role in the story they fill. Their language is shown to be poetic, terse, ungrammatical, formal, simple, long winded, technological, slangy—whatever is appropriate.

The Martian thug will sound like a thug even if he has green skin and purple eyes, and the slave on the far side of the galaxy will not sound the same as his master. If you want to see this skill at its best, examine the C. S. Lewis space novel *That Hideous Strength*, in which a Cambridge philologist journeys to far planets and returns to help defend earth. Language itself becomes a weapon.

Now let's assume that, with great labor and much pondering, you have assembled the dialect of each of your characters. Most speak quite standard English, with the occasional idiosyncrasy or dropped "g" that is easily captured in print. But you have one character, one on whose shoulders so much of the weight of the story rests that you can't delete him, no matter how much trouble he is giving you, and he is—must be—fresh from the Highlands of Scotland. What do you do with *his* dialect?

First and foremost, accept that you aren't going to be able to reproduce his speech perfectly: without the special resources of a phonetic alphabet, that's impossible.

Even Professor Higgins, when he wanted a precise copy of a dialect, cut a phonograph record. If you wonder why, try putting down on paper what an actress does with Eliza's pronunciation of "flowers." Is it "flo-ow-ah-ahs"? Or perhaps "fl-ah-ow-ahrs"? Or maybe "fl-uh-ow-ahr-ahs" is closer?

Before you try to solve the problem of your Scots laddie in any such fashion, think of yourself as a reader. If you ever encountered a character who is mumbling something strange like "Dooyuhunnerstanmih?" wouldn't you hastily shut the book? And resolve never to touch another of that author's? Of course you would, and very sensible of you, too. An attempt at facsimile speech is not the way to go.

So at one and the same time you must accept the lamentable fact that you cannot capture on the ordinary printed page the way your characters would in reality sound, and the equally necessary fact that you must convince your readers that that is precisely what you have done. Pseudo-authenticity—a fake with flavor—therefore must ever be your aim.

Fortunately there are time tested tricks (as there always are in any confidence game which has been practised as long as this one) which provide the answer. First, write out your character's speeches and thoughts, using whatever combination of letters and punctuation marks seem to you to indicate the most accurate reproduction. Then keep the rhythm of the words and the structure of the grammar as unchanged as possible, and alter nearly all the oddities back to standard spelling and vocabulary, leaving no more than one or two in a sentence to infer the obliterated rest.

How many and which ones will require your nicest judgment; the safest rule is fewer rather than more.

Tennyson could start a poem, "Wheer 'asta beän saw long and meä laggin' 'ere aloän?" and be applauded. Alas, them days have gone forever. The modern reader doesn't want to be slowed down, and will accept only what he can read at a glance.

Always remember, too, that in reproducing dialect, consistency is a jewel that you dare not lose. If a character starts by saying "deown" for "down," he must always do so.

(And he will almost surely also say "teown," "freown," "peownd," "reownd," "seownd" and "weound" too. See what you've let yourself in for?)

This is so important and so easy to become muddled about, especially if you are dealing with a large number of characters, that it may be well worth while to make a brief dialect glossary for each character.

Head a sheet with a character's name, in a column on the left set the standard spelling of the word, and in the right put the version your character uses. You'll end up with something like this:

Mike:

| am not, is not, isn't, are not, aren't: | ain't |
| yes: | yeah |
| of: | o' |

Then you can readily go over each speech, word by word, during the rewrite process, and make sure that you haven't had Mike say, 'I'm not going" on one page and "I ain't comin'" on another.

If all this sounds like an awful lot of work, it is, luv, it is. But if you truly have the sound of a dialect in your head, if you labor long and hard in the mighty vineyard of idiom and vocabulary, and if you are willing to rewrite and rewrite until you loathe the very thought of your keyboard and are ready to give every floppy disc to the puppy to chew on, then someday you will receive the reward of the faithful servant.

Your editors will accept your pages without a demur, and reviewers will praise the accuracy of your characterization. You may even hear a murmur in your ear, "I hae been tryin' tae tell ye how tae do it for a fort-nicht an' mair, ye silly gossoon," and you will find yourself replying, humbly, "I'm sorry. I didn't know how to listen. But I do now."

How to listen, write, alter, and thus succeed.

• • • • • • • • • •

Some of L.B. Greenwood's favorite dialogue

Chaucer records the mishap of a lover who has been pleading at a girl's window. Will he go away for a kiss? Yes, he agrees eagerly. So she opens the window, and, in the deep dark, he indeed kisses something—her "naked ers." "Tehee!" quod she, and clepte the wyndow to."

Written nearly six centuries ago, and yet sweet Alison's merry impudence rings through the years and the language changes.

The god of thunder and the goddess of the moon meet in Guy Gavriel Kay's *The Summer Tree*, concerned with the ongoing battle of good and evil. She is the one who might well appreciate a mere mortal's sacrifice, and he one who might appreciate that appreciation. She has turned the moon red and sent it to stand directly over the tree.

"Lady," said the God, muting the thunder of his voice, "Lady, this you have never done before."

"It was needful," she replied, a chiming on wind...

"Why did you speak to my sacrifice?" A slight reproach.

The Lady's voice grew deeper, woven of hearth smoke and caves. "Do you mind?" she murmured.

There came a sound that might have been a god amused. "Not if you beg forgiveness, no. It has been long, Lady." A deeper sound, and meaningful. There was a silence, then she was finest lace again, cajoling: "I have interceded, Lord, will you not do so?"

"For them?"

"And to please me," said the moon.

"Might we please each other?"

"We might so."

A roll of thunder then, Laughter.

What more is there to say?

In H. R. Percy's *An Innocent Bystander*, the lower class protagonist has arrived in London, "burdened down with luggage and bemused by the jostling crowds," and hears a voice shout: "Hello! You're Jesus, aren't you?"

He is leaning out of the first-class carriage window beckoning to me and shouting.

I stare up at him nonplussed, ready to be resentful. *More* resentful, that is...

Then he gives a great bellowing laugh. "Aren't you for Jesus College?"

"Oh. Oh, yes."

"Well, better wriggle your arse, man. You'll get left behind."

To bear him out, the guard blows a piercing blast not four feet from my ear and shouts, "Orl abawd!"

"Here, hop in here with me. Glad of the company." He climbs down and grabs my luggage (having, I discover later, paid a porter handsomely to carry his own).

In and out of the character's mind with such a deft slight of hand we never notice the transition.

L. B. Greenwood is the author of four published novels and several novellas, short stories and articles. Holding a BA and MA, she has taught English at universities and has given workshops in creative writing from coast to coast.

# Keep it Simple

*by Beatrice Fines* ───────────

There can be a number of reasons why your manuscript comes back with a little printed slip or a kind note that makes you feel better but still says "no thanks." Sometimes you have simply sent your story to the wrong market. On the other hand, perhaps the editor didn't like your language.

I'm not talking about the inclusion (or lack of) certain four-letter words. It may be that you have neglected to K.I.S.S. The majority of today's magazines use a K.I.S.S. style. So did Lincoln, Churchill, Hemingway, Steinbeck, and a host of others whose words are long remembered and often quoted.

K.I.S.S.?

**Keep It Simple, Stupid!**

A hundred years ago, speakers and writers were wont to use as many polysyllabic words as they could and string them together in paragraph-long sentences. Their aim seems to have been to impress the illiterate masses with their superior knowledge. Politicians, business executives, lawyers, teachers and others have reverted to the verbosity of earlier times. Each group is busy coining new words to add to its own particular jargon, too. Keith Dryden, writing in the *Western Producer* some time ago, called it "verbal overkill." It's pomposity at its worst. It can kill any story.

Here's an example used by Mr. Dryden in his article, "Meaningful Dialogue." Please wade through:

"In establishing inter-personal relationships and verbalizing this issue with the French, I said Britain would persist in the international, inter-military violent interaction irrespective of the course they pursued. The evaluation of our position by the

French generals, communicated to the prime minister and his cabinet (at that point in time unable to interrelate effectively among themselves) was that within the ball park of three weeks England would have her neck wrung like a chicken, as it were. We cannot help but emphasize that this extrapolation of the contemporary position is an exaggeration of the first order."

Here's the way Winston Churchill actually said it in 1940:

"When I warned the French that Britain would fight on alone whatever they did, their generals told the prime minister and his divided cabinet, 'in three weeks England will have her neck wrung like a chicken.' Some chicken, some neck."

The next quote is from a letter sent to me by the senior analyst in the "Systems and Procedures Department" of an institution which shall mercifully remain anonymous. It contains 107 words. Read it, even if you find it painful, then re-write, using K.I.S.S.

"The Blank Company has accepted the invitation of the Industrial Systems Study Group to be the pilot company in an ongoing study to test a system for measuring the productivity of company departments with a view to improving the utilization of departments and controlling the cost factor. The study will be initiated by Mr. Joe Blow, within the next month, and will be under the auspices of Mr. Blow and Mr. Bellow of the Systems Study Group. The study envisioned will provide information on a continuing basis that will allow the company to evaluate the performance of the various company departments to other companies."

Count the words in your simplified version. I got the paragraph down to seventy-nine words without, I am convinced, losing one iota of the message.

As a second exercise you might like to try the "Fog Index" on both paragraphs, yours and theirs. This index was introduced by some reading researchers more than four decades ago. It is often used by newspapers and magazines to find the approximate number of years of education their readers need for easy understanding of their publications. It works this way.

Take a sample of writing about one hundred words long. Find the average number of words per sentence. Then count the number of polysyllables (words of three syllables or more) in your sample. Omit capitalized words, verbs made into three syllables by a change of form (for example "producing"), and other relatively simple three syllable words like "department." Add the average number of words per sentence to the number of polysyllables and multiply the result by 0.4. The number you get indicates the approximate number of years of education required of the reader.

Using the paragraph as quoted (and my own judgment of genuine polysyllables), I arrived at a fog index of 19.0. I got 9.6 on my rewritten version. Newspapers aim at about 9. An index of 19 is probably fine if you write exclusively for Ph.D.s. On the other hand, perhaps even they would appreciate a little K.I.S.S. once in a while.

Using the fog index will not tell you whether your writing is good or bad. There are too many other factors. But if you have a high index, it may be time to examine your work for signs of verbal overkill and catch it while it's curable. Are you saying "at an early date" when you could say "soon"? Do you tack on "program" when you speak of research, and "conditions" when you mention the weather? Are words like "oriented," "interrelated," "optimized," and "systemized" creeping into your vocabulary? Take care!

We must stop this polysyllabic and contrived presentation of the English language, re-evaluate our position and re-establish the priorities brought forward by those contemporary communicators whose methods of presentation have given us a substantial investment of intelligence and imagination and a heritage that should be monitored regularly for optimum use.

And if you read through that last paragraph without wincing, things are more serious than I thought.

Beatrice Fines has taught creative writing in adult continuing education classes and has participated in Manitoba's Artists in the Schools Program. Beatrice's sixty short stories and over two-hundred articles have been published in Canada, the United States and Great Britain.

# Keep it Tight

*by Fred Kerner* ─────────

"To be or not to be?" asks Shakespeare's Hamlet. How much more simply could that be put? The longest word is three letters, yet the impact is as strong as any editor could ask for from a writer.

The Bard could have written, "Should I act upon the urgings that I feel, or remain passive and thus cease to exist?" Poetic, yes, but what impact does it have?

Simplicity of language is not only reputable, but perhaps even sacred. The Bible opens with a sentence well within the writing skills of a lively fourteen-year-old: "In the beginning God created the heaven and the earth."

The magic of words lies in the power they have, when properly chosen and arranged, to convey to other people what we wish them to know of what is in our minds. Every word we write goes out as an errand. Skill in saying what we mean so as to get the result we desire is not a literary frill around the edges of social life or business. It is an essential part of life, our only means of intellectual contact with the world around us.

It may be that you are capable of putting together a sentence as intricate and as glittering as a necklace for Cleopatra. But your eloquence should be the servant of the ideas in your head. As a writer, your rule might be that which Kurt Vonnegut—a fine stringer-together of words—promulgated.

"If a sentence, no matter how excellent, does not illuminate your subject in some new and useful way, toss it out."

Some people think that writing style is like the geometer's "straight line," which is not anything anyone has ever seen. In fact it is not a line at all, but simply the straightness of a line. Others believe that style can be seen and developed. They say it is a pattern in words expressing some idea of the writer's mind within a beautiful fabric.

Some writers, as we all know, have the ability to beautify the commonplace and to illumine the dingy and the sordid.

Bear in mind—when you are choosing words and stringing them together—how they sound This, you may think, seems absurd: readers read with their eyes. But actually they hear—in their inner ear—the words they are reading.

The worship of big words and ornate phrases isn't confined to academic surroundings. A notable collecting place for stuffed shirts, linguistically as well as literally speaking, is government. Ottawa and the provincial capitals have become repositories for the windiest and stuffiest purveyors of gibberish.

Assuming that you know what you want to say here are four basic rules to follow in making your writing clear, simple and fluent:

### 1. Before you begin to put a sentence on paper, complete it mentally.

Beginning a sentence without knowing how it will end results in wordiness and vagueness.

### 2. Make your sentences short.

If you follow Rule 1, writing short sentences will almost become automatic. But keep your writing fluent by avoiding the choppiness of making all your sentences approximately the same length.

### 3. Use words and phrases that are natural.

Avoid words like *prognostication* when you can say *forecast*, or *communication* when you can say *letter*. There are times long words are needed, but they shouldn't be used simply because they are long. And the same applies to phrases: "It has been brought to the writer's attention..." is a clumsy way of saying, "I have been told..."; or "Acquaint us with the facts..." instead of "Tell us...".

### 4. Study your own writing and do your own editing.

This will enable you to improve the readability of your work and help you to avoid poor writing the next time. But do your editing after you have finished writing, not while you are in the midst of it.

Because it is a permanent record, the written word must express the writer's ideas clearly. When a child misuses a word, you laugh, sympathize and admire him for trying. When an adult misuses a word, you may laugh but you do not admire or sympathize. So it is essential that to become a good writer, you learn to use the right word, and use it correctly.

There are two ways of appraising the rightness of a word: by its effectiveness in saying exactly what you wish it to say, and by its sound or its appearance. Some words, though acceptable or passable in conversation, are not legal tender in writing. (Similarly, other words, properly and effectively used in writing, seem pretentious in conversation.)

Quite often the choice between a right and a wrong word is not dictated by a book of reference but by the writer's perception. Most everyone with some education knows how words that are associated with the commonplace grate on the eye or ear when used in more formal or more tender communication.

Good word-use doesn't come without effort. That effort need not be strenuous, but it must be sustained. If you listen and read critically, your word knowledge will increase rapidly. It isn't always easy to choose the right word. But if you are willing to concede that one word can be better than another, you are on the right road.

It is not always possible to mark one word as right, another as wrong. But if you use the words you know well, and then carefully check your dictionary for words that are even slightly unfamiliar, you are well on the path to writing right.

The language is filled with words that can be confused. Look at three words like *apt*, *liable* and *likely*. There are subtle differences. And how about *infer* and *imply*; few words offer more confusion than these two. Yet their correct use requires only a few moments of study. The same applies to *less* and *fewer*, *affect* and *effect*, *allude* and *elude*, *averse* and *adverse*, *flout* and *flaunt*. The list goes on and on.

A large-sized volume could be filled with the hackneyed phrases that should be avoided. Just think how tired these expressions are:

"The right to a fair shake."

"The land of opportunity."

"She moved to greener pastures."

"By any stretch of the imagination."

"It remains to be seen."

"He saw the handwriting on the wall."

"The argument fell on deaf ears."

When a cliché such as one of the above comes to mind easily, discard it and look for a fresh approach. Remember some of the great originality that has come from writers of the past, writers whose work you have admired.

"Always do right," wrote Mark Twain; "you will gratify some people and astonish the rest."

"God is subtle but not malicious," wrote Albert Einstein.

And Emerson wrote: "Climb to Paradise on the stairway of surprise."

How simply put; how expressive; how un-hackneyed.

Shun artifices and tricks and fashions. Gain the tone of ease, plainness and self-respect. Write frankly what you have thought out in your own brain and have felt within you.

To write well is no gift of the angels, nor is it the outcome of striving audaciously to be different. The first thing demanded of the literary craftsman is that he or she be clear; then eloquence and harmony follow.

Your purpose as a writer is to convey an idea with the smallest possible obstacle to the flow of thought between mind and mind.

So keep it simple.

Keep it fresh.

Keep it tight.

And keep writing. Remember, a professional writer is an amateur who didn't quit.

Fred Kerner has, as an editor, guided hundreds of writers through the finer points of written expression. He is currently developing a unique lexicon that will, he hopes, help thousands of others to create magic with their words.

# Make Every Word Count

*by Robert H. Jones*

lthough I started writing for outdoor magazines in the mid-1970s, it was not until I began freelancing to *The Vancouver Sun* newspaper in 1981 that I learned the meaning of "making every word count." Outdoor section editor Phil Hanson specified a maximum of 1,000 words, with a preference between 600 and 800. As payment was by the word, I split the difference and submitted four 800-word articles. When my first piece was published, it did not appear to have been edited, but for some nagging reason seemed shorter and easier to read. After comparing the article to a carbon copy of its original, I realized several words had been cut. Upon marking them with a red pen, I discovered it had been reduced by nearly 100 words. I pondered those results for quite awhile, then took my red pen to the remaining three carbon copies, plus four more originals about to be mailed. All were cut dramatically, retyped, then mailed. When I met Hanson for the first time a few weeks later, he commented that I had "learned fast."

In 1983, editor Burton Myers asked me to write a column for *Ontario Out of Doors*. Although given free rein regarding topics, I had to stay within 600 words. I was dubious about being able to develop a plot; write a catchy lead; introduce various characters; describe surroundings and situations; then bring everything to a meaningful conclusion with so few words. It proved, however, simply a matter of writing a story, then massaging it—over and over—until the word counter on my Kaypro II said it was 600 words. Precisely. Writing those "Leftovers" columns was fairly easy; massaging them was not. Entire paragraphs, which seemed so lyrical and important while being created, were replaced with one or two words—or deleted. Some columns took three days to write, while others (not many) were finished in three hours.

I discovered dialogue can replace descriptive narratives that ramble. By establishing a flow, the use of "said," "replied," and "answered" is required only often enough to avoid confusion. I also learned repetitive words or phrases can be rewritten to reduce their numbers. In most cases, common terminology can be shortened by removing or replacing a word or two: "In spite of" becomes "Despite"; "Do not forget to" becomes "Don't forget to".

Some of the easiest words to remove are "that," "the," "and," "I," and "my." To demonstrate this (assuming you are using a word processor), use the Search and Replace command to replace "that" with **. If your manuscript already has asterisks in it, choose symbols like >>, ++, ##, [].

"That was the truck that hit that fire hydrant!" becomes "** was the truck ** hit ** fire hydrant!" Seeing an abundance of asterisks is a good indication you are overusing "that." Scan the entire manuscript, then see what can be rewritten to reduce the number of asterisks. When satisfied, go back to Search and Replace, then convert the remaining asterisks back to "that" (capitalizing where necessary.)

Search and Replace will indicate other repetitious words, but avoid confusion by thinking about them before converting. For example: type a space before and after "I" and "the" to prevent words like "In," "It," "then" and "other" from appearing as "**n," "**t," "**n" and "o**r" (words starting a paragraph or followed by punctuation will not change).

I could go on, but I think you get the idea. Besides, my word counter just revealed this writing tip is now 600 words. Precisely.

Robert H. (Bob) Jones presently writes a 1,200-word fishing column for *BC Outdoors* and a 600-word humor column for *Real Outdoors*.

# Techniques
# of Fiction

# Write a Winner

*by W. D. Valgardson* —————

So, you want to write a winning story. What's the first thing to do?

Don't try to write a winner. That is don't waste your time checking out who the judges are. What do you do if you discover that there's one from Newfoundland, one from Manitoba and one from the Yukon. Further research shows one writes children's stories, the other writes science fiction and the third romance novels. The solution then is to write a story about a Newfoundlander who falls in love with a Manitoban and they both go to the Yukon where they search for a lost child. All this, of course, takes place in the future. That's the kind of nonsensical hodge-podge I sometimes hear from people who want to know more about the judges so they can "psych" them out.

That's a kind of high school attitude that should be left in high school.

Instead, just write the best story you can.

There are two basic principles to follow in writing a winning story. Write what you know about. Write what you care about.

What? You don't want to write what you know about? Why not? It's boring. You want to write about something exotic in Papau New Guinea. Have you been to Papau New Guinea? You've read three articles in National Geographic. How would you like a slap in the head? How would you like to get up, right now, and go into the bathroom and look in the mirror. See that person? That person is not boring. That person is interesting. Now, look that person in the eye and say, out loud, "You are an interesting person." That wasn't loud enough. Say it, out loud. "You are an interesting person." Repeat this procedure every time you go into the bathroom for the next seven days. You can add the following lines as the week progresses. "What you think and feel and believe are worth writing about. The people you know are worth writing about. The place where you live is worth writing about." Keep saying these until you believe them.

You see, every place is exotic. Every place is interesting. Over the years I've had innumerable visitors from Europe stay with me. Writers, editors, academics from Ukraine, Russia, Scandinavia, Britain.

They're blown away by Goldstream Park and fascinated by Chemainus with its painted buildings and overwhelmed by our shopping malls. Just as I'm blown away and fascinated and overwhelmed by what they show me when I visit them.

I don't know any kings or queens, nor do I need to. The fishermen and farmers and store keepers and hockey players and insurance agents have all the virtues and weaknesses necessary to make good subjects for short stories. They are honest and dishonest, vain and humble, generous and stingy. They are everything. Their passions lead them to acts of bravery and cowardice, to love and murder.

To be a convincing author, to create a convincing narrator, you have to be an expert in the area in which you write. Therefore, don't write about the world. Write about a world. All of us have many a worlds: family, friends, work, hobbies, sports, school, clubs. We are the experts of these worlds. We know their secrets. We know their rituals. Who but you knows what goes on in your condo complex? Who but you knows the politics around Christmas dinner when the family gathers?

It is critical that you are an expert of the world you create in your story.

If you are not, you'll be found out and quickly dismissed. Once, I was shown a novel a writer had worked on for three years. This was when I was living in the United States. The first page of the novel had a group of American hunters stalking moose in the deep, primeval forest outside Moosejaw, Saskatchewan. Did I need to read further to dismiss the book? Do I need to eat every last mouthful of a badly cooked meal to know it's bad?

Writing about a world that you know intimately—serving on a PT boat in WWII or working for a year at McDonald's—means that no one can steal your work.

This is an issue that comes up every year at the workshop. To obtain advanced standing, new students have to apply by portfolio. Every year some of them apply for advanced standing but don't want to show me their portfolios. Why? Because they're afraid that I'm going to steal their stories, sell them and become instantly rich and famous. This past year was no different. A young man stood there, desperately hanging onto his portfolio, assuring me that the stories were every bit as good as he said they were and there was no need for me to read them because they weren't copyrighted and he didn't have an agent or a lawyer yet. I point out to him that our more spectacularly successful graduates—W. P. Kinsella, Eden Robinson, Richard Van Camp, Gail Anderson-Dargatz, Tom Henry—are all writing about specific worlds I know nothing about. To try to write WPK's stories, I'd need to learn a vast amount about baseball. To write Eden's stories I'd have to know what it's like to be female, native and grow up in Kitimat. To write Richard's stories, I'd have to understand what it's like to be Dene and live in the Northwest Territories. To write Gail's latest book, I'd have to know a terrible amount about living on a farm. To write Tom's essays, I'd need to know Metchosin country life and people as if they were my home and neighbours, as they are his.

I then suggested the following: that I'd tell him an idea for one of my stories and he could steal it if he wanted. Father and two sons. Sons hate brutal father. Love each other. Father's behaviour causes one son to die.

Other son takes revenge. Now, go write that from the point of view of a Lutheran fundamentalist, Icelandic-Canadian, commercial fishing, Manitoban.

He got the point. At least, he let me read his portfolio.

Remember, you're not writing for the stupidest, most easily pleased, most easily conned reader. Nor are you writing for someone constrained by loyalty or besotted by lust. That means that what your mother thinks of your story or your boyfriend/girlfriend thinks of your story is of absolutely no importance. The test is what does the most intelligent, most knowledgeable reader think of the story. Will there be a detail here or there that will ring false and destroy the credibility of the narrator for them?

If you really don't believe that getting the details right, and are not just avoiding the hard work of writing successful stories, then the next time you need a lawyer, or an open heart surgeon, stick to your beliefs. Choose one who doesn't care to be encumbered with getting the details right.

The second half of writing a prize winning story is writing about a world you care about. If you don't care about it, why should anyone else? If you don't care about it, how do you expect to get others to care? Remember, that art, dance, music, film, writing, reach us first through our emotions.

They make us feel, then they make us think. First we cry and laugh. Then we ponder. As I read through a pile of manuscripts, looking for one that I'd like to publish in Canadian Author magazine, I'm not impressed by cleverness. The story that gets set aside for another look is the one that takes me into a world and makes me feel. Not because it's tried to manipulate me with melodrama or adverbs and adjectives that tell how to feel, but because it briefly makes me care.

Short stories are brief. There is much to be done in them if they are to be successful but before craft or art, there is the right attitude. Without that both craft and art fail.

W. D. Valgardson is the author of numerous books and plays. He has recently written two children's picture books: *Thor* (Mr. Christie Award Winner) and *Sarah and the People of Sand River*. He is a member of the Department of Writing at the University of Victoria.

# Design Your Dialogue

*by Betty Millway*

D ialogue is, by definition, conversation. From the writer's standpoint it is the representation of conversation in writing.

"But how do you write dialogue?" the beginner might ask. "Mine never seems real and I can't seem to put it in the right places."

This same novice is probably capable of writing imaginative narrative around and about his or her characters, of steering the story to a satisfactory conclusion. However, without dialogue, those characters mostly remain shadowy, background figures, not fully employed.

Given the power of speech they will come to life and tell much of their story themselves.

There are beginners who have no difficulty in putting words into their characters' mouths. For such, the initial hurdle to dialogue is no problem. They fall at the second. All their characters speak in exactly the same way which, on analysis, often proves to be more or less the writer's own way.

If you have not decided how your characters should speak you have omitted a vital ingredient of their makeup; an ingredient no less important than their appearance, manner, and mannerisms; one that could reveal at least as much about them as any other component.

For ideas on how people talk, eavesdrop a little. Listen to some of the many conversations taking place around you, at home, in restaurants, planes, trains, buses, places of business and of entertainment. You will hear conversations between people of like minds and differing minds, educated and uneducated, trivial and profound. The speakers will have their individual accents, mannerisms, peculiarities, some obvious, most more subtle but all part and parcel of their personalities.

Analyze the speech styles of your family and friends, under varying circumstances. Notice similarities and differences, the topics introduced and discussed, the language—formal or casual, appropriate or otherwise—the touches of humor; whether, in fact, the exchanges rate as conversation or whether they are inconsequential comments, chit-chat, or babblings. All this is the raw material from which you, the imaginative, creative writer, will fashion speech styles for your characters.

Tailoring speech to a character's dimensions does not mean that this aspect of his personality, any more than any other, must, as a matter of course, be blatantly unusual. An exception might be the deliberate intention to create a "character"—a caricature, perhaps—a Uriah Heep, forever washing his unctuous hands in the air, the 'umble son of an 'umble mother from an 'umble abode; an Alfred Jingle with a remarkable style of verbal shorthand. Time has immortalized many such "characters" but not in principal roles. The very unusual, however entertaining in brief appearances, loses its charm if invoked too often and arbitrarily.

Dialogue, by the writer's choice of words, the length, brevity, on occasion the interrupted or unfinished phrase or sentence, can convey a whole range of emotions while requiring little or no expository linkage.

Consider the following passage from an essay by Cornish writer C.C. Vyvyan, which appears in an anthology *My Cornwall*:

> "Good day," she (the tourist) said and put on an intimate smile addressed to each one of them (the fishermen).
>
> "Good day," one or two or them replied and then looked to a ship on the horizon.
>
> "Taking a nice rest, I see," she said brightly.
>
> There was a dead silence. It seemed as if the eloquence of Ignatius and the animated attention of the others had been turned off suddenly by a switch. "You poor dear men," she said, "you must have a dreadful life always at sea on dark nights while we sleep snug in our little beds."
>
> The men sat still as images.
>
> "You poor darlings," she went on, "working so hard to get our food." Then rather nervously, trying to break the silence, "He! He! He! I daresay if you'd only talk you'd have some dreadful tales to tell of your dangers and adventures."
>
> "Miss," said Ignatius, as he took his black pipe from his mouth and spat respectfully into the road before he said what he had to say; "Have 'ee ever looked out o' your front door an' seen comin' in the bay a boat with waun man instead o' two? I seen un waunce and I never shall forget it. 'Tis oogly thing fur to see.

The wimmen, they was tremblin' all over the beach, all except the waun woman who saw her own man in the boat an' when he come in shore he said, 'Iss friends, Joe's gone with the pots'."

The emotional impact of this conversation is intensified by the contrast between the bright, brittle superficiality of the tourist and longer, slower serious periods of Cornish-accented English.

The fisherman's speech should not, by the way, be confused with dialect. It is accented English which, spoken, might be difficult for the unaccustomed ear to understand. Written, it is perfectly intelligible.

True dialect would require similar handling to speech in a foreign language which, to all intents and purposes, it is. No matter how many foreign languages you, the writer, may have at your command, the likelihood of your readers having matching abilities is extremely slim. As a general rule, it might be best, therefore, to limit the use of other tongues to single words or short phrases that serve to create the illusion without unduly frustrating the reader. Dialogue in English but written in or close to idiom of the foreign language has much the same effect.

Sir Arthur Grimble, in his book *Return to the Islands*, uses both methods:

"Bon te rine ngaia! (The pick of mankind, he!)" I prompted her. She leaned forward to lay a hand on mine: "Somebody told you that? Yes, the very crest of the tree of beauty. No man was ever so beautiful or kind as Tangaro. My eyes saw only him that night. Every gesture of my dance was made for him." She laughed: "My sister's husband praised me at the end for the excellence of my keteikai (gestures). That made me happy, for my heart said, 'What this man tells me here, Tangaro is thinking too, alone in his canoe-shed.'"

Conversation between characters supposedly speaking in a language native to them but foreign to the reader (once that point has been established) should be reproduced as speech between comparable English-speaking characters. Only when they are supposedly speaking in a language foreign to *them* should their English be "broken."

Bearing these points in mind, good dialogue will depend on the writer's ability to slip into each character's skin as occasion demands, to think, as *he* would think, to express thoughts in *his* terms.

There is really no substitute for practice. It might be a worthwhile exercise to review some of your own long passages of narrative and rewrite them using dialogue wherever possible or reasonable.

What is "reasonable" amounts to selecting the appropriate points at which to introduce dialogue smoothly and naturally. It is a matter of timing.

It might help to consider what happens in a movie. The characters are not constantly speaking. Rather, there are sequences in which nothing is said, but the characters are occupied in performing various tasks or making movements suitable to the occasion. Their manner may indicate anxiety, anger, boredom, impatience, grief—any of a number of emotions. There will be long shots, close ups; the camera may follow the actor; it may focus on something he sees which the viewer is expected to note, some clue, perhaps, to what is to follow. However, if this sequence is too prolonged, the viewer's interest is likely to diminish rather than grow. He has been prepared for action/speech. If his attention is to be held the director must determine the right moment at which to move from the buildup to the action. This is timing.

In a written story, the narrative corresponds to the silent sequences of the film. You are setting or developing the scene, as the case may be, and leading your reader into the next piece of action dialogue. The action may be mild or violent or at any level in between, the dialogue ranging appropriately. At all events, however inconsequential or otherwise as far as the characters are concerned, you will have created an opportunity to tell through your characters, overtly or by implication, some item of interest or importance to the story's development and, therefore, to the reader.

This does not imply that every single word uttered by the characters must be loaded with significance. At the same time, they are not allowed the luxury of dialogue that is totally devoid of meaning, that tells the reader nothing, that leads nowhere.

Dialogue gives you, the writer, an opportunity to express by means of your characters, your own pertinent theories and philosophies and thus add depth to your story. This needs deft and sensitive handling. Anything, particularly something of this nature, dragged in by the short hairs will read and sound exactly what it is, painful and contrived.

Your most profound thoughts might be made to emerge as random mutterings from the least intellectually astute member of your cast or, equally, from a character who has already given some indication of his turn of mind. The decision must be yours. Since you have created the characters it is up to you to make them work for you. They can keep your story moving when pure narrative might slow it down. Their conversations can fill in necessary background that will throw light on the whys and wherefores of their behavior and attitudes and the reason for telling the story.

When only a lone character is in the picture, how are long passages of narrative to be relieved?

Let this performer speak some of his thoughts, significant ones along with those of little consequence. Monologue in moderation provides a legitimate change of pace.

A brief passage of dialogue may effect a smooth transition from one scene and sequence of events to another. This device is especially useful in short and short-short stories where progress must be maintained with an economy of words, as in the following:

> With admirable fortitude Roddy endured yet another delay while Len Chester and the boys cooled off in the lake (just off the road).
>
> "The sidehill gouger is nocturnal in habit, I understand, Chester. That means we should establish camp and be settled in before nightfall," he warned Len as the tracks finally got on the road again.
>
> "Still plenty of time, sir. We're in good gouger country right now but I thought we'd make for the Okanagan valley as planned. There's a fine campsite on the lakeshore, close to the best gouger pasture in the district."
>
> At the campsite, Roddy's tent was pitched...

An uneventful journey between two scenes of action has been accomplished in a short but informative exchange between the two principal characters. It suggests mild impatience and concern over delays on Roddy's part, a soothing casualness on Len's, with a hint of going along with Roddy's rather incredible delusion. The whole would have been conveyed much less easily in narrative of comparable wordage.

How much dialogue should there be in a story?

Enough to do the job. As much or as little as the story requires, which is usually more than the novice is inclined to allow. A reasonable amount would be twenty to thirty percent. The publication you have in mind for your story might have specific requirements—one of a number of reasons for studying the market you hope will accept your work.

When using dialogue, guard against giving your characters long, unbroken speeches to deliver. Except when addressing a meeting or recounting an incident to an interested party, one seldom speaks more than a sentence or two without a break or interruption of some kind. Perhaps it will be a comment or question from another member of the group, perhaps we will pause—for effect, sometimes—while we light a cigarette, search in purse or pockets for some article or other associated with our subject, or any other reason for a break that you can imagine. Often such a pause will result in the conversation taking a new direction. The writer is free to manufacture such a situation in order to steer his dialogue in the right direction for the purpose of the story. Such breaks are invaluable when, for some good reason, a single character must say a large amount at one time. They help to preserve the idea of the circumstances surrounding the speaker and the effect of his words on his listeners.

If it appears contradictory to you to demand naturalness in dialogue while at the same time insisting that—unlike everyday spoken conversation—it must meet specific requirements, and must appear to be spontaneous when it is, in actuality, planned, then you have grasped the principle of dialogue.

Apply this principle and, with practice, your own well-directed imagination and cultivated sense of balance and timing will combine to give the ring of authenticity to your designed dialogue.

(A note for the curious: a "sidehill gouger" is a mythical animal unique to the drylands of British Columbia. It is said to have shorter legs on one side of its body so that it can walk along the sidehills, creating the horizontal paths that can be seen throughout the BC south Interior.)

Betty Millway is a west-coast short-story and article writer. She enjoys helping other writers on the local and national level.

# Write the Short Story

*by Bess Kaplan* _____

**W**hat makes an editor buy one story, reject another? What type of magic is necessary to ensure the first rather than the second? Is it luck? Is it hitting him with it at the right time, when he's just had a reconciliation with his wife? Or what?

Not having a hotline to the editor of any magazine, I can't vouch for the luck theory, but I can offer a few thoughts on the subject of what a short story ought to be, and the various components that make up most successful stories. Before I do, though, let's look at some of the things a short story is not. It's not an essay, an article, a character study, a day-in-the-life-of rambling inner monologue. Yet many writers keep submitting manuscripts that are a mish-mash of the above and think they've written a story.

A story is—or should be—a dynamic compressed view into the life of a character at a moment in time when he faces a crisis. We show what led to the crisis and how he resolves his problem. End of story. In the showing of it, we reveal our main character, his strengths and weaknesses, his thought processes, providing insights to the reader who may gain an understanding of this particular element of human nature... which, I believe, is what short stories are all about.

How do you do this? It certainly sounds complicated and much too difficult when put in such a technical way. That word "crisis" for instance. It brings to mind all sorts of sorrows and might stop a new writer in his tracks. A crisis can be any problem facing any character. It can be about a job, a date, an anniversary. It can be about a new driver and his first accident. (Will he have the courage to get behind the wheel of a car again? Or should he throw away the keys?) It can be humorous.

A short story I once sold was about an old woman who owned a dilapidated three-suite house. She kept intercepting visitors to the main character's duplex. I told the story in the first person and showed how the main character finally foiled the old woman. Another story that sold to the same market was about an elderly confirmed bachelor who was accosted by a scheming widow who kept plying him with lemon meringue pies. How he accepted her ministrations while still evading her intentions was my main theme, the crisis erupting at the point where she moved in for the kill. Any problem that needs surmounting constitutes a story's crisis, and they can be found anywhere.

But merely having a crisis to write about is not enough. After all, short stories are about people, and people are the subjects most interesting to other people. The element of a story, even more important than a crisis, is the main character or protagonist. The character in fact is the story, because without him or her, there is no emotional involvement on the part of the reader (and editor) and no reason to care whether the protagonist will solve his dilemma or not.

Because of the importance of your main character to the success of your story, he or she should be chosen with care. Not only chosen but nurtured, fed, embraced, devoured by the writer. You should finally know the protagonist so well that you wear his skin, pull his head on over your own, see through his eyes, smell through his nose, think with his brain, and love and hate all those that he loves and hates. Only then can you be sure of the way your main character will act in any given situation, knowing his motivations and the depths of his feelings. Viewing the scene from above, or from the outside, holding him at arm's length, will cause the reader to do the same, if at all. But when you don your main character's body you see it all so clearly—the thing he must do to get out of the fix he's in.

Of course, once you're inside his head, you get his viewpoint, another important part of any short story. Viewpoint—seeing the situation from a particular character's point of view—can be done either in the first or third person. There are advantages and drawbacks to both. In the first person, you must be careful to give only that information the character would logically know, or find some other but equally vivid way (through dialogue for instance) of having this information brought to the character's (and the reader's) attention. But you may let the reader in on your main character's thoughts, emotions and reactions, since you're walking around inside his head, as it were. In the third person, while you're still close to the main character, you can show the larger scene and even "milepost" events to come without losing his perspective, but now you see him rather dispassionately, as you would perhaps a friend. In other words, in the first person, you are the main character, and can express his emotions with more impact, using the "I" as though it were a telescope, focusing on his thoughts and actions. In the third person, you point him out to the reader as That Man, the one in that group, and pull the reader in closely. We stand beside the main character, not inside him, although we still get his viewpoint. But beware of jumping from character to character, expressing each one's thoughts, scattering your shot. The impact of a story is weakened this way.

Sometimes it's difficult to know what character in your story should be the spokesman; whose viewpoint, in other words, would best do the job. Analyzing your story, separating the theme from the characters may help set the writer on the correct path. Whose story is it? Who had the narrow escape? Should it be the agent or the victim? Sometimes a minor character steps up to the microphone and takes charge, telling it as he saw it happen to the main character (especially if the main character must die in the end). "Move me, make me care!" Dorothy Powell, a writer who has acted as judge in many short story contests, replied when asked what guidelines she used in picking the winners. "Make the characters so real, that their problems become my problems."

How do you make characters real? Books have been written on this subject, but in a thimble, it's this: make your characters human, with all the complexities of humans, their virtues and faults (but lovable faults, please!). We're all made up of so many sides that even a so-called simple character would stump a computer.

In making your character seem real, you must mix in a dash of mannerisms to set him apart (does he limp, or swagger or hold his head to one side while he muses? Is he a neat dresser... revealing character... or a slob?). Does he eye the ladies; is she a flirt; does he speak with a cigarette bobbing from the corner of his mouth, or chew on a toothpick? Just a smattering of this kind of detail draws a picture in the reader's mind and stamps our man or woman as this or that type. But it's the small detail that rounds him out from a drawing to a living, breathing person who then steps off the page and begins to direct traffic.

Sometimes you have to let your main character do his thing, and not yours. Sometimes he becomes so real that he knows better than you how his story should be told. If you have your perfect ending but he doesn't care for it, something went wrong somewhere, maybe with your idea of his character. All you can do then is retrace your steps to see where you missed the turning-point, and if possible, revise either your protagonist or your ending, to make it believable.

Revelation of character, that's what the short story is all about; and the ways we do this are through action and dialogue. He speaks and we know the man, by what he says and the words he uses. They must be consistent with his character, and logical as befits a person of his schooling (or lack of it).

There is no room in the short story for meaningless dialogue. Every word must count, must move the story forward to its logical conclusion. The same is true of action. Showing your man as he sets about to right the wrongs in his life involves the reader emotionally. The reader wants to see him. You have the reader on your side (if you made your main character sympathetic; with villains, that's another story).

In brief, if you have a strong protagonist, a crisis to overcome, the empathy necessary to identify with your creation, an eye for the telling detail, a fast-paced opening paragraph, a gripping tale to tell and a little bit of luck, then in hardly any time at all you should find something really nice in your mailbox from some discerning editor.

Bess Kaplan, a Winnipeg-based freelance writer, has edited a weekly newspaper . She has also written numerous short stories, magazine articles and a radio play. Her novels include *Corner Store* and *Malke Malke*. She is currently working on a non-fiction book.

# Payment in Copies?

*by Beatrice Fines* _____

T he listing information in the writers' market book is encouraging. Here's a magazine which publishes fiction, up to 4,000 words in a wide variety of genres and uses 40 stories a year. It has been in existence for 20 years—no here-today, gone-tomorrow operation this. Some rather well-known writers are named as contributors. Surely, your story will be well received. But the last line in the description reads "Payment in copies". So you frown and keep on looking for a suitable market. Or do you?

You spent weeks writing this story. You dreamed about it, researched it, wrote it, re-wrote it, struggled with it, revised it again and after many hours of dedicated service to it, finally came to love it. It's been out searching for a home five times. You have received two printed rejections with no comment, two with "Sorry, we're over-stocked" and one very complimentary RWKN, (Rejection With a Kind Note), followed by "but..." In spite of all that, you know it's a good story. It deserves an audience. It could find one in the magazine that pays in copies. But after spending all that time and effort and postage, don't you deserve more than payment in copies?

Although I usually try to make my writing pay in hard cash, I have submitted stories to outlets that pay in copies. Sometimes I send stories that have been rejected by other magazines for various reasons, (or no reason at all). Sometimes I have just felt that a story belonged in that particular magazine and would not likely find a home elsewhere. Besides, I strongly believe that many of these small magazines offer much more than just their copies in payment.

First, you have the satisfaction of seeing your work in print and knowing that someone out there will read it. Second, you have another magazine's name to add to your list of credits. Third, since "payment in copies" magazines usually take only first rights, you can try the story on the market again. It may get more attention the second time around because it has already received one editor's approval.

Many of the "payment in copies" magazines are university or college based and attract discriminating readers, including the editors of other magazines—a plus. Because their budgets are limited these magazines are often printed on cheap stock with matte stock covers and line drawings. Though the outer appearance is not impressive, one such magazine regularly gives me several hours of good reading. A recent issue contained nine short stories, 33 poems and short biographical notes on the contributors. The poems and stories came from 11 Canadian and 12 American cities. One story came from Auckland, New Zealand. Since all contributors received their "payment in copies" the book has been more widely distributed than you might expect.

Reading the biographical notes I learned that many of the writers had an impressive publishing record in other places. Some are teachers or professors and others identified themselves simply as writers. The magazine has been in existence for 25 years and gives every indication of staying around for another 25.

Similar publications are listed in *The Canadian Writer's Guide* and in the *American Writers' Market* books. So before you relegate any story to the bottom drawer of your desk, explore some of the magazines that reward you only with copies and satisfaction.

Beatrice Fines has taught creative writing in adult continuing education classes and has participated in Manitoba's Artists in the Schools Program. Beatrice's sixty short stories and over two-hundred articles have been published in Canada, the United States and Great Britain.

# Write the Novel

*by W.G. Hardy*

Except for the long haul involved (sixty thousand to one hundred thousand words or more) the novel is easier to write than the short story. There is more space; shifts in place, time and point of view are not restricted; and there is freedom in structure. What is required is pertinacity. In my experience, if the hard work is done first, the actual writing becomes comparatively easy.

The first thing to remember is that you can choose from among many types of novels. To list a few: there is the historical novel; the regional; science-fiction; the novel about contemporary life, including the novel of social protest and the semi-autobiographical novel.

To decide which type is to be your canvas is one of the first jobs you undertake. A second task is to determine exactly what you want to write about. One method is to put down your own special interests or bits of knowledge (interest in wildlife, your experiences as a pioneer or a rancher or as the wife of a businessman). It is a cliché that any intelligent person has a novel waiting in his or her own experiences or reactions. One trick is to know how to omit the dull and ordinary and to dramatize what is striking (e.g. meeting a grizzly bear, the serious illness of a loved one or being in an automobile accident). So, jot down the potentially dramatic incidents of your life and of the lives of your relatives and friends.

Keen observation is an obvious way to pile up ideas. It is again a cliché that stories are all around you, if you develop the "seeing eye" and your imagination. Here, a notebook for striking characters and incidents is invaluable, and also the device of imagining people and their probable reactions in unusual situations, overtaken, for example, by a menacing hitchhiker, an airplane disaster or burglars.

Reading and analyzing books to put down what you like or don't like and, above all, what devices the authors use to produce these reactions is another source of ideas. So are book reviews and analyses of motion pictures.

From these methods you are likely to discover a plethora of ideas. Choose the one which is most compelling to you.

Let's suppose you have decided what to write about, perhaps, a semi-autobiographical novel. Your choice now is between first or third person narration.

Many successful novels have been written in the first person. First person narration does give the reader a sense of intimacy. But it is fraught with limitations, the most obvious being that nothing can be written except what the narrator has personally seen or experienced. You may, of course, use letters or reports from other people or say: "I suppose he thought I was an idiot," and other cop-outs to circumvent this difficulty. It is still an important limitation.

In third-person narrative, on the other hand, you may shift the time, the place and the point of view (i.e., the person through whom events are being seen or experienced) as often as you like. There is more freedom in structure and in getting inside the psyche of your characters.

Your next job is to write a brief résumé (two hundred to five hundred words) of what you want to say to your reader. Out of this résumé there should emerge incidents, characters and your theme. Theme sounds technical. It isn't. It is merely the chief message or messages you want to communicate to your readers.

The characters who inhabit your story are important. Apart from genres in which plot is dominant (e.g., the detective story), the novel is primarily about people. They must be real people, not cardboard outlines. If you are writing about contemporary life, the best method, perhaps, is to meld the characteristics of two or three people whom you know into one fictional character. Similarly, in the historical novel you may base your historical and fictional characters on real-life people whom they seem to resemble. People have not really changed too much since history began.

I would suggest that you paint your people in dramatic colors. Above all you must give them depth. One device is to write an in-depth description of each of your characters, how he or she grew up, what influences molded each of them and what the family (parents, brothers, sisters, uncles, aunts, cousins) of each was, so that finally you know each of your people thoroughly. Remind yourself that, in writing these people into your novel, you will have to become each of them in turn.

Perhaps I might digress at this point to review the major methods of characterization. There is third person description by the author. In Herman Wouk's *The Winds of War* the wife of the principal character is described in these words: "At 45 Rhoda Henry remained a singularly attractive woman, but she was rather a crab."

A second method is through the words and actions of the character. A third is by the reactions of other characters in the story to the person being described (e.g. someone says: "He's a nut—dangerous, too").

The three methods may be used to describe any character.

At some point in your preparation the time-span of your novel needs to be determined, whether, for instance, it is to cover ten days or ten years. Similarly with your place-range. Is it to be, for example, from Toronto to Hawaii or to revolve around an Ontario or Alberta farm?

At this point, you are ready to expand your résumé into your "story-line," that is to write (from two thousand to ten thousand words) the story you want to tell. Certain cardinal principles enter here. Since all art is selection, discard what doesn't fit your theme and eliminate dull troughs. Don't be afraid to melodramatize. You know that what really happens often doesn't make a good story unless you "touch it up." For incidents, draw upon real-life facts or experiences such as a violent thunderstorm, a riot, a tidal wave, or even a church picnic, and use devices to make the events dramatic. Remind yourself that clash is the essence of drama.

There is clash between man (man here includes women and men) and nature, man and God or authority. There is also man versus man and man versus himself. Clash is linked with broken action in which obstacles are placed between a person and his goal. To make broken action dramatic, the goal must be a vital one. For example, a bush pilot sets out to rescue a man who will die if he isn't flown at once to a hospital but is faced by a blizzard, a failing engine, a half-frozen lake for a landing place and so on. Such obstacles give you broken action, suspense and dramatic action. Essentially, what you do is to raise the question: "Will the pilot succeed or won't he?"

In your storyline, however, I would suggest that you leave room for your characters to help write your novel.

One more preliminary should be mentioned. No matter what you are writing about, careful research is necessary. If you are writing a detective story, police and court procedures must be authentic. If you are at a semi-autobiographical novel, reaching back into horse-and-buggy days, you must know on which side of a buggy or cutter the driver sits. Triple-check every fact, ancient or modern, that you are using. Books in libraries are an obvious source for research.

With these preliminaries completed you are now ready to begin your novel. But where to begin? My suggestion is to begin at a high point, and to raise a question so that the reader asks: "What happens next?" It is a good device, also, to start with physical motion, actual or implied, or with dialogue.

Another problem in the beginning of a novel is how to "set the stage," that is, how to let the reader know the time, the place, who the people are, why they are where they are and what their relationships to each other are; and still keep the story moving. Dialogue can do part of it, but make sure, by reading it aloud to yourself, that all your dialogue sounds like authentic speech. In any case, you should feed in what your reader needs to know, unobtrusively and bit by bit. Some authors try two or three beginnings to see which "feels right." Prologues or forewords are acceptable to set your scene.

Questions often asked by neophyte novelists are: "How do you know where to end chapters? How many chapters should there be? What should be the length of each chapter?" There are no hard and fast rules. In general, each chapter ought to conclude a unit of time, emotion or allied events and should lead naturally into the next chapter. You may also begin a new chapter by writing: "While this was going on in Toronto, in Vancouver... etc." or "At this moment Betty was thinking of Harry" or by a shift in time. Chapter length may vary from a page to, say, ten pages. The number of chapters depends simply on the length of the story you tell.

You will have to decide whether your approach is to be romanticist (the world as you'd like it to be or as you think it ought to be) or realistic (the world as you think it really is). Both approaches vary in type or intensity. Realism, for example, can be pathological (emphasis on the morbid, ugly, pornographic or chaotic) or what may be called "Greek realism," that is the good and bad in people and the world. Whichever approach you use, every action—whether physical or emotional—of your characters should be motivated and should also be consistent with the characterization of each person.

In the modern novel, description is generally woven in to set or change a mood or to give local color and verisimilitude. In structure the chronological method is the easiest. Even here, you will find that you may be using "flashback," that is, through the characters' minds and words you will be returning to events that precede the time-span of your novel. Flashback can be used for the whole novel as in Thornton Wilder's *Bridge of San Luis Rey*. James Joyce's *Ulysses* is regarded as the *ne plus ultra* of the "stream of consciousness" novel in which the events and feelings are put through the major character's mind. You may also use alternating chapters to move from one level of time back to a previous time as in Ross Lockeridge Jr.'s *Raintree County*. The novel has few restrictions in respect to structure. Use that form which tells your story best.

As far as style goes, the best advice, possibly, is to have something to say and to say it as simply and directly as you can. This advice does not preclude the use of metaphors and similes. They make your writing vivid. But, as every editor will tell you, avoid clichés, that is expressions which have been around so long that they are dull and tarnished coins. Instead, try to find a fresh approach.

A final suggestion is that in the first writing you should not stop to polish or revise but go right through to the end, leaving the rough or the parts that you merely outline until later. Otherwise you may never get beyond the first few pages. However, if you leave wide margins on your pages, when you are re-reading what has been written in previous days, you can put down ideas as to what you will do with these parts later. When you have reached the end of your novel, that is the time to revise and revise until your work is as nearly perfect and professional as you can make it. Be your own sternest critic.

---

W.G. Hardy, scholar, sportsman and author, was professor of classics at the University of Alberta from 1920 to 1964. He won the Governor General' s Medal at the University of Toronto and in 1974 became a member of the Order of Canada. He served as president of the Canadian Amateur Hockey Association and the Canadian Authors Association. But he was best known as a writer; the author of five historical novels, one modern novel, four histories, two textbooks and numerous articles and short stories.

# The Modern Romance Novel

*by Gail Hamilton*

Today, even the briefest scan of the fiction shelves will reveal the boom in romance novels that now generate up to fifty percent of all mass-market paperback fiction sales. Twenty percent of romance readers say they read one romance a day. Forty percent say they read one every two days. True addicts have been known to spend up to $150 a month to satisfy their craving. Naturally, any such seemingly voracious market is going to attract the attention of the fiction writer. The question is where to begin.

First, you must decide whether you really want to write a romance novel. Lack of genuine interest in the genre, coupled with the assumption that a book can be tossed off on spare weekends to pay for the canary's chow, will only lead to disaster. The craft requirements are just as rigorous as in any other form of novel. The market, due to its very size, is intensely competitive. The mostly mythical formula is present only to the extent that usually excessive violence and bloodshed are excluded and the heroine and hero make a permanent romantic commitment at the end.

Having discovered that one's heart is, so to speak, in the right place, the next stop is, once again, the bookstore. One of the best ways to keep up with the romance field is to examine carefully the many different choices shouldering each other off the shelves. Besides all the regular lines, there are romances geared for teenagers (squeaky clean self-discovery stories), romances that deal exclusively with the problems of married couples, romances about those who are winning their second chance at love, and, of course, all those splendid historicals glittering with the panache of another era.

Book lengths can vary from fifty thousand words up to more than one hundred twenty-five thousand. The new author might be wise to attempt the shorter length first, since the longer works require a much greater all-round complexity in order to maintain reader interest. For anyone unused to working with a novel, even a short romance can be quite a sustained project to take on.

Samples of as many as possible should be acquired and read. Only in this way can one gain a solid feeling for the needs and trends of the genre. And time should be spent only on the most up-to-date issues, markedly different from those ten – to twenty-year-old books so temptingly available at the rummage-sale counter.

After deciding which line is the most attractive to you, you can then write to the editorial department for tip sheets, which most publishers are happy to provide. Tip sheets will briefly outline the audience at which the line is aimed, the length of the book, and whether the publisher wants a complete manuscript or is willing to look at sample chapters accompanied by character sketches and an outline. This latter method of submission can save a lot of time and frustration. An editor can tell whether a book is on the right track before an author expends all the effort necessary to finish the work.

Also given are suggestions about how the plot might be developed, whether the book length indicates a sub-plot and what clichéd characters and situations are to be avoided at all costs. Many old-fashioned stock devices—such as the scheming, totally evil other woman or those convenient bouts of amnesia—produce apoplexy in editors today. As in any novel, nothing can replace a warm-hearted, well-told tale with characters one can root for who are involved in a powerful conflict which builds to a suspenseful, carefully orchestrated climax. Characters ought to have iron-clad motivation for what they do. Both protagonists should be introduced quickly and the temptation to do lengthy flashbacks strongly resisted. Editors like plenty of action in the plot and there's even a tendency to combine romance with intrigue and mystery as long as the romance remains the dominant theme.

Hints about the heroine and hero may come as a surprise to those whose acquaintance with the genre consists of a few adolescent forays at summer camp. To maintain its ongoing appeal, the romance novel has had to keep apace of the times—times which have brought a growth of feminism along with a much increased role of women in society outside the home. No one is interested any more in a helpless nineteen-year-old waiting for a father figure to sweep her off into a state of perpetual dependency. Today's women want to read about heroines more like themselves. The modern heroine is mature, usually twenty-five or older. She is successful in whatever field of endeavor she has chosen. She has had sexual experience. Maybe there are even children and a divorce in her background. She does not blush, cry, run away from her problems or crumple under stress. She does not fall for men who are macho, domineering or violent. She is a strong individual in control of her own life.

The corollary of this is that the hero can now really be human. While he is secure in himself and doing well in life, he is not afraid to show his vulnerabilities, make mistakes, recount his innermost thoughts or express tenderness toward the heroine. He does not demand that the heroine give up her separate integrity in order to devote herself exclusively to him. He supports her career efforts, her diverse interests, and allows her full scope to develop herself in whatever direction her individuality dictates.

Formerly, the story has nearly always told from the heroine's point of view. Now, there is a growing interest in the hero's point of view. Readers want to get inside him, know what he is thinking too. In this way, the hero's character may be more completely developed and the narration given a much broader perspective.

Sexual encounters may take place at any time between the hero and heroine. These encounters, however, are always a portrayal of healthy, loving emotion between two equal individuals and are in no way to be confused with pornography, which is a form of hate literature against women.

Very important to the romance novel is the setting, which can add that element of glamor and escape sought by the readers. The writer need not, however, suppose that some entrancing foreign background is always de rigeur. One should write about what one is familiar with. To the rest of the world out there, one's own home ground can be quite exotic. The story can take place anywhere as long as the writing, woven with sensuous detail, makes the setting come alive with all its vividness in the reader's mind. For the setting, the professions of the main characters, or any other aspect of the book, one can't skimp on research. Lack of authenticity is spotted at once and will quickly doom a manuscript.

Since contact with other professionals always provides a boost to the spirit, a writer might keep on the look out for local meetings and seminars or join one of the rapidly proliferating romance writers' organizations. The largest is probably Romance Writers of America, though it is a U.S. based group which includes Canadian members in its northern chapters. The frequent newsletters provide interesting author profiles, market news and the latest information about workshops and conferences. In Canada, a number of groups are now beginning to provide all the same services to romance writers as does the American organization. More general associations, such as the Canadian Authors Association, take care to include romance writing in the yearly program of meetings, blue-pencil days and conference topics. Also, one can subscribe to newsletters designed especially for the romance writer or reader, but the subscription price can make one wonder whether the data provided is really worth it.

The rapid evolution of the romance novel is perhaps the seed of a genuine literature for women. After all, where else is there such a body of writing written largely by women, about women and for women? Where else can women—in such large numbers—begin to see their own concerns, thoughts and emotions expressed, their own sexuality recognized in a warm and positive manner? The true excitement is for the future as each romance writer takes a part in shaping this ever new and promising form.

Gail Hamilton has taught high school, written advertising and camped across the Sahara to Timbuktu. To date, she has produced nine romance novels and adapted the immensely popular *Road to Avonlea* TV series, published a reference book for charitable organizations and is still going strong.

# Construct the Mystery Plot

*by Fred Walker*

The mystery has been described, by literary greats who don't know what they're talking about, as the sort of story in which no sooner does the curtain go up than a body falls out of the closet. In fact, most mystery plays begin with a bit of business before the murder. But *only* "a bit." If nobody has done anything illegal by the end of the first scene, your show is in trouble.

Use the 2-2-2-2 rule in fiction. A reader first reads the first two lines, then the first two paragraphs, the first two pages and the first two chapters. Read your first draft, stopping yourself at those points. If it isn't interesting in any of these places, you've already lost 'em. Rewrite, or cut that dull opening and start closer to the crime.

## The detective.

A detective should be moral without being boringly perfect. Give your hero at least one flaw—and I mean a character flaw like vanity, not a physical weakness. It goes without saying that the hero must be intelligent, but he shouldn't be such an intellectual that he loses the sympathy of the audience, nor should he be an expert on everything. Make sure there's at least one point on which he needs advice from another character. But be careful. A detective who always just happens to have an old war buddy who knows "all about this stuff" and who happens to be in town for the weekend and who happens to owe him a favour is almost as annoying as one who already knows everything.

A sidekick is not essential, but is very useful as someone to whom the detective can talk out of the presence of the suspects, so we can find out what he's thinking (remember the central premise of the mystery—that a character thinking is more interesting than a character emoting.) A sidekick should be a character in his own right, not just a toadying appendage of the hero. Give him unique traits, and avoid the temptation to make him stupider than the hero. Your hero will seem all the smarter, if he outsmarts smart people. Writing books will tell you your sleuth needs a private motive— "this time, it's personal." Nonsense. He's a detective. He doesn't need a motive to solve a crime any more than a doctor needs a motive to treat a patient. The exception is the gifted amateur, who's not a cop or a licensed private investigator.

### The villain.

The character who needs a motive is the villain. In art, crime is always rational. It needn't be a motive that makes sense to you and me, but it must make sense in the twisted mind of the villain. If your mystery is based on a true crime, do not invent new crime scene facts. Do not pin the rap on any person still living. Either support the findings of the real police, or use a clearly fictional villain who illustrates the *type* of unknown person you think was responsible, or accuse some long dead person at whom the facts really point. Do not attribute a theory of the case to a real detective who is positively known not to have supported it.

If your crime itself is fiction, you have greater freedom and more work ahead of you. The villain can be anyone you like. Broaden your plot by having at least one lady suspect. Conspiracies also work well on stage. They are also harder to guess.

### The solution.

There are three types of solution, in descending order.

1. Realistic—the villain is an ordinary person who knew the victim well and to whom much evidence points.

2. Sensational—the villain is powerful, or a celebrity, or a conspiracy, and the evidence comes as a revelation.

3. Surprise—the villain is a character you met in the last ten pages, or someone who hasn't been mentioned since the first scene, or who you were told was dead, or who is supposed to have spent the whole story posing as somebody else.

Be honest to the historical period. I have read novels in which 18th century thief-takers use fingerprints, and Victorian gaslight chillers in which Freudian psychology is used to "profile" the killer! Eighteenth century detectives used informants and rewards, 19th century detectives relied on eyewitness descriptions and uncovering the motive, and 20th century detectives sneer at human frailty and trust test tubes, photographs and blood typing.

Red herrings? Please don't use them. Rely, instead, on a genuinely mysterious crime and ambiguous evidence. Old fashioned "tricks"—like the 1st chapter doesn't count because it was somebody's dream—are thankfully out of fashion. In particular, don't bring the corpse back from the dead unless it's a comedy. Death, at least, must be final and certain, or there is no reason for the reader to have any faith in the writer.

How should the villain be caught? *Not* by luck, even in comedy. Here's where you *can* use trickery. Entrapment won't hold up in a real courtroom, but it still works on stage, especially if the villain outsmarts himself. If the detective pretends to suspect somebody else, it can fool the reader, too. But you have to time it right—a false solution has to come close enough to the end of your story that everyone will think it's the real solution. Don't use The Blurt, in which the villain slips up and conveniently says something that only he would know. Acceptable endings include:

1. The Brag—the villain is tricked into boasting of his deed in front of a witness, or to a pal who's wearing a wire.

2. The Glass Slipper—some clue known to belong to the real criminal, such as a bloody shoe, is elaborately tried on each suspect in turn, fitting only one.

3. The Lineup—self-explanatory.

4. The Broken Alibi—two people who claimed to be together when the murder took place are proved to be lying. Often, the villain is the one who was not previously considered a suspect! Variation—someone who claimed never to have visited the crime scene before is proved to have been there: see The Blurt.

5. The Trap—the detective falsely announces that he already knows the identity of the criminal, and will announce same at some future date. He then waits to see who will turn up to try to kill him. There are a hundred variations, in which the detective dupes the villain into incriminating himself by pretending something to provoke a guilty reaction.

6. The Bluff—my favourite. "It's all over Rocky. Your buddy just confessed." "That SOB! He swore he'd never tell! How'd you break him?" "I didn't. You have the right to remain silent..."

### The peroration.

All of which takes us to The Peroration, the big speech where the detective explains everything. A typical peroration goes on, with interruptions and flashbacks, for about seven pages, in both fiction and scripts. Some do's and don'ts:

Don't make the explanation *overly* complicated.

Don't make the detective go on impossibly long without a sip of water or any objection from the people he's accusing!

Don't base the conclusion on something ridiculous, like a feather found on the floor or a theory that the villain swung in through the window on a vine. (These from real plays!)

Don't have the villain pull a revolver and make a break for the French doors.

Do make the truth surprisingly elegant and simple.

Do let the villain make the case for his innocence.

Do base the conclusion on real facts, pointing unmistakably at a particular person.

Do write another mystery, because I want to read it!

Frederick A. Walker has written two published mystery plays, *I Love My Work*, about Jack the Ripper, and *The Roswell File*, about a hardboiled private eye. He has acted in *A Few Good Men*, *Ten Little Indians*, *Dracula* and many other mystery plays.

# The World of Science Fiction

*by Brian M. Fraser*

D on't try writing science fiction unless you like to read it. Otherwise, your lack of knowledge about the genre or your lack of enthusiasm for what you are writing will show through.

You may have heard that science fiction offers the perfect starting ground for a beginning writer because it is one of the few markets that still publishes short stories. And it is always much easier to learn by writing short stories than investing time in long novels.

This is not necessarily true. Unless you know what kind of short stories the market is seeking, no short piece of fiction will sell. So you must read science fiction, study the kind of stories being published, analyze the market, and determine what themes or styles are suitable for each magazine or publisher.

One of the first things you will discover is that science fiction is mostly an American genre. Most of the major SF magazines are published in the United States, and most of the hardcover and paperback publishers which produce SF lines are located south of the border.

This is not to say that there are not SF publishers elsewhere. In Britain, a great deal of science fiction is being published, in both hardcover and paperback, but our distance from this market puts us at a disadvantage. And although some Canadian publishers occasionally put out a future-oriented or SF title, they do not regularly publish science fiction.

At any rate, the centres of SF publishing are certainly in the eastern United States. It is no problem for Canadian writers to learn this market however; through the publication and distribution of U.S. materials on our newsstands, Canada can be considered an extension of the American reading public.

In any major Canadian city, you should be able to find a well-stocked magazine rack carrying the SF magazines. You can then buy them, read them, and understand their needs.

In addition to this research, which will tell you what is being accepted and published currently, there are sources you can study to better understand what is considered good SF.

There are a number of "World's Best" and "Best of the Year" short story anthologies which can give you a good idea of the calibre of stories—including themes, writing style, and scientific content. And the Hugo and Nebula Awards, given each year by the fans and the Science Fiction Writers of America, are also excellent indicators.

Your study of the SF genre will quickly tell you, for instance, when an alien being has been portrayed effectively and believably or is just another Bug-Eyed Monster. Even with a technical background, you'll know when the scientific explanation of a planet's atmosphere, gravity, and physical characteristics have been well researched. You'll soon know, too, if your story idea is original or just another overworked cliché.

This reading research is important, and it will go beyond just reading other people's stories. You will have to do additional research into the physical sciences—biology, physics, geology, communications—and the soft or social sciences such as psychology, anthropology, archaeology, and history.

Meanwhile, by writing actual stories, you will be developing the discipline of regular working habits and a feel for what works in fictional form. This will polish your skills of writing narrative and dialogue, developing characters, and integrating a complex future background into your story without slowing the plot.

In combination with your analysis of effective writing from the books you are reading—in both science fiction and mainstream literature—and general observation of life around you, you will translate the human experience into fictional situations and tell stories about people with whom the reader can identify, because science fiction stories are about people, too. In fact, without human conflict, without individuals, there is no story.

Preparation for a career in science fiction is not an overnight task, but then neither is the effort required by an historical novelist, a biographer, a nonfiction author, or any other kind of writer. Each day, with study and practice, the writer learns his craft.

Science fiction is a genre on its own, demanding some study before you can make much headway in the market. There is no shortage of texts or how-to books that deal with the subject. They are all worth reading and can help you avoid obvious mistakes.

A very basic primer is *Notes to a Science Fiction Writer* by Ben Bova, former editor of *Analog*, the leading SF magazine. Mr. Bova practises what he teaches in this primer, using some of his own published stories to show how character, conflict, background, and setting must be integrated in a good science fiction story.

Similar in principle—and highly recommended—a paperback titled *Those Who Can: A Science Fiction Reader*, edited by Robin Scott Wilson, carries short SF stories together with the author's own comments on the major literary elements: plot, character, setting, theme, point-of-view, and style.

*The Craft of Science Fiction*, edited by Reginald Bretnor, is a text for the more advanced writer, one who perhaps has the basic skills of story construction but would like to apply them to the complexities of writing science fiction. Chapters by accomplished SF authors discuss the building of believable aliens, the creation of planets which do not conflict with known physical laws, and the development of effective words and alien languages.

*Writing & Selling Science Fiction*, published by *Writer's Digest* in cooperation with members of the Science Fiction Writers of America (SFWA), contains basic information for the beginner.

*Science Fiction Handbook, Revised: How to Write & Sell Imaginative Stories*, by L. Sprague and Catherine de Camp, is a revision of the book of the same name originally published in 1953. De Camp gives some practical tips on studying the history of science fiction, on learning who your readers are, and on plotting in advance. Finally, if you can obtain it, *Of Worlds Beyond*, edited by Lloyd Arthur Eshback is a re-issue of a 1947 symposium of essays on writing SF by such masters as Robert A. Heinlein, John W. Campbell, A. E. van Vogt, and others. Although somewhat dated, the book gives an insight into the working methods and philosophies of writers and editors who directed the shape of the genre.

Brian M. Fraser teaches the art of science fiction to university students.

# The Quest for Good Fantasy

*by Fred Walker*

**F**antasy is based on creativity, escapism, quest and romance.

**Creativity** means that you have to ignore what your grade school teacher told you. How many youngsters have had promising imaginations drummed out of them by a school insistence that everybody should write about what they know? In Fantasy, you write about what you *don't* know. William Shakespeare never visited Denmark. Edgar Rice Burroughs never went to Africa. And J.R.R. Tolkien never went to Middle-earth, for the simple reason that it doesn't exist.

**Use your imagination.** Make it up. Imagine it. Speculate freely. Invent. What will you need to invent? It depends on your setting. You can use a real place and time, like medieval Europe, or just an imaginary time, like the 24th century or the days of Atlantis, or an imaginary place and time, like Alpha Centauri in a parallel history-stream where ancient Egyptians have colonized the universe. There are only two rules: you must make it interesting, and you must make it consistent. Invent your world in detail, more than you think you will need. It's a good idea to take lengthy notes before you begin your plot, on such subjects as maps of your imaginary landscape, flora and fauna, races and religions, politics, art and culture, and, most importantly, the prior history that over several centuries has led up to the situation in which your characters now find themselves.

**Quest** means a journey, preferably a long and adventurous one. In serious literature, the quest is a symbol of the character's interior journey. In popular fantasy, it's something much more important—a dangerous and exciting trip someplace. Naturally, such adventure requires a motive. Keep in mind the advice of Lucy to Snoopy: "If you want people to read your book, you should have the characters fighting over something important." Characters don't go on quests to "find themselves," they go on quests to find the stolen key to the Temple of Poseidon, or something of similar power and worth. This type of device is called the "macguffin" in mystery or spy fiction. In fantasy it is often called the "holy grail." The "holy grail" of your quest should be colourful, interesting and of great importance. Something that your reader can't wait to saddle up and cross deserts and mountains to find—because fantasy is also about vicarious experience.

Which brings us to **Escape.** Fantasy is not realistic, *and this is not a fault*. Realism was invented about a hundred years ago, and is probably a passing fad. For 6,000 years of the human experience, the vast majority of imaginative literature from every culture on Earth has been escapist. Ulysses and Moses, King Davis and King Arthur, Roland and Beowulf. The sin of the 20th century is not that it invented Willy Loman, but that it insists that any character who does not resemble Willy is for that reason alone a bad character with a story that is not worthwhile. The 20th century has succeeded in brainwashing us into believing that every form of literature that ever existed except that of our own times has no real value, and is only for children. Reality sucks. Help your reader escape from it, and that means give him a story he wants to follow and characters whose heroism he will want to identify with.

**Romance** means *not* that your characters will fall in love (though they might), but that their adventures will be episodic and larger than life. This is the original meaning of the term "romance"—an exciting, unrealistic tale. Aristotle pronounced that "of all plots, the worst are the episodic" and it's important to know just what he meant. After all, as a fantasy writer, you will be doing something as subversive as disputing the Aristotelian foundations of our culture—you might as well be doing it on purpose. An episodic plot is one in which each episode, or event, is just what is supposed to have happened next. It is the primal storyteller's "and then ... and then." By calling these plots the worst, Aristotle meant that good plots should have logical cause and effect relationships. That each event causes the next event, and has in turn been caused by something prior. This level of authorial control will ruin your fantasy. It is important to remember that *when Aristotle was writing, the fantasy novel hadn't been invented yet*. Aristotle was writing about tragic plays, mostly, with the occasional nod to epic poetry. You're doing something different—and Aristotle just might have been wrong.

As your characters travel though one magical kingdom after another, they will have a series of fascinating adventures. In a good novel, *some* of these adventures will grow from prior events and decisions. Taking the left hand fork will get them robbed by forest outlaws, the knight's drinking will get him in trouble when pixies put a sleeping spell on his wineskin. But other events should be truly random, completely out of anybody's control, including the author's. An avalanche as they cross the Mountains of Peril, or getting mistaken for cutpurses in the City of Thieves. A fantasy does *not* presume the ultimate rationality of life and art, and the total control of the writer's relentless purpose. In the words of our esteemed prime minister, when he took the job he now holds: "Hang on! It's going to be a Hell of a ride!"

One last point about **Magic**. Control it. There's nothing heroic about a hero who can make bad guys disappear by casting a spell. And there's something really silly about heroes who only remember that they can fly in the last chapter, when it could have saved them a dozen times before. Magic can be a little unpredictable, but it can't be completely arbitrary or you're into lazy storytelling. The best advice for a novice is to state clearly in the first chapter just what is and is not possible in your world. Levitation? ESP? Shape-shifting? Curses? Vampires? Werewolves? Dragons?

Since nobody knows, make it up!

Fred Walker holds a Ph.D. in English Literature from Queen's U. His doctoral thesis explained the style of Tolkien, C.S. Lewis and Charles Williams. He has written two published fantasy stories, *The Chrononauts*, about time-travel, and *Dragons of the Ring*, which includes vampires. He has also toured a one-man show called *Proconsul of Mars*.

# Where Humour has its Start

*by Alex Mair*

I am about to make a prediction—which is a very dangerous thing to do. I am going to predict that if you sit down to write a deliberately humorous piece, you're going to fail.

I say that because humour, true humour, is always in the treatment, never in the topic.

Dorothy Parker once said that humour has wit in it. Wisecracking is just callisthenics with words. Neil Simon's advice to writers and actors in training was "Never play for the laugh in a line, play for the life."

Howard Lindsay and Russel Crouse wrote a play which set a record for continuous performances on Broadway. It was a smash comedy hit. They made it into a movie, starring Cary Grant. It was the funniest film to hit the screen in years. It told the story of two little old ladies who lived in a Brownstone house in New York, lured lonely old men in off the street and poisoned them by putting arsenic in the home-made elder-berry wine they served them, then buried the bodies in the basement with the aid of a retarded nephew. Funny, you ask? It was—after the treatment that Lindsay and Crouse gave the story line. They called it *Arsenic & Old Lace*.

Neil Simon is considered by many to be the funniest playwright that ever wrote for the American theatre. Take any Neil Simon play, rough out the story line and hold it up to the light and check it for lumps. *The Odd Couple*? It's a story about two lonely men, one of whom has been thrown out by his wife because he is an absolute slob and is destroying the family. He settles in to make a life with a man who has been thrown out by his wife because he is a fastidious neurotic and he's driving the rest of the family out of their minds.

Humour is a tool that helps you to get people to read what you write, listen to what you say, and agree with what you think. Erma Bombeck was the love of every newspaper reader's life, but it was the treatment she gave her topics that made gems out of every column. Did she complain about the way her kids dressed? Of course not. She said that her son came to her and asked how he should dress for Halloween. She told him he should just wear what he always wore, and go as a wino.

One of the best pieces of advice for any humourist, and for any writer for that matter, came not from a writer, but from a photographer. He taught photography at a community college, and to assess the kind of students he had in a class, he would load them all on the school bus, take them out to a National Park nearby and turn them loose. He made sure each student had a camera loaded with black and white film, and his only guideline was shoot pictures of anything you like. The next day the films would be processed in the darkroom, printed the day after that, and on Friday he would critique the students choices of their pictures.

He said that, invariably, the student who took the best picture never went more than fifteen paces from the door of the bus. It would be a photograph of a dandelion gone to seed, or a drop of moisture on the end of a leaf. The instructor used to say that the successful photograph is one which, when he looked at it, made him say, "You know, I've seen that a hundred times, but I've never looked at it in quite that way before."

Isn't that equally true of a successful piece of writing? And if you can treat your topic with insight, and with freshness, you make readers see things from a fresh angle. They laugh, and they like you for making them laugh. Just think of Erma Bombeck's son and his Halloween costume.

E.B. White once said that humour must not professedly teach, and it must not professedly preach if it would live forever. It need only speak the truth, he said, then very quietly added, "And I notice that it usually does."

As Simon said, "Don't play it for the laugh, play it for the life!" My mother spent her declining years in a nursing home, and there weren't all that many things to laugh at. The Director stopped me on my arrival one day, and explained that a local orchestra had come in the night before to entertain the residents. It was a small group, playing what you might call oom-pah music. Lots of accordions and violins. The residents loved it. They recognized the tunes, and they remembered some of the lyrics, singing along with the band. But, the Director explained, it got a little emotional because the leader looked into the audience and recognized an elderly lady as the mother of a friend of his, and he hadn't realized that she was still alive. At the end of that selection, he unclipped his accordion, put it down on the stage and went down and knelt beside her wheel chair. He looked her right in the eye and said, "Hi. Do you know who I am?"

And she looked back at him for a long time and then said, "No. But I'm sure if you'll check at the front office they'll be able to help you."

Humour is simplicity raised to an art form. Back to Dorothy Parker again. She once reviewed a book in 18 words. "This is not a book which should be tossed aside lightly. It should be hurled with great force."

Humour can hurt—and the trickiest kind of all is ethnic humour. My father came to Canada from Scotland when he was 15. That was in 1911, and he never lost his accent. In the mid-fifties after the Hungarian revolt, many of the Hungarian refugees ended up in our city, some working in the department where my father was Master Mechanic. I remember him saying to me one day, "You know, some o' they Hoongarians have been oot here for a whole year and they still speak wi' an accent."

Ethnic humour can be cruel while attempting to be funny. Have you heard the one about the three Irishmen who went ice fishing and were run over by the Zamboni machine? Substitute Scots, English, Norwegian, in fact any ethnic group for Irish, and it's still mean-spirited and a put down.

If humour is so tricky, why use it at all? Because when used properly, when used with skill and good taste, it can give your writing a cutting edge in a way that nothing else can. When it works, it *really* works.

Do what the successful photographer does. Climb a ladder and take your picture looking down. Kneel down and shoot your picture looking up. Show the reader the familiar from a fresh angle. And if you've done your job, the reader will look up from the printed page and say, "You know, I've seen that situation a hundred times before, but I have never thought about it from quite that angle."

Humour can help you to do your job effectively, the job of making the reader listen to what you have to say, and to think about it.

Humour is a powerful tool. Use it well, but use it wisely. You might just leave them with a smile on their faces and a thought in their heads, and isn't that what you started out to do in the first place?

Alex Mair has written, spoken, and taught at the University and College level, always with a touch of humour. He is the author of *How To Speak In Public, How To Be A Great M. C.* and a wide variety of historical works. Eleven years of daily broadcasts on CBC radio were followed by a daily newspaper column for five years. He continues to be in demand as a speaker.

# Become Your Own Literary Critic

*by Nancy Smith*

A s a student of English literature I have, on several occasions, attempted to weigh the value of literary criticism to writers in Canada. Why are students of English literature taught to read for theme and symbol, while plot and character are secondary? And why aren't more creative writers attuned to the importance of literary criticism? Greater attention to theme and symbol may well be the key to success for the creative writer.

In pursuit of this idea, I have perused some of the contemporary self-help books on the subject of creative writing in the local book store. Some ignored literary devices altogether, others mentioned them as an aside, another suggested only "mature" writers could hope to master these techniques. Jack Hodgins' book, *A Passion for Narrative*, explained the use of literary techniques in building a story clearly and succinctly, stressing the importance of adopting these devices. Hodgins explains that experienced authors say their literature operates on many levels, so each reader will find something in it.

I like that sudden sensation I get when I recognize a pattern within a story or a reference to another book—the way in which stories can converse with one another, as I think Roland Barthes points out in *The Pleasure of the Text*. On the other hand, I appreciate an author who is discrete enough not to point out my dullness in missing yet another signpost. The story still makes sense whether or not I recognize the hidden subtleties of it.

Some will argue that it isn't necessary to think about literary devices, that they come out of the writing naturally; stories have their own density. Of course, this is also true. However, let's pretend for a moment that we want to be the best. We want to know what it takes to be considered a master like Alice Munro, Margaret Atwood, Carol Shields.

A prominent literary critic, Harold Bloom, in *The Western Canon* defines the canon as works that are "authoritative in our culture." Works must be an amalgam of the following: "mastery of figurative language, originality, cognitive power, knowledge, exuberance of diction." Perhaps our writing will not measure up to Shakespeare's, however, if we are aware of these devices and how they may be used in our own literature, the chances of finding our books on the syllabuses in schools are improved. Teachers and professors introduce thousands of readers to worthwhile writers every year. How do they decide which writers are worthwhile? They look for literature that connects to life through the masterly use of literary techniques.

In addition, writers need to be in touch with the whole heritage of literature. Northrop Frye wrote *The Great Code: The Bible and Literature* because he realized that the student who does not know the Bible does not "understand a good deal of what is going on in what he reads." Could we say the same of writers about their creations? Perhaps writers will not appreciate the influences on their own literature?

About myth in literature Frye said: "Most of this is held unconsciously, which means that our imaginations may recognize elements of it when presented in art or literature, without consciously understanding what it is that we recognize." So, too, may writers' work be mythological because of the way they have lived; that is to say, much of what they understand about life may find its way into their writing without their necessarily being aware of it. The subject matter chosen for exploration may be tapping into something much more universal. How will they know whether their themes are relevant to a larger audience, if they haven't read for themselves about the driving forces in literature over the centuries? As Frye suggested, "One of the practical functions of criticism is, I think, to make us more aware of our mythological conditioning."

Great writers acknowledge each other intertextually; they realize that literature, like any other discipline, is built upon and adds to the work of others. Likewise, the kind of materials used will affect the quality of the product. Allow yourself to make connections between your literature and that of others where it comes naturally. If done tastefully and unobtrusively, you are not "putting on airs" by making reference to another author or reworking themes from Greek myth. Macauley and Robie say it succinctly in their book *Technique in Fiction*: "three kinds of things can carry symbolical meanings: an object, an event, and a character. The all-important requirement is to keep the name tag invisible."

An example of myth being applied to Canadian literature is shown by Kathleen Wall in her book *The Callisto Myth From Ovid to Atwood*. In it she compares Atwood's *Surfacing* to the Callisto myth in which the nymph Diana eventually is turned into the Great Bear constellation. You missed the reference to the stars in her novel, you say? Wall finds enough in Atwood's novel nevertheless to make a convincing argument. However, you might ask yourself these questions: Was Atwood aware that she was using a feminine archetype? Or was this novel the result of her need to express herself, a culmination of her own experiences, her imagination, what she had read, as well as all of those other influences? Either way, the reader benefits from the depth of the text.

To be in control of your writing you should be aware of the many ways in which you can bring your message into greater focus, the ways in which you can draw your reader in, or play with their assumptions about reading. As an editor once pointed out to me: "Whether or not we achieve recognized status and have our works taught in secondary and post-secondary institutions, we probably want wide readership and long shelf-life for our work. With that in mind, we need to understand and use appropriately the literary devices that add depth and resonance to our stories."

Read the Greek myths; read the Bible; read anthropological and psychological texts. Look for patterns; become an amateur literary critic. It might pay off.

Nancy Smith's poetry has appeared in various literary magazines. A radio play was short-listed for the CBC's literary competition. She is currently completing a graduate degree in English and American Literature at Harvard University Extension School.

# Theatre, Screen and Radio

# Traditional Play Construction

*by Don Wetmore*

A successful play gets two affirmative nods, the first from the producer who will buy it, the second from the audience. Both kudos are heaven for the playwright—but to get the first is the crucial test.

Although theatre today, as with the other arts, continues to look with hope for new forms, in order to pass the first test the neophyte playwright should try to absorb all he can about traditional play construction. Later he can break out into freer form—if he has the courage.

The "well-made" play may no longer impress critics, who have seen everything anyway, but producers still rely on it because it continues to hold audiences.

The great technical clichés are exposition, the unfolding of character, the intensifying of conflicts, the rising action, the suspense of crises, the excitement's climax, the satisfaction in denouement, the dialogue that reveals and pushes forward. Still great stuff.

If any of these giant traditional "ribs" is overlooked in an intelligent attempt to construct new form, I think you should be warned that the compensation has to be terrific.

So, if you'll try to write a well-constructed play, here are the "ribs" again, and a few old-fashioned ideas about how to put some flesh on them.

## The exposition.

An explanation, usually early in the play, of the oft-advised five Ws (Who, What, Where, When, Why) so that the audience is adjusted to what they are looking at and what they are supposed to know. Well—don't put all the Ws in one person's mouth. Be inventive about explaining things the natural, easy way. If you must use a narrator, give him or her the strong dramatic function used in *The Glass Menagerie, Our Town, I Remember*

*Mama*, or *A Man For All Seasons*. Maybe you can save a "W" for a surprise or a puzzle—but don't confuse. Begin at the start, the middle, or the end of the story; but begin where you think you might get immediate interest. Study the openings of *Hamlet*, *Ghosts*, *Butterflies Are Free*.

### The unfolding of character.

As the action rises, people get more and more interesting and their clashes with each other or within themselves get more absorbing.

Partially characterize immediately—even if the first picture is a stereotype. Do it in that person's speech, not by someone else's description. For instance, a woman makes her first entrance wearing a new dress and is questioned about it. Here are five *different* reactions:

"I got it cheap!"

"It's heavenly!"

"I'm going to defy mother and wear it."

"I wish it were pink."

"My father bought it and I hate the thing."

And here are men being asked for a charity donation as we first see the asker coming through an office door:

"How much?"

"What's it for?"

"I'll be glad to."

"See my wife."

"I gave at home."

"Go to Hell!"

After you've established the core of the character, begin to define the outline and dig for and develop all pertinent facets of the personality.

In a play, nearly every character has a flaw—minor or major; what the writer does with the flaw can be fascinating. Think of the delightfully flawed characters in *The Importance of Being Earnest*. Even Romeo and Juliet have the fatal flaw of too impetuous a love.

Characters must unfold, develop, and grow larger than life—act more slowly, more quickly; feel more deeply, more exuberant; think more steadily, more exasperatingly. Paint in broad strokes; add the subtleties as you go along. Give actors "juicy" parts; give them something to hold onto, hold back, reveal, explode.

You must have believable reasons (motivation) for development and changes in character. This is part of the creative excitement. Without believable character motivation, all the Ugly Duckling, Cinderella or Scrooge stories become mere fairy tales, and the horrifying changes in the lead character in the late Agatha Christie's *The Mouse Trap* (theatre's longest-run play), would not be accepted. What a challenge to have your butler first announce, "Dinner is served, Madame," then motivate him to roar at the end, "Come and get it!" J.M. Barfie almost did that.

### The conflicts in a rising action.

A play, as it rises toward a climax, is a series of conflicts, transitions and actions that build in interest.

Let's be clear: There are three kinds of conflicts—intellectual (clashes of ideas), emotional (clashes of feelings), physical (clashes in movement). Use all three, but not necessarily together as in this example: "Who's right, you or I? I want to be free! Let me pass!" The actor saying this line must go through three transitions—and will love it.

But to get sustained audience interest and to see action increase, build the line into dialogue with a touch of rhythm:

SHE: Who's right, you or I?

HE: (*trying to embrace her*) I only said you should stay.

SHE: (*looking away*) Not after this! I want to be free!

HE: (*quickly blocking her*) You think for a minute I'll let you?

SHE: (*forcing*) I don't care! Let me pass!

HE: No! (*He strikes her*)


(Stage directions help the writer visualize it first—but most are omitted later.)

While this example is dramatic, the technique is equally effective for comedy—the gentleman kisses, not strikes. Read it again as comedy.

Of course, the scene would be much more stimulating if the dialogue were worth listening to—it isn't! But the here-contrived lines serve to show how conflicts and transitions may be built up.

Most plays, even short ones, have a secondary story. Longer plays have more, like threads weaving the warp and woof of a pattern, each with its series of conflicts, each pushing the interest forward, yet each linking with the main story. Study the various stories in such plays as *The Crucible* and *Private Lives*.

The meaning of action is what *appears* to be happening. But it's more than story (plot), more than physical movement; action is growth and development of thoughts and feelings of the characters in the play. One can speak of "inner" and "outer" actions. The playwright who gets *both* "going" at the same time is succeeding.

### The suspense of crises.

Note the plural—when ideas or emotions come in conflict we are in suspense as to what follows. In the previous example, we ask (a) What happens after the man strikes the woman? (b) What happens after he kisses her if both are married to other persons?

Keep several crises in mind when planning. The more suspense in a play, the more entertaining.

### The climax and denouement.

Note the singular—the final grand crisis and its resolution. Throughout the play at various crises we are never sure how things will turn out; but at a climax the result is terminal. This is the big scene, the scene to which the play has been building. In crime drama on television, it's the chase; on the stage it's more often a determination of who or what will triumph. Don't stint in writing this scene, perhaps overwrite— and tighten up later. Above all, write the scene for actors; do not write it to justify nor test your ingenuity. Visualize every moment and "hear" everything said; give the actors your best lines, your best thinking, your best feelings.

The way a writer handles a climax depends upon the kind of play he or she is writing. In farce or melodrama, the climax can be a melange of movement (*A Flea In Her Ear*, *The Desperate Hours*); in comedy, the charm of good people overcoming a final obstacle (*Candida*, *The Cactus Flower*); in drama, the triumph of right and/or humanity (*The Doll's House*, *The Winslow Boy*, *Leaving Home*); in tragedy, final destruction and catharsis (*Juno and the Paycock*, *Death of a Salesman*, *The Ecstacy of Rita Joe*).

The climax should complete the story satisfactorily, with all major questions answered and all motivations explained. It should contain an assurance that crises are finished, for better or worse.

There may be minor explanations and decisions still to disclose; these are best dealt with swiftly in a denouement. The old literal definition of denouement is "an untying"; more often the writer uses this last quick scene to untie unresolved knots or tie up loose ends. Many plays do not need a denouement in this sense; they end with the climax. But some suspense writers use the denouement for a "twist," a twist that has to be as clever as it is in *Witness for the Prosecution*, *Arsenic and Old Lace*, and *Sleuth*. However, if there is anything to be said or done after the climax, do it in a short scene with a devised impact and a good last line on which to bring the curtain down.

### Dialogue.

Think of a play as a piece of fiction in spoken form. Everything needed, if the plot were to have been a novel, has to be spoken, even descriptions if they're not obvious. If you aren't keen about listening to the way people talk—in life, on the stage, screen, radio—stick to the novel form. A play needs a writer with an ear receptive to and capable of accurately repeating idiom, inflection, emphasis, rhythm, phrasing, style, the beat in repartee, and the sound of poetry.

One interesting job is trying to keep the speeches characterized. Alice should never speak like the Queen of Hearts unless she has a reason. Men and women don't usually talk in the same way. Compare the language given to Juliet's nurse with Mercutio's speech pattern. Not all playwrights succeed in this, but the good ones try and the best succeed admirably.

While revealing character, dialogue should build crises, each speech giving the cue for a stronger reply:

"I'm going to town,"

"To pay the rent?"

"No. To buy golf clubs!"

"Naturally!"

…and the comic fight is on.

Avoid "literary" words and phrases; the lines should be easy to speak. An actor can't do much but camp-up a line like "This room has an arcane atmosphere," but he'll make a selling point with "Brrr, it's creepy in here!"

Weigh the effectiveness of your dialogue against the value of the blank paper you type it on. A two-hour play uses a mere hundred typed pages to tell as much as a four-hundred-page novel. Cherish your space and be drastic with the blue pencil. Delete to get impact. And have faith that an actor's gesture can convey more than paragraphs of prose.

Comedy must have speed and succinctness—drama, clarity and humanity—tragedy, compassion. Write them all larger than life, and with energy.

## *What have you got to say?*

While the great plays have something to say, many successful plays don't necessarily; they are just written for entertainment.

Plays meant to entertain usually tell a story. Are you stumped for a story? If you'll think hard about people, ideas and emotions all in conflict, a story is bound to come. Motivations will, too; and motivations make plots.

By then you may have hit on a theme. *The Glass Menagerie* has the theme "Selfish people unknowingly shatter other people's lives"; *Barefoot in the Park* has the age-old theme "The course of true love never runs smooth." Reducing your play in this way to a maxim may be helpful in planning and might keep you from wandering. But don't cling to it. Creativity needs space and freedom to soar.

If you have many things to say, scatter them around—as that master craftsman Bernard Shaw did so brilliantly, and Eugene O'Neill so movingly.

But if you feel deeply about something or vastly amused by it, get absorbed in your theme and write it at fever pitch. Later, when you look back and revise, think again about humanity and character. Because what you have to say will not be listened to if the characters are pasteboard.

Don Wetmore (1907-01-23 to 1992-09-07) was a Nova Scotia playwright, actor, director, musician and educator. He was founder of the Nova Scotia Drama League, founding member of the Writer's Federation of Nova Scotia, and National President of the Canadian Authors Association. All of Don Wetmore's 26 plays were produced, and several chronicled Nova Scotia history.

# Action on Stage

*by Gregson Winkfield* _____

The house lights dim, the curtain rises, the young man proclaims, "I'll hang myself if she marries that senile old duffer!"

Out in the audience, we have learned almost all the background information to the play immediately. There is a girl, and the young man before us is in love with her. She appears to be promised to an old man and it looks as though she is going to marry him. We surmise, from experience of the comedy formula, that the young man will try every trick possible to woo her away from his adversary, and we guess he will succeed. We settle back in our seats to enjoy the performance that has so far revealed one line of dialogue.

How do playwrights create the kind of plays that keep audiences coming back to see them? The answer is that they have learned one simple lesson, and that lesson has taught them *what* they are doing, and why they are doing it. They have learned what is at the heart of the theatrical experience.

In the past, experimental groups have tried many innovations: plays without writers, directors, backstage technicians, audio and visual equipment, plays without music, designers, or even costumes. The results of these experiments have made clear that, after all the trappings are taken away, what is left is the essence of theatre:—something that happens only between the player and the audience.

It's what is happening between the player and the audience that the playwright must understand. At the root of that understanding are three premises, each having *action* in common: the plot is subordinate to the action; working on the action itself is the correct approach to characterization; and action on the stage is always in the continuous present tense (the present participle,—*ing*).

As we saw in the opening of both our play and our article, the plot is the simple telling of facts. The audience and the actors follow the tale of the young lover's attempts to win his girl. But they are not mainly concerned with the story-line, since the shape—the genre—already indicates the appropriate ending (some genres, like murder mysteries, are excluded from this comment, as they are usually nothing but plot). The actors must naturally make the story clear, but their main area of concentration, like that of the audience, is on action, both physical and psychological, revealed through the spoken word, which alone supplies the real drama. It is this real drama that brings the audience back to see the play whenever it is performed.

In order to find out what is meant by *action*, let's look in on the playwright as he writes his opening lines. This is his first draft, so he is merely sketching out the necessary facts. As he goes along, he will embellish the characters instinctively, although at the moment he knows very little about them.

He visualizes the curtain's opening and the Lover and his Friend on stage. Let's say the playwright wants the audience to know that there will be a later scene in which the Lover and the girl will meet for the first time. At the moment, he is concentrating only on giving that information. The scene might begin as follows:

LOVER: I've got to see her before she decides to marry that old guy.
FRIEND: Yup.
LOVER: She's visiting her aunt this evening. Let's find a way to bump into her. Accidentally, you might say.
FRIEND: Okay.

Okay. He's got the information across, but it's boring. Usually most of a first draft is written as badly as this. But it doesn't matter. The plot is now on paper and the fun can begin. Perhaps the playwright thinks the first action should come from the Friend, and to find out what that is, he asks a most important question, 'What is the Friend do*ing*?' (Notice the present participle.) *The answer must be on both physical and psychological levels.* What the Friend is doing physically is listen*ing* patiently, or wait*ing* to hear plans, and so on; what he is doing psychologically— another way of asking, What is he experienc*ing*?—might be any number of things. If he's amused, for example, he might be teas*ing*:

**Draft 2:**

LOVER:   I've got to see her before she decides to marry that old guy.

FRIEND:   Almost a necessary preliminary I'd say.

LOVER:   You would, would you? Just listen. She's visiting her aunt this evening, so it shouldn't be too difficult to bump into her.

FRIEND:   Good idea! Let's take the car.

Perhaps the last line was a little too biting for the kind of relationship needed between the two men. However, they were doing something—an improvement. Notice the rewrite of the Lover's dialogue, 'You would, would you? Just listen'. It was a totally spontaneous reaction from a character the playwright wasn't even working on. The Lover simply responded to the Friend's new *psychological action*: teasing.

By now, the playwright is becoming aware that the Lover is entirely too sure of himself for a man in the throes of passion. He decides that maybe it would be better if the Friend had the information about the girl and her aunt (changing the plot). This should help both the Friend's character and the Lover's distraction (changing the physical action). He tries another draft, this time with the Friend advis*ing* and the Lover distractedly attend*ing*:

**Draft 3:**

LOVER:   I can't believe she's going to marry that old guy!

FRIEND:   She will, if you don't get to her first.

LOVER:   Thanks a lot! I don't keep you around to make me miserable.

FRIEND:   I heard a rumour—

LOVER:   Why can't you say something encouraging? . . . What did you say?

FRIEND:   I heard a rumour that she's going to visit her aunt this afternoon.

LOVER:   What good's that to me?

FRIEND:   You could, er, bump into her.

It's better, but not quite satisfactory. The Lover needs to be even more passionate. He should barely heed the Friend at all. This time he will change the Lover's psychological action; he will be agoniz*ing*:

**Draft 4.**

LOVER: I'll hang myself if she marries that senile old duffer! How could she do this to me?

FRIEND: She's never met you.

LOVER: Don't split hairs, you imbecile! Help me.

FRIEND: She's seeing her aunt this evening.

LOVER: Good for her! And while she's doing that I'll be jumping off the roof.

FRIEND: A bit premature. Perhaps you should meet with her first and, if that fails, jump off the roof.

LOVER: Yes, I will. I'll hang myself, and then jump off the roof.

FRIEND: Perhaps we could arrange it for seven o'clock?

LOVER: I'm going to do it now!

FRIEND: I'm speaking about the meeting with what's-her-name.

LOVER: What's that? A meeting? You mean you can arrange a meeting? Oh! once she meets me, she'll change her mind.

And so it goes on. The number of drafts you write is up to you. It pays to bear in mind, however, that the writer who saves time by not working will find that audiences will save time by not coming.

A valuable rule of thumb is to work at the play until you're sick of it. This sounds ridiculous, I know, but you don't really know what you can do until you've reached that stage. When that point is reached depends upon the type of writer you are. Neil Simon says he can write one in a year, Shakespeare seems to have averaged about two a year, Noel Coward could write one over a weekend, while the average for most playwrights seems to be about two years.

Each draft you write contains some residue of the *action* from the preceding drafts. This is why a particularly good play can have so many interpretations. An actor will 'discover' that the Friend is teasing the Lover and will experiment with this action throughout the rehearsals. The result might be that the Friend is more intelligent than the Lover in one production of the play, and more mature in another. But, the actor cannot put anything into the character that you didn't write into him, so the more determined you are to reveal a particular trait in a character, the more you must *concentrate on what he is doing* to reveal that trait.

If we look away from our hypothetical playwright to the works of an acknowledged master, we can see how even a rather banal plot can bring audiences back time and again simply to experience the action.

Take Shakespeare's *Richard III*. Richard wants to be king. That's simple enough, but hardly the stuff that glues you to your seat. The real fascination for the audience is in watching Richard the Game Player in the act of decid*ing* his next wicked move.

Another example from Shakespeare demonstrates how even a silly plot can become a powerfully moving dramatic experience because of the intense physical and psychological action. The story concerns a man who believes a flimsy lie about his wife and kills her without trying to find a reasonable explanation. Only an idiot would believe such a lie, and nothing proves more conclusively than this play that it is character-in-action, not plot, that makes a play work. *Othello* succeeds because Shakespeare focuses so intensely on what a jealous man *does* that his central character becomes a symbol of jealousy itself. At various times during the play Othello is either fight*ing* his own terror, sens*ing* his own torment, indulg*ing* in passion, and so on. The theatre-goer shares in this action, which the actor brings to life through his focus on the continuous present tense.

As Shakespeare needed a *consistent* character from the beginning to the end of the play, so do you. Focus on your character's dominant personality trait so that his every action reveals this trait. Othello is possessed by the devils of jealousy, so we always find him either yield*ing* to or contend*ing* with these devils. This is the essence of his character. In an art form we must necessarily select and stylize the people we create. Concentration by the playwright on one kind of continuous action is a way to get this refinement.

All that's left to say in conclusion is this: don't let a belief that you can't think of anything to write about stop you from writing. Plots are nothing to worry about. If you can't think of one, steal one. There are only 36 anyway! Most of Shakespeare is folk tale. If you're that worried, adapt the basic plot of a short story you like and get it on paper in play form. Then, for as many drafts as possible, concentrate your energies on what each character is doing physically and experiencing psychologically. If the character is a 'thinker', he must be attend*ing* to an idea or a problem almost all the time; if he is emotional, he must be feel*ing* or adapt*ing* his emotions constantly; if he is violent, then he is hat*ing* his enemy or lov*ing* his hatred. Such is the continuous action we come to the theatre to share, because we are all one in the experience of it. If your dialogue ensures that continuous action engages your audience, they will return again and again to your plays.

Gregson Winkfield is a director and playwright. He has written two plays for radio and seven plays for stage, four of which have won awards. He has also published essays on theatre, and poetry. He is currently artistic director of Upper Canada Playhouse in Morrisburg, Ontario.

# Make Dialogue Work for You

*by Don Wetmore*

**A**good textbook on technique can recharge the writing battery ready for ignition. Why not go back to relearn that "dialogue must be faithful to character"... "born on the lips of the moment"... "push the inner and outer action forward"... and similar truths? To interest you in such a semiannual exercise, here are some considerations that first struck me from texts and later were confirmed by drama producers.

Even with exposition, dialogue should have a character-objective, otherwise the bones of the exposition show. Compare "Who's knocking? Who's outside?" with "Who's knocking? Who's outside? We don't let strangers in."

Dialogue must reveal character. Compare "Grandpa's sitting with the hippies" with "Grandpa's sitting with the hippies, of course!" Or "You must have listened to many a burial service," with "Oh, aye—words, words, words."

And dialogue must sound like the characters. Obvious comparison is "I wish John were here" with "Too bad John ain't here." A more subtle comparison is "I'd say so" with "Definitely so." Which sex said which line?

And if a character has dominant traits, bring them out in his or her speech. If you write a full description of a character for your own use, it's surprising how often the description will indicate the kind of speech you need for that character—sometimes telling you the words spoken. I once included in a character description the sentence "She's more than a shrew, she's a fiend." The epithets cropped up and were effectively used several times in the script. And this is a good place to remind you that if you say a character is witty, you'd better make sure that occasionally he says some witty things.

Never pad dialogue. One of its functions is to ensure an adeptness of illumination or communication. Note the better impact when the words in parenthesis are omitted: "(Not yet) But this is monstrous! (How much longer must we wait?) (All the) Volcanoes (in the world) are less eruptive than she! (in a rage)."

However, actors need lines that are rounded out enough for them to modulate. This is very important in radio drama. No actor can do much with "And be in on it, too—you old schemer!" But he'll ring out the noun if it's "And be in on the kill—eh?—you old schemer!" Again— "We agreed" is a dull speech. But— "We agreed, darling, we agreed." has an insistence an actor will appreciate. Compare the sound of "Aha, you're afraid of her" with the sound of "Aha, don't tell me you're afraid of her." And use words that make effective sounds. Compare "Give me time to get my breath" with "Give me a second to catch my breath." This difference may not be as noticeable in fiction as in the theatre or on radio or television, but many fiction addicts "hear" the dialogue they read silently. Don't you?

Beware of hidden tongue-twisters and alliterations. Read your dialogue aloud to check this. How impossible to say naturally: "Since she started, she's stowed away stacks of stamps." Equally impossible if: "I insist that some political analysis can fit this theoretic victory into a development pattern."

Speeches should connect when possible. The following is crude: "People are still searching the ruins. I've lost my son." But a smooth connection improves it: "People are still searching the ruins. I've no need to search anymore. I've lost my son."

Questions and exclamatory phrases have impact. Compare "The water's over the causeway. Look at the waves. The road's gone." with "Look... the waves... over the causeway! Where's the road gone?"

Rhythm and beat don't belong exclusively to music and poetry. Perhaps the following examples explain. The first has no sense of rhythm and no satisfying, conclusive stresses. The second is sharper— has rhythm and punch. Read them aloud.

| | |
|---|---|
| DAVID: | You speak to him and then… |
| ELLEN: | You speak to him. I won't be here. |
| DAVID: | You stay where you are. Why won't you be here? |
| ELLEN: | I'm going away. I'm leaving you both. |

| DAVID: | Just speak to him! |
| ELLEN: | You speak to him. I won't be here. |
| DAVID: | Why? Where are you going? |
| ELLEN: | I'm leaving you both. |

Keep the dialogue natural-sounding. Don't get clever or colorful too often or your dialogue will remain a mere ornament. Avoid any taint of the literary. Oscar Wilde and Bernard Shaw got away with it, but they were writers of their time and you're a writer of your time. Today a convincing reality is the essential quality. The most serious criticism you can have is that your dialogue sounds contrived. How can you be sure? Study the dialogue of writers of merit. And listen, listen, to other people's talk. In time your ear will get attuned and won't fail you. Don't worry that the colloquial might cheapen your work. Dialogue must sound real. Compare "So that's why money figures in delaying your marriage" with "Oh, that's it—why you won't marry. Money!"

Yet, dialogue can strengthen style. It can be an aspect of style—provided that basically it sounds real for the theme, the setting, the time, the characters, and the purpose of the play or story. Think of Henry James, Conrad, Hemingway, J. M. Barrie, Ionesco, Neil Simon. And why not Shakespeare?

After noting all of the above, you'll likely now want to avoid dialogue. If you're a playwright, you can't. If you write fiction, that would be a pity. Writing dialogue is a special obligation—and enjoyable because it's often delightfully overwhelmed by mood yet responds satisfyingly to carpentry and polish.

Dialogue is the only way in which your characters can communicate the essence and vitality of their personalities. So, when characters begin to assert themselves—begin to demand to be heard—they'll force you to use dialogue. Be grateful to them, and have a good time.

Don Wetmore (1907-01-23 to 1992-09-07) was a Nova Scotia playwright, actor, director, musician and educator. He was founder of the Nova Scotia Drama League, founding member of the Writer's Federation of Nova Scotia, and National President of the Canadian Authors Association. All of Don Wetmore's 26 plays were produced, and several chronicled Nova Scotia history.

# The Workshop's the Thing

*by Robert Shipley* _____

I f you are already writing plays for the Neptune Theatre in Halifax, The Playwright's Co-op in Montreal, Toronto's Passe Muraille, or Edmonton's Citadel, we congratulate you. But if, like most aspiring playwrights, you are looking for a chance to try out your ideas, you might want to consider workshops.

For a writer, the advantages of the workshop approach are manifold. While experienced playwrights have already developed a sense of the way the dialogue sounds, how the pacing works, and the possibilities of handling a critical moment in the plot, the beginner has to learn what works and what doesn't.

For a writer who has just the outline of a story, the process of building up the texture of the drama is even more challenging. In a workshop, a writer solicits the help of a group of people to cooperate in playmaking.

And not least of all considerations, workshops can be a way for developing dramatists to make some money on the way to future fame and fortune.

Workshops, of course, are not for everyone. If you are going to ask others to participate in your work you have to be willing to let them both criticize and make suggestions. That, after all, is the reason they're there. Workshops are no place for overly sensitive writers who are very protective of their work. Such writers will end up alone with their plays and can make all the final decisions about form and content. In the workshop phase however there has to be open season on ideas.

Whom can writers entice into this kind of volatile creative cauldron? It could be a group of friends, actors and other writers who want to trade the favor around. While they have expertise to offer, these people also have their own well developed ideas about staging, dialogue and so on. The cauldron could end up with too many cooks in a stew.

A better suggestion is to work with less opinionated people who have fresh imaginations: students! Classes of senior elementary or high school students are not mere substitutes for real actors but are creative allies in their own right.

Now this is also where making money comes into the picture. If the potential benefits to the students can be sold to school boards, the mutual gains multiply.

Where drama is being taught as a subject, the teachers may welcome the opportunity for their classes to see a work in progress and to participate in its creation. Where the subject matter of the writer's play relates to the curriculum—history, law, family studies, or civics, for example— the chance for the students to role-play can enrich their studies. Many provincial arts agencies and school boards have funds and programs for bringing artists into schools. It is through such programs that writers may turn their experimentation into paying work.

The actual techniques of workshopping are limited only by imagination. A few basic starting points can be given but it is up to each practitioner to develop a modus operandi. If a working script has been completed, the writer can simply give it to the workshop participants and let them run with it while he or she observes, makes notes, and perhaps suggests new directions from time to time. In a more structured situation, the writer might actually have alternate scripts or might rewrite on the spot.

Where only an idea and outline have been completed, improvisation is the basic method. Here the writer explains the situation and perhaps the characterization, and then lets the participants make up the play as they go. This is particularly exciting for students who are learning about the subject involved. An aspect of the writer's play might concern racism. The students would be asked to do some background reading and then play the parts of, say, a minority-group landlord dealing with a white anglophone tenant. The results, as was said at the beginning, can be volatile but the process is certainly exciting.

In the workshop approach writers must remember two important things. First, they have to be in control and know where they are going. Ironically it takes a good deal of preparation to plan spontaneity. The writer has to have plenty of ideas and research material to feed into the boiling pot of the workshop or the participants will lose interest. The second important factor is for the writer to be able to recognize relevant ideas as they unfold within the group and encourage them to develop. What might start as horseplay among exuberant boys might be the germ of some very effective stage business. An off-hand comment might become a classic line.

For some great inspiration on the subject of workshop theatre have a look at the video *Listening to the Wind*. It features the work of James Reaney, one of Canada's greatest playwrights and a pioneer in theatre workshops. The video is available from Lockwood Film & Video, 365 Ontario, London, ON N5W 3W6 Phone (519) 434-6006, and was made for Vision TV in 1997 by Mark McCurdy and Nancy Johnson.

For the aspiring but not-yet-recognized playwright, workshops can be a proving ground for untried ideas, a learning experience, and a source for that elusive cash that keeps us all going.

Robert Shipley has published several books on Canadian history. He returned to university in 1990 to study and teach urban issues. His is also active in the local community in the Waterloo Region of Ontario.

# Resurrect Your Kinfolk

*by Don Wetmore*

Have you a folk lode to mine? I wasn't blessed with colorful kinfolk, but at least there was Great Great Great Grandfather, and I expect he belongs in a book. He came over in the mid-1700s and cleared a farm. He also cleared himself with three maidens and wed them—one at a time, of course. With their considerable help he produced 28 children, and we've spread around since then, for better or worse. In his will he left a cow to his eldest daughter— "she being already married and disposed of." I expect that if his book gets written, it should be from the viewpoints of the three wives, and include the thoughts of the daughter—after the cow died.

Mainly I've re-created folks of the past through drama. And, like any other writer, I've met them by mining the lode of village, town, and county histories, memoirs, family papers, genealogies. I've tried plays about big historical figures but they've always finished with a dull thud, while the ones about ordinary folks, and written for ordinary folks in the audience, have been rewarding.

I devised one play for the bicentennial committee of a town in Nova Scotia. Another was first a radio play and then expanded for a local theatre group to stage. They both opened my eyes. I found out that modern audiences can be completely nostalgic about people like themselves who lived before them, and that they warmly identify with them. I also discovered a wealth of fascinating characters buried in old records.

The bicentennial play called for long research, much dull reading. Then I started to visualize. These people lived; they felt emotion; they went through crises. Where are the hints of this? In time the stories came out from behind the statistics, from behind brief mentions in memoirs. I began to see what might live again when put into drama.

I read, for instance, that the leading 1765 settler built a jail in the cellar of his house, and the first occupant was his young grandson for stealing apples—surely a pleasant scene if Grandma is on hand to defend the culprit. Grandfather's son was a rebel and he called his apple-minded child George Washington, then he left Nova Scotia for the independent States. Grandfather brought up the boy, changed his name to George William, and in time the young man was offered a seat in the British House of Commons. Such are the dramatic whims of fate that tantalize a writer.

I find delights in footnotes, one of which briefly mentions that the village caught fire on a Sunday morning from some carelessness in Mistress Gogan's kitchen while she was churning. The reverend preacher regretfully dismissed his congregation as the flames licked the church steeple, but was heard to remark as they went out that he wondered why Mistress Gogan was churning when she should have been sitting in her pew. Could a writer ask for a luckier hint of character? The descendants of this determined gentleman, watching him impersonated on the stage, responded gleefully.

I keep imagining how it might have been. An old record tells me that an entire family clan of twenty-eight people all came on one ship. Nothing new here—but then look at their arrival date—December 23— snow, ice cold; I wonder what happened. So I set up a kindly neighbor, hysterical at the thought of housing more than two dozen souls in her small cabin; place the little candlelit room far over on one side of the stage and the deep snow and forest gleaming in the moonlight across the rest of the stage expanse—and then they appear in twos and threes, stumbling, sliding, laughing, the children singing carols, and the tiny warm space gets more and more crowded, people sit on each other, the walls bulge, and the hostess collapses.

Ripples of consoling pleasure run through the modern audience watching, especially among the women.

I start seeking clues in ages, tabulating the "begats" and looking beyond the perpetual "was born in": "Matthew Archibald was born in 1747." Eighteen pages farther on: "Janet Fisher was born in 1750." Thirty-three pages later: "Matthew Archibald married Janet Fisher in 1767 and their children were born in ...." With patient arithmetic I discover that Matthew was twenty when he married, and Janet only seventeen—then find that the spirited lad went off by ship to claim his girl in New Hampshire and brought her back on the return trip. So what kind of a reception do they get? The whole village turns out, of course. And the young men of Matthew's age make an arch of their flintlocks above the gangplank, and as the young couple walk under it they pull the triggers, bang-bang, and all the children scream and run and cover their ears and the musician starts a song and the older folks dance; and the curtain comes down—satisfactorily—on Act One, all due to arithmetic.

Or am I faced with the moment when at last the courier comes with the official deeds for the settlers' lands—the moment they have been waiting for. I know I must have the names read out—that's what this commemorative play is about. But I dread the scene—the dull reading of more than forty names of the original grantees who founded the town. I have the courier stand on a stump, and put a spotlight on him and dim the other lights, and then pray—will it come off? But it does. The modern audience of descendants hushed—expectant—waiting to hear their names called, or the names of their neighbors. And all realize that drama and life abide together.

Then, finally, the deaths. Where do I start selecting? For, of course, they all died.

These scenes of action are valid. Because they happened or could have happened that way, they come off believably. The people, too, seem real and identifiable. When we watch them, we say, "They were very like us."

In a play, of course, the people must talk. Regrettably little is recorded of anything that was talked about, or how. I sighed before tackling the memoir on which I based the second folk play. There was not a line of dialogue in it. I could skip the research—it was all there—but nobody spoke! So I kept thinking of the people—of the characters—and the more strongly I visualized them as the author recalled them, the more easily I heard their voices. They asserted their own way of speaking. They began to use the vocabulary and the phrasing they might have used. They composed their own dialogue.

The memoir recalled Cape Breton rural life in 1902. The people were Scottish, and the author loved them for their virtues and their foibles. He depicted them clearly, forcefully. He adored his grandfather; he described him as a staunch upright Catholic. One day a wealthy cousin came to visit. Grandfather lost no time in reminding the cousin that it is easier for a camel to pass through the eye of a needle than for a rich man to enter the kingdom of heaven.

I had to put this in speech. Here, then is what Grandfather composed for me.

> And don't think to say that the needle which Christ meant was but a hole in the wall of Jerusalem whereby a small camel could go through it—or a large one if it was stoopin'. Christ said—an ordinary needle! Mother—bring me yer strawberry

cushion needle. We'll show this heathen that naught but a thread can enter without strain an eye such as that. I do not approve of men like you, Cousin Aleck, and I think it iss pity, indeed, that you need.

Village conversation at that time was bound to touch on the new interest in science. The memoir specifically mentions Marconi and Bell. Something like this might have been heard across a dinner table:

And I haff been told, Mr. MacNeil, that the Eyetalian Marconi over to Glace Bay hass been tryin' out a machine he calls a wireless. It sends messages through the sky in little balls o' fire from vessel to vessel across the ocean .... For that matter, our Professor Bell at Baddeck hass wanted to put a machine into the air to make it fly. As if God meant men to fly .... He hass also been experimentin' with sheep's teats—they say he wants to improve the breed. Why should a sheep haft only one or two lambs, why not three or four? It will depend on the teats, thinks the professor. He iss a very great man, that Dr. Bell, inventin' sheep's teats and telephones.

Every village had its fey crone, and Old Betsey is recalled lovingly. It is easy to give her dialogue; she was a storm in petticoats; her speech would reflect this. One of her weirdest fancies was that she had a treasure of gold in the gulch back of her little house. But at night, with a great noise, the evil fairies stole from it. Of course the fairies were the village children tormenting her. But she never failed to appear—angry, outraged—standing above the gulch, roaring down at their darting shadows, and venting a lovely theatrical curse:

Damn ye imps o' Satan! Ye robbers an' ye thieves—ye bogies an' warlocks! Get awa' from me gold! I heard ye de night—wid yer tappin' an' scrapin'—yer shuffles an' yer crowbars! I calls down de wrath o' Mary Mother o' God on yer evil schemes! May Satan tak' ye back ta where ye come from—and God damn ye ta Hell's eternal fire an' de flames that'll burn ye alive fereffer!

Or you are impressed by what Grandmother stored in her larder. You stage a ceilidh—a Highland frolic. In the midst of festivities Grandmother will stop, stricken by apprehension, and you characterize her almost in one speech, as she ticks off on her fingers:

Ooo, now, ooo... haff we enough for all? Boiled herrin' and mackerel... hot sodabread and molasses... Queen puddin' and Cabinet puddin' and custard puddin' and curds... pound cake and oatmeal cookies... and a side o' mutton in the barrel. There's hot tay on the hob for all events. Aye, ye—we haff enough. Come—eat!

This has been a way of mining the folk lode, and perhaps suggests one to you—a way to cope with action and speech. The real events that happened, or might have happened, have the drama of life in them. The characters, because they lived, can be clear enough to tell you how they might have talked.

They were real people; they were like us. It's sad to leave them silent—buried under the forgotten pages of family records and genealogies. They could come alive again—in vignettes, short stories, novels, plays, or poetry. What they ask from the creative writer is just the warmth and humanity they lived by—and a matching imagination.

Don Wetmore (1907-01-23 to 1992-09-07) was a Nova Scotia playwright, actor, director, musician and educator. He was founder of the Nova Scotia Drama League, founding member of the Writer's Federation of Nova Scotia, and National President of the Canadian Authors Association. All of Don Wetmore's 26 plays were produced, and several chronicled Nova Scotia history.

# Questions the Artistic Director Will Ask About Your Script!

*By Fred Walker*

## Does it have an interesting title?

Believe it or not, this really matters. Don't count on the poster—it will just say "X, a drama by Y. March 14-17. Tickets $20." Ask yourself: If I saw this title on a marquee, would I lay down 20 bucks and go in?

### How Long Is It?

I am astounded by the number of budding playwrights who have never bothered to estimate the running time of their show. A one-act play should run between 30 and 50 minutes. A full-length play should be "two hours traffic of the stage." If you've written a three hour play, you'd better be Shakespeare. And if you've written a 90 minute play, the audience may glance at their watches and wonder if they got their money's worth. One act plays are often entered in drama festivals, where each company is given one hour total, including putting up and striking the set. Anything longer than 50 minutes is, therefore, impractical. And there is simply no market for a 15 minute play. Use it for kindling. To estimate running time, assume one and one-half minutes of acting per page. Better yet, read your script aloud with a watch in your hand.

### How many sets do we have to build?

If the answer is one, and if the set you describe sounds cheap and easy to construct, your play will almost certainly get read. It is often difficult to find excuses for everybody to keep coming into the same room. One way around this problem is to design an abstract set, which depends on the audience's imagination to take them anywhere from London to Thebes.

## How many actors? How many women?

Professional companies want plays with small casts, since they have to pay the actors. An amateur theatre generally wants a cast of six or eight. If your cast size is in double digits, your play is unlikely to be produced.

See if all those minor characters are really necessary. A phone call can take the place of a messenger. Or maybe your doctor character can also "dabble" in oil painting. If several of your characters never meet, actors can double up on roles.

Please write decent roles for women. Play after play has either no female parts at all, or two: a bitch, and the pretty girl who gets saved by the hero. Any play with a cast of six, including three or four strong women, will get read.

## What about music?

I am truly astounded by the number of playwrights who include stage directions like, "enter the cast, singing *I'm Getting Married in the Morning*". You can't do this. You can't use music without obtaining permission from the creator or an appropriate licensing agency.

## Does it have a plot?

Remember Aristotle's definition of drama as characters in *action*. Something has to happen. People will ask the artistic director what the play "is about". He doesn't want to say "it's about life", or "it's a personal piece", or "it's non-linear self-expression". He wants to say "it's a comedy", or "it's a murder mystery". It's hard to sell a play that consists of characters preaching at the audience.

## Is it offensive?

Nudity is never appropriate on stage. Got that? Never. Violence may be necessary in a war story or murder mystery. Most artistic directors now understand that realistic dialogue often includes swearing. But every audience includes three or four people who will stand up and walk out if they hear even one swear word.

Racism and sexism will only fly if it is clear that the point of the play is to mock the idiocy of the racist or sexist character.

## Does it require any special effects?

A good play should depend on script and acting, not falling chandeliers. Modern over-protective fire regulations can forbid an actor to light a cigar, or enter a dark room with a lit candle. It is easier to buy a real gun to kill somebody than it is to get permission to use a fake gun in a play. If your play does not have any special effects, it will get read.

## Is it any good?

Please notice that this is the *last* question any artistic director asks. Never count on mere quality to get your play a fair reading. If it is impossible to stage on a reasonable budget, and if it is 10 pages long, it will not get read.

Dr. Frederick Walker has been involved in theatre for many years, as an actor, director, artistic director, and that guy who tears your ticket at the door. He has written two published plays, *The Roswell File* (about ufos) and *I Love My Work* (about Jack the Ripper). He has also written a number of performed but unpublished children's plays, and has served on the executive of the Gloucester Players. He is currently writing sketch comedy for television.

# Write Theatre and Arts Reviews

*by Michael Lasser*

R eviewing theatre and arts performances for a newspaper means you have to be opinionated, outspoken, and disciplined—on demand—especially if you're writing as a freelancer for a daily newspaper. Deadlines require you to do your best work quickly and to length, without much opportunity to polish. You don't get to bed until you're finished, and you rarely start to write much before 11:00 p.m. or midnight. At least some of the time, the presses downstairs are waiting for you to finish before they turn out tomorrow's first edition.

In other words, I'm talking about being a reviewer rather than a critic. Criticism is more considered and more leisurely, and lets you wear your learning a little more heavily. A review is a pointed first response based on what you just saw, enriched by your knowledge of the field and your ability to write confidently and vividly on command. You don't need to convince a single reader, but every reader needs to understand what you thought. Sometimes you'll find you've changed your mind three or four days later. Too late. By then, you've moved on to the next opening.

If you have the right temperament and a sufficient body of information about one of the arts, reviewing can be exhilarating. It can also provide something approaching a steady, though hardly a lavish, second income. Best of all, you get to write about something you love, and you know a wide audience will read it. You go to the theatre without paying (either the ticket will be complimentary or your newspaper will pay for it), you get one of the best seats in the house, and then somebody pays you to say what you think. Did I hear somebody whisper the word "racket"?

You even have the pleasure and occasional irritation of knowing that people are taking what you write very seriously. I've had my dinner interrupted in a restaurant by a stranger who went to see a play because I liked it. She hated it. Despite that woman's assault, writing reviews is liberating for the simple reason that you really don't have to be right.

Sometimes getting hired is harder than doing the work. Most of the time, regular staff members write most of the reviews, even on a suburban weekly. But one writer may not be able to handle all the new movies or art openings. If you notice more than one person writing a single kind of review, your local paper may be ready to add a freelance writer.

There's a trade-off here. There are more movies than dance recitals, for example, and larger audiences for movies than dance. There are also more people who can write about the movies. If your field is film, you'll have more competition but also more work to divide up between you. Dance is the opposite—but at least you'll probably have the field to yourself.

To get started, you should have an area of the arts about which you are both knowledgeable and enthusiastic. One without the other won't do. You're probably going to be writing for a readership that numbers in the tens of thousands or more, and you don't want to be caught with your ignorance showing.

Since you're not writing for *The New York Times* with its seemingly unlimited space and highly sophisticated readership, don't use it as a model for your reviews. Look in your own city's paper, and other similar cities' as well, to find some good reviews. What makes them good? What combination of style, opinion, clarity and organization works best? Do you know where the reviewer stood? Do you know why? Did the review have a point of view? How long are the reviews? What can you learn from them about completeness and conciseness?

Once you've thought about what makes a review good, attend some performances or exhibits. Then go straight home to write the reviews. Don't go to bed until you finish. You need to be able to work well when you're tired and under pressure. Practise.

Once you've written and polished a number of reviews within the space of a few weeks, send copies with a cover letter to your paper's features editor, explaining what you want to do, summarizing your qualifications, and saying you'll call for an appointment. Date the reviews so that the editor can see how you work under several deadlines at the same time.

For some reviewers, writing the review actually begins in the theatre. I dare not trust my memory of what I'm seeing. I cling to my program and my three-by-five-inch spiral notebook for dear life. I make one brief note to a page, scrawled quickly in the dark. During intermission, I go over my notes and expand on them briefly so that I don't forget what they mean. I also try to set a theme for the review by the end of the first act. It may change—there's another act to see—but I want to have a tentative frame of reference within which I'll be watching that second act.

Generally, you write about the play first and then the performers and technical people. But it's also true that your opening should try to take both the play and the production into account. It's not essential to organize this way, but most reviews do, for the simple reason that it works.

Here is the opening sentence of a review:

"Though it starts with a married couple reaching climax in the dark—not your typical TV fare—the first act of Robert Shaffron's *Survival of the Fittest* turns out to be little more than a sitcom for grownups."

This is a good opening, I believe, because it establishes a theme and point of view immediately, it is direct and attention-getting, and it is as much a newspaper lead as it is a statement of opinion.

Here's a review that breaks the rules because it is for a one-man show featuring an actor whose range and vitality made him more important than the play:

"Gregary Harrison is a dynamo, a non-stop parade that shuffles, swishes, and stampedes its way across the Downstairs Cabaret Theatre's stage in his one-man show, *Big Wind on Campus*."

For a recent production of *As You Like It*, I realized that while I would have preferred a more sophisticated approach to the play, the company was trying to reach a broad audience. I had to review the production on those terms while still suggesting my own preferences. For my second paragraph, I wrote:

"Rochester's first professional performance of Shakespeare in 13 years is exuberant and rambunctious rather than witty or thoughtful. It's more interested in the play's rampant theatricality than its alternately buoyant and pungent language. Though some of the cast's younger actors struggle with Elizabethan English, their vitality fits the high jinks that director Eberle Thomas has devised for them..."

Too many reviewers fall into the trap of plot summary. You can't ignore the story but that's not why people are reading you. A broad, even incomplete summation will do. If you haven't mentioned the production somewhere early in the review, you might be writing too much about plot, and not enough about what you thought.

As a reviewer, you're not all that different from every other theatre-goer—caught up in the play, wanting to love it—but another part of you has to be evaluating what's going on at the same time. Some people learn the trick easily; some never do. If you're one of those who can, you possess the reviewer's temperament.

Now go convince an editor.

Michael Lasser is the theatre reviewer for the Rochester Democrat & Chronicle. His nationally-syndicated public radio program, Fascinatin' Rhythm, won a 1994 George Foster Peabody Award. He writes about the performing and visual arts for a wide range of national and regional magazines – ranging from *American Legion* to *American Scholar.*

# Transformation—a Writer's Greatest Act of Magic

*by Sheldon Oberman* _____

ere's a great exercise for a writer: Take something you've written—something good or maybe not so good—and try it in a new medium. Turn a poem into a radio script, turn a narrative into a dramatic monologue or try reworking a short story into a film treatment or a play. You may discover its true form. You may also discover a new field for your creativity. At the very least, the exercise may give you insights for the next draft of your story.

As writers we need to keep playing with the form of things. All art is transformation. We reshape reality by turning experiences into books, plays, poems. I learned this best when I joined a theatre group and we were given drama exercises: mime, improvisation—constantly creating new characters, new situations, new worlds without end. It was great training for writing.

I learned to turn stories into plays as a school teacher with my students. Some of my friends learned by creating skits as camp counsellors. Often we used stories we had written, sometimes we just improvised with a rough sketch.

Recently I had to learn the art of transformation in a fuller way when I was commissioned to turn my published children's story into a script for the stage. In *The Always Prayer Shawl*, Adam receives a prayer shawl from his grandfather as a boy. It changes just as he does, until years later he passes it on to his own grandson. Based on my grandfather's life, the story described a life cycle and the transmission and transformation of Jewish tradition.

Turning a 1,000-word book into sixty pages of dramatic action and dialogue—well, that was, as they say, another story altogether. However, your future film, radio or play script may begin with a simple story no longer than a 1,000-word children's book. Scripts, with an even shorter "treatment," are often first hawked by a writer.

Try this at home: Dramatize a scene from your short story, novel or narrative poem. Remove yourself so that you are no longer translating or interpreting or explaining the story and the people in it. Cut everything away but the characters' words and actions.

The set is minimal—a mere suggestion will do; let your imagined director take care of it. The atmosphere will be set later with some clever lighting, a bit of music and sound effects, so don't be concerned about that either. Let the characters loose to express themselves by themselves. And if you have to be in the story as the narrator, then make yourself a character as well. The voices and actions may seem weak and awkward at first but they will become stronger and more vital with time and exercise. Try a single scene for a start.

For my part, I had to write many new scenes. I only had two with any dialogue or detailed action in my original story. I also needed a second character as a balance and contrast. That turned out to be Miriam, a firebrand social activist who challenged Adam and also loved and married him. There was a central "prop" with its symbolism and transformative power: the prayer shawl. Most of this was only briefly indicated in the original story. Much was developed from scratch.

In other words, to dramatize a simple storyline one needs many, many other words and actions. This does not have to be done alone. You may have organizations in your area to help you. In my case, once the local community theatre group to which I had submitted my story commissioned me to rewrite it as a play, it turned out that the local playwrights' organization had a grant to provide me with a mentor. The mentor was terrific, as were others whom I approached for advice and support. A year down the line, I had a working script and a week-long workshop with five actors, a director and a technical person. I did rewrites every night until my play was performed to a small test audience. Once it was solid, it had a professional début.

Even as I write this, a local playwrights' group is running a Sunday afternoon drop-in for anyone who has a script and wants to share it with other writers. Some people at that table haven't anything more than a couple of sketched-out scenes. There are a few empty chairs—maybe one for you.

Transferring your skills to film, radio and video is not as difficult as you might think. There are courses available, but there are also chances to try out "on the ground floor" without great pressures. I got to write a ten-minute script for a local film co-op. Writer friends of mine created stories for a video co-op. My first film was based on a story that wasn't very good on paper but was almost okay on film. (We had a better time making it than anyone had watching it.) The people who gave us our "breaks" were also amateurs—film and video makers who could produce or run the technical end but were not writers. Some had stories that needed shaping, others just had a camera, film and a crew all waiting for "Action!" There is probably a notice on a co-op bulletin board right now for a volunteer writer willing to join some motley crew. You might have a story they'd be happy to try out.

Did anything come of our films and videos? Nothing to impress Hollywood, but it gave new life to my writing, and some of those friends eventually became professionals in the industry.

Similarly, I learned to write for radio when CBC advertised a contest to join a week-long course training writers. Radio producers are always willing to read someone's treatment.

These media have plenty of technically skilled people but are often short on writers. However, don't expect to be paid in advance and in the cases of co-ops, don't expect anything but a share of the doughnuts during the shoot.

Transforming your written story into another medium can help you grow as a writer. It's a fresh form for your talents. If I had originally written the story as a play I'd have been just as challenged to turn it into an children's book. I learned a lot about writing for the stage. I also learned about writing more dramatically for the page. Most of all I relearned something about this work we are all in. We may separate ourselves into specialties such as poetry or prose or scriptwriting, but first of all we are "at play" as artists.

And if we are playing—we can play at any game we want.

Sheldon Oberman is a writer, film maker and storyteller. Among his ten books are *The Always Prayer Shawl*, an award winning children's book and *This Business With Elijah*, set in Winnipeg's North End. He travels extensively, speaking and giving workshops on writing out of personal and family experiences.

# Write for Radio

*by Alex Mair* _____

T here are two reasons why you might consider writing for radio. There is a market out there that you might be able to tap. There are also some aspects to writing for radio that are marvellous lessons applicable to any field of writing you might wish to explore. Let's look at the market situation first.

To discover where you might sell your material in your area, listen to the radio in your area. That's sounds simplistic, true, but it's amazing what you can learn by doing just that. You might find that one of your local stations has a seasonal program dealing with outdoor living. Have you got a favourite technique for making a hole in the ice when you're ice fishing? Have you developed a way to get a beginner up on water skiis for the first time? Do you know more about good picnic spots in your area than the host does on this show?

That's just one example, and the idea behind suggesting it was to get you to listen, really listen, to what the stations in your community are carrying. And more important, what they are buying from freelancers.

One more thought on the market situation. Don't just listen for what they are buying now. Think about what they should be buying to make their programs more interesting and informative for listeners like you.

There was a day when Canadian radio, with the exception of the CBC, consisted of a mellow-voiced host who introduced records and read the news. Not any more. Television is an entertainment medium, and radio is growing more informational in nature all the time.

Think about it. This might just be the market for you.

Now you have started thinking about writing for radio, let's explore some of the techniques that will make your material saleable.

If you talk to program producers, or anyone working regularly in the industry, they will all make roughly the same comment. They will tell you in their own way, that people don't write the way they talk. In radio, this isn't just important—it's vital.

You're not quite sure what this means? Listen to a typical newscast. The portion prepared by the news writers is recognizable. The style flows, is conversational. Then they cut to a voice clip from someone, and all too often, the person being interviewed sounds stiff, uncomfortable, and perhaps a bit preachy. Just because they have a microphone in front of them doesn't mean that they have to use big words and long sentences.

### Write for the ear.

A wise editor once said that there was a big difference between writing for the eye and writing for the ear. This may be a tricky point to explain, but we had best try, because it's very important.

**Read your material out loud.** You have to breathe, and if you have introduced a long, clumsy sentence, you're going to find it. And having found it, you can fix it.

**Use lots of punctuation.** A voice that makes pleasant listening is a voice with lots of expression. When you're writing your script, those punctuation marks are your way of putting the expression down on paper. Then, when you're delivering the material, the punctuation marks are your reminders for the expression you want built into it.

**Use alliteration.** It sounds good, and a good sound is what you're after. "The portion prepared by the news writers…" has a ring to it, in contrast with "the copy written by someone in the news department".

**Sound as though you're enjoying yourself.** The next time you have some friends in, try an experiment. Have people take turns turning their backs to the group and reading the same paragraph from a paper or a magazine twice. With one of the readings, tell them to smile. For the other reading, tell them to frown, but not let anyone know which is which. You'll be surprised. Without fail you can tell when the readers are smiling their way through the paragraph. This little trick can be of use in any speaking situation. Try it—use it—it's a dandy suggestion.

### Avoid potential problems.

Up to now we've been dealing with a list of "do's". Now for a short list of "don'ts."

**Don't use objectionable language.** Objectionable means in bad taste. If you don't know what bad taste is, you're in trouble.

**Don't use slang.** Having said that, I will confuse the situation by saying use slang if it fits the idiom. It can add credibility to what you're saying. If you're making a reference to a remark made by a teen-ager across the supper table, think about the way teen-agers talk. You may be drawing their attention to the need for a haircut, and the response is going to be—"Cool it." Teen-agers don't say, "Approach the question of the length of my hair with a measure of caution." Cool it is slang, true, but it fits. It sounds right.

**Don't fuss over things that have been talked to death already**. Look for something fresh, different, new. And we're all looking for something optimistic, happy, or funny, whether we realise it or not. Keep that in mind when you're casting about for ideas.

**Don't use a stereotyped opening.** How many times have you heard someone say, "And that reminds me of a funny story." And what do you do? You stop listening, don't you. The seven deadliest words on radio or television? "And now a word from our sponsor."

If you were a producer looking over manuscripts for Christmas stories and you came across one that began, "I will never forget that December night, thirty-two years ago, when my brothers and sisters and I trooped through the thigh deep snow and the twenty-seven below temperatures for the whole three mile hike to the church hall for my very first Christmas concert, and…"

And that's about as far as the producer is going to read, too.

**Let the listener do a little of the work.** Paint the mental picture, of course, but let the listener fill in some of the details. "The Schoolboys Band was on parade, and I marched along with my bass drum strapped to my chest. Filled with pride, yes, but couldn't see a thing ahead of me over the top of the drum. And at that point, Herbie Dofka, a clarinet player who was marching in front of me, dropped his music book and did what anybody else would do He stopped, and bent down to pick it up." And you hold it right there. Every listener fills in their own ending, and they'll love you for it.

**Don't neglect the other four senses.** And at the same time, show 'em, don't tell 'em!

You could say that your wife yelled from the kitchen, asking you to take out the trash. But wouldn't it have more impact if you said, "My wife parted her delicate lips, and in a voice easily audible in Mazatlan, suggested I take out the garbage because the canary was starting to gag."

### Really listen.

And finally, let's get back to the matter of listening, really listening. It's the best way to improve your appreciation of technique, and at the same time it's a great way to sharpen your appreciation of the market. If you want to find out what CBC radio is buying, listen to what CBC radio is using. It's just that simple.

For a change of pace and a great learning experience, go down to the basement and dig out some of those old 33 1/3 rpm record albums of the great stand-up comics of 35 years ago, Bill Cosby, Bob Newhart, and Phyllis Diller and listen to them with your new set of ears. When Newhart is paying tribute to the driving instructor, you're there in the seat beside him. When Cosby gets his tonsils out, you're in the next bed. Be aware of the amount of work they leave *you* to do, listen to their delivery, their pacing, their phrasing, and learn.

It's fun.

Alex Mair's writing and voice was heard twice daily on CBC radio local and network programs, including Radio International from Montreal, from the late 1960s until 1981. He then wrote a daily newspaper column for five years. He continues to write and narrate a local history item on CBC AM out of Edmonton on a weekly basis.

# Children and Young Adults

# Write for Children and Young Adults

*by Karleen Bradford* ———————

Y ou want to write, and figure writing for children would be the easiest way to start, right? Wrong. Unless you specifically want to write for young people, don't bother trying. Writing children's and young adult fiction is not an easier version of writing for adults. It's just as demanding, requires just as much work, and just as much talent and commitment. Madeleine L'Engle believes emphatically that if a book is not good enough for adults, it's certainly not good enough for children. (And if you don't know who Madeleine L'Engle is, run, don't walk to your nearest library or bookstore and pick up *A Wrinkle In Time*, then go on from there to the rest of her books.)

Basically, a children's book is a book like any other, the only difference being that the story is told through the viewpoint of a young person, rather than an adult. I once had a skeptical and slightly patronizing person ask me, "Why in the world would a thirteen-year-old who can read at an adult level want to read a kids' book?" I answered, "Because a thirteen-year-old doesn't always want to read about adults. Sometimes they want to read about people their own age, with their own interests and problems."

So, you begin with a sincere desire to write for young people. (And by "write" I mean tell stories to children, not instruct them, or teach them, or try to pass on moral concepts to them. Some of these things may happen in a good, well-told tale, but that's not the purpose, and if it is, the normal kid will spot it in an instant and your book is toast.)

Then, if you haven't done so already, you read as much as you possibly can of the kind of book that you want to write. Learn who the best writers for children and young adults are, and read, read, read them. If it's not a joy to do this, you're not a children's writer. Find something else. I once asked a would-be writer for children in one of my writing classes what children's books she had read.

"Oh, I don't read children's books," she replied.

"How in the world do you expect to write children's literature if you don't read it?" I asked.

She didn't get it, and dropped out of the course the next week.

I don't believe in rules for writing, but here's a rule anyway: Don't write down to children. Use the same vocabulary, the same tone, and the same intelligence that you would if you were writing for adults. If Beatrice Potter can say that "the effect of eating too much lettuce is 'soporific'", (*The Tale of the Flopsy Bunnies*), you can use most of the big words you know. If you feel some word is really too unusual, try to clarify it in the context of what is going on in your story.

I can't resist putting in another rule: No cute, talking animals. Break this rule if you wish. *Watership Down* is a perfect example of what can happen if you do, but if you do break it, make sure your manuscript is as good as *Watership Down*.

We are not talking here about picture books. Picture books are another whole kettle of fish, and in some ways are more aligned to poetry than prose fiction. Picture books often do have cute little talking animals, but again, if you're going to do that, make sure you have stories that are as good and as original as the *Franklin* books by Paulette Bourgeois. Picture books are not easier to write than full-length books. In many ways they are much harder. Granted they have fewer words, but every single word is a polished gem that is absolutely necessary to the story. If writing a picture book is your goal, again, read as many as you can. Read them aloud to any children you can corral, and see which ones work and which ones don't. Figure out why they do or don't. And read books about writing picture books. There is no formula for the stories, heaven forbid, but there is a formula for the presentation, length, etc., and you should know this. And don't have your daughter or your best friend illustrate it. With very few exceptions, this will be the kiss of death for your manuscript. Picture book illustration is an art all its own, with its own rules, and publishers usually deal with artists whose work they know. By submitting artwork with your story, you're just giving an editor an extra possible reason for rejecting it.

Now, enough of rules and don'ts. Here's what you will need to write a manuscript that will knock the socks off an editor.

First of all: characters that are real people, not two-dimensional paper dolls. Get to know your characters as well as you know your own children, or yourself. If you don't have a supply of young people of your own, spend time with nieces or nephews, or children of friends.

Volunteer at your local school or library. Eavesdrop and observe. Know how your characters talk, what they eat, how they dress, what they think and believe in. Know them so well that if you inadvertently try to make them say or do something "out of character", they'll just refuse.

Secondly, the plot. A story without conflict is rarely a story. The conflict can be physical, emotional, psychological, whatever, but your main character has to have a problem. And bring this problem on as soon as you can. I submitted a book to my agent a few years ago. She and her husband went over the manuscript with me. He pointed out that the story of Goldilocks doesn't really get interesting until the bears arrive.

"And in this book," he said, "the bears don't come in until page 65."

I got the point, and got those bears in by the second page.

It is absolutely important that your main characters solve the problem themselves. Don't let an adult step in and do it for them. In this way your character or characters will be different people at the end than they were at the beginning. They will have faced challenges, solved them and overcome them themselves. They will have changed and grown. Young people reading your book will face those challenges with them, and exult with them when they win out. This doesn't mean that children's books always have to have a happy ending. The world doesn't work that way, and kids know it just as well as we do. The sick kid doesn't always get better. The abusive home situation doesn't always get resolved. Sometimes friendships are irretrievably damaged. But your hero or heroine has learned how to cope. How to face up to and deal with the problem. The ending is not a conventionally happy one, but it is positive. (Forget *Alice's Adventures in Wonderland* and do not, I most emphatically repeat, do not, have your character wake up and find out "it was all a dream!" That's a cheat and a cop-out and your readers will hate you for it.)

Finally, write the story that's inside your head, and that you just have to write. It's not a story for kids—it's a story for you, written out of the feelings and memories of the child you once were. Another time when someone asked me why I wrote for children my daughter, who was about 12 at the time, broke in.

"She writes for kids because her own mind never grew up," she stated in a matter of fact tone.

In a lot of ways she was right. Writers for children remember what it was like to be young. They know very well that it wasn't the best time of their lives. They remember the pains, the anxieties, the fears. They also remember the joy of new discoveries. One of the main reasons I write for children, (which I explained to my friend when my daughter would let me get a word in edgewise), is because it's exciting to me to write about a young person who is experiencing something for the first time, whether it is something as emotional as love, or loss, or as terrible as war.

Don't worry about what age group will read your book. If it's good enough you'll have readers from 4 to 40+ writing to tell you how much they enjoyed it. Revise it, polish it, make it the very best you can, then send it out and start on the next one.

Good luck. Remember, a writer's greatest talent is sheer stubbornness. (And be prepared for all your dear friends and relatives who, after you're successful, will ask you when you're going to write a "real" book.)

Karleen Bradford is the award-winning author of 13 books for children and young adults, including *WRITE NOW!, How to turn your ideas into great stories.* (Scholastic Canada, 1996.)

# You Can Write for Children!

*By Margaret Springer*

P rofile of a children's writer: Female. Young mother or middle aged matron. Time on her hands. Tells bedtime stories to her own children, then writes them down. In public, a funny lady with bright blue shoes and a Mary Poppins personality.

Myth.

Profile of a children's story: Scampering squirrels. Hopping bunnies. Sweet children who live with Mommy and Daddy in a neat little house. An active boy. A cute sister. A moral, and a prize at the end, awarded by the Mayor.

Myth.

Those of us who write for children are of every age, gender, size, shape, personality, and quirk, and the writing we do is equally varied. We don't all love children, though we respect them. It is NOT easier to write for this particular audience, nor is it more difficult. It is simply a separate, challenging genre, with its own sub-genres.

And you can do it.

You were once a child yourself.

You are interested in writing (or you wouldn't be reading this).

You are open to new markets, and to new avenues for your creativity.

Think for a moment about your own childhood. What do you remember? Was it all wonder and love and happiness—one long endless perfect summer? Or do you also remember the pain of being left out sometimes? The fight you had with your best friend? Your fear of the neighbourhood bully? Your frustration at not being able to master a new skill? Your anxiety while waiting in the wings for your part in the school play?

Such conflict and emotional turmoil is at the heart of good fiction for any age. Human feelings are the same whether we're six or ninety-six;

only the way we deal with them changes as we mature. I have a poor memory for the things and names and dates of my childhood, but the feelings are still vivid, and it's that well that I draw from in my writing. You can, too.

A few years ago my husband and I were selling our house and buying another, and at the last moment one of the deals hit a snag. Our lawyer had promised to phone as soon as he had news. I sat at my desk. I'm a pro, I kept telling myself. I can write even if I don't feel like it. But I kept looking at that phone, willing it to ring, worrying.

Finally I knew what I had to do. I took that feeling—the agony of waiting and uncertainty—and I translated it to a child's world. I wrote a story about a young child of divorced parents, waiting for his dad to arrive to take him for the weekend. A blizzard is blowing, and the dad is hours late...

That story, which sold on its first time out to *Single Parent* magazine, absorbed me so much that when my phone finally rang, for an instant I was annoyed by the intrusion. (And yes, it all worked out OK.)

Good writing for any age, for the reader and for the writer, depends on this emotional resonance, this feeling of identity with the main character.

"Without it," author/illustrator Ian Wallace points out, "the reader is left with an accumulation of words and a series of images."

In children's fiction the main character will be someone about the readers' age, or a little older. That person will be believable, in a believable setting, and will struggle with and overcome a story problem —or preferably both inner and outer problems—by his or her own efforts in the end.

The ending will be satisfying, with subtle character growth; not necessarily 100 per cent happy, but probably hopeful and realistic.

There will be an underlying theme, and values to impart, but character growth will be subtle. I try to write something that children will eagerly read on their own. Moralistic stories are like medicine, unpalatable even if slightly sweetened, and kids don't take medicine unless they have to. A good goal is to write stories that nourish, but that taste so good they won't even know that it's good for them.

What about age ranges, and reading levels? I have a confession to make here. While I have written and published for every age from preschoolers to young teens, I don't worry about vocabulary and reading levels. Perhaps it's because I'm a writer, not a teacher.

My usual approach is to imagine my audience, which is one child: a laid-back teen, an engrossed eleven year old, a seven year old sounding out the words, a squirmy pre-schooler. Word lengths get progressively shorter, plots less complicated and within the realm of experience of the child, language and sentence structure more simple.

Teen/YA (Young Adult) is transitional writing. It's so close to adult that there's little difference except perhaps in main character, viewpoint, or theme. The challenge here is to treat your teen characters as equals, and to speak in their voice.

At the other end of the spectrum, the younger the audience, the closer writing comes to poetry. Writing for the very youngest is the most difficult form of all. (If you don't believe this, because it always looks so easy, try it some time.)

Many writers focus on their own children as a target audience— but children grow up. I visualize one reader, but I write for the child within myself, or, as Janet Lunn puts it, "to the person inside me listening to the story". Occasionally I check child guidance books to remind me what kids are like at various ages. (These are, incidentally, a gold mine of plot ideas.)

For subject matter, the choice is almost endless. Young readers enjoy realism, mysteries, adventure, animal stories. They like fantasy, science fiction, historical fiction, teen romance. Religious stories have their place.

Humor is always in demand. You can choose magazine or novel length, picture book or easy reader.

Are you a nonfiction writer? There's a strong market for accurate and interesting nonfiction which doesn't talk down to young people. Childhood is a time when everything is new, when the world is full of mysteries. What's your hobby? Your work? Your area of expertise? What excites your enthusiasm?

There's a particular need today for good writing about science and technology. When I was a university reference librarian, if we didn't understand a subject we searched out a children's book about it. Isaac Asimov labels himself "an explainer", and if you can explain things simply and clearly, your manuscripts will soon find a home.

Good nonfiction uses many fictional techniques. It's important to grab the reader in the first sentence, using a lively style. (You're competing with TV, video games and the computer for this child's time.) Avoid being encyclopedic; if your writing has the faintest whiff of textbook, it will soon be set aside. Include weird, little known facts, and tell kids what they don't already know. For biography, focus especially on the person's childhood. Did they have trouble making friends? Were they awkward? What was their family like?

And don't think you can skimp on research. For 900 word articles, I've worked through a pile of books, magazine and newspaper sources as high as if I were writing an adult research paper. "Writing nonfiction," says science writer Margery Facklam, "is like putting together a puzzle. When you dump all the pieces on the table, it seems impossible to fit them together at first. But then you begin to sort and select, and once the border is locked in place, once it is defined and enclosed, the fun begins."

You prefer poetry? The market is more limited here. Stories in rhyme are particularly difficult to sell, and rhymed alphabet books are almost impossible, unless extraordinarily good. The best advice I've read comes from author Barbara Steiner: "Write poetry for yourself. If you should discover that it speaks perfectly to children, you may want to market to those publications that aim at a young audience."

For the past few years, besides my own writing, I've read and critiqued thousands of manuscripts written by other adults for children. If I had one thing to say to prospective children's authors it would be: "Read it aloud, and polish it until the language sings." When we read, we don't see with our eyes as much as we hear with our inner ear. The rhythms and sound and music of words is what singles out, from a pile of good manuscripts, that one which stands out as special and publishable.

"Children," writes author/educator Claudia Lewis, "are no less receptive than adults to language that is art as well as communication. Primarily they want what we all want when we open a book—words that can work a little magic, a language strong enough to hold emotion."

So what is the profile of a children's writer? For that you can look in the mirror, because the person you see there has that potential. You will need talent, which can be developed. Persistence, certainly. A willingness to learn your craft. Most of all, faith in yourself.

The process is whatever works, whether that means using detailed outlines, winging it, or some combination of the two. Find your own way. The final manuscript is what counts.

Writing for children? You can do it! I challenge you to try.

Margaret Springer is an award-winning author of dozens of published stories, articles and poems for children. Her book credits include *A Royal Ball* (Boyds Mills Press) and *Move Over, Einstein* (Penguin UK, 1997). She also teaches writing and gives workshops.

# Entertain Young Readers

*by Bert Williams* _____

suspect that some people who have never written for children think that the way to go about it is by surveying the young to discover their current interests and then combining the two most popular topics into one story, using a vocabulary of not more than six hundred words.

Combining dinosaurs and space travel could certainly be done in this age when so much is written to order, but not by me. While I have the greatest affection for dinosaurs, I care not at all for space travel. I couldn't write anything I viewed as science fiction because I don't enjoy reading the stuff, and any moderately bright six-year-old would catch me out by the top of page two, because I'd undoubtedly place the retro-rockets on the wrong end of my space ship.

I am convinced that children (like the rest of us) read primarily by interest rather than by vocabulary. If they do not care what happens to the people in the story, then a word a page is too much to ask of them. If, however, they're caught up in the excitement of the quest and the adventures of the hero, then they'll race through it though it has a vocabulary to match *Webster's International* dictionary, and a cast of characters larger than the Toronto telephone directory. I write simply, which saves a lot of worrying about whether or not you're writing down to your reader.

I know it's trite to say I write to please myself, but I don't know any other way of doing it. My books are about the things that interest me, because this is the only way I can interest anybody else. I tell the kind of story I enjoy reading—about decent people undertaking important and arduous tasks for noble reasons.

One of the charges to which I plead guilty is that my writing is very moral. It certainly is. I wouldn't be writing if I didn't think I had a viewpoint that should at least be considered by someone struggling towards maturity. Young people want categorical statements made for them, statements they are not yet capable of making for themselves, which they are free to accept or reject. Further, I believe that every worthwhile creative work has a message, although I don't think it need necessarily spring at the reader from every page.

Most of us who write fiction do so because we can't help ourselves, because if we could, we'd all be writing non-fiction, which usually sells so much better. Therefore, since we can't help it, I think we should only spend our time on those stories that are in our souls and that we have to put down on paper for our own peace of mind.

I prefer writing about the past, because it allows both the reader and me to stand back and take a more detached view of society, but also because I find nothing there as unreal as the present. The period I write about is determined by my thinking and reading of the moment, but it really doesn't matter. What really concerns me is *people*, their stresses and strains, fears and worries, which are much the same whether they be cavemen or Vikings, Indians or contemporary Canadians.

By the way, if you're thinking of writing a children's book because you don't think you're ready to write an adult one, forget it. The only legitimate reason for attempting a children's book is because it's the best form for what you have to say. It happens to suit me ideally, because I'm concerned with what I consider the most difficult journey in the world, the one from childhood to adulthood. Children need all the help they can get in learning the human ethic. I realize it's out of style, but I still believe in the traditional virtues of loyalty, truth, honor, duty, patriotism and courage.

The writer must have the traditional freedom of the creative artist to choose the setting and period for his own work. What makes a work Canadian is the peculiar view we share of the world. I'd like to see that silly term "Canadiana" dropped, for I can't imagine going into the libraries of other countries and finding shelves of "Norwegiana" or "Romaniana." A work is either Canadian or it is not, and by that I mean anything written by a citizen or an inhabitant of this country.

In doing my research, if I choose a historical setting, I use the following alphabetical headings:

• **Animals**—any, both domestic and wild, they were familiar with.

• **Calendar**—their entire system of time keeping.

• **Cities** (where applicable)—type, size, layout, major buildings, etc.

• **Clothes**—what they wore, what they were made from, and how they got them.

• **Education**—what they thought they should pass on to their young, and how they went about it.

- **Family**—size, organization, importance of parents, and sexes, etc.
- **Food**—what they ate and how they prepared it.
- **Games**—any amusement, entertainment or sports they had.
- **Government**—how they ruled themselves or were ruled by others.
- **Houses**—size, method of construction, materials, decorations, furnishings.
- **Medicine**—how they treated illnesses, wounds, etc., and what member of the society was responsible for this service.
- **Law**—the written or unwritten rules they lived by, and who interpreted them.
- **Names**—their system of naming themselves, along with a list of names and nicknames I draw upon for my characters.
- **Other**—any information I've collected that might find its way into the story, but doesn't fit under any of the other headings.
- **Plants**—the domesticated and wild varieties they knew.
- **Plots and Phrases**—any stories or plot developments I may want to include, plus speeches for my characters, usually with the intention of revealing themselves or of shedding light on others.
- **Religion**—their deities, what they stood for and believed in.
- **Society**—the organization of their society, the social classes they were divided into, and under what conditions mobility was possible.
- **Speech**—the way they worded what they said, to help set the atmosphere of the period, and to distinguish certain characters.
- **Trade**—their business techniques, the goods they produced and traded, and what they received in return.
- **Travel**—their means and methods of transportation, including provision for stopping over while away from home.
- **War**—their weapons and tactics, and their feelings about it.
- **Work**—what they did for a living.
- **Wisdom**—any scraps of wisdom to indicate what they thought mattered about life, which may often be worked into the story.

If my setting is Canada today, the only category I would have to use would be Plots and Phrases, adding only necessary research related to that particular story.

There are similarities between children's and adult fiction, but the former is far more stylized. The difference (especially today when the adult novel often hasn't any form at all) might be compared to writing poetry in free verse or the sonnet form. Among these constants, it seems to me (although a children's writer of genius may break them) are:

• A hero (or heroine) who is himself a child, possessed of a strong inherent moral sense;

• He (or she) is suddenly faced with an abrupt change in life, brought about by some external disruption that casts him out into the world on his own;

• He often has only a single parent (or none at all), and whoever is responsible for him is handicapped or ineffectual;

• He encounters during the course of the story adults who are unmitigated villains, and learns they must be dealt with, both for his own safety and for the preservation of his society;

• He faces a moral dilemma alone, unable to turn to others for help, and he must decide the action necessary to safeguard those he loves and the beliefs he has come to hold;

• In this crisis he manifests extraordinary courage, daring, selflessness and determination.


C. S. Lewis once said that "No book is really worth reading at the age of ten which is not equally (and often far more) worth reading at the age of fifty...the only imaginative works we ought to grow out of are those which it would have been better not to have read at all."

It goes without saying, of course, that any book should have a strong central idea, some originality of presentation, good writing, careful plot development, as well as characterization, motivation, humor, and a satisfying ending in which the hero has at least succeeded in learning something about himself that he didn't realize before.

I have no special knowledge of children, but it seems to me that children are much as they have always been—humble, proud, courageous, cowardly, dominant, submissive, curious, easily satisfied, eager, indifferent, searching, contented, compliant and willful, all in the same breath. There is no typical twelve-year-old, any more than there is a typical forty-year-old. If you write a story that's important to you—in an interesting way—there are bound to be a number of young people who will enjoy it.

I prefer writing dialogue to description, because it's more immediate, more life-like and, fortunately, more in tune with other media of the moment. Somewhere early in your story, you'll have to have an expository chapter to set the scene and the characters, and the objective of the contest, and later on you'll need one or two more for contrast with your action chapters. But keep the action going. I always recall C. B. DeMille's advice on film-making: "The way to make a film is to begin with an earthquake and work up to a climax."

I prefer writing action, both for its own sake, and because it moves the story along more rapidly. After the climax, I finish the whole thing off very quickly, because I prefer being asked why I close off so quickly rather than why I dragged it out so long.

As you can see, I don't worry about tying up every last little detail, because I think that after every book there should be an unwritten chapter, to be completed by the imagination of the reader. Reading and writing is a partnership, and I believe if I've done my share, the reader should do his too.

Bert Williams is the author of several novels for young readers, as well as a contributor to historical journals.

# Write a Picture Book

*By Margaret Bunel Edwards* _____

**W**henever I browse through a bookstore, I am amazed at the number and variety of picture books on the shelves. They are there because they are popular with both parents and children, so this is a publishing area which is receptive to the writer and to the artist. If you are a combination of both, you have it made.

Before you begin, consider the following suggestions carefully. They will help you realize your goal of being a published picture book author.

Decide on the exact age for which you plan to write. This is important because the difference in development between a three-year-old, at home or in day care, and a five-year-old, in kindergarten, is enormous.

Study children within the chosen age group. Every writer should know his or her audience, of course, but it is essential with young children. I review picture books for the *Canadian Book Review Annual* and I see that more and more books are being written by nursery school teachers. These men and women observe young children daily and use, for plots, the activities and conflicts they see taking place in their schools. Young mothers often have books published, also based on personal experience.

If you don't have close contact with today's young child, watch children's programs and take note of what television producers are doing to interest and educate youngsters.

Spend some time thinking of your own childhood, concentrating on the early years. The world has changed and the world for young children has changed but a small child still has the basic, instinctive needs to be loved, to feel secure, to make friends, to play, to be part of a family.

Which brings us to a change in the definition of the word "family". Families now encompass single parents, working mothers, day care workers, live-in nannies and single people who adopt children. These are all part of a child's experience and these circumstances and characters appear in today's stories.

Let us look specifically at writing for children three to five, since this age group is just graduating from pictures with a few words, to books with a simple plot.

These children are curious about their surroundings. They are full of wonder at the things they see and hear. They bubble with life and are active and creative.

Your plots will not be complicated. As a writer, you should have a real desire to help children learn as they enjoy books. The plots will be easy to follow and have happy little surprises and lessons in them. Every child needs to be taught kindness, honesty and helpfulness and these ideas appear often in published stories.

General information can also be included in your stories. Other lands have customs that interest small children. Multicultural books are very much in demand. Teachers, librarians and parents need them for information about and understanding of different customs and cultures. Editors are anxious to receive well-written, knowledgeable manuscripts to publish to fill this need.

Of course, all information should be presented in a bright, easy way. Let your little reader feel the sting of the sleet on his face as he slides down the hill. Let her smell the chocolate cookies baking in Grandma's kitchen. Let her hear the music at the skating rink or see the shadow of the lost puppy and taste the cool lemonade. This kind of graphic writing is a must for the very small child.

The picture book story has a beginning, a middle and an end. The main character is interesting and appealing, he or she has a reason for whatever is happening and the ending is either surprising or satisfying, or both.

Themes for these stories are very simple. A theme is hidden in the plot so that the child will not think he or she is being preached to, or scolded. Lessons such as, be brave, respect the rights of others, obey your parents, tell the truth, help others—are all used, over and over again.

Now for the mechanics of getting started. Picture books are 32, 48, and occasionally, 64 pages in length. This has nothing to do with literary merit and everything to do with the printer. One of these sheets, using both sides, translates to eight picture book pages so the books are made up of units of eight.

After you allow for the title page, dedication, publisher's information and first page, you have about 25 pages for your story and its accompanying pictures.

Start by taking four sheets of 8 1/2 x 11 paper and folding them in half. After cutting along the crease, again fold the sheets to form a small book. Number the pages, 1 to 32, and this becomes your working model.

I begin writing on page five or six. As the story unfolds, I make sure that each page tells of something that can be illustrated. At one time, I submitted my story in this format but, on the advice of an editor, I send it now as a standard manuscript, with each paragraph representing a page. I still do the rough work on the mock-up book, though, because it is an easy, visual way to be certain the artist has scenes she can illustrate.

A word about the illustrations in a picture book. This is NOT the concern of the author. Publishers have illustrators they use and they DO NOT WANT to see sketches by your friends or relatives. The exception to this rule is if you are a professional artist and have written the story also. In this case, you include photographs of your illustrations, along with your story manuscript and a covering letter stating your qualifications. In it, briefly describe your training as an artist and any experience you may have in the illustrating field.

Study the picture books in the library. They will give you a sense of the style and rhythm popular with small children. You'll see how rhyme and alliteration are used, how dialogue furthers the plot. Humorous touches are popular and a simple mystery or puzzle is an added delight.

Read your work aloud. You'll soon know if your sentences are too long or if your story line is not clear. You'll also be pleased when your words sing and your figures of speech add colour and appeal to your work.

When you've finished, put the work aside and start on a new project. After a week, go back to your book and re-read it several times. You now have a fresh perspective as you look for descriptive verbs or stale statements and clichés.

Markets for children's picture books are listed in *The Canadian Writer's Guide*, the *Writer's Market* and the *Children's Writer's & Illustrator's Market*. An excellent source for market updates is CAN-SCAIP, the Canadian Society of Children's Authors, Illustrators and Performers.

When you are ready to submit your manuscript, be very sure of the editor's name and its spelling. Editors change frequently so check the *Publishers Trade List Annual* at your library for up-to-date information.

Keep your covering letter short. Tell why you wrote the book, how people who have read it have reacted to it, and why you chose that particular publisher.

Tell something about yourself, as well. The editor wants to know about your experience with young children, your hobbies and your interests, as well as your writing credits. Be brief and to the point.

Sometimes you are asked to revise on speculation, before a contract is offered. The choice is yours. If you think the editor is really interested, fine, but remember, the majority of manuscripts revised on speculation are never published.

As you study picture books at the library, you will see that there are re-told fairy tales, the ever popular alphabet books, concept books and rhyming stories. The range is wide and complex. I have tried to give you only an uncomplicated over-view to help you begin.

If you decide to specialize in writing picture books, I recommend the publication *Writing Books for Children* by Jane Yolen.

This is a clearly written, comprehensive volume which discusses every category of children's fiction and non-fiction books, and will be a great help to you. Good luck!

Margaret Bunel Edwards is the author of two picture books and teaches a writing course in this field. Her young adult historical novel, *The Ocean Between*, was short-listed for the Geoffrey Bilson Award.

# Non-fiction for Children

*by Elma Schemenauer* _____

Travel photographers Sybil and Sam provide photographs for Publisher A's series of children's books on communities around the world. Sybil and Sam ask Publisher A to let them write some books in this series.

"What do you know about writing for children?" asks Publisher A.

"Why not give us a chance?" say Sybil and Sam. "We've written successfully for adults."

"You're on," replies the publisher.

Sergio teaches religion to children's classes organized by his church. He develops songs, games, puzzles, "chalk talks," and other support materials to help present the basic curriculum he has been given. At an authors' group to which he belongs, Sergio meets an editor from Publisher B, which publishes a church magazine. Impressed with Sergio's work, the editor invites him to try writing a children's column for the magazine.

Sigrid teaches mathematics in a rural Alberta school. Educational Publisher C, whose representative Sigrid meets at a math conference, asks her to review a manuscript for a proposed mathematics textbook. Sigrid makes good suggestions, even drafting activities and exercises she would like to see added to the textbook. As a result Publisher C invites Sigrid to join its author team. She and the other math authors go on to write a multi-textbook series.

Stories like these abound. The above accounts illustrate a few basic principles about getting published as a writer of children's non-fiction:

• There are many ways to break in. Sending a proposal and/or manuscript to a publisher on speculation is the standard method for getting started, but it's certainly not the only one.

• Many opportunities exist for authors of children's non-fiction in textbook and other educational writing (which, by the way, is quite often more lucrative than trade, or non-educational, writing). Unlike the fiction writer, who may mainly approach trade publishers, the non-fiction writer should be sure to investigate educational publishers as well.

• It's useful to join an authors' association. CANSCAIP—the Canadian Society of Children's Authors, Illustrators, and Performers—is a particularly good one for children's writers. Through its newsletter, monthly meetings, and other means, this organization offers moral support, advice, contacts, and methods of promoting members' work.

• It's helpful to attend events at which you are likely to meet publishers. Educators' conferences, book launchings and book fairs are good places to start. That way you become aware of what publishers are doing for children. Another way of increasing your publishing awareness is to read periodicals such as *Canadian Author*, *Canadian Writer's Journal*, *Quill & Quire*, and *CANSCAIP News*.

• Once a publisher shows an interest in you for any reason, you may be able to use that contact to get published. If, like Sigrid, you are asked to review a manuscript, do an outstanding job. If like Sam and Sybil, you are asked to provide photography or some other service, you can perhaps use your inside track to wangle an authorship contract.

Tactics like these may seem like taking unfair advantage, but they're not. The publisher of children's non-fiction, particularly educational books, prefers to work with a responsive, reliable person who will do accurate research, get along with editors, and meet deadlines. If you've shown yourself to be that (and, of course, if you can write), why shouldn't the publisher work with you rather than an unknown from the "slush pile"?

So suppose you've caught the eye of a potential publisher, or you've decided to simply go ahead and write children's non-fiction on speculation. How is this type of writing different from any other? Perhaps you, like Sybil and Sam, have written for adults but not for kids. What points might you keep in mind as you launch into your masterpiece about life in a Bedouin tent community, Norwegian fjord, or Montreal suburb?

Let's start with a word about research in adult-oriented sources. This is almost always a mistake. Non-fiction for children, if it's any good, has a way of zeroing in on the basics, stating information in colorful ways, and highlighting human interest. This is what you need at the beginning. You can always use adult books for reference later, to fill in any gaps.

If you go to the adult sources first, they may lead you into a mind set that will make it difficult to narrow your topic sufficiently or present it simply enough for children. If you model your masterpiece on a doctoral thesis, the kids will never get into it.

Having done your research you sit down with all those notes and references and start writing. A handle is the first thing you need. Give children a reason for reading. Tie your topic to their lives in some fresh exciting way. Remember, children's minds don't easily jump around in time and space the way adult minds do. Kids simply haven't lived long enough for that. The following, for example, might be an arresting opening for an adult article or book: "Egyptian queen Cleopatra and Elizabeth I, Queen of England hundreds of years later, both had difficulties in their love lives."

An opening like that would be hopeless in children's writing. It jumps around in time and space without sufficient explanation, and there's also a problem with the concept. Children are much more likely to relate to a concept such as making friends at school, playing with toys, or obtaining a pet—something that is part of their own everyday lives. They aren't interested in the private lives of unknown adults. In your opening, then, make sure to start where children are. If you do, you can lead them a long way from that point. If you don't, they may just stop reading right there.

It's a good idea to use concrete, specific words in any kind of prose writing, and it is especially important when you're writing for children. Children aren't as sophisticated as adults in relating to abstract terms such as *courage* or *peace*. They relate better to concrete symbols such as a lion for courage or a dove for peace. Nor do children relate as well to generalizations as adults. Be specific. Instead of writing, "Nando wears his cap wherever he goes," it's much more interesting to say, "Nando wears his baseball cap to the playground, to school, and even to the dentist's office."

Most authors are motivated at least partly by emotions. For example, why would Alison write a children's article about the discovery of insulin or the election of Ottawa's first woman mayor unless the event evoked feelings of excitement, fascination, and probably national pride in her own heart? Sadly, many authors who desperately want to share important feelings with children freeze when they're in the vicinity of a typewriter or word processor. Some of these authors will tell you with tears in their eyes how excited they are about what they have written. Yet when you read the story or article, it turns out to be stiff and flat. You wonder how it could ever be expected to bring a tear or smile to anyone's eye.

Somehow, by whatever means, such writers need to learn to let their emotions flow through the printed word. This is essential in children's writing. If you "keep children company" in your writing, sharing your emotions and evoking reciprocal emotions in them, they will want to read what you have written. This is as important in non-fiction as in fiction. Search creatively for places to convey emotion, even when giving straight information. For example, instead of writing, "The one-legged runner Terry Fox began his attempted crossing of Canada in April 1980," consider conveying your feeling that what Terry Fox did was courageous and dramatic by saying, "In April of 1980 Terry Fox, with only one leg, bravely set out to run across Canada."

If you need to state, for example, the size of an animal, you could write, "The narwhal was five metres long," or you could convey humor and whimsy about this unusual animal by presenting it in a more interesting way: "The narwhal, at five metres, was about the length of an average living room."

In the past some educators, authors and publishers used mathematical "readability" formulas and word lists to determine grade levels of writing for children. Such formulas have now fallen into disfavor among many because, too often, they caused people to lose sight of literary quality.

What most reading formulas measure is syllables per 100 words (there should be relatively *few* for children) and sentences per 100 words (there should be relatively *many* for children). In other words, use short words and short sentences.

People now realize that even this is too arbitrary and mechanical a rule to follow slavishly. However, it's still useful as a general guide for children's non-fiction provided the author keeps firmly in mind other less-easily measured, far more important factors including: narrowing the topic sufficiently; tying the topic to childrens' experiences; using concrete, specific words; and expressing yourself in ways that evoke answering emotions in young readers.

A former teacher, Elma Schemenauer has written over 50 books, many for young people. Titles include *A New True Book: Canada, Yesterstories, Hello Montreal, Hello Edmonton*, and *Jacob Jacobs Gets Up Early*.

# Advice From An Editor

*by Larry Muller* ⸺⸺⸺⸺⸺⸺⸺⸺⸺⸺⸺

A s a publisher/editor talking to writers, I am reminded of Brendan Behan's comment about critics. He said they were like eunuchs in a harem: they saw the trick done every night but couldn't do it themselves.

It may be sheer insecurity, but I have a horrible feeling that writers may have the same attitude toward editors and publishers. Unfortunately, however, an editor today is lucky if he sees the "trick" done two or three times a year never mind every night.

C. S. Lewis, one of the really great writers for children, observed that in the realm of imagination we must meet children man to man—no patronizing or idolizing—and that really the only area in which we are superior to them is in our ability to communicate.

If you were to see the vast majority of manuscripts coming into publishing houses today, you would have to conclude that we are not communicating very well.

If everyone has at least one book in them, then just about everyone feels they have two or three children's books in them—a conviction made absolutely ironclad by their own personal market research. After all, your children or grandchildren or neighbor's children have all at one time or another sat in rapt attention while you whomped up a story for them.

It may well be so. But there may be other factors. You may simply have a comfy knee or a full cookie jar, or they like you very, very much.

The unfortunate result of this situation is that most of us either think it is unworthy of the attention of a serious writer or we do not bring our best creative, imaginative and emotional energies to bear on the task of writing for children because we believe, quite simply, that it is "kids' stuff."

Writing for children is one of the most demanding, and certainly most rewarding, areas in the whole of literature. And it is about as easy to "whomp up" a good children's story as it is to "whomp up" a brace of Petrarchan sonnets.

Thanks to the information explosion and television, children's writing now covers an extremely wide spectrum and rises through many reading and interest levels. Just about everything of interest to an adult, in a different form, can be made interesting to a child. So it is extremely difficult to talk about it as though it were a clearly defined and limited area.

It comprises fairy tales, animal stories, cartoons, puzzles, jokes, ghost stories, how-to books, science, space, professions, machines, horses, etc., etc., etc.

But certainly in the best children's writing we expect to find those qualities by which we judge adult literature: adequate themes, good style and structure, powerful characterization, vigorous pace and a satisfying resolution.

A special requirement of children's literature is a compact form. This does not mean a mindless watering down as though children were idiots. It does mean sticking to essentials and a vigorous presentation. Children need swift passage with no unnecessary words or ideas to impede their progress. What Beatrix Potter called a chaste style is also essential: strong, simple, evocative words. And certainly a gripping opening.

Writing less instead of more is no easy task. Was it not Bernard Shaw who stated that he wrote a book because he did not have time to write an article?

Questions that are always asked of a children's story among others are: Does it have a good central idea? Does it have a definite appeal for its audience? Is it original in conception and presentation? Does it call the imagination into play? Does it increase understanding of human actions and motives? And the final one is, always, does it leave a strong impression on the mind?

Children's literature should always be a door and not a wall—a door through which the imagination can flow again and again.

I don't really want to embark on the Pilgrim's Progress of the do's and don'ts for the writer. Even if an editor gave complete and detailed instructions that were to be followed meticulously, it probably wouldn't work. Words are, after all, vessels for life and imagination. If there is no life and imagination in them, no surprise and delight they would simply be like an engine without pistons, perfect on the outside, but one that simply would not work.

What I would like to do in the form of a few colossal generalizations is touch upon those areas that I feel have been inhibiting good writers from becoming good writers for children.

The main task is to communicate effectively—and to do this you must know whom you are communicating with. This is our problem, as adults. We forget the real nature of childhood. Too many adults recall childhood as a mental Tahiti—a flowered refuge where we remember nice comfortable, cute things. We drown in the nostalgia for a delicious, uncomplicated, secure existence. And even if we look at children around us, we may see them as fortunate little beings free of the worries and anxieties that oppress us as grown-up people. This is, of course, nonsense. If we recall our own childhood honestly, we can surely remember periods of intense sadness, joy, longing, desire, loneliness, etc. Things that struck our funny bones and made us laugh insanely for days on end to the intense annoyance of our parents. As children we encountered the most profound things in the universe—love, and death, and fear, and delight, all probably in a more intense form than we know them now.

And if it turns out that we cannot recall our childhood clearly then I think it is safest to regard it as the medieval or at least early renaissance stage of human existence—a vivid, vigorous, hustling, brawling, terrifying, outrageously funny, cruel, vindictive, colorful stage. A period of earth-shaking discoveries and fascinating possibilities—gargantuan appetites, strong convictions and unshakable attachments. (Did your mother ever try to throw away your favorite teddy bear because you washed it in a stagnant pond? Did you ever get sick from eating too much ice cream?)

We should, therefore, see childhood as a time of intense emotions, powerful experiences, terrible vulnerabilities and great sensuousness—qualities that make adulthood insipid in comparison. With this view in our minds we would not dare serve up pap.

And look at the context of this seething mental and physical activity! Children are clearly restricted to home and street and, later, school. Certainly they are told what to do, where to go, when to do it, and so on. Later, when they are in school they encounter a whole new set of pressures and restrictions. They are worried about acceptance by their friends, whether they will measure up to what their parents and teachers expect of them, and a whole range of fears, insecurities and needs that they cannot cope with effectively because they have not the backlog of experience necessary to cope with them. And all through it, their minds and their imaginations are far larger than the physical and social environment in which they find themselves. To sum it all up, they are intelligent, sensitive, very energetic human beings living very complex lives.

This is the clue for the writer. For she, above all other people, can take that tremendous potential, that ceaseless energy of the child's mind, the great flux of its experience and make sense of it. She can open up whole new realms of sensation and understanding.

Quite simply the writer can give the child freedom—freedom to pass from the restrictions of the everyday and experience exhilarating new worlds. And by freedom I do mean escape. A good story can free a child to experience imaginatively what she or he could never hope to experience in his or her immediate surroundings. It enables him to see and understand what he otherwise might only feel.

The writer can take the raw materials of a child's life and needs and present them back to her in a form that will help her better understand herself and her world and realize her potential as a human being.

Writing can enrich by giving the child new ways of looking at things. It can make bearable emotions such as loneliness and rejection. It can give understanding of beauty and love and fear. It can expand competence by reassuring the child of his own powers. It can overcome insecurities and inadequacies (stories about people who have overcome tremendous handicaps, are one example). It can answer the need to love and be loved, (many animal stories are responses to the child's need to love and come into a relationship with other creatures). Social stories can enhance the child's ability to cope with a situation in which he find himself. Stories can supply insights to what families are all about and help him better to understand his own. All in all, writing for children can increase their humanity—give them a mirror for their world to help them to meet real situations in their own lives.

But to do this the writing must be full of life and power. Perhaps the surest way of making your writing a living and compelling experience is to write only what you really know and care about. If you do not care about the characters you create, if you are not immensely fascinated by their natures and their problems, how on earth can you expect a reader, even a very young and innocent one, to be interested?

Basically you write for yourself—and hope children will respond. If you don't, you will have stereotyped characters and situations of no interest. No one likes boring, superficial people. As adults we avoid them like the plague. How much more intolerable is boredom when we encounter it in the pages of a book which purports to grasp our attention and interest?

While I am on the subject of character, one other tip—the Greeks used to say that character is fate. This is as true of children's stories as it is of Greek tragedy. From the nature of the man springs the tribulations, disasters and delights he encounters. In children's writing you will be able to develop only two or three aspects of character. But make these striking aspects, and let them anticipate, and in a way compel, the incidents that befall the protagonist. Toad of Toad Hall in *The Wind in the Willows* is, I suppose, the perfect example.

And for heaven's sake, do not be afraid of emotion in your writing. Good children's literature will never fail to excite fear, joy, hatred, desire, compassion, resentment, anger, forgiveness and all the other ingredients that give life savor. You should not really tell a story—what you should be doing is sharing an experience.

This is particularly important because emotions are the bricks and girders of fantasy. And fantasy is the link between the world of everyday experience and great sweeps of imagination. Maurice Sendak, who is surely one of the outstanding creators of children's books of our time, stresses that fantasy must always be rooted ten feet deep in reality. No matter how exotic the situation, no matter what the nature of the protagonist—animal, vegetable, mineral or extraterrestrial—it must be one to which the reader can readily respond. It must present a completely satisfying universe operating consistently within its own framework and laws. Animals or ogres, space men or leprechauns, can all work out their separate destinies—but they must be ones which the reader can instantly share.

Fantasy has always been the core of children's literature—and in contrast with adult fantasies it is usually a rich and impressive experience because it usually deals with good and evil. It is replete with magnificent confrontations involving great doses of cruelty, beauty, pity, and terror. It is the stuff that literally enthralls the mind and makes it reluctant to switch back to the everyday. Fantasy in children's literature fertilizes the imagination with the symbols and archetypes which we encounter again and again in our reading lives.

And while we are on the subject of fantasy, if you have a moral or didactic message, show it but don't tell it. Whatever convictions you have will shine through what you create; don't bother hammering the message home. Remember Huckleberry Finn? He did not condemn. He saw the world for what it was—and allowed it to condemn itself.

And I must not forget to mention the great common denominator of children's reading: humor. Children love to laugh—as do we all. I am sure none of us can forget the agonizing pain in our sides we suffered over Laurel and Hardy, and Abbott and Costello when we were kids. The sense of the ridiculous is never stronger nor more robust than among children. They love to follow up all the ridiculous implications of a funny situation—especially if it is one they can relate to from their own experience.

Now one last test before you send your manuscript off for readers and editors to sprinkle cigarette ashes over it and drip coffee on it.

Put it away for two weeks or a month; then take it out and READ it—right through, listening to the words you have used, letting the characters speak and act for themselves—letting the plot build up. C. S. Lewis observed that no book is worth reading at the age of ten that is not equally (and often far more) worth reading at the age of fifty.

Whatever you find factitious, dull or shallow as an adult, will almost certainly have the same effect on a child. And no amount of cuddly furry things and tinselly brightness will redeem it.

What is your reward for going through all this rigmarole and trouble? Probably not riches. What you will have is the satisfaction of having created a sub-universe that other minds and imaginations will find utterly convincing. Best of all you will have reached human beings at their most exciting stage and have given them mental riches at the time they most need it. You will have spoken to children and they will have listened.

F. C. Larry Muller has been active on the Canadian children's writing scene for more than 30 years as a writer, editor and publisher. He is currently president of Scholastic Canada Ltd., a leading publisher and distributor of children's books. He was the 1996 winner of the Canadian Authors Association's Allan Sangster Award.

# Is it Ready to Publish?

*by Adrian Peetoom*

So you've finished your manuscript—well done! All writing, even writing to family and close friends, is "venturing into enemy territory," as one wit has described it. Writing is tough. Good writing is tougher. A manuscript has even more dimensions of vulnerability, since it aims to be made public. I get an image of a snail that has finally reached the middle of a busy highway, and wonders whether it's been worth it coming this far, with so much further to go.

You've suffered a bit. I don't mean the kind of suffering people allude to when they simply expect artists to be misfits—poor, drug-crazed, alcoholic, unkempt, their bodies ill-fitting in second-hand clothes, their personas ill-fitting in a materialist and impersonal culture. You've written one draft, then another, revised some more, and the more you revised the worse you thought it got, until finally you woke up in the middle of the night from a dream that had you autographing copies of your book—stark naked.

It is true that Canadian publishers are publishing more children's books. Only twenty-years ago you could count the number of children's books published in Canada in one year on your fingers. Now hundreds of new titles are published each year.

Aha, you say, I knew that, and that's why I completed my manuscript. We're on to a good thing. Teachers are getting used to classrooms being filled with authentic children's books. The new generation of parents is buying more and more books for their children. There's a growing market here, and there must be lots of opportunity to make some extra money. Maybe I can retire early and write full-time!

Let's try to put things in some sort of perspective. Every educational publisher will now make sure that its anthologies for language programs contain stories, poetry, and other writing of the highest quality. In fact, teaching guides recommend the use of real books at every turn.

This contradiction shows us that all is not as rosy as you may think. Knowing what I know about the costs of typesetting, making color separations, printing and binding, and about the sales record of children's books, it would be my guess that the majority of children's books published in recent years were unprofitable.

So there you are, holding your manuscript, and you look at it and say, "What do I do now?" Well, the first thing you do not do is convert any hope of earnings from this healthy children's book market into non-refundable tickets for a world cruise. Wait until you see cold hard cash.

Next, you have to deal with the realization that, though you know your manuscript is perfect, others may be a little harder to convince. I offer the following story:

One particularly trying day, an acquisitions editor for a successful Canadian publishing firm sat knee-deep in brown mailing envelopes and wrote...

"It's got to be said, if only to make me feel less frustrated and less tired from all the wasted effort. I read at least 20 manuscripts each week that hopeful authors/illustrators suggest we turn into picture books. That's about 1,000 over 52 weeks. We publish about ten in a good year. Many of the 1,000 should never have been sent. Which ones?"

I freely offer you a checklist. If your manuscript has any or all of the following characteristics, please think five times before you send it:

1. The events take place on sunny days in spring, with flowers and bees and butterflies all around.

2. Any paragraph starts with "suddenly."

3. Mothers are angels.

4. Fathers are strong.

5. Animals talk to people.

6. Inanimate objects talk to people.

7. Unicorns are important.

8. Grandpa died.

9. Grandma is weekend hostess for one or more grandchildren.

10. Your own children and all the neighborhood children and the whole class liked the story when you read it to them.

11. There is a monster in the closet.

12. There is a monster under the bed.

13. You've always wanted to write, and now that you are retired after a lifetime of teaching, you've decided you're going to do it, damn it.

14. Your story contains a good moral.

15. The events of your story happened to you in real life.

16. You want to communicate an important truth to children.

17. You've kept big words out.

18. You've kept swear words out because you don't think nice kids use them.

19. You have not read at least 177 different picture books in the last 177 days, and thought critically about each one.

20. You have not read a lot of picture books aloud to children.

21. Your manuscript is good for children.

22. Your manuscript will teach children about life.

23. This one is really tough: the language you use describes, observes and concludes. It does not present a universe of the imagination in which the reader happily judges for himself or herself what to see, smell, hear, touch, taste, take part in and conclude.

24. Your manuscript uses rhyme.

25. Your manuscript uses rhythm.

26. Your manuscript is about the alphabet.

27. Your manuscript is about numbers.

28. Your manuscript is about shapes and colors.


There is an important postscript. Children's books are about miracles—so there is always a chance. Probably you should never have sent your story in, but you did. And the next thing you know you have a publisher, a contract, an advance, good reviews, and solid sales. And you'll start writing all over again—with utter contempt for this checklist!

I can hear you thinking: Who asked you, anyway? So far, all you've told me is that my manuscript is probably lousy, and even if a publisher deigns to accept it, he'll take all the profits.

The truth is that I think it's absolutely terrific that you've written your manuscript. If you have not yet done so, I urge you to get started. Honestly! What I wanted to do first is to destroy two fallacies.

1. Nothing you do is really worth anything unless you get paid for it.

This is the first and greatest lie! The second is:

2. No writing meant for a public is worth much unless it is published by a commercial publishing company.

If you've written a good story, it deserves to be published. Publish it yourself, give it to children, read it to children. Children deserve to be read to, and to have their own stories written and read. They need to be encouraged to experience the joy of reading and writing, so that they will love it as much as you do.

There is only so much room for the commercial sort of publishing, with contracts, advances, national publicity, royalties, interviews by Peter Gzowski. No Canadian publisher can afford to publish more than two or three dozen of the thousands of children's manuscripts they receive each year. So please do submit your best work to publishers, but do not consider acceptance, or lack thereof, proof of anything. Publication is not the mark of a writer. Producing genuine text that struggles to explain and to relish life —that is the mark of a writer.

If your stories bring joy to readers, especially if those readers are children, you are a writer.

Adrian Peetoom authored and co-authored over 15 books during his career in educational publishing. He also translated a book of Dutch poetry and an account of persecuted Christians in Siberia. In addition, he has written numerous articles for a variety of journals, most notably the *Christian Courier* (formerly *Calvinist Contact*).

# Poetry

# The Craft of Poetry

*by Peggy Fletcher* ——————————

A s we approach the year 2000, the role of the poet is quickly evolving to embrace the Information Age. The Internet and its multi-media cousins hold a promise of new and exciting changes for creating poetry. Where in the past, poets could only hope to reach a few hundred supportive readers, the electronic stage now offers global opportunities. Its prospects are both mind-bending and sobering. Attention to craft is more important than ever.

Contemporary poetry, like all modern art, is of a progressive nature. Its content is governed largely by its age; its style, form and imagery by the skill of the poets living within that era. Without craftsmanship, great poetry could never be born; without change, the poetic language ceases to have effect. Indeed, it might become an obsolete voice.

As we come to the end of the 20th century, we need to review what has happened to the craft of poetry since poets such as T. S. Eliot, Ezra Pound, Amy Lowell, Walt Whitman and others questioned the romantic voices of the past and turned poetry and its methods upside-down. These poets discarded certain devices and styles which were then in vogue. They sought a more concrete form, free of forced rhyme, archaic words and thought.

They employed dramatic new imagery that was less obscure. It was terse and ironic, and had more impact on the reader. A line such as T. S. Eliot's "the yellow fog which rubs its back upon the window pane" was born, along with even more startling images such as Carl Sandburg's "stuff of the moon runs on lapping sand."

Largely discarded was the end rhyme with which most people were familiar. Gone too, were the safe and romantic nature poems of the Victorian age. Inversions for the sake of rhyming, and poetic terms such as 'ere, t'was, e'en and other contractions were no longer acceptable.

As decades passed, poetry and its craftspeople became bolder. In some instances, the poetry they wrote was deemed inaccessible. Whereas William Wordsworth's song "To a Daffodil" was easily fathomed, Dylan Thomas' highly lyrical lines "now as I was young and easy under the apple bough / about the lilting house and happy as the grass is green" made readers vaguely uncomfortable. It seemed the poet was breaking more rules than he should. Sound and intensity became increasingly important. How the words looked on the page took on new meaning.

Free verse continued to dominate North American poetry styles during the middle decades of the century. The Black Mountain Poets in the United States and the Tish Movement in British Columbia brought a new economy of words as reflected in William Carlos Williams "The Red Wheelbarrow".

This economy was adopted by Canadian poets Raymond Souster in his 'Six Quart Basket' and George Bowering in his longer poem 'For W.C.W.' Added to this was the effect of dropping capitals and eliminating punctuation in the manner of e. e. cummings, all of which had an impact that is still being felt today. Intensely personal and graphic expression became more common.

Despite the strong American influence, Canadian poetry had a unique voice of its own. E. J. Pratt's The Shark became a classic with its lines "His fin / like a piece of sheet iron, / three cornered, / and with a knife edge, / stirred not a bubble / as it moved with its baseline on the water."

These words are evocative of a northern scene. So too, the lines from A. J. M. Smith's The Lonely Land "Cedar and jagged fir / uplift sharp barbs / against the gray / and cloud piled sky." Earle Birney's North of Superior captured "the rhythm of trees / wild where they clutch at pools."

Different regions of Canada produced outstanding poets in both official languages. A. M. Klein, a Quebec poet, led a Montreal movement which included younger poets Louis Dudek, Irving Layton and Dorothy Livesay. Livesay, a Winnipeg native, developed a strong feminist voice. From her *Unquiet Bed* came lines such as "The woman I am / is not what you see / I'm not just bones / and crockery." Her honest approach to sexuality opened the door for freer expression.

French Canadian poet Saint-Denys Garneau's sparse " I am a bird cage. / A cage of bone with a bird," reflected mood and economy in its translation. This was followed by strong and unique voices of Quebec's Anne Hebert and Manitoba's Gabrielle Roy. Other regional poets Eli Mandel, Elizabeth Brewster, Jay MacPherson, P. K. Page, Ralph

Gustafson, Ann Wilkinson and Margaret Avison bridged the past to the present. Poetry journals began to flourish and readers were startled by James Reaney's Anti-Christ as a Child and the protest poetry of Milton Acorn who said "I've tasted my blood too much / to love what I was born to."

As the heady Sixties waned, younger poets John Newlove, Gwendolyn MacEwen, Patrick Lane, Margaret Atwood and Pat Lowther invaded the poetic scene with new and daring assaults on the language of the day. Leonard Cohen turned to music and his recording of Suzanne became better known than his beautifully lyrical "As the mist leaves no scar / On the dark green hill / So my body leaves no scar / On you, nor ever will." Alden Nolan in his Bull Moose left images burned into our Canadian consciousness. And bill bissett and the Four Horseman brought poetry and sound to the exciting level of performance art. This in turn opened the door for more poetry readings and coffee house slams.

Even the long discarded practice of using end rhyme and set forms is making a comeback, and offering new challenge.

The Formalist movement is seeing more sonnets, haiku, quatrains, ballads, villanelles, and other strict forms return and gain back respect in both the printed journals and e-zines found on the World Wide Web. More than ever the poet needs to be grounded in the history of good craftsmanship, and what constitutes fine poetry.

The craft of poetry is not a mysterious one. When poets compose poems and the words seem to flow from nowhere, it is actually a clear example of the subconscious mind busy at work while we go about our daily business. The senses are used to absorb life around us. Children learn quickly through taste, touch, smell, hearing and seeing. In a way, poets retain this child-like sensitivity. They are more aware of their world and like to translate this into imaginative language which we call the poetic muse.

Some aspiring poets claim that the past and its poetic traditions have little relevance in today's fast moving world.

They will insist the important thing is to create, not to publish. But until communication is made between reader and poet, there is no poem; only a stillborn idea resting solely in the mind of a individual. Publication either by print or electronic means brings the creation of poetry special satisfaction and meaning.

Few poets are satisfied completely with their work. If they were, their poetry would not mature or improve beyond the apprentice stage. Most poets continue to learn by reading work from the past, as well as that of their contemporaries. They strive to practice economy of word, and to find new ways of expressing themselves, and stretching the imagination to its outer limits. A fine example of this kind of crafting is found in the conversational poems of Al Purdy through lines such as "No, my grandfather was decidedly unbeautiful / 250 pounds of scarred slag."

For those who despair that the teaching of poetry has lagged behind the sciences and computer age, one has only to link up with the many poetic voices on the Internet to realize that poetry is far from dead. It is evolving as it should into a brand new century. Canadian poets have a chance as never before to have their words widely recorded in the Information Age. They can join their global versifiers as purveyors of the muse. For those still practicing their art by more conventional means, the print medium still remains the most potent avenue for well crafted poetry. The road ahead is an exciting one, and the maps have already been drawn. Whether you climb aboard the global train or take that familiar path to small and intimate audiences, your words can be to paraphrase Keats "a thing of beauty."

Peggy Fletcher, former editor of *Canadian Poetry* and *Mamashee*, has had four poetry books and a short story collection published. Her work has appeared internationally. She has won awards for her poetry and playwriting. Also a visual artist, she lives in Sarnia, Ontario.

# Meld Music and Message

*by Bernice Lever*

**A**s good poetry is a true blend of sound and sense, good poets strive for that perfect mix of tones and vocabulary.

How do you invite your muse in for a visit?

There are as many ways to summon that inspiration as there are different types of writers. Some writers just close their eyes and meditate, shutting out distractions around them, while others set themselves tasks to complete. Since memories, experiences and flashes of insight happen at random times, be certain you always carry a notebook and pencil with you throughout your day. Dorothy Livesay recommended paper and pen on your night table to jot down dreams or nightmares before they fade away.

Good poets are alive to all their senses: sound, smell, sight, taste and touch. Also they often note details of their environment that can be used later. Here are several ways to awaken your senses:

Take a walk in the fall woods, or along a stormy seashore, or high in an alpine meadow.

Sip wine to your favourite music on a comfy couch.

Trace your lover's face with your fingertips.

Push a veteran's wheelchair through a farmer's market.

Dance and sing in a strange culture in a foreign land, or to a video in your own front room.

Then jot down your feelings. Describe that scene and one new character encountered. Let these simmer until your subconscious pokes you into writing that connected poem.

Some poets find unconnected words or images while flipping through books or magazines. You can open your dictionary at random, three or five times, then try to connect the words you discover in the upper right hand corners. What pattern does your mind develop with these words?

When looking for words, you can try several types of brainstorming, such as those described in *Branching* by H.A. Klauser and *Clustering* by G.L. Rico. In "freefall", W.O. Mitchell suggests a method of continuous writing for a set period of time, say, ten to thirty minutes. You do not stop writing or typing on a topic once you start on it. You just keep your words and phrases flowing. If your topic seems to run dry or your mind goes blank, just write lists of names of people, animals, colours and more. In this very act of forced writing and creating, your mind will eventually release buried thoughts and feelings that you have not been able to write about consciously. In freefall writing (or in any first drafts), do not worry about sentence structure, spelling, grammar, agreements or such, just let your writing flow for a unified piece. As singer David Campbell says, "There is beauty deep down inside every one of us." Grammatical errors can be and should be corrected later, but an interrupted flow is not easy to turn on again.

Writers, especially poets without the pressure of deadlines, need to give themselves permission to write. You should write often, at a certain time of day, or at least, your special time alone each week. If you have no new inspirations or visits from your muses, use that time for revising and marketing your poems. Poems need to be rewritten and pondered over ten times each, even if you later discover that version two or four was the best one. Yes, a poem can become over-worked, dull and dry, so keep your "work in progress" versions for comparison. After years of editing, and heeding the advice of other good poets or rare editors, you will develop critical skills that will tell you when a poem is ready for public eyes and ears.

Sometimes you may want to avoid the white paper and empty computer screen, and just talk into a tape recorder for ten to twenty minutes or more. Then listen and re-listen with eyes closed. Are there phrases or sentences you wish to save on paper or disk? Whether you work alone or in a group, reading your poems aloud will produce rewarding editing changes.

Writing exercises explore technique and allow your skills to grow. Often poets need to create a dozen new beginnings to develop what will eventually become one or two fine poems. Just do not expect great or even good poems every day you write. You have to work many dull rock and slag heaps before you uncover gold veins. Just keep mining your memory and exploring your imagination.

Discovering who you are and what you want to say to the world is a poet's lifelong career. As you revise and polish rough notes and first drafts of poems, you are learning about yourself and then honing your poems to their sharpest edge. Within your style, you are developing your "trademark" poetic voice. One that will be unique and apart from each poem's narrative voice: first person singular, omnipresent, etc. Whatever you believe, your focus and values in life, your unanswered questions and philosophy, will shape your themes and slants and biases in your poems.

Read widely of poets both living and dead world-wide all the years that you write . Choose a few who please you, and then try to imitate and/or to parody them by writing your versions of a few of their poems. This exercise gives you vocabulary control as well as helps to define your own voice. By trying to write or to sing like another poet, you learn who you are and are not. Comparing and contrasting yourself with your favourite poets can aid you in shaping your own distinctive voice. Such exercises should also help you spot unintentional echoes of those you admire that will need editing from your poems from time to time. Your personality will choose most of the content, detail and message of your poems.

Your vocabulary and the way you use language will be the major components of your poetic voice. All poets need and use their dictionaries and thesaurus to expand the number of words they understand, but your best poems are those that spring from your own speaking vocabulary. I could use my reference books to write: "cool iridescent carrageen / clambering, clinging clumsily / over clammy creviced coves." to describe Irish moss, only to lose my reader in tongue-twisting vocabulary that calls too much attention to itself. Being too cute or too clever with words turns a possibly good poem into silly or sad crap.

Good poets know that each word has its own history of meanings and emotional effects. Poets delight in the different connotations and denotations of words. In the 1990s, not even the gays have a "gay time" as did the "flappers" in the 1920s. What teenager today, reading poems on the Internet, knows the word "flapper"? Yes, words are the writer's "building blocks", but to me they are more like ice cubes. If the poet sets the right words next to each other, a poem or rainbow-emitting ice sculpture is created. But if words are chosen and placed carelessly, the would-be poet is left with a shapeless puddle of muddy music and message.

Whatever your poem is about, you will need some concrete imagery to anchor your thoughts and feelings. There should be some literal meaning or descriptive words from the five senses. Good poets use specific, definite words, not just "a summer's day," but "an ice-cold-watermelon black-seed-spitting day." Poets reach readers by actual details (even when invented) because readers have emotional memories attached to each of their interactions with the five senses. So readers immediately start to compare their reaction or involvement with watermelons to those in the poem. Hurrah! Your reader is involved in your poem. So whether your poem is about Art experienced or life on Mars in the year 2200 AD, your poem will be more effective with intelligent use (never overkill) of real or imagined sensory data.

Metaphors and other poetic devices are the poet's arrows to reach a reader's heart and brain. These can be as gentle as the one my student once wrote, "the sound of silence is one freckle forming." Or they can be as powerful as Irving Layton's lines in 'If Whales Could Think'. "Just then the harpoon / slammed into his side / tearing a hole in it / as wide as the sky." For excellent use of language, read his 'Keine Lazarovitch: 1870-1959', or Lorna Crozier's 'Inventing the Hawk'.

Do you recognize your own cadence? Poets spend time changing the alignments in their poems trying to achieve the best rhythm and sound effects for their poems. Some try to start and to end lines with strong verbs and nouns, while others want whole poems to flow as one forever sentence. Do you question your poems as to whether it wants waltzing, marching or jazzing words? Do your readers find your poetic voice recognizable without your written signature on your poem. Perhaps you want an ironic fun rhythm to undercut your harsh message? Your poems will still have your voice even in different tempos.

Poets should attend readings by contemporary poets and/or listen to tapes, as it is too easy to get stuck in the music of the Romantic poets of the 1800s! For sound effects in your poetry, explore and test rhyme, slant-rhyme, alliteration, assonance and more. Puns and allusions can also add richness to your musical mixture. Whether you are writing song lyrics or not, you need some mastery of the sound values of words.

Can you name the mood or tone of each of your poems? Somehow poems grow from your sweetest dreams and your scariest nightmares. You will need all of your imagination and learned poetic skills to control the emotion—choose which one and at which level—that you wish to share in each poem. Obviously, in a long narrative poem, a poet can move the reader to tears, then anger, to laughter, and back, but a good poet gets an emotional response in pieces of any length. Poems are wonderful vehicles for poets and their readers to develop and to understand their emotions. Can you really share a feeling with others that you cannot put into words? Some people do with music or painting or dance. Sensitive poets are open to their own feelings and are aware of the range in other people's. Yes, poems can be used to jar the complacency of the readers, but the brain recalls best what the heart felt first.

Power in poetry comes from its compression and complexity. Great poems have several layers of possible meanings as the good poets use allusions and delusions, and many more poetic techniques to create word holograms that seem to change as you grow with experience! For example, Margaret Avison's "Snow" provides new riches on each re-reading, as does Clifton Joseph's "Black on Black". Poetry lives as an oral tradition; even when reading the screen or the page silently, readers want to "hear" your voice.

Through public workshops, college courses or your own home study with a few library books, there are ways to understand and to develop the many skills needed to create good poems. Today, some take part in Internet workshops, but these lack the tone of voice and facial expressions of the personal contact, so it may be trickier to give honest but kind criticism although the chat mode of back-and-forth comments could help clear up misunderstandings. At a local workshop, read your poem aloud or have another speak it. If you live in an isolated community, swap voice cassettes. If you own a video camera and recorder, perform for each other. Video cassettes and VCRs are wonderful devices for seeing and hearing how well you project your poem. You should at least listen to yourself before you have a radio or TV interview or reading. Each of these individual or shared experiences of your poems can let you grow as a poet.

There are many exercises or techniques that you can use to help focus or improve an early draft of a poem. Try giving the reader your same message through the voice of your grandmother or grandson, your enemy or your lover, a prisoner on death row or an astronaut on the moon, a 1800s pioneer or 2100s colonist on Venus, or from a new immigrant on your block. From the changes you make, you can start to discover who you are, and whether using your own viewpoint for that particular poem is the most effective one.

Sometimes the most wonderful metaphor you have ever created is the very one you need to eliminate! If a poem seems perfect in its first draft, try lining up in two columns all the subjects (mainly nouns and pronouns) with their verbs. O.K., you can have a third column of direct objects. For this exercise, ignore all descriptors: adjectives, adverbs, similes and metaphors as well as connectors: prepositions and conjunctions. Next compare your bare bones or poem skeleton of two or three columns with your full poem. Are your verbs and subjects in the most intriguing order? Should you have started at the middle and worked in circles to the beginning and ending like ripples from a meteor hissing into a cold lake? How many of the descriptor words of the first version add excitement, clarity and depth? Discard as many as possible, then add drama and rhythm with some new ones. Is the second poem better?

If not, try another route to "polishing your rough gem" of a poem. If you can't cope with eliminating many of your words, try cutting your sentences into phrases and clauses. Next scatter these in random patterns on the table top, then push them into patterns of long and short lines. Is this trick showing you a more arresting poem? Perhaps just one part of your original is stronger in this changed order. Try printing your poem with your non-writing hand while creating it, as this slows down your inscribing speed.

Another playful way to vary your voice or alignment in poems is to write on narrow rolls of adding machine paper for short lines, and then re-write the same poems in long lines of 14-inch-wide ledger paper. Which version seems more "you"?

Sometimes just filing your creations away for a few weeks will help you evaluate your lines objectively. All our creations, at birth, seem awesome! There are many books, workshops, cassettes—both voice and video—and writer's magazine columns to give you many more ideas about how to improve your poems. One line, even a single word, from these exercises or practice word games may launch a flood of feeling, flowing words that create your true poem.

Just keep going deeper inside yourself and reaching further outside to other poets, until somewhere in the middle, you recognize you—the poet—with your own unique voice and individual style. You will meld your music with your message.

Bernice Lever, a Canadian Authors Association member for more than 25 years, has been leading creative writing workshops and clubs for 30 years. She teaches English at Seneca College in the Toronto, Ontario area. Editor of *Waves* (1972-1987), her sixth book of poems is *Things Unsaid*, Black Moss, 1996.

# Poetry for Children: Create an Emotional Adventure

*by Lola Sneyd*

don't write for children, I write for the child in me. This child is fascinated by the sight, sound, smell and feeling of words that bounce around in my imagination, arranging and rearranging themselves as they create word pictures.

A bonus is having a child tell me or write to me that a certain poem "is my favourite one," and then share a "private one" of their own with me. When classrooms of students use my poems for choral reading, in dramatic sketches, create computer posters or a calligraphy art show with them, that's when I feel as if I am the luckiest person in the world.

I've been writing all my life, especially poetry, and had my first article on nature published in a national magazine at eleven, and many poems published in high school magazines. Nevertheless, as an adult, it was years before I had the courage to submit my work to publishers. Somehow I had not yet learned to have confidence in my own talent.

I enjoy visiting schools, encouraging the students to believe in themselves as writers, to go with their ideas—silly, funny, ridiculous, happy, sad, lonely, angry, unusual... I urge them to get that split-second idea down, let it simmer, jot down all their thoughts about it, choosing the exact words to create the image they want. I suggest each student should try to be original, this is what gives the poem "sparkle", the excitement felt when that student first caught that poem-idea. It is the reason that poem may be published, and will be read and remembered by readers. This encouragement is vital, and should be used instead of negative, hurtful comments that can crush a child's creativity and fragile feelings of self-worth.

To write for children, Claudia Lewis, in *Writing for Young Children*, says: "Begin by tearing off those top layers of yours." Become a child again. Remember a vivid experience you had as a child, see things with fresh eyes and with all your senses. Listen to children, view things from a child's world, be curious and state your ideas simply.

Merely mastering the techniques of writing poetry will not insure that your poetry will be enjoyed by children. You need to enjoy reading their kind of poetry yourself, to delight in the rhythm of the words and the ideas as you did when you were a child. Then you may write the kinds of poems they treasure, too.

Above all, write for the child inside of you.

Lola Sneyd is a poet, short story writer, journalist and teacher of Creative Writing and Writing for Children, (adult and children students.) She has written five books for children, writes for and about all ages, and is published in Canada, U.S., England and Australia. Her first book of poetry for children, *The Asphalt Octopus*, has been reprinted three times.

# Get Paid for Your Poetry

*by Lola Sneyd*

**W**riting poetry is fun, and many poets tell about the "high" they get when they've completed a fantastic, inspiring, stupendous...(take your pick, or add your own adjective) poem. They ride this crest of elation for weeks or months only to be plummeted to earth with a rejection slip. The lament then is: "I just can't get published!"

After hearing this so many times I've reached the conclusion that the difference between writing poetry and not getting it published and writing it and getting it published is just old-fashioned work.

Writing poetry may be fun, but marketing poetry is work.

Keeping accurate records is time-consuming and boring work and not very creative (I'd rather write any day), but if you're serious about becoming a published (and paid) poet and are willing to work, here are some suggestions and short-cuts to help you get your brain-child in print.

Where do you find markets for your poetry? Everywhere. Libraries, bookstores, schools, doctors' and dentists' offices. *The Canadian Writer's Guide* and the *Writer's Market* are just a few places to begin your search.

Leaf through magazines wherever you find them and study the poems in them to see if the editors use the type of poem you write. (Unlike article and story writing, which is being taught in creative writing classes all over the country, poetry is such a personal art, even the best teachers of these classes hesitate to teach it. Many say they know what a good poem is but don't know how it is done.)

If you write your poem in the style that is being published (slanting) you usually find you've lost it and the result isn't you, so the sensible thing to do is to find a market that uses your kind of writing.

What kind of poem do you write? Is it light verse, juvenile or adult humor, nature, haiku, free verse, inspirational, religious, greeting-card verse, song lyrics, literary, sports, retired man or woman, etc.?

There are specific markets for all types of poetry, from literary quarterlies, newspaper letter pages, school textbook anthologies, jingle contests to electronic e-zines.

How do you find these markets?

Besides checking all the periodicals that cross my path (like a bee drawn to honey, writers zero in on all published matter within theft range), about once a year I go through the poetry markets in *The Canadian Writer's Guide* and the *Writer's Market*, making a list of possible markets and rates of pay for my type of poems. Then I narrow the field to the ten best prospects and write a short note requesting sample copies of their publications.

When these arrive—and nine out of ten times they come almost by return mall, frequently with an encouraging handwritten word of welcome from the editor—I study them to see if these might be future markets. If so, I send in four to six poems, neatly typewritten, double-spaced, one poem to a page with my name and address in the top left-hand corner, plus a stamped, addressed return envelope, being sure to enclose the proper amount of appropriate postage or International Reply Coupons.

To keep track of submissions some poets use cross-indexed file cards with the title and first line and the possible markets. Others, like myself, keep a lined notebook with the titles of poems listed down the left hand side of the page, and lines ruled about a half-inch apart from top to bottom of the rest of the page. Across the top of the page in these spaces I write the markets. As I send out a poem, I jot down the date under the market in ink, and in pencil I put small check marks under the possible future markets.

When a poem is returned (don't read "rejected") I put "R" for returned, and the date under the submitted date.

If it is sold, I put "**SOLD**" in bold red letters, the date and payment beside the poem.

As quickly as possible, I get those returned poems back in the mail to the next market I've checked in pencil, and I keep doing this. As I said, selling poems is work, plus persistence. Poems in a returned envelope, sitting in a desk drawer gathering dust, won't ever be published.

What are your chances of being published in that national monthly magazine that you see on all the newsstands? Very small. Twelve issues a year that use only one or two poems in each issue equals at most only a couple of dozen chances out of thousands of poems submitted. Weekly newsmagazines or periodicals and newspapers that have poetry corners or use poems as fillers are excellent markets.

As all writers know, Canada has relatively few markets for freelance writing and few mass-circulation poetry markets. Almost every state in the United States has more markets than all of Canada. Britain is another good market for poets. Investigate farther afield than your own backyard. The markets are there if you'll look for them.

Some reasons why poems are rejected are:

• Too-long verse. You'll sell short verse to periodicals quicker than long ones. Twenty lines (and usually fewer) is the limit for most publications.

• Too-long lines. Try to express yourself in short lines. It may give your poems new movement and vigor. Periodicals use narrow columns and your poems must fit the column.

• Avoid "just good reporting." Good, factual reporting is an essential element of good poetry but when you've written something especially well, stop and ask yourself, "What of it?" If your answer is original and has impact, you may have the makings of a poem.

• Avoid tired verse. Write with freshness, life and vigor, and avoid the clichés and bromides.

• Avoid parodies. Too many poets do this and it annoys many editors because you're copying.

To be published and paid, write, write and write. Not just in your head, but on paper. The more you write, the more you'll develop a way with words, a way of writing that even though you may have agonized over it, looks easy and free. See how your words look on paper, say them aloud. Are these the exact words that best convey your meaning? (A dictionary is a poet's best friend.) Don't be afraid to rewrite. All writers do this.

When your poem says what you want it to say—is you—then submit, submit and submit until you've found the right market for this creation that gave you that "high."

Good luck and happy pay cheque!

Lola Sneyd is a poet, short story writer, journalist and teacher of Creative Writing and Writing for Children, (adult and children students.) She has written five books for children, writes for and about all ages, and is published in Canada, U.S., England and Australia. Her first book of poetry for children, *The Asphalt Octopus*, has been reprinted three times.

# Newspapers and Periodicles

# Fame on the Community Weekly

by Lola Sneyd ⎯⎯⎯⎯⎯⎯⎯⎯⎯⎯⎯⎯

I have been frequently asked, "Why do you write for a local weekly when your field is poetry and writing for children? Isn't it time consuming and not very rewarding?"

My answer is, why not be a big frog in a little pond? I've been one for many years and am enjoying it now as much as I did when I first started.

Some of the finest human-interest writing is done in local newspapers, and some articles are reprinted in national publications.

One that was reprinted was an article, with photographs, of our local Brownies presenting a wheelchair to The Canadian Cancer Society in memory of Cathy, their nine-year-old Brownie friend who had died of leukemia. This chair was obtained by saving Dominion Store cash register tapes and is now in constant use. One of the first to use it was our 18-year-old star lacrosse player, Tony, a hero and inspiration to the young people in our local lacrosse club. Tony died a few months later and his teammates, sixteen-to-eighteen-year-olds, donated much needed play therapy equipment to the Children's Ward at Princess Margaret Hospital in Toronto in his memory.

Who but a friend of these young people would know of these stories and could write so that people across the country would become involved with The Canadian Cancer Society and have an appreciation of what great kids there are today. (Letters to the Editor, "praise in print," speak volumes and are an unexpected gift, a tangible reward to a big frog.)

Perhaps as a local writer you'll never achieve international fame, but music to a writer is recognition (plus a regular pay cheque), and no matter where you go—shopping, at school, at a game or at church—someone will come up and say, "I didn't know that about George, or Mary. How interesting!" Or because your name is in the local paper, they recognize it in a book or a magazine at school, the library or in a Sunday School pub-lication and meet you on the street with, "My kids got a kick out of your poem, or story!" As Jackie Gleason used to say, "How sweet it is!"

All is not sweetness and light, however. There are the letters saying you got the date wrong, misspelled a name, or spelled convener with an "or." You do get blamed for any and all typographical errors, but where else do you get instant feed-back?

When it comes to writing humor, the weekly writer has it made:

• A turtle named George lays seventeen eggs and the kids make money selling "male" turtle eggs. Their hand-lettered signs read: *Start your own ecology project. Be the first on your block to hatch your own turtle.*

• An ad on a telephone pole at the Lake Ontario beach across the street from our home: *Found—lower dentures—on the beach on Saturday night.* (By a mermaid taking a skinny dip by the light of the full moon?)

• The fascinated three-year-old exclaiming to the children watching their pet beagle give birth to ten young, "Look how she unplugs the pup-pies!" And the knowledgeable five-year-old brother retorts, "You mean cuts the cord. You can't unplug a puppy. It's not a toaster!"

Like all writers you're always listening, on streetcars, local buses, on boardwalk or window-shopping strolls—and always jotting down thoughts and observations. But how many writers see these jottings in print the next week?

A big frog does.

A weekly deadline means you've got to produce, daily if possible, or you'll develop writer's cramp on the weekend.

Impossible, you say? Not at all, because the well of ideas never runs dry. Of course, it does help to have a family whose activities reach into every facet of life, but for writers who don't have an active family, just look around you. Personalities and happenings are everywhere:

• The visit of grade eight students to the Senior Citizens' meeting, hearing history from living pioneers. The boys and girls became volun-teer bakers for the afternoon tea-time, swapping recipes and making last-ing friendships.

• The Senior Citizens staging variety shows, including a lively can-can, to raise funds for young lacrosse players.

• The High School Smelt Derby in a freezing drizzle which proved that not only the show, but school spirit, must go on.

• The beginning of girls' lacrosse, with the first ever Golden Horseshoe Girls Lacrosse League tournament held at the Canadian National Exhibition. It drew a record twenty-two thousand spectators and not one of the giant daily papers even mentioned it. These articles are part of the history of the C.N.E., and these tournaments a regular feature each year. (Being manager of the winning team, with daughter Nancy the captain, made this an easy "I was there" article to write.)

• The nonagenarian making the Guinness Book of Records for the second time, once at eighty-one and again at ninety-four by scoring a hole-in-one at the same hole and with the same golf-buddy.

Lola Sneyd is a poet, short story writer, journalist and teacher of Creative Writing and Writing for Children, (adult and children students.) She has written five books for children, writes for and about all ages, and is published in Canada, U.S., England and Australia.

# Plan a Weekly Newspaper Column

*by Gerald Walton Paul* ⎯⎯⎯⎯⎯⎯⎯⎯⎯

Since 1984, I've written over five hundred 1,000-word pieces for my weekly *Kingston Whig-Standard* column (circulation 30,000). Though religion has trouble getting ink these days, my column on religion has survived over a decade.

As a columnist, I've learned plenty from poets, novelists, dramatists, essayists, non-fiction authors, short story writers and the rest. Having incorporated their wisdom into the art of column writing, I have something valuable to give in return.

Writing a regular column has seven parts: planning, researching, outlining, incubating, writing, editing and responding to readers. Each is joined to the next one. Reader-response to a published column—the end of the process—influences the planning of future columns—the start of the process. Each part adds skill, energy and motivation to those that follow. The result? Writer's block happens rarely, if ever.

Before beginning to write a column, we need to consider a few "givens." Columnists bring all their experience, knowledge, and their personal identities to their desks. I am a generalist with a specialty. The base on which I draw for the process of writing a weekly column is deep in religion and broad in other fields of knowledge.

There is something he has never caught. / Something that makes him stand here / every evening, casting, casting / and reeling in. Like Lorna Crozier's angler, I spend the planning stage fishing for ideas.

To enable me to meet weekly deadlines, each September I strike 53 tentative themes for the following calendar year. Useful planning tools include: *Farmers' Almanac*, *A Book of Days for the Literary Year* edited by Neal T. Jones, and a variety of books and calendars on the four seasons. By the time I've entered topics for major holidays—New Year's, Valentine's, St. Patrick's, Mother's Day, Father's Day, Canada Day,

Labour Day, Thanksgiving and Remembrance Day—plus extras for Lent, Easter, Pentecost, Advent and Christmas—themes for half the year's columns are in place.

I generate titles as soon as possible. Titles may evolve from general themes, dictate the parameters of preconceived themes, or suggest fresh themes. They may be evoked by collections of poems, clichés and quotations; lists of images from my journals, sermons, speeches; tear-sheets from newspapers and periodicals. These collections of classical and contemporary "triggers" are catalysts for creating themes and sharpening them to titles.

For the remaining themes, I fish in my filing system. In 40 years, I've filed over 15,000 three-by-five index cards. My collection constitutes the best quotes, images and anecdotes from reading, experience and imagination. I group the 15,000 cards by means of elastic bands under 200 paired categories. These include: chance and providence, the going and the goal, freedom and order, wonder and awe, vices and virtues, comedy and tragedy, love and hate, hope and despair, faith and doubt, memory and imagination, good and evil, annuals and perennials, comfort and courage. My angle of vision influences what I put on the cards and the accumulated cards influence my angle of vision. The product is creativity and speed. In a day or two, I can plan an entire year of columns without any irritation.

Besides banks of index card files, I have an old fishing box labelled "Fish File." Into this go fresh index cards produced from recent encounters and from insights gleaned from reading. During the planning stage, to fill out a year's supply of themes I often "Go fish!"

Then, too, a three-tiered open table, my "Fresh Rack," sits on top of a bookcase. When I read papers, magazines and letters I cut or tear out material with potential to trigger a topic. These are placed on the bottom tier. As this tier fills, I select promising resources for upcoming columns and raise them to the second tier. Best bets eventually arrive on the top deck. From this group I select the rest of the year's topics. Resources that stay on the bottom I eventually discard.

In addition to index cards, Fish File and Fresh Rack, legal-size files covering my major areas of interest provide easy access to historical and timeless material. Categories in these files are the same as those in the index files.

After planning, the next step is researching, focused on an upcoming theme. The purpose of focused research is to find a sharp angle for treating a general theme. In successive years, researching the general topic I've listed simply as "a Mother's Day piece" has produced the following focused columns: "My Mother-in-law", "To Unknown Mothers", "Critique of Mother's Day Sermons", "Readers' Perception of Mother from Reader Responses", "Mother's Religious Legacy to Me".

While researching, columnists are hunters searching for game that tickles their fancy (and hopefully that of their readers). Lead time for this should be a minimum of a month. I always keep my nose to the news. If I see a subject such as "turbot" getting a lot of ink in April, even though the theme planned for July was "Fishing in the Bible", I'll move it up to spring rather than wait to use it in summer.

When a particular subject dominates the news, that is the time to write about it. It would be a mistake to stick to the plan and write a column on every topic entered on my annual planning pad. As well, time has a way of filtering out subjects that a columnist doesn't feel like writing. Unless some excitement is evoked by the thought of writing on a particular topic—gun registration, for example—there's no use tackling it. While many alternative subjects are chosen for columns, it's surprising how many of the original tentative themes end up under my byline.

Every writer needs to plan. The very act of planning supplies the energy as well as the formula to generate new ideas to replace those that do not succeed.

Without focused research, a sharp angle would never emerge and this year's Valentine's Day column would only echo last year's. Re-telling "the old, old story" may be important for some readers, but for the columnist, unless a fresh way of seeing comes into play, boredom creeps in, and writers' block is seldom far behind.

The next step in the writing process is that of outlining. In outlining a column, as in playing a round of golf, a game plan is essential. In the beginning I had pages and pages of outlines. I'd use numerous directional headings. At the keyboard, I was forever turning pages of outlines, trying to find where I should go next.

Currently, I work with a single uncluttered page. My mini-outline is confined to four headings: Lead, Slant, Body, Ending. With time, I end up with a bare-bones written outline, all on one page with headings highlighted. The mind freely chooses not only the story line but all the ingredients needed to stick with the theme. Outlining, I've learned, is not just the product of thought but the creator as well.

Leads are miniature maps. Hitting upon a lead prior to outlining can just about write the column. When focused research is adequate, the lead usually leaps into mind. The lead provides focus, energy and limits. An outline without a lead is worse than no outline.

The next step in the column-writing process is that of incubation. The most productive period of incubation is after outlining and before writing. Because of the short deadline the columnist faces, the incubation phase is abbreviated to a day or two.

While incubating, I try to spend as much time as possible alone. Talking about the piece at this stage squanders creativity. After working on the outline for the next column, I head for the nearby Rideau Trail. Now and then, a lead sentence comes to mind, absorbing as by osmosis the rhythm of my step. The motion of walking brings the body as well as the mind and emotions into the writing process. I call this "embodiment of the column." Nothing is as concrete as bodily movement. Without it writing can become ethereal, abstract, uninspired, perhaps even impossible.

"Good writing," wrote Ralph Waldo Emerson, "is a kind of skating which carries the performer where he would not go."

I used to follow a detailed outline and glacially slowly proceed to write and edit at the same time. The result was often a ragged article. I soon learned to separate writing and editing and to write fast and long one day and to edit at leisure the next. It's a real time-saver in the long run and that's important for a columnist. Writing quickly liberates the writer from robotically following the outline. By postponing editing, ambivalence of attention vanishes: I'm committed to writing. The result is a piece that flows rather than one that limps along.

More important, by writing quickly, one not only expresses what the writer knows but discovers things about the subject that at the conscious level were formerly unknown. I call this "the going is the goal." In writing quickly, we tap reservoirs of rhythm, form and content. We also access imagery we didn't know was there. Writers should be like skaters: They should go partly where they want to go and partly where the skates take them.

Editing a column—the sixth step—is like weeding a rose garden so as to display the order, unity and beauty of the roses while exorcising anything that might break the spell.

For me, editing is the easiest part of the writing process. Having written long there is much to cut. Before cutting line by line, I rearrange paragraphs so that they have a logical, aesthetic or dramatic order. I work with the image of gardening. I imagine myself laying out beds with flowers of similar or complementary shape, colour, height, texture and fragrance. The flow's the thing. I seek coherence: Things must hang together.

While editing paragraphs, I keep in mind the title, angle, mood, theme and rhythm of the column. Digressions, padding, repetitions, overkill, ego-trip anecdotes, cryptic analogies and opaque illustrations—all are deleted. In *speaking*, I tell listeners what I'm going to tell them, tell them, then tell them what I have just told them. But in *writing*, once is enough.

In line-by-line editing, I use the image of a gardener using a Whipper-Snipper in wild abandon. I whipper-snip adjectives, spare verbs, bisect complex sentences, and follow the gardener's motto, "Keep it simple, stupid!" Readers buy newspapers for their own edification, not to admire the columnist. By the time I've edited for four hours, the 2,000-word piece I wrote at a fast clip has shrunk to a 1,000-word column ready to upload to the *Whig-Standard*.

Feedback is important to the writer. I get responses by telephone, correspondence, letters to the editor and through personal encounters. I analyze these responses to discover what the readers feel. Responding to readers completes the process.

When I feed wild birds, they enhance my life with their beauty and song. When readers send me their responses, I am nourished and become a better writer, thanks to their contribution.

As a columnist, these seven steps and their accompanying images—planning/fishing, researching/hunting, outlining/golfing, incubating/walking, writing/skating, editing/gardening, responding/bird-feeding—not only keep me writing but keep me healthy and happy as well. Writers, whatever their genre, who adopt this imaging method of writing, will find writing easier, faster, more pleasurable and more saleable than ever before.

Gerald Walton Paul is a United Church minister who, while serving urban congregations and university campuses, managed to write occasional articles and columns for periodicals and newspapers. Since 1983, he has been a full-time freelancer. An amateur naturalist, he also contributes articles on the natural world to magazines and newspapers.

# The Art of the Article

*by Beatrice Fines*

The article—by any name: travelogue, editorial, news feature, personality profile, essay—gives you more scope than any other kind of writing you may try. Make it long or short, funny, serious, even scholarly, but make it accurate and make it flow. Your article may come straight out of your own experience, or you may write on a subject about which you know nothing in the beginning, if you do your research carefully and thoroughly.

An example of the "off the top of the head" kind of article is one I did criticizing the crowded, look-alike building that goes on in most suburban housing developments. To research it, about all I had to do was take a look around me, and express my feelings. I did make a couple of phone calls to check on zoning by-laws.

At the other extreme was an article on Driver Education in Manitoba about which I knew nothing. Research for this started with a couple of phone calls and continued with interviews with gentlemen from the Manitoba Motor Vehicles Branch, who sent me home loaded down with brochures and statistical analyses; and with managers of commercial driver-education schools, who did the same. (Incidentally, when I get that kind of co-operation from people, I say "thanks" by letting them know exactly what I am going to say that concerns them, either by reading that part of the article to them over the phone, or by sending them a carbon. This not only makes friends, it also prevents mistakes. I am referring, of course, to situations where you are dealing with facts, not opinions.)

Whether the knowledge needed comes out of your own head, the heads of others, or a pile of papers, books and brochures, the next step is to decide what aspect of the subject to explore, what slant to take, and what to say first, second and third. In the article on suburban development my contention was that builders have little regard for the natural beauty of an area, and crowd too much into too little space. I used a somewhat satirical style. After describing an undeveloped area (the one I happen to live in), I told what a developer would probably do to it in words like these:

> "...they could fill up the creek and the hollows where the pussy willows grow and clear the bush in a couple of afternoons with the right kind of equipment. By taking out a dozen or so big oaks they'd have room for three or four high-rises, back to back. The alfalfa field to the east would make a good site for a shopping centre and nothing compares to the fragrance of asphalt on a good hot day..."

In the second article I wanted to tell how the commercial schools and the government-sponsored driver education programs in the high schools are run, what laws govern them, how driver-teachers are trained, what the pupils pay, how insurance companies regard driver education, with some statistical reports of the accident records of trained drivers as compared to those who have not had driving lessons, and to take a look at how we may learn to drive in the future. I did not slant this article either "for" or "against," but simply reported what I learned. My style was straightforward, and the problem in writing this piece was "what do I say first?"

I usually find writing the lead, "what I say first," the most difficult part of any article. Although you don't have to spell out the 5 Ws, bang, bang, bang, as in news reporting, the lead must indicate what the article is about, and it should be as bright and clear as a photograph. It's one of the places where the article writer may borrow a technique from the short story writer, and start with characters, dialogue, even a problem situation.

The lead may pose a question: "Are we running out of oil?" or make a surprise statement: "In spite of what many citizens may believe, the Red and Assiniboine rivers are cleaner today than they were in the 1930s," which is one I used in an article.

Once the lead is written, the rest of the material must be organized and presented in the most interesting and natural sequence. When there are several aspects to explore, as there were in the piece on driver education, I usually write each facet of the article separately and then try to arrange the various paragraphs in the best order. After I organize my material, I read it aloud and re-work it until I am satisfied it flows as smoothly as possible.

To increase interest, you can't beat putting people in your article. Use dialogue or quotes, and "humanize" your material as much as possible.

Put yourself in, if the subject is personal. If you must include "cold facts" warm them up as much as possible. For instance, you may say the state of Virginia produces five hundred thousand tons of ham a year, or you could find out what the weight of the ham in an average sandwich is, and come up with something like this: "Last year the state of Virginia produced enough ham to give every man, woman and child in the United States sixteen ham sandwiches." Or, if you must say that the Republic of Togo is roughly twenty-one thousand square miles, add that it is approximately the same size as Nova Scotia.

When your article is finished, read the beginning and the ending. They should balance each other. The beginning should show what you mean to say, and the ending should show that you have said it.

Writing an article is work, often hard work. But it can be rewarding. That's what I meant to say in the beginning. Is that what I said?

Beatrice Fines has taught creative writing in adult continuing education classes and has participated in Manitoba's Artists in the Schools Program. Beatrice's sixty short stories and over two-hundred articles have been published in Canada, the United States and Great Britain.

# Seasonal Articles—Plan Ahead

*by A. C. Stone* _____

T he air conditioner had just suffered its annual breakdown and I was about to have mine. I opened a window to trade some of the stifling air inside the house for some of the even warmer air outside. The dull clatter of my neighbor's lawnmower rose to a full-throated roar. The muffled shrieks of his kids in their pool grew to riot proportions. I closed the window...better suffocation than distraction.

Back at my word processor I tried to write something funny about Christmas. Visions of sugar plums did *not* dance through my head.

Topical humor, like any other seasonal material, must be written months in advance, whether you're in the mood or not. There isn't much you can do about unsuitable or uninspiring weather, but you must plan your articles and get them out, regardless. I find making a list at the beginning of each year helps a lot. For example:

• Begin in January by rising above your New Year's hangover. Think about July: The annual battle with crab grass begins. Is there a neighbor on your street whose lawn is immaculate? What kind of revenge can you plot so that you'll be spared the invidious comparison every time you pass?

• For February, if you can remember to buy your beloved a Valentine Day card, fine. But think August: Summer will be in full swing and so will the swimmers. Describe the frustrations of installing a pool; the problems of maintenance; or the trouble you have with the neighbors who think you run a free playground. Or how about that brother-in-law who only comes around when both the refrigerator and the pool are full?

• To be sheltered from the March winds, reflect on September: Describe the photos you took on your vacation last summer. (e.g. "This is a slide of Billy feeding peanuts to the monkeys the day we visited the zoo. Billy is the one wearing the cap. This is a picture of Billy at the

Doctor's getting his finger stitched.") Or, what about all of those interesting people you met while you were away? You know, the ones you invited to drop in if they were ever in the neighborhood. What happened when they took you up on the invitation?

• Put up your umbrella against April showers and forget the Easter rabbit. You're writing for October: The Halloween we observe is a combination of customs imported from other countries. A little research will tell you how it all started. Use that as a base, add a twist to bring it up to date and you've got an October article. (e.g. Given our current labor/management climate we could eliminate ghost stories and scare kids with some of the meatier strikes we've known.)

• Take a few minutes of a day in May—say, after you've put the screens up and look forward to November: It's time to replace the storm windows and clean up the back yard. (Idle thought: When the leaves of Brown come tumbling down, why can't they stay on his lawn?)

• So it's June and your daughter is getting married. As far as editors are concerned, it's December: Christmas cards—who invented them? Who do you send them to and why? Do you discriminate when it comes to who gets what kind of card? Have you ever sent a card out of guilt when you received one from someone you'd forgotten? Or, carols: Write some parodies. Lord knows, Rudolph can stand some competition. Or even Letters to Santa: Give Santa some suggestions for all those people who are too busy to write to him themselves.

• It may be July to the rest of the world, but in your house, where the air conditioner just quit, it's January: Write a list of resolutions that famous people might have made. (e.g. Benjamin Franklin: "I'm going to quit flying kites in thunderstorms. A guy could get killed that way.") Or, cross-country skiing is enjoying a surge of popularity. Your fictionalized efforts to master the sport could provide a column.

• In August, at the cottage, you'll be the only person thinking of February: Most people don't realize that there were actually two St. Valentines or that many of our current customs evolved from ancient fertility rites. Compare what they did then to what we do now. Or you might explore the changing viewpoint of senders of valentines, from elementary school (where every kid sends one to every other kid) to marriage (where it usually takes a little judicious prompting by the wife). But if St. Valentine doesn't turn you on, try Groundhog Day, the traditional indication of spring. List all of the other ways you can tell how long winter will last. (e.g. If your six-year-old falls off her toboggan and tears the seat out of her snowsuit, and you know she'll outgrow a new one before next winter, count on two more months of ice and snow.)

• Now that September is here at last and the kids are back at school, you'll have time to get ready for March: Spring cleaning should be good for at least a thousand words. What do you keep; what do you throw out; what do you find when you remove twelve months worth of dust? Of course, decorating can also be discussed at this time of the year. If you've ever tried to hang you own wallpaper you've got the material for a humor piece. (Idle thought...didn't Hitler start out as a paperhanger or something like that?)

• As soon as Thanksgiving Dinner is over, get back to your computer and type April: You can bounce your humor off the gardeners in April. Compare flowers to personalities. Who plants what? Or describe your losing battle with the weeds/rabbits for possession of the vegetables you planted.

• For the writer of articles, dreary November is really May: Once the sun starts to shine the natives get restless. Joggers lace on their Adidas and eighteen-speed addicts dig their bikes out of garages. Describe your efforts as a novice jogger/cyclist. The punishment your body absorbed, the clever way you outwitted the dog that thought you were a postman, and the attitude of your non-exercising friends can all be used for laughs.

• Somewhere in the crush of Christmas shopping, you'll have to shift your mental gears into June: This is open season for girl watchers. A review of fashions, past and present, and their effect on the devotees of this sport could be interesting. Or turn the idea around and describe the vagaries of male summer attire. You might, on the other hand, try a well-told story of a vacation trip, from a slightly jaundiced viewpoint, emphasizing the problems you ran into, which can also be milked for a laugh or two.

• Well, now it's January again. Time to make another list... and think about—Dominion Day. (What *are* we calling it now, anyway?)

A. C. Stone is a freelance writer from Windsor, Ontario whose work has appeared in more than 70 US, Canadian and UK publications.

# Specialized Magazines

*by Harold C. Griffin*

T he writer had complied with all the requirements that usually commend a submission to an editor. His manuscript was typed cleanly, with none of the irritating handwritten changes that make editing difficult, and its spacing allowed for revision. The photographs, and the line drawings offered as alternative illustrations, were adequately identified. The accompanying letter set out his personal background with an admirable economy of words.

He had overlooked only one thing, but it was enough to reduce his efforts to naught. By falling to study the publication to which he was submitting his work, he had sent a series of columns on the sport of angling to a paper published exclusively for commercial fishermen.

The editor of that magazine had, for many years, received submissions from freelance writers who seemingly equated the word fisherman with angler or sports fisherman. All of them waste not only their own time, but the editor's too, for each of them must be written a letter pointing out the mistake.

There's no excuse for this. Listings in a number of directories available at most public libraries, define the field of interest and requirements of all newspapers, magazines and journals of any consequence—and the special interest publications far outnumber those of general interest.

Freelance writers are frequently advised to become specialists in one or more fields, preferably those corresponding to their own inclination and experience. In this, they are merely following the long accepted practice of daily newspapers with their own writers assigned to marine, labor, business and other specialized fields.

A writer who has established a reputation as an authority, be it locally or nationally, in a particular field has a greater likelihood of being accepted or receiving an assignment than the writer who tries to cover a wide range, dashing from one field to another as opportunity seems to beckon. As a specialist the professional writer has an advantage because the experts in their field fill the pages of specialized publications with some of the dullest of all contemporary writing. But even the finest writing can't conceal shallow knowledge.

All this might seem to be axiomatic, but too many writers are unaware of it.

As specialized journals directed to a particular trade or industry, trade publications are reflecting the trend already well advanced in the daily newspaper field.

They are read by the management and supervisory personnel of the larger corporations, by small operators and individual tradesmen interested in new techniques, new equipment and developing trends in a given industry. Most of them have small staffs—perhaps only an editor—to process the mass of material they receive between issues, and they rely heavily on prepared papers delivered to conferences and releases for copy.

On the face of it, there would seem to be scant opportunity for the freelance writer. In fact, the writer who can discern the trend, its possibilities and consequences, lift it imaginatively from the jargon and dry as dust exposition of the experts and bring it to life, is likely to excite the interest of any editor looking for a new approach. But this presupposes that the writer knows his field, has studied the publications catering to it and is familiar with their particular needs.

Freelance writers complain constantly that editors don't answer their inquiries, don't return their manuscripts promptly, don't explain their reasons for rejection, and sometimes these complaints are justified. But editors of specialized publications, sifting through the piles on their desks and working against a deadline to produce the next issue, usually have neither the time nor the staff to undertake a correspondence course for freelance writers.

Trade magazines, however, are not the only specialized publications that offer a market to writers who themselves are prepared to specialize.

It's no accident that the most successful magazines in the western provinces are those blending our pioneer history with hunting, fishing, rockhounding and other outdoor pursuits. It's a publishing recipe that has a wide appeal at this period in our economic and social development.

After all the books and articles that have been published in recent years about the history of British Columbia, Alberta, Saskatchewan and Manitoba, it might seem that we have exhausted the stories of our past.

I don't think so. Perhaps they lie in thesis form, unread except by university students researching for their own theses, but I know of several major figures, of events that made headlines in their day, waiting to be retrieved from obscurity by writers able to see history not with the eyes of the past but with those of the future.

Whether a page from history, a social issue or a new industrial technique, an in-depth grasp of the subject and a fresh and imaginative approach provide the best introduction to specialized publications. But if you find the subject dull yourself, don't attempt it. The chances are that the editor already has an expert's version to which no amount of polishing will bring a shine.

London-born Harold Griffin has been an editor, journalist and author since the 1920s. He has edited a BC weekly labor newspaper and *The Fisherman*, organ of the United Fishermen and Allied Workers Union. He is now retired and living in Vancouver, BC.

# How-To's That Sell

*by Catherine Lazers Bauer* ————————

**T**here's a how-to in your writing repertoire.

Everyone is an expert at something. Look to your experience and expertise and discover a gold mine of article ideas.

In my twenty-two years of teaching writing, I've known the steady thrill of seeing student work appear in print, and one of the things I've learned is that a well written how-to article is a perennial favorite with editors.

What do you do well? Raise kids?

Debra, the busy mom of seven small children, regarded writing class as a panacea for pandemonium. Soon she was selling fillers like ice cream cones in August. She wrote a how-to on the subject. "If you have a house full of kids and aren't selling fillers," she admonished, "you 're just not listening."

Another good listener wrote a moving piece on helping a friend in tears. It sold to *Ms*. She used the popular list format to spell out the standard condolences that hinder rather than help, then shifted those responses to approaches that are constructive and comforting.

In our complex, technological age, readers devour how-to's to help them solve social, economic, political and marital problems. Books, magazines and newspapers are filled with self-help how-to information.

There are two main types of how-to pieces: the how-to make or build article and the problem-solving article.

## The how-to make or build article.

This type of article tells the reader exactly how to build a gazebo, a boat, a toy or a patio. It may explain how to make a quilt or a family scrapbook, or host an unusual party. It details procedures step by step, giving precise instruction, leaving nothing to chance. It's hard to beat a chronological time sequence when organizing a how-to. It's disconcerting to learn that the activity explained in point ten should have preceded that in point five.

Your instructions will be the reader's guide in carrying out her own project, so strive to write with clarity. Avoid abbreviations. If you must use an unfamiliar term (such as dulcimer or wok), include a definition. Take nothing for granted. Avoid vagueness (medium-low oven). Clarify!

Tom, an attorney and avid fisherman, sold "The Compleat Urban Angler" to *Denver Magazine* for a three-figure pay cheque. Grace made patchwork skirts for her granddaughters and sold a how-to, with a photograph of the girls proudly displaying Grandma's handiwork, to *Stitch and Sew*.

"Don't throw away those knit scraps," she advised her readers. This creative seamstress also wrote an article about an original wall-hanging of a family tree. The pattern and photograph she included helped sell the piece.

Speaking of family trees, an elementary school teacher sold "How To Trace Your Family Tree" to *Bend of the River*. Her article told readers how to get started and how to organize their research. It included notes of caution about practices that lead to blind alleys and result in a frustrating waste of money and time.

A bank teller sold "Sausage Made Simple—Five Easy Steps" to *Women's Circle*. A school bus driver who loves deer hunting sold venison recipes to the food pages of his local newspaper.

If you study published how-to's, you will notice the popularity of lists. An electrician sold "Ten Things to Check Before Calling the Serviceman."

Ethel insisted she had no expertise to draw upon, but she was able to sell "Ten Ways To Use Ten Minutes" to *The Chicago Daily News*. It was a clever essay on what to do while waiting in line, or sitting in the car waiting for your youngsters.

Georgia, an excellent gardener, sold a how-to on vegetable gardening to *Colorado Homes & Lifestyles*. Another student of mine interviewed a neighbor who had a magnificent garden with thirty-one-thousand plants. That article produced a handsome cheque from *House & Garden Magazine*.

If you are a do-it-yourself person, feature your own projects. If not, interview neighbors, relatives or friends about their endeavors. Science, mechanics, home, garden, and farming magazines, as well as the home and lifestyle editors of newspapers, often publish how-to's.

### The problem-solving article.

These present solutions for the frustrations in human relationships, and other everyday dilemmas. The problem can be stated in the title: "How To Get Along With Your Mother-in-Law," or "How Well Do You Communicate?"

No one has all the answers, but readers anxious for ideas will be satisfied with suggestions that improve their know-how, showing them how others solved similar problems.

Ruth, a real estate agent, sold "Being In Control" to *Ohio Realtor*. It was picked up for reprinting in National Realtor. Ruth's opening established her premise: "If I could name one quality a real estate person must possess, it would be control." She then went on to describe a quiet, pleasant, efficient way to keep buyers and sellers contented and relaxed, making the entire operation profitable for everyone.

A tennis-pro sold an article to *World Tennis*. A retired drilling foreman for Mobil Oil sold a technical how-to on cement squeezing to *Drilling Magazine*. Perhaps your how-to would fit best in a trade magazine or professional journal.

### Clip and compare.

The next time you stand in front of a magazine stand, take a good look at the teaser headlines on magazine covers. See how many of them are how-to's of one kind or another, then start thinking about what you can share with readers.

As you read, clip articles with how-to titles. After collecting about twenty-five how-to's of each type (how to build, and problem solving), place them in two labelled folders. When you're ready to begin your own, study these first. Note how they're constructed. How does the lead grab your attention? How many anecdotes are used? Are the sentences and paragraphs long or short? How does the piece end?

When you write your own article, remember your task is to communicate, not impress. Eliminate excess words, garbled phrases. Everyday language usually works best.

Read your piece out loud. How does it sound? Does it flow? Is it easy to follow? Does it make sense?

If you were an editor, would you buy it? If not, why not?

Tailor your article for the market so you don't waste time—yours and the editor's. And always remember to include a stamped, self-addressed envelope. It's the mark of a professional.

Catherine Lazers Bauer has sold more than 500 essays, articles and stories to more than 100 national, regional and literary publications. She has taught writing classes for over 20 years, most recently at the University of Colorado, Denver.

# How to Break Into Reader's Digest

*by Lynne Schuyler*

'd like to share a few tips for breaking into *Reader's Digest* magazine based on my own experience writing 16 original features for the magazine. Some of these pointers come from the magazine's own excellent set of guidelines that will be sent to you if you write for them—check a recent issue of the magazine for the address.

The old saw about studying the magazine you want to write for couldn't be truer in this case. If you're serious about breaking into *Reader's Digest*, you should be grabbing issues off the newsstand and reading *everything* in them, from cover-to-cover. You can also find back issues of the magazine in your library, or at second-hand book stores. Read at least a dozen or more issues. Note the variety of topics and, no matter how regional any article may seem, its universal appeal.

Soon you'll recognize how writers handle the wide variety of subjects published in the magazine. What you're seeing is not necessarily "formula writing" but tried and true methods that work, methods that are used in the top magazine markets. (In fact, you'll notice the reprints feature the same kind of writing styles used in *Digest* originals.) By now, after all this reading, you should be able to pinpoint an article's "universal" appeal, that special "something" that speaks to readers across the country.

Look at how the lead paragraphs are structured; how subjects are brought into sharp focus, how they are dramatically framed and supported by fact. The more you read the magazine, the more you'll recognize *Reader's Digest* subjects all around you.

A few words here about finding ideas for the magazine: they are everywhere. Sometimes you become aware of a compelling story through friends or through involvement in an organization you belong to; some of my articles have stemmed from nothing more than a one paragraph item in my local newspaper. Forget the story that's playing the headlines, unless you personally know the subject and he or she has agreed to work with you exclusively. The competition for headline stories is fierce, and if it's a story the *Digest* is interested in they are likely to assign it to a senior writer who has a proven track record.

Did I say something about reading the magazine? Oh, yes, here it is again. Even when I'm in the midst of a *Digest* assignment, I'm busy wading through back issues. Why? It helps me to understand how other writers have tackled difficult story ideas, to see how they have effectively worked around obstacles.

*Reader's Digest* is always on the lookout for good dramatic stories, but they must be of the type where it's "human courage and not machines that manage the drama." A person should not have gotten into a life threatening situation from their own "damfoolishness." Years ago, I picked up on a dramatic story about a family lost in the mountains in February. All the ingredients for a good story seemed to be there: the father had to struggle through the rugged bush and snow to get help for his family. But a few phone calls later, I learned that he was actually trying to sneak his family across the border. Not only was he involved in illegal activities, but he nearly killed his family. It's up to you to check out a story thoroughly, ensuring to the best of your ability that it will hold up under close scrutiny.

Whatever story you decide upon, does it have enough action, events, and vivid anecdotes to maintain a tight, fast paced narrative for 2000-3500 words, maybe more? I usually write about 3500 words which are then cut back to 2500. (This process fills the editors in on background information that may not always make the final cut).

More important, is your subject willing to work with you? As the writer, you can expect to spend long hours interviewing, researching, digging for facts and more facts. Subjects need to understand that an interview for a *Digest* piece can take days, perhaps longer. A writer must be able to ferret out those anecdotes that richly illustrate a person or point and provide the wealth of details that *Digest* readers have come to expect.

In one particular story, it literally took me months to elicit a telling detail about my subject's life. But it was crucial to the story: it explained how it brought her to a turning point in her life; it was the "hook" that the story hung on. It took a lot of questioning and gentle persistence on my part until she felt comfortable enough to reveal her innermost feelings. (But a writer may not always have the luxury of time and must be adept at making subjects feel comfortable enough to talk freely). In this case, the "hook" that took me months to uncover became the angle used by *People* magazine and *Chatelaine* when they sent writers to cover the story many months after my article appeared.

Will your story be as interesting a year or more from now as it is today? It has to stand the test of time; sometimes it can take a year for an article to appear in print. Is your story the kind that will leave readers with a good feeling? A solution to a problem? Renewed faith in mankind? Or a different way of looking at pressing issues of today? You get the idea—and will understand it even better if you've been reading those back issues!

Pick an editor's name from the magazine's masthead and establish a relationship with him or her. Be professional and polished in your approach, send your best ideas. Spend some time doing good research. It'll not only help you focus your idea, but it should tell you if there is enough there for a feature length article.

It's rewarding to work for *Reader's Digest*, The pay is top notch (expect to work very hard, though!) and the satisfaction is enormous to see your by-line in one of the world's best known magazines. In my work with the editors, I've been encouraged, prodded and pointed in new directions and ways of thinking. As a result, I've produced better work through this team effort. The skills I've honed working for *Reader's Digest* magazine have stood me well with other publications; editors have complemented me on the rich detail woven throughout my articles.

So, pick up those back issues, read the magazine, send for guidelines, and approach an editor with your best idea. Stay alert to the many possibilities out there. I guarantee it'll be worth the effort!

Lynne Schuyler is a British Columbia Interior writer who loves to discover exciting human interest stories. She is a frequent contributor to *Reader's Digest* and, at last count, has had 16 original articles published in various international editions of the *Digest*.

# The Payoff in Travel Writing

*by Lyn Harrington*

Y ou can make your travel pay off handsomely. It's a matter of recognizing the many-sided nature of the subject.

More often than not, the beginner breaks into print with a travel story. Why? Because often it is his first literary effort, the first time he has been moved to set it down on paper, and he's conscientious about it. Again, it may be because his travel writing has a freshness and enthusiasm lacking in previous attempts. A third reason is that it is meaty. Most beginners' articles are too thin. This has nothing to do with the number of words, but rather with the lack of information and a failure to see more than one aspect of a subject. The travel article, on the other hand, is likely to be packed with crisp impressions. Therefore it appeals to the editor.

A common fault of amateurs is that of giving a chronological account of a journey. It's the lazy, orderly way of writing, but it makes dull reading. If you crowd in every last detail, you cannot do justice to any one part. Either you sell all your material at once or, something that is more likely, you can't persuade anyone to buy it.

People insist on entertainment with their information. Your written experiences can serve the useful purpose of suggesting places to go, things to do and see, interesting routes to follow, how to travel with pleasure and safety.

If you want your travel to pay off, you must look upon it as a business, not strictly a pleasure trip. This calls for advance planning, much as a salesman lays out his route, lines up prospects, and learns as much about each as possible.

You should consider travel from more than a scenic aspect. Anyone gets tired of rapturous descriptions of roads, caves, beaches, buildings. But how about national sports, unusual ways of fishing or hunting, music, art? There's another array of travel articles in way-stations, hotels, motels, trailer camps, youth hostels, igloos, or the black tents of Arabia.

The term *travel* can be stretched to cover a world of subjects, each with a group of journals eager for the information you dig up. Just as an example of how big a subject it is, take one sub-division—transportation by water. From there you can go into barges, canals, ice-boating, sailing, marine telephones, customs, harbors, freighters, radar, shipboard etiquette, famous travelers, dugouts, marine mysteries. Multiply by the other forms of transportation, from Indian travois to turbo-jets, and you've more subjects than you could cover in a lifetime.

By planning ahead, you work on a tighter schedule than by merely hoping some interesting material will cross your path. It is a good idea to discuss a forthcoming trip with a few editors, offering ideas and accepting suggestions. This cuts down rejections, and gives confidence in asking for interviews and information later on. Chats with editors may result simply in "See what you can pick up for us"—which is a green light. Quite often the result is an assignment, and on rare occasions a side trip on an expense account, which is a break for self-supporting freelancers.

Many magazines limit their area of interest; *Arizona Highways*, for example. Your problem is to locate such markets, and write to their specifications. No matter where you travel, watch out for new markets, regional publications to which you might sell local material.

Study, too, the local papers and magazines. A visit to the public library reading-room will certainly offer a few new titles. These are often an excellent market for material picked up on your travels and sold on the spot. Items that are too localized for publication in national magazines are just right for regional ones.

Business journals appreciate outside material, even though they may have correspondents in different areas. If you strike an idea while travelling or visiting, send it to the editor of the local or national business journal. The worst that can happen is that you don't get paid. You generally do.

Consider magazines for special-interest groups: education and schools; religious publications; nature; farm papers; sports; fashions; and, not least, the homemaking magazines. The age level for which you prefer writing may also indicate material that is salable.

Bone up ahead of time. Your mental packing is much more important than your wardrobe. Before leaving home, learn what you can about the towns, historic sites, scenic attractions, local industries, literary background, of the area you are visiting. Such research serves as a springboard for questions, increases your observation and pleasure, and makes the finished article more colorful reading. A small amount of historical lore worked in with a light hand seems acceptable to editors.

So you are prepared with jottings as to what you may expect along the way, and perhaps a file of clippings. Say you're heading for a dude ranch. It's only smart to learn something about branding, roundups, loco weed, and stampedes before you set out. Your clipping file may yield a reference to rodeo superstitions—ask questions on the spot, to round out your information. If your lore is still lean, dig some more when you reach a library. But *always* have some first-hand knowledge of your subject.

It's just as well not to leave everything until you get home. Put the information down on paper the evening of the day you get it, since figures and names and data can become very elusive. Type your notes while your handwriting is still legible, and rough out your articles. It certainly isn't a fun way to spend an evening, but it pays off.

You may, in fact, have more material than you can use in one article. That extra knowledge shines through your written words. And in itself it may be sufficient to launch another article for a different market.

If you have chosen a subject on which you can get little information, either aim it at a market that takes short items, or shelve it. Even established authors have to throw out cherished ideas.

Cross-country travel makes it possible to do a series of articles, say, on provincial capitals, national parks, or out-of-the-way corners of the country. In addition, it gives complete coverage and better balance to whatever travel material you're writing about.

Travel can provide background material for fiction, and may turn into books. In fact, you might remind yourself that your home town is a foreign spot to many readers, a strange and glamorous place, representing "travel" to others.

To the editor and to the reader, then, the average trip means little. It is the interesting individual items that win acceptance.

Byproducts will account for far more sales than any attempt to "tell all." The handicraft you bought has a story behind it. The primitive peoples you met, and the personalities (but beware of "characters"). The bird sanctuary, or the thousand-year-old forest. The fascinating old churches, covered bridges, or pioneer mills—these are the things that will make your travel pay off.

Lyn Harrington was an active member of the Canadian Authors Association, and the author of numerous articles and books, including her 1981 CAA history, *Syllables of Recorded Time*.

# Religious Periodicals

*by Margaret Bunel Edwards* ————————————

W hen was the last time you read a Sunday School paper? Or a religious magazine? If it has been a decade or two, you may be surprised to learn that these formerly conservative, sometimes sentimental publications now discuss the drug scene, women's liberation, abortion, social unrest and pre-marital sex with candor and common sense.

Writing for religious periodicals is an exciting challenge to anyone who has a desire to communicate their opinions on topical subjects and who has the foresight to study the magazines in which they hope to have work appear. The editors of these papers are sincerely interested in manuscripts from new writers. They need material in volume, they seldom employ staff writers and the freelancer is assured a warm and sympathetic reception.

So let us first define the term, "Sunday School papers." It refers not only to the take-home pamphlets given the four-year-old, but encompasses periodicals aimed at juniors, teens, young adults, older adults and senior citizens.

Since each age group is included, you have the widest possible choice of audience for your work. Due to such a range, it is most important that you read carefully before you begin to write. This *Guide* as well as the several U.S. market volumes list in detail the markets open to you as a freelancer. Check such categories as "Juvenile," "Teen," and "Religious." Note the names of editors who send copies of back issues and write for the ones that interest you. These papers will be your study material and as you read, you will become aware of certain necessary information.

For one thing, you will see that the religious field, like the secular, is divided into the "slicks" and the "pulps." Very simply, the difference is this: the "slicks" publish a fast moving, ethical story, often with no mention of religion as long as acceptable moral standards are incorporated in it. The "pulps," by contrast, are interested only in conversion. The main characters in these stories are usually instrumental in bringing someone into the church or have some outstanding religious experience of their own.

There is also a division as to Roman Catholic, Jewish and Protestant publications, but with the ecumenical movement more and more widely accepted, there has been a shading of these divisions. A well-written story or article can be sold to any denomination, with no slanting to a specific creed. Everyone is interested in reading of a successful solution to a universal problem.

Keep in mind that your material should be suitable for family reading. Your hero will sit down and have a soft drink instead of a cocktail. He does not light a cigarette and the dialogue is free of profanity.

Also, there are still a few taboos which must be respected. The Church of Jesus Christ of Latter Day Saints does not permit tea or coffee drinking to be mentioned in its stories. Unity Press wants no reference made to meat eating. Alluding to dancing and theatre-going is contrary to the principles of some of the more fundamental denominations. An editor's guide sheet lists his requirements and the serious writer should note them well.

Obviously, not every age group or magazine will appeal to you, as a writer. But there will be many whose stories and articles strike a responsive note and these are the ones to which it is logical to direct your work.

There is almost no subject you cannot write about, within the bounds of good taste. I have seen fiction dealing with abortion, an unwed mother, drugs in the high schools and teen-age selfishness. All stories gripped the reader's interest and the authors presented flexible, possible solutions to problems.

Their style illustrates yet another change in the Sunday School papers over the past two decades. They are no longer authoritative in tone but give the reader the option of working out a problem for himself or herself.

There are radical changes taking place within many of the church denominations. For example, the role of women in the church is being discussed at length. Their desire to become full partners with priests, and administer the sacraments, is a very controversial issue. Many articles have been written about this situation and freelancers will no doubt continue to write about it.

Also, the acceptance of homosexual men and women into the ministry is of primary interest and the topic of essays and articles.

However, several aspects of religious writing have remained constant. Every story and article published in this field must have a definite theme. Nothing is used unless it inspires the reader, illustrates a useful truth or instructs in an unobtrusive way. At no time may the writer preach, rather than entertain. And upbeat, hopeful endings are almost the rule here.

There is a plus value to writing for the religious periodicals which should not be overlooked. Many editors are willing to consider material on a simultaneous submission basis because their papers are denominational and they are not competing for readership.

This means that payment for your work is often substantially multiplied. Although you are paid from one cent to four cents per word generally (some pay a little more), you will find that, financially, it is well worth your while to write for these editors when you are able to sell the same story five or six times to separate papers.

Remember, the publishers of Sunday School papers and religious magazines have one universal characteristic: they are looking for entertaining material which inspires or instructs. They want to show their readers how to overcome difficulties, how to find courage in an often hostile world, how to be optimistic despite personal disappointments.

Stories and articles with these upbeat themes are always popular. Share your optimism, your experiences and your solutions and you will soon find yourself sharing in some welcome acceptances.

Margaret Bunel Edwards writes both adult and juvenile material for religious publications. Her inspirational and humorous essays are frequently reprinted by many denominations.

# The Living Profile

*by Elizabeth St. Jacques*

W e love to read about successful people, to find out what makes them tick, how they act, how they succeeded. And because we're so interested, more publications than ever are carrying stories about such people. For the writer interested in opening the door to a new market, the profile could well provide the key.

The ideal candidate for a profile is usually someone outstanding in a particular field, one who has an unusual job, or hobby, or style of living, or someone whose life or work serves as an inspiration or a model for others. On the other hand, an infamous person also makes good copy for a profile.

Once you've done some preliminary research on your candidate you should find out which markets would be interested in your profile. The surest way is to study the magazines. Guidelines supplied on request by magazines may not show you all that is expected in style, mood and slant, but the magazines themselves will. So beg, or borrow copies, or visit your library to study several back issues. List from four to six potential markets. Then query one editor at a time about your profile idea.

Studying magazines will also indicate what type of profile they use. Basically there are three kinds: entertaining, inspirational, and educational. Although each differs in presentation, all three require the laying of similar groundwork which we'll discuss first.

In every profile, your main objectives are to create a vivid image of your subject, to concentrate on a specific angle, and to inform accurately and clearly. The most important step toward achieving these objectives is the interview with the subject in which you observe the person at close range. Contact your subject by telephone or letter for an interview. (You may have to go through a public relations office.) Make sure to specify the length of time you'll need for the interview (and stick to it). Then carefully prepare a list of questions, some aimed at clearing up any contradictions you may have discovered in your basic research.

Before the interview you must make arrangements to obtain a photograph. Some publications send their own photographers, so check with your editor first. If you handle your own photography, find out if the magazine requires a model release and have one on hand for your subject to sign after the session. (It's wise to take two cameras with you _ one for black-and-white and the other for coloured photographs. Then you'll be well prepared should you wish to include your subject in other profiles or articles.)

Use a tape recorder during the interview if possible; it will not only guarantee correct quotations but will provide greater freedom for you to concentrate on questions, and make mental notes about your subject's appearance, mannerisms and reactions.

Home in on the angle you are interested in, gently steering your subject back to it at every opportunity. But don't be obsessed with holding the line; sometimes brief diversions can lead to unexpected information which could give material for spin-off articles later. (Remember, too, if you're writing about a celebrity you must find a fresh angle.) Be observant and attentive, but try to relax; it will make the interview easier for both you and your subject.

After the interview, ask for exclusive rights to the story. This means the person agrees not to give it to anyone else for at least three months. A statement to that effect should be ready for his or her signature.

You may be called upon to write intelligently on a subject about which you may know very little. Become as well informed as you can: learn special terminology, talk to and read about people involved in the field.

Depending on the market, your research could take anywhere from several days to months. For example, when *The New Yorker* wants an in-depth profile of, say, a world-famous musical conductor, the writer spends three months interviewing his family, friends, and colleagues; another two months travelling with the conductor, attending rehearsals and performances; and an additional two months gathering details and actually writing—a total of seven months.

Researching notorious persons could take even longer because the person will try to avoid you at every turn; getting information from any source will seem next to impossible. You will need all your ingenuity to hurdle the obstacles in the way of your research.

We advise you to read how other writers came through for their editors. An excellent example can be found in Hayes B. Jacob's book,

*Writing and Selling Non-fiction* in which he details every difficult step of the way for his revealing profile of Oral Roberts, the faith healer.

You'll probably have more than enough information after you've assembled all your research and interviews, but don't be overwhelmed by it. Stick to your angle, select only what is pertinent. Whatever you can't use now, file away for the future.

To make your subject come alive for readers, show, rather than tell, the person's habits, mannerisms, physical appearance, opinions, and character. This rendering of character can be accomplished by relating observations of others who know your subject well, and by your own well-crafted descriptions of his or her reactions in different circumstances.

To add color and sparkle, sprinkle your profile with plenty of quotations and anecdotes, but make sure they are accurate. Avoid embarrassment and possible legal implications by making sure quotations and facts are correct.

Apart from creating a vivid image, make your subject believable. That is, don't make the person too bitter or too sweet; work for a balanced picture.

Beginners to profile writing might be interested in the brief profile which can be done after conducting only a few interviews. But be forewarned: brevity doesn't give licence for carelessness, nor does it mean the profile will be a snap to write. The shorter the profile, the faster the pace and the tighter the writing. Therefore it may be more difficult to write than the longer piece. Whatever the length, take your time and try to create an honest image.

Before submitting your profile to the editor, write to your subject (and anyone else you plan to quote) for verification of quotations. Along with a stamped, addressed return envelope, enclose a letter containing the person's quotes and your request for his or her signature of approval. Please note: only quotations need to be verified with them; your editor is the only person who should see the completed manuscript.

The next important consideration is the function the piece will serve. Let's look at the various types of profiles.

The entertaining profile uses a light breezy style. Readers will be interested in the person simply because he or she is a well-known figure, or because the story promises to satisfy their curiosity or to amaze or amuse them. An example is Jennet Conant's three-thousand-word profile of famous Cover Girl model, Christie Brinkley, in *Redbook* (Dec. 1993). Lighthearted and humorous with serious overtones, this profile makes for a delightful and entertaining reading.

Shorter profiles can be found in such publications as *The Toronto Star* which once ran a story of about three hundred words concerning a seventy-nine-year-old woman who hunts mountain lions and captures rattlesnakes. Such bizarre details would pique the curiosity of most readers.

Although the entertaining profile has a limited demand, you'll find newspapers, supplements, tabloids, as well as general and special interest publications such as *The National Enquirer*, *Country Woman* and *People Magazine* interested in your offerings.

The inspirational profile has been popular down through the years because of the message of courage it delivers. It offers strong reassurance and positive direction that perseverance and faith pay off, even under the most trying circumstances. You will find an increase in inspirational profiles during depressed economic and tense political times; people need to know others have survived similar difficulties.

On the other hand, an inspirational profile can deal with a simple testimony of one's faith, whether it concerns faith in God, in oneself, or in others. For instance, Jeanne Marie Laskas' story in *Good Housekeeping* (April 1997) profiled Ginny Jones, a 39-year-old single woman, who adopted three seriously handicapped children , and shows her remarkable courage and faith in helping these children.

A wide range of markets including newspapers, women's magazines, travel and sports publications use inspirationals. Styles and lengths vary for this kind of profile, so again we stress the importance of studying the markets to learn where your profile could fit in. For starters, check out *Guideposts*, *Homemaker's*, *The HighGrader* and *Our Family*.

The educational profile, also very popular, instructs its readers and motivates their personal development. Of course the profile must be entertaining, too, in order to capture the readers' interest in the subject they may wish to emulate.

For example, numerous profiles have been written about poet/ songwriter Leonard Cohen but those appearing in literary publications concentrate not only on his intriguing personality but also on his writing routine and techniques. In that respect, then, the profile serves an educational purpose. For examples, consult *Canadian Author*, *Family Times*, *American Forests* and *Wildlife Photography*.

The same is true of exposés of unsavory people. Although it may be entertaining to read about such people, the intention of exposés is to educate readers about the way the subjects have achieved their notoriety and to raise public awareness of the issues at stake.

If profile writing interests you, it could open doors to new markets. Certainly, there are ample choices to keep you happy, busy, and prosperous.

Elizabeth St. Jacques, author of eight books, has been a writer for thirty years, her work published in ten countries. Currently, she is Associate Editor of *SIJO WEST*, Poetry Editor of *Canadian Writer's Journal*, Contributing Editor with *Small Press Review* and a Book Review Editor with *Albatross* (Romania). Her profiles have appeared in *Canadian Living*, *Our Family*, *Sunday Digest*, *Purpose* and others.

# Write Book Reviews

*by Teresa Pitman* ————————————————

I'm the woman with the armful of books who is always in front of you in the library check-out line. I'm the one who can't resist buying the latest releases in the book store—and then picks up a couple more from the clearance table on her way out. I read while I'm brushing my teeth, and when I'm washing the dishes. And I never watch TV without an open book in my hands.

Like most writers, I'm an incurable reader. But I've found a way to turn all that reading into some extra income and a useful introduction to magazine editors. The secret is simple: I write book reviews.

You might be surprised to discover how many publications use book reviews. Many newspapers do, for example. Our local paper only publishes twice a week, but they were delighted to have my book review column for their entertainment section every Friday. Big-city papers often have an entire section of book reviews, although these may be harder to break into. Magazines use book reviews, too.

In reviewing, as in writing articles, it is essential to know who the magazine's readers are, and what topics they will be interested in reading about. The more specialized magazines can be your best bets if you find a book that fits their field. Readers often look to these magazines for information on specialized books that isn't available to them anywhere else.

How do you get the books to review? This sounds like an expensive proposition, especially if you are considering hardcover books. But publishers are actually eager to have their books publicized. Once they know you are reviewing, they will send you catalogues (with order forms) and copies of anything they think you might be interested in. The majority of the books I review in my column come to me this way. Sometimes I will hear about a new release, and call the publisher to request a review copy. They are usually happy to cooperate.

Magazine editors also receive books from publishers, and will assign these to their established reviewers. These may be very specialized or technical books, so if you have expertise in a particular area, you might call or write the editor of the appropriate magazine and ask to be put on the list.

There are other potential sources. Our local bookstore often hosts "meet the author" sessions and will give me a copy of the featured author's book to review; the chief librarian has invited me to visit the "back room" where the new books are kept before they go on the shelf and to borrow any that interest me; the writers I meet in various writers' associations send me copies of their latest books.

When I write reviews, I try to keep three important points in mind.

1. Remember the reader! The purpose of the book review is to give readers a clear idea of what the book is about. (This means, by the way, that you must *read* it—all the way through.) I always try to tell the reader exactly what the book is about, what topics it covers, and why it is interesting or worthwhile (or not interesting and not worthwhile).

2. Let the book speak for itself. I like to include at least one quote that illustrates the book's style and approach. I might also list some chapter titles or quote from the author's introduction, if these will more clearly reveal the contents of the book.

3. Don't be afraid to be personal. This is, after all, a review. Tell your readers what *you* liked, what offended *you*, what moved *you*, what fell flat—and then tell them why. Sometimes *your* background should be included as well, when you have experience with the subject matter of the book, so that the reader understands your perspective. But be brief!

I've found real benefits in writing book reviews. The pay is not high—my weekly column is carried by two local papers, and they each pay me $35 a column. Magazines generally pay $35-$50 for a review. However, since reviews are usually short (500-600 words or so), they don't take long to write—and remember, you get to keep the books!

There are other benefits, too, for the serious writer. After I had sold two reviews to *Great Expectations*, a Canadian magazine for new mothers, the editor invited me to submit article ideas. I've had at least one article in every issue since then. And when I was interested in writing for *Today's Seniors*, a publication for senior citizens, I sent copies of reviews I had done on books about retirement living. I'm now one of their regular contributors.

Book reviews can be your introduction to the editors you'd like to write for. I've also found that reading the publisher's catalogues keeps me up-to-date with the current trends in book publishing—and when I get my novel finished, I know exactly to whom I'll send it.

But the best part of becoming a book reviewer is that I no longer feel guilty. I can read in the bath, read at the dinner table, read while I'm riding my exercise bike, and never feel the slightest twinge of guilt. After all, I'm not just reading—I'm working on my column!

Teresa Pitman has published more than 400 magazine and newspaper articles; her work is seen most frequently in *Today's Parent*, *Great Expectations* and other parenting publications. Her first book, *All Shapes and Sizes*, was published by Harper Collins in 1994 and her next will be published in early 1998. Teresa has also won awards for her short fiction and has had several stories for children published.

# The Essay: a Personal View

R. G. Condie

# **W**hat is an essay?

Defined by default, if it is short, and isn't poetry, fiction, straight journalism, or biography, it's probably an essay. An essay reveals a writer's personal views, and can be formal or informal. It can instruct, debate, influence, excite emotions, or simply entertain. Some non-fiction books are really long essays—or each chapter is an essay in itself.

An article in the newspaper is a fact-driven essay. The editorial in that same newspaper is an essay that may be fact driven, but voice a strong opinion. A column in that same newspaper may be opinion driven, but voice a few facts for support.

A good speech is a verbal essay. A political speech may be an essay or fiction, depending on the topic and the speaker. A doctoral thesis, often longer than most essays, is still a fact and opinion driven essay; usually formal to the extent that it follows a rigidly prescribed format. The three minutes Andy Rooney takes at the end of *60 Minutes* is less formal, but still an essay.

In all cases, the writer espouses a point of view. Whether the essay finds its way onto a written page, is played as a voice-over on television visuals, or hawked by a speaker, there will be a point of view, and most often, a personal point of view.

The essay writer who presents his work as an article, is not required to present opinions at odds with his point of view. The writer arranges his selection of fact-supported points, in hopes that his reader will reach the same conclusions, without being coerced. However. While ignoring opposing conjecture or opinion is acceptable, to leave out or distort pertinent opposing facts, is poor journalism. The writer who does so will find his future essays received with skepticism, by editors and readers both.

In science, anything unproven, even if it is highly possible, is theory. In essay writing, anything unproven is opinion. The essay writer must make clearly understood and defined distinctions between proven fact, and opinion. This holds true, even if the opinion is well supported. In essay writing, the personal integrity of the writer is often more valuable to his readers, than either his topic, or his writing technique. Opinions from believable people, are believed. Opinions from writers who have disregarded truth in the past, are not believed.

What you have just read is an essay.

### Know your topic.

Knowing what to research, and how to research it, is imperative for the essay writer. Columnists are the most readily identifiable full time essay writers. To think of topics for a column, every month, or week, or day, requires a broad range of knowledge and interests. To produce a regular column requires research.

For example, writers whose essays explore outer space, can discuss the theory of the big bang from a perspective of personal opinion, drawing from the few actual facts available, to make a reasonable hypothesis. However, if they wish to discuss bright lights in the night sky viewed from Toronto on April 17, 1996, at 11:00 p.m., then they need facts.

I looked out that night and saw an especially brilliant light, reminiscent of a recent comet. Research proved to me that it was Mars, at Galactic longitude 221:52:20, latitude 47:42:50. Looking overhead at that same night-sky quadrant, I could also see the moon, six other planets, plus bright stars such as Sirius, Capella, Vega, Altan and Deneb.

Research tells me that Sirius, 8.6 light years away, is only slightly brighter than Deneb, 543 light years away. Depending on the point I wished to make, all these facts and thousands more are available for that one night, at that one particular time, in that one view of my night sky. Before I do a cunning essay on how bright sights light my night, I had better do my research. I had better know my topic. In this case, my information comes from a highly informative computer CD-ROM encyclopedia of visible heavenly bodies.

Over centuries, the names and position of stars, planets, and comets have been verified by repeated sightings. The writer can safely use these "facts," and draw hypotheses from them. Other "facts" are not really facts, but conjecture so oft repeated that they seem like fact. If your research turns up a "fact" which challenges your own good sense, ask questions, and never use such facts to sustain an essay's argument.

Modern technology has placed enormous stores of information at the finger tips of a writer with Internet-capable modem connections, or facsimile machines. In large cities, most libraries have phone-in information lines to complement their resource books, tapes, and discs.

Major businesses usually have public relations departments to answer journalists' questions. Just be forewarned. PR people are more interested in putting a positive spin on information than in providing simple facts. Even their "facts" often require careful scrutiny. Finally there are government agencies probing almost every topic you might find of interest. Ask your question of the minister in charge, and let him or her pass it down. You are more likely to get a swift answer going from the top down.

An essay writer has no excuse for failing to display supportive information.

### Package your information.

The effective essay writer is often the one who spends the most time researching potential markets. Regardless of how well written or researched a piece on the benefits of socialism, it is unlikely to find a home in William F. Buckley's right-wing journal. Even undeniable economic benefits of strip mining will not likely find a forum in *Harrowsmith*. Pro-choice essays won't be published in Pro-life publications.

Successful publishers target a market and cater to that market. Editors know they aren't hired to offer arguments that their readers are wrong. More often, they are seeking to reassure their readers that they are right.

It isn't sufficient to know the general viewpoint of a publication. Especially with complex subjects, a successful publication offers readers a consistent slant or spin to their diet of assurance. For this they are rewarded with good subscription lists. Advertising keeps a publication healthy. Being able to deliver a consistent subscription list of readers to these advertisers, on a regular and dependable basis, encourages consistent advertising investment in that publication. Given this reality, a writer always has a choice. He can write essays specifically slanted and directed at identifiable markets, or he can write what he wants, then try to find a market that wants it. The situation isn't right or wrong, good or bad. Just realistic.

For the essay writer/journalist, there are other formats, but the most effective is often the simplest:

Tell your readers what you are going to tell them.

Tell them.

Tell them what you have told them.

Defuse possible dissenting opinion in the body of your essay. For example, if you quote a politician, even one such as Winston Churchill, offer a second reliable opinion, or well-researched facts. *Reader's Digest* will publish articles on the dangers of smoking. Knowing some readers will undoubtedly be smokers, *Reader's Digest* anticipates the personal arguments smokers might provide. Always anticipate and answer argument with facts.

Finally: If, as an essay writer, you are choosing a particular side in an on-going argument or debate, pick a side and stick to it in each essay.

### Rewrite! Edit! Polish!

Words that come freely to the page directly from the mind or heart, are hard to change. Unfortunately, these original words are usually disorganized, less than explicit, and rambling.

Even the most hardened professionals hate to have their words edited. The best way to avoid a blue-pencil nightmare is aggressive self-editing. Writers who edit their own work, will rarely have to cringe while a stranger does it for them. This is especially true if that editing leads to rejection.

Here are some tricks to rewriting. Leave your work to percolate by itself for at least three weeks before your first review. Don't even look at it. When you finally go back to it, you will read what you have written, not what you intended to write.

Read your work out loud, especially to non-related friends. The added stress of reading to others will point out awkward passages. You will run out of breath in those that are too long. You will stumble on sentences that need punctuation. You will hear repetitious phrases, and note any lack of involvement by listeners. These are all prompts to editing.

Review each passive verb. Where possible, rewrite your sentence using active voice. Select powerful verbs rather than letting the modifiers carry the weight of meaning.

Where you need three commas in a sentence, juggle it so it only needs two. But beware of the comma splice.

Make certain you are saying exactly what you want to say. If not, use your thesaurus to find the specific word your sentence demands.

A piece that includes simple misspellings tells editors you didn't consider their time valuable enough to polish your work. That's what they get paid for, right? Wrong!

First they are paid for choosing your work, then for editing. Make a friend, not an enemy. Check your spelling. If you can't do it yourself, borrow or rent someone who can. I would consider *your* instead of *you're*, *to* instead of *too*, and even *there* instead of *their*, all typically unacceptable errors. Look also for simple things like january, instead of January, and lack of space between a comma and the next word.

Aside from mechanics, make only those changes that advance your logic, or improve the flow of writing. Never make changes just to do it differently.

Finally. When you have rewritten your essay to the best of your ability, stop writing, and start selling. If you need a rule of thumb, always do at least two rewrites, but never more than four. Analyze your work. This will force you to do the complete job immediately, instead of in infinite stages. Sooner or later you must finish writing.

### Writing essays for contests and editors.

If you are writing for a publication or a contest, read everything you can find that has been published or chosen before. If it is a newspaper or magazine, read the most recent copies and carefully note how the material is presented. If you write for a contest, get copies of former winning entries. Many contests offer publication to the winners. Borrow or buy at least the previous two volumes.

For newspapers and magazines, ask for writer's guidelines. Follow them. For contests, read all the contest rules. If anything is unclear, send a self-addressed stamped envelope (SASE) and ask for an interpretation. Then follow the rules. This seems so self-explanatory, but it is really incredible how many writers ignore the rules of contests they enter. Since most contests require an entry fee, not following the rules is just throwing your money away. It wastes your time, and the time of the first-line evaluators.

Editors, and those who run writing contests, are not simply fussy. They have a reason for setting down contest parameters. Essay writing contests usually have strict word count limits. Contest rules mirror the realities you will encounter in the marketplace.

Any writer hoping to sell essays, columns, or articles as they are often called, must accept the reality of word restrictions. Publishers have space restrictions when they block out a magazine or newspaper. The only way publishers and editors can organize a publication, is to advise the writer how much space is available for his or her contribution. In newspapers, news will take a set amount of space. This may encompass three or thirty stories, but the space is set. Regular columns are set. Book, play, movie, and music reviews are set. Regular features are set. Only advertising space can be expanded. Any writer who thinks close enough is good enough, won't be asked for a second submission.

Margin size, type size, line spacing, page numbering and manuscript identification or non-identification, are all for a purpose. Writers ignore these requirements at their peril. In a contest, their work may never get to a judge. In business, the work may be rejected before being read, and future work declined.

Anyone unable to live with the simple discipline of a writing contest, will probably have difficulty in the marketplace.

Finally, if a contest requires an application and a fee included with your submission, include them. The fee may cover everything from administration, to evaluation, to publication costs. If you require the return of your manuscript, enclose a self-addressed stamped envelope (SASE). If you require a receipt of acknowledgment, enclose a self-addressed stamped card.

Think of following rules as simple courtesy to editors. Most will respond in kind.

A good working relationship is always one where both parties are willing to recognize the problems of the other.

### Recommended reading:

Any current *Writer's Market,* by Writer's Digest; *Essays on the Essay* by A.J. Butrim; *The Art of the Essay* by L. Fakundiny; *The Observing Self. Rediscovering the Essay* by G. Good; *The Contemporary Essay, 2nd Ed.* by Donald Hall; *The Canadian Style Guide* by Secretary of State.

Essays by the following writers; Charles Lamb, Robert Louis Stevenson, G. K. Chesterton, J. B. Priestly, Ralph Waldo Emerson, Henry Thoreau, Edgar Allan Poe, Jean-Paul Sartre, James Thurber, and E. B White.

R.G. Condie is a published author whose non-fiction, fiction and poetry has appeared in a wide variety of magazines and newspapers. He is also the Canadian Authors Association's Metro Toronto Branch writer-in-residence.

# How to Write a College Essay

*by Fred Walker*

I f the topic hasn't already been assigned by your professor, study the reading list and pick something (the professor may give the class a short list of acceptable topics.) It must be something you know a lot about, or can easily research, and it must be something about which you can pretend to have a strong opinion. Notice I wrote "pretend." In fact, you will rarely have any opinion about the topic of any college essay. And when you do, your real vehemence will probably get in the way.

Consult the official style sheet *before* you begin a first draft. This will minimize rewriting later. And follow it *blindly*. It doesn't matter how stupid the rules are. You must do anything the professor wants in order to get your degree. So prostitute your writing style. In particular, never use slang, never use humour, and never write in the first person.

The most important paragraphs are the first and last, so polish them until they shine. A good Introduction (as it's called) captures the reader's attention, explains your methodology and includes a clear thesis statement. A thesis statement is the one sentence that, in firm declarative fashion, states the contention you will try to prove. "Hamlet has an oedipus complex." It should be sufficient to demonstrate thorough knowledge of a topic without arbitrarily taking a side, but, due to the adversarial presumptions of our society, it isn't. Of course, the notion that somebody's freshman essay is ever going to "prove" anything about topics that have been debated by scholars for centuries is downright laughable. In picking a thesis statement, you are looking for a contention that you can intelligently support, whether you believe it or not—and it's better that you don't. You are also looking for something that will let you show off what you know. For example, if you know a lot about the life of the author, don't pick a thesis that will force you to spend most of the essay discussing the morality of war, on which you have little expertise.

Instead, pick a thesis like "Literary influences gained from his Oxford education determine the plot of Tolkien's *Hobbit*."

The second part of your essay is called The Body. There's not much I can tell you here—it's your argument, and you'll have to make it for yourself. Paragraphs shouldn't be too short, or it will look like journalism. Big, fat paragraphs look more academic. Use correct spelling and grammar. And use appropriate quotations. You will quote three types of sources: the text itself, critics who agree with you, and critics who disagree with you. The first two are self-explanatory. But the third is perhaps the most important. Quote critics who disagree with you, so you can devote a few paragraphs to proving them wrong. This helps you pad for length, and demonstrates that you aren't afraid of contrary opinions. The body will be 80 per cent of your final length—make it good. And always remember two things: 1) your professor has already read the book. 2) your professor is looking for proof that *you've* read the book.

The final part of your essay is the Conclusion. Again, one paragraph, this time a little longer. Do not engage in lengthy summary here. This is your final impression, your final chance to leave a good impression. Polish, polish, polish. Most importantly, include a concluding statement, summarizing that which you have *really proven*, not just guesses or hunches. Then, flip back to the front of your draft—it is truly astonishing how few students bother to do this—and make sure *your conclusion is exactly the same as your thesis*. If it isn't, change your *thesis*.

Now, do your research. That's right. *After* the first draft. If you don't have enough knowledge of the topic to write a draft without going to the library first, then you should have picked another topic. Having double checked your sources, you then go back to the draft and fix any errors you made. You may also want to alter your thesis, if you have found through further research that it's untenable. But you will usually find out that you were right. And if not, so what? No professor is naive enough to think that you really believe your thesis statement—it's just an excuse to show off what you know, and to prove you can intelligently and eloquently defend a position. First draft first, research follows. If the critics agree with you so much the better. But at least they haven't told you what to think.

Endnotes give sources for quotations, facts and ideas. Quotations are simple enough. Include a note every time you quote some source directly, no exceptions. The others are judgement calls, and you will have to get a few low marks before you discover just what this professor calls "common knowledge" and what he considers an obscure fact or an original idea. Put vanity aside. On most academic topics, it probably isn't possible for you to have an original idea, so don't worry about it. The bibliography should include a list of every book you read in preparing your essay, whether you wound up quoting it or not. Some sources are, for some reason, considered unacceptable by academia. Never admit you read the newspaper, or watched a television documentary, or saw it in a well-researched movie. And never admit you read Coles Notes. For that matter, never read Coles Notes, and you won't have a problem.

Finally type the second draft, have *somebody else* check it for spelling mistakes and typos (the professor will believe you think "the" is spelled "hte" and deduct a mark) and submit it on time. That won't be hard. The "first draft first" method takes about two weeks from conception to proofreading. If it *isn't* ready on time, do two things: 1) stop drinking so much, and take your education seriously. 2) Ask for an extension. Most professors will give you an extra week without even asking for a reason. It is much better to hand in a good essay late than a lousy one on time.

Fred Walker wrote numerous college and high school essays in acquiring his Ph.D. in English literature from Queen's U. He has also marked many as a professor and assistant professor, and has taught essay writing at the university level.

# Shoot First—Market Later!

*by Murphy Shewchuk*

With a little care in the beginning and careful editing and marketing afterward, there can be gold in the films you expose. Here are ten steps to improve your photographic output and income.

**1. Shoot First.** It may be a cliché from a western movie, but it is as valid now as it was a century ago. Shoot first means carrying your camera on your hip, on the car seat next to you, or safe, but handy on your boat—and then using it at the slightest provocation. Film is cheap. You may have to wait years for a better sunset or another moose to tiptoe past your punt.

**2. Shoot with care.** While we're hung up on wild-west clichés, it's safe to say that the man who shot first, but wild, may not have lived to make the last shot. Line it up, hold it steady—and squeeze. Use a faster shutter speed or a tripod if the photos you have been bringing home have even the slightest amount of unplanned motion blur. Lead your subject. Line up on the eyes of your meandering moose or the ski tips of a downhill racer.

**3. Give 'em room.** Every living thing has a space that it will fight to protect. Take your close-up shots if you can, then back off and leave a little space in the frame for the one who pays the bills to add a message. Advertisers will pay well for your quality photograph if you have room in the picture for their product. Cover photos also need room for magazine names and the blurbs that convince the newsstand buyer to part with a buck. If you want publishers to part with a buck, give them room.

**4. KISS.** Keep It Simple and Saleable. Saleable photographs usually have a clear sense of direction—a visually simplistic approach to a scene that may be very complicated to achieve. Waltz around the scene until you can eliminate the distraction such as the clichéd tree growing out of your subject's head. Adjust your depth-of-field to blur distracting backgrounds or foregrounds.

**5. Edit.** You can throw back the small fry when you are on a fishing trip, but you're stuck with your photos until you get them back from the processor. Then make the harsh decisions. Use an eight-power magnifier to carefully check your slides, then destroy the stuff that does not meet your standards. And keep high standards.

**6. Label.** You can buy laser printer labels (Avery #05667) that are 1¾ inches wide by ½ inch high (4.4cm x 1.3cm). With your computer set to an eight point font such as Arial Narrow, you can get three 30-character lines of data on each label. Stick them to the slide mounts. You will have enough information to satisfy many buyers or prompt your memory when you need to write a caption.

**7. File.** You now have a saleable image, but it won't bring you any money if you can't find it. Slide storage is an important part of the process. Archival grade clear polyethylene sheets that hold up to 20 slides each are available for 35 cents to 50 cents each in bulk. These can be used to store as well as ship your precious transparencies.

I use clear plastic "Keep Boxes" with fifteen compartments that each hold about 30 slides for a total 400 to 500 per box. With the boxes organized by main subject and labeled file cards separating the sub-groups, I can access almost any slide in less time than it takes to turn on the computer. Develop a system that works for you and keep it up to date.

**8. Market.** Mere selling may have worked for the western cattle barons, but in this competitive field, creative marketing is essential to make money. Start off by making your photo subjects aware that you have good photos that may be useful in their advertising or promotion. If the photographs have been published, send them copies of the publication. If your subject is of community or regional interest, send copies along with your promotional material to local city and Chamber of Commerce public relations people. Don't forget any other group that may be interested in paying for the use of photographs that present them in a favorable light.

**9. Price right.** Price your product to give you a fair return for your efforts. Don't give away your creative output—your photographs—to the lowest bidder. If you're not sure what your photographs might be worth, check the publications of ASMP—The American Society of Media Photographers, Inc. 14 Washington Rd, Suite 502, Princeton Junction, NJ 08550-1033 (phone 609 799-8300 fax: 609 799-2233). At the time of writing, ASMP had Web pages at <http://www2.asmp.org/asmp/> and a publication listing at <http://www.ndgphoenix.com/asmp/pubs/publications.html>. If they have moved, try a Web search for "ASMP".

You may also want to contact CAPIC - The Canadian Association of Photographers & Illustrators in Communication, 100 Broadview Ave., Suite 322, Toronto, ON M4M 2E8 (phone 416 462-3700, fax 416 462-3678 or e-mail <capic@astral.magic.ca> to inquire about their latest publications. You can also find them on the Web at <http://capic.org/>.

Do your research, then set prices that reflect your skills and the marketplace.

**10. Follow up your marketing.** One sale can lead to another if you regularly remind your customers that you are still in the business. Keep them informed of additions to your stock as well as awards you have won or new directions you are taking. Personal visits, telephone calls, business cards, simple brochures and Christmas cards are all part of the scheme of marketing your image as well as your photographic images.

We may not live in the old wild west, but we can learn a little from the old-time snake oil promoters when it comes to creating and marketing our photographic images.

Murphy Shewchuk is a freelance writer/photographer with nine books, hundreds of newspaper and magazine articles and over 1,000 photographs published. He is an active member of the Outdoor Writers of Canada, the Periodical Writers Association of Canada and the Canadian Authors Association.

# In the Picture

by Robert H. Jones ————

**M**ost editors of outdoor publications prefer package submissions—a manuscript plus an assortment of colour slides and/or black and white (B&W) photographs. Rather than hire a photographer, many outdoor writers learn the basics of shooting their own photographs in order to make their product more marketable. A few advance to the point where they become known equally well for their images and their prose. Conversely, some photographers take up writing in order to make their images more marketable, and become very successful as weavers of tales.

Photography can be exciting and challenging: wildly-leaping muskies; cock pheasants rocketing skyward; bald eagles diving to pick up a fish from the water's surface. However, in the production of how-to-do-it articles, I am confronted with nothing more thrilling than a work bench cluttered with blobs of lead, fish hooks, pieces of wood, scraps of metal, feathers, and other assorted debris. Nevertheless, there are challenges to this type of photography: layouts, positioning, backgrounds, camera and lighting angles, depth of field, exposure times, plus a multitude of problems associated with colors and contrast.

My photo studio, workshop and fly-tying room are one; complete with dust, grime and cobwebs. Several projects might be under way at any given time, but when the workbench is required for photography, it must be cleaned off to avoid a busy background—clutter that detracts from whatever is being portrayed.

As several sequential pictures may be required, how-tos are usually shot in black and white, which is cheaper to reproduce than colour. However, as some editors prefer a colour shot of the finished product, both techniques will be covered.

There are two basic types of how-to photography: vertical and horizontal. My verticals are shot from a standard tripod with the subject in front of the lens, while horizontals are shot straight down, with the subject under the lens.

Whether vertical or horizontal, some things are the same: To increase clarity and contrast, a backdrop of some sort may be used. Whatever the material, it should be in contrast to the subject to make it stand out: dark subjects on light backgrounds and vice versa.

Some colors virtually disappear against certain backgrounds, particularly while shooting B&W. Avoid combinations like blue on green, red on brown, yellow on orange, or pale colors on light or neutral backgrounds.

Backdrops I have accumulated over the years include cloth, burlap, carpeting, woven bamboo, paper, cardboard, textured and painted wood paneling, and sheets of translucent plastic. If the subject is intricate, detailed or has a soft outline, a plain backdrop is chosen; if the subject is symmetrical or clean-lined, a textured background might be used.

For most vertical B&W work, a drop curtain of cloth is used. It consists of yard-wide lengths of pure white and dark green polyester rolled back-to-back on a length of round wooden dowel. The roll is suspended from a ceiling-mounted bracket located directly over and to the rear of the workbench. Changing the backdrop from light to dark is simply a matter of reversing the dowel, then unrolling the curtain.

For close-ups of lures or flies, 12 x 12-inch sheets of white, black or coloured felt are used. The sheets are stored flat in a cardboard box measuring 2 x 13 x 13 inches. If a vertical background is required, the desired colour is fastened to the side of the box with a spring clip. The box is then stood on edge and positioned for best effect. This can be effective for shooting a fly clamped in a vise, or a single lure suspended by its nose.

The secret to sharp photographs is a perfectly stationary camera that is fired with a cable release. Also important is the depth of field—areas on the subject itself, or in front of or behind it, that remain in sharp focus. The smaller the lens aperture, the more depth of field, and vice versa. If the subject has a fairly flat plane, it may be advantageous to throw the background out of focus; in which case the aperture is opened wider. In the long run it is best to determine beforehand which aperture setting produces optimum results. This is accomplished by shooting a test role of film with any lenses intended for this type of work.

When shooting B&W, I prefer a Mamiya C330 Twin Lens Reflex camera loaded with a 12-exposure roll of Kodak Verichrome Pan 125 film. This is usually sufficient for most projects, and the medium format 2¼ x 2¼-inch negatives are a pleasure to work with in the darkroom.

For close-ups, an 80mm lens is used. This is a near macro that permits focusing within 10 inches of the subject. For a different perspective or increased depth of field, a 135mm lens is used. The tripod is positioned at least seven feet back from the subject, which is the minimum focusing distance for that lens. The basement floor has permanent marks on which to set the tripod's feet, and the bench top is marked to indicate extremes the subject can be moved to the right or left.

Up to three adjustable reflector lamps with 200 watt, incandescent bulbs are used for B&W lighting. Light readings are taken with a handheld, Gossen Lunasix 3 meter, and in most cases I work with only an incidental reading. Positioning of the lights depends on the subject, and whether or not shadow sculpting is desirable. If a light-coloured background is used, one or two lamps may be aimed on the backdrop, and only one on the subject.

For B&W macro shots, a 35mm OM-1 Single Lens Reflex is used with Ilford 50 ASA film. This slow film provides virtually grain-free prints. The through-the-lens light meter is used in conjunction with the Lunasix 3. Lenses used include a 50mm macro, and macro-zooms of 28-105mm and 70-210mm. For extreme close-ups, a 2X doubler may be used, or the camera and one of the lenses may be attached to a bellows unit.

For colour, a 35mm OM-4 SLR is used with either Fujichrome 50 or 100 daylight film. The internal spot metering system is used to determine the best exposure time (up to eight readings can be computed and average out), but this is cross checked with the Lunasix 3.

For colour close-ups or macro shots where back lighting is not required, a ring flash and reflector provides even light with no shadows. If light control is desired, blue photo-floods are used in the reflector lamps. In many cases the project is simply carried outside and shot in natural light: in direct sunlight for highlighting or shadow sculpting, or in a shaded area for subdued lighting with no shadows.

The secret to producing good slides and photographs is the same as for good writing: set high standards, then settle for nothing less. This means learning to use all of your photographic equipment properly, and equally as important, to throw away every slide or negative strip that fails to meet your self-imposed standard.

Robert H. (Bob) Jones is the author of *Tangled Lines and Patched Waders* (1995) and *Dull Hooks and Squeaky Reels* (1997), both published by Horsdal & Schubart. He has won numerous awards for his book and magazine writing. He resides in Courtenay, B.C., with Vera, his wife of 40 years, who is also a writer.

# Capture Winter Photographs

*by Murphy Shewchuk* —————————————————————————

**W**inter is the most difficult season of the year for the amateur and professional outdoor photographer. It is often the season of jammed equipment and dark, dull photos. Yet with care and attention, your photographic images can be well worth the extra trouble.

The two major difficulties I associate with winter photography are independent of your choice of camera or film. They afflict all sorts of cameras from the simple disposable to the complex boxes full of electronics. They have much more to do with winter temperature and light than your skills or budget.

Equipment problems due to cold temperatures are of primary concern, often receiving considerable publicity in the photo magazines. However, I think many photographers over-react when they put their equipment away until spring. I find that the best solution is to keep equipment warm and dry. (We photographers also appreciate similar treatment.)

Carry your film and spare batteries in an inside pocket. Protect your cameras and lenses from extreme cold and condensation. I carry my gear under my parka whenever possible. When this is not safe due to the risk of equipment damage or a cracked rib during a ski fall, I use a small backpack similar to those used by ski patrols. I pack my equipment carefully, using plenty of Ziploc® type bags. Then I add my spare clothing as an insulation and shock barrier around the gear. This arrangement allows my body warmth to keep my equipment above the ambient outdoor temperature while the pack and the plastic bags serve as a vapour barrier for any perspiration I may develop.

The second most pressing problem that I associate with winter photography is dealing with that essential ingredient, light.

Obtaining proper, controlled exposure is a challenge. Grey snow is a common result when built-in light meters are fooled by the high reflectance of sunlit snow. In order to compensate for the fact that your scene is not green grass and blue sky, you have to take control of your camera. You must coerce it into thinking that the scene is darker than the light meter measures. This may mean going to manual exposure or using the exposure compensation features that most adjustable cameras have.

I use several methods to obtain a true reference reading. On a clear day I take my readings by first aiming the camera at the blue sky in the opposite direction from the sun. I know that if I were shooting a black and white picture, I would like the sky to have a touch of grey or "colour." I also use a piece of medium colored clothing or, if the air is not too cold, my bare hands as a reference, opening one more stop than the meter indicates. The key word is "open." That means using a lower f-stop number or increasing the exposure time by one or two steps.

On one particularly sunny day I made the mistake of closing one stop and, after a day on the Kane Valley ski trails, I almost cried over the dark, lifeless results.

Once I have established my reference, I bracket my shots, sometimes deliberately over- or under-exposing for special effects. Alpine photographs and photos taken from an aircraft or helicopter require even greater compensation. Under these conditions, I usually try to get a representative exposure reading before getting airborne. Otherwise, I often find it necessary to open my aperture two or three stops more than my meter indicates.

If your camera doesn't allow you to over-ride the meter, you may be able to fool it by adjusting the film ASA down one or two steps. If you are using 200 ASA film, set the camera to 100 ASA while taking outdoor winter photographs, but don't forget to change the setting back when you move indoors.

Another lighting problem is shadows. At our northern latitudes, sun and shadows go together in the winter months. Add white snow and the shadows become a much more dominant part of the photograph than they are in summer.

I try to make shadows work for me. I avoid getting my own shadow in the picture, then I try to use shadows to lead into my subject. Shadows can emphasis rabbit tracks across new snow or give a lone skier much more character. To make the best use of shadows often requires trackless snow. This requires careful planning so that I do not mess up the scene while trying to determine my best point of view.

Capturing winter on film is a cinch, from my point of view, if I only keep temperature and light under control.

Sounds easy, does it not?

Murphy Shewchuk is a BC Interior writer/photographer whose award-winning photographs have appeared in nine books and hundreds of magazine and newspaper articles.

# People and Places Past

# Write Your Memoirs

*by Ruth Latta*

W henever I mention to other writers that I teach a course called "Life Writing: How to Write Your Memoirs," I invariably encounter one of two common reactions:

"Memoirs are all very well for old codgers who want to ramble on about the good old days," say the practical ones, "but I'm not over the hill yet, and I'm trying to write something commercial. Who would buy my life story? I'm not Sheila Copps or David Suzuki."

Then there are the "literary" types who assume supercilious little smiles. They know that autobiography is raw, naive, self-indulgent, possibly even dishonest—and certainly not art. They imply, whatever they say, that we all have lives and that if the best an author can do is to plunder his own, then he hasn't done anything terribly special.

Ordinary people, amateurs, write their memoirs for a variety of reasons: because leaving a written document is one route to immortality, at least with family and friends; because they know deep down that their personal experience of war or depression or the '60s is a part of history; and because they see writing as a means of figuring out what life was all about anyway (as in the words of the old song, "What's it all about, Alfie?").

These reasons could certainly apply to professional writers as well, but the aspiring professional has other concerns uppermost in mind. "Real" writers, as we all know, earn money and get published. "Real" writers can hear Dr. Samuel Johnson's oft-quoted statement ringing in their heads, "No one but a fool writes except for money."

The truth is that writers must be fools; they must take chances, be a little bit crazy, do things to stimulate their creativity, write for the love of it. Take poets, for instance. I have met many people who consider themselves poets, but poetry by definition is not a profitable form of writing.

My publisher won't touch poetry unless it's in combination with something else such as a diary/planner or a cookbook. Poets write for the joy of it, or for art's sake. May not any writer do the same thing?

Creative people know that there's more to their work than churning out words for bucks. I forget which famous writer said that 50 per cent of what he wrote was publishable and marketable and 50 per cent was not, but that he didn't know which 50 per cent was which until he got it all down on paper. It's best to approach a life-based story as a labor of love and, if by chance, it turns into something marketable, that's an extra.

"If I wrote my autobiography, who would read it?" you may ask. I have no way of knowing since I don't know you, but I do know that seemingly ordinary lives sometimes take twists and turns which are often interesting to other people.

Take, for example, *Out of Africa*. Those of you who haven't read the book by Isak Dinesen may have seen the movie. It is important to realize that when Karen Blixen (the author's real name) went out to live on a coffee plantation in Kenya, she was not yet a well-known writer, but a planter's wife whose plantation had failed. Not until she moved back to Denmark did she write of her life in Africa and create the book so well-known today. Similarly, when a young woman named Laura went to teach kindergarten in the Yukon at the time of the Gold Rush, she had some aspirations as a writer but had no idea that her experiences there would become a publishable memoir. Eventually, she married and had children; her son, Pierre, became successful as a journalist, and he helped her get the work published in her mature years. The result was *I Married the Klondike* by Laura Berton.

Many people want their memoirs only as private art, as a personal and family document; however, if one has something interesting to say and can say it well, one may be able to break into print with it. Here are some people who did:

Dr. James Wiley, an Ottawa pediatric orthopedic surgeon, wrote about the funny and grim aspects of his work in *You Just Can't Hardly Believe It!* Margaret Robinson's account of growing up in a rural Ontario village at the turn of the century, *Burnstown Remembered*, is another enjoyable read. *No Time Off for Good Behaviour*, the war memoirs of H.E. Woolley, who spent three years in a prisoner of war camp during World War II, was successfully published recently.

Another example of an ordinary person who found a publisher for her memoirs is a friend of mine, Muriel Newton-White, a painter and writer of children's books who has achieved a certain fame in Northwestern Ontario, where she lives, although she isn't known nationally. Her book, *The Cold Wind in the Winter* may be read on several levels. It has been described as "biography"; however, it can be read as a children's novel about a five-year-old girl in the Depression; it is also a portrait of the artist as a young child, interested in shapes and colors, forming pictures in her mind which she will later translate into oils and watercolors. Finally, those who know her and her community can read the book to encounter her family, whom they knew in real life, and to see if her life was like theirs back in the 1930s. A sequel, *The Pleasant Summer Days*, was published a year later.

Ottawa Valley residents are aware of broadcaster Mary Cook's popular books about her girlhood in Renfrew County: *One for Sorrow, Two for Joy* and *The View from the West Hill*.

Obviously, these people asked themselves: "What aspect or period of my life is most interesting?" and, at some stage, "How can I present it in a way that will interest a publisher?" Clearly, publishable autobiographies are not mere random reminiscences, but are constructed with some art and design; they have form. The linear, objective, historical autobiography which traces the path of career success is not the only form of autobiography; life writing may be a children's novel, a self-help book, a series of anecdotes linked by theme, setting or character, or some other form entirely.

In urging flexibility as to form, I am supported by William Spengemann, an "expert" on autobiography as a literary genre. In *The Forms of Autobiography*, he contends that—with so much fiction frankly autobiographical in form, content or both, and with so much fiction being experimental—an autobiographer should feel free to adopt the form which best expresses his or her life and its meaning.

His assertion has been supported by two quite different writers. Poet Ezra Pound, when urged to start writing his autobiography, pointed to his shelf of published poetry and said, "That's my autobiography." A similar view was expressed by rock and roll singer Chuck Berry, who contends that his compositions like "Maybelline" and "Johnny Be Good" are more directly autobiographical than his unghosted autobiography, because they came more spontaneously from his inner self.

Spengemann makes some radical statements to do with autobiography that are potentially interesting to "literary writers." "Biographical facts are not necessary to autobiography," he claims. Novels and fiction address the same problems of self-definition that tax autobiographers, in that both concern the realization of the self. Both autobiographers and fiction writers shape the past to serve the present and are using memory and imagination. His book contains an interesting discussion of how part of *David Copperfield* is autobiography. And, of course, we are all aware of "autobiographical novels," some of them more autobiographical than others. Scholars have spent a great deal of time and ink showing how, to name two examples, James Joyce's *Portrait of the Artist As a Young Man* and D. H. Lawrence's *Sons and Lovers* are derived from the lives of their authors. There is much fact in such works, but they are regarded as great novels, not only because of the authors' skill and innovation in presenting the narrative, but also because the authors labelled them fiction, not fact.

Robertson Davies once said in an interview that, "The first requisite of good autobiography is *not* that the author should have an interesting life, but that he should be able to write." Skills of writing which come into play in fiction have a place in non-fiction as well.

The person who says, "I'm going to take my entire life and put it down just as it was and make a book of it," is in serious danger of producing a piece of writing that lacks focus. The best thing to do is to determine a theme, that is, a sense of what your life is all about, a thread which will run through the whole story and provide unity. What might a theme be? Well, it might be the value of love of some kind. It might be a commitment to a religion or to a political movement. It might be pursuit of an art, it might be overcoming a disadvantage, whether physical, mental, social, economic or family related. It might be the beauty and happiness of life long ago, or quite possibly, it might be the difficulty or tragedy or horror of life in some past time. Then you would focus on the experiences that are pertinent to that subject. Or you could think of the process as singling out the main plot of your life, and then the subplot. If you turn out to have more than one book inside you, then write one at a time.

Once you have established the connecting element, I would suggest starting, not with your infancy or your ancestors, but with an incident or experience that is part of the plot, which stands out in your mind and which you can dramatize for the reader in a vivid way. Eventually, you may find that you have ten or fifteen sections to arrange however you see fit.

Of course, if you want to begin at the beginning and do a complete memoir there's nothing wrong with that; it is a way to collect your thoughts and material. Once it is done, you can extract from it for other purposes. In helping an elderly woman with her memoirs, I realized that several sections might be of interest as independent articles.

Another friend completed an autobiography of several hundred pages, primarily to leave to his children, and from this he has extracted, arranged and expanded material which he is making into short stories, several of which have been published in little magazines. In his case, it was useful for him to have the entire book-length, directly autobiographical work to spread out in front of him to go through—it is like looking over a forest and singling out the best trees to use to build a hand-crafted piece of furniture. He was able to see that certain childhood incidents had bearing on subsequent events; having the whole life story to extract from made it easy for him to create nice parallels and do foreshadowing.

Writers often hear it said that only the beginner, wet behind the ears, writes autobiographical work. Related is the notion that the writer should get the autobiographical stuff out of his or her system in order to go on to write something truly creative and artistic. Also stressed is the necessity of distancing yourself from life events before one can transform them into art. While there may be some truth in all that, I think it's wrong to dismiss all autobiographical writing as bad writing, simply because of preconceived notions about it being undigested and unstructured.

One of the clichés most frequently thrown at beginning writers is, "Write about what you know." It's valid advice, but not a simple process. Examining one's life may be more complicated or traumatic than one expects, but "the foul rag and bone yard of the heart" may be transformed into art.

Ruth Latta is the author of three books, most recently *A Wild Streak* (General Store, 1995). Her fiction, poetry and articles appear in US and Canadian publications. She lives in Ottawa with her husband and her cats.

# Write A Family History

*by Betty Dyck*

I begin my workshops with an anecdote about the *Mennonite Game*. When I married into the Manitoba Mennonite community, I soon learned to appreciate this "game" At an initial meeting people trace back their lineage beginning with the East and West Reserve (east and west of the Red River where Mennonites settled in Manitoba), the year of emigration and thence to Europe. The game continues until you finally connect with one relative, no matter how distant, that you both call cousin/aunt/uncle. Once that's settled you can comfortably continue to visit. You have established your place in the order of things. You belong. My hope is that my written family history will give our children a strong sense of belonging.

Many people have become hooked on leaving a written heritage for their children. You will have a head start if as parents you kept loose-leaf or scrap books of their activities. After our children left home, I gathered all the material collected throughout the years into individual three-ring binders for them. This included report cards, school pictures, Brownie, Beaver, Girl Guide and Scout merits, baptismal, musical and graduation certificates, plus captioned photographs. These books are indispensable in rounding out our family history.

Time, patience and perseverance are the main ingredients necessary, and are usually found once your children have left home. Begin with the time worn adage of writers—with what you know—and work backwards.

Genealogical charts play an important role in registering time frames for story telling. We have one on the Dyck side and recently we acquired others regarding my ancestors, one of which dates back to the 1700s when the first McLeod of our clan landed in Newfoundland. These will appear in the appendix.

A family tree is much like a winter elm if it contains only names. How much better to add the green leaves of summer by providing brief histories of each member. My father-in-law's obituary tells of his 47 years teaching in southern Manitoba. As well, Grampa Dyck loved music and singing. He lead a young people's band in which his children all played musical instruments.

From the video tape of my husband's retirement in 1985, our grand-children will learn that their Grandad Dyck spent 37 years teaching and sang in church choirs from the time he was 17. So teaching, the love of music and the ability to sing are part of our children's heritage.

In any project memory plays a large part. Special family celebrations throughout the years may give you clues. As we age, memory needs a jump start. My journal, begun in 1976, has proved invaluable.

Once you exhaust questioning relatives and collecting memorabilia from them, your next step is a visit to your local genealogical society who will direct you to available sources such as provincial and national archives. Principal sources for genealogical research in Canada are divided into the following categories: census records, vital statistics (births, deaths, marriages), wills and records of land holdings, estates, military service and immigration. Baptismal and marriage certificates often lead to learning about localities where further information might be on record.

Libraries have back-issues of newspapers on microfilm. Through inter-library loan, microfilmed newspapers from most Canadian cities can be forwarded to your local library. To begin your research, politely approach librarians for assistance.

A formula for asking effectively is:

1) Tell why you need the information.

2) State your project clearly.

3) Give a summary of information already collected.

Once your research is completed, write succinctly. The most important element is to record your story. Think about the words you are using—familiar words in short, simple sentences with active verbs. Write directly to the point. Good writing is like geometry where the shortest distance between two points is a straight line—the shortest distance to a written point is the fewest words. In order not to overwhelm yourself, consider the project a series of chapters or short stories, not as a whole book. Liberal use of family anecdotes makes for pleasant reading.

My outline is my guide, but it is flexible. You may find the need to change your outline several times as you work with the material.

Originally I planned to put published articles and poems drawn from family events in an appendix, but later believed they were better suited for inclusion in relevant chapters.

If you have a computer, it generally has a spell checker, but you also need to be conscious of consistency in spelling, capitalizing and style. One way to insure word consistency is to select a specific dictionary and stick to the spellings therein.

I decided to tell our story in the first person, acknowledging other sources. For instance regarding my grandfather's sparse diary of his Boer War service, I found a letter in the *St. John Globe* written by a soldier travelling on the same troop ship. The letter gave an authentic picture of the ocean voyage from St. John, New Brunswick to Cape Town, South Africa. My grandfather was an avid letter writer, so it is entirely possible that he wrote something similar to my grandmother. I also found journalists' accounts of the train trip and marches through the African countryside. These additions will give our children graphic descriptions of the lives of grandparents in times past.

Writing a family history is a personal project and there are as many ways to tackle it as there are people. Still, it is helpful to have some kind of guideline with which to work. And there's always the chance that once you have completed your family history, you can use the research to write another book. Such a book might hit the best seller list as did David Macfarlane's *The Danger Tree* when it won the Canadian Authors Association literary award for non-fiction in 1992. More recently, Macfarlane's book was made into a TV documentary.

Good writing and good luck.

•••

**A Proposed Chronological Outline for a Family History**

**Preface:**

Your reason for compiling this family history. This will be prepared after you have made the decision of the scope of the history—whether it is to be a joint (paternal and maternal) family history or just one side of the family.

**Acknowledgments**

Thanking others for their assistance in compiling the family history.

**Chapter 1**

Paternal family background as far back as you have been able to research up to grandparents:

- country/places/dates of births/deaths,
- social, political, economic, religious aspects that influenced their lives,
  - education/occupation,
  - marriages/other special celebrations,
  - health/diseases/accidents,
  - special visitors to the home,
  - family lore—stories passed on from generations.

**Chapter 2**

Maternal family background. (as above).

**Chapter 3**

First twenty years of paternal grandparents' lives and how they met and married:
  - childhood, health, diseases, accidents,
  - associations with brothers/sisters,
  - unusual happenings, religion,
  - occupation, financial condition, education, etc.

**Chapter 4**

First twenty years of maternal grandparents' lives and how they met and married (as above).

**Chapter 5**

Birth and first 20 years of father's life/or until marriage to mother (as above) and add more details concerning:
  - health,
  - school days, schools attended, teachers, courses,
  - activities (scouts, etc.),
  - achievements (in music, sports, etc.),
  - influences of home and other people.

**Chapter 6**

Birth and first 20 years of mother's life or until marriage to father (as above).

**Chapter 7**

How parents met, early married life:
  - occupations, places lived,
  - associations,
  - travel with children,
  - accomplishments.

## Chapter 8

Bring family history up to the present. This could include your own marriage, children and grandchildren.

### Epilogue

If you find you have something more to add that does not fit into any other category.

### Pictures

Could be placed in text in approximate appropriate places or bunched. It is popular to have a picture section with captions one-third and two-thirds throughout the book. This allows for an uninterrupted read of the story. The picture section can be seen at leisure or referred to as one desires.

### Appendix

• Lists of names, dates and places of births/deaths as far back as you have researched. Although some or most of this will appear in the text, it will be available for quick reference.

• Maps indicating places of origins, especially if the towns have disappeared from modern maps.

•Certificates of births, baptisms, marriages, university degrees, other achievements, deaths, etc.

### Endnotes

If you wish to give sources for quotes from printed and copyrighted material.

### Bibliography

If you wish to list a variety of printed sources from which you found helpful information to round out your own family history.


**Note:** This is to be treated as a general outline to be adapted to the type of family history each individual is planning to compile.

Betty Dyck is the Winnipeg-based author of three non-fiction books, editor of two church histories, and freelance writer who conducts workshops for the CAA Manitoba Branch.

# Write Biographies

*by Douglas Waugh*

Almost any one of the five billion people alive today could be a subject for a biography. And if you add to that number all of those of whom there is some historical record, the supply of candidates becomes almost limitless. There is something of interest in almost every human life.

### Choose a subject.

Whoever you choose to write about, it should be somebody to whom you are attracted. You don't need to *like* your subject, but it is important that you find her interesting. Your work will be easier and more fun if you choose a subject from a field with which you are familiar. Thus, a retired soldier might choose a military figure, a writer another writer, and so on. Because my field is medicine, I have chosen medical subjects. It is also a big help if there is plenty of readily accessible archival information.

### Support.

Writing a biography can be costly, particularly if it requires travel, long-distance calls, photocopying, and so forth. If your subject is a Canadian, you might be eligible for a grant from the Canada Council. A political party or a wealthy family may give you a generous subsidy if you want to write about one of their giants, though if you accept such support, there may be strings attached. In specialized situations, such as the history of medicine, there are agencies like the Hannah Institute that are dedicated to supporting medical biographies.

### Research.

Research will be the most time-consuming part of your task. Not only will you need to dig out information about your subject's life, correspondence, letters, press reports, obituaries, and the like, you will also need to dig out details of the time in which she lived.

Family background is an important part of any biography. Readers want to know the kind of family from which your subject came, whether there were distinguished or infamous relatives, and what factors in upbringing seem to have been important in the evolution of personality and character. A visit to the family homestead or churchyard and interviews with surviving kin can be rewarding. Much of this can be done by phone using a tape recorder and telephone pickup. Old newspapers from the time(s) and place(s) in which the subject lived can help place her in the society of her time and town.

"To whom it may concern" letters, to the editors of newspapers or professional journals, can be used to solicit information from any who may have known your subject. In biography writing, you have to gather your information where you can find it, and often one bit will lead to others.

In your research, don't rely only on your memory. Wherever possible, make photocopies or tape recordings. Always note the essential reference data so that it can be found again. Reference to the publications should include volume, number, pages, year, and publisher. An archival reference might include title, box number, folder number, year, and names of correspondents. I make a habit of dictating notes to myself during archival searches. This might not suit everyone, but I couldn't survive without it.

One of the trickiest bits about biographical research is knowing when to quit. With many subjects, there is almost no limit to the amount of available information. One bit leads to another—on and on, forever. Imagine doing a biography of Sir John A. MacDonald, Sir Wilfred Laurier, or William Lyon Mackenzie King! The biographer must sift through mountains of material and then must be *extremely* selective.

Apart from writing talent, the most important tool of the biographer is a capacity to exercise judgment in the selection of material to be included or omitted. No matter how much material you are able to accumulate, there will always be gaps—some aspects of your subject's life will remain forever unknown. Half of an obviously important exchange of letters may be missing; the subjects may have dropped from sight for a week, a month, or a year—always at a time critical to your story. When a gap can't be filled, you have to decide whether to leave it blank, or to fill it with speculation (which is acceptable as long as you warn the reader).

### The writing.

It is best not to decide on the structure of your biography until your research is finished, or nearly finished. If you start with a predetermined plan, you may find yourself tempted to ignore bits that don't fit. In general, the data should determine the structure, not the other way around.

The most important rule to remember about the writing of biographies is that good writing cannot salvage shoddy research any more than meticulous research can make bad writing publishable.

Before the writing begins, you need to decide the sequence in which you want your material to appear. The rule here is to remember that a biography is about a *person*. The thread of that person's individuality must be continuous and unbroken throughout the narrative. Even though you have to provide a background for certain events, you shouldn't drop your main character while you do this. Worst of all is to set the main character aside for a whole chapter while you set the stage for a later chapter. As a rule of thumb (remember rules are made to be broken!), your main character should appear on every page of published text. There are various ways of accomplishing this, the most common being some variation of "Meanwhile, back at the farm…"

Early in your writing, it is a sound plan to identify the points of conflict or tension in your subject's life, particularly if these lead to a change in her behaviour or attitudes. Like a novelist, you may decide to bring this in by an oblique allusion in an earlier chapter. Remember, your subject's reaction to crisis or calamity can make fascinating reading.

For the early part of your subject's life, it is often easy and prudent to follow a strict chronology. The subject is born, grows up, goes to school, makes friends, interacts with parents, siblings, playmates, etc. This may continue until she is established on her final career pathway.

However, in the course of a career, most of us become engaged in a number of activities that either go on simultaneously or overlap with one another over long periods. Here a pattern of strict chronology can make for tedious, verbose writing. It may be best to break out major activities and follow them separately for a chapter or two or more.

A tricky part of biography writing can be that of getting your character off the stage. There are no magic formulas for this. It need not happen by having her die, although this is a frequent ending. Another way is to send her quietly off to a nursing home or to live with offspring, or you may decide it is best to leave her at the scene of a final triumph.

## Footnotes and references.

Finally, there is the question of footnotes and references. Some biographies have neither. The advantage of the footnotes is that it enables you to include information that, while relevant, is not absolutely essential to the main thread of your story—it simply clarifies or amplifies. References, on the other hand, tell where you got your information. My preference is to combine footnotes and references in a section of *Notes* at the end of the book, listed chapter by chapter. This makes it possible to intermingle references with anecdotal information in a way that can be almost as readable as the main text. This is best settled in discussion with your publisher, although it helps to have a "best method" in mind when you enter such negotiations.

While I haven't become rich through biography writing, it has been the most stimulating and rewarding activity I've ever undertaken. I wish you well when you try it.

Douglas Waugh had a checkered career that took him from railway labourer to army medical officer to Dean of the Medical Faculty at Queen's University. From the time of his professional retirement in 1983 until his death in April, 1997, he had been a columnist, book author and speech writer. Several of his essays have been reprinted in *Reader's Digest*.

# How to Interview for a Life Story

*by Sheldon Oberman*

G athering a life story can be a wonderful experience as well as an honor for both the interviewer and the person interviewed. It strengthens the bonds between generations and enriches both family and community. When members of a class undertake such a project, it can connect the school to families in very special way.

### A good interview establishes a comfortable rapport with sincere interest in someone's life story.

You can gather a life story in different ways—*objectively* in the manner of a reporter, historian or academic researcher or else more *subjectively* in a personal search for roots or as a storyteller looking for a good tale. For me, what began as a personal recollection of my grandfather's life led to my writing a children's book, *The Always Prayer Shawl*. Whatever your purpose, it is important that the interview itself is satisfying for everyone.

### The right question asked in the right way brings out great treasures—not highly priced objects but the stories and insights that give events and objects their personal value.

I suggest it is best to gather both the hard facts, as well as personal insights. The facts establish the objective reality, the subjective impressions provide the ring of truth.

Be patient. An answer may seem quite short even dismissive but it may be an initial response that can lead to a longer and fuller account. Your quiet nod or further question may encourage your subject to go beyond generalities or cliché responses and deeper into memory.

*A general question can open a whole world. A specific question can bring it to life.*

Switch between general and specific questions. A general question can be overwhelming, leading to abstractions.

Question: Was the Depression difficult for your family?

Answer: It sure was. But we learned the value of hard work. People pulled together, not like today...

However a general question can introduce specific questions.

Questions: Did you have to go to work? Where did you work? What was that like? How much did you earn? What did you miss most by leaving school?

The list of questions is a guideline and starting point to stimulate memories. Adapt it to the person and the situation. Let your subject "warm up" and recall things naturally. Once a story begins, add your own questions to encourage details. One story leads to another. Return to this question list as needed.

Video or tape recording may be better than taking notes. You can always transcribe it if desired. Test and set up equipment beforehand so you can have a natural discussion. (Set the camera on a stand aimed at you both in a familiar comfortable setting.)

*Life story questions.*

**A**. What was your mother's family like?

1. What were the names of your mother's parents?
2. When and where were they born? Where did they live?
3. How did they make a living?
4. What are your clearest memories of them?
5. Do you recall anything either one said to you? Or did for you?
6. Who else in that family do you remember? What was he/she like?
7. Do you know your ancestry before your mother's grandparents? Do you know other family stories about any of them?
8. What was it like for them during... (various historical events of the time—war, immigration, Depression, natural disaster, political changes.)
9. Did they have any special traditions? Are any still followed?
10. Do you have any special objects or mementos of any of them? Does the object have a story? (If not an object, perhaps there's a place or activity reminiscent of a family member.)

11. Where are the other members/branches of the family now?

12. What was your mother like? (Appearance, personality, habits, common expressions, interests, work, special memories of her.)

**B**. Ask similar questions on the father's side.

**C**. What was it like for you as a child?

1. When were you born? Where did you grow up? (Country, name and size of city or town, neighbourhood, kind of home.) How was that place different from here? What did you bring with you?

2. What were your parents like? Describe them—appearance and character, way of making a living.

3. How many brothers and sisters did you have? What were their names and the order of their birth? (Ask for possible dates of birth.)

4. Who were you closest to in the family? Describe that person or persons. What would you do together that was special?

5. What kind of family chores did you do?

6. What jobs did you get outside the family? What did you earn?

7. Where did you go to school? How was your education different from today? What was better? What was worse? Did you have any special teacher? How did that person help you?

8. How was your life then different from a child's today?

9. What were your clearest memories of childhood?

- kinds of food - who made it, where and how? - pets, hobbies, sports

- your favourite toy, bike or car

- favourite joke or game or practical joke.

- special movie, book, radio programs or songs

- favourite place in the house / the neighbourhood / the area (perhaps a fishing hole, a vacation spot or a hideaway) - how did your family spend a typical day or evening?

- family time - game, picnic, different holidays, gifts, visits, traditional event, entertainment, storytelling.

10. Do you recall any stories told by your family? (These can be family stories or folk tales) Do you remember folk songs or lullabyes?

11. Who were your friends, heroes, role models?

12. Did you ever get into trouble? What happened?

13. What did you want to be when you grew up?

14. Were you ever given any important advice or predictions?

**D**. Adulthood

   1. When did you first leave home and why?

   2. What kind of jobs did you have? What did you have to learn to succeed at them? Were any very difficult? Exciting? Unusual?

   3. Did you travel? How old were you? What did you see?

   4. Did you ever meet anyone famous?

   5. Were you ever present at a historic moment?

   6. Did you ever receive any kind of award or honour?

   7. Did you ever feel you were in great danger or in great need?

   8. Did you ever help someone who was in great danger or need?

   9. Who helped you the most in your family. Outside your family?

10. What was your family's first car?

11. When did you first ride in a plane?

12. When did you meet the one you married? Where and how? What impressed you at that time? When did you decide to marry? What convinced you it was the right decision? How did the proposal go? What was the wedding like?

13. What was your first home? What was your first car?

14. How did you make a living at the time?

15. What was it like to raise a family? (Discuss each child.)

16. Who were your family friends? What family events, vacations do you remember best as the children were growing up?

**E**. The Present

   1. What did your brothers and sisters do later in their lives?

   2. Things have changed greatly since you were a child. What do you think are important things that have not changed?

   3. Do any members of your family have your traits? Which traits? Does anyone in your present family have traits of your parents or grandparents? Who? Which traits?

   4. If you could be any age again, which age would you be? Why?

   5. If you could go anywhere in the world where would it be? Why?

   6. If you could talk to any person you ever knew, who would it be? What would you talk about?

   7. Is there anything that you regret not doing?

   8. Is there anything you are especially proud of?

**Note:** Record the person giving a tour of his/her home and memorabilia or record the person going through photos, family trees or mementos as they stimulate memories. Consider interviewing a friend or relatives of the person to get insights and more stories about the person.

### After the interview.

The person may continue thinking about your questions afterwards. Leave the question sheet. Call back. You may learn more. Use the next opportunity to clarify details.

### Gather your own life story.

The questions we ask of others we can also ask of ourselves. Ask yourself these questions to recall and organize your own early memories. I used similar questions to recall details from my own past which led to me writing *This Business With Elijah, interconnected tales set in Winnipeg's immigrant Northend.*

My children's illustrated book, *The Always Prayer Shawl,* (Boyds Mills Press) was inspired by a specific question. In preparation for my son's Bar Mitzvah I came across my grandfather's prayer shawl. I wrote the story to explore why my grandfather's tallis was so important to me and to "introduce" my grandfather to my son. In the book a grandson asks a simple general question—"Grandfather, were you ever a kid like me?" The book tells his life story with the shawl as its central symbol. Later, when I adapted the book into a play, I used such questions to develop characters and scenes.

Sheldon Oberman is a writer, teacher and storyteller. He has published eight books for children and adults. He presents stories, addresses and workshops for schools and conferences.

# How to Write the "Life Story" of a Building

*by Sheldon Oberman*

I took a tour of Toronto's Casa Loma, a "castle" built in 1912 by Sir Henry Pellatt. My tour guide was a good storyteller with colourful descriptions about Sir Henry's life, his times and the construction of Casa Loma.

The tour guide's story of the building gave life to the entire historical period—how the rich and poor lived; how they worked, played, their homes, their clothing and vehicles, what the city was like to live in and walk through at the time, and the exciting rise and fall of Sir Henry Pellatt himself.

### A single detail can spark a great idea.

One detail struck me; Sir Henry offered the people of the city a dollar for each field stone they brought for his wall. He bought 250,000 of them. This historical fact inspired by the presence of the actual building combined with a personal observation—I noticed there was only one white stone in the wall. It inspired a story—*The White Stone In The Castle Wall*—about a Scottish immigrant boy who struggles to bring that white stone to Casa Loma and what he learns about the value of work. It was published by Tundra as a children's book. The illustrations of the boy's journey to Casa Loma also function as a visual walking tour of old Toronto from the poorest neighbourhood to the wealthiest.

### Set a fictional tale or "news" story in an actual local building.

Learn about a famous local place or even a neighbourhood fire hall, theatre or house. Take a tour, read local history books, old newspapers or have a visit from someone who knew the area at the time. It is useful to think about the potential story before a tour or a talk. With some preliminary information, you can ask better questions. Combine historical information with a sense of how people lived at the time. Stories will be richer in both history and colourful detail if it comes from a real sense of place.

### *Try your own house or locale.*

You can create a great story set in your own area, especially if it has some history. Who was there years ago? Consider how people lived there when a certain interesting building was new. Imagine an exciting event that might have happened in the rooms, the yard and street.

With careful research and your own vivid imagination, the story of a building can spring to life in your hands, whether as an article, poem, or story.

Sheldon Oberman is a writer, teacher and storyteller. He has published eight books for children and adults. He presents stories, addresses and workshops for schools and conferences.

# Preserve Oral History

*by Sarah Yates* ———————————————————

A dozen years ago, I wrote a theatre history based on a series of interviews, originally in tape form. Because I was on a limited budget, I made the tapes, transcribed them and reused them for other projects or subjects. Those tapes that had been saved were poorly labelled. After five years during which I had not reused the backup documentation, I destroyed it. I needed the space.

When the Manitoba Archives later wrote to ask for assistance in documenting these interviews, I was frustrated. I had lost my chance at fame. But, more seriously, I had destroyed some original research which might have proven valuable to the archives and future researchers.

You may not want to donate your tapes to the archives immediately because you might turn them into a radio program or use them to imbue a character in faction or historical fiction with the flavor of authenticity. You would, nevertheless, be wise to consider preserving the interviews you have collected.

Invaluable assistance and advice about the collection and preservation of this material can be obtained from the public archives. Every province in the country has at least some archivists engaged full time in the collection and preservation of oral history. Many of them have literature available on the subject. Consultation is part of their mandated responsibility. I have found every archivist to whom I have gone for information and assistance to be helpful and co-operative.

"Empathy is the most important thing about any oral history interview," according to Gilbert Comeault, Head Archivist of Manitoba's Provincial Archives.

"Getting to know the person—to develop rapport and to understand his or her attitudes and outlook is critical," he added. "Never forget why you are conducting the interview. Get into the person's body and mind and know his way of looking at a situation. The idea is not to be a Crown prosecutor.

"It is important to have quality interviews for long-term preservation and to provide a greater variety of application for late use. So, a quality tape may be used for broadcast or as an insert in a film. In the short-term, however, one of inferior quality may serve the need."

The questions most likely to concern the writer are: What if you cannot afford a good tape machine? Is it worth recording the interview? Or, is it worth saving and offering to the archives if you could not use the best quality machine?

Although answers to these questions vary greatly between one archivist and the next, if the content of the interview is good, the archives can transcribe it onto a format that can be saved. Perhaps most important is to speak to your local archivist prior to embarking on any long-term project. You may also consider contacting the National Archives in Ottawa. Examine the possibility of interest and support.

Though not many provinces make direct grants, tax benefits or some project money from other indirect sources may be available. By all means, examine the possibility.

Despite the fact that the validity of oral history has been questioned by those who believe the written text is less subject to personal bias, the benefits to a writer in judging a situation assisted by on-the-spot taped coverage are unquestionable. Nothing can replace either the immediacy or the validity of personal recall. When you are asked to prepare a story on a person or situation which has historical relevance, call your local archivist about the availability of interviews already recorded and preserved.

Comeault is firmly convinced about the validity of oral history as a record. "More and more people will come to understand and treat information contained on film, video and audio tapes as mirrors of our society, like any other textual records."

Many people think that the collection of anecdotes and stories is an easy task. Nothing could be further from the truth.

A lot of preparation is necessary since you, as interviewer, determine the text of your tape. The real challenge is to provide stimulus to your interviewee through knowledge. Know your subject. At least one month of research would be needed for a six-month or thirty-person project. Prepare simple biographies of the people to be interviewed and learn the "lingo" and the technical terms necessary to question people intelligently. An oral historian needs to establish, in an hour, the character of the person being interviewed and his or her place in society.

You will need a good tape recorder, adequate preparation, a willing subject, and a lot of time. Comeault estimates that to conduct, transcribe, catalogue and record one hour may cost between $250 and $500 including contact, research, and travel time. It can be expensive to do the job well. Although this sum is beyond reach of the majority of writers working on a one-time only project or story, it does give you an idea of the enormousness of the task facing archivists actively involved in the collection of oral history tapes.

The relationship between the interviewer and the interviewee necessarily affects what is said and how. The people interviewed can best describe their feelings and circumstances. Try to elicit their responses, insights and interpretations and not to interject, interpret or alter. Always be aware of your own bias.

Note the conditions of the interview and the person being interviewed. Was he or she hesitant or rambling? Where did the interview take place? What did it entail?

Flexibility, resourcefulness, and sensitivity to the person being interviewed and to the situation being described are critical for a successful oral history interview.

The sound quality of the tape is important.

Some important practical tips to consider include:

• Before starting the interview, test your machine to be sure it is in working order with tape heads cleaned, microphone clear. Use a plug into an electrical circuit with a backup battery. If you are using cassettes, use good quality C-60 because they provide better quality recording and are much less susceptible to stretching, breakage and print-through than the C-90.

• Don't rely on the counter on the tape machine; use a stop-watch. You won't want to interrupt the interview at a critical or sensitive point.

• If possible, work in stereo to record both questions and answers with maximum clarity. Use two microphones, with each person having his or her own. This can also allow for the separation of voices for transcription and in broadcasting where the interviewer's voice must be isolated.

• Find a quiet area for recording. The sound of traffic, air conditioners, or other people in the room talking is distracting and can destroy the value of your tape. Put the tape recorder midway between the two of you, but within your reach so you can maintain control of it.

• Before starting the interview, discuss some of the points you will cover. Surprise is not always most conducive to recall. Relax your interviewee and explain what you are trying to do.

• Prepare an agreement form to be signed by him or her, releasing the interview for immediate or future use. If access is to be restricted, it is best to specify a limited time-period. Sample forms can be obtained from most archives.

• After you have set up, do a trial run. Ask a question, tape the reply and play both back to check the sound level and other technical aspects of the recorder.

• Leave a small amount of tape blank at the beginning and end of the reel or cassette. This is where the wear and tear occurs.

• Include a brief biography at the beginning of the tape, explain where you are, who you are, the circumstances of the interview, the person being interviewed, and the main subject of the interview.

• Listen to the tape after you have completed your interview. Make notes about questions you neglected to ask.

• Immediately after your interview, label your tapes clearly. If you have used a cassette, break the seal so it cannot be erased accidentally.

• Ask questions that elicit more than a simple "yes" or "no." So you might ask, "What did your family do on Sundays in the country?" rather than, "Did you go to church on Sunday after you moved to the farm?"

• Be sensitive to your interviewees. They are not simply memory machines. Some memories may elicit painful or emotional responses. Body language is important. Remain alert and attentive.

• Do not plan to record for much more than an hour. If you have more information to collect, plan another session.

In Canada, the sponsoring institution such as the archives or the company for whom you are preparing the history, has the copyright on the interview after it has been recorded and stored. Be sure that you have proper forms signed which release the interview for use after a specified date. In the U.S. both the interviewer and the interviewee have copyright.

Oral history is an intriguing way to learn to develop the art of listening, to collect stories, learn history, and even develop another kind of expertise which is stimulating and enjoyable.

Sarah Yates, a member of the Periodical Writers Association of Canada, has been a professional freelance writer, editor and researcher for more than 20 years, publishing across Canada, in the US, England, France and Hong Kong. Her children's books include *Can't You be Still?* (1992), *Nobody Knows!*(1994) and *Here's What I Mean to Say...*(1997). She has also written two textbooks for Lerner Publications in Minneapolis.

# Publishing a Hungarian Anthology

*By Susan Romvary*

**"N**o other history shines as much as the Hungarian Nation's history. The whole civilized world is indebted for the heroic historical actions of the Hungarian people." – Theodore Roosevelt addressing the Hungarian Parliament, April 2nd, 1910.

The Hungarian Literary Association of Montreal celebrated the mille-centenary of the Magyars settlement in Hungary with a commemorative trilingual anthology—English, Hungarian, French—written by enthusiastic, talented authors and artists from around the globe. The millecentenary was important to Hungarians throughout the world as this event marked their nation's foundation and their blueprint for the future. Eleven-hundred years with a Christian cultural background has created a nation that is typically Hungarian, but characteristically European.

This anthology portrayed an image of the Hungarian country and the Hungarian battle-torn nation throughout the centuries. The authors gave us a rendition of the Hungarian past, from their ancestors to the present, from their humble peasants to their revered scientists, inventors, writers, musicians and artists.

To chronicle 1100 years of Hungarian history could fill several volumes, but this anthology sampled the country's memories, humor, art and achievements. It is a tribute to the courageous participants of the 1956 Hungarian Revolution and Hungarian accomplishments in the world—a gift and a legacy for future generations.

Adapted from the Preface of *Visszatekintés / Looking Back / Regard sur le passè*

## Background

Forty years have passed since the suppression of the 1956 Hungarian Revolution, which I fled with my family to Canada—in order to be freed from the communist terror. The terrible pain of being homeless was worsened by the fact that I did not speak the language of my adoptive country. This also hindered my hope of future assimilation. To be a homeless stranger is a painful experience. I am sincerely grateful to Canada for its immigration policy regarding the Hungarian refugees. We were not only offered a new home, but could keep our language, culture and interest in our historical heritage.

This policy of understanding made the foundation of the Hungarian Literary Association of Montreal possible. Its main goal was, and still is, to keep our literary language alive and help us cherish our cultural heritage. With the talented writer and poet, Éva Puskás-Balogh, as its President, the Hungarian Literary Association realized a farfetched dream: to publish a trilingual historical anthology for the millecentennarium of the Magyars settlement in Hungary—the only one in the world published for this occasion.

## Questions and answers

The creation of this historical Hungarian anthology will certainly interest other ethnic groups. In order to get more detailed information about this work of art, I interviewed Éva Puskás-Balogh—whose experience could give creative and essential help for future undertakings in the field of ethnic anthologies.

## Question:

Why did the Hungarian Literary Association of Montreal publish this commemorative anthology?

## Éva:

In 1996, Hungarians celebrated the 1100th anniversary of the Magyars settlement in Hungary. This settlement was the foundation of our nation's development. For us it is an important jubilee that was celebrated by Hungarians all around the world.

In honour of eleven hundred years filled with history, the Hungarian Literary Association decided to celebrate this special event with a commemorative book. Our undertaking was a monumental task as we chose to make it a trilingual issue.

We received stacks of manuscripts and researched articles—thousands of pages—to make our selections as interesting to young and old, Hungarians and Canadians alike.

**Question:**

How and when was the final decision made?

**Éva:**

In the Spring of 1996 at our executive meeting, we debated among ourselves: how should the Hungarian Literary Association of Montreal celebrate this anniversary? We knew that there would be art exhibits, concerts, folks dances etc., but we also knew that nobody was publishing, or intended to publish a commemorative book for this occasion.

We voted for an anthology—to leave a legacy for future generations. The Hungarians gave so much to the world in the fields of art, literature, music, science and sport. It was time to honor their achievements. We précised these accomplishments, as it would take several volumes to list them all.

Time and funds limited us. We only had a few months to plan, solicit contributions, select our final contributors, and publish this anthology. Since the Government refused our request for a grant, we had to raise the funds necessary to print our book as well.

**Question:**

How did you plan the book? What procedure did you follow?

**Éva:**

If I told you it was a difficult job, it would be the understatement of the year. The proper description would be that this book was a frustrating and exciting undertaking for us all. At the beginning the team felt that we were in total chaos, because the book actually was conceived in my mind's eye, and just like a symphony, we had different sections to work on, one by one, and only at the end would we all see the total picture of this anthology.

To establish our guidelines, at the beginning of this mammoth undertaking several of our members and authors, including myself, contributed our publishing experiences and points of views. To make this a near "perfect" edition we used this combined knowledge which helped us tremendously in eliminating many problems.

In my mind's eye, I had envisioned a magnificent testimonial for all Hungarians to be proud of. Unfortunately vision and reality came down to dollars. We had to cut the material to less than 200 pages. Also colour pictures became a cost issue—sadly, we had to leave many out.

Our selection came down to fifty contributions: art, poetry, historical and personal accounts. To balance our Hungarian legacy we fashioned the contributions into the following sections:

Our Heritage; Our History; A Blink To The Past; Our Pride; Canada; My Country.

It had taken us months to read the material. We selected, discarded, contacted authors, asked for diskettes, and we cringed at the articles typed on old fashioned typewriters. As this publication was planned as a trilingual book, we had to use three different computers, each loaded with the necessary software, different fonts and alphabets.

Computers are sophisticated and useful instruments—and just as frustrating. Our computers had a habit of crashing, and many times we had to start our jobs over again. We also used a scanner to transfer faxed manuscripts, printed manuscripts, including the ones typed on old fashioned typewriters, and some graphics into a computer format.

Our art director's biggest challenge was the historical maps and Arabic letter transcription into our book. Some computers "don't want to speak Arabic". We overcame our technical difficulties, and as you can see, we have the maps and Arabic letters in the right places.

To complete this work the Art director put in at least three thousand hours, the English and French editors about one thousand hours each. After eight thousand working hours, I gave up counting. We all have regular jobs—we used nights and weekends to work on the book.

This was a labour of love. The excitement never left us. This "high" carried us through the sleepless nights, weeks and months—we rarely felt tired. We are proud of the book's design, the editorials, the art and the graphics. We are grateful to our contributing authors and artists. Their magnificent work and uniqueness makes this anthology very special.

## Question:

What advice would you give to others about publishing an anthology?

## Éva:

The question is very difficult to answer as each publication presents a different problem. If it's an anthology, the editor must be aware of the authors' personalities, their special talents, and make the best use of their uniqueness.

Our anthology was published as a non-profit undertaking. If the funds were available in advance, it would have freed up time to work on the book in lieu of soliciting funds for the publication.

The effort, the challenges, the frayed nerves—that was the easy part of the book: we were in control.

The most important task has just begun.

Promotion!

We may have published the best anthology ever written, we believe in our work and we have expended all or most of our energy to get it to the printer—however, if the public is not aware of its existence, if it is not promoted—the effort, the challenges, the frayed nerves are all for nothing.

Susan Romvary is a Montreal-based published writer of humorous stories about being an immigrant in Canada. *Zsusa Not sa Zsa, Balance With a Smile* was translated into French.

# New and Non-Traditional Markets

# Newsletters That Get Noticed

*by Ann Douglas* _____

f you're anxious to produce a newsletter that will enhance—rather than detract from—the image of your business, keep these tips in mind:

## Find a focus.

Launching a newsletter without knowing who it is targeted to and what it is supposed to accomplish is like taking your marketing dollars and tossing them out the window: if they happen to land in the right hands or produce any results, it's purely by chance. Unless you're a die-hard gambler, this is no way to promote your business.

## Choose a name.

Your newsletter's title and subtitle should immediately tell your readers who the publication is for and what it's about.

## Get graphic.

If it looks like junk mail, it's going to get treated like junk mail. Do whatever you can to distinguish your publication from everything else that crosses your readers' desks. A graphic designer can help you to come up with a workable layout and style for your newsletter and prevent you from producing a product that might detract from—rather than enhance—the image of your business. You could also use the templates available in many of the more advanced word-processing and publishing programs.

## Make it simply irresistible.

Design an attractive envelope that demands to be opened. It is false economy to use plain brown envelopes if most are likely to be recycled unopened. Newsletters arriving without an envelope may be mistaken for ad mail and so be ignored.

### Make it digestible.

Choose a format that enables your readers to scan through the articles quickly so that they can focus their attention on items of particular interest to them.

### Be polished.

A spelling error in the headline on page one acts like a death sentence for your newsletter. Your credibility—and the reader's interest—are lost immediately.

### Stay topical.

Because newsletters can be produced in such a short period of time, your readers will expect your newsletter to contain new information and leading edge ideas. Don't write about the product you launched last winter; give your readers a sneak-peek at the new items you're bringing out this season.

### Capture your readers' interest.

Make sure that your newsletter contains information of genuine interest to your readers, not just yourself. The last thing your readers want to wade through is a four-page-long advertisement for your business.

### Encourage action.

Encourage your readers to become involved with the publication by including at least one response device. Include a customer survey, order form, or reader reply card.

### Be regular.

To be effective, a newsletter should be issued at least four times per year. If you publish less frequently, you're carelessly sidestepping a valuable opportunity to build relationships with your readers.

### Stay on target.

There's no use sending your newsletter to people who would never even consider purchasing products or services from your company. The idea of a marketing newsletter is to sell (or re-sell) your business to potential and existing customers. This means getting your newsletter into the hands of the very people with whom you hope to do business.

### Get the most bang for your buck.

Use your newsletter in creative ways above and beyond a basic mailing. For example, if your newsletter has been designed to promote your accounting business, leave copies in the reception areas of local banks, law firms, and business consulting services. If your newsletter's purpose is to promote your line of office furniture, include it in your company's promotional packages, and hand it out at trade shows.

Ann Douglas is the President of Page One Productions Inc., a communications company based in Peterborough, Ontario. She is also an accomplished journalist whose work has appeared in *The Chicago Tribune*, *The Globe and Mail*, *Cottage Life*, *Canadian Living*, and numerous other publications. She can be contacted via e-mail at pageone@oncomdis.on.ca.

# Gaglines For Cartoonists

*by Allen Melton*

There are only two reasons why anyone would consider entering the zany world of the cartoon gagwriter: (1) fun and (2) profit. But what better reasons could one want? Writing cartoon gags requires a minimum of equipment and monetary investment—and enjoys a surprisingly large market.

Dozens of top cartoonists buy cartoon gags from people just like you and me, sitting at home scribbling their gags at the kitchen table, or jotting down ideas that come to them while riding the bus to work. The gags are extremely important to these cartoonists; no matter how good their drawing is, they will not sell a cartoon unless the gag is funny.

Many people ask, is it difficult to write cartoon gags? At first, it seems so. My first efforts for a school newspaper were amateurish, but there were a few that were actually funny. Gagwriting, like driving on the highway or playing the guitar, is something that improves with practice. Finally one day the newspaper cartoonist looked up from a batch of cartoon gags I had handed him and said, "Why don't you send these to professional cartoonists and make some money on them?" I had learned that cartoon gagwriters, like all other writers, are made, not born.

Another frequently asked question is, where do you get cartoon gags? Or, how do you come up with them? That's simple. You get them from everyday life. You get cartoon gags at home, at work, at church, on the golf course, at the zoo, at the grocery store—anywhere and everywhere there are people. You simply observe life from a humorous point of view.

Ordinary people can get into the funniest predicaments—your daily newspaper comic section will give you an idea of how many gags you can get simply by watching the everyday antics of your own family. Everyone knows a zany, unconventional character or two, either in your own family, at work, or socially. You can gain a wealth of comic gags by watching these characters in action. In addition, you probably stumble into some interesting situations yourself. Keep a small notebook handy for jotting down ideas no matter where they come to you.

Also, by gleaning ideas from current events from the newspaper, you can come up with the topical, up-to-date gags that cartoonists so enjoy.

What material sells? In short, anything that is funny and saleable will bring you bucks. Cartoonists (and their editors and readers) like gags that are off-beat, unusual, fresh, and surprising. Be original, and go for the belly laugh. Borderline gags that are merely "cute" or mildly amusing, probably will not sell. It is better to be a little bit wild and crazy, rather than too boring.

Cartoonists look for two things, especially:

(1) Make your gags as visual as possible, and

(2) be brief.

Cartoonists like captionless gags the best of all, the kind where the picture conveys the entire gag. This type of gag is most in demand, the hardest to write, and brings top prices. The writer who can consistently supply captionless gags that are genuinely funny is worth his weight in gold to a cartoonist.

In those gags which do require a caption, make the picture and caption work together in presenting the cartoon. For example, I sold one gag to a cartoonist in which a bleary-eyed, near-sighted man says "Good morning, Dear!" to a set of false teeth sitting on a mantelpiece. In this cartoon, both the picture and the caption are required to carry the joke. Neither one standing alone would be sufficient.

Illustrated jokes, i.e. cartoons which consist of two people sitting around cracking jokes, have their place in the world of cartooning—but these have to be very funny in order to sell.

Send cartoon gags that are up-to-date. Computers are very modern and "in," and so are things like VCRs, three-wheelers, space cartoons, and aerobics. Worn-out gags and obsolete gags are not in demand. Make sure you reflect today's language in your gags.

Of course, certain things remain constant through the years. Gags about family, work, sports, church, taxes, and school are always appreciated. Risqué gags remain popular (although the humor must exceed the spice).

Be as brief as you possible can. Cartoonists receive many gags through the mail—sometimes as many as a hundred a day—and your gags will receive a more serious reading if your descriptions are brief. Also, cartoons pack more of a punch if the caption is snappy and straight-to-the-point. Do not suggest a setting or background; let the cartoonist's own imagination and experience take care of this. (For example: "Man sitting in easy chair reading newspaper. Woman with a frown on her face washing dishes. Woman says to man..." can be condensed to "Woman to man:").

Try each punch line several different ways until you arrive at the shortest, funniest, and most effective way of saying it. Study the market and analyze what is selling. Study your own gags and figure out why they hit—or missed. Avoid heavy gruesome humor, and be joyful—have fun. Stay in good taste—don't insult religions, nationalities or races.

Consider the markets. The bible of the cartoon gagwriter is *Writer's Market*. You can find it in most bookstores or your local library, and a new, updated version comes out every year. There are thirty to fifty cartoonists listed in there every year, and they hold from five to fifteen hundred gags each year apiece. Some cartoonists work with only one or two gagwriters a year, others may work with a hundred or more. Publications and newsletters printed especially for cartoonists and gagwriters, such as *Cartoon World*, are also a source of markets.

And don't ignore local outlets. Cartoonists for local newspapers and magazines are often in need of gags.

Study the needs of the various cartoonists, and slant your gags toward them. Some cartoonists direct their talents toward the "general" markets, which pay more and don't require you to be too technical in your knowledge and language. Others concentrate on the trades, technical journals catering to various occupations. There are more than fifteen thousand of these and they are published for all types of professions, from bus drivers to businessmen to doctors.

Many cartoonists either already have their own cartoon strip or panel, or are trying to get one started. They welcome good ideas from writers that will help them on these projects.

Make your submissions neat and professional in appearance. Type your gags on 3 inch by 5 inch white index cards, only one gag to a card. In the upper left-hand corner type an identification number. In the upper right corner, type your name and address. Skip a line or two and type the gag. Use pica or elite type, black ribbon only. Keep the ribbon fresh, and the type clean. Retype any gags that have too many errors.

If you are working with a computer word processor, most printers won't handle 3 inch by 5 inch cards. Instead, consider using 5 inch by 8 inch cards and printing two submissions per card. The larger cards can then be cut to the conventional size with a paper cutter before you send them out.

Send ten to twenty gags at a time. You can send a one-page letter with your first submission to each cartoonist, listing your previous writing credits and qualifications, and telling a little about yourself.

*Always* enclose a stamped, addressed return envelope. When sending to a cartoonist in the United States, include return postage in U.S. stamps. The stamps can be affixed to the return envelope. If you have no U.S. stamps, buy sufficient International Reply Coupons from your postmaster to cover return postage.

Cartoonists usually return rejected gags within one or two weeks. When they decide to try one of your gags, they may hold it for two years or longer, circulating it to their various markets. Cartoonists get anywhere from $10 to $300 for each cartoon, and the gagwriter generally gets a twenty-five to forty percent commission on each sale.

The realities of the gagwriting business can be summed up simply: writing humorous gags for cartoonists is a serious business.

There is much competition, and cartoonists are selective because their editors are. On the bright side, keep in mind that there is always a demand for good gagwriters who can come up with fresh material that is genuinely funny. Cartoonists are constantly on the lookout for new talent. More women should enter the gagwriting field because many top magazines welcome submissions with a woman's viewpoint.

Few gagwriters make a living from writing cartoon gags, but it can be an exciting, fun-filled, profitable hobby. Hard work and persistence pay off. The main secret is to keep writing and submitting. So if you decide to enter the wacky, offbeat world of the cartoon gagwriter, I must first give you a warning: it's habit-forming!

Allen Melton has written gags for a number of professional cartoonists.

# Write and Sell Greeting Card Ideas

*by Donna Gephart* _____

Greeting card companies pay between $50 and $150 for a single card idea without artwork. That means a ten-word card idea paying $100 brings the writer a whopping $10 per word.

So, what are you waiting for? Sit down and write some blockbuster greeting cards. Right? Wrong!

Selling greeting cards begins with figuring out what your boss (the editor) needs from you. *The Writer's Handbook* lists greeting card companies, their addresses, and general requirements for free-lance submissions. You'll need even more information about each company, though, if you want them to send you a cheque.

So buy some #10 (business-size) envelopes and stamps and mail each company that interests you a self-addressed, stamped envelope for their guidelines. I can't stress strongly enough: Don't mail ideas to a company until you've studied their guidelines! You'll notice each company has a different style and tone. Some companies want risqué ideas, with copy that gets right to the point:

*Outside:* On Valentines Day, all you ever think of is SEX, SEX, SEX!

*Inside:* Thank God!

(Kalan)

To compete with professional greeting card writers, after studying guidelines and before writing, you must analyze greeting cards for sale on store racks. Take note of the format. Is it a riddle?

*Outside:* A riddle for your birthday: What are the four favorite animals a woman likes to keep around the house?

*Inside*: A jaguar in her garage, a mink in her closet, a tiger in her bed, and a jackass to pay for it all!

(Kalan)

Perhaps it's a twist on a cliché, like the following:

*Outside:* And yet another birthday, but remember—you're not getting older, you're getting better...

*Inside:* at getting older!

(Oatmeal Studios)

Some cards feature lists:

*Outside:* Another birthday and you haven't lost a thing...

*Inside:* except maybe some hair, your waistline, and a few too many brain cells! Happy Birthday, anyway!

(Kalan)

As you study published greeting cards, make a note of the subjects that are popular. Does a card make fun of the recipient's graying hair...

*Outside:* A little gray hair makes you look distinguished...

*Inside:* it distinguishes you from young people!

(Oatmeal Studios)

Or compare love life to the hustle and bustle of Christmas?

*Outside:* What do sex and Christmas have in common?

*Inside:* You eagerly await the big event and when it finally comes it's loads of fun and excitement, but both seem to end too quickly, leaving you with a good feeling and a big mess to clean up! Merry Christmas.

(Kalan)

How does the card achieve its desired effect? Would it make the recipient smile, gasp in surprise, or nod in agreement?

Study greeting cards in stores not to copy them, but to avoid copying them. When I was an editor at Kalan, I often had to reject ideas because they were too similar to what was already on the market or in Kalan's own line.

Just as you wouldn't write a novel without reading several, it is necessary for you to take written or tape-recorded notes or buy greeting cards to study at home.

When you're done the research you've arrived at the fun part, the addictive part, the part that gives you a mental high: Writing!

Here you can be your own boss. Set up a work schedule. Arrange times when you will do nothing but create greeting cards. Set yourself a quota. For example, promise yourself not to leave your desk until you've written ten greeting card ideas.

Your tools will include the following: sample cards, guidelines, books of quotations, a dictionary, thesaurus, and lists. You should brainstorm lists of everything from the physical effects of aging to activities performed at Christmas. Pairing items from lists and finding humorous connections is what makes an effective, saleable greeting card.

Imagine you are writing to a particular person. Most greeting cards are personal communications and shared experiences. Since women purchase 90 per cent of all greeting cards, if you're not female, try to think like a woman when writing messages. If you are a woman, think about what delights or annoys you. More than likely, many other women have similar thoughts and feelings.

A few days after writing up your ideas, revise them and type the best ones onto 3 x 5 index cards, one per card, in the following format:

*Outside:* A wine your age would be fine vintage.

A car your age would be classic.

A dog your age would be...

*Inside:* DEAD!

(Kalan)

Your name, address and phone number should appear on the back of each index card.

Mail a batch of up to twenty card ideas along with a self-addressed, stamped envelope to the company you've carefully selected. For your records, keep a copy of each card sent out, and a cover card noting the date, name of company, and code number of each card sent. (Code numbers should be kept simple: For instance, B-256 would be the 256th birthday card you've written.)

Your cover card, which could also be typed on an index card, would look like this:

Date        Birthday Ideas: #1,43,61,96,101,130,142,196

      Company name and address

(blank space to note company's response)

What happens to your ideas once they're received at a card company? When I worked as an editor, I was the first person (and sometimes the last) to review submissions. Kalan receives approximately 50 envelopes per week. Of these, some contain requests for guidelines; others include ideas from established writers, but most submissions are from new writers.

Every submission will be read, since the editor's purpose is to find and nurture talent and ultimately get salable cards for publication.

Be persistent with your writing and marketing. A response from an editor may encourage you to send more greeting card ideas, even though your first submissions are rejected. Five reasons greeting cards get rejected:

1. The tone and style are not right for the company.

2. The idea might be a great gag or joke, but not a personal communication to express a universal feeling.

3. The topic is too obscure. There is a limited need for cards about divorce, diet, new home, etc. Your best chance of selling is to write the types of cards that are constantly in demand. According to the National Greeting Card Association, the most frequently purchased cards are for birthdays, Christmas, and Valentine's Day.

4. As for humor, what you and your mother may find funny may not appeal to a particular editor.

5. Last and most significant, your idea can be hilarious and original with universal appeal and still be rejected because of a company's space and budget constraints. Therefore, something rejected by one company may be purchased by another.

The greeting card industry is always changing. If you keep abreast of these changes and make the most of every word in the greeting card you write, you may become part of a vast, profitable field.

Try one or more of these potential greeting card markets:

**Amberley Greeting Card Co.,** 11510 Goldcoast Dr.,
Cincinnati, OH 45249-1621  Phone: (513)489-2775 Fax: (513)489-2857

**Art a deux Ltée, 3417 Bertrand Road,** Missisauga ON L5L 4G5
Phone: (905) 828-7399 or (888) 278-3672

**Carol Wilson Fine Arts Inc.,** PO Box 17394, Portland, OR 97217-0394
Phone: (503)261-1860 Fax: (503)255-6829

**Gibson Greetings Inc.,** 2100 Section Rd, PO Box 371804,
Cincinnati, OH 45222  Phone: (513)841-6600 Fax: (513)841-6739

**Innovisions Inc.,** 2nd Floor West, 1802 W Cuyler Ave.,
Chicago, IL 60613-2402  Phone: (312)244-9275 Fax: (312)244-9278
**Kalan, Inc.,** 97 S Union Ave., Lansdowne, PA 19050-3027

**Oatmeal Studios Inc.,** PO Box 138, Rochester, VT 05767-0138
Phone: (802)767-3171 Fax: (802)767-9890

**Paramount Cards,** PO Box 6546, Pawtucket, RI 02860
Phone: (401)726-0800 Fax: (401)723-0220

**Pets And People Cards,** PO Box 8985, Portland, OR 97207-8985
Phone: (503)241-1313

**Pillow Talk Cards,** 601 Minnesota St., San Francisco, CA 94107-3045
Phone: (415)282-3200

**Rockshots, Inc.,** 9117 77th St., Jamaica, NY 11421-2807
Phone: (718)296-4486

Additional information may be available from:
**Greeting Card Association,** 1407 Military Trail, Toronto, ON M1C 1A7
Phone (416) 281-8147

Donna Gephart is a freelance writer who has worked as a greeting card editor, has sold gift books and written humor for national magazines. She continues to write for the greeting card market from a base in Jupiter, Florida.

# Write Technical Material

*by Bruce Madole*

D o you remember those incomprehensible instructions you wrestled with last year while trying to assemble your child's Christmas present? Do you remember the company policy manual that left you more confused then enlightened? If you have ever been faced with an illogical, illiterate set of instructions which proposed to tell you how to do something, but didn't, you have probably also entertained the notion that, "I could do better myself." If that thought has crossed your mind, read on. You may be on the way to becoming a technical writer.

Technical writing involves writing about technical and business subjects from bicycle-repair booklets to corporate manuals and nuclear missiles. There is almost no limit to your subject matter.

Many technical writers drift into this field because their jobs have required them to write about their own area of technical knowledge. They have progressed from technical specialization to technical writing. There are, however, a growing number of technical writers whose first love was writing and who have succeeded as "generalists" in technical writing through careful research in their chosen subjects.

### Journalist's essential questions.

If you already have an area of technical competence, you have a good start toward technical writing. If you are coming to the field of technical writing equipped with little more than talent, a word processor, and the desire to learn a new skill, the journalist's list of essential questions should help you overcome most of your research difficulties.

Although these six basic questions are designed to cover the essential elements of a news story, they are equally suited to research by the technical writer.

• Who—Find out who is doing what; identify the people involved in a procedure, policy, etc.

• What—Break the description of the actual task or procedure into logical steps. Pay careful attention to the sequence of details. Root out false assumptions by asking for explanations whenever you don't understand something. Detailed research is required.

• How—Identify the tools, materials, information, etc., required to carry a task from start to completion.

• Where—Describe the specific location of the process or flow of work from one place or process to another.

• When—Identify exact times, conditions (i.e. if... then). Determining when a step in the sequence should take place may involve a mass of logical alternatives, each of which must be followed through to its conclusion.

• Why—Explain the reason for a policy or procedure. Give context and authority.

### Be prepared for several drafts.

Your purpose in asking all of these questions, many of which overlap, is to eliminate as many false assumptions as you can about your subject matter. You need to gain a complete and detailed picture of the task, process, operating procedure, or whatever your subject matter may require.

The company for whom you are working should provide you with access to all the people you need to interview as well as documents and manuals. The more you are being paid, the quicker your employer will put the necessary resources at your disposal.

After you have finished the interviewing and data gathering, you will produce the first of many drafts. While the average for a technical piece is three drafts, it is not unusual for a technical writer to produce up to twenty drafts before the final one is approved for publication. Occasionally the process of preparing another draft will involve supplementary research, but more often the managers and executives who have to approve publication will want to suggest changes for political reasons. Don't let these changes discourage you—they are a part of the job.

After each draft is written, it must undergo the test of practical application. Arrange for someone to follow your description through, "taking it literally." If your reader can't make sense of the work, or if it doesn't reflect reality, another draft will be required.

Write simple sentences in the active voice. Avoid compound sentences. Be logical. Your readers will not be insulted if you write in a simple, logical style; after all, they are reading your material in order to learn something, not to admire its poetic impact. In this respect, the technical writer carries a greater burden of responsibility than any other kind of writer—people have been killed by following poorly worded instructions. The technical writer's challenge is to write in such a way that the directions cannot possibly be misunderstood.

### Standards may be available.

One of the tools used to simplify technical writing is the set of rules known as a manual standard. This set of rules will specify a set pattern to organize materials, to punctuate sentences, to present diagrams on a page, and so on. Sometimes a company will buy a commercially developed standard. These commercial standards may be several hundred pages thick, and are generally more of a hindrance than a help. If a company actually has a manual standard, look at some of their published material to discover how closely the manual standard is being followed, and do likewise.

If you have to develop your own manual standard, be sure the format you adopt will permit you to revise pages easily without having to republish the whole work.

### A contract is important.

Technical writing is not something you can do "on spec," unless you are attempting to show a manufacturer how well you could explain his products. (This approach can be useful to gain a contract.) A contract is usually necessary, even if it is only in the form of a letter, signed by both parties, stating the conditions of your employment and the hourly rate. (Avoid fixed-rate jobs.) Like any entrepreneur, you will have to avoid pricing yourself out of the market, although certain markets are much more tolerant than others—particularly data processing and the provincial and federal governments.

Technical writing also covers the area of employee publications for corporations and newsletters for organizations, so do not neglect these markets either.

Finally, remember that in the technical writing business, the writing is what counts.

Bruce Madole is President of Bruce Madole & Associates Inc., a communications consulting firm.

# Write for Government

*by Gill Foss*

Why would a freelancer want to work for the government? A panel of experienced writers from across the country was asked this question. The reply was loud and clear: If you produce a consistently high standard of work, the return is steady employment, often paid at above the private sector rate. For those with an interest in politics and public policy issues, this work would be ideal.

How can a freelancer who wants to write for the government find contract work? The panel's collective response to this question forms the basis of the following article.

## Research the departments.

If you are starting from scratch and would like general information about the federal government you can phone the Canada Can Help line at 1-800-667-3355. Although that number is really a referral point for services and programmes, the helpful internal researchers can provide phone numbers for individual departments. There is also a main federal web site for those with Internet access. The address is: <http://canada.gc.ca>

With a call to the relevant departmental library you can request a copy of their Annual Report which will provide a guide to the internal functioning of the department and the areas where freelance work may be available.

Similar access can be found for provincial governments at the back of local telephone books.

## Assess self-marketing opportunities.

Some members of the panel made their first contact by letter, others used the "cold call" technique (just pick up the phone and go from there) but there are two other options at the federal level. One is to advertise in

*The National Writing and Editing Services Guide.* The other, to list your-self on the Net via the government's Open Bidding Service.

### • The National Writing and Editing Services Guide.

This publication offers three options depending on the amount of financial exposure with which you are comfortable.

All suppliers are offered a free alphabetical listing on the basic Key Word Database. You send a business card, indicate if you have employ-ees and the type of services offered. Beside each service list your hourly rate. Other information required is the type of software used and your subject and topic areas of expertise. This registry is only circulated on special departmental request.

For more in-depth exposure opt for a structured half-page listing at a cost of $80 which includes a short company profile. This guarantees cir-culation to 8,000 federal government departments and carries all infor-mation provided for the basic listing.

The third option is to place an advertisement formatted to your own specifications. The choice is either a half-or full-page, two-colour pro-motion available for $350 and $625 respectively. For registration forms phone (613) 991-5791, fax (613) 991-5870 or write:

Government of Canada

Public Relations and Print Contract Services Sector

350 Albert Street, 4th floor

Ottawa, ON K1A 0S5

Although very few of the freelancers contacted had received work directly through this publication, several had found it an advantage to refer to their listing when applying for contract work.

### • The Open Bidding Service (OBS).

This is an on-line alternative through which you can search for daily updates of public and private sector contract information and order bid-ding documents. It lists international opportunities and also provides software for IBM/compatibles, DOS or Windows, for downloading.

The annual subscription for OBS Internet access (web site: http://www.obs.ism.ca) is $130 with unlimited usage for a fee of $12 a month. Call 1-800-361-4637 or (613) 737-3374. Or write:

The Open Bidding Service

P.O. Box 22011

Ottawa, ON K1V 0W2

Only one respondent reported using this service. Most viewed it as more appropriate for companies offering a full range of project expertise.

Replies from those with provincial government contracts indicated none was aware of any parallel listing services for those seeking freelance employment at that level.

### Consider what you have to offer

What will be expected is the ability to work to deadline and deliver a focused product in which every fact must be justified. All the relevant details may not be provided. In this case you will also be responsible for the accuracy of the necessary research. Therefore it is important to know your strengths.

If you have a special area of expertise, it would be prudent to approach a department in a similar field. It is good to have an edge on the competition. It is definitely an asset to have a CV that shows you have in-depth experience as a writer or editor. With governments, federal or provincial, professionalism is paramount. If you hope to work on small contracts, offering yourself as a sole contractor will likely be acceptable. If the work you seek requires complete project management you would be wise to team up in partnership with others who can provide the services outside your own expertise such as research skills, graphic design or translation.

### Target your marketing.

The two most likely departments to have freelance work to offer are Communications and Research. The busiest time of year is between January and March. Bear this in mind when making your first inquiries.

The areas involved in programme delivery and development are often in need of writers. The type of work available is varied and can include producing newsletters, reports, executive summaries, brochures, fact sheets, magazine articles, the design of web pages and, for the more experienced, ghost writing or speeches.

Only those who have a proven track record within a department can hope to receive a speech-writing contract. If you are in that category, the appropriate Minister's Press Secretary is the person to contact.

No matter how you finally make contact, in all cases it is helpful to talk first with the department's Public Relations Manager or the Director of Public Affairs. That is, unless you have a personal contact.

### Network for personal contacts.

Networking, as the word itself says, requires work. The more effort you put into it, the better will be the result. It can be as varied as being visible as a professional writer in your local community, joining the local Chamber of Commerce, Rotary Club, or active business group. Alternatively, join a professional writers' organization. Seek out others who have already broken into the field you wish to enter. Discuss your credentials with your new contacts. Offer to sub-contract should they find themselves on project overload. Work your way into becoming an insider. Several of the panel received assignments through word-of-mouth. The person with whom they usually worked had nothing available, but passed their names to colleagues looking for help.

Another avenue is to apply for a position with a company which specializes in government contract work. These organizations are listed in the yellow pages of all local phone books under a heading such as "Writers" or "Writing Services". If your ability is its own advertisement, the contacts you make in the process of your corporate work may lead to the offer of individual assignments.

No matter which avenue you chose, diligent networking is essential if you are to keep on top in the contract market.

### Study the contract system.

Don't price yourself out of the market. Most individual contracts come in at under $25,000. Some departments expect a quote by the day, others by the hour. The hourly rates quoted range from as low as $25 to a more usual $45-$50. One respondent, writing for the provincial government of BC, quoted the top of the range at $75 per hour for a 7.5 hour working day when more than the basic writing skills were offered. This is where networking comes in again. Find out what is acceptable.

If your work is respected in a department you may be offered the chance to bid on a new contract. Remember to keep in mind that you are, in effect, working for a committee where approval is a multi-level process. Allow for numerous revisions and occasionally complete re-writes. One panelist suggested quoting twice what you would charge for a similar private sector project to compensate.

### Accept the Public Service culture.

If you are asked to take a writing/editing test when you first apply for a contract, don't take this as a professional insult. Think positive. What the department wants to know is whether you can produce quality work with speed and accuracy to meet their requirements. The fact that you can provide first-rate copy when you have a month to research the article doesn't matter if you will be expected to produce a three-page report to the same standard in 24 hours.

As mentioned in the previous section, the public service works like a committee with a hierarchical mentality. Everyone involved in the assessment of a project may have a different bias. Hence the reminder to include the cost of several revisions when estimating your bid.

Most freelancers chose that lifestyle to keep some semblance of ownership over their existence. If you decide to work on contract for any government you are unlikely to avoid a return to office politics. Be prepared to control your frustrations. Remember the repeat work—and the paycheque.

Gill Foss is an award-winning writer/editor with *Reader's Digest* among her clients. She chairs the National Awards Committee of the Canadian Authors Association, has been a CAA Regional VP, and Ottawa Branch President. Gill has programmed two national writers' conferences and teaches as a subject specialist for a consulting company.

# Copyright on the Web

*by Lesley Ellen Harris*

Y ou're in the planning stages of your company's Web site. You want to display on your home page the art commissioned for your annual report cover. You may want to show internal memos or documents prepared by employees, freelance writers and photographers. And you'd like to add clips from a training video based on a script you prepared for a client, plus links to related sites. But before you go any further, make sure you own the rights to these works. Just because you paid someone to create art for the report doesn't mean you have the right to run these works on your site. In most cases, the types of material used on Web sites are protected by copyright under Canadian law. If you own the copyright to these works you can reproduce, publish and transmit them in any manner. But if you don't, you have to get permission—and possibly pay a fee.

## How do you know if you own the copyright to a work?

Consider the following:

• If employees created the work as part of their duties on the job, the employer owns the copyright. For example, internal memos and policy documents written by employees belong to their employers.

• If photographs, portraits and engravings are commissioned, the person commissioning these specific kinds of works owns the copyright.

• Other types of commissioned work, besides photographs, portraits and engravings, belong to the people who created them—for example, the freelance writer or company commissioned to write the video script (though that company wouldn't have rights to the video itself).

• Contracts, preferably written ones, can reverse any of the above conditions. For example, a contract can ensure that employees own copyright in their works, or that someone who commissions an article from a freelance writer owns the copyright.

• If the author of the works has been dead for 50 years, the work is considered in the public domain and can be freely used without obtaining permission or paying a fee.

### Obtain permission.

If you don't own copyright or at least electronic or Web site rights to a work, legally you need permission from the copyright holder to use that work on your site. When asked for permission, the copyright holder may ask for payment for that work. The amount will have to be negotiated. Because the electronic media are new, no industry standards have been established for appropriate fees.

Whether you own the rights to copyright works or licence certain rights so you can place works on you Web site, you still have to respect the moral rights of the creator. Under the Canadian Copyright Act, authors of a copyright work have the right to have their names appear on it, to use a pseudonym, or to remain anonymous.

Also, authors can prevent certain uses that may harm their reputations—for example, modifications of the works or uses in association with a service, cause, product, or institution. Unlike copyright rights, moral rights cannot be transferred to a company or licencee. However, authors can waive their moral rights and agree not to exercise them. If you require a waiver, it is a good idea to have it in your agreement.

From a legal point of view, it's generally believed that you don't have to get permission to have links on your Web site to information and copyright materials on other sites. This is based on the notion that when you create a link, you generally do not reproduce a copyright work and, therefore, do not have to obtain permission. (Some people may disagree with this). But if you "borrow" a copyright work from another site, you would require permission.

### Protect your copyright.

What can you do to protect copyright material in your site from being reproduced without permission? Works on your Web site may be protected by copyright but it is almost impossible with today's technology to allow free access to browse your Web site and then require payment for downloading information in it. Some lawyers would argue that by placing works on the site, you are granting an implied licence allowing others to download, print out, and forward the copyright material in your site. If you want others to use the works, you might want to state that you are in fact allowing them to reproduce the copyright works in your site (assuming you have the rights from other copyright holders to do so).

If you don't want others to download, forward, or print out copyright materials from your site, post "loud" copyright notices but don't be surprised if you are ignored. Don't despair, though: in the future, the Internet will probably offer various ways to track the use of materials and compensate copyright holders. Until then, a notice is your best bet.

Lesley Ellen Harris is a Copyright & New Media lawyer and the author of *Canadian Copyright Law* (second edition, 1995, McGraw-Hill Ryerson). She can be reached at (416) 226-6768 or at <Copyrtlaw@aol.com> or <http://www.mcgrawhill.ca/copyrightlaw>.

# Avoid The Seven Deadly Sins of Cyberspace Marketing

*by Ann Douglas*

B efore you invite the world to your web page, take a few moments to ensure that you have avoided the seven deadly sins of marketing in Cyberspace:

## 1. Sacrificing content in favour of glitter.

Having a lot of flashy graphics can help you to attract traffic to your web page, but content is what brings people back. Make sure that your graphics help to reinforce your key marketing messages rather than simply distracting or annoying your visitor.

## 2. Neglecting to offer anything of value.

It doesn't take a sophisticated Internet user more than a second or two to evaluate what's available on your web page. If your web page contains an ever-changing smorgasbord of genuinely useful information, then someone visiting it has a reason to return. However, if you're simply dishing up self-promotional drivel your reader will seize the first available opportunity to make his or her escape.

## 3. Boring people to death.

One person's trash is another person's treasure. That's why it's important for you to make it easy for people to travel around on your web page in whatever way they see fit. Rather than having all of the pages linked in a linear, book-like fashion, design links that will allow people to move, for example, from page two to five to six—quickly and easily.

## 4. Wasting their time.

When you're selecting graphics for your web page, keep in mind how frustrating it is for someone visiting your site to sit and wait for each dot of an elaborate photograph to appear on screen. I've stumbled across the odd site with complex graphics that take upwards of a minute to create. While I might put up with sluggish images on my first visit, I'm less likely to make a return trip. That's why it's so critical to ensure that the graphics used on your page are capable of being recreated in a matter of seconds.

## 5. Failing to update your material.

Your web page should be constantly changing. After all, if it stays the same week after week—month after month—your visitors have no reason to come back. While you'll likely want to continue to offer certain types of material on an ongoing basis, it's generally wise to add new material frequently.

## 6. Failing to let your personality shine through.

There's no excuse for being bland on the World Wide Web. Use lively graphics, evocative language, and an innovative structure. After all, the name of the game in Cyberspace is to stand out from the crowd.

## 7. Failing to let people know where you are.

Your web page has to be found in order to be appreciated. That's why it's critical that you register your web page with each of the major Internet search engines. Fortunately, this is not nearly as difficult or as painful as it sounds: a simple visit to <http://www.submit-it.com> is all it takes to register your web page with 10 of the most widely used search engines in one fell swoop.

Once you've learned how to avoid these seven deadly sins, you'll be well on your way to tapping into the amazing opportunities that await your business in cyberspace.

Ann Douglas is the President of Page One Productions Inc., a communications company based in Peterborough, Ontario. She is also an accomplished journalist whose work has appeared in *The Chicago Tribune*, *The Globe and Mail*, *Cottage Life*, *Canadian Living*, and numerous other publications. She can be contacted via e-mail at <pageone@oncomdis.on.ca>.

# Will Web Magazines Change Publishing's Style?

*by Paul Lima* —————————————————————————————————

I was seven years old when I published my first magazine. Using a stubby pencil, I meticulously printed articles about members of my family and illustrated the articles with crayon art. I only produced one copy of the magazine but my entire family read *The Lima News*. I had great fun doing it, and words have been an important part of my life since.

After graduating from university with a major in English, I worked as a copywriter and magazine editor before becoming a freelance writer. While I dreamt of publishing a literary magazine, I lacked the time and money—especially money—necessary to do so. The cost of designing, printing, distributing and promoting a magazine seemed prohibitive. So I put my dream on hold—until the development of the World Wide Web.

The Web has changed the face of publishing. Anybody with a computer, modem, access to the Internet and a few megabytes of Web space can publish an electronic magazine (e-zine)—or almost anything else—on the Web. But can they make money from it?

Published quarterly, my literary e-zine, *Maple Syrup Simmering*, is one example of online publishing. But there are thousands, perhaps tens of thousands, of e-zines—general interest, literary, computer, fashion, entertainment and more—published around the world on the Web.

The first issue of *Maple Syrup Simmering* was, admittedly, a chaotic site. In retrospect, more time should have been spent on site design. However, on the Web, you can revise after publishing. With feedback from visitors and help from assistant editor Lorina Stephens, (we "met" in an online writing forum and discovered we shared a passion to publish a literary magazine) I reorganized the e-zine.

Since January 1995, we have published writers from across Canada and the USA and from Moscow and the Philippines. Over a thousand people visit the publication monthly—again, mostly from Canada and the US, but also from England, Japan, New Zealand and Russia. And we won have Web site awards from *eye weekly*—the first Canadian publication to establish a serious presence on the Web—and several other self-proclaimed Web site judges.

When launching our publications, we bypassed paper because an e-zine is less expensive and easier to publish than is a magazine. There are no postal or printing costs, and formatting manuscripts for uploading consumes less time than desktop publishing. When Internet Direct, a Toronto-based Internet service provider, donated web space to us, our publishing costs were reduced to nil. When was the last time a pulp and paper company provided a magazine with free paper for life, for a year or even for one issue?

We have a rate card and accept advertising but advertisers have not beaten a path to our door. Yet. This is no surprise as our focus has been on soliciting manuscripts and producing the site. However, when set up "Friends of Maple Syrup Simmering" seven sponsors made donations. While we have not been able to pay contributors—most literary magazines pay "contributor copies" only—four sponsors supported our recent OH-OH! Canada writing contest enabling us to pay the winner and two runners-up.

Does web publishing on this scale herald the demise of print magazines? No. But in small steps, the Web is altering the dynamics of publishing. According to the *Masthead* Tally, 10 literary and arts magazines were launched in 1994, but only three in 1995. No doubt other new publishers, like me, skipped print and went straight to the web. And while existing literary magazines intend to continue with the print versions, publishing online editions has its benefits.

Within a week of launching its Web site *blood & aphorisms* received four new subscriptions: two from overseas. Publisher Tim Paleczny describes the Web as "a directory that exposes anyone anywhere [with access to the Web] to the hard copy version of our magazine." And *Shift*'s editor, Evan Solomon, considers *Shift Online* "an intellectual prosthesis" enabling him to publish material he can't fit into the paper version of *Shift*.

The Web has also had an effect on scholarly journals as financially hard-pressed publishers and libraries have discovered the joys and ease of electronic publishing. (The Royal Astronomical Society of Canada recently cancelled its *Journal* in part because professional astronomers can now publish their research findings in electronic journals.)

All this has a ripple effect on traditional print publishing: film houses, paper companies, printers, mailing houses, the post office, wholesalers and retailers. Perhaps the biggest change, though, affects publishers who must now compete with each other and with the masses who can launch publications in cyberspace and reach the online the global village.

Even thought I'm still learning the online publishing ropes, I consider *Maple Syrup Simmering* a relative success. It's attracting writers and readers, costing me nothing but time and I'm having great fun doing it. Eventually, I still hope to profit from it.

Postscript: This article was originally published in the July 1996 issue of *Masthead*. After a two-year run publishing his online magazine, Paul Lima was breaking even but still saw no potential for profit. He shut down his magazine but continues to work as a freelance writer. He also teaches Creative Writing and Freelance Writing courses by E-mail. E-mail: <tiko@idirect.com>; Web page: <http://web.idirect.com/~canuck>.

# A Sample of E-Zines

*by Paul Lima, John Oughton and Murphy Shewchuk*

H ere is a small selection of the thousands of e-zines out there. It has been compiled with the help of Paul Lima and John Oughton. John, in turn, credits Leilani Wright for some of the leads to the Web sites.

These were checked prior to going to press, but as the World Wide Web is a volatile network of thousands of computers, many of the listings may have changed by the time you attempt to locate them. A search engine such as AltaVista <http://www.altavista.digital.com/> may help you locate hundreds more potential electronic publishers for your work. The Ejournal SiteGuide <http://www.library.ubc.ca/ejour/> can also be a good starting point.

It should be noted that many of the comments below are by Paul Lima or John Oughton. Others were quoted directly from the respective Web sites. Except for alphabetizing the listing, no attempt has been made to classify them in any way.

If this is your first time using a web browser to search for information, the web address (URL) is the information between the chevrons < >. Punctuation and case is usually critical. If your browser says it can't find the site, double-check your typing before giving up.

### *(poundpoundpound)*
<http://www.teleport.com/~mimz/pound/call.html>

### (pronounced "Pound-Pound-Pound") is a new e-zine devoted to becoming a forum for... for what, exactly? Well, for the kind of good writing that doesn't really fit into any one category, and therefore, often falls through the cracks.

Agnieszka's Dowry

<http://www.enteract.com/~marek/asgp/agnieszka.html>

Special Instructions: "click on the ladybug." Best viewed with Netscape. Uses poetry and short prose. Displays texts in "rooms with unique graphic formats and interconnected poems."

*Alsop Review, The*

<http://www.hooked.net/~jalsop/>

Jaimes Alsop, who lives, works and writes in Northern California, is the editor of The Alsop Review. He describes his e-zine as "a showcase of the best poets and writers available on the World Wide Web."

Articulata

<http://www.mightymedia.com/articulata/>

"Interactive poetry site on the WWW that allows poets to publish and control a sample of their own poetry on the web... also interactive collective poems."

Aspiring Writer

<http://www.connet80.com/~aspire/>

Simply put: a place for new and published writers.

*Atlantic Unbound*

<http://www.theAtlantic.com/atlantic/>

Atlantic Unbound is at once The Atlantic Monthly's home on the Web and an evolving online publication.

*B&A New Fiction*

<http://www.interlog.com/~fiction/>

Since its inception in 1990, b&a's publishing mandate has been to publish new writing, to promote new and emerging authors, and to do it all with distinction. Assisting publisher Tim Paleczny with the magazine and e-zine are a number of volunteers committed to a principle that new fiction deserves a place in popular literature. Published in Canada.

*Blue Moon Review, The*

<http://www.TheBlueMoon.com/> or <http://1q.com/bluemoon>,

A triennial online review of the literary arts.

*Cross Connect*

<http://tech1.dccs.upenn.edu/~xconnect/>

\'kros-ke'nekt\

1: (wiring term) The connection running between wiring terminal blocks linking two physically different bodies together. 2: A triennial electronic journal for contemporary art and writing based in Philadelphia at the University of Pennsylvania.

*CyberStage Online*

<http://www.cyberstage.org/>

CyberStage Online is the digital edition of CyberStage Magazine. It's a resource centre for the world of art and technology.

*E.S.*

<http://www.shmooze.net/es/>

E.S. is a not-for-profit e-zine dedicated to providing an open environment for artists of all types from around the world.

*Eclectic Literary Forum*

<http://www.pce.net/elf/home.html>

ELF: Eclectic Literary Forum. "A Top Mainstream Market for Poetry in 1997" Check the site for Writer's Submission Guidelines. Publishes Fiction Poetry and Essays.

Ejournal SiteGuide

<http://www.library.ubc.ca/ejour/>

Ejournal SiteGuide: a MetaSource

Provided here is a selected and annotated set of links to sites for ejournals, which in turn provide links to individual titles and/or to other collections of links. In no instance does this site guide point directly to individual electronic periodicals. Includes an alphabetic list — direct links to 36 sites.

Electronic Poetry Center

<http://wings.buffalo.edu/epc/>

The Electronic Poetry Center is a collaborative effort involving the University Libraries, the Faculty of Arts & Letters, and the Poetics Program, Department of English, at the University at Buffalo.

*Enterzone* _
<http://ezone.org:1080/ez/>
Enterzone is published quarterly and distributed electronically from the ezone.org web site, which is itself, in turn, hosted by AALN. ISSN No. 1090-0020

*eScene*
<http://www.etext.org/Zines/eScene/>
Note: eScene is just one of many electronic magazines at The Etext Archives.

Etext Archives
<http://www.etext.org/>
The Etext Archives (est. 1992) are home to electronic texts of all kinds, from the sacred to the profane, from the political to the personal. Our duty is to provide electronic versions of texts without judging their content.

*FUGUE*
<http://www.uidaho.edu/LS/Eng/Fugue/>
FUGUE c/o English Dept. University of Idaho. Fugue is a biannual digest of multi-genre fiction, poetry, and nonfiction.

*Grain Magazine*
<http://www.sasknet.com/corporate/skwriter/GRAIN_Homepage.html>
Grain Magazine is an internationally acclaimed literary journal, publishing the freshest poetry and prose from Canada, the US, and abroad. Grain Magazine is an arms-length committee of the Saskatchewan Writers Guild.

*GRIST On-Line Magazine*
<http://www.thing.net/~grist/>
Leads to several other publications. Includes GRIST On-Line Magazine

*Gruene Street:*
<http://ebbs.english.vt.edu/olp/gs/gruene.html>
An Internet Journal of Prose & Poetry, Gruene Street is published quarterly. Fiction, poetry, essays, and reviews are accepted year-round.

*Gutter Press*

<http://www.salzmann.com/gutter/>

Welcome to the most exciting source of dangerous fiction and radical literature on the Web.

*Highbeams*

<http://www.beloit.edu/~highbe/>

Highbeams is published and posted quarterly at Beloit College, Beloit, Wisconsin. Unsolicited manuscripts (poetry, fiction, and prose) are invited.

*Hungry Mind Review*

<http://www.bookwire.com/hmr/homepage.html>

Hungry Mind Review. An Independent Book Review.

*InterText*

<http://www.etext.org/Zines/InterText/>

Publishing fiction on the Net since March 1991. InterText is a bimonthly online magazine. It is a free publication, and currently has no sponsors. As a result, InterText cannot pay its contributors.

*Kudzu*

<http://www.etext.org/Zines/Kudzu/>

Kudzu is a digital quarterly magazine dedicated to bringing you the best in fiction, poetry, and essays.

*Lady in the Radiator*

<http://www.etext.org/Zines/TLITR/>

The Lady in the Radiator, an Online hypertext version of a print journal containing art, photographs, poetry, and interviews.

*Literary Review, The*

<http://www.cais.com/aesir/fiction/tlr/>

The Literary Review, published by Fairleigh Dickinson University, includes fiction and poetry by writers from such areas of the world as Russia, Latin America, Japan, and North Africa, highlighting a new international theme with each issue. (Included music when checked in early, 1997.)

MindSpring

<http://www.mindspring.com/content/arts.html>

MindSpring Enterprises, Inc. is a starting point for a variety of on-line literary resources.

*Mississippi Review*

<http://sushi.st.usm.edu/mrw/>

The Mississippi Review is a monthly literary magazine, winner of the 1995 GNN Best of the Net Award in literature, rated as a Top 5% Site by Point Communications, and by Lycos, recognized as a Planet Earth Ultimate Site and a Magellan 4-Star Site, and published by the Center for Writers at The University of Southern Mississippi.

*Morpo Review, The*

<http://morpo.novia.net/morpo/>

The Morpo Review, an electronic literary journal which is published on a bi-monthly basis.

The Morpo Review is seeking submissions of poetry and short, unhinged essays and short stories for future issues.

*NWHQ*

<http://www.knosso.com/NWHQ/>

This is nwhq, a web-journal of hypertexted literature and art that is constructed somewhat like a labyrinth wherein works grow over time.

*Occasional Screenful, The*

<http://www.ssc.upenn.edu/~lszyrmer/scrnsub.html>

The Occasional Screenful is an edited electronic magazine of short poetry published at unpredictable intervals.

*Paris Review*

<http://www.voyagerco.com/PR/>

*Parsec*

<http://icewall.vianet.on.ca/comm/parsec/>

Canada's national science fiction, fantasy and horror magazine contains articles on upcoming and current movies and television shows in the three genres. It also offers interviews with such authors as Terry

Pratchett and Kevin Anderson, book reviews, animation reviews, Star Trek profiles, and fiction by Canadian authors and illustrations by Canadian artists.

*Planet Magazine*

<http://www.etext.org/Zines/planet/>

Planet Magazine is a FREE, award-winning electronic quarterly of short science fiction, fantasy, poetry, horror, and humor. Wild SF, Fantasy, Horror, Humor, Poetry—On-line since January 1994!

Positively Poetry

<http://iquest.com/~e-media/kv/poetry.html>

This is a homepage created by a 14 year old who is interested in writing and reading poetry. Positively Poetry is designed for children from the ages of 5 to 15 to share their artistic abilities in writing poetry with people around the world.

*PRISM international*

<http://edziza.arts.ubc.ca/crwr/prism/prism.html>

PRISM welcomes submissions from both established and unknown writers living anywhere in the world. We print short fiction, poetry, drama, translation and creative non-fiction. Our only criteria are originality and quality.

*QWERTY*

<http://www.unb.ca/web/QWERTY/>

QWERTY is a non-profit literary and visual arts magazine published by ICEHOUSE PRESS in Fredericton, New Brunswick, Canada. It's existence is made possible through the support of the University of New Brunswick English Department and Graduate Student's Association.

*RealPoetik*

<http://www.wln.com/~salasin/rp.html>

RealPoetik is the little magazine of the vernacular, quotidian, witty and postmodern. Think of it an attempt to invent an english lit (small e) for the last decade of the Twentieth Century. And the beginning of the Twenty First.

*Recursive Angel*

<http://www.calldei.com/~recangel/>

Recursive Angel specializes in the cutting edge of poetry, fiction and art. Our goal is to publish experimental works of all genres and promote the arts in this new forum of technology.

*Salmagundi*

<http://www.emf.net/~jgm7/maya/salmagundi/salmagundi.html>

Salmagundi was an electronic literary journal that strove to bring you quality poetry, fiction, essays, and art. We tried to focus on pieces that experiment with genre boundaries and with the hypertext format. These are the three existing issues of Salmagundi, before it was abandoned by its staff.

*Shift Online*

<http://www.shift.com/>

The online edition of Canada's media magazine. Founders Evan Solomon and Andrew Heintzman want to "inject new life into the moribund state of general interest magazines in this country." "Shift is about redefining what it means to be Canadian in a global culture. It is about taking down artificial barriers between high and low culture. It is about giving space to contemporary and intelligent voices that seek to make sense of the present and invent the future."

*Stand Magazine* (Online edition)

<http://felix.vcu.edu/~dlatane/stand.html>

Stand Magazine is an independent quarterly of new writing founded in 1952 by the poet Jon Silkin. Stand is an international magazine of poetry, short fiction, reviews, criticism and occasional short plays.

*Switched-on Gutenberg*

<http://weber.u.washington.edu/~jnh/>

Switched-on Gutenberg: A Global Poetry Journal. Submissions by e-mail include up to three poems of any subject or form.

Texoma Poetry Society

<http://www.grayson.edu/ecampus/texpoet.htm>

This Is Not Art

<http://cac.psu.edu/~dwm7/notart.htm>

This Is Not Art: An Experiment in Literary Brevity. In fact, we publish micro-fiction (250 words or less), micro essays (250 words or less), short poetry (we prefer ten lines or less), and other abbreviated language experiments, only. Please send your best brief work.

*Verbiage Magazine*

<http://www.boutell.com/verbiage/>

Verbiage Magazine: A short fiction magazine, which pays (modestly) for material. Submissions should be fiction. Submissions should be prose. Verbiage does not print poetry.

*Writer's Block*

<http://www.niva.com/writblok/index.htm>

Writer's Block is always looking for submissions. The Editorial Calendar describes themes for the upcoming year along with suggested topics. Please note that all submissions will be edited for length, style, grammar, and adherence to theme. No payment will be made in exchange for publication; however, a brief but descriptive byline will be attributed. Submissions should not exceed 2500 words.

*ZIPZAP*

<http://www.dnai.com/~zipzap/>

ZIPZAP accepts ALL types of writing—literature, experimental, sci-fi, cyberpunk, anything, everything. Artwork in the form of slides, .gifs, .tifs, .bmps, or photographs of paintings, collages, sculptures, cartoons, hypertext word & image pieces. Traditional, contemporary, postmodern diction and illustrations. We accept poetry, photography, interviews and reviews, etc. If we like it, we'll publish it.

*ZYZZYVA*

<http://www.cais.net/aesir/fiction/ZYZZYVA/>

ZYZZYVA: the last word: West Coast writers and artists only. This means currently living in AK, HI, WA, OR, or CA.

# The Writer's Reference Shelf

# CAA: Three-quarters of a Century

*By Robert Collins*

f words could kill, the Canadian Authors Association would have dropped dead long ago. Few literary organizations have endured so much ridicule and abuse, for so little reason.

Over its 75 years, periodicals from *Saturday Night* to *Canadian Forum* to the *National Home Monthly* have taken pot shots at it. CAA members have been labelled "little old ladies in tennis shoes" and "old ladies crying over their rejection slips." A *Toronto Star* reporter once stooped to poking fun at members' names ("Vinia was there and Fanny was there and Bluebell and Una...").

To this day some members smart over F. R. Scott's 1927 poem, "The Canadian Authors Meet," depicting "virgins of 60 who still write of passion" twittering at literary tea parties. Actually Scott was taunting a certain Montreal poetry club but, given the poem's title, CAA took his arrow straight in the heart.

Hugh Garner, never one to mince words, called CAA "a receptacle for aborted literary non-talent" composed of "literary loonies" and "senile amateur writers and poetasters." In a kind of sweet justice, William Arthur Deacon, literary editor of the Toronto *Globe and Mail* and a longtime CAA member, once bought Garner a membership. The prickly author attended one meeting and, predictably, trashed it in print.

Yet most of the hecklers, illogically, have attacked CAA for steadfastly doing exactly what it set out to do in 1921: catering to aspiring writers as well as professionals. The association, as writer/broadcaster Harry Boyle once put it, has "persisted with the admirable notion that those who ardently desire to write are as important in their own way as those who write."

"CAA has never been given adequate recognition for its decades of yeoman service to Canada's writing community," adds British Columbia author Andreas Schroeder, "notably its remarkable care and feeding of this country's apprentice writers."

The mix of professionals (full "members") and apprentices (now called "associates") has always bred dissent. The 1972 founding of the Writers' Union of Canada—for published authors only—was in part a reaction to some professionals' distaste for that mix. There have been calls within CAA to drop the associates or, at least, put them into a peripheral ghetto. But the original mandate prevails. In recent years the membership roster has remained steady at about 700 with approximately 50 life members and the remainder evenly split between full "members" and "associates".

The amateurs' presence has not deterred many of Canada's finest writers from lending their names and influence to the Association. Recent members include Margaret Atwood, Karleen Bradford, Robert Munsch, Cora Taylor, W. D. Valgardson and L. R. (Bunny) Wright. Over the years the more than 25,000 members have included Pierre Berton, Will Bird, Marjorie Wilkins Campbell, Helen Creighton, Robertson Davies, Paul Hiebert, Constance Beresford Howe, John Patrick Gillese, W. P. Kinsella, Thomas Raddall, Joseph Schull, Stuart Trueman and Scott Young. And in defence of "little old ladies": Montreal's Vi Bercovitch, who died not long ago at age 96, was a CAA stalwart and had recently published her first book of poetry.

From the beginning, the CAA had a strong reservoir of professional talent. Founders included literary heavyweights Stephen Leacock, Nellie McClung, B. K. Sandwell (later editor of *Saturday Night*), Bliss Carman and Duncan Campbell Scott. Ten months later, Mazo de la Roche, Robert W. Service and Vincent Massey were among the 423 on board.

The CAA's prime mission at its first meeting in Montreal on March 11, 1921, was to overhaul Canada's antiquated copyright laws. But it also vowed "to act for the mutual benefit and protection of Canadian authors and for the maintenance of high ideals and practice in the literary profession."

Then, even more than now, few writers could survive on their writing. The early membership was laced with learned professors who had written a book or two (13 of the first 19 presidents adorned their names with "Dr.") but earned their livings in academe. First president John Murray Gibbon was public relations manager for the Canadian Pacific Railway. He had written two novels (and would win the 1938 Governor General's Award for nonfiction) but claimed the real reason he got the job was that he could travel Canada on a railway pass and not cost the CAA a cent.

That was important. Although the authors put on a brave showing at their first gala dinner—men in dinner jackets and wing collars, women in bead-spangled gowns—the association then (as now) lived on a shoestring. The initial membership fee was $5. The earliest correspondence appeared on Gibbon's CPR letterhead until the CAA could afford its own. Until the 1930s, delegates went to conferences on rail passes. In the depths of the Depression the annual budget was around $2,000. When the Canada Council began dishing out money to arts organizations, CAA received nothing. Apart from some convention funding the Council has consistently turned down this country's senior writers organization: too many of its members are deemed non-professional.

Yet the achievements of its professionals stand up in any company. Founding member Rev. Charles W. Gordon of Winnipeg, writing as Ralph Connor, produced 22 novels and books of short stories over 40 years, while holding a full-time job as pastor. By 1926 his books had sold over six million copies on five continents. (Despite that, he died poor, having lost his fortune in bad investments.)

Another founder, Arthur Stringer, turned out 65 books: an outpouring of fiction, poetry, biography and literary criticism. Mazo de la Roche, after joining CAA, wrote 28 novels and books of short stories. In 1927 her *Jalna* won the $10,000 Atlantic Monthly Press prize.

Toronto member Gwethalyn Graham twice won the Governor General's Award for fiction. Her second winner in 1944, *Earth and High Heaven*, sold 600,000 copies in its first six months and screen rights went for $100,000. Her sister, Isabel LeBourdais (Toronto branch president in 1952-54), wrote a sensational best-seller, *The Trial of Steven Truscott*, in the mid-'60s.

A random sampling of the current membership turns up some notable success stories:

Toronto's Paulette Bourgeois has written 32 children's books in the last 10 years, including 17 in the popular Franklin the Turtle series, which just by itself has sold six million copies.

Waterloo's David Chilton, the financial expert who self-published *The Wealthy Barber*—hoping to sell maybe 5,000—caught North America's fancy and went into megasales.

And there is Dan Ross of Saint John, N.B., an international phenomenon still relatively unknown in CanLit. Before his death in November, 1995 at the age of 83, Ross had published more books than any other Canadian, or most other authors on earth: 356 novels (plus more than 600 short stories). He had begun full-time writing at 50. At his most prolific he wrote 20 books a year; even at the end of his career he was turning out three annually. His sales are astronomical; *China Shadow*, on the New York Times best-seller list in the '70s, sold more than two million.

Despite being snubbed by the Canada Council, and with membership fees still substantially lower than those of, say, the Writers' Union of Canada, CAA has a record of solid achievement. In 1961 Dr. Leslie Gordon Barnard, a past president and accomplished short story writer, eloquently listed some of the "intangible benefits that to my mind have mattered most: the encouragement of an older writer to a younger; the shared excitement of a creative idea; the market tip that pays off; the word of timely advice; not least, the linking of mind with mind, of province with province, so that the Canadian scene is dotted with friendships."

Timothy Findley reiterated that point in a 1986 article: "From the outset, one of the CAA's greatest accomplishments has been to help form a sense of community among writers." A National Newsline survey in 1984 invited members to tell what about CAA was most important to them. They chorused "contact with the outside"; "breaks the isolation"; "fun, fellowship, food for thought"; "to meet and chat informally with other writers"; "invaluable support and friendship."

To many members, local branches are the heart and soul of the CAA. Their seminars, workshops, meetings and news-letters are invaluable sources of information and fraternity. Past president Cora Taylor credits the CAA with the encouragement that led to her first novel, the best-selling prize-winning *Julie*. In the 1980s, a Vancouver teenager, Evelyn Lau won prizes for fiction and non-fiction in student writing competitions in the CAA-published *Canadian Author*. Today Lau too is a best-selling author. Even veteran member Fred Kerner, already a professional journalist when he joined the association in 1945, says, "CAA opened doors for me and made me aware of markets I needed to know."

The CAA's first tangible achievement in 1921 was Canadian Authors Week, bringing writers to public attention en masse for the first time in the country's literary history. With publishers and booksellers the association next launched Canadian Book Week, which continued until 1957.

In the early '20s, the CAA urged Canadian universities to set up courses on Canadian literature (virtually non-existent then). The initial response was cool; educators weren't keen on taking advice from such lower life-forms as writers. Undaunted, the CAA brought CanLit to national attention in 1937 by creating the Governor General's Awards. It administered them until 1960, when the Canada Council latched onto what was clearly a good thing. In 1973 the CAA set up a new awards program of its own.

In 1946, in a surge of postwar accomplishment, the association drew up a standard contract for authors, began exploring the possibility of a Public Lending Right and even wrung a concession out of the tax man— prodded by a persuasive CAA brief, the federal government agreed to permit authors to average their income tax over a three-year period.

Over the years CAA has produced at least a dozen editions of *The Canadian Writer's Guide*; launched a series of anthologies, including a tribute to cultural aspects of the Olympic Games in Montreal and another marking the International Year of the Child; helped celebrate Canada's centenary with *A Century of Canadian Literature/Un Siecle de Litterature*, and produced a one-time booklet on careers in writing for secondary schools. By its very existence and longevity, the CAA has provided the impetus (and many members) for most other writer groups in Canada. As Robertson Davies once said, "The Writers' Union stands on the shoulders of the Canadian Authors Association."

All through the years, the CAA's national magazine, *Canadian Author* (and its earlier incarnations) have presented inspiration and counsel, telling over and over how to write, how to sell, how to deal with editors, how to cope in this lonely profession. Its backbone has always been the tireless low-profile contributors but its bylines have included such respected names as Ralph Allen, Ross Annett, Arthur S. Bourinot, Marjorie Freeman Campbell, Thomas Costain, Merrill Dennison, Ralph Gustafson, Hugh MacLennan, E. J. Pratt, Thomas Raddall, Frances Shelley Wees, Scott Young—a veritable *Who's Who* (Or Ever Was) in Canadian writing.

None of which is to say the CAA is without warts. In its early years "there was a slight air of genteelism ...." Robertson Davies told the 1989 conference. "In those days in Canada, writing was still regarded as a somewhat dilettante pursuit."

That attitude persisted into the 1940s. Writer Keith Edgar, in a 1945 article in *Canadian Author & Bookman*, complained that newcomers at CAA meetings were asked, "What do you write?" If he or she was selling confessions or detective fiction to the slicks, the association's establishment arched their eyebrows: That wasn't literature.

"Or our writer goes down to attend a meeting," Edgar added. "He listens to a musical recital, someone reads a poem, someone talks about vague trends in literary art and a nice social time is had by all. But does anyone mention writing? Does anyone mention current problems of authors? Does anyone touch upon the need for revision of our copyright laws? Or the income tax laws...?"

Lyn Harrington in her 1981 CAA history, *Syllables of Recorded Time*, confirmed that the mid-'40s were "a period in Toronto branch history when F. R. Scott's derisive poem could fairly apply." Nor was Toronto's the only offending branch; subsequently the national executive injected some new blood into the organization.

In the mid-'80s the CAA Fund to Develop Canadian Writers was launched with the help of a $10,000 gift from philanthropist Lionel Gelber. The fund, an independent entity, provides financial aid (within or outside the CAA) to projects that meet its criteria: encouraging and educating young writers.

"Living on the brink of financial disaster for six decades is not pleasant, and several times we have nearly foundered," president Hal Lawrence told the 1987 conference. (One meagre consolation: while other organizations today are bemoaning the loss of grants and having to tighten their belts, austerity is already second nature to the CAA).

"The CAA has never been at its best in matters of business," concluded Robertson Davies at the 1989 conference, "but it has shown astonishing spirit and inventiveness and tenacity in clinging to those things which are so deeply necessary to literature, and which may be called things of the spirit."

After three-quarters of a century that spirit endures.

Robert Collins has been a staff writer with *Maclean's* and *Readers Digest* and editor of *Toronto Life*. The latest of his 13 books is *Who He?: Reflections on a Writing Life*.

# A Guide to Grants for Writers

*by Karleen Bradford* _____

The number of writers applying for grants in Canada today is growing steadily. The number of grants is decreasing. That's the bad news. But there is still a lot of good news. There are grants out there, and writers are receiving them. But applying for them takes skill and know-how. It's a talent all on its own, and one writers would be wise to learn before throwing themselves into the maelstrom.

The most important thing to do, before anything else, is to learn as much as possible about the preparation of an effective grant application and, please, don't waste your time and others' by applying for grants for which you are not qualified. Study the application forms carefully. Then follow the requirements stringently. Make the effort to prepare everything requested as carefully as you can, and be sure it is presented in as professional a manner as possible.

Many grant applications will ask you for a sample of your writing. Choose carefully. This will be the most important aspect of your application. Juries will base their decisions mostly on it. Keep to the word or page count requested. Prepare the piece with as much nit-picking care as you would when you send it off to a publisher. Even if your manuscript is in the first-draft stage, polish the sample until it is as perfect as you can make it. The sample does not necessarily have to come from your first chapter. Choose a selection that will give a good idea of who your characters are, and what the problems are that beset them.

Let the jurors know that your theme is a meaningful one, and that you are capable of exploring it.

In the same way, if your work is non-fiction. The topic with which you are dealing will be of equal importance with the quality of the writing. Juries must be convinced that your project is of vital importance.

In either fiction or non-fiction, you are usually quite at liberty to send a selection taken from various pieces of work, unless requested otherwise but, if you are applying for a work-in-progress grant, it goes without saying that you send a sample from that work. Again, even though the work may still be in progress, make certain that the sample is a finished, polished piece of writing.

If a description of your project is required, prepare this with as much care and thought as you would prepare the sample of writing. The same points will be important. You must convince the jurors of the importance of your work and of your ability to do it. The quality of the writing in this sample must accurately reflect the quality of the writing in your work itself.

Send references only when requested. The same thing goes for blurbs or reviews of previous work.

In short—find out what the rules are, follow them, and be professional.

Good luck! (And if you don't succeed at first...you know what to do.)

The following is a list of grants available to writers across Canada at the time of publication:

### The Canada Council For The Arts
### Grants for Professional Writers

Editor's Note: The Canada Council Grants for Professional Writers in Creative Writing and Literary Nonfiction underwent major changes just as the 12th Edition was going to press. The following is a summary of the new program details as they were available at press time:

• The former "A" and "B" grant levels and the Literary Arts Development Program have been discontinued. Grants are now available in fixed amounts of $5,000, $10,000, $15,000 and $20,000.

• The entry level is one book published by a professional publisher or two major publications in literary journals or recognized magazines.

• $15,000 and $20,000 grants are available only to writers who have a minimum of two books published by professional publishers.

• One deadline per year: October 1.

For further information contact:

Silvie Bernier, Writing and Publishing Section Officer.

Toll-free: at 1-800-263-5588, ext. 5537, or call directly at (613) 566-4414, ext. 5537. Fax: (613) 566-4410. E-Mail: <silvie.bernier@canada-council.ca>.

### First Peoples Words: Printed and Spoken

This program provides assistance for the creation, production and dissemination of First Peoples literary and oratory arts. The Individuals' Component is for First Peoples writers and storytellers. Value of grants up to a maximum of $4,000. One deadline per year: May 15.

For further information contact:

Louise Castonguay.

Toll-free: at 1-800-263-5588, ext 4573, or (613) 566-4414, ext. 4573.

Fax: (613) 5660-4410.

### Alberta

Alberta residents may apply for the following grants:

Junior Writer: $4,000

Intermediate Writer: $11,000

Senior Writer: $25,000

Special Projects: $5,000

For further information and guidelines, please contact:

The Alberta Foundation for the Arts,

5th Floor, Beaver House,

10158 103 Street,

Edmonton, AB, T5J 0X6

### British Columbia

Assistance is available to professional British Columbia creative writers for specific creative projects. Funding, up to a maximum of $5,000 during one fiscal year, is intended to assist creative writers by providing time to work on the proposed project.

Eligible genres include drama, fiction, juvenile, non-fiction and poetry.

For further information contact:

Walter K. Quan, Coordinator, Arts Awards Programs.

P.O. Box 9819, Stn Prov Govt,

Victoria, BC, V8W 9W3.

Tel: (604) 356-1728. Fax:(604) 387-4099

## Manitoba

Grants to Individuals:

Major Arts Grant to support personal creative projects of six to ten months in duration, with a maximum award up to $25,000.

Writers "A" Grant is available to support concentrated work on a major writing project. Designed to assist professional Manitoba writers who show a high standard of work and exceptional promise. This grant covers living expenses only and is worth up to $10,000.

Writers "B" Grant is available to support concentrated work on a major writing project. It is designed to assist published professional Manitoba writers in the early stages of their careers. This grant covers living expenses only and is worth up to $5,000.

Writers "C" Grant is available to support manuscript development by an emerging writer. Covers any combination of living, research or travel expenses up to $2,000.

Short-Term Project Grants are available to published professional Manitoba writers to support projects of short duration related to current artistic work or significant career opportunities. Maximum award is $1,000.

For further information contact:

Pat Sanders, Writing and Publishing Officer.

525-93 Lombard Avenue,

Winnipeg, MB, R3B 3B1.

Tel: (204) 945-0422. Fax: (204) 945-5925.

## New Brunswick

Creation Grant available for professional artists for the research, development and execution of original projects in the arts. Maximum grant is $6,000 per two-year period.

Documentation Grant available for professional artists to provide support for original documentation of arts activities, arts products or art history. Preference given to proposals concerning New Brunswick art or artists. Maximum grant is $6,000 per two-year period.

For further information contact:

Arts Branch, Department of Municipalities, Culture and Housing,

P.O. Box 6000,

Fredericton, NB, E3B 5H1.

Tel: (506) 453-2555.

## Newfoundland and Labrador

Project Grants support production costs, operating costs. Travel costs and study costs relating to a specific project to be undertaken by an artist, arts group or organization. Less established artists, groups or organizations may be considered in this category as determined by Council.

For further information contact:

Newfoundland & Labrador Arts Council

P.O. Box 98, Station C,

St. John's, NF, A1C 5H5.

Tel: (709) 726-2212. Fax: (709) 726-0619.

## Nova Scotia

The Assistance to Established Writers' Programme will no longer be administered by the Cultural Affairs Division. Funding for individual creative projects is being devolved from the Nova Scotia Department of Education and Culture, Cultural Affairs Division to the newly-created Nova Scotia Arts Council/Conseil des arts de la Nouvelle-Ecosse.

For further information contact:

Nova Scotia Arts Council

P.O. Box 666, Halifax Central P.O.,

Halifax, NS, B3K 2T3.

Tel: (902) 422-1123.

## Ontario

### The Ontario Arts Council

The Ontario Arts Council is reviewing all granting programs at the present time. At the moment, grants for writers include Arts Writing, Works in Progress and Writers' Reserve.

The Arts Writing program offers assistance to Ontario writers in the creation of criticism, commentary and essays on literature. The arts and media. In Category A, writers may apply for up to $3,000 a project. In Category B, writers may apply for up to $1,500 a project.

Grants to writers for Works-in-Progress are intended to assist with the completion of book-length works of literary merit in poetry and prose. The value of each Works-in-Progress grant will be $12,000.

The aim of the Writers' Reserve program is to assist talented new, emerging and established Ontario writers in the creation of new work. Writers' Reserve grants are available to writers upon the recommendation of an Ontario book publishing company or periodical that has been designated a Third-Party Recommender by the Ontario Arts Council. The maximum assistance to a writer through this program in one fiscal year is $10,000. (However, any one publisher's total recommendation for any single writer may not exceed $5,000 in one fiscal year.)

For further information contact:

The Ontario Arts Council,

151 Bloor St. West.

Toronto, ON, M5S 1T6.

Tel: (416) 969-7450. Toll free: 1-800-387-0058.

**The Toronto Arts Council**

Applicants must have resided in the City of Toronto for at least two years prior to the date of application. Grants are for the creation of new work or for work-in-progress in the area of literary arts:

$1,500 for writers whose work has never been published or produced.

$4,500 for previously published or produced writers.

For further information contact:

Nalo Hopkinson at (416) 392-6802, ext. 208

## Prince Edward Island

Maximum grant available to an individual artist is $3,000. Travel and study grants of up to $1,000 are also available. Residency requirements are 6 of last 12 months.

For further information:

Prince Edward Island Council of the Arts,

P.O. Box 2234,

Charlottetown, PE, C1A 8B9

(Or: 94 Great George Street,

Charlottetown, PE, C1A 7I9)

Tel: (902) 368-4410.

## Québec

Type "A" and Type "B" Grants are available for writers of novels, poetry, books for young people and short fiction.

The value of Type "A" Grants is up to $25,000 for long term projects, and up to $9,000 for short term projects. The value of Type "B" grants is up to $20,000 for long term projects, and up to $7,000 for short term projects.

For further information contact:
**Québec Office:**
Conseil des arts et des lettres du Québec
79, boul. Rene-Levesque Est, 3e etage,
Québec, QC, H1R 5N5.
Tel: (418) 643-1707. Toll-free: 1-800-897-1707. Fax: (418) 643-4558.
**Montreal Office:**
Conseil des arts et des lettres du Québec
500, place d'Armes, 15e etage,
Montreal, QC, H2Y 2W2.
Tel: (514) 864-3350. Toll-free: 1-800-608-3350. Fax: (514) 864-4160.

## Saskatchewan

Creative Grants available to assist Saskatchewan's artists and emerging artists. "A" Grants of up to $20,000, "B" Grants of up to $12,000, and "C" Grants of up to $4,000.

Professional Development Grants available to assist individuals from Saskatchewan to pursue excellence in the arts through study in a formal setting or in an informal setting such as apprenticeships or mentorships. "A" Grants of up to $10,000, "B" Grants of up to $7,500 and "C" Grants of up to $4,000.

Research Grants available to assist individuals from Saskatchewan to pursue research in the arts such as general research, independent curatorial research and research on new techniques or new technologies. "A" Grants of up to $5,000, "B" Grants of up to $3,500 and "C" Grants of up to $1,500.

For further information contact:
Saskatchewan Arts Board,
3rd Floor. T.C. Douglas Building,
3475 Albert Street,
Regina, SK, S4S 6X6.
Tel: (306) 787-4056. Toll-free: 1-800-667-7526. Fax: (306) 787-4199.

## Yukon

Grants up to $5,000 for "A" level artists, up to $2,500 for "B" level artists. "A" level artists should have some national prominence and "B" level artists should have had a least some local recognition. One year continuous residency in the Yukon prior to application is a requirement.

For further information:
Laurel Parry, Arts Consultant Arts Branch,
Yukon Tourism, Government of Yukon,
Box 2703,
Whitehorse, YT, Y1A 2C6.
Tel: (403) 667-5264 or Toll-free: 1-800-661-0408. Fax: (403) 393-6456.

Karleen Bradford is the author of thirteen books for children and young adults. She has been assisted in the writing of some of these by Canada Council Short Term Grants, and a Canada Council "B" Grant. She has also worked in schools in Ontario under the Ontario Artists in the Schools Grants program.

# Contests and Awards Available for Writers

*Researched and compiled by Gill Foss* _____

T he following listings cover only those contests and awards offered in Canada. All information has been checked for accuracy at time of publication but may change without notice due to relocation, market fluctuations and sponsorship cutbacks. Although this section includes over 250 contests, awards and fellowships—many more than the previous edition of *The Canadian Writer's Guide*—it in no way represents all available contests or awards. Sources carrying updated information include *Quill & Quire*, Wordwrights Canada *Contest Calendar*, a number of web sites/bulletin boards and the reference section in public libraries.

The information included for each listing does not necessarily carry the full entry requirements due to space limitations. In all cases, requesting a complete set of rules would avoid disqualification due to failure to comply with all criteria.

Common submission information:
- Entries must be typed or sent as computer/word processor print outs.
- Paper should be standard 8.5" x 11" (or metric equivalent).
- Prose submissions should be double-spaced, single-sided.
- Poetry submissions single-sided but spacing/formatting at dis cretion of the poet.
- Title should be repeated on top of each page subsequent to title page.
- Pages should be numbered consecutively.
- Entry fee must be included with submission as cheque or money order.

- Multiple entries usually require multiples of the entry fee.
- Deadline date is usually "as postmarked".
- One-time publication rights only granted (if applicable).
- Copyright remains with contestant.
- "Blind judging" means manuscripts must not show your name. Entrant's name, address, phone number and titles/categories of submission should be included on a separate sheet enclosed with the material entered.
- SASE (self-addressed, stamped envelope) must be included if requesting further information, winners list etc..
- UNESCO definition of a book: 48 pages of literary content excluding front and back material. Chapbooks do not meet this standard.
- All contests/awards listed are offered annually unless otherwise stated.

Prize money won should be included in taxable writing income which can be set against related expenses. Awards named on a résumé increase a professional profile.

### Beware:

Occasionally, contests offer prizes for amateur contributions but send back non-winning entries saying the piece (usually poetry) will be included in a proposed deluxe (expensive) anthology if the author agrees to purchase a copy. Make sure you think the benefit is worth the expense.

### E-mail and Web page addresses:

Editor's note: We have included e-mail and web page addresses whenever they where available. However we would like to point out that the volatile nature of the Internet and the World Wide Web means that these could have changed by the time you read this publication. Be particularly careful with your address entry, but if you still fail to get through, use a Web search tool such as AltaVista <http://www.altavista.digital.com> to find the new address.

## Eleanor Abram Prize for Fiction

Department of English Language and Literature
Brock University
St. Catharines, ON  L2S 3A1
Prize: $75.
Awarded for the best work of fiction in *the Harpweaver*, a publication of the
Department of English Language and Literature.

## Milton Acorn Poetry Award

Island Literary Awards
PEI Council of the Arts
115 Richmond Street
Charlottetown, PE  C1A 1H7
Phone: (902) 368-4410
Prizes: a flight for two between any two points (excluding Boston) covered
by Air Canada/Air Nova; $200; $100.
Open to original, unpublished poetry to a maximum ten pages per entry by
Island residents only. Multiple entries permitted. Material having previously
won any award is ineligible. Blind judging. Entry fee: $8.
Deadline: 15 February.

## The Acorn-Rukeyser Chapbook Contest

Unfinished Monument Press
237 Prospect Street South
Hamilton, ON  L8M 2Z6
Phone: (905) 312-1779. Fax: (905) 312-8285.
Prize: $100 and publication.
The manuscript (up to 30 pages), which may contain both published or
unpublished poems, must be within the People's Poetry tradition, as exem-
plified by the work of Milton Acorn and Muriel Rukeyser. Entry fee: $10.
Deadline: 31 October.

## Alberta Romance Writers Association
## Professional Development Award

Alberta Romance Writers Association
223-112th Avenue S.W.
Calgary, AB  T2R 0G9
Phone: (403) 282-6676.
Prize: $250 to be applied towards any type of professional advancement.
The Association also offers a variety of in-house awards.

## Alberta Screenwriting Competition

The Television and Film Institute for Screenwriters
441-10045 156 Street
Edmonton, AB  T5P 2P7
Phone: (403) 497-4304. Fax: (403) 497-4330.

E-mail: <tfinst@picasso.ab.ca>
Prizes: $3,000 in each of two categories.
Open to Alberta writers only, for either long-form feature scripts or half-hour teleplays for children. All work submitted must be original, unpublished and without options. Collaborative scripts are permitted but all contributing writers must be Alberta residents. Entry fee: $35. Deadline: mid-September (date not set at time of publication).

### The John Alexander Media Awards
Public Education Department
Multiple Sclerosis Society of Canada
250 Bloor Street East, Suite 1000
Toronto, ON  M4W 3P9
Phone: (416) 922-6065.
Prizes: $500 print media; $500 broadcast media.
Awarded to encourage excellence in writing and broadcasting about MS for the lay audience. Topics can include understanding of the disease, research, treatment, coping, and activities of the Multiple Sclerosis Society of Canada. Each category is open to work in either official language but only one piece in each category will win. Entries must have been published or aired between 1 September and 31 August of the competition year. Entry form required. Deadline: 31 September.

### Algoma District Poetry Contests
Michi-Mook Publishing Enterprises
Sault Ste. Marie, ON  P6A 2A4
Phone: (705) 946-5746.
### 1. Chapbook Competition
Grand prize: 100 copies of winning chapbook professionally produced (value $800).
Open to traditional forms of poetry, free verse and prose poetry up to 20 pages. Entry fee: $50. Deadline: 31 March.
### 2. Northern Anthology Contest
Prizes: $100; $75; $50.
Open to traditional forms of poetry, free verse and prose poetry. Entry fee: $5 per poem. Deadline: 31 March.

### *Amethyst Review* Writing Contest
Marcasite Press
23 Riverside Avenue,
Truro, NS  B2N 4G2
Phone: (902) 895-1345. E-mail (inquiries only): <amethyst@atcon.com>
Web site: <http://www.amethyst@atcon.com>
Prizes: $50 poetry; $50 prose.
Awarded for unpublished work: poetry to 200 lines/poem; prose to 5,000 words. Themes change for each contest. Guidelines essential.
Deadline: 31 January.

## R. Ross Annett Award for Children's Literature
Writers Guild of Alberta Awards Program
Percy Page Centre, 3rd floor
11759 Groat Road N.W.
Edmonton, AB  T5M 3K6
Phone: (403) 422-8174. Fax: (403) 422-2663. Calgary office phone: (403) 265-2226.
Prize: $500 and a leather-bound copy of the winning book.
Open to residents of Alberta who have lived in the province for 12 of the previous 18 months. The books may have been published anywhere in the world, 1 January–31 December. Deadline: 31 December. Only books published 15–31 December are permitted to meet the delayed submission date: 15 January.

## ARC Poem of the Year Contest
P.O. Box 7368
Ottawa, ON  K1L 8E4
Prizes: $1,000; $750; $500. All prizes include publication in Autumn issue.
Awarded for unpublished poems to a maximum of 100 lines. Up to four poems may be submitted. Entry fee: $12 (which includes a one-year subscription to the magazine). Blind judging. Deadline: 27 June.

## Atlantic Journalism Awards
The School of Journalism
University of King's College
6350 Coburg Road
Halifax, NS  B3H 2A1
Phone: (902) 422-1271. Fax: (902) 425-8183.
Web site: <http://www.ukings.ns.ca/aja/aja.html>
Prizes: $300/winner of individual categories, citation-of-merit certificates to two runners-up in each category.
Awards available in eight categories. Eligibility restricted to journalists writing in the Atlantic Region for work in print, radio and television. Entry form required (available on Internet site or from School). Entry fee: $20.
Deadline: 31 January.
Deadline for Journalist Achievement Award: 1 March.

## Atlantic Writing Competition
Writers' Federation of Nova Scotia
1809 Barrington Street, Suite 901
Halifax, NS  B3J 3K8
Phone/fax: (902) 422-0881.
E-mail: <writers1@fox.nstn.ca>
Web site: <http://www.ccn.cs.dal.ca/culture/WritersFedWFNS-home.html/
Prizes by category:

**Novel:** $200; $150; $100.
**Non-fiction Book:** $200; $150; $100.
**Short Story:** $100; $75; $50.
**Poetry:** $100; $75; $50.
**Writing for Children:** $150; $75; $50.
**Radio Play:** $150; $75; $50.
**Youth Writing (Short Story):** $150; $75; $50.
Open to writers in the Atlantic provinces only. Entry fee: $15 per entry or $10 per entry for WFNS members, students or seniors. Further details required. Deadline: 23 August.

### Backwater Review Editor's Choice Awards (Poetry/Fiction)
Backwater Press
P.O. Box 222, Station B
Ottawa, ON K1P 6C4
Prizes: $100 and publication.
Contest entries must be original, previously unpublished work. Poetry contest: submit five poems. Entry fee: $9 (which includes one-year subscription). Deadline: 31 January. Fiction contest: submit one short story or play. Entry fee: $9 (which includes one-year subscription). Deadline: 31 July.

### Baha'i Poetry Calendar
White Mountain Publications
Baha'i Poetry Calendar Competition
P.O. Box 5180
R.R. #2
New Liskeard, ON P0J 1P0
Prizes: small cash awards and five free calendars.
Nineteen winning entries will appear in the calendar. Poems should reflect on aspects of Baha'i life or address the inspiration given by its teachings to everyday living. Work must be original, unpublished, up to 32 lines of 44 characters and typed. Entry fee: $5 per poem. Deadline: 31 May.

### The Alfred G. Bailey Prize
Writers' Federation of New Brunswick
P.O. Box 37, Station A
Fredericton, NB E3B 4Y2
Prize: $400.
Open only to residents of New Brunswick for an original, unpublished poetry manuscript of at least 48 pages. Individual poems published or accepted for publication may be included. Deadline: 14 February.

### The Herb Barrett Award
Hamilton Haiku Press
237 Prospect Street South
Hamilton, ON L8M 2Z6

Prizes: $75; $50; $25. All prizes include publication in an anthology.
Open to writers of short poems in the haiku tradition up to four lines and not
necessarily 17 syllables. Published or unpublished work judged on originality, haiku style, content and technical mastery. Entry fee: $10 (1 to 2 poems);
$15 (3 or more). Deadline: 30 November.

## The Shaunt Basmajian Chapbook Award
Canadian Poetry Association
P.O. Box 22571
St. George Postal Outlet
Toronto, ON  M5S 1V0
Prize: $100 and publication, plus ten copies of the chapbook.
Entry should be a manuscript of poems up to 24 pages which may contain
both published and unpublished work in any style or tradition. Complete
entry rules required. Entry fee: $10. Deadline: 30 November.

## BC Historical Federation Awards
c/o 7953 Rosewood Street
Burnaby, BC  V5E 2H4
Award: the Lieutenant Governor's Medal for Historical Writing. Other monetary awards and certificates of merit will be presented for valuable books
prepared by groups or individuals.
Any book presenting any facet of BC history, including biography, published
the previous year is eligible. Attention to quality presentation, fresh material,
appropriate illustrations, an adequate index, table of contents and bibliography will be noted. Reprints or revisions of books are not eligible. Send two
copies of each book which then become the property of the Federation.
Deadline: 31 December.

## The Geoffrey Bilson Award for Historical Fiction for Young People
c/o The Canadian Children's Book Centre
35 Spadina Road
Toronto, ON  M5R 2S9
Phone: (416) 975-0010. Fax: (416) 975-1839.
E-mail: <ccbc@1global.com>
Web site: <http://www.1global.com/~ccbc>
Award: $1,000.
Open to Canadian writers only. Send for further details.

## Blood & Guts Horror Story Contest
c/o Bad Moon Books
Pinecrest P.O. Box 84052
Ottawa, ON  K2C 3Z2
E-mail: <spider@freenet.carleton.ca>
Prizes: $100 and publication in a Bad Moon Books chapbook with print run
of 250. Top ten submissions receive an honourable mention in the final

publication. All entrants receive a copy of the publication.

Here is your chance to show the world the dark corners of your mind. A chance to run your work up the gallows and see if people scream. Stories 5,000–20,000 words. Send for complete guidelines. Entry fee: $10 for up to three stories. Deadline: 31 July.

### *Books in Canada* Student Writing Awards

*Books in Canada*
427 Mount Pleasant Road
Toronto, ON M4S 2L8
Phone: (416) 489-4755.
Prizes: $500; $250; three honourable mentions in both levels.

Undergraduate level: entrants must be enrolled as a full-time student at a Canadian university or community college. High school level: entrants must be OAC students at a Canadian high school graduating either in the year of entry or the following year. Open to one submission per student of either a piece of short fiction to 2,500 words, or a book review to 1,500 words, judged as a single category on creativity, thought and originality. Entrants must agree to one-time publication in *Books in Canada*. Blind judging. Include name, address and phone number of educational establishment and student identification number. Keep copy of submission.
Deadline: 20 February.

### Joseph Brant Award

The Ontario Historical Society
34 Parkview Avenue
Willowdale, ON M2N 3Y2
Phone: (416) 226-9011. Fax: (416) 226-2740.
Prize: framed certificate and copy of citation acknowledging the winner's contribution to the heritage community.

Awarded for the best book on multicultural history in Ontario published during the previous three years. Entry form required. Deadline: 30 October.

### Ann Connor Brimmer Award

c/o Thomas Riddall Public Library
Halifax Regional Library
32 Glendale Avenue
Sackville, NS B4C 3M1
Prize: $1,000.

Open to residents living in Atlantic Canada for an outstanding children's book for readers up to age 15. Entries may be fiction or non-fiction (except textbooks), but must be in print and accessible. The book must have been published in Canada between 1 May and the following 30 April. Nomination forms available from above address. Deadline: 31 April.

## Georges Bugnet Award for Fiction
Writers Guild of Alberta Awards Program
Percy Page Centre, 3rd floor
11759 Groat Road N.W.
Edmonton, AB T5M 3K6
Phone: (403) 422-8174. Fax: (403) 422-2663.
Calgary office phone:(403) 265-2226.
Prize: $500 and a leather-bound copy of the winning book.
Authors must have been resident in Alberta for 12 of the previous 18 months. Awarded for a novel published anywhere in the world, 1 January–31 December. Deadline: 31 December. Only books published 15–31 December are permitted to meet the delayed submission date: 15 January.

## John Bullen Prize
Canadian Historical Association
395 Wellington Street
Ottawa, ON K1A 0N3
Phone: (613) 233-7885. Fax: (613) 567-3110.
Prize: $500.
Awarded for the best doctoral thesis accepted for the degree between 1 October and 30 September of the previous two years if the topic is Canadian history, or 1 October to 30 September of the current year if in a field of history other than Canadian. Submission details required.

## Burnaby Writers' Society Competition
6584 Deer Lake Avenue
Burnaby, BC V5G 3T7
Phone: (604) 435-6500.
Prizes: $200; $100; $50.
Open to all BC writers. Categories vary: announcement in March. Send SASE for current guidelines. Deadline: 31 May.

## Calendar Competitions (Haiku and small poems)
White Mountain Publications
P.O. Box 5180
R.R. #2
New Liskeard, ON P0J 1P0
Prizes: a small cash award and five free calendars in each competition.
There are four calendars each with its own competition: Writer's Calendar; Soaring Spirits; Love Lines; and Burnished Pebbles. Poems must be titled, original, previously unpublished, 32 lines or less and typed, one per page, in black on white 8.5"x11" (or metric) paper. Line width of more than 44 characters may be broken at the discretion of the editor (thereby becoming two separate lines). Further details required. Entry fee: $5 per poem. Deadline: 30 April (except Burnished Pebbles: 31 March).

## Calgary Writers Association Contests

c/o P.O. Box 68083
7750 Ranchview Drive N.W.
Calgary, AB  T3G 3N8
Phone: (403) 242-3130.
Open only to Alberta writers.

### 1. Arrol Award for Non-fiction

Prize; $100 and permanent certificate. At winner's choice article may be printed in *Write Angels* Special Edition.

Open to non-professional writers not previous winners of the award. Subject matter "open" but writer must identify target publication(s) for article on separate sheet of paper. Judging will be applied accordingly. One submission per contestant per year of unpublished work.

Entry fee: $10 (includes copy of *Write Angels* Special Edition). CWA members enter free. Deadline: 15 April.

### 2. Poetry Contest

Prizes: $50; $25; $25. All with publication in *Write Angels* Special Edition.

Open to one entry per year of up to three poems or total of 60 lines of unpublished work. Any style/subject. Contest format required. Entry fee: $5. CWA members enter free. Deadline: 15 March.

### 3. Short Fiction Award

Prizes: $75 and publication in *Write Angels* Special Edition; $50 with publication, space permitting; $25 with publication, space permitting.

Open to one unpublished short story to maximum of 2,500 words. Contest format required. Entry fee: $10 (includes copy of *Write Angels* Special Edition). CWA members enter free. Deadline: 1 March.

## Canadian Association of Journalists (CAJ) Awards

Rm 316B, St. Patrick's Bldg.
Carleton University
Ottawa, ON  K1S 5B6
Phone: (613) 526-8061. Fax: (613) 521-3904.
E-mail: <cf408@freenet.carleton.ca>
Prizes: $1,000 in each category.

Categories available: open newspaper/wire service; community newspaper; magazine; open TV (under 5 min.); open TV (over 5 min.); regional TV; radio news (under 10 min.); radio news (over 10 min.); photojournalism; conflict analysis; student award. Entry form required. Entry fee (CAJ and conflict analysis awards): CAJ members $25 per entry; non-members $50 per entry. Entry fee (Student Awards of excellence): CAJ student members free; non-members $20. Deadline: CAJ awards (inc. photojournalism award), 31 January; Student award, 28 February.

## *Canadian Author* **Okanagan Short Story Award (quarterly)**
Fiction Editor
c/o P.O. Box 419
Campbellford, ON  K0L 1L0
Prize: $125 and publication in the magazine.
Offered for the best original, unpublished story submitted for each issue.

## The Canadian Authors Association (Niagara Branch) Prize for Poetry
*the Harpweaver*
Department of English Language and Literature
Brock University
St. Catharines, ON  L2S 3A1
Prize: $50.
Awarded for the best poem published in *the Harpweaver*'s one yearly issue.

## Canadian Authors Association Awards
The Administrator
Canadian Authors Association
P.O. Box 419
Campbellford, ON  K0L 1L0
Phone: (705) 653-0323. Fax: (705) 653-0593.
E-mail: <canauth@redden.on.ca>

### 1. CAA Air Canada Award
Award: two tickets to any one of Air Canada's destinations at winner's choice.
Open to a Canadian writer under the age of 30 by end of April of that year. Entry only by nomination received from a recognized writer's organization or a publisher. Submissions should include a brief letter indicating the reason for the choice of nominee, including writer's date of birth, a current CV, and samples of the writer's work with reviews if available. Full-length works are not required. Deadline: 31 March.

### 2. CAA Awards for Drama/Fiction/Poetry
Check for continued availability of these awards.

### 3. CAA Lela Common Award
Award: $2,500 and an engraved silver medal.
Open to books of historical non-fiction, on Canadian topics, by Canadian authors. Biographical works are eligible. Entries must be English-language literature for adults (not "young adults") and must have been first published in the previous year. Translations are not eligible. Deadline: 15 December.

### 4. CAA Jubilee Award
Award: $2,500 and an engraved silver medal.
Open for a collection of short stories by one Canadian author. The stories must be English-language literature for adults (not "young adults"). All must have been first published as a collection the previous year. Translations are

not eligible, nor are books published at the author's expense.
Deadline: 31 December.

### 5. CAA Vicky Metcalf Body of Work Award
Award: $10,000.
Open to authors of work inspirational to Canadian youth, with at least four books published. Application forms available from the Administrator. Deadline: 31 December.

### 6. CAA Vicky Metcalf Short Story Award
Award: $3,000 (plus $1,000 for the editor if the story is published in Canada).
Open to writers of stories inspirational to Canadian youth. Application forms available from the Administrator. Deadline: 31 December.

### 7. CAA Student Writing Contest
P.O. Box 32219
250 Harding Blvd.
Richmond Hill, ON  L4C 9R0
E-mail (inquiries only): <bfarrar@learn.senecac.on.ca>
Prizes: $500 best story, $500 best poem. Four honourable mentions in each category.
Open to students between 12 and 21 who are Canadian citizens or landed immigrants. Short story to a maximum of 2,000 words. Poems up to 30 lines. All winners will receive a one-year subscription to *Canadian Author* magazine and be invited to a CAA meeting. Write for entry form. If list of winners required, include SASE with entry. Entry fee: $5 per story or set of three poems, with no limit on number of entries submitted. Deadline: 22 March.

### Canadian Ethnic Journalists' and Writers' Club Awards
24 Tarlton Road
Toronto, ON  M5P 2M4
Phone: (416) 488-0048.
Prizes: a plaque and a certificate of acknowledgment from the Federal Government.
Open to ethnic journalists working in print, radio or television. Also open to mainstream journalists writing on ethnic topics with accuracy and cultural sensitivity. Deadline: end of February.

### The Sierhey Khmara Award
Prize: as above.
Awarded for an outstanding contribution to multi-lingual journalism. Deadline: end of February.

### Canadian Farm Writer's Federation Writing/Broadcasting Awards
Fundraising Chair/Office of Research
University of Guelph
Guelph, ON  N1G 2W1

Phone: (519) 824-4120. Fax: (519) 821-5236.
E-mail: <owen@ornet.or.uoguelph.ca>
Web site: <http://www.uoguelph.ca/Research/cfwf>
Prizes: $300; $200; $100.
Offered in ten categories for stories about production agriculture: news release; radio; TV; best feature; editorial; column; news story; daily press reporting; weekly press reporting; targeted publication writing.
Deadline: mid-June.

**The Canadian Forest Service-Sault Ste. Marie Journalism Award**
Canadian Science Writers' Association
P.O. Box 75, Station A
Toronto, ON M5W 1A2
Phone: (416) 928-9624. Fax: (416) 960-0528.
E-mail: <cswa@interlog.com>
Prizes: $750 for winner in each of two categories: newspapers and magazines.
Open to writers in English or French who have a news story, feature or editorial in a weekly, periodical or magazine published in Ontario. Topics must promote a better appreciation and understanding of Ontario's forests either rural or urban. Material must have been published between 1 January and 31 December of the previous year. Write for further details and entry form.
Deadline: 14 February.

*Canadian Living*'s **Short Fiction Contest**
P.O. Box 7750
Station B
North York, ON M2K 2Z9
Prize: $1,000. Five runners-up will be announced in the same issue.
Open to residents of Canada 18 years of age or older. Entries must be original, unpublished, to a maximum of 2,500 words and submitted only by the author. Publication in December so topic must speak in some way to the events readers share at that time of year. Should evoke human values, hopes and dreams. Multiple entries are allowed but each must be mailed separately. Send for complete guidelines and entry form. Entry free.
Deadline: 15 July.

**Canadian National Playwriting Competition**
c/o Theatre BC
307-1005 Broad St.
Victoria, B.C. V8W 2A1
Three awards: $1,500 (full-length); $1,000 (one act); $750 (special merit).
Open to all professional and non-professional playwrights resident in Canada. Write for complete entry requirements.

## Canadian Nurses Association Media Awards
Public and Government Relations Manager
Canadian Nurses Association
50 Driveway
Ottawa, ON  K2P 1E2
Phone: (613) 237-2133 ext. 204. Fax: (613) 237-3520.
Prizes: nine awards of excellence and three certificates of merit.
Entries accepted from magazines, regional and national daily newspapers, national and local television and radio. Entries must have been published or aired in Canada for a general Canadian audience in the previous year. Work written in other than the two official languages is accepted if accompanied by a translation in English or French. Entry form required but no entry fee. Deadline: early January.

## Canadian Poetry Chapbook Competition
The League of Canadian Poets
54 Wolseley St.
Toronto, ON  M5T 1A5
Phone: (416) 504-1657. Fax: (416) 703-0059.
E-mail: <league@io.org>
Prizes: $1,000; $750; $500; five honourable mentions. The first prize winner's entry will be published.
Open to Canadian citizens and landed immigrants. Submit poetry manuscripts of 15–24 pages with not more than one poem per page. All winners will receive a copy of the winning chapbook. No electronic or fax submissions. Write for complete rules. Deadline: 1 March.

## *Canadian Writer's* Journal Awards
P.O. Box 5180
RR #2
New Liskeard, ON  P0J 1P0
Prizes: $100; $50; $30 (in each category), plus publication in the magazine.
Poetry deadline: 30 June. Short fiction deadline: October (date to be announced).

## Cavendish Tourist Association Creative Writing Award for Young People
Island Literary Awards
PEI Council of the Arts
115 Richmond Street
Charlottetown, PE  C1A 1H7
Phone: (902) 368-4410
Prizes: $75; $50; $25 (in each of three categories).
Open to all Island elementary, junior and senior high school students.
Entries may be on any topic to a maximum of five pages of poetry or a five-page short story per entry. Blind judging. No entry fee.
Deadline: 15 February.

## Certificates of Merit Awards for Regional History
Canadian Historical Association
395 Wellington St.
Ottawa, ON  K1A 0N3
Prizes: certificates of Merit.
The Regional History Committee of the Canadian Historical Association solicits nominations for meritorious publications or exceptional contributions by individuals or organizations to regional history. Write for more information. Nominations and supportive documentation should be submitted to the representative for the appropriate region: Atlantic, Quebec, Ontario, The Prairies, British Columbia, or The North (Yukon and NWT).
Deadline: 31 December.

## Chalmers Play Awards
Chalmers Awards Office
Ontario Arts Council
151 Bloor Street West
Toronto, ON  M5S 1T6
Phone: (416) 961-1660. Fax: (416) 961-7796. Toll-free: 1-800-387-0058.
### 1.The Floyd S. Chalmers Canadian Play Awards
Four prizes: each $10,000.
Awarded to the writers to recognize the creation of original plays produced in Metro Toronto by any professional theatre company in Canada. Complete information available on request.
### 2.Chalmers Canadian Play Awards: Theatre for Young Audiences
Two prizes: each $10,000.
Awarded to original plays given their Toronto area premiere production during the calendar year. The plays must be intended for school-age audiences from primary to OAC levels. Nominees chosen by a jury. Complete details available on request.

## Chapters/*Books in Canada* First Novel Award
*Books in Canada*
427 Mount Pleasant Road
Toronto, ON  M4S 2L8
Award: $5,000.
Awarded for a published first novel by a Canadian citizen or landed immigrant, in English or translation from French. Unpublished manuscripts are ineligible. Write for more information. Deadline: 1 December.

## Lina Chartrand Poetry Award
*Contemporary Verse 2*
P.O. Box 3062
Winnipeg, MB  R3C 4E5
Phone: (204) 949-1365.

Prize: amount of interest accrued over the year on a fund established to finance this award (in 1996, $400), plus publication in *CV2*.

The award is given to recognize a distinguished contribution by an emerging writer to *CV2*'s endeavour to promote women's writing. The winning poet is chosen from those whose work has been published in the magazine during the year.

### The City of Calgary W.O. Mitchell Book Prize

Writers Guild of Alberta Awards Programme
Calgary Office
305-223-12 Avenue S.W.
Calgary, AB  T2R 0G9
Phone: (403) 422-8174.
Or: Calgary Awards Program, Public Information Department
Phone: (403) 269-8844.
Prize: $2,000.
Awarded to recognize achievement in literary book writing (fiction, poetry, non-fiction, children's literature and drama) by residents of Calgary.
Deadline: 31 December.

### The City of Edmonton Book Prize

Writers Guild of Alberta Awards Programme
Percy Page Centre, 3rd floor
11759 Groat Road N.W.
Edmonton, AB  T5M 3K6
Phone: (403) 422-8174. Fax: (403) 422-2263.
Prize: $2,000.
Awarded for fiction, poetry or drama in published form, written for adults or children. The subject must deal with some aspect of the City of Edmonton and be by a writer 18 or over, or by a group. Entry fee: $10.
Deadline: 14 March.

### City of Toronto Book Awards

c/o City of Toronto Corporate Communications
City Hall, East Tower, 22nd floor
Toronto, ON  M5H 2N2
Awards total: $15,000. Each finalist (usually five or six) receives $1,000 and the winning author is awarded the remainder (usually $9,000 to $11,000).
These awards honour authors of books of literary merit that are evocative of Toronto. Entries may be fiction or non-fiction for adults and/or children. Textbooks, reprints and manuscripts are not eligible. Books must have been published between 1 January and 31 December of the previous year.
Submit five copies of the book, along with your name, address and phone number. Deadline: 31 January.

## CLA Book Awards
c/o CLA Membership Services
200 Elgin St., Suite 206
Ottawa, ON  K2P 1L5
Phone: (613) 232-9625. Fax: (613) 563-9895.
### 1. Book of the Year for Children
Chairperson
Book of the Year for Children Award Committee
Award: a handsome medal.
Open for an outstanding children's book published in Canada by a Canadian citizen or permanent resident. Creative writing regardless of format, including anthologies and collections suitable for readers to age fourteen.
Deadline: 31 December.
### 2. CLA Young Adult Canadian Book Award
Chairperson
Young Adult Canadian Book Award
Award: a leather-bound book with the award seal embossed on the cover.
Available to recognize the author of an outstanding English-language Canadian book, by a Canadian citizen or landed immigrant, published in the preceding calendar year, which appeals to young adults 13–18. Entries must be a work of fiction in either hard cover or paperback.
Deadline: 31 December.

## Codyco Poetry Contest
10 Eagle Lane
Dartmouth, NS  B2V 2G5
E-mail: <codyco@atcon.com>
Web site: <http://members.tripod.com/~codyco/index-2.html>
Prize: $100 and publication on the Net.
Poems to a maximum of 31 lines. Send for entry categories. Entry fee: $5/one poem; $7/two poems; $10/three poems. Deadline: 26 February.

## Nathan Cohen Award
The Awards Chair
The Canadian Theatre Critics Association
25 George Street, Suite 701
Toronto, ON  M5A 4L8
Phone/fax: (416) 367-8896.
Prize: $500 and a framed certificate in each category.
Awarded to recognize high critical standards of theatre criticism in two categories: long review (reviews, profiles and other theatrical features 1,000–4,000 words and short review (up to 1,000 words). All work must have been published the previous year. Send for complete contest rules.
Entry fee: $10 per piece. Deadline: 4 March.

### Confederation Poet's Prize

Prize: $100

This is a contributor's prize awarded for the best poem published in *ARC* magazine the previous calendar year. No submissions accepted.

### Connaught Medal for Excellence in Health Research Journalism

Canadians for Health Research
P.O. Box 126
Westmount, PQ  H3Z 2T1
Phone: (514) 398-7478. Fax: (514) 398-8361.
Prize: medal and $1,500 bursary.
Open to journalists whose articles must have appeared in Canadian newspapers or magazines during the previous calendar year. Selection criteria include accuracy of content, impact, presentation, originality and creativity. Deadline: 14 February.

### *Contemporary Verse 2* Short Fiction Contest

P.O. Box 3062
Winnipeg, MB  R3C 4E5
Phone: (204) 949-1635.
Prizes: $200; $100; $50; plus payment for publication.
Entries must be original, unpublished and up to 1,000 words. Blind judging. Entry fee: $18 (includes a one-year subscription). Deadline: 31 May.

### Marianna Dempster Award

Nova Scotia Branch
Canadian Authors Association
c/o 15 MacRea Avenue
Dartmouth, NS  B2Y 1Z4
Phone: (902) 466-2558.
Prize: $100 to author plus book award seals to either author or publisher at author's choice.
Open to Nova Scotia writers only. Awarded for the best children's book for the age group up to ten years, published either in the year of the award or the preceding one. Deadline: 30 March.

### Brendon Donnelly Award for Children's Literature

Calgary Writers Association
c/o P.O. Box 68083
7750 Ranchview Drive N.W.
Calgary, AB  T3G 3N8
Phone: (403) 242-3130.
Prizes: $400 (to be applied to some form of "education" and used within 12 months); $100 book certificate. Published, or excerpted, in Special Edition of *Write Angels* and name inscribed on the Brendon Donnelly Trophy.

Open to all Canadian residents. One submission of unpublished work per contestant per year. Categories change. Contest format required. Entry fee: $15 (includes copy of *Write Angels* Special Edition). CWA members enter free. Deadline: 1 April.

### Bill Duthie Booksellers' Choice Prize
West Coast Book Prize Society
700-1033 Davie Street
Vancouver, BC  V6E 1M7
Phone/fax: (604) 687-2405.
Prize: $2,000.
Presented to the originating publisher (with head office and creative control in BC or Yukon) and author of the best book in terms of public appeal, initiative, design production and content. Entry fee: $25. Deadline: 24 December.

### Wilfred Eggleston Award for Non-fiction
Writers Guild of Alberta Awards Program
Percy Page Centre, 3rd floor
11759 Groat Road N.W.
Edmonton, AB  T5M 3K6
Phone: (403) 422-8174. Fax: (403) 422-2663. Calgary office phone: (403) 265-2226.
Prize: $500 and a leather-bound copy of the winning book.
Open to residents of Alberta who have lived in the province for 12 of the previous 18 months.
Books may have been published anywhere in the world 1 January -
31 December. Deadline: 31 December. Only books published between 15-31 December are permitted to meet the delayed submission date:15 January.

### Sheila A. Egoff Children's Prize
West Coast Book Prize Society
700-10033 Davie Street
Vancouver, BC  V6E 1M7
Phone/fax: (604) 687-2405.
Prize: $2,000.
Awarded to the best book written for children 16 years and younger. Author and illustrator must be BC or Yukon residents or have lived in either for three years out of the last five. The book can have been published anywhere. Entry fee: $25. Deadline: 24 December.

### Arthur Ellis Awards
Crime Writers of Canada
3007 Kingston Road, Box 113
Scarborough, ON  M1M 1P1

Phone: (416) 782-3116. Fax: (416) 789-4682.
E-mail: <ap113@torfree.net>
Web site: <http://www.swifty.com/cwc/cwchome.htm>
Value of awards not available at time of printing.
Awarded for the best crime book in the following categories: novel by a pre-
viously published author; true crime; first novel; short crime story; play with a
crime theme; crime genre criticism/reference/anthology; and juvenile story.
Initial publication must be in the preceding year. Open to all residents of
Canada. No entry fee. Deadline: 31 January.

### The Marian Engel Award

Open to a female Canadian writer for a body of work with hope of future
contributions. Recipient selected by the Writers' Development Trust. Entries
by mail not accepted.

### The Hubert Evans Non-fiction Prize

West Coast Book Prize Society
700-1033 Davie Street
Vancouver, BC  V6E 1M7
Phone/fax: (604) 687-2405.
Prize: $2,000.
Awarded to the BC or Yukon author of the best original non-fiction literary
work (philosophy, belles lettres, biography, history etc.). Quality of writing
and research are major considerations. The book may have been published
anywhere. Entry fee: $25. Deadline: 24 December.

### *Event* Creative Non-fiction Contest

The Douglas College Review
P.O. Box 2503
New Westminster, BC  V3L 5B2
Phone: (604) 527-5293.
Prizes: $500 to each of three winners, plus publication payment.
Open to unpublished manuscripts to 5,000 words which explore the creative
non-fiction form. Contest format. Include SASE and phone number. Material
submitted or accepted for publication elsewhere is not eligible. Entry fee:
$16 (includes one-year subscription to magazine). Deadline: 15 April.

### Tom Fairley Award for Editorial Excellence

Fairley Award Coordinator
c/o Editors' Association of Canada
35 Spadina Road
Toronto, ON  M5R 2S9
Phone: (416) 534-7168. Fax: (416) 975-1839.
Prize: a mounted certificate.
Open to nomination only by the publisher or editor for excellence in free-
lance work in English or French during the calendar year. Any type of editing

on any type of written project is eligible. Deadline (nominations): 24 February. Deadline (supporting documentation): 3 March.

## Wallace K. Ferguson Prize
Canadian Historical Association
395 Wellington St.
Ottawa, ON  K1A 0N3
Phone: (613) 233-7885. Fax: (613) 567-3110.
Prize: $1,000.
Awarded to a Canadian citizen or landed immigrant for an outstanding scholarly book in a field of history other than Canadian, published during the past year. Diaries, textbooks, edited collections of essays, translations, or books of documents are not eligible. Write for further submission information. Deadline: 15 December.

## *Fiddlehead* Writing Contest
The *Fiddlehead* Campus House
P.O. Box 4400
Fredericton, NB  E3B 5A3
Phone: (506) 453-3501. Fax: (506) 453-4599.
Prizes: $300 best poem; $300 best story.
Themes vary each year. Ten pages per entry. Blind judging. Entry fee: $18 (includes one-year subscription). Deadline: 15 December.

## The Sheree Fitch Prize
Writers' Federation of New Brunswick
P.O. Box 37, Station A
Fredericton, NB  E3B 4Y2
Phone/fax: (506) 459-7228.
Prizes: $150; $100; $50.
Open to residents of New Brunswick 14–18 years old as of 1 January of contest year. Fiction in 1997, then alternating between poetry and fiction. Fiction entries no more than 15 pages (4,000 words). Poetry up to 100 lines or five poems. Original, unpublished work. Deadline: 14 February.

## Lionel Gelber Prize
Prize Manager
c/o Applause! Communications Inc.
398 Adelaide Street West, Suite 1007
Toronto, ON  M5V 1S7
Phone: (416) 504-7200. Fax: (416) 504-5647.
E-mail: <applause@idirect.com>
Prize: $50,000.
Awarded for a non-fiction title in the field of international relations, available in English or English translation. All entries must be submitted by the publisher. Deadline: 31 May.

### The Giller Prize
c/o Kelly Duffin
21 Steepleview Crescent
Richmond Hill, ON  L4C 9R1
Phone: (905) 508-5146. Fax: (905) 508-4469.
Prize: $25,000.
Awarded to the author of the best first edition, full length novel or short story collection by a Canadian citizen or permanent resident, published in English (either originally or in translation). In the case of translation, the original work must have been Canadian authored. No self-published books are eligible. For publication date eligibility request submission package.

### John Glassco Translation Prize
The Literary Translators' Association of Canada
3492, rue Laval
Montreal PQ  H2X 3C8
Phone: (514) 849-8540.
Prize: $500 and a one-year membership in the Literary Translators' Association of Canada.
Awarded for a first book-length literary translation into either English or French, from any language, published the previous year. The work must be by a Canadian citizen or landed immigrant. Deadline: 15 February.

### God Uses Ink Contest
*Faith Today*
M.I.P. Box 3745
Markham, ON  L3R 0Y4
Phone: (905) 479-5885. Fax: (905) 479-4742.
E-mail: <ft@efc-canada.com>
Web site: <http://www.efc-canada.com>
Prizes: $150 each for book categories; $100 each for other categories.
Categories: Short story; Novel; Third-person, non-fiction article; Personal essay/article; Non-fiction book; and a sixth category that changes annually.
Open to material by Canadian Christian writers published anywhere in the world during the previous year. Publication can be in Christian or secular media. Entry form must be attached to each single piece entered to limit of three. Entry fee: $20 /book; $10/article or story. Deadline: 1 April.

### Goldbook Literary Prize
Philip Murphy
501 Cambridge Street S.E.
Medicine Hat, AB  T1A 0T3
Phone: (403) 526-2524. Fax: (403) 526-8020.
E-mail: <Authmag@aol.com>
Web site: <http://members.aol.com/authmaga/authors.htm>

Prize: minimum $100 and one-year membership (value $100). Runner-up prizes vary in value.

Open to *Author Magazine* members only, writing all types of fiction, poetry, essays and commentary. To be eligible for prizes entrants must have progressed through publication in the preceding three sections of the magazine (Blue, Bronze, Silver).

## Government of Newfoundland and Labrador Arts and Letters Competition

The Secretary
Arts and Letters Committee
P.O. Box 1854
St. John's, NF  A1C 5P9
Phone: (709) 729-5253. Fax: (709) 729-5952.
Prizes: $600; $300; $100. Awarded in two divisions.

Junior division: 12–18 years; Senior division: 19 and over. For original works of fiction, non-fiction, poetry or drama by residents of Newfoundland or Labrador. A gold medal may be presented for outstanding achievement in any category. Deadline: 14 February.

## The Governor General's Awards for Literature

Canada Council
Writing & Publishing Section
350 Albert Street
P.O. Box 1047
Ottawa, ON  K1P 5V8
Phone: 1-800-263-5588. Fax: (613) 566-4410.
Awards: $10,000 in each category.

For the best book of fiction, non-fiction, poetry, drama, translation, children's literature and illustration in English and French. Open only to Canadian citizens. Deadline: 15 August.

## Short *Grain* Writing Contest

Editor
*Grain* magazine
P.O. Box 1154
Regina, SK  S4P 3B4
Phone: (306) 244-2828. Fax: (306) 244-0255.
E-mail: <grain.mag@sk.sympatico.ca>
Web site: <http://www.sasknet.com/corporate/skwriter>
Prizes: $500; $300; $200; Honourable Mentions in each category.

**1. Postcard Story:** a work of narrative fiction in 500 words or less.

**2. Prose poem:** a lyric poem written in prose paragraph(s) in 500 words or less.

**3. Dramatic Monologue:** a self-contained speech given by a single character in 500 words or less. Write for complete rules. Deadline (all categories): 31 January.

### The Great Canadian Haiku Contest
c/o *Geist* Magazine
103-1014 Homer Street
Vancouver, BC  V6B 2W9
Fax: (604) 669-8250.
E-mail: <geist@geist.com>
Prize: Great Canadian Haiku Trophy plus unspecified cash and merchandise.
Reminder: a Canadian haiku has three lines of five, seven and five syllables each. In addition, a Canadian haiku almost always makes reference to the Great Canadian Season: winter. Maximum entry is five haiku. Entry fee: $5. Deadline: midnight, 21 December.

### The Great Canadian Story Contest
*Storyteller* Magazine
43 Lightfoot Place
Kanata, ON  K2L 3M3
Prizes: Not available at time of printing.
Open to Canadian citizens (at home or abroad) or residents, submitting original fiction of 2,000–6,000 words which must contain a uniquely Canadian element (theme, setting, institution, politics, social phenomenon etc.). Stories will be judged on their literary merit and entertainment value, those with an uplifting or positive theme are preferred. Complete guidelines available on request. No entry fee. Deadline: 15 April.

### Roderick Haig-Brown Regional Award
West Coast Book Prize Society
700-1033 Davie Street
Vancouver, BC  V6E 1M7
Phone/fax: (604) 687-2405.
Prize: $2,000.
Awarded to the author(s) of the original book which contributes most to the enjoyment and understanding of British Columbia (people, history, geography, oceanography etc.). The author must reside in BC. Location of publisher unimportant. Entry fee: $25. Deadline: 24 December.

### Harbourfront Festival Prize
410 Queen's Quay West
Toronto, ON  M5V 2Z3
Prizes: total $11,000.
For a Canadian writer in mid-career for his or her contribution to Canadian letters and for efforts on behalf of other writers. By invitation only. More information available on request.

## The Hawthorne Society Poetry Contest

The Hawthorne Society
1051 Roslyn Road
Victoria, BC  V8S 4R4
Prize: $500, publication in Society's award-winning series of chapbooks and a public reading.
A selection of poems from runners-up will be published in the annual *Hawthorne Anthology*. Open to all Canadian residents who have not yet published a book-length collection of verse. Contestants send 12–30 previously unpublished poems in a single-spaced manuscript including a suitable title. Blind judging. Further details available on request. Entry fee: $25. Deadline: 30 April.

## The Robert C. Hayes StoryBook Script Writing Contest

Script Writing Competition
StoryBook Theatre
3530 11A Street N.E., Bay #3
Calgary, AB  T2E 6M7
Phone: (403) 291-2247. Fax: (403) 291-9677.
Prize: $100, script workshop and possible stage production of the work.
Open to scripts for children's entertainment (ages 3–7 with parent appeal), never previously produced on stage. Approximate length 60 minutes or several 10–20 minute playlets to one hour total. Deadline: 15 September.

## The Heaven Chapbook Prize (biennial)

Manitoba Writers' Guild Inc.
206-100 Arthur Street
Winnipeg, MB  R3B 1H3
Phone: (204) 942-6134. Fax: (204) 942-5754.
E-mail: <mbwriter@escape.ca>
Prize: $250.
Awarded biennially to a Manitoba writer. Next offered in 1998 for chapbooks published in 1996 and 1997. Deadline: 15 December.

## The John Hirsch Award

The Manitoba Writers' Guild Inc.
206-100 Arthur Street
Winnipeg, MB  R3B 1H3
Phone: (204) 942-6134. Fax: (204) 942-5754.
E-mail: <mbwriter@escape.ca>
Prize: $2,500.
Awarded to the most promising writer living in Manitoba who has a publication or production track record but has not yet received national or international recognition. Eligible genres include fiction, poetry, creative non-fiction and playwriting. Complete information available on request.

### Hoffmann-La Roche Awards for Excellence in Vitamin Nutrition Journalism

Canadian Science Writers' Association
P.O. Box 75, Station A
Toronto, ON  M5W 1A2
Phone: (416) 928-9624. Fax: (416) 960-0528.
E-mail: <cswa@interlog.com>
Prizes: Three of $1,000.
Open to Canadian citizens or residents of Canada writing in either English or French whose work has been published during the preceding year. Full details and entry form available on request. Deadline: 15 February.

### HOLLYWOOD NORTH Feature Screenplay Competition

Canadian Screenwriters Alliance
24 Watts Avenue
West Royalty Industrial Park
Charlottetown, PE  C1E 1B0
Phone: (902) 628-3880. Fax: (902) 368-1813.
E-mail: <evie@isn.net>
Prizes: $500, representation by Canadian Screenwriters Alliance, and a conference pass; other finalists receive a conference pass and mini critique by an industry professional.
Open to writers who have not yet earned money writing for TV or film. Work must be the original work of applicant(s) and in Motion Picture Industry standard screenplay format. All scripts entered must be registered with a writers' guild. Full details and entry form available on request. Entry fee: $30/script. Deadline: 31 December.

### The Hope Writers' Guild Poetry Contest

P.O. Box 1683
Hope, BC  V0X 1L0
Phone: (604) 869-9848.
Prizes: $200; $100; $50; three Honourable Mentions.
Submit up to three unpublished poems, any style, any theme, to 100 lines in total. No poems returned. Entry fee: $5/poem or $10/three poems. Deadline: 31 July.

### The Amelia Frances Howard-Gibbon Award for Illustration

Chairperson
Amelia Frances Howard-Gibbon Award Committee
c/o CLA Membership Services
200 Elgin St., Suite 602
Ottawa, ON  K2P 1L5
Phone: (613) 232-9625. Fax: (613) 563-9895.
Award: a handsome medal.

Awarded to a Canadian citizen or permanent resident who is the illustrator of an outstanding children's book for ages up to 14 years, published in Canada during the previous calendar year. Award nominations accepted from CLA membership and publishers only.

## Humanities and Social Sciences Federation of Canada Scholarly Book Awards
410-151 Slater Street
Ottawa, ON  K1P 5H3
Phone: (613) 234-1269. Fax: (613) 236-4853.
E-mail: <secaspp@aspp.hssfc.ca>
### 1. The Harold Adams Innes Prize
Prize: $1,000.
Awarded to the best English-language book published in the field of Social Sciences.
### 2. The Jean-Charles Falardeau Prize
Prize: $1,000.
Awarded to the best French-language book published in the field of Social Sciences.
### 3. The Raymond Klibansky Prize (English)
Prize: $1,000.
Awarded to the best book in English in the field of Humanities.
### 4. The Raymond Klibansky Prize (French)
Prize: $1,000.
Awarded for a collection of scholarly works.
Complete information for all awards available on request.

## IODE Book Award
The IODE Municipal Chapter of Toronto
40 St. Clair Avenue East, Suite 205
Toronto, ON  M4T 1M9
Phone: (416) 925-5078.
Prize: $1,000.
Open to the author or illustrator of a children's book written by a Canadian citizen and published in Canada. Deadline: 1 December.

## IODE Violet Downey Book Award
National Chapter IODE of Canada Head Office
40 Orchard View Blvd., Suite 254
Toronto, ON  M4R 1B9
Prize: $3,000.
Awarded for the best children's book of at least 500 words. Deadline: 31 January.

## International 3-day Novel-Writing Contest
Anvil Press
204-A, 175 East Broadway
Vancouver, BC V5T 1W2
Prize: Publication of winning novel.
Start writing 12.01 a.m. on Saturday of Labour Day weekend and stop at or before 12 midnight the following Monday. Novels must be submitted in contest format. No paper clips, staples or folders. Participants may use the rest of the week to have manuscripts typed or to convert disk to hard copy. Finished novel must be accompanied by a non-legal statement signed by a witness confirming novel's completion over the Labour Day weekend. Two-person collaborations accepted. Outline only permitted prior to contest. Entry form required. Non-refundable entry fee: $25. Registration deadline: 30 August. Deadline (manuscript submission): Saturday after Labour Day.

## The Laura Jamieson Prize
Chairperson
Laura Jamieson Prize
c/o CRIAW/ICREF
151 Slater Street, Suite 408
Ottawa, ON K1P 5H3
Phone: (613) 563-0681. Fax: (613) 563-0682.
E-mail: <criaw@worldlink.ca>
Web site: <http://www.worldlink.ca/~criaw>
Prize: laminated certificate.
Awarded by the Canadian Research Institute for the Advancement of Women for a non-fiction feminist book by a Canadian author. Given on an alternating basis for work in each official language published during the previous two years. (In 1997 it will be given for the best English-language book imprinted 1995 or 1996).The work must advance the knowledge and/or understanding of women's experience; it may be theoretical, a monograph, or an edited collection drawn from any discipline, or be multi-disciplinary. Deadline: 1 June.

## The Joker is Wild Humour Contest
c/o Valley Writers' Guild
P.O. Box 32
Spencerville, ON K0E 1X0
Prizes: $75; $50; $25. Awarded in each of two categories. Winning entries will be published in *The Grist Mill*.
Open to writers in Eastern Ontario/Western Quebec only, for unpublished work in English. Humorous verse to 40 lines. Humorous prose to 750 words. Submit two copies of each piece: one with name, address, and phone number, the other anonymous. Entry fee: $3/entry. (Make cheque or money order out to: Valley Writers' Guild.) Deadline: third Friday in February.

## The Jane Jordan Poetry Contest
96 Rochester Street
Ottawa, ON K1R 7L8
Phone: (613) 235-2783.
E-mail: <az241@freenet.carleton.ca> or <dk983@freenet.carleton.ca>
Prizes: $250; $150; $100; and publication in *Bywords* magazine.
Open to poets resident in the National Capital Region writing in English.
Poems, any subject or style, must not exceed 100 lines. No restriction on
number of poems submitted. Blind judging. Entry fee: $2 per poem (Make
cheque or money order payable to: the TREE Reading Series.)
Deadline: 28 February.

## Journey Prize
McClelland & Stewart
481 University Avenue, Suite 900
Toronto, ON M5G 2E9
Phone: (416) 598-1114. Fax: (416) 598-7764.
Prize: $10,000.
Awarded to a new and developing writer of distinction. Winner is selected
from among the nine stories in the *Journey Prize Anthology*, itself compris-
ing selected submissions made by literary journals across Canada.

## Kalamalka New Writers Competition (biennial)
Kalamalka Press
7000 College Way
Vernon, BC V1B 2N5
Phone: (250) 545-7291. Fax: (250) 545-3277.
E-mail: <kalpress@okanagan.bc.ca>
Prize: publication and marketing of the book, royalty payments at 10 per
cent of retail value, ten free copies and a book launch in Vernon, BC, with
travel and accommodation included.
Open to Canadian citizens and landed immigrants who have not yet published in book form in any genre. Entrants must have a substantial collection
of poetry. The poems may have been previously published in anthologies or
periodicals. Contact for next deadline.

## Kingston Literary Awards
Kingston Regional Arts Council
P.O. Box 1005
Kingston, ON K7L 4X8
Prizes: Up to value of $1,000 total.
Open to residents of Frontenac, Lennox and Addington, and Leeds-Grenville
for an original story to 2,000 words. Limit one per entrant. Computer printout
accepted but not fax entries. No entries returned. Blind judging.
Entry fee: $5. Deadline: 31 March.

## Henry Kreisel Award for Best First Book
Writers Guild of Alberta Awards Program
Percy Page Centre, 3rd floor
11759 Groat Road N.W.
Edmonton, AB T5M 3K6
Phone: (403) 422-8174. Fax: (403) 422-2663. Calgary office phone: (403) 265-2226.
Prize: $500 and a copy of the winning book.
Open to writers in Alberta who have resided in the province for 12 of the previous 18 months. The books may have been published anywhere in the world, 1 January–31 December. Submit eight copies. Deadline: 31 December. Only books published 15–31 December are permitted to submit to delayed deadline: 15 January.

## The Cecilia Lamont Literary Contest
c/o White Rock and Surrey Writers' Club
1334 Johnston Road
White Rock, BC V4B 3Z2
Phone: (604) 536-8333.
Prizes: $75 plus engraved plaque; $50 plus certificate; $25 plus certificate; three Honourable Mentions.
Open to BC residents only. For poetry, short stories (fact or fiction), and articles previously unpublished for a fee. Maximum length: prose 1,000 words; poetry 36 lines. Entry fee: $6 per piece ($5 each if 4 or more entered). Deadline: 31 October.

## Gerald Lampert Memorial Award
The League of Canadian Poets
54 Wolseley Street, Suite 204
Toronto, ON M5T 1A5
Phone: (416) 504-1657. Fax: (416) 504-0059.
E-mail: <league@io.org>
Prize: $1,000.
Awarded to a Canadian citizen or landed immigrant for a first book of poetry conforming to the UNESCO definition, published in the year of entry. Entry fee: $15 per title. New deadline: 31 December.

## The Herb Lampert Student Writing Award
Canadian Science Writers' Association
P.O. Box 75, Station A
Toronto, ON M5W 1A2
Phone: (416) 928-9624. Fax: (416) 960-0528.
E-mail: <cswa@interlog.com>
Prize: $750.
Open to any student science writer who has a science article published in a

student or other newspaper or magazine, or aired on a radio or TV station in Canada. Write for more information and entry form.

**Archibald Lampman Award**
ARC
P.O. Box 7368
Ottawa, ON  K1L 8E4
Award: $400.
Awarded for the best book of poems published by a resident of the National Capital Region in the previous calendar year. Deadline: 28 February.

**Fred Landon Award**
The Ontario Historical Society
34 Parkview Avenue
Willowdale, ON  M2N 3Y2
Phone: (416) 226-9011. Fax: (416) 226-2740.
Prize: framed certificate accompanied by a copy of the citation acknowledging the winner's contribution to the heritage community.
Awarded for the best book on regional history in Ontario published during the past three years. Entry form available on request. Deadline: 30 October.

**The Stephen Leacock Memorial Medal for Humour**
Stephen Leacock Associates
c/o 203 Martin Drive
Orillia, ON  L3V 3P4
Phone: (705) 325-6546.
Prize: $5,000 and a silver medal.
Awarded for the best book by a Canadian citizen or landed immigrant, published during the previous calendar year with humour as the major element of its content. Anthologies are not eligible. No part of the entered book must have been previously published in book form. Submit ten copies. Entry fee: $25. Prefer to receive entries in September/October.
Deadline: 31 December.

**Stephen Leacock Poetry & Limerick Awards**
The Orillia International Poetry Festival
P.O. Box 2307
Orillia, ON  L3V 6S2
Web site: <http://bconnex.net/-poetry> (for winners list only. Available 31 May.)
Prizes: Poetry: $5,000; $1,000; $500. Junior Poetry: $150; $75; $25.
Limericks: $1,000; $500; $200.
Multiple entries accepted. Put name and address on reverse of each page (include e-mail address if available). Poetry category: unpublished poems to 50 lines. Entry fee: $5/poem. (Junior entrants under 16 as of 31 December.) Limerick entry fee: $10 for 3 limericks. No e-mail entries accepted.
Deadline: 31 January.

## Literary Writes

Federation of BC Writers
890 West Pender Street, Suite 600
Vancouver, BC  V6C 1J9
Phone: (604) 688-2057. Fax: (604) 683-8269.
E-mail: <fedbcwrt@pinc.com>
Web site: <http://www.swifty.com/bcwa>
Prize: not listed.
A genre-specific competition open to BC writers only. Send SASE for rules.
Opens September.

## The Dorothy Livesay Poetry Award

West Coast Book Prize Society
700-1033 Davie Street
Vancouver, BC  V6E 1M7
Phone/fax: (604) 687-2405.
Prize: $2,000.
Awarded to the author of the best work of poetry. No anthologies or "best of"
collections. Author must be a resident of BC or Yukon or have lived there
three of the last five years. Entry fee: $25. Deadline: 24 December.

## Pat Lowther Memorial Award

The Canadian League of Poets
54 Wolseley Street, Suite 204
Toronto, ON  M5T 1A5
Phone: (416) 504-1657. Fax: (416) 703-0059.
E-mail: <league@io.org>
Award: $1,000.
Given for a book of poetry by a woman who is a Canadian citizen or landed
immigrant. The book must conform to UNESCO definition and have been
published in the year of submission. If its contents are "selected" or "collect-
ed", it must contain at least 50 per cent new material. If submitted in a lan-
guage other than English, it must be accompanied by a translation.
Entry fee: $15. New deadline: 31 December.

## Sir John A. Macdonald Prize

Canadian Historical Association
395 Wellington Street
Ottawa, ON  K1A 0N3
Phone: (613) 233-7885. Fax: (613) 567-3110.
Prize: $1,000.
Awarded by the Canadian Historical Association for the non-fiction work of
Canadian history "judged to have made the most significant contribution to
an understanding of the Canadian past". Diaries, textbooks, edited collec-
tions of essays, translations, or books of documents are excluded. Authors

of eligible books are encouraged to ensure their publishers submit their works. Deadline: 15 December.

**C. B. Macpherson Prize** (biennial)
The Canadian Political Science Association
1 Stewart Street, Suite 205
Ottawa, ON  K1N 6H7
Phone: (613) 564-4026.
Prize: $750.
Awarded to the best book published, in English or French, in the field of political science during the previous two years. Books must be single-authored. No text books, edited texts or collections of essays will be considered. Deadline for next submission: 10 December, 1997.

***Malahat Review* Contests** (biennial)
Editor
*The Malahat Review*
University of Victoria
P.O. Box 1700
Victoria, BC  V8W 2Y2
Phone: (250) 721-8524.
E-mail: <malahat@uvic.ca>
**1. Long Poem**
Prize: $400 plus $25 per printed page for each of two winning entries.
Blind judging. Entry fee: $25 (includes a one-year subscription). Deadline: 1 March, **1999**.
**2. Novella Contest**
Prize: $400 plus $25 per printed page for the winning entry.
Blind judging. Entry fee: $25 (includes a one-year subscription). Deadlines: 1 March, **1998**; 1 March, **2000**.

**Manitoba Branch CAA Contests**
Manitoba Branch
Canadian Authors Association
208-63 Albert Street
Winnipeg, MB  R3B 1G4
Phone: (204) 947-0512.
**1. Adult and Young Writer's Short Story Contest**
Prizes: $25–$200. Awarded in each category.
Open only to Manitoba residents for original, unpublished stories in the following categories: Adult; Junior Division (grades 7-9); Senior Division (grades 10-12). Check for entry fee and deadline.
**2. Non-fiction and Poetry Contest**
Prizes: $25-$200.
Open only to Manitoba residents for original, unpublished works of non-fiction

and poetry in Adult and Young Writer categories. Check for entry fee and deadline.

## McNally Robinson Awards
c/o Manitoba Writers' Guild Inc.
206-100 Arthur Street
Winipeg, MB R3B 1H3
Phone: (204) 942-6134. Fax: (204) 942-5754.
E-mail: <mbwriter@escape.ca>

### 1. Book for Young People Award
Award: $1,000.
Presented to the writer of the young person's book judged the best written by a Manitoba author and published in the calendar year of the award. Eligible writers must have resided in Manitoba for three out of the last five years as well as one of the past two. Deadline: 16 December. Only books published 16–30 December will be accepted at late deadline: 31 December.

### 2. Book of the Year Award
Award: $2,500.
Open to Manitoba residents for non-academic titles published in English during the year of submission. Residency requirement: three of the last five years including one of the last two. Books written by more than one author are eligible if all authors meet the residency requirements. Deadline: 16 December. Only books published 16–30 December will be accepted at late deadline: 31 December.

## The Michenor Award for Meritorious Public Service Journalism
The Michenor Awards Foundation/La Fondation des Prix Michenor
*The Ottawa Citizen*
1101 Baxter Road
P.O. Box 5020
Ottawa, ON K2C 3M4
Prize: handsome bronze casting on a marble base.
Entries must come from a senior member of the news organization. Complete details available on request. Entry fee: $25. Deadline: 1 February of the following year.

## The Gordon Montador Award
Awarded by The Writers' Development Trust for a non-fiction book on contemporary social issues. Shared jointly between writer and publisher. Juried by Canadian booksellers. Judged on work and promotion. Entries by mail not accepted.

## Lucy Maud Montgomery PEI Children's Literature Award
Island Literary Awards
PEI Council of the Arts
115 Richmond Street
Charlottetown, PE C1A 1H7

Phone: (902) 368-4410.
Prizes: $500; $200; $100.
Open only to Island residents for a story written for children 5–12 years of age. One story, maximum length 60 pages, will constitute one entry. Multiple entries permitted. Blind judging. Entry fee: $8. Deadline: 15 February.

## Montreal Grand Prix Book Award

Service de la culture
5650 rue d'Iberville, 4e etage
Montreal PQ  H2G 3E4
Phone: (514) 872-1160. Fax: (514) 872-1153.
E-mail: <paul_langlois@ville.montreal.qc.ca>
Web site: <http://www.ville.montreal.qc.ca/culture/>
Prize: $10,000.
Offered by the City of Montreal to the author or co-authors of a work of creativity, analysis, anthology or literary/artistic/socio-historic reference in either official language published by an author or editor in the city of Montreal. Phone for deadline.

## {m}Öthêr Tøñgué Press

290 Fulford-Ganges Road
Salt Spring Island, BC  V8K 2K6
Fax: (250) 537-4725.
Prizes: $400; $200; plus publication of both as special Limited Edition chapbooks.
Awarded to the two best Canadian manuscripts of unpublished poetry in English. Submit 10-15 typed, numbered pages with title and brief biography. Blind judging. Write for complete details. Entry fee: $20.
Deadline: 30 November.

## The Dora Mavor Moore Awards (DMMA)

Executive Director
Toronto Theatre Alliance
720 Bathurst Street, Suite 403
Toronto, ON  M5S 2R4
Phone: 1-800-541-0499. Fax: (416) 536-3463.
E-mail: <tte@idirect.com>
Web site: <http://www.tta/ucalgary.ca/tta/>
Prizes: Each winner receives a bronze statue.
There are two categories in which the writer receives an award for the outstanding new play, musical or revue and one for the outstanding new play only, namely the large, mid-size and small theatre divisions. Productions which open 1 May–30 April of the following year are eligible for consideration for the DMMA of a given season. Those which preview during this period but do not officially open until after 30 April will be eligible for the DMMA of the following season. Complete details available on request.

## Morguard Literary Awards
Real Estate Institute of Canada
5407 Eglington Avenue West
Toronto, ON  M9C 5K6
Phone: (416) 695-9000. Fax: (416) 695-7230.
Awards: $2,000 (one in each category.)
Offered to encourage excellence in real estate journalism. One for practising industry writers, the other for academic writers. Entries must be previously unpublished articles or speeches of 3,000–6,000 words. Deadline: 15 April.

## Muriel Morrison Awards
Peterborough Branch
Canadian Authors Association
P.O. Box 2134
Peterborough, ON  K0J 7Y4
Prizes: individual keeper plaque and autographed book by a CAA author suitable for the grade level in each of three categories.
Open to primary, junior, and intermediate grades in Ontario only. Entrants must submit one piece of original creative writing. No restriction on format or length. Registration forms available from the branch.
Deadline: 31 December.

## National Capital Writing Contest
To locate information flyers and to obtain current Convenor's address, Phone: (613) 829-8220. Fax: (613) 829-4616.
Prizes: $100 (cheque); $50 (gift certificate); $25 (gift certificate). Prizes awarded in each of three categories.
Organized by the Ottawa Branch of the Canadian Authors Association, co-sponsored by *The Ottawa Citizen* and six independent bookstores. Open to writers in the National Capital Region working in English. Alternate years poetry/prose. (1997 is poetry). Deadline: 15 November.

## National Canadian Playwriting Competition
The Director
Canadian Playwriting Competition
Ottawa Little Theatre
400 King Edward Avenue
Ottawa, ON  K1N 7M7
Phone: (613) 233-8948.
Awards: total $1,800 and include medals.
Open to professional and non-professional playwrights who are Canadian citizens or landed immigrants for a one-act play in English. Entry fee: $35.
Deadline: 31 May.

## National Magazine Awards
National Magazine Awards Foundation
109 Vanderhoof Avenue, Suite 207
Toronto, ON  M4G 2H7
Phone: (416) 422-1358. Fax: (416) 422-4762.
Awards: President's Medal $3,000; Gold Awards $1,500; Silver Awards $500; Honourable Mentions.
Now offered in 30 categories with individual information available on request. Deadline: January (exact date to be announced).

## National Newspaper Awards
NNA Secretary
890 Yonge Street, Suite 1100
Toronto, ON  L6M 1Z6
Phone: (416) 923-3567. Fax: (416) 923-7206.
E-mail: <bcantley@fox.nstn.ca>
Web site: <http://www.nna-ccj.ca>
Prizes: $1,500; $250 for each of two runners-up in each category.
Open to all writers whose works have first appeared in a Canadian daily newspaper during the preceding year. Selected for entry at editor's choice. Categories: Features, Criticism, Sports, Business Reporting, Enterprise Reporting, Spot News Reporting, Editorials, Columns, Cartoons, Photography, and Design. Deadline: 7 January.

## National Poetry Contest
The League of Canadian Poets
54 Wolseley Street
Toronto, ON  M5T 1A5
Phone: (416) 504-1657. Fax: (416) 703-0059.
E-mail: <league@io.org>
Awards: $1,000; $750; $500.
Open to all Canadians. Poems must be unpublished, up to 75 lines, any subject, type or style. Winners and 50 runners-up will be published in a soft-cover anthology for national distribution. Copyright remains with poet. Entry fee: $6 per poem. Deadline: 31 January.

## The Hilda Neatby Prize in Women's History
Canadian Historical Association
c/o The Hilda Neatby Prize Committee
395 Wellington Street
Ottawa, ON  K1A 0N3
Phone: (613) 233-7885. Fax: (613) 567-3110.
Prize: $50 (English); $50 (French).
Awarded to encourage publication of scholarly articles in women's history and gender history as it relates to women, in Canadian journals and books.

Any original, academic article published in Canada during the preceding year is eligible for nomination. Send nominations and three copies of the article. Deadline: 1 February.

### Nepean Public Library Short Story Contest
Communications Office
Nepean Public Library
101 Centrepointe Drive
Nepean, ON  K2G 5K7
Phone: (613) 727-6646.
Prizes: $500; $250; $100.
Available to residents of the Regional Municipality of Ottawa–Carleton over 18 years of age writing in English. Work must be original, unpublished and up to 2,500 words. Entry fee: $5. Deadline: 1 April.

### New Muse Award
P.O. Box 596, Station A
Fredericton, NB  E3B 5A6
Phone/fax: (506) 454-5127.
E-mail: <jblades@nbnet.nb.ca>
Prize: Publication as a trade paperback by Broken Jaw Press.
Open to poetry manuscripts of 50–65 pages of which individual poems may have been published. Entrants must not have published a first full-size poetry book (UNESCO definition). Entry fee: $15. Deadline: 31 March.

### *New Voices* Playwriting Competition
Theatre PEI
550 University Avenue
Charlottetown, PE  C1A 4P3
Phone: (902) 566-0321. Fax: (902) 566-0420.
Prizes: $1,000 (full length); $400; $200; $100 (one-act); $50 (best one-act comedy).
Open to professional and non-professional writers born or resident in Prince Edward Island submitting original work not previously produced or awarded a prize. Maximum of two plays per category. Winner of first prize in any *New Voices* category will be ineligible in that category the following year. Entry fee: $5 per play. Deadline: 15 February.

### Niagara Poetry Competition
Competition Chair
CAA Niagara Branch
P.O. Box 56
Welland, ON  L3B 5N9
Prizes: $100; $50; $25.
Open to all writers in the Niagara peninsula. Results in the publication of an anthology. Write for submission details.

## The bpNichol Chap-Book Award
316 Dupont Street
Toronto, ON  M5R 1V9
Prize: $1,000.
Offered for the best poetry chapbook (10–40 pages) in English published in Canada during the previous year. Poet or publisher must submit three copies. Deadline: 30 March.

## Northern Ontario Poetry Competition
White Mountain Publications
Northern Ontario Poetry Competition
P.O. Box 5180
R.R. #2
New Liskeard, ON  P0J 1P0
Prizes: Small cash awards will be given to first-, second- and third-place winners.
Open to all residents of Northern Ontario whose postal codes begin with "P". Poems must be titled, previously unpublished, of up to 50 lines (including title) of 44 characters and typed. (Co-sponsored by Canadian Authors Association Temiskaming Branch.) Entry fee: $3 per poem.
Deadline: 31 March.

## Nova Scotia Student Writing Contest
Canadian Authors Association
c/o 85 Collins Grove
Dartmouth, NS  B2W 4G3
Prizes: $50; $25; a book (suitable to the age of contestant) in both English and French categories.
Open to Grade Six students in Nova Scotia only, writing in either official language, as advertised in *The Teacher*. Three pieces per classroom may be entered either as essays or fiction stories of 200–300 words, or narrative or descriptive poems of 40–60 lines. Each entrant whose work is of a sufficiently high standard will receive a certificate of recognition. Deadline: 1 March.

## Howard O'Hagan Award for Short Fiction
Writers Guild of Alberta Awards Program
Percy Page Centre, 3rd floor
11759 Groat Road N.W.
Edmonton, AB  T5M 3K6
Phone: (403) 422-8174. Fax: (403) 422-2663.
Calgary office phone: (403) 265-2226.
Prize: $500 and a leather-bound copy of the winning book.
Open to writers resident in Alberta for 12 of the previous 18 months. Books may have been published anywhere in the world, 1 January–31 December. Deadline: 31 December. Only books published 15-31 December are permitted to submit by the delayed date: 15 January.

### The *Ottawa Citizen* Non-fiction Award

The Co-ordinator
*Ottawa Citizen* Award for Non-fiction
399 Sunnyside Avenue
Ottawa, ON  K1S 0S3
Phone: (613) 730-5620.
Prize: $1,000.
Offered for a non-fiction book written by a resident of the *Citizen*'s circulation area, professionally published in English the previous calendar year. Edited anthologies not eligible. Submit three copies. Deadline: 7 February.

### PEI Feature Article Award

Island Literary Awards
PEI Council of the Arts
115 Richmond Street
Charlottetown, PE  C1A 1H7
Prizes: $500; hand-carved stone lamp; $100.
Open to Island residents for one original feature article intended for print or broadcast per entry. Work can be either unpublished or published within the last twelve months. No length limit. Multiple entries permitted. Blind judging. Entry fee: $8. Deadline: 15 February.

### People's Political Poem Contests

*People's Poetry Letter*
P.O. Box 51531
2060 Queen Street East
Toronto, ON  M4E 3V7
Prizes: $300 and book prizes in each contest, plus publication in *People's Poetry Letter*.
Five winning poems selected in each contest. All entrants receive a year's subscription to *People's Poetry Letter*. Entries limited to two per contest. Form required. Entry fee: $15. Deadlines: 15 February; 15 April.

### Periodical Writers Association of Canada Magazine and Newspaper Writing Contest

Director
PWAC National Office
54 Wolseley Street, Suite 203
Toronto, ON  M5T 1A5
Phone: (416) 504-1645. Fax: (416) 703-0059.
E-mail: <pwac@cycor.ca>
Web site: <http://www.cycor.ca/PWAC>
Prizes: $2,000; $1,000; $500.
For unpublished manuscripts of 1,200–2,500 words by a Canadian writer of non-fiction. Future contests will be held in the fall. Deadline: not available at time of printing.

## Periodical Marketers of Canada Canadian Letters Awards

1007-175 Bloor Street East
South Tower
Toronto, ON  M4W 3R8
Phone: (416) 968-7218. Fax: (416) 968-6182.
Prizes: two awards of a statuette plus $5,000 grant to the educational institution of the winners' choice.
This award, which replaces the PMC Authors Awards, recognizes achievement in writing, publishing and administration of literary and literacy programs in Canada. No external submissions accepted.

## Playwrights Union of Canada Monologue Competition

54 Wolseley Street, 2nd floor
Toronto, ON  M5T 2P3
Phone: (416) 703-0201. Fax: (416) 703-0059.
E-mail: <cdplays@interlog.com>
Web site: <http://www.puc.ca>
Prize: $500.
Open to all playwrights and writers for a monologue in English up to 75 lines, not previously published or produced in any format. The winner and ten Honourable Mentions to be published in *CanPlay*, PUC's bi-monthly news magazine. Entry fee: $10 per monologue. Deadline: 31 January.

## Pottersfield Portfolio Compact Fiction/Short Poem Contest

Competition Judges
Pottersfield Portfolio
P.O. Box 27094
Halifax, NS  B3H 4M8
Phone/fax: (902) 443-9178.
E-mail: <lcolford@is.dal.ca>  or  <saundc@atcon.com>
Prizes: $150 in each category.
Poetry limit of 20 lines with three unpublished poems per entry. Prose limit of 1,500 words with two unpublished stories per entry. Blind judging. Entry fee: $20 (which includes one-year subscription to the magazine).
Deadline: 14 February.

## *Prairie Fire* Writing Contests

423-100 Arthur Street
Winnipeg, MB  R3B 1H3
Phone: (204) 943-9066.
All entry fees ($24) include a one-year subscription to the magazine.
**1. Poetry**
Prizes: $300; $200; $100.
Up to three poems of no more than 30 lines per entry. Deadline: 30 June.
**2. Two-Minute Tales (or A.S.A.P.'s Fables)**
Prizes: five of $100.

Up to three pieces of postcard fiction or prose poetry of no more than 500 words. Deadline: 31 September.

### 3. Short Fiction
Prizes: $300; $200; $100.
One story per entry to a maximum of 3,000 words. Deadline: 30 November.

### 4. Long Short Story
Prizes: $300; $200; $100.
One story per entry to a maximum of 20,000 words. Deadline: 31 December.

### 5. Science Fiction
Prizes: $350; $250; $150.
One story per entry to a maximum of 3,000 words. Deadline: 28 February.

### 6. Creative Non-fiction
Prizes: $300; $200; $100.
One work per entry to a maximum of 3,000 words. Deadline: 30 April.

### Prickly Poetry Contest
Filedelphia
60 King Street West
Dundas, ON  L9H 1T8
Phone: (905) 627-8960. Fax: (905) 627-0776.
E-mail: <file@interlynx.net>
Web site: <http://www.the-web.net/filedelphia>
Prizes: amounts vary up to $300, and include publication in literary magazine and in an anthology published by Filedelphia.
Open in two categories (under 15 years of age, and 15 and over) for poems up to 40 lines. Looking for rants, bitches and complaints that can be humorous or serious. No geographical restriction on entry but winners should be able to attend the Dundas Cactus Festival (mid-August) at own expense, to perform their poetry. Arrangements will be made to read work of those unable to attend. Deadline: 1 August.

### The Prism Awards
90 Venice Crescent
Thornhill, ON  L4J 7T1
Phone: (905) 881-2507. Fax: (905) 881-8703.
In Western Canada phone: (403) 932-24331 or fax: (403) 248-3730.
For entry forms phone: (905) 451-1725 or fax: (905) 451-2035 in September.
Prizes: $500 and a trophy to winner in each of five categories.
Open to unedited, original stories in two age ranges: children 7–10 and 11–14. Judged on original thought and perspectives on life. Story categories, which include one for work in French, change annually.
Deadline: 26 January.

### *PRISM* Short Fiction Contest
*PRISM international* Short Fiction Contest
Creative Writing Program
University of BC
E462-1866 Main Mall
Vancouver, BC  V6T 1Z1
Phone: (604) 822-2514. Fax: (604) 822-3616.
E-mail: <prism@unixg.ubc.ca>
Web site: <http://www.arts.ubc.ca/crwr/prism/prism.html>
Prizes: $2,000; $200 to each of five runners up.
All entrants receive a one-year subscription to *PRISM*. All winners will be paid for publication at $20/page. Entry fee: $15 plus $5 per story.
Deadline: 1 December.

### Le Prix litteraire des caisses populaires (biennial)
c/o The Manitoba Writers' Guild Inc.
206-100 Arthur Street
Winnipeg, MB  R3B 1H3
Phone: (204) 942-6134. Fax: (204) 942-5754.
E-mail: <mbwriter@escape.ca>
Prize: $1,000.
Offered to the Manitoba writer whose published book or produced play is judged best French-language work. The author's contribution to Franco-Manitoban literature may be taken into consideration. Deadline: 20 January.

### QSPELL Awards
1200 Atwater Avenue
Montreal, PQ  H3Z 1X4
Phone/fax: (514) 933-0878.
E-mail: <qspell@total.net>
1. Fiction; Non-fiction; Poetry
Prizes: $2,000 in each category.
### 2. QSPELL/FEWQ Best Book Award
Prize: $500.
To support English-language writing by Quebec residents who have lived in the province for three of the past five years. Entry fee (both awards): $10.
Deadline: 31 May.

### The Thomas Head Raddell Atlantic Fiction Award
The Writers' Federation of Nova Scotia
1809 Barrington Street, Suite 901
Halifax, NS  B3J 3K8
Phone: (902) 423-8116. Fax: (902) 422-0881.
E-mail: <writers1@fox.nstn.ca>
Prize: $4,000.

Awarded by the Writers' Federation of Nova Scotia in conjunction with The Writers' Development Trust, for a work of outstanding adult fiction (novels or full-length collections of short stories) in either official language. Anthologies not accepted but works can have been co-authored. Open only to residents of the Atlantic Provinces. To enter, send four copies. No entry form required. Deadline: 19 April.

### Regional Municipality of Ottawa–Carleton Book Awards
Arts Office
Regional Municipality of Ottawa–Carleton
Ottawa–Carleton Centre
111 Lisgar Street
Ottawa, ON  K2P 2L7
Phone: (613) 560-1239. Fax: (613) 560-1380.
Awards: $2,000 (English); $2,000 (French).
Alternates between fiction and non-fiction. Criteria: literary merit, published within the previous two calendar years and written or co-authored by residents of the Regional Municipality who are Canadian citizens or landed immigrants. Application forms available on request. Deadline: 20 January.

### The David Adams Richards Prize
Writers' Federation of New Brunswick
P.O. Box 37, Station A
Fredericton, NB  E3B 4Y2
Phone/fax: (506) 459-7228.
Prize: $400.
Open only to residents of New Brunswick for a collection of short stories, a short novel or a substantial portion of a longer novel (not to exceed 30,000 words). Work must be original and unpublished, although some individual stories may have been previously in print. Complete details available on request. Deadline: 14 February.

### The Evelyn Richardson Memorial Literary Prize
The Richardson Trust
c/o Writers' Federation of Nova Scotia
1809 Barrington Street, Suite 901
Halifax, NS  B3J 3K8
Phone: (902) 423-8116. Fax: (902) 422-0881.
E-mail: <writers1@fox.nstn.ca>
Prize: $1,000.
Awarded to the writer of a non-fiction book who was born, or lived for the past year, in Nova Scotia. This is the province's highest formal recognition of non-fiction writing. No formal entry form. Send four copies of the book. Deadline: 19 April.

## The Riddell Award
The Ontario Historical Society
34 Parkview Avenue
Willowdale, ON M2N 2Y3
Phone: (416) 226-9011. Fax: (416) 226-2740.
Prize: framed certificate accompanied by a copy of the citation acknowledging the winner's contribution to the heritage community.
Awarded for the best article on Ontario history published during the award year. Entry form required. Deadline: 30 October.

## Ringwood Award for Drama
Writers Guild of Alberta Awards Program
Percy Page Centre, 3rd floor
11759 Groat Road N.W.
Edmonton, AB T5M 3K6
Phone: (403) 422-8174. Fax: (403) 422-2663. Calgary office phone: (403) 265-2226.
Prize: $500 and a leather-bound copy of the winning book.
Open to writers who have been resident in Alberta for 12 of the previous 18 months. Plays may be unpublished but must be registered with the Writers Guild of Alberta or the Alberta Playwrights' Network Drama Award Production Registry. Anthologies are eligible.
Deadline: 31 December.

## Rogers Communications/Writers' Trust Fiction Prize
c/o The Writers' Development Trust
24 Ryerson Avenue, Suite 201
Toronto, ON M5T 2P3
Phone: (416) 504-8222.
This is a new award. Contact for entry criteria. Details not finalized at time of printing.

## The Romance Writers of America, Inc.: RITA, Golden Heart and Janet Dailey Awards
RWA Headquarters
13700 Veterans Memorial, Suite 315
Houston, TX 77014-1023 USA
Phone: (281) 440-6885. Fax: (281) 440-7510.
Web site: <http//www.rwanational.com>
All contestants must be RWA members in good standing. The RITA awards recognize the best in published romance/romantic novels. The Golden Heart awards recognize outstanding manuscripts by unpublished writers. The Janet Dailey Award recognizes a romance novel which addresses a social issue.
The following RWA chapters in Canada offer their own competitions: Hamilton, ON; Ottawa, ON; Toronto, ON; Edmonton, AB; Vancouver, BC; Vancouver Island, BC.

**Room of One's Own Literary Competition** (semi-annual)
*Room of One's Own*
P.O. Box 46160, Station D
Vancouver, BC  V6J 5G5
Web site: <http://www.islandnet.com/Room/enter>
Prizes: $300; $150; $75. Prize winners and runners-up published in special issue.
Open to women writers for work in the first person. Poetry (4–5 pieces) to 70 lines per poem. Short fiction and creative non-fiction to 3,000 words. Include 40–60 word bio on separate page. Submit in contest format with name, address, phone number and e-mail address if applicable. Send SASE. Manuscripts not returned. Full details and contest updates on web site.

**RTNDF Scholarships for Journalism Students**
c/o RTNDA
2175 Sheppard Avenue East, Suite 310
North York, ON  M2J 1W8
**Ernest Bushell Memorial Scholarship:** $1,500
**Dr. G.R.A. Rice Scholarship:** $1,500
**Canadian Corporate News Scholarship for Top 1st Year Student:** $1,500
**Eric Murray Scholarship for Visible Minorities:** $1,500
**Barbara Frum Scholarship for Interviewing:** $1,500
**RTNDA Scholarship for overall winning entry:** $2,500
The above assistance is offered by the Radio Television News Directors Foundation to students a) enrolled in a broadcast journalism course at a college or university; b) enrolled in a college or university programme with a broadcast journalism option; or c) enrolled on a college or university programme and actively involved in news at a radio or TV station on or off campus. Team entries are not eligible. Entry form and guidelines required. Deadline: 19 May.

**The Sandburg–Livesay Anthology Award**
Unfinished Monument Press
237 Prospect Street South
Hamilton, ON  L8M 2Z6
Phone: (905) 312-1779. Fax: (905) 312-8285.
Prizes: $100 and anthology publication; anthology publication.
Poems entered may be published or unpublished, up to 80 lines, and must be in the People's Poetry tradition as exemplified by the work of Carl Sandburg and Dorothy Livesay. Write for complete rules. Entry fee: $10 for up to ten poems. Deadline: 31 October.

**Saskatchewan Book Awards**
P.O. Box 1921
Regina, SK  S4P 3E1
Phone: (306) 569-1585. Fax: (306) 569-4187.

Prizes: $1,000 and a certificate (authors); certificate and gold seals to affix to books (publishers).

Categories: First Book (Brenda Macdonald Riches Award); Book of the Year; Non-fiction; Children's Literature; Fiction; City of Regina Award; Poetry.

Open to Saskatchewan book authors. Books may be entered in as many categories as desired. Entry fee: $15 per title per category. Contact for entry forms and deadline details.

## Saskatchewan Writers Guild Awards

P.O. Box 3986
Regina, SK  S4P 3R9
Phone: (306) 791-7740. Fax: (306) 565-8554.
E-mail: <swg@sk.sympatico.ca>

### 1. Story Scholarship

Award: $200.

Given to assist a writer whose project has an obvious Saskatchewan setting to attend the Saskatchewan Writers/Artists Colony.

### 2. Literary Awards

Under review at time of printing. Contact for next deadline and programme status.

### 3. Scholarships

The Guild offers the following awards to help writers attend the Sage Hill Writing Experience workshops: John V. Hicks Scholarship; Jerry Rush Scholarship; Saskatchewan Playwrights Centre Scholarship. Amounts of bursaries vary each year. Check for availability.

## *Scenes* Contests

P.O. Box 51531
2060 Queen Street East
Toronto, ON  M4E 3V7
Phone: (416) 690-0917.

### 1. Short fiction

Prize: $200 and publication in *Scenes* for winner of each contest.

Open to previously unpublished fiction by Ontario writers to a maximum 1,500 words. Excerpts from novels and novellas are eligible but please include a brief introduction. No limit to number of submissions. Entry form required. Blind judging. Entry fee: $10 per story.
Deadlines: 21 January; 21 March.

### 2. Poetry

Prizes: $200 and publication in *Scenes* for winner of each contest.

Open to Ontario poets for previously unpublished poems to 50 lines. No limit to number of entries. Entry form required. Blind judging. Entry fee: $10 ($5 for each additional entry). Deadlines: 15 May; 15 July.

## Ruth Schwartz Awards for Excellence

Ontario Arts Council
151 Bloor Street West
Toronto, ON  M5S 1T6
Phone: (416) 969-7450. Fax: (416) 961-7796. Toll-free: 1-800-387-0058.
E-mail: <info@arts.on.ca>
Web site: <http://www.ffa.ucalgary.ca./oac/index.html>
Awards: $3,000,(shared); $2,000 (individual).
Awarded for work in either English or French. The shared award is for the author and illustrator of a children's picture book published in Canada. The individual award is for a book for young adults. Entry details under review. Contact for new deadlines.

## Science in Society Contests

Canadian Science Writers' Association
P.O. Box 75, Station A
Toronto, ON  M5W 1A2
Phone: (416) 928-9624. Fax: (416) 960-0528.
E-mail: <cswa@interlog.com>

### 1. Journalism Competition

Prize: $1,000 for the winner in each of nine categories.
Open to Canadian citizens or residents of Canada, writing in English or French, for work in print or electronic media which has appeared in a Canadian publication or has been broadcast on a system licensed in Canada during the previous year. Contact for complete details. Deadline: 31 January.

### 2. Book Awards

Prizes: $1,000 to winner in each of two categories.
Science writing intended a) for the general public; b) for and available to children. Open to Canadian citizens and residents of Canada writing in English or French for work published that year. Entry form required. Deadline: 15 December.

## Carl Sentner Short Story Award

Island Literary Awards
PEI Council of the Arts
115 Richmond Street
Charlottetown, PE  C1A 1H7
Phone: (902) 368-4410
Prizes: $500; $200; $100.
Open to residents of PEI only, for one short story per entry. Multiple entries are permitted. Blind judging. Entry fee: $8.
Deadline: 15 February.

## Slice of Life Short Story Writing Contest
P.O. Box 599
Fort Langley, BC  V1M 2R9
Prizes: $150 and publication; $50 and publication; Honourable Mentions published in future issues.
Open to unpublished fiction, any genre, to 2,000 words. Each entry needs separate envelope marked "Contest". Blind judging. Entry fee: $10.
Deadline: 30 September.

## The Donald V. Smiley Prize (biennial)
The Canadian Political Science Association
1 Stewart Street, Suite 205
Ottawa, ON  K1N 6H7
Phone: (613) 564-4026.
Prize: $750.
Awarded to the best book published, in English or French, in a field relating to the study of government and politics in Canada. Entries may be single or multi-authored. Text books, edited texts and collections of essays will be considered. Deadline for next submission:
10 December, 1997.

## Dave Smith Playwriting Award
The Coordinator
Dave Smith Playwriting Award
Ottawa Valley Book Festival
305 St. Patrick Street
Ottawa, ON  K1N 5K4
Phone: (613) 565-7991.
Prize: $1,000.
Open to authors in Eastern Ontario and Western Quebec writing in either official language. Plays written within the previous five years are eligible even if already produced or published. Limit one script per year per entrant. No previously submitted script may be entered in future years without special invitation by the jury. Four typed/printed copies required.
Deadline: 21 February.

## The Edna Staebler Award for Creative Non-fiction
Award Administrator
Office of the President
Wilfrid Laurier University
Waterloo, ON  N2L 3C5
Phone: (519) 884-0710. Fax: (519) 894-8202.
E-mail: <kwardrop@machl.wlu.ca>
Prize: $3,000.
Awarded for an author's first or second published book which employs a literary rather than a journalistic approach. It must have a Canadian location

and significance, demonstrate first-hand research, and reflect the writer's personal discovery or experience. Books published during the previous calendar year only are eligible. Entry form required. Deadline: 30 April.

## Starving Romantics Poetry Competition
The Director
93 Charnwood Place
Thornhill, ON  L3T 5H2
Phone: (905) 731-8055. Fax: (905) 477-7390.
Prizes: $125 plus select recitation at various Toronto literary venues; $50 plus recitation; $25 plus recitation; 4th to 10th—one free entry the following year.
Submission may contain up to five unpublished poems which will be judged individually. Enclose SASE. Blind judging. Entry fee: $5 per poem. Deadline: 31 July.

## Stephan G. Stephansson Award for Poetry
Writers Guild of Alberta Awards Program
Percy Page Centre, 3rd floor
11759 Groat Road N.W.
Edmonton, AB  T5M 3K6
Phone: (403) 422-8174. Fax: (403) 422-2663.
Calgary office phone: (403) 265-2226.
Prize: $500 and a leather-bound copy of the winning book.
Open to writers who have been resident in Alberta for 12 of the previous 18 months. Books may have been published anywhere in the world, 1 January–31 December. Deadline: 31 December. Only books published 15-31 December permitted to meet the delayed date: 15 January.

## Lilla Stirling Memorial Award
Nova Scotia Branch
Canadian Authors Association
c/o 15 MacRea Avenue
Dartmouth, NS  B2Y 1Z4
Phone: (902) 466-2558.
Prize: $100.
Open to Nova Scotia writers only. Awarded for the best, recently published children's book for the age group eight years to young adults. Entries may be fiction, non-fiction or verse. Include name, address, phone number. Entry fee: $10 per entry. Deadline: 30 March.

## sub-TERRAIN Writing Contests
204-A, 175 East Broadway
Vancouver, BC  V5T 1W2
Phone: (604) 876-8710. Fax: (604) 879-2667.
Entry fees include a four-issue subscription to *sub-TERRAIN*

## 1. Creative Non-fiction Contest

Prize: $250 plus publication in the next issue.

Open to essays, wailings, rants, polemics, monographs, memoirs etc. of 2,000–4,000 words.. Entry fee: $15. Deadline: 1 August.

## 2. Last Poems Contest

Prize: $200 plus publication in the next issue. Runners-up receive complimentary book prizes plus publication in subsequent issues.

Maximum four poems per entry. All entrants get a four-issue subscription to *sub-TERRAIN*. Entry fee (one-time only): $15. Deadline: 31 January.

## 3. Short Story Contest

Prize: $250 plus publication in the next issue.

Open to unpublished fiction to 2,000 words. All entrants get a four-issue subscription to *sub-TERRAIN*. Entries must be accompanied by SASE to ensure notification of results and (if desired) return of story. Please attach sufficient postage. Entry fee: $15 with extra $5 per story for additional entries. Deadline: 15 May.

## *Sunday Star* Short Story Contest

StarPhone: (416) 350-3000 and press category 2747 (for touch-tone phones only).

Awards: $10,000; $3,000; $1,000.

Offered for original, unpublished stories up to 2,500 words by a Canadian citizen or landed immigrant over age 16. Call for complete contest rules. One submission per person. Entry fee: $5. Deadline: 31 December.

## The J.J. Talman Award

The Ontario Historical Society

24 Parkview Avenue

Willowdale, ON  M2N 3Y2

Phone: (416) 226-9011. Fax: (416) 226-2740.

Prize: framed certificate accompanied by a copy of the citation acknowledging the winner's contribution to the historical community.

Awarded for the best book on Ontario's social, economic, political or cultural history published in the past three years. Entry form required.

Deadline: 30 October.

## Theatre Night in Merrickville Playwriting Competition

P.O. Box 177

Merrickville, ON  K0G 1N0

Phone: (613) 283-2058.

Prizes: $25 and performance during summer production; $15; $5.

Open to the community as well as members of TNIM for original, unpublished work not submitted elsewhere. Plays must run between 20 and 40 minutes, be suitable for outdoor production and family audience. Local setting preferred. Blind judging. Full entry details important. Entry fee: $5 (free to TNIM members). Deadline: 31 March.

### *Tickled by Thunder* Writing Contests
7385-129 Street
Surrey, BC  V8W 7B8
E-mail: <Larry_Lindner@mindlink.bc.ca>
Web site: <http://mindlink.bc.ca/LarryLindner/Thunder.html>
Intended to help beginning writers succeed through contests and publication.

#### 1. Fiction Contest
Prize: 50 per cent of all entry fees (minimum $100) plus publication in *Year's Best Fiction* chapbook.
Theme is open. Limit 2,000 words. Entry fee (subscribers): one free story, each additional entry $5. Entry fee (general): $10 per entry. Deadline: 15 February.

#### 2. Poetry Contests (4)
Prize: 50 per cent of all entry fees (minimum $25) plus publication in *Year's Best Poetry* chapbook and "chapvideo".
Theme, length and style open. Entry fee (subscribers): three poems free, additional entries $2 per poem. Entry fee (general): $5 per poem. Deadlines: 15 February; 15 May; 15 August; 15 October.

#### 3. Article Contests (4)
Prize: $5 plus courtesy copy of magazine.
Open to subscribers of the magazine only, for articles related to writing, maximum 2,000 words. Entry: free. Deadlines: 15 February; 15 May; 15 August; 15 October.

### Trillium Book Award
Ministry of Citizenship, Culture and Recreation
c/o Cultural Programs Branch
77 Bloor Street West, 2nd floor
Toronto, ON  M7A 2R9
Phone: (416) 314-7745. Fax: (416) 314-7460.
Prize: $12,000 to winner in each of two categories with $2,500 to winners' publishers.
Awarded to recognize writing excellence in both the English and French languages by authors residing in the province of Ontario. Open to books of any genre, except for anthologies and translations, submitted by the publisher. Deadline: 13 December.

### The University of Western Ontario President's Medal Awards
These awards are administered by the National Magazine Awards Foundation as part of their annual literary competition. (See National Magazine Awards).

## The Valley Writers' Guild Contests

c/o Mario Carini

R.R. #4

Kemptville, ON  K0G 1J0

For all VWG contests send two copies of entry, one with name, address, and phone number, the other anonymous.

### 1. Fiction Contest

Prizes: $50; $30; $20; five Honourable Mentions.

Open to unpublished short stories, literary or genre, in English up to 2,000 words. Limit one story. Entry fee: $5. Deadline: first Friday in February.

### 2. Non-fiction Contest

Prizes: $50; $30; $20; five Honourable Mentions.

Open to unpublished literary essays, memoirs, articles etc. in English to 2,000 words. Limit one submission. Entry fee: $5. Deadline: first Friday in May.

### 3. Poetry Contest

P.O. Box 32

Spencerville, ON  K0E 1X0

Prizes: $50; $30; $20; five Honourable Mentions.

Open to unpublished poetry in English, any style, single spaced to 60 lines. Limit four poems. Entry fee: $2/poem. Deadline: first Friday in November.

## VanCity Book Prize

c/o BC Book World

3516 West 13th Avenue (rear)

Vancouver, BC  V6R 2S3

Phone: (604) 877-7641. Fax: (604) 877-7639.

Prize: $4,000 ($3,000 to author and $1,000 to BC women's charity of choice).

Presented for the best BC book pertaining to women's issues, published anywhere in the world. Author can be male or female but must have resided in BC for three of the past five years. Submission by publishers. Deadline: 15 May.

## Viacom Canada/Prentice Hall Trust Non-fiction Prize

c/o The Writers' Development Trust

24 Ryerson Avenue, Suite 201

Toronto, ON  M5T 2P3

Phone: (416) 504-8222.

This is a new award. Contact for entry criteria. Details not finalized at time of printing.

## The Herman Voaden National Playwriting Competition
Drama Department
Queen's University
Kingston, ON  K7L 3N6
Phone: (613) 382-2774. Fax: (613) 382-6268.
E-mail: <hannaca@post.ca>
Web site: <http://www@queensu.ca/drama/>
Prizes: $3,000; $2,000; $1,000. (The first- and second-place winners will also receive a one-week workshop and a public reading of their works by a professional company.)
Open to Canadian citizens and landed immigrants for one full-length, adult play in English not previously produced or published. Submit two copies. Blind judging. Send for complete guidelines. Entry fee: $30.
Deadline: 31 January.

## The Bronwen Wallace Award
c/o The Writers' Development Trust
24 Ryerson Avenue, Suite 201
Toronto, ON  M5T 2P3
Phone: (416) 504-8222.
Prize: $1,000.
Open to writers under 35. Alternates between short fiction to 2,500 words and poetry. (1998 is for poetry.) Work entered must have been unpublished in book form but have appeared in a least one independently edited magazine or anthology. Do not staple. Send top sheet with personal information. Blind judging. Entries will not be returned.
Deadline: 15 January.

## The Jon Whyte Memorial Essay Prize
The Writers Guild of Alberta Awards Programme
Percy Page Centre, 3rd floor
11759 Groat Road N.W.
Edmonton, AB  T5M 3K6
Phone: (403) 422-8174. Toll-free: 1-800-665-5354.
Prize: $2,000, publication and broadcast.
Open to Alberta writers aged 18 and over for an essay of up to 2,800 words. Themes change each year. Deadline: 30 November.

## The George Wicken Prize for Canadian Literature
*Essays on Canadian Writing*
3483, rue Peel, suite 23
Montreal, PQ  H3A 1W8
Phone: (514) 398-8326. Fax: (514) 398-8220.
E-mail: <ecw@sympatico.ca>

Web site: <http://www.ecw.ca>
Prize: $200, publication of essay and a one-year subscription to ECW.
Awarded to the graduate or undergraduate student who submits the best previously unpublished critical essay of up to 9,000 words on any aspect of Canadian literature. Work already submitted or accepted for publication elsewhere is not eligible. Proof of student status (photocopy of ID card sufficient) must accompany entry. Deadline: 30 June.

### The Ethel Wilson Fiction Prize
West Coast Book Prize Society
700-1033 Davie Street
Vancouver, BC  V6E 1M7
Phone/fax: (604) 687-2405.
Prize: $2,000.
Awarded to the author of the best work of fiction. No anthologies. Open to residents of BC/Yukon who have lived there three out of the past five years. Entry fee: $25. Deadline: 24 December.

### Winner's Circle Short Story Contest
Metropolitan Toronto Branch
Canadian Authors Association
33 Springbank Avenue
Scarborough, ON  M1N 1G2
Phone/fax: (416) 698-8687.
E-mail: <caamtb@inforamp.net>
Prizes: $500; 4 runners-up $125 each; ten Honourable Mentions.
Stories must be unpublished and 1,500–3,500 words. All winners receive a certificate, publication in *Winner's Circle* and a free copy of the book. Uses one-time rights for first publication only. Entry fee: $15 per story. Deadline: 30 November.

### Write on the Edge Student Playwriting Contest
Playwrights' Montreal Workshop
P.O. Box 604
Postal Station Place d'Armes
Montreal, PQ  H2Y 3H8
Phone: (514) 843-3685. Fax: (514) 843-9384.
E-mail: <pwm@web.net>
Prize: $100 and both a professional workshop and public reading of the script plus a one-year membership in the Playwrights' Montreal Workshop awarded to four scripts.
Open to post secondary students in Quebec or the Ottawa area. Eligible work: one or two scripts of any length, on any topic, never professionally produced. Winners must be prepared to attend the workshop and public reading of their play in Montreal in late March. Deadline: 1 February.

## WriteNow!
*Ottawa Citizen* Contests
P.O. Box 84083
Pinecrest Post Office
Ottawa, ON  K2C 3Z2
Prizes: $300; $200; $100.
Open to residents 16 years of age and over in the *Citizen*'s distribution area writing in English, for original, unpublished work. Topic changes annually. One submission per author. Blind judging. Entrants grant the right to the *Citizen* and other members of SouthamStar Satellite Network to publish their entry (one-time rights only) and to use the author's photo, name and brief biography. No *Citizen* or Southam employees or those they live with may enter this contest. Deadline: 14 March.

## Writer's Block Writing Contest
P.O. Box 32
9944-33 Avenue
Edmonton, AB  T6N 1E8
Prize: $150 plus publication.
Open to previously unpublished stories and poems to 5,000 words. All genres and styles eligible. Write for further details.

## Writers' Federation of New Brunswick Literary Competition
P.O. Box 37, Station A
Fredericton, NB  E3B 4Y2
Phone/fax: (506) 459-7228.
Prizes: $200; $100; $30.
Open only to residents of New Brunswick for poetry, non-fiction, fiction, and children's literature (poetry or prose). Deadline: 14 February.

## Writers Guild of Alberta Book Awards
See: R. Ross Annett Award for Children's Literature; Georges Bugnet Award for Fiction; Wilfred Eggleston Award for Non-fiction; Henry Kreisel Award for Best First Book; Howard O'Hagan Award for Short Fiction; Gwen Pharis Ringwood Award for Drama; and Stephan G. Stephansson Award for Poetry.

## The Writers' Union of Canada Contests
24 Ryerson Avenue
Toronto, ON  M5T 2P3
Phone: (416) 703-8982. Fax: (416) 703-0826.
E-mail: <twuc@the-wire.com>
### 1. Short Prose Competition for Developing Writers
Prizes: $2,500; $1,000.
Open to Canadian citizen or landed immigrant writers not published in book form. Entries must be non-fiction or fiction prose of 2,000-2,500 words in

English and unpublished in any format. Entry fee: $25.
Deadline: 3 November.

**2. Writing for Children Contest**

Prize: $1,500.

Open to Canadian citizens or landed immigrants writing in English who have neither been published in any format nor have a publishing contract. Submit writing for children up to 1,500 words. Entry fee: $15. Deadline: Canada Book Day (mid-April).

## FELLOWSHIPS AVAILABLE TO WRITERS

### The Atkinson Fellowship in Public Policy

Atkinson Fellowship Committee
One Yonge Street, 6th floor
Toronto, ON  M5E 1P9
Phone: (416) 869-4034. Fax: (416) 865-3619
Award: a $65,000 stipend and up to $25,000 in expenses.

Awarded for a one-year project to research a relevant public policy issue resulting in publication of a series of articles which the journalist is then free to develop into a book. It is open to all full-time Canadian journalists in any of the print or broadcast media. Preference will be given to those who have already achieved some distinction in reporting on policy issues. The deadline for applications is mid-March.

Further information required.

### FOCAL Media Fellowships

55 Murray Street, Suite 230
Ottawa, ON  K1N 5M3
Phone: (613) 562-0005. Fax: (613) 562-2525.
E-mail: <focal@focal.ca>
Web site: <http://www.focal.ca>
Prizes: five $10,000 grants to be used at the media fellows' discretion during a two-month sabbatical, and return economy air fare to the country of tenure.

Fellowships available to experienced Canadian journalists, editors and producers in print and electronic media. Awarded for two-month stay in a Latin American or Caribbean country to research a topic previously identified and proposed to FOCAL. Application form required.

Deadline: 31 March.

### The Michenor Foundation Study-leave Fellowships

Michenor Foundation Administrative Office
29 Madawaska Drive
Ottawa, ON  K1S 3G5
Phone: (613) 234-7480.

Award(s): one or more of $20,000.
Available to cover four-month periods of study-leave. Provided for mature, mid-career Canadian journalists. Designed to foster journalism that promotes the public interest and demonstrates values beneficial to the community as a whole. Write for complete details.
Deadline: last day of February.

## Southam Fellowships for Journalists
Office of Admissions and Awards
University of Toronto
315 Bloor Street West
Toronto, ON  M5S 1A3
Phone: (416) 978-7956. Fax: (416) 978-6089.
Prize: eight months' salary to a maximum of $4,900/month, all university fees and travel expenses for Fellow and family to and from Toronto.
Open to full-time news or editorial employees with at least five years' experience. No educational prerequisites. Tenable for one academic year, Sept–May, at the University. of Toronto. No credit or degree is granted. Write for brochures and application forms.

*[The CAA Publications Committee thanks all those whose ready response made the preparation of these sections possible.]*

Gill Foss is an award-winning writer/editor with *Reader's Digest* among her clients. She chairs the National Awards Committee of the Canadian Authors Association, has been a CAA Regional V.P., and Ottawa Branch President. Gill has programmed two national writers' conferences and teaches as a subject specialist for a consulting company.

# Organizations of Interest to Writers

*Compiled by Murphy Shewchuk* _____

Alberta Romance Writers
Association
223-112th Avenue S.W.
Calgary, AB  T2R 0G9
Tel: (403) 282-6676

Assoc. acadienne des artistes
professionelles du NB
140, rue Botsford, Pièce 10
Moncton, NB  E1C 4X4
Tel: (506) 852-3313.
Fax: (506) 852-3401

Assoc. des écrivains acadiens
du NB
140 rue Botsford
Moncton, NB  E1C 4X4
Tel: (506) 856-9693.
Fax: (506) 857-3070

Assoc. Journalistes Independents
4034 av. de Lorimier
Montreal, QC  H2K 3X7
Tel: (514) 523-9845.
Fax: (514) 523-1270

Assoc. of American Publishers
220 East 23rd St.
New York, NY  10010

Assoc. of Book Publishers of
British Columbia
100 W. Pender, Ste.107
Vancouver, BC  V6B 1R8
Tel: (604) 684-0228.
Fax: (604) 684-5788

Authors Guild, Inc., The
330 West 42nd St. 29th Fl.
New York, NY  10036
Tel: (212) 563-5904.
Fax: (212) 564-8363
E-mail: <staff@authorsguild.org>

Authors League of America
234 West 44th Street
New York, NY  10036

Automobile Journalists
Association of Canada
970 Eglinton W
Toronto, ON  M6C 2C5
Tel: (416) 785-8475.
Fax: (416) 785-1377

Burnaby Writers' Society
6584 Deer Lake Avenue
Burnaby, BC  V5G 3T7
Tel: (604) 435-6500

Calgary Writers Association
PO Box 68083,
7750 Ranchview Dr. N.W.
Calgary, AB T3G 3N8
Tel: (403) 242-3130

CAN:BAIA
54 Wolseley St., 2nd Fl.
Toronto, ON M5T 1A5
Tel: (416) 369-9040

Canada Council for the Arts, The
350 Albert St. P.O. Box 1047
Ottawa, ON K1P 5V8
Tel: (613) 566-4414.
Fax: (613) 566-4410
E-mail: <silvie.bernier@canada-council.ca>

Canadian Association of
Journalists (CAJ)
Rm 316B, 1125 Colonel By Dr.
Ottawa, ON K1S 5B6
Tel: (613) 526-8061.
Fax: (613) 521-3094
E-mail: <cf408@freenet.carleton.ca>

Canadian Authors Assoc. -
Alberta Branch
#1604 - 11111 87 Avenue
Edmonton, AB T5G 0X9
E-mail: <caa@freenet.edmonton.ab.ca>

Canadian Authors Assoc. -
Manitoba Branch
208 - 63 Albert Street
Winnipeg, MB R3B 1G4
Tel: (204) 947-0512
E-mail: <ilmoore@mb.sympatico.ca>

Canadian Authors Assoc. -
Metropolitan Toronto Branch (ON)
33 Springbank Ave
Scarborough, ON M1N 1G2
Tel: (416) 698-8687.
Fax: (416) 698-8687
E-mail: <caamtb@inforamp.net>

Canadian Authors Assoc. -
National Office
Box 419,
Campbellford, ON K0L 1L0
Tel: (705) 653-0323.
Fax: (705) 653-0593
E-mail: <canauth@redden.on.ca>
Web Page:
<http://www.CanAuthors.org/national.html>

Canadian Authors Assoc. -
Niagara Branch (ON)
P.O. Box 56
Welland, ON L3B 5N9

Canadian Authors Assoc. -
Nova Scotia Branch
c/o 15 MacRea Avenue
Dartmouth, NS B2Y 1Z4

Canadian Authors Assoc. -
Okanagan Branch (BC)
#20, 1304 Ellis St.
Kelowna, BC V1Y 1Z8

Canadian Authors Assoc. -
Ottawa Branch (ON)
c/o Gill Foss
30 Hexham Road
Nepean, ON K2H 5L1
E-mail: <gillfoss@netcom.ca>

Canadian Authors Assoc. -
Peterborough Branch (ON)
P.O. Box 2134
Peterborough, ON K0J 7Y4

Canadian Authors Assoc. -
Temiskaming Branch (ON)
Box 5180
New Liskeard, ON  P0J 1P0
Tel: (705) 647-5424 or
1-800-258-5451.
Fax (705) 647-8366
E-mail: <dranchuk@aol.com>

Canadian Authors Assoc. -
Vancouver Branch (BC)
726 Parkside Road
West Vancouver, BC  V7S 1P3
Tel: (604) 922-6983

Canadian Authors Assoc. -
Victoria & Islands Branch (BC)
c/o Russ Harvey
2325 Pacific Avenue
Victoria, BC  V8R 2V6
E-mail: <caa@islandnet.com>

Canadian Children's Book
Centre, The
35 Spadina Rd.
Toronto, ON  M5R 2S9
Tel: (416) 975-0010.
Fax: (416) 975-1839

Canadian Copyright Licensing
Agency (CANCOPY)
6 Adelaide St. E., Ste 900
Toronto, ON  M5C 1H6
Tel: (416) 868-1620.
Fax: (416) 868-1621

Canadian Ethnic Journalists' and
Writers' Club
24 Tarlton Road
Toronto, ON  M5P 2M4
Tel: (416) 488-0048

Canadian ISBN Agency, National
Library of Canada
395 Wellington St.
Ottawa, ON  K1A 0N4
Tel: (819) 994-6872.
Fax: (819) 953-8508
E-mail: <isbn@nlc/bnc.ca>

Canadian Magazine Publishers
Association (CMPA)
130 Spadina Ave., Suite 202
Toronto, ON  M5V 1L4
Tel: (416) 504-0274.
Fax: (416) 504-0437
Web Page:
<http://www.cmpa.ca>

Canadian Music Publishers
Association
56 Wellesley St. West, Ste 320
Toronto, ON  M5S 2S3
Tel: (416) 926-1966.
Fax: (416) 926-7521
E-mail:
<cmpa.inquiries@cmrra.ca>

Canadian Poetry Association
P.O. Box 340, Stn B,
London, ON  N6A 4W1
Tel: (519) 660-8976
E-mail: <resource.centre@
onlinesys.com>

Canadian Science Writers'
Association
P.O. Box 75, Stn A
Toronto, ON  M5W 1A2
Tel: (416) 928-9624. Fax: (416)
960-0528
E-mail: <cswa@interlog.com>

Canadian Screenwriters Alliance
24 Watts Avenue, West Royalty
Industrial Park
Charlottetown, PE  C1E 1B0
Tel: (902) 628-3880.
Fax: (902) 368-1813
E-mail: <evie@isn.net>

Canadian Society of Children's
Authors, Illustrators and
Performers (CANSCAIP)
35 Spadina Rd.
Toronto, ON  M4S 2M7
Tel: (416) 515-1559.
Fax: (416) 515-7022

Canadian Theatre Critics
Association, The
25 George St., Suite 701
Toronto, ON  M5A 4L8
Tel: (416) 367-8896

CAPIC
100 Broadview Ave., Suite 322
Toronto, ON  M4M 2E8
Tel: (416) 462-3700.
Fax: (416) 462-3678
E-mail: <capic@astral.magic.ca>

Children's Writers & Illustrators
of BC
3888 West 15th Avenue
Vancouver, BC  V6R 2Z9
Tel: (604) 224-3260.
Fax: (604) 224-3261

Crime Writers of Canada
3007 Kingston Rd., Box 113
Scarborough, ON  M1M 1P1
Tel: (416) 782-3116.
Fax: (416) 789-4682
E-mail: <ap113@torfree.net>

Editors' Association of Canada
35 Spadina Rd.
Toronto, ON  M5R 2S9
Tel: (416) 975-1379.
Fax: (416) 975-1839

Federation of British Columbia
Writers, The
Ste 600, 890 West Pender St
Vancouver, BC  V6C 1J9
Tel: (604) 683-2057.
Fax: (604) 683-8269
E-mail: <fedbcwrt@pinc.com>
Web Page:
<http://www.swifty.com/bcwa>

Federation of Canadian Artists
1241 Cartwright St.
Vancouver, BC  V6H 4B7
Tel: (604) 681-8534.
Fax: (604) 681-2740

Federation Of English-Language
Writers of Québec (FEWQ)
#3 1200 Atwater
Montreal, QC  H3Z 1X4
Tel: (514) 934-2485

Island Writers Association (P.E.I.)
P.O. Box 1204
Charlottetown, PE  C1A 7M8
Tel: (902) 566-9748.
Fax: (902) 566-9748

League of Canadian Poets, The
54 Wolseley St., Ste 204
Toronto, ON  M5T 1A5
Tel: (416) 504-1657.
Fax: (416) 703-0059
E-mail: <league@io.org>

Literary Translators' Association
of Canada, The
3492 Avenue Laval
Montreal, QC  H2X 3C8
Tel: (514) 849-8540.
Fax: (514) 849-6239

Manitoba Writers' Guild Inc.
#206 100 Arthur St.
Winnipeg, MB  R3B 1H3
Tel: (204) 942-6134.
Fax: (204) 942-5754
E-mail: <mbwriter@escape.ca>

National Writers Association
1450 S. Havana, Ste. 424
Aurora, CO  80012

National Writers Union, The
873 Broadway, #203
New York, NY  10003
Tel: (212) 254-0279.
Fax: (212) 254-0673
E-mail: <nwu@netcom.com>

Ottawa Independent Writers
265 Elderberry Terrace
Orleans, ON  K1E 1Z2
Tel: (613) 841-0572.
Fax: (613) 841-0775
E-mail: <ac615@freenet.
carleton.ca>

Outdoor Writers of Canada
P.O. Box 1839
Peterborough, ON  K9J 7X6
Tel: (705) 743-7052.
Fax: (705) 743-7052

PEI Writers' Guild
P.O. Box 2234
Charlottetown, PE  C1A 8B9
Tel: (902) 894-9933.
Fax: (902) 961-2797

Pen International, Canadian
Centre
#309-24 Ryerson Ave.
Toronto, ON  M5T 2P3
Tel: (416) 703-8448.
Fax: (416) 703-0826
E-mail: <pencan@web.apc.org>

Periodical Writers Association of
Canada
54 Wolseley St, Suite 203
Toronto, ON  M5T 1A5
Tel: (416) 504-1645.
Fax: (416) 703-0059
E-mail: <pwac@cycor.ca>

Playwrights Union of Canada
54 Wolseley St. 2nd floor
Toronto, ON  M5T 1A5
Tel: (416) 703-0201.
Fax: (416) 703-0059
E-mail: <cdplays@interlog.com>
Web Page: <http://www.puc.ca>

Poets & Writers
72 Spring St., Rm. 301
New York, NY  10012

Saskatchewan Writers' Guild
P.O. Box 3986
Regina, SK  S4P 3R9
Tel: (306) 791-7740.
Fax: (306) 565-8554
E-mail: <swg@sk.sympatico.ca>

SF Canada
11759 Groat Rd., 2nd Fl.
Edmonton, AB  T5M 3K6

Society of American Travel
Writers
1155 Connecticut Ave.NW,#500
Washington, DC  20036

Society of American Travel
Writers - Canadian Chapter
135 Crescent Road
Toronto, ON M4W 1TB
Tel: (416) 925-9286.
Fax: (416) 925-0116
E-mail: <gdhall@astral.magic.ca>

Society of Graphic Designers of
Canada, BC
VMPO Box 3626
Vancouver, BC V6B 3X6
Tel: (604) 877-6404

Society of Graphic Designers of
Canada, ON
P.O. Box 813, Adelaide St. E.
Toronto, ON M5C 2K1
Tel: (416) 360-6486.
Fax: (416) 862-1161
E-mail: <gdcont@web.apc.org>

Union des écrivaines et ecrivains
québecois
3492 avenue Laval
Montreal, QC H2X 3C8
Tel: (514) 849-8540.
Fax: (514) 849-6239

Union Des Encrivain(e)s Quebec.
3492 rue Laval
Montreal, QC H2X 3C8
Tel: (514) 849-8540.
Fax: (514) 849-6239

Victoria Writers Society
P.O. Box 6447, Depot #1
Victoria, BC V8P 5M3
Tel: (604) 920-7154

West Coast Book Prize Society
700 - 1033 Davie St.
Vancouver, BC V6E 1M7
Tel: (604) 687-2405

Writers Alliance, The
12 Skylark Lane
Sony Brook, NY 11790

Writers Guild of Canada
35 McCaul Street, Ste 300
Toronto, ON M5T 1V7
Tel: (416) 979-7907.
Fax: (416) 979-9273
E-mail: <wgc@io.org>

Writers' Alliance of Newfoundland
& Labrador
PO Box 2681
St. John's, NF A1C 5M5
Tel: (709) 739-0630.
Fax: (709) 739-5215

Writers' Development Trust, The
24 Ryerson Ave., Suite 201
Toronto, ON M5T 2P3
Tel: (416) 504-8222

Writers' Federation of New
Brunswick
P.O. Box 37, Station A
Fredericton, NB E3B 4Y2
Tel: (506) 453-1366.
Fax: (506) 459-7228

Writers' Federation of Nova
Scotia
1809 Barrington St., Ste. 901
Halifax, NS B3J 3K8
Tel: (902) 423-8116.
Fax: (902) 422-0881
E-mail: <writers1@fox.nstn.ca>

Writers' Guild of Alberta (Calgary)
305 223-12 Ave. S.W.
Calgary, AB T2R 0G9
Tel: (403) 269-8844

Writers' Guild of Alberta
(Edmonton)
11759 Groat Rd., 3rd Fl.
Edmonton, AB T5M 3K6
Tel: (403) 422-8174.
Fax: (403) 422-2663

Writers' Union of Canada, The
24 Ryerson Ave.
Toronto, ON M5T 2P3
Tel: (416) 703-8982.
Fax: (416) 703-0826
E-mail: <twuc@the-wire.com>

Writers' Union of Canada, The
(Vancouver Chapter)
3102 Main St., 3rd Fl.
Vancouver, BC V4A 3C7
Tel: (604) 874-1611.
Fax: (604) 874-1611

## *E-mail and Web page addresses:*

Editor's note: We have included e-mail and web page addresses whenever they where available. However we would like to point out that the volatile nature of the Internet and the World Wide Web means that these could have changed by the time you read this publication. Be particularly careful with your address entry, but if you still fail to get through, use a search tool such as AltaVista <http://www.altavista. digital.com> to find the new address.

# Literary Agents in Canada

*by Deidre Hill*

I n Canada, the listing of literary agents is still small, but is definitely growing. As we progress into the high tech multimedia, multifaceted publishing world of the 21st century, the specialized knowledge and insight of an agent will be needed more than ever to effectively promote a writer's work and to meet the publisher's needs.

Although there are always exceptions to every generality, a review of the market listings and discussions with individual agents have created the following impression of how best to approach a literary agent. It is worth noting that these same guidelines apply when dealing directly with a publisher.

### *Return postage is necessary.*

Very few literary agencies will return inquiries or manuscripts that have not been submitted with a self-addressed return envelope accompanied by sufficient postage (SASE) to cover the full weight of the shipment. In the case of material originating from a US or foreign source, the postage can be in the form of International Reply Coupons, but because of the high cost of Canadian postage, these should be double the normal mailing fees. A short note can be added to your covering letter if the return of your manuscript is not required.

### *Query letters serve as an important first step.*

Although there are a few exceptions, most agents will not read unsolicited manuscripts. In most instances the preference is to first receive a detailed query letter (with SASE). If interested in the subject matter, then the agency will ask for more information which may be in the form of sample chapters or the complete manuscript.

### Never submit first drafts.

Prepare your query letters and manuscripts as cleanly and as perfectly as possible. As in any other business, first impressions are extremely important. Remember that you are also selling a product. To quote one agency, "We are not impressed by the credentials of a writer—amateur or professional—or by his or her pitching techniques, but by his or her story ideas and ability to build a well-crafted script."

### Representation is a personal service business.

It is worth noting that most agents do not use freelance readers to help evaluate manuscripts. Evaluation is usually a very personal matter and is the basis from which the agent decides to expend the considerable energy needed to promote a work. They may call on specialists in certain fields, such as technical non-fiction, to assist with the assessment of a manuscript.

### Fees may be charged.

An agent's time is his or her stock in trade. Most agencies earn a large part of their income from the fees they receive as a percentage of the royalties or other earnings from published or, in the case of film or drama, produced work. In general, these fees are 15 per cent of the authors income for domestic sales and 20 to 30 per cent for foreign sales and lecturing.

Once an agent decides to represent your work, most prefer written contracts which can be binding for a fixed period, often two years. Some agencies charge writers an additional amount for photocopying, courier, postage, telephone/fax "if these are excessive."

Finding publishable material can be very time-consuming and this is often considered part of the agency's cost of doing business. However, providing the author with written evaluations and suggestions for improvement is often beyond the scope of normal agent duties and fees may be charged for this work. Individual agency fees vary widely. One agency mentioned a fee of $200 for a 200 page double-spaced manuscript. Another charges a fee of $395 to read the manuscript and produce a three or four page constructive critique. Still another agent was in the process of re-evaluating her fee structure.

Because of changes in the literary marketplace and space limitations, we have chosen not to list specific fee structures. In all instances, you should ask for clarification of the agency's fee structure with your first letter of inquiry (accompanied by an SASE, of course).

The following list of agents is offered to begin your search. New agencies' businesses are often short-lived; long-time agencies often form new partnerships; policies and needs change. An updated listing of Canadian literary agents is maintained on the CAA web site at: <http:www.CanAuthors.org/national.html> or can be obtained by sending a request with SASE (#10 business envelope) to Canadian Authors Association, P.O. Box 419, Campbellford, Ontario, K0L 1L0.

Deidre A. Hill, a member of the Canadian Authors Association Victoria & Islands Branch, has been published in local and national publications regularly since Spring 1996. She is the founding Editor of a storytellers' newsletter, *Word Weavers*. She planned to continue her study of literature and storytelling by entering university in the fall of 1997.

**Acacia House Publishing Services Ltd.**
51 Acacia Rd.,
Toronto, ON M4S 2K6
Phone/Fax: (416) 484-8356
Contact: Frances Hanna
Notes: Specializes in contemporary fiction—literary or commercial (no horror, occult or science fiction); non-fiction in all categories but prefers business/economics—in the trade, not textbook area; children's books, but very few picture books; young adult, mainly fiction. Handles film and TV rights. Prefers previously published writers. Strong consideration given to those with three or more published books. Does consider unpublished writers of outstanding talent. Query with outline (with SASE). Does not read unsolicited manuscripts. Represented *Chicken Little Was Right* and sequel, *Whatever Happened to Jennifer Steele?*, (St. Martin's Press, USA); *Goodbye Mom and Apple Pie*, by Robert Collins (McClelland & Stewart, Canada).

**Alpha Translations Canada Inc.**
38 Stoneshire Manor,
Spruce Grove, AB T7X 3E3
Phone: (403)962-7821. Fax: (403)962-6517
Email: <atc@alpha01.com>
URL: <http://www.alpha01.com>
Notes: Alpha Translations Canada Inc. is a Canadian-based Translation and Language Consulting Agency, offering a wide range of services to companies in North America and Europe. This service focuses on the language combinations of German-English and English-German, but also offers translation services for French, Spanish, Italian and Portuguese. They specialize in technical, legal and commercial translations and act as a literary agency, selling the foreign language rights for books.

**Aurora Artists Inc.**
207 - 3 Charles St. W.,
Toronto, ON M4Y 1R4
Phone: (416) 929-2042. Fax: (416) 922-3061
Notes: Interested in film scripts and stories. Does not consider children's illustrated books.
Does not accept unsolicited manuscripts—inquiries only. Represented CBC movie, *Giant Mine* by Martin O'Malley.

**Author Author Literary Agency Ltd.**
P.O. Box 34051,
1200 37 St. SW,
Calgary, AB T3C 3W2
Phone/Fax: (403) 242-0226
Contact: Joan Rickard
Notes: Considers juvenile, New-Age, scholarly fiction and non-fiction books. Prefers adult material. Not interested in poetry or screen plays. Please do not submit individual short stories or magazine articles. Will consider book-size short story collections. No reading fee—prefers complete manuscripts. SASE necessary for any reply. Represented Kim Kinraid's best seller, *Ice Breaker*.

**Authors' Marketing Services Ltd.**
200 Simpson Ave.,
Toronto, ON M4K 1A6
Phone: (416) 463-7200. Fax: (416) 469-4494
Email: <authors_lhoffman@compuserve.com>
Contact: Larry Hoffman.
Notes: Seeks full-length fiction—specializes in thrillers and romance novels. Also considers non-fiction books in a wide variety of fields. Negotiates domestic and foreign rights. Handles film and TV rights when book is represented. Represented *Yes you Can!* by Dr. M. Nagler (Stoddart); *Dark Shadow*, by Veronica Shaw (Ballantine).

**The Bukowski Agency**
125B Dupont St.,
Toronto, ON M5R 1V4
Phone: (416) 928-6728. Fax: (416) 963-9978
Contact: Denise Bukowksi
Notes: Specializes in adult trade fiction.
Query first (with SASE). Does not read unsolicited manuscripts. Film & TV rights represented for material agency handles. Prefers book proposal as per guidelines for non-fiction; synopsis & sample for fiction. No reading fees. Commission plus disbursements.

## Canadian Speakers' & Writers' Service Ltd.

44 Douglas Crescent,
Toronto, ON M4W 2E7
Phone: (416) 921-4443. Fax: (416) 922-9691 (call ahead)
Contact: Matie Molinaro or Paul Molinaro
Notes: Trade non-fiction; adult education; how-to books; professional books; novel-length fiction; juvenile fiction; short story collections; stage plays; and screenplays. Specializes in architecture, art, autobiography, and biography. No unsolicited manuscripts: inquiries only. Does not return material without SASE. Agency also provides non-client contract consultation services. Not taking new clients at publication date.

## Leo J. Deveau & Associates

Comp A1, Site 11, R.R. 2,
Wolfville, N.S., B0P 1X0
Phone: (902) 542-3908. Fax: (902) 542-7686
Email: <ljdeveau@fox.nstn.ca>
Contact: Leo J. Deveau
Notes: Literary agent services for screenplay writers. Representation in all major markets. "I am strictly focused on representing screenplays for television and film production. In terms of submissions, I prefer a query with sample scenes, a story outline and/or treatment, with a bio on the author."

## Great North Artists Management Inc.

350 Dupont St.,
Toronto, ON M5R 1V9
Phone: (416) 925-2051
Contact: Ralph Zimmerman
Notes: Interested in screenplays, stage plays and teleplays.
Reads multiple submissions, if requested by the agency. Can supply ghost-writers/collaborators if required. Great North is also a packager for scripts for television, film and stage.

## Dale Harney Productions

10737 St. Gabriel School Road,
Edmonton, AB T6A 3S7
Phone: (403) 463-4924. Fax: (403) 463-3079
Email: <dhprod@planet.eon.net>
URL: <http://www.ualberta.ca/~nscotten/magic.html>
Contact: Dale Harney
Notes: The husband and wife team of Dale and Lynda Harney bring over twenty years as performers, writers and producers to their literary agency. They are interested in well developed, original and innovative screenplays.

They are not interested in novels. Query first by e-mail or letter (with SASE). Do not query by telephone. They reply to all written queries. Manuscripts must be registered with the Writers Guild before being sent to Dale Harney Productions by mail. Do not send manuscripts by e-mail. No reading fee. "Be patient." Tip: "The quality of writing is judged by the synopsis we receive." (Dale Harney)

**Helen Heller Agency Inc.**
892 Avenue Rd.,
Toronto, ON M5P 2K6
Phone: (416) 481-5430
Contact: Helen Heller, Daphne Hart
Notes: Specializes in fiction and non-fiction trade books. No unsolicited manuscripts. Query first by letter with SASE.

**Inga Hessel Literary Agency**
304 - 180 Bruyère St.,
Ottawa, ON K1N 5E1
Phone: (613) 241-1769
Contact: Inga Hessel
Notes: Interested in children's books, novels and scientific texts. One-person operation. Charges a reading fee for assessment work. "Reads every manuscript."

**Charlene Kay Agency**
6 - 901 Beaudry St.,
St.-Jean-Sur-Richelieu, QC J3A 1C6
Phone: (514) 348-5296
Contact: Louise Meyers
Notes: Louise Meyers is particularly interested in real-life stories and bio-graphical movie scripts. She also considers: action/adventure; biography/autobiography; family saga; fantasy; psychic/supernatural; and science fiction. Query first, prefers a written synopsis accompanied by an SASE or International Reply Coupons.

**Kellock & Associates, Ltd.**
11017 80th Ave.,
Edmonton, AB T6G 0R2
Phone: (403) 433-0274
Contact: Joanne Kellock
Notes: Seeks non-fiction books, juvenile books and novels. Query with outline plus three sample chapters. Does not return on-spec long-distance calls—a query letter is much more appropriate. Joanne Kellock stressed that publishers of science fiction/fantasy and mystery books are looking for

writers that can produce a series of such books, as it takes several books to develop character and author recognition. Charges a reading fee to new writers. Criticism is also provided for the fee. Represented *Song Bird* (picture book), by Tololwa M. Mollel (Clarion Books, New York); *Do You Want Fries with That.*, by Martyn Godfrey (Scholastic, Canada).

## Jessica Lane Productions

P.O. Box 493,
Dundurn, SK S0K 1K0
Phone: (306) 492-2343. Fax: (306) 492-2253
Email: <10432.3347@COMPUSERVE.COM>
Contact: Jessica Lane
Notes: Jessica Lane is mainly interested in trade fiction and non-fiction books. On the fiction side, she prefers mystery and romance. For non-fiction, she leans toward New-Age and health subjects. Query with sufficient Canadian postage.

## Anne McDermid & Associates

78 Albany Ave.,
Toronto, ON M5R 3C3
Phone: (416) 533-9879. Fax: (416) 533-3953
E-Mail: <105361.3577@Compuserve.com>
Contact: Anne McDermid
Notes: Seeks general fiction and non-fiction manuscripts. Film and TV scripts. No children's books or "coffee table" books. Please do not make inquiries by telephone—written (with SASE) or e-mail correspondence is a much better way to deal with literary inquiries.

## Northwest Literary Services

2699 Decca Rd.,
Shawnigan Lake, BC V0R 2W0
Phone: (250) 743-8236
Contact: Brent Laughren
Notes: Interested in non-fiction and juvenile books, novels and short story collections.
Brent Laughren specializes in working with new and unpublished writers. Query with outline/proposal. Charges reading fee for unpublished authors. Reading fee includes short evaluation. Offers various related editorial services at negotiated rates. All fees, if charged, are authorized by the writer in advance.

### The Pamela Paul Agency Inc.,

253 High Park Ave.,

Toronto, ON M6P 2S5

Phone/Fax: (416) 769-0540

E-mail: <ppainc@interlog.com>

Contact: Pamela Paul

**Notes:** This agency has a small list representing screen writers and book authors—primarily literary fiction. No unsolicited manuscripts. Address written inquiries to the attention of Sue Munro. Include SASE. List includes Cable Ace and Governor General award winners.

### Bella Pomer Agency Inc

22 Shallmar Blvd., Penthouse 2,

Toronto, ON M5N 2Z8

Phone: (416) 781-8597. Fax: (416) 782-4196

Contact: Bella Pomer

Notes: Handles quality fiction, mystery fiction and general interest non-fiction. Not accepting new clients.

### Rosoph Book Services

631 Smart Ave.,

Montreal, QC H4X 1T2

Phone/Fax: (514) 488-3395.

Contact: Samuel Rosoph

Notes: Specializes in British books and books about antique clocks.

### Beverley Slopen Literary Agency

131 Bloor St. W., #711,

Toronto, ON M5S 1S3

Phone: (416) 964-9598. Fax: (416) 921-7726

Email: <slopen@inforamp.net>

WEB: <http://www.slopenagency.on.ca>

Contact: Beverley Slopen

Notes: No unsolicited mss, query first with SASE. No software, no film or TV rights handled. Canadian authors only. Look for Beverley Slopen's "The Insider" column: <http://www.digitalbookworld.com>.

**Carolyn N. Swayze, LL.B**
**Authors' Representative**
WRPS Box 39588
White Rock, BC V4A 9P3
Phone: (604) 538-3478. Fax:(604) 531-3022
E-Mail: <cswayze@direct.ca>
Contact: Carolyn N. Swayze
Notes: Literary fiction, some genre fiction (mysteries and suspense), and commercial non-fiction. Handles a limited children's list. Does not accept poetry, scripts, screenplays or essays. Please inquire in writing, enclosing a brief bio, short synopsis of the available work and, if fiction, the first 50 to 100 pages. For non-fiction please include an outline, sample chapter and market research. Always enclose SASE.

**Westwood Creative Artists Ltd.**
94 Harbord St.,
Toronto, ON M5S 1G6
Phone: (416) 964-3302. Fax: (416) 975-9209
Contact: Administrator, Hilary Stanley or President, Bruce M. Westwood (416) 964-1406
Notes: General trade fiction & non-fiction for international marketplace; Canadian authors only. No unsolicited mss, query first with SASE. Handles film & TV rights. No reading fee.

# Selected Canadian Periodical Markets

by Sandra E. Weatherby _____

The most interesting change to periodical listings since our last publication is the addition of E-mail and Web sites. Writers could reach periodical publishers by telephone, fax machine, Canada Post. Now many also can be reached by sending an E-mail message. Many publisher's also have Web sites where writer's guidelines are posted, saving the writer and the periodical publisher considerable time and expense.

There are now six ways to communicate. What? You only counted five! There is still the best and truest contact and that is face-to-face. It is still the best means of communication and one that helps build true working relationships.

Another significant change as part of computer technology is the way writers can deliver their submissions. Many writers are submitting their magazine articles, short stories and poetry on inexpensive floppy disk, accompanied by a paper printout. These are mailed in a large 9 x 12 envelope, but the SASE is a #10 business envelope. Writers are instructing the publishers to shred the printout after processing or rejection. The smaller envelope (SASE) is for the publisher's reply and (hopefully) a cheque. The saving in postage expense compensates for the cost of printing a new copy of the work for presentation to another market. Please notice among the fee schedules that many publishers are also paying a higher rate for manuscripts submitted with disks than those where just the paper printout is submitted.

Another trend that I observed while researching the periodical markets is the number of publications that do not pay writers, either in cash or copies. New writers may appreciate the honour of having their work published in such periodicals as they often encourage beginning or unpublished writers to submit. However, I feel we must seek some financial remuneration, even if it is an honorarium or a free copy of the publication. I advise all new writers to ask for payment. Even if it is a small amount, ask for it.

Sandra E. Weatherby has been an award winning journalist/photographer for the last seventeen years. She has sold freelance stories and photos to many Canadian magazines, journals, and daily newspapers.

ABILITIES Magazine
Canadian Abilities Foundation
489 College Street, Suite 501
Toronto, ON M6G 1A5
E-mail: <able@interlog.com>
Web site: <http://indie.ca/abilities/>
Contact: Lisa Bendall, Editor/Coordinator.
Category: Special Interest.
Non-fiction: Yes. Fiction: Yes.
Poetry: Yes. Graphics: Yes.
Notes: Published quarterly by the Canadian Abilities Foundation. Circulation 50,000. *Abilities Magazine* focuses on the lifestyles of Canadian people with disabilities. Contains information and inspiration about disabilities, challenges, coping strategies, new trends, technology, policies, employment, education, travel, health, transportation, recreational activities. Invites submissions in all genres 500 to 2,500 words. Fees vary and paid on publication. Send for guidelines with SASE and study back issues, $14 ea. before submitting queries or manuscripts.

ABORIGINAL VOICES
116 Spadina Ave. #201
Toronto, ON M5V 2K6
Tel: (416) 703-4577. Fax: (416) 703-4581
E-mail: <abvoices@inforamp.net>
Web site: <http://207.96.159.10/clients/abc/cmall/abvoices/>
Contact: Millie Knapp, Editor.
Category: Special Interest.
Non-fiction: Yes. Fiction: Yes. Poetry: Yes. Graphics: Yes.
Notes: *Aboriginal Voices* is the magazine of evolving Native American Arts. It is dedicated to covering the arts and culture of North American Native people from a Native perspective.

ABOVE AND BEYOND: An Inflight Magazine
PO Box 2348,
Yellowknife, NT X1A 2P7
Tel: (403) 873-2299. Fax: (403) 873-2295
Contact: Jake Ootes, Editor.
Category: People and Places.
Non-fiction: Yes. Fiction: No. Poetry: No. Graphics: Yes.
Notes: Published quarterly, circulation 25,000. This in-flight magazine for First Air and Air Inuit carries articles about Arctic areas including the Northwest Territories, Arctic Quebec and Greenland. Articles of 1,000 to 1,500 words are invited about Arctic people, communities, lifestyles, tourist and commercial services, music, entertainment and special events in the Arctic. Pays $300 per article, $15 for photos on publication. Submit on speculation. Guidelines available.

ABSINTHE
PO Box 61113 Kensington
Calgary, AB T2N 4S6
E-mail: <amathur@acs.ucalgary.ca>
Web site: <http://www.ucalgary.ca/~amathur/absinthe.html>
Contact: The Calgary Women of Colour Collective.
Category: Literary/Arts.
Non-fiction: Yes. Fiction: Yes. Poetry: Yes. Graphics: Yes.
Notes: Published twice a year, *Absinthe* is an arts magazine for literary prose and visual/graphic arts. Its mandate is to support and encourage minority races of colour who are working in the arts. Seeks articles, fiction, prose, poetry, graphics, photos, and illustrations pertaining to people of colour. Advise study previous copies $10ea, send SASE for guidelines/queries.

ACADIENSIS: Journal of History in Atlantic Region
University of New Brunswick,
Campus House,
Fredericton, NB E3B 5A3
Tel: (506) 453-4978. Fax: (506) 453-4599
E-mail: <acadnsis@unb.ca>
Web site: <http://hoshi.cic.sfu.ca/calj/Acadiensis/>
Contact: Gail G. Campbell, Editor.
Category: Scholarly.
Non-fiction: Yes. Fiction: No. Poetry: No. Graphics: No.
Notes: Published twice a year, circulation 900. *Acadiensis* is dedicated to the four Atlantic provinces, in English and French. Uses original academic research articles, reviews, and library bibliographies. Does not pay. Guidelines available.

ACCESS: The Rock Radio Magazine
109 Morse Street, 2nd floor
Toronto, ON M4M 2P7
Tel: (416) 465-9718. Fax: (416) 465-9718
E-mail: <access@castlecom.net>
Web site: <http://www.accessmag.com/>
Contact: Deith Sharp, Publisher/Editor.
Category: Music.
Non-fiction: Yes. Fiction: No. Poetry: No. Graphics: Yes.
Notes: Published six times a year. *Access* focuses on rock music, concerts, profiles, new records, news, views, dance, blues, stage. Query for guidelines.

ALIVE, A Canadian Journal of Health and Nutrition
7436 Fraser Park Drive
Burnaby, BC V5J 5B9
Tel: (604) 435-1919. Fax: (604) 435-4888
Contact: Rhody Lake, Editor.
Category: Special Interest.
Non-fiction: Yes. Fiction: No. Poetry: No. Graphics: Yes.
Notes: Published 12 times a year. 84 pages colour glossy. Circulation 205,000 and is distributed through Canadian Health Food Stores. *Alive* supports the united grass root effort for production of whole, organically grown food and nutritional supplements. Articles cover natural and alternative health remedies, products, services, supplements, herbs, exercise, food recipes and Calendar of Events. Queries welcome. Guidelines available.

ALPHABET CITY Magazine
PO Box 387, Station P
Toronto, ON M5S 2S9.
Category: Arts.
Non-fiction: Yes. Fiction: Yes. Poetry: Yes. Graphics: Yes.
Notes: Published twice a year. Circulation 5,000. *Alphabet City Magazine* covers a single theme in every issue involving every artistic expression on the subject. It employs essays, poetry, prose, visual arts and mixed media from diverse cultures. Query with SASE, guidelines available. Back copies $18.

ALTERNATIVES JOURNAL
Faculty of Environmental Studies,
University of Waterloo,
Waterloo, ON N2L 3G1
Tel: (519) 888-4545. Fax: (519) 746-0292
E-mail: <ndoucet@fes.uwaterloo.ca>
Web site:<http://www.fes.uwaterloo.ca/Research/Alternatives/>
Contact: Nancy Doucet, Managing Editor.
Category: News & Opinions.
Non-fiction: Yes. Fiction: No. Poetry: No. Graphics: Yes.
Notes: Published quarterly, circulation 4,000. Established in 1971 as Canada's first environmental magazine. *Alternatives* provides scholarly reporting about international environmental issues. Articles are well researched for professionals, researchers, activists, and general public. Invites features, 3,000-4,000 words, short news reports, 500/1,000 words, humour, book reviews, 750/1,000 words and essays 2500-3000 words. Does not pay. Contributors guidelines available.

AMETHYST REVIEW, THE
Marcasite Press,
23 Riverside Ave.
Truro, NS B2N 4G2
Tel: (902) 895-1345
Web site: <http://users.atcon.com/~amethyst/>
Contact: Penny Ferguson and Lenora Steele, Co-Editors.
Category: Literary.
Non-fiction: Yes. Fiction: Yes. Poetry: Yes. Graphics: Yes.
Notes: Published by Marcasite Press twice a year. Publishes short shorts, poetry, fiction and creative non-fiction in themes up to 5,000 words. Fees vary but pays on publication plus one contributor's copy. Sample copies available for $6.

ANARCHIVES, THE
PO Box 108 Station P
Toronto, ON M5S 2S8
Tel:(416) 812-6765
E-mail: <media@tao.ca>
Web site: <http://www.tao.ca/>
Contact: Jesse Hirsh, Publisher.
Category: Literary.
Non-fiction: Yes. Fiction: Yes. Poetry: Yes. Graphics: Yes.
Notes: Published by TAO Communications. Interested in creative expressions of the desire for freedom.

ANGLICAN JOURNAL
600 Jarvis Street, Room 224
Toronto, ON M4Y 2J6
Tel: (416) 924-9192. Fax: (416) 921-4452. Voice mail: (416) 924-9199
E-mail: <anglican-journal@ecunet.org>
Contact: David Harris, ext. 306; Janet MacMaster, ext. 304.
Category: Special Interest.
Non-fiction: Yes. Fiction: Yes. Poetry: Yes. Graphics: Yes.
Notes: Published 10 times a year, circulation 265,000 This journal contains news and features from across Canada and the world. Although published by the Anglican Church of Canada, all denominations and faiths are included. Invites news, articles on social and ethical issues for a national audience. Pays $200 to $500 for 600-1,000 word/features and $75 to $200 for news stories, $35 book reviews (plus the book). Query for back issues and guidelines.

ANNALS OF SAINT ANNE DE BEAUPRI, THE
PO Box 1000,
St. Anne de Beaupre, PQ G0A 3C0
Tel: (418) 827-4538. Fax: (418) 827-4530
Contact: Father Roch Achard, Editor.
Category: Special Interest/Religion.
Non-fiction: Yes. Fiction: Yes. Poetry: Yes. Graphics: Yes.
Notes: Published 11 times a year. July/August combined. The *Annals* invites spiritual expository articles of general interest, inspirational and personal experience. Buys 30 manuscripts/year at 500-1500 words. Pays 3-4 cents/word. Religious fiction; buys 20 manuscripts/year at 500-1500 words. Pays 3-4 cents/word. Poetry overstocked until 2000. Photos vary and negotiated individually. Write for guidelines with SASE, free back issue.

ANTIGONISH REVIEW, THE
St. Francis Xavier University
PO Box 5000,
Antigonish, NS B2G 2W5
Tel: (902) 867-3962. Fax: (902) 867-2389
E-mail: <tar@stfx.ca>
Web site: <http://www.stfx.ca/publications/t-a-r/>
Contact: George Sanderson, Editor.
Category: Literary.
Non-fiction: Yes. Fiction: Yes. Poetry: Yes. Graphics: Yes.
Notes: Published quarterly, circulation 800. This literary review invites poetry, fiction and critical articles from anywhere in Canada and the world, 1,500 to 4,000 words. Pays $100-$200 for articles, $100 for reviews, $15 for poems, plus two copies. Guidelines available, samples $3.

ANTIQUE SHOWCASE
202-103 Lakeshore Road
St. Catharines, ON L2N 2T6
Tel: (905) 646-7744. Fax: (905) 646-0995
E-mail: fiocca@trajan.com>
Contact: Mr. Fiocca, Editor.
Category: Special Interest.
Non-fiction: Yes. Fiction: No. Poetry: No. Graphics: Yes.
Notes: Published nine times a year. This magazine is for antique lovers and collectors. Articles cover specialized information, periods, history, values, with extensive photo/illustrations. Regular features cover museum exhibitions and acquisitions, book reviews and the most comprehensive show calendar available. Writers submitting articles must be experts or have a background to support their work. Queries welcome. Guidelines available.

ANTIQUES!
55 Charles Street W., Suite 2402
Toronto, ON M5S 2W9
Tel: (416) 944-3880. Fax: (416) 944-3872
E-mail: <dylmaa@cylcorp.dylex.com>
Contact: Marni Andrews, Publisher/Editor.
Category: Special Interest.
Non-fiction: Yes. Fiction: No. Poetry: No. Graphics: Yes.
Notes: Published six times a year, circulation 4,000. *Antiques!* magazine is about quality collectibles in Canada and Abroad. The editorial emphasis is on accurate, carefully researched reports yet presented with clarity and style to assist the novice to the most seasoned collectors with information. There is an interesting mix of trends, trivia, features and columns for freelance writers to submit articles, 1,200 – 2,000 words, pays five cents per word. Guidelines available.

APPLIED ARTS Magazine
885 Don Mills Road, Suite 324
Don Mills, ON M3C 1V9
Tel: (416) 510-0909. Fax: (416) 510-0913
E-mail: <app-arts@interlog.com>
Contact: Publisher: George Haroutiun, Editor: Sara Curtis, Assist Editor: Chris Ovsenny.
Category: Visual Arts

Notes: Published five times a year, circulation 15,000. Targets communications arts market spotlighting the work of graphic design, advertising, photography and illustration professionals, features outstanding examples of their work. Carries profiles and interviews. Pays 60 cents/word on acceptance for 1,000-2,500 words. Fees vary/negotiated. Query, responds in 30 days.

ARACHNE: A Literature Journal
Laurentian University,
Ramsey Lake Road,
Sudbury, ON P3E 2C6
Tel: (705) 675-1151 Ext 4341. Fax: (705) 675-4870
E-mail: <bkrajews@nickel.laurentian.ca>
Contact: Bruce Krajewski, Editor.
Category: Scholarly.
Non-fiction: Yes. Fiction: Yes. Poetry: Yes. Graphics: Yes.
Notes: published twice a year, circulation 1,000. Essays about literature, film, philosophy, religion, art history, law, classics, history and rhetoric, 5,000 to 7,500 words. Does not pay. Guidelines available.

ARC: Canada's National Poetry Magazine
PO Box 7368
Ottawa, ON K1L 8E4.
Contact: John Barton, Rita Donovan, Co-Editors.
Category: Literary.
Non-fiction: Yes. Fiction: No. Poetry: Yes. Graphics: Yes.
Notes: Published twice a year since 1978. Seeks reviews, articles, interviews related to Canadian poets and poetry. Uses B&W photographs (eight per issue). Pays $25 per page. *Arc* hosts a yearly contest with cash prizes. Write for details, back issues and query with SASE.

ARCH-TYPE
255 - 40 Orchard View Blvd.,
Toronto, ON M4R 1B9
Tel: (416) 482-8255. Fax: (416) 482-2981
E-mail: <arch@indie.ca>
Web site: <http://indie.ca/arch/archtype.html>
Contact: The Editor.
Category: Special Interest.
Non-fiction: Yes. Fiction: Yes. Poetry: Yes. Graphics: Yes.
Notes: Published six times a year by Advocacy Resource Centre for the Handicapped (ARCH), *Arch-type* provides current, well-researched information of interest to disabled and non-disabled readers. Issues surround defending the rights of people with disabilities. Queries welcome.

ARCTIC
The Arctic Institute of North America
The University of Calgary
2500 University Drive NW
Calgary, AB T2N 1N4
Tel: (403) 220-7518. Fax: (403) 282-4609
E-mail: <anail@ucdasuml.admin.ucalgary.ca>
Contact: The Editor.
Category: Scholarly.
Non-fiction: Yes. Fiction: No. Poetry: No. Graphics: Yes.
Notes: Published quarterly, *Arctic* is a multidisciplinary journal of circumpolar research. The articles are written by those working in research areas of the arctic region as a means of sharing information with peers or relevant studies in northern areas of the world. Papers are original, relevant scholarly topics of inquiry. Book reviews, letters to the editor and profiles of significant northern people, places and things are featured. Does not pay. Guidelines available.

ARTFOCUS
PO Box 1063, Station F,
Toronto, ON M4Y 2J7
Tel: (416) 925-5564. Fax: (416) 925-5564
E-mail: <Info@artfocus.com>
Web site: <http://www.artfocus.com/>
Contact: Pat Fleisher, Publisher/Editor.
Category: Visual Arts.
Non-fiction: Yes. Fiction: No. Poetry: No. Graphics: Yes.
Notes: Published quarterly with circulation 6,000. Features of 1,500 to 2,000 words and shorter articles 500-600 words about art, galleries, museums, reviews and previews, and profiles plus contemporary artists, collectors and dealers, art technique, new equipment, supplies and some commentary on controversial issues. Fees range from $50 to $200 on publication. Query first. Guidelines available.

ARTICHOKE
901 Jervis Street, #208
Vancouver, BC V6E 2B6
Tel: (604) 683-1941. Fax: (604) 683-1941
Contact: Paula Gustafson.
Category: Visual Arts.
Non-fiction: Yes. Fiction: No. Poetry: No. Graphics: Yes.
Notes: Published three times a year. *Artichoke* is about the visual arts of western Canada. Features, interviews, critical reviews about the fine arts, architecture, applied arts and decorative arts, cultural politics and art trends in Canada. Articles 500 to 2,500 words. Pays approximately $75 per article. Guidelines and back issues $15 with SASE.

ARTS ATLANTIC
145 Richmond Street
Charlottetown, PE C1A 1J1
Tel: (902) 628-6138. Fax: (902) 566-4648
Contact: Joseph Sherman, Editor.
Category: Visual Arts.
Non-fiction: Yes. Fiction: No. Poetry: No. Graphics: Yes.
Notes: Published three times a year with circulation 2,700. Atlantic Canada's award winning arts review magazine featuring reviews, reports, fine arts, cinema, video, performance, literature, and controversial topics about the Canadian arts culture scene. Reviews are 600-800 words, features are 1,200 to 3,000 words. Pays $75 for reviews, 15 cents/word and up to $400 for features on publication. Query by mail, phone or fax. Guidelines available.

ATHLETICS Magazine
1185 Eglinton Avenue East, Suite 601
North York, ON M3C 3C6
Tel: (416) 426-7215. Fax: (416) 426-7358
E-mail: <ontrack@io.org>
Web site: <http://www.io.org/~ontrack/>
Contact: John Craig.
Category: Sports.
Non-fiction: Yes. Fiction: No. Poetry: No. Graphics: Yes.
Notes: Published nine times a year. *Athletics Magazine* covers all Canadian areas of track and field, road racing, running, cycling, marathons, long distance, obstacle courses and major competitions around the world as well as Canada. Features are about prominent athletes, coaches, teams and organizations. Rank lists and other details included. Guidelines available.

ATLANTIC BAPTIST
Box 756
Kentville, NS B4N 3X9
Tel: (902) 681-6868. Fax: (902) 681-0315
Contact: Editor.
Category: Special Interest/Religion.
Non-fiction: Yes. Fiction: No. Poetry: No. Graphics: Yes.

AUTHORS: An On-line Periodical for New Writers
501 Cambridge Street S.E.
Medicine Hat, AB T1A 0T3
Tel: (403) 526-2524. Fax: (403) 526-2524
E-mail: <authmag@aol.com>
Web site: <http://members.aol.com/authmag/authors.htm>
Contact: Philip Murphy, Publisher/Editor.
Category: Literary
Notes: *Authors* has discontinued its pulp version and is *ON-LINE* on the Internet. This literary magazine focuses on the development of writers on the Internet. These submissions are also entries for the monthly *ON-LINE* Contest prize of $100. There is a $15 entry fee. This site also reports other resources for writers.

AZURE
2 Silver Avenue
Toronto, ON M6R 3A2
Tel: (416) 588-2588. Fax: (416) 588-2357
Contact: Nelda Rodger, Editor.
Category: Special Interest
Notes: Publishes bimonthly, circulation 12,000. Specializes in areas of interest to Canadian designers, architects and visual artists. Covers developments in graphics, interior and industrial designs, Canadian arts and world arts, reviews, resources and profiles. Pays on publication. Guidelines available.

B&A NEW FICTION
(Formerly *Blood & Aphorisms*)
PO Box 702, Station P,
Toronto, ON M5S 2Y4
Tel: (416) 972-0637
E-mail: <fiction@interlog.com>
Web site: <http://www.interlog.com/~fiction/>
Contact: Tim Paleczny, Publisher, Dennis Boc, Editor.
Category: Literary.
Non-fiction: Yes. Fiction: Yes. Poetry: Yes. Graphics: Yes.
Notes: Published quarterly, circulation 2,000. This journal is dedicated to new and emerging writers, but also publishes established writers. Seeks innovative new styles in all genres. Articles 500 to 4,000 words. Pays $20 per page plus one-year subscriptions. Guidelines available.

BACKWATER REVIEW
PO Box 222, Stn B
OTTAWA, ON K1P 6C4
Contact: L. Brent Robillard, Editor.
Category: Literary.
Non-fiction: Yes. Fiction: Yes. Poetry: Yes. Graphic: Yes.
Notes: *Backwater Review* is a journal of contemporary writing and reviews, published twice a year. Subscriptions: $9 year (add $5 outside Canada). The magazine is professionally printed in a saddle-stitched, digest-format with black and white photography on a glossy cover. Backwater's goal is to provide a forum for new writers and a dynamic and enjoyable venue for readers. All styles accepted and encouraged. Submit up to five poems or two short stories along with cover letter and brief introduction. Drama, essays and photography also welcome. Emphasis on craft. Payment for publication is two issues of contributor's work. Annual poetry and fiction contests.

BC BOOKWORLD
3516 West 13th Avenue
Vancouver, BC V6R 2S3
Tel: (604) 736-4011. Fax: (604) 736-4011
E-mail: <bcbookworld@msn.com>.
Category: Literary
Contact: Alan Twigg, Publisher; Katja Pantzar, Editor.
Non-fiction: Yes. Fiction: Yes. Poetry: Yes. Graphics: Yes.
Notes: Published quarterly, circulation, 50,000 copies. *BC Bookworld* promotes BC authors and books through interviews, profiles, reviews, photo spreads, opinion/commentary. Covers bookstores, authors tours, and the entire literary scene. Fiction and Poetry are featured in articles about authors only. Articles 500 to 800 words. Payment is negotiated when assignment is confirmed. Query first.

BC BUSINESS Magazine
4180 Lougheed Highway, Suite 401,
Burnaby, BC V5C 6A7
Tel: (604) 299-7311. Fax: (604) 299-9188
Contact: Bonnie Irving, Editor.
Category: Business
Notes: published 12 times a year, circulation, 26,000. *BC Business Magazine*'s mandate is to inform readers of the latest trends shaping the BC business environment. Articles of 1000 to 2500 words about business owners, managers, entrepreneurs, professionals as profiles, success stories, innovative techniques and banking/economics. Pays on publication; rates vary. Guidelines available.

BC OUTDOORS
780 Beatty St., Suite 300,
Vancouver, BC V6B 2M1
Tel: (604) 606-4644. Fax: (604) 687-1925
E-mail: <oppubl@istar.ca>
Contact: Karl Bruhn, Editor or Ms. Roegan Lloydd, Assistant Editor.
Category: Outdoor Recreation.
Non-fiction: Yes. Fiction: No. Poetry: No. Graphics: Yes.
Notes: Published eight times per year, circulation 40,000. Primarily interested in BC sport fishing, hunting and camping subjects. Buys one-time rights, uses photographs with articles. Query in writing with SASE. All submissions must be accompanied by an SASE.

BC SPORT FISHING
909 Jackson Crescent
New Westminster, BC V3L 4S1
Tel: (604) 521-4901 or (604) 683-4871. Fax: (604) 683-7716
Contact: Rikk Taylor.
Category: Sports / Outdoor Adventure.
Non-fiction: Yes. Fiction: No. Poetry: No. Graphics: Yes.
Notes: Published six times a year. This magazine is for the sport fisherman with eight to 12 adventure features in each issue. Fresh water fishing in lakes, rivers and streams are listed for best locations. Saltwater fishing opportunities are covered. Features are written by the best freelancers in the west. Guidelines available with SASE.

BC STUDIES: The British Columbia Quarterly
University of British Columbia
#165 - 1855 West Mall
Vancouver, BC V6T 1Z2
Tel: (604) 822-3727. Fax: (604) 822-9452
E-mail: <bcstudie@unixg.ubc.ca>
Contact: Carlyn Craig, Business Manager/Editorial Assistant.
Editors are R. Cole Harris and Jean Barman.
Category: Scholarly Journal.
Non-fiction: Yes. Fiction: No. Poetry: Yes. Graphics: Yes.
Notes: Published quarterly *BC Studies* is devoted to all aspects of human history in BC. Articles 1,000 to 3,000 words about subjects from anthropology to the economy are carefully researched and clearly presented; book reviews, 500 to 2,000 words are in-depth analysis of current titles; bibliography—an overview of recent publications—by theme. Average article 25 to 30 double-spaced pages (6,000 to 7,500 words). Disk required at publication. Does not pay but contributors may obtain a free guideline with SASE.

BC WOMAN
704 Clarkson Street
New Westminster, BC V3M 1E2
Tel: 604) 540-8448. Fax: (604) 524-0041
Contact: Anne Brennan, Editor.
Category: People and Places.
Non-fiction: Yes. Fiction: Yes. Poetry: Yes. Graphics: Yes.
Notes: Published 12 times a year. Circulation 33,000. *BC Woman* celebrates the achievements of BC women through articles, profiles, discussions of issues, finance, politics, business apparel, cuisine, and opinion/advice columns. Fiction and Poetry are also featured each issue. Photographs, artwork of BC women artists also included. Pays 10-30 cents work for 800-3000 words 30 days following publication when assignment has been pre-negotiated. Query first. Guidelines available.

BEAUTIFUL BRITISH COLUMBIA

929 Ellery Street

Victoria, BC V9A 7B4

Tel: (250) 384-5456. Fax: (250) 384-2812

E-mail: <ed@bbcmag.bc.ca>

Web site: <http://www.beautifulbc.com/bbc/>

Contact: Brian McGill, Editor-in-Chief or Anita Willis, Assistant Editor <trav@bbcmag.bc.ca>.

Category: Special Interest.

Non-fiction: Yes. Fiction: No. Poetry: No. Graphics: Yes (Photography).

Notes: Published quarterly with four seasons. Publishes articles about British Columbia focusing on geography and travel. Articles 1500 to 2500 words that are well-researched, and photo spreads by established BC freelance writers and photographers. Pays 50 cents per word and up for negotiated assignments. Query first. Guidelines for writers and photographers available.


BEAVER, THE

167 Lombard Ave., #478

Winnipeg, MAN R3B 0T6

Tel: (204) 988-9300. Fax: (204) 988-9309

E-mail: <beaver@cyberspc.mb.ca>

Web site: <http://www.cyberspc.mb.ca/~otmw/cnhs/cnhs.html>

Contact: Christopher Dafoe, Editor.

Category: People and Places.

Non-fiction: Yes. Fiction: No. Poetry: No. Graphics: Yes.

Notes: Published bimonthly. Historical well-researched, informative articles about Canada receive honoraria of $500 to $600 on publication for 3000 to 4000 words. Unpublished journals and letters are sought. Guidelines are available.


BENEATH THE SURFACE

McMaster University Society of English

Dept. of English,

Chester New Hall, McMaster Univ.

Hamilton, ON L8S 4S8

Contact: Editor change every four months.

Category: Literary.

Non-fiction: Yes. Fiction: Yes. Poetry: Yes. Graphics: Yes.

Notes: Published twice a year. Accepts manuscripts up to 3,000 words, multicultural/ethnic, experimental, fantasy, feminist, gay historical, horror, humour/satire, lesbian, literary, mystery/suspense, psychic/supernatural/occult, science fiction, and pays in contributor's copies. Avoid formula fiction. Send printouts of manuscript, biographical information, cover letter and disk.

BLACKFLASH
12 - 23rd Street E.,
Saskatoon, SK S7K 0H5
Tel: (306) 244-8018. Fax: (306) 665-6568
E-mail: <ac010@sfn.saskatoon.sk.ca>
Web site: <http://www.io.org/~wallace/bfindex.html>
Contact: Monte Greenshields.
Category: Photography.
Non-fiction: Yes. Fiction: No. Poetry: No. Graphics: Yes.
Notes: Published quarterly, circulation, 1,500. Dedicated to Canadian photography and photographers in critical articles, profiles, news, innovative techniques and markets/contests. Pays $100 to $250 for 1,500 to 2,500 words. Accepts proposal outlines only. Guidelines and back issues available at $2.50 each.

BLUEGRASS Magazine
#1-231 Victoria Street
Kamloops, BC V2C 2A1
Tel: (250) 374-3313. Fax: (250) 374-0304
Contact: The Editor.
Category: Music.
Non-fiction: Yes. Fiction: No. Poetry: No. Graphics: Yes.
Notes: Published six times a year, *Bluegrass Magazine* is Canada's only national bluegrass publication. There are 14 regular columnists who keep readers attuned to the Bluegrass news heartbeat in North America, where to find bands and concert events. Submissions are invited for articles, 1,000-2,500 words; record reviews, 500 to 750 words; interviews, profiles, and regional events, 750 to 1,200 words. Send SASE for guidelines. Article proposals only.

BOOKS IN CANADA:
The Canadian Review of Books
427 Mount Pleasant Road
Toronto, ON M4S 2L8
Tel: (416) 489-4755. Fax: (416) 489-6045
E-mail: <binc@istar.ca>
Contact: Gerald Owen, Managing Editor.
Category: Literary & Scholarly.
Non-fiction: Yes. Fiction: No. Poetry: No. Graphics: Yes.
Notes: Published nine times a year, circulation 8,000. *Books in Canada* provides spirited commentary on over 400 books each year, children's novels, non-fiction and poetry plus profiles and interviews with Canadian authors. Pays 12 cents per word on publication for assigned articles. No unsolicited submissions. Query first, always. Study back issues, send SASE for guidelines.

BORDER CROSSINGS

393 Portage Ave., Suite Y300,

Winnipeg, MB R3B 3H6

Tel: (204) 942-5778. Fax: (204) 949-0793

Contact: Meeka Walsh, Editor.

Category: Arts & Culture.

Non-fiction: Yes. Fiction: Yes. Poetry: Yes. Graphics: Yes.

Notes: Published quarterly, Circulation 4,000. Covers contemporary arts in Canada and internationally. Topics include architecture, dance, fiction, film, painting, photography, poetry, politics and theatre. Accepts reviews, feature articles, book reviews, artist profiles, and photography and pays a negotiated fee on publication.


BORDER/LINES

183 Bathurst Street, #301

Toronto, ON M5T 2R7

Tel: (416) 504-5249. Fax: (416) 514-8781.

Category: Arts & Culture.

Non-fiction: Yes. Fiction: No. Poetry: No. Graphics: Yes.

Notes: Published quarterly. *Border/Lines* teeters along the edges of genders, literature, science, multiculturalism, mass communications, and political culture. It is eclectic and diverse. It seeks excellence in articles, exquisite style, communicating the cutting edge in every theme and pushing a subject to its limits. Query before submitting.


BOUDOIR NOIR

PO BOX 5, Station F,

Toronto, ON M4Y 2L4

Tel:(416) 591-2387. Fax:(416) 591-1572

E-mail: <boudoir@boudoir-noir.com>

Web site: <http://boudoir-noir.com>

Contact: Robert Dante or Diane Wilputte, Editors.

Non-fiction: Yes. Fiction: No. Poetry: No. Graphics: Yes.

Notes: Quarterly magazine about leather fetish, consensual SM lifestyles, publishes non-fiction only. They prefer stories that focus on people rather than abstract fetishes or issues. Pays $25-$50 for feature articles for 500 to 1,000 words. Photos one-time use $10. Some expenses paid if negotiated at time of story assignment. No simultaneous submissions.

BRIARPATCH

2138 McIntyre Street,

Regina, SK S4P 2R7

Tel: (306) 525-2949. Fax: (306) 565-3430

Contact: George Martin Manz, Editor.

Category: News and Opinion.

Non-fiction: Yes. Fiction: No. Poetry: No. Graphics: Yes.

Notes: Published 10 times a year, Circulation 2,500. This award-winning magazine publishes investigative, activist journalism on issues concerning Saskatchewan and Canada not published in mainstream media. Short critical articles 600 to 1,100 words on politics, environment, agriculture, aboriginal and women's rights and labour. Pays in free copies only. Query for back issues and guidelines.


BRICK: A Writer's Journal

Box 537, Station Q

Toronto, ON M4T 2M5

Contact: Linda Spalding and Michael Ondaatje, Editors.

Category: Literary.

Non-fiction: Yes. Fiction: Yes. Poetry: Yes. Graphics: Yes.

Notes: Published three times a year. *Brick* is dedicated to be accessible to writers, poets, artists, photographers and illustrators. Submissions are welcome for features, 1,000-3,000/words, literary reviews, 750-1200/words, short essays, interviews, 1,000-1,750/words, photographs, sketches, art/concepts, send photocopies on spec. Submit queries, SASE for guidelines by mail. Payments vary.


BUILD AND GREEN

Studio D, 2922 West 6th Ave.

Vancouver, BC V6K 1X3

Tel: (604) 730-1940. Fax: (604) 730-7860

Contact: Leonard Wexler, Publisher/Editor.

Category: Special Interest/design/building/gardening.

Non-fiction: Yes. Fiction: No. Poetry: No. Graphics: Yes.

Notes: Published 10 times a year. *Build and Green* is Canada's hands-on magazine of design, building and gardening. They invite articles about installations, e.g. solariums, flooring, greenhouses, fences, benches & arbors, gardens, lawns, etc. They also consider articles about design, technology, law, finance, computers, or any field connected with design, building or gardening. Queries welcome.

BUSINESS ACCESS (ACCHS AUX AFFIAIRES)
Suite 200, 16 Concourse Gate
Nepean, ON K2E 7S8
Tel: (613) 727-5466. Fax: (613) 727-6910
E-mail: <MarionS@nortext.com>
Contact: Marion Soublihre, Editor.
Category: Business.
Non-fiction: Yes. Fiction: No. Poetry: No. Graphics: Yes.
Notes: Published quarterly, circulation 500,000. *Business Access* in a national publication going to small and medium sized businesses in Canada. Articles should focus on advice, how-to, tips, resources, success stories, strategies and entrepreneurial encouragement for business owners. Pays 30 cents per word for 750 words max. Query, back copies, guidelines available.

BUSINESS EXAMINER
1824 Store Street
Victoria, BC V8T 4R4
Tel: (250) 381-3926. Fax: (250) 381-5606
E-mail: <be@busex.bc.ca>
Web site: <http://www.busex.bc.ca>
Contact: Woody Turnquist, Publisher or Bjorn Stavrum, Editor.
Category: Business.
Non-fiction: Yes. Fiction: No. Poetry: No. Graphics: Yes.
Notes: Published by Island Publishers 24 times a year, the first and third Tuesday of each month. Circulation of South Island edition, 14,000; North Island edition, 10,500. Directed towards business owners, managers, entrepreneurs and professionals. Topics cover business trends, tourism, profiles of people and companies shaping the business environment on Vancouver Island particularly. Pays 35 cents/word on acceptance of 1,000 to 2,500 word. Query first.

BUSINESS QUARTERLY
Richard Ivey School of Business,
University of Western Ontario
London, ON N6A 3K7
Tel: (519) 661-3309. Fax: (519) 661-3838
E-mail: <asmith@novell.business.uwo.ca>
Web site: <http://www.business.uwo.ca/~bq/bqhome.html>
Contact: Angela Smith, Publisher/Editor.
Category: Business.
Non-fiction: Yes. Fiction: No. Poetry: No. Graphics: Yes.
Notes: Published quarterly, circulation 9,000. This is an educational/professional development journal for senior executives. Articles 2,000 to 3,000 words invited. Does not pay. Guidelines available.

C Magazine
PO Box 5, Station B,
Toronto, ON M5T 2T2
Tel: (416) 539-9495. Fax: (416) 531-7610
E-mail: <cmag@istar.ca>
Contact: Dawn Weaver, Editor/Publisher.
Category: Visual Arts.
Non-fiction: Yes. Fiction: No. Poetry: No. Graphics: Yes.
Notes: Published quarterly, circulation 4,500. *C Magazine* provides a forum for contemporary art and criticism of issues surrounding art in Canadian culture. Features range from 500 to 2,500 words, reviews 500 words maximum plus graphics/photo spreads of original artist's projects. Payment varies $100 and up on publication. Guidelines provided.

CAMERA CANADA: A Forum for Photographers
1140 South Dyke Road
New Westminster, BC V3M 5A2
Tel: (604) 524-5039. Fax: (604) 524-5039
Contact: Marilyn McEwen, Editor.
Category: Special Interest.
Non-fiction: Yes. Fiction: No. Poetry: No. Graphics: Yes.
Notes: Published twice a year by the National Association for Photographic Art, (NAPA). Circulation 6,000. NAPA is a non-profit organization committed to promotion of photography as an art form. Articles cover camera handling techniques, reports on new processes, personal experiences and showcases emerging photographers and their portfolios, method and philosophy. Articles 2-6,000/words. Does not pay but queries welcomed. Guidelines available with SASE.

CANADA JOURNAL
Ruland Communications Inc.
12 Lawton Boulevard
Toronto, ON M4V 1Z4
Tel: (416) 927-9129. Fax: (416) 927-9118
Contact: The Editor.
Category: News & Opinion.
Non-fiction: Yes. Fiction: No. Poetry: No. Graphics: Yes.
Notes: Published six times a year. This is Canada's unofficial ambassador to Europe providing German speaking Europeans with information about business and travel opportunities in Canada. Regular features range from real estate, investment, politics to the economy. Submit queries with SASE.

CANADA QUILTS
PO Box 39, Station A
Hamilton, ON L8N 3A2
Tel: (905) 523-5828. Fax: (905) 523-1200
Contact: The Editor.
Category: Special Interest.
Non-fiction: Yes. Fiction: No. Poetry: No. Graphics: Yes.
Notes: Published five times a year. *Canada Quilts* covers news, events, and reviews of original quilting patterns, designed by Canadians. Features cover how-to instructions for novices. Regular columns: "Guildbuilding" addresses Guild management, "CQM Yesterday" discusses antique quilts, and historical perspectives, "Pro-File" features Canadian quilters who teach, lecture or write. Pay varies with or without photos. Query with SASE. Guidelines available.

CANADIAN AMATEUR PLAYWRIGHTS' CATALOGUE
c/o Questex Consulting Ltd.
8 Karen Drive, Guelph ON N1G 2N9
E-mail: <slater@net2.eos.uoguelph.ca>
Contact: Keith Slater, Publisher/Editor.
Category: Playscripts.
Non-fiction: No. Poetry: No. Fiction: No. Graphics: No.
Notes: CAPCAT is a cooperative play publishing venture inaugurated under the auspices of the Waterloo-Wellington Branch of the Canadian Authors Association. For a low fee, plays will be evaluated, if accepted, published in CAPCAT. (If rejected, comments for improvement/partial refund.) Royalties at 10% of playscript sales and 50% of per performance rights are paid annually. Queries welcome.

CANADIAN ANTIQUE POWER
PO Box 120
Teeswater, ON N0G 2S0
Tel: (519) 392-6733. Fax: (519) 392-6731
Contact: The Editor.
Category: Special Interest.
Non-fiction: Yes. Fiction: No. Poetry: No. Graphics: Yes.
Notes: Published six times a year. *CAP* is a source book for antique farm implements featuring articles on restoration projects, steam and antique show reports, histories of Canada's farm machinery companies and reprints of century-old operators' manual and agricultural history items. Query before submitting.

CANADIAN ART
70 The Esplanade, 2nd floor
Toronto, ON M5E 1R2
Tel: (416) 368-8854. Fax: (416) 368-6135
Contact: Richard Rhodes.
Category: Visual Arts.
Non-fiction: Yes. Fiction: No. Poetry: No. Graphics: Yes.
Notes: Published quarterly. *Canadian Art* is designed for the gallery visitor, art collector, artist, designer, architect and general reader. Visual graphics with articles display paintings, sculptures, films, photography, architecture, design, videos and television. Profiles of prominent artists and critical analysis of art/culture. Query with SASE.

CANADIAN AUTHOR
Subscription and business correspondence to:
Canadian Authors Association
Box 419,
Campbellford, ON KOL 1L0
Tel: (705) 653-0323. Fax: (705) 473-4450
E-mail: <canauth@redden.on.ca>
National Web site:
<http://www.CanAuthors.org/national.html>
Editorial queries to:
Doug Bale, Editor
Canadian Author Magazine
776 Colborne St.
London, ON N6A 3Z9
E-mail: <DougBale@netcom.ca>.
Category: Literary.

Non-fiction: Yes. Fiction: Yes. Poetry: Yes. Graphics: Yes.
Notes: Published quarterly, circulation 3,000. *Canadian Author* is Canada's oldest, most respected national writers' magazine. Features articles on the business of writing and the writing life, plus profiles of the people who influence Canadian literature (800-2800 words, $30-$60 per page). One fiction story (2,000 to 3,000 words) selected each issue for Okanagan Award. Pays $125 on publication. Book reviews pay $20, poetry $20-$30 per page. Written queries only with SASE. Guidelines available. Sample copies available for $5 from Campbellford office.

CANADIAN BAPTIST
195 West Mall, Suite 414
Etobicoke, ON M9C 5K1
Tel: (416) 662-8600. Fax: (416) 662-0780
Contact: Larry Matthews, Editor.
Category: Special Interest/Religion.
Non-fiction: Yes. Fiction: No. Poetry: No. Graphics: Yes.
Notes: Published 10 times a year for members of Baptist Churches in Canada. Accepts articles with or without photos about faith, society, social issues, ethical issues, church politics, philanthropy, and justice. Pays negotiated fees. Written queries only.

CANADIAN BIKER
Box 4122
735 Market St.
Victoria, BC V8T 2E2
Tel: (250) 384-0333. Fax: (250) 384-1832
E-mail: <canbike@islandnet.com>
Web site: <http://www.islandnet.com/~canbike/canbike.html>
Contact: Len Creed, Publisher/Editor.
Category: Sports.
Non-fiction: Yes. Fiction: No.
Poetry: No. Graphics: Yes.

Notes: Published eight times a year, circulation 25,000. Subscriptions $27 year. This motorcycle magazine features interviews, narratives, in-depth articles about foreign country tours, events, racing, vintage and custom motorcycling. Sport enthusiasts are offered a wide range of new products and resources. Preferred length 500 to 1,500 words on 3½ inch disk with hard copy and minimum of two photos—captioned. Payments vary on publication. Guidelines available.

CANADIAN BUSINESS ECONOMICS
Canadian Association for Business Economics
PO Box 828, Station B
Ottawa, ON K1P 5P9
Tel: (613) 238-4831. Fax: (613) 238-7698
Web site: <http://www.cabe.ca>
Contact: Andrew Sharpe, Editor.
Category: Business.
Non-fiction: Yes. Others: No.

CANADIAN BUSINESS
777 Bay Street, 5th Floor
Toronto, ON M5W 1A7
Tel: (416) 596-5475 Toll Free 1-800-465-0700. Fax: (416) 599-0901
Contact: The Editor.
Category: Business.
Non-fiction: Yes. Fiction: No. Poetry: No. Graphics: Yes.
Notes: Published monthly. *Canadian Business* offers professional development for executives in Canada's top businesses. Information provides guidance, insight, reliable trends, strategic ideas that affect business climate. Every area of relevance is covered with excellence in writing style. Query for guidelines.

CANADIAN CHILDREN'S LITERATURE
Department of English,
University of Guelph
Guelph, ON N1G 2W1
Tel: (519) 824-4120, Ext 3189. Fax: (519) 837-1315
E-mail: <ccl@uoguelph.ca>
Web site: <http://www.uoguelph.ca/englit/ccl/>
Contact: Gay Christofides, Administrator.
Category: Children.
Non-fiction: Yes. Fiction: No. Poetry: No. Graphics: Yes.

Notes: Published quarterly, circulation 1,000. Scholarly articles of criticism and reviews of Canadian literature for children and young adults as professional development for teachers, librarians, academics and parents. Articles, reviews, illustrations, photos, also covers film, electronic media, videos and computer mediums. Articles 2,000 to 8,000 words. Seeking articles on Entertainers, The Holocaust, Discourses of Self and Science. Does not pay, but promotes writer's name in ad/lit and bookmarks. Guidelines and back issues available.

CANADIAN COIN NEWS
103 Lakeshore Road, Suite 202,
St. Catharines, ON L2N 2T6
Tel: (416) 646-7744. Fax: (416) 646-0995
E-mail: <bret@trajan.com>
Web site: <http://www.trajan.com/coin/>
Contact: Bret Evans, Editor.
Category: Special Interest.
Non-fiction: Yes. Fiction: No. Poetry: No. Graphics: Yes.
Notes: Published semi-monthly by Trajan Publishing Corp., circulation 13,000. *CCN* is a tabloid magazine for Canadian collectors of coins and paper money. Pays one month following publication. Fees negotiable. Prefers electronic queries.

CANADIAN COWBOY COUNTRY
355 Yellowhead Highway #316
Kamloops, BC V2H 1H1
Tel: (250) 314-1506. Fax: (250) 314-1508
E-mail: <cowgirl@mail.netshop.net>
Web site: <http://www.canadiancowboy.com>
Contact: Carla Dornan, Publisher, Sherril Siebert, Editor.
Category: Special Interest/Western cowboy cultural heritage.
Non-fiction: Yes. Fiction: Yes. Poetry: Yes. Graphics: Yes.
Notes: Published bimonthly, 5000 circulation to BC, Alberta and Saskatchewan. *Canadian Cowboy Country* provides a diverse western content uniquely focused on cowboy culture, such as rodeos, ranching, western lifestyles, memoirs, entertaining adventure stories and profiles, colourful photos spreads, spirit of the west, fashion, western trends and decor, arts and entertainment, music and western events calendar.

CANADIAN DIMENSION
301- 63 Albert Street
Winnipeg, MB R3B 1G4
Tel: (204) 957-1519. Fax: (204) 943-4617
E-mail: <info@canadiandimension.mb.ca>
Web site:
<http://www.canadiandimension.mb.ca/cd/index.htm>
Contact: Michelle Torres.
Category: News & Opinion.
Non-fiction: Yes. Fiction: No.
Poetry: Yes. Graphics: Yes.

Notes: Published bimonthly, circulation 3,000. *CD* is a magazine for optimists who want to make a difference in Canadian society and the world. Articles about environment, peace politics, labour movement, popular culture, Aboriginal peoples, minority races, women's issues, and alternative philosophies, radical ideas, are invited. Can pay honorarium for 600 to 2,000 words, poetry, photos and graphics/arts. Guidelines available.

## CANADIAN ETHNIC STUDIES

University of Calgary

2500 University Drive, N.W.

Calgary AL T2N 1N4

Tel: (403) 220-7257. Fax: (403) 282-8606

E-mail: <frideres@acs.ucalgary.ca>

Contact: Dr. J. S. Frideres and Mary Anne Morel, Co-Editors.

Category: Scholarly.

Non-fiction: Yes. Fiction: Yes. Poetry: Yes. Graphics: Yes.

Notes: Published three times a year. Circulation 1,000. This journal focuses on all ethnic groups in Canada and issues of concern to them. Immigration, inter-group relations, history, cultural life and artistic expressions. Articles, memoirs, fiction, poetry, illustrations, photography relevant to this ethnic group, all invited. Guidelines available.

## CANADIAN FICTION MAGAZINE

PO Box 1061,

240 King Street East

Kingston, ON K7L 4Y5

Tel: (613) 548-8429. Fax: (613) 548-1556

Contact: Managing Editor of Quarry Press.

Category: Literary.

Non-fiction: Yes. Fiction: Yes. Poetry: Yes. Graphics: Yes.

Notes: Published quarterly, circulation 1,500. Dedicated to new Canadian fiction, translations from French, Chinese, Polish, Ukrainian, Ojibway, Coast Salish Indians, Japanese, Spanish, German, Italian, Greek, and other languages spoken in Canada. Publishes short stories, novel excerpts and innovative/experimental fiction, illustrations, photos, manifestos, memories, articles. Pays $10 a page on publication. Guidelines available.

## CANADIAN FOREIGN POLICY Journal

The Norman Paterson School of International Affairs

Rm. 106, Social Sciences Research Building,

Carleton University,

1125 Colonel By Drive,

Ottawa, ON  K1S 5B6

Tel: (613) 520-5756. Fax: (613) 520-3981

E-mail: <epotter@ccs.carleton.ca> or <prourke@ccs.carleton.ca>

Contact: The Editor.

Category: Business.

Non-fiction: Yes. Fiction: No. Poetry: No. Graphics: Yes.

Notes: Published three times a year. *Canadian Foreign Policy: The Practice and Policies of Canada's International Relations*, contains fully referenced articles on topics such as trade, investment, defence, intelligence, foreign aid, immigration, multilateralism and Canada's primary bilateral relationships. Query with SASE.

CANADIAN FORUM

804-251 Laurier Ave. West

Ottawa, ON K1P 5J6

Tel: (800) 567-3393 or 1-800-567-3393. Fax: (902) 425-0166

Contact: Duncan Cameron, Editor.

Category: News & Opinion.

Non-fiction: Yes. Fiction: Yes. Poetry: Yes. Graphics: Yes.

Notes: Published 10 times a year, circulation 10,000. *Canadian Forum* covers every aspect of Canadian politics, national and international affairs, economics, and business. It also carries substantial articles on the arts, literature, film and high quality fiction and poetry. Articles 2,500 to 3,000 words. Pays honorarium of $100 per article, $50 per review, on publication. Send SASE for guidelines.

CANADIAN GARDENING

130 Spy Court

Markham, ON L3R 0W5

Tel: (905) 475-8440. Fax: (905) 475-9506

Contact: Lis Primeau, Editor.

Category: Home and Garden.

Non-fiction: Yes. Fiction: No. Poetry: No. Graphics: Yes.

Notes: Published seven times a year, circulation 130,000. This magazine is dedicated to the home gardener. Invite articles about garden design, tips and techniques on gardening, Canadian climate, plants, species, profiles, products, seed catalogue lists, and seasonal plantings. Pays on acceptance for 1,000 to 2,500 words at $400 to $700, with or without photos. Query with outlines. Guidelines available.

CANADIAN GEOGRAPHIC

The Royal Canadian Geographical Society

39 McArthur Avenue

Vanier, ON K1L 8L7

Tel: (613) 745-4629. Fax: (613) 744-0974

E-mail: <editorial@cangeo.ca>

Web site: <http://www.cangeo.ca/>

Contact: Rick Boychuk, Editor.

Category: People and Places.

Non-fiction: Yes. Fiction: No. Poetry: No. Graphics: Yes.

Notes: Published six times a year by the Royal Canadian Geographical Society, circulation, 245,000. Widely used in secondary schools, colleges and universities as teaching resource. Describes/illuminates with colour photography all aspects of Canada, people, places, natural resources, wildlife, landscape, sciences, archaeology to zoology. Pays $1.00 per word on acceptance for 2,000 to 3,500 words. A large paid circulation—a very lucrative freelance opportunity. Written queries; back issues and guidelines available.

CANADIAN HISTORICAL REVIEW
University of Toronto Press/Journals Division
5201 Dufferin Street
North York, ON M3H 5T8
Tel: (416) 667-7781. Fax: (416) 667-7881
E-mail: <journals@gpu.utcc.utoronto.ca>
Web site:
<http://library.utoronto.ca/www/utpress/depthome.htm>
Contact: The Editor.
Category: Special Interest.
Non-fiction: Yes. Fiction: No. Poetry: No. Graphics: Yes.

Notes: Published quarterly. *CHR* covers a broad spectrum of Canada's history, scholarly articles, reviews, research with bibliographies of recent historical publications. Query for guidelines with SASE.

CANADIAN HOME PUBLISHERS
511 King Street, West, Suite 120
Toronto, ON M5V 2Z4
Tel: (416) 593-0204. Fax: (416) 591-1630
E-mail: <homepub@inforamp.net>
Contact: Cobi Ladner.
Category: Special Interest/Decorating.
Non-fiction: Yes. Fiction: No. Poetry: No. Graphics: Yes.
Notes: *Canadian Home Publishers* covers home decorating, painting, wall-papering, texture coverings, antiques, modern furniture, designs, colour complements, creative solutions to difficult structures and general service, products and information about home decorating. Pays an honorarium for well-written articles with colour photos. Submit on diskette please. Queries welcome.

CANADIAN HORSEMAN
225 Industrial Parkway South
PO Box 670 Aurora, ON L4G 4J9
Tel: (905) 727-0107. Fax: (905) 841-1530
Contact: Lee Benson, Editor.
Category: Special Interest.
Non-fiction: Yes. Fiction: No. Poetry: No. Graphics: Yes.
Notes: Published six times a year, circulation 10,000. *Canadian Horseman* features the Western riding style and covers everything about care of the horse, training, grooming, farm management, feeds, grazing, husbandry, competitions, techniques of riding style, and service and special equipment, meetings, calendars, trails and outdoors recreation. Pay negotiated for 500 to 1,500 words and photos. Guidelines and back issues available.

CANADIAN HOUSE AND HOME
511 King Street West, Suite 120
Toronto, ON M5V 2Z4
Tel: (416) 593-0204. Fax: (416) 591-1630
E-mail: <mail@canhomepub.com>
Web                                    site:
<http://www.canadianhouseandhome.com/>
Contact: Cobi Ladner, Editor.
Category: Home and Garden.
Non-fiction: Yes. Fiction: No.
Poetry: No. Graphics: Yes.
Notes: Published eight times a year, circulation
130,000. Features Canadian decorators, designers,
architects, creative decorating, how-to articles, with
photo spreads. Fees are negotiable, 300 to 1,000
words with colour photos. Query, guidelines and
back issues available.

CANADIAN JOURNAL OF HISTORY
ANNALES CANADIENNES D'HISTOIRE
University of Saskatchewan
Department of History
9 Campus Drive
Saskatoon, SK S7N 5A5
Tel: (306) 966-5794. Fax: (306) 966-5852
E-mail: <cjh@duke.usask.ca>
Web site: <http://www.usask.ca/history/cjh/>
Contact: Christopher A. Kent.
Category: Scholarly.
Non-fiction: Yes. Fiction: No. Poetry: No. Graphics: Yes.
Notes: Published three times a year. Circulation 2,000. *CJH* carries original scholar-
ship from all fields of history except the history of Canada. Articles and reviews
cover themes and controversies in historical writing. Does not pay. Query with
SASE for guidelines.

CANADIAN JOURNAL OF SOCIOLOGY

Dept. of Sociology, University of Alberta

Edmonton, Alberta, T6G 2H4

Tel: (403) 492-5941. Fax: (403) 492-5941

E-mail: <cjscopy@gpu.srv.ualberta.ca>

Web site: <http://www.ualberta.ca/~cjscopy/cjs.html>

Contact: Susan A. McDaniel, Editor

Assistant Editor: Joanne Milson—E-mail: <Joanne.Milson@UAlberta.CA>.

Category: Scholarly.

Non-fiction: Yes. Fiction: No. Poetry: No. Graphics: No.

Notes: Founded in 1975, the *Canadian Journal of Sociology/Cahiers canadiens de sociologie* is a leading source of information on Canadian society, as well as new trends in the discipline internationally. The *Journal* is dedicated to publishing high-quality, original articles representing a wide spectrum of sociological topics, perspectives and approaches.


CANADIAN JOURNAL OF WOMEN AND LAW

575 King Edward Ave.,

Ottawa, ON K1N 6W5

Tel: (613) 562-5800 Ext-3473. Fax: (613) 562-5124

E-mail: <cjwlrfd@gtn.net>

Contact: Lucille Beland for English and Nitya Iyer French, Co-Editors.

Category: Scholarly.

Non-fiction: Yes. Fiction: No. Poetry: No. Graphics: No.


CANADIAN LAWYER

240 Edward Street

Aurora, ON L4G 3S9

Tel: (905) 841-6480. Fax: (905) 841-5078

Contact: The Editor.

Category: Special Interest.

Non-fiction: Yes. Fiction: No. Poetry: No. Graphics: Yes.

Notes: Published 10 times a year. *CL* covers the contemporary Canadian law scene, provides mandatory reading for those in legal professions. Subjects pertain to trends and developments, law firm mergers and expansions. Scholarly articles about cases, social issues from a legal perspective and news in latest legal technology markets. Query first with SASE.

CANADIAN LEADER, THE
PO Box 5112, Station F
Ottawa, ON K2C 3H4
Tel: (613) 224-5131. Fax: (613) 224-5982
E-mail: <leader@scouts.ca>
Web site:<http://www.scouts.ca/>
Contact: The Editor.
Category: Special Interest.
Non-fiction: Yes. Fiction: No. Poetry: No. Graphics: Yes.

Notes: Published 10 times a year. *Canadian Leader* is a magazine for adult members of Scouts Canada. It operates as a resource for leaders to use for activities, games, songs, crafts, the environment and the outdoors. Writers focus on the development of character, self-reliance, good citizenship, survival techniques, crafts, relationships and all areas of general interest for adults who work with young people. Query with SASE.

CANADIAN LIVING
25 Sheppard Ave. W,
North York, ON M2N 6S7
Tel: (416) 733-7600. Fax: (416) 733-8683
Contact: Bonnie Cowan, Editor
E-mail: <canadianliving@sympatico.ca>
Web site: <http://www.canadian-living.com/>.
Category: People and Places.
Non-fiction: Yes. Fiction: No. Poetry: No. Graphics: Yes.
Notes: Published 13 times a year, circulation 586,000. This popular mass-market Canadian life-style magazine focuses on a wide range of popular general interest articles for the family. Country/city homes and gardens, seasonal styles in fashions, decorating, crafts, health, fitness, contemporary living, pets, family relationships, travel and parenting. Fees vary on original manuscripts 300 to 2,000 words with photos. Guidelines available.

CANADIAN PUBLIC ADMINSTRATION
ADMINISTRATION PUBLIQUE DU CANADA
150 Eglinton Ave, East, #305
Toronto, ON M4P 1E8
Tel: (416) 932-3666. Fax: (416) 932-3667
Contact: The Editor.
Category: Special Interest.
Non-fiction: Yes. Fiction: No. Poetry: No. Graphics: Yes.
Notes: Published quarterly, *CPA* focuses on public policy and is a refereed, scholarly, examination of structures, processes, outputs and outcomes of public policy. This publication reaches management related to executive legislative, judicial and quasi-judicial functions in all spheres of government. Query with SASE.

CANADIAN PUBLIC POLICY
ANALYSE DE POLITIQUES
School of Policy Studies
Queen's University,
Kingston, ON K7L 3N6
Tel: (613) 545-6644. Fax: (613) 545-6960
E-mail: <beach@quedn.queensu.ca>
Web site: <http://qsilver.queensu.ca/~cpp/>
Contact: Charles M. Beach.
Category: Scholarly.
Non-fiction: Yes. Fiction: No. Poetry: No. Graphics: Yes.
Notes: Published quarterly. Circulation 10,000. *CPP* is a leading journal of public policy targeted for academics, government officials, business community, and students in professional training. *CPP*'s forum of ideas result from research, policy criticism and policy proposals. Topics cover every aspect of government policy pertaining to capital gains exemption, pensions, employment equity, right-to-die controversy, Canada's Green Plan, tax distribution and programs for women and children. Query first with SASE.

CANADIAN RAILWAY MODELLER
1453 Henderson Hwy #28103
Winnipeg, MB R2G 4E9
Tel: (204) 668-0168. Fax: (204) 669-9821
E-mail: <morgant@infobahn.mb.ca>
Web site: <http://www.infobahn.mb.ca/cdnrwymod/>
Contact: Morgan B. Turney, Editor/Publisher.
Category: Hobby Magazine.
Non-fiction: Yes. Fiction: No. Poetry: No. Graphics: Yes.
Notes: *Canadian Railway Modeller* is a colour glossy magazine with a distribution of 4,000, published bi-monthly. Articles are Canadian content written by railway modellers. Query about articles.

CANADIAN SELECT HOMES
Telemedia Publishing
25 Sheppard Avenue West, Suite 100
Toronto, ON M2N 6S7
Tel: (416) 218-3528. Fax: (416) 733-3566
Contact: The Editor.
Category: Special Interest.
Non-fiction: Yes. Fiction: No. Poetry: No. Graphics: Yes.
Notes: Published eight times a year. *Canadian Select Homes* presents great ideas about home renovation and decoration. Filled with coloured photographs of home interiors, how-to techniques illustrated, plus other topics relevant to home lifestyle, gardening tips, food and entertainment, household appliances, furniture and supplies. Query by mail with SASE.

CANADIAN SHAREOWNER
1090 University West Suite 202
Windsor, ON N9A 5S4
Tel: (416) 766-3021. Fax: (416) 767-6926
Contact: The Editor.
Category: Business.
Non-fiction: Yes. Fiction: No. Poetry: No. Graphics: Yes.
Notes: Published six times a year. *Canadian Shareowner* is about sound investing education and stock analysis. Features and articles assist in well-informed investment decisions. Every issue highlights two stocks for study. Other articles examine the merits of stocks and how to apply the Stock Selection Guide. Freelancers who are well-informed about the stock market are invited to submit queries. Guidelines available with SASE.

CANADIAN SPEECHES: Issues of the Day
194 King Street, Box 250
Woodville, ON KOM 2T0
Tel: (705) 439-2580. Fax: (705) 439-2646
E-mail: <speeches@lindsaycomp.on.ca>
Contact: The Editor.
Category: Special Interest.
Non-fiction: Yes. Fiction: No. Poetry: No. Graphics: Yes.
Notes: Published 10 times a year. Each issue of *Canadian Speeches* contains over 12 speeches given by informed leaders in government, national and foreign affairs, economics, business, law, education and the arts and sciences. Speeches are completely intact. Please query with SASE before submitting.

CANADIAN SPORTSCARD COLLECTOR
202-103 Lakeshore Road
St. Catharines, ON L2N 2T6
Tel: (905) 646-7744. Fax: (905) 646-0995
E-mail: <fiocca@trajan.com>
Web site:<http://www.trajan.com/trajan/collectibles/>
Contact: The Editor.
Category: Special Interest.
Non-fiction: Yes. Fiction: No. Poetry: No. Graphics: Yes.
Notes: Published 12 times a year. This magazines is Canada's most complete sports collectibles and price guide. It carries a range from vintage to newest hockey cards, O-Pee-Chee baseball cards, CFL football cards. Beehive photos, insert cards, non-sport issues and much more. Query before submitting.

CANADIAN SPORTSMAN, THE
PO Box 129,
25 Old Plank Road
Straffordville, ON N0J 1Y0
Tel: (519) 866-5558. Fax: (519) 866-5596
Contact: Gary Foerster, Editor.
Category: Sports.
Non-fiction: Yes. Fiction: No. Poetry: No. Graphics: Yes.
Notes: Published every two weeks, circulation 5,500. *The Canadian Sportsman* is about harness racing in Canada. News and features about riders, owners, tracks, horses, breeders racing statistics. Fees negotiable and queries invited.

CANADIAN STAMP NEWS
202-103 Lakeshore Road
St. Catharines, ON L2N 2T6
Tel: (905) 646-7744. Fax: (905) 646-0995
E-mail: <newsroom@trajan.com>
Web site:<http://www.trajan.com/trajan/stamp/>
Contact: Ellen Rodger, Editor.
Category: Special Interest.
Non-fiction: Yes. Fiction: No. Poetry: No. Graphics: Yes.
Notes: Published six times a year, circulation 9,500. *Stamp News* is the collectors choice, filled with the latest news and collecting tips from experienced philatelists. Current auction results, new releases from around the world and up-to-date show listings. Query before submitting. Fees negotiable. Guidelines available.

CANADIAN THEATRE REVIEW
Dept. of Drama, Queen's University
Kingston, ON K7L 3N6
Tel: (613) 545-2104.
Contact: Natalie Rewa, Editor.
Category: Performing Arts.
Non-fiction: Yes. Fiction: Yes. Poetry: Yes. Graphics: Yes.
Notes: Published quarterly, circulation 1,200. *C. T. Review* publishes plays, scripts, and features about playwrights, actors, directors, designers, costume designers, play-houses, and trends, techniques, tips, services, courses and calendars, and is thematic by issue. Fees negotiable for 1,500 to 3,000 words. Must send printout plus IBM WordPerfect diskette. Guidelines and previous issues available.

CANADIAN THOROUGHBRED

225 Industrial Parkway S.

PO Box 670

Aurora, ON L4G 4J9

Tel: (905) 727-0107. Fax: (905) 841-1530

Contact: Susan Jan Anstey, Publisher.

Category: Special Interest.

Non-fiction: Yes. Fiction: No. Poetry: No. Graphics: Yes.

Notes: Published six times a year, circulation 5,000. Horse racing in Canada with news, features, owners, pedigrees, stable product updates, jockey profiles, and calendars of events and travel. Query/send for back issues, guidelines.

CANADIAN WOMAN STUDIES JOURNAL

212 Founders College, York University,

4700 Keele Street,

North York, ON M3J 1P3

Tel: (416) 736-5356. Fax: (416) 736-5765

Contact: Luciana Ricciutelli, Editor.

Category: Literary.

Non-fiction: Yes. Fiction: Yes. Poetry: Yes. Graphics: Yes.

Notes: Published quarterly, circulation 4,000. This is a bilingual feminist journal with a wide range of topics within the articles, essays, fiction, poetry, and experimental writings, reviews on books, arts, films, music, politics, profiles etc. 500 to 2,000 words. Does not pay. Guidelines are available.

CANADIAN WORKSHOP

130 Spy Court

Markham ON L3R 5H6

Tel: (905) 475-8440. Fax (905) 475-9246

E-mail: <nstn4303@fox.nstn.ca>

Contact: Hugh McBride, Editor.

Category: Special Interest.

Non-fiction: Yes. Fiction: No. Poetry: No. Graphics: Yes.

Notes: Published monthly, circulation 113,000. This magazine showcases woodworking projects complete with lists of materials, diagrams, and step-by-step instructions. Other features cover home repair, renovation ideas, maintenance tips, product reviews, toys and projects to make for children. Please contact the editor first before sending manuscripts. Pays $800 on acceptance for features 800-2,000 words; $300 for 800-word articles. Guidelines and back issue are available for $2.

CANADIAN WRITER'S JOURNAL

Box 5180 New Liskeard, ON P0J 1P0

Tel: (705) 647-5424  Toll Free: 1-800-258-5451.

Fax: (705) 647-8366

E-mail: <dranchuk@aol.com>

Contact: Deborah Ranchuk, Editor.

Category: Literary.

Non-fiction: Yes. Fiction: Yes. Poetry: Yes. Graphics: Yes.

Notes: Published quarterly, *CWJ* began 1983 in Victoria BC, moved to New Liskeard in Sept. 1996. *CWJ* provides professional development for Canadian writers in all gen-

res. Pays honorariums for Non-fiction How-To articles 400-2,000 words, book reviews 250-500 words, of small Canadian Press, self-published titles on writing related subjects. Fiction published in *CWJ* are winning contest entries in Annual Short Fiction Competition each Fall. Poetry previously unpublished, haiku, senryu, tanka, sijo and renga max 5. Premium paid for electronic/disk acceptances. Pays on publication plus one copy. Send SASE #10 size for details.

CANADIAN YACHTING

395 Matheson Boulevard E.,

Mississauga, ON L4Z 2H2

Tel: (905) 890-1846. Fax: (905) 890-5769

Contact: Graham Jones, Editor.

Category: Sports/Outdoors.

Non-fiction: Yes. Fiction: No. Poetry: No. Graphics: Yes.

Notes: Published six times a year, circulation 15,000. *Canadian Yachting* is about sailboats, sailing, adventures, regattas, racing, keelboat and dinghy sailors. Features are 2-3,000 words and pay $400 to $600; 1,200-2,000 words pay $200-$250 after publication. Query first after reviewing back issues.

CANNABIS CANADA

504 - 21 Water Street,

Vancouver, B.C. V6B 1A1

Tel: (604) 669-0969. Fax: (604) 669-9038

E-mail: <muggles@hempbc.com>

Contact: Dana Larsen, Editor.

Category: Special Interest/Gardening.

Non-fiction: Yes. Fiction: Yes. Poetry: Yes. Graphics: Yes.

Notes: Published monthly, circulation 8,000. This tongue-in-cheek sassy magazine is for the cannabis consumer and those interested in drugs and drug policy. They have a mandate to bring an end to prohibition and censorship in Canada and worldwide. The magazines is published on tree-free cannabis hemp paper. Send for back issues.(Paper not for consumption). Articles 700 to 2,500 words. Pays 3/4 cents per word on publication, depending on the quality.

CAPILANO REVIEW, THE
2055 Purcell Way
North Vancouver, BC V7J 3H5
Tel: (604) 984-1712. Fax: (604) 983-7520
E-mail: <erains@capcollege.bc.ca>
Web site: <http://www.capcollege.bc.ca/departments/tcr/tcr.html>
Contact: Elizabeth Rains, Managing Editor.
Category: Literary/Scholarly.
Non-fiction: Yes. Fiction: Yes. Poetry: Yes. Graphics: Yes.
Notes: Published three times a year. Circulation 1,000. Est. 1972. *The Capilano Review*, winner of five National Magazine Awards, features poetry, prose and fine art by Canada's most innovative writers and artists. They are interested in new voices and wild visions, new art, and experimental prose. Pays $50-$200 per page on publication for up to 6,000 words. Please read back copies, available for $8.50, before submitting your manuscripts. Guidelines available for SASE.

CARP NEWS
27 Queen Street East, #702
Toronto, ON M5C 2M6
Tel: (416) 363-5562. Fax: (416) 363-7394
Contact: David Tafler, Publisher/Editor.
Category: Special Interest/Lifestyle.
Non-fiction: Yes. Fiction: Yes. Poetry: Yes. Graphics: Yes.
Notes: CARP is an acronym for Canadian Association of Retired Persons. The circulation is membership based for fifty-plus lifestyles. It is printed six times a year. *CARP* won an award in 1996 in the Mature Media category.

CASCADIA
1001 Wharf Street, 3rd floor
Victoria, BC V8W 1T6
Tel: (250) 388-4324. Fax: (250) 388-6166
Contact: Carolyn Camillei, Editor.
Category: Travel & Tourism.
Non-fiction: Yes. Fiction: No. Poetry: No. Graphics: Yes.
Notes: (Previously published as *Two Nation Vacation*.) Published annually, circulation 60,000. A vacation guide to promote and encourage travel to and around the region known as Cascadia. (Oregon, Washington, British Columbia, Alberta) Articles 1,000 to 2,000 words. Pays 25 cents per word on publication. Query first.

CATHOLIC INSIGHT

PO Box 625, Adelaide Station

36 Adelaide Street East

Toronto, ON M5C 2J8

Tel: (416) 368-4558. Fax: (416) 368-8575

E-mail: <interim@idirect.com>

Contact: Alphonse de Valk.

Category: Special Interest/Religion.

Non-fiction: Yes. Fiction: No. Poetry: No. Graphics: Yes.

Notes: Independent, published 10 times a year. Circulation 3,500. Comprehensive coverage of a wide range of issues of interest to Catholic Canadians. Covers politics, culture, spiritual life, family values, contemporary social issues with ethical and ecumenical perspective. Queries with published tear-sheets accepted. Prefers articles of 750 words. Payment negotiable on publication. Guidelines available.


CENTURYHOME

12 Mill Street South

Port Hope, ON L1A 2S5

Tel: (905) 885-2449 or 1-800-361-1957. Fax: (905) 855-5355

Contact: Joan Rumgay, publisher.

Category: Home & Garden.

Non-fiction: Yes. Fiction: No. Poetry: No. Graphics: Yes.

Notes: Published eight times/year, circulation 40,000.

*CenturyHome* showcases vintage homes, renovating/decorating how-to with illustrations, landscaping/gardening, furnishings/antiques plus country crafts and formal art providing diversity for tastes and budgets. Articles 1,000 to 1,500 words, fees vary but paid on publication. Study back issues available for $3.50. Guidelines available with SASE.


CHANCES

155B Front Street South

Orillia, ON L3V 4S6

Tel: (705) 327-0076. Fax: (705) 327-0076

Contact: Sandi Clarke, Editor.

Category: Special Interest.

Non-fiction: Yes. Fiction: Yes. Poetry: Yes. Graphics: Yes.

Notes: One pony-tab format publication. It features general interest topics, adventure, outdoors, table faire, northern women, music, homes, computing, touring, travel, nostalgia, memoirs and gaming industry (chances).

CHART

41 Britain St., #200

Toronto, ON M5A 1R7

Tel: (416) 363-3101. Fax: (416) 363-3109

E-mail: <chart@chartnet.com>

Web site: <http://www.chartnet.com>

Contact: Nada Laskovski, Publisher/Editor.

Category: Special Interest (Arts and Culture).

Non-fiction: Yes. Fiction: Yes. Poetry: No. Graphics: Yes.

Notes: Published monthly (12 times a year) ; Canada's music and youth culture magazine; includes B&W and colour photographs, original art where applicable, cartoons. Established 1990.

Covers new music for high school/university audience. Canadian bands, independent/alternative music, campus radio, pop culture. Reviews and articles. "Although we pay for most articles, it is only a token amount." Guidelines available.

CHATELAINE

777 Bay Street, 8th Floor

Toronto, ON M5W 1A7

Tel: 1-800-268-6812 Toronto: (416) 596-5523 Fax: 596-5516

Web site: <http://www.canoe.ca/chatelaine>

Contact: Rona Maynard, Editor.

Category: Canadian Women's People and Places.

Non-fiction; Yes. Fiction: Yes. Poetry: Yes. Graphics: Yes.

Notes: Circulation: 900,000. Published monthly by Maclean Hunter Publications Ltd. Covers current issues, personalities, lifestyles, health, relationships, travel and politics. Runs features of 1,500 to 2,500 words pay rates starts at $1,250, columns of 500 words on parenting, health, nutrition and fitness pays $350 up. All articles expected to be deeply researched, accurate with rich details. Features on beauty, food, fashion and home decorating written by staff and editors only. Buys first North American serial rights in English and French (to cover possible use in French-language edition). Pays on acceptance. Query first with brief outline. Guidelines available.

CHESTERTON REVIEW, THE
1437 College Drive
Saskatoon, SK S7N 0W6
Tel: (306) 966-8962. Fax: (306) 966-8917
Contact: The Editor.
Category: Literary.
Non-fiction: Yes. Fiction: Yes. Poetry: Yes. Graphics: Yes.
Notes: Published quarterly, *The Chesterton Review* is dedicated to the Communitarian Tradition of thinkers of the 20th Century. Subjects such as detective fiction, modernist culture, theological crisis, ethics and economics in combinations of literary, theological, sociological, economical are being accepted for publication. Fees vary and pays on publication. Become familiar with past issues before submitting query proposals. Guidelines available with SASE.

CHICKADEE
179 John Street, Suite 500
Toronto, ON M5T 3G5
Tel: (416) 971-5275 Fax: (416) 971-5294
E-mail: <wiredowl@owl.on.ca>
Web site: <http://www.owl.on.ca/chick/chick.html>
Contact: Carolyn Meredith, managing Editor.
Category: Youth & Children.
Non-fiction: Yes. Fiction: Yes. Poetry: Yes. Graphics: Yes.
Notes: Published 10 times a year with a circulation of 110,000. Content focusing on nature and science for children three – eight-year-olds. Designed to entertain and educate with photographs, illustrations, fiction, poetry, animal puzzles, science experiments and pullout poster. Pays $250 on acceptance for 800-900 words. Avoid anthropomorphic and religious material. Guidelines available.

CHRISTIAN WEEK
300-228 Notre Dame Ave.,
Winnipeg, MB R3B 1N7
Tel: (204) 943-1147. Fax: (204) 947-5632
E-mail: <editor@christianweek.org>
Web site: <http://www.christianweek.org>
Contact: Doug Koop, Editor.
Category: Special Interest/Religion.
Non-fiction: Yes. Fiction: Yes. Poetry: No. Graphics: Yes.
Notes: Published biweekly (24/yr), *CW* is a national, trans-denominational newspaper, written from an evangelical perspective, covering events and issues concerning Canadian Churches. Vigorous religious journalism committed to historic Christianity. Pays 10 cents per word on publication plus expenses for phone, fax, courier charges. Pays $8 per photo. Half of CW content by freelancers. Queries welcome. Guidelines available.

CHRYSALIS: National Health & Healing Magazine
28 Ross Street,
Barrie, ON L4N 1E9
Tel: (705) 722-5328. Fax: (705) 722-5328
E-mail: <chrysals@mail.transdata.ca>
Contact: Linda Straiko, Editor.

CLAREMONT REVIEW, THE
4980 Wesley Road
Victoria, BC V8Y 1Y9
Tel: (250) 658-5221. Fax: (250) 658-5387
E-mail: <aurora@islandnet.com>
Contact: Bill Stenson, Co-Editor.
Category: Literary.
Non-fiction: Yes. Fiction: Yes. Poetry: Yes. Graphics: Yes.
Notes: Published twice a year, circulation 500. Dedicated to publishing the fiction, poetry, and short drama of emerging young writers aged 13 to 19. Introduces some of the best student writing in Canada. Submissions may be between 200 and 5,000 words. Payment only if grants are available. All submissions given serious responses. Guidelines available.

CLASSICAL MUSIC
PO Box 45045,
Mississauga, ON L5G 4S7
Tel: (905) 271-0339. Fax: (905) 271-9748
E-mail: <classical-musica@inforamp.net>
Web site: <http://www.cmp.ca/pa3.html>
Contact: Anthony Copperthwaite, Publisher.
Category: Performing Arts.
Non-fiction: Yes. Fiction: No. Poetry: No. Graphics: Yes.
Notes: Published quarterly, circulation 7,000. Features classical music news, profiles of musicians, composers, orchestras, record cuts, performance reviews, history of music/instruments, photo features. Pays on publication 2,500 to 3,000 words/$300. Short articles, 100 to 200 words/$50. Send $5 for writers guidelines.

COAST MAGAZINE

PO Box 65837, Station F

Vancouver, BC V5N 5L3

Tel: (604) 254-2331. Fax: (604) 254-9220

Editorial Queries: Fax: (604) 731-7255

E-mail: <coastmag@eworld.com>

Contact: Allan Main, Publisher, Steven Threndyle, Editor.

Category: Outdoor.

Non-fiction: Yes. Fiction: No. Poetry: No. Graphics: Yes.

Notes: Published eight times a year. *Coast* is an outdoor recreation magazine, with features 200 to 2,500 words about kayaking, snowboarding, skiing, rock climbing, river rafting, mountain biking, hiking, touring, back-packing, and skydiving. Calendar of meets, events. Query for guidelines.

COASTAL GROWER

1075 Alston Street

Victoria, BC V9A 3S6

Tel: (250) 360-0709 Toll Free: 1-800-816-0747 Fax: (250) 360-1709

E-mail: <grower@islandnet.com>

Web site: <http://www.islandnet.com/~grower/homepage.html>

Contact: Mary Mills, Editor.

Category: Special Interest/Gardening.

Non-fiction: Yes. Fiction: No. Poetry: No. Graphics: Yes.

Notes: Published nine times a year by Greenheart Publishing Ltd. The magazine contains articles about west coast gardening from a personal perspective. "Our writers are gardeners first." Unsolicited articles 200 to 2,500 words pays $50 to $150 on publication. Queries welcome. Guidelines available.

COLLECTIBLES CANADA

103 Lakeshore Road, Suite 202,

St. Catharines, ON L2N 2T6

Tel: (416) 646-7744. Fax: (416) 646-0995

E-mail: <bret@trajan.com>

Web site: <http://www.trajan.com/trajan/collectibles/default.ehtml>

Contact: Bret Evans, Editor.

Category: Hobby.

Non-fiction: Yes. Fiction: No. Poetry: No. Graphics: Yes.

Notes: Published seven times a year, circulation 12,000. *Collectibles Canada* is a guide to limited-edition collectible art. A forum for club news and classifieds. Articles on collector plates, figurines, limited edition lithographs, new products and interviews/profiles about Canadian artists are welcome. Pays vary for 750 to 1,500 words. Pays a month after publication. Query by phone, fax or e-mail.

COMMON GROUND (Vancouver)

3091 W. Broadway#201

Vancouver, BC V6K 2G9

Mail: Box 34090, Station D,

Vancouver, BC V6J 4M1

Tel: (604) 733-2215 1-800-365-8897. Fax: (604) 733-4415

Contact: Joseph Roberts, Publisher & Senior Editor.

Category: Environment and Health.

Non-fiction: Yes. Fiction: No. Poetry: No. Graphics: Yes.

Notes: Published 10 times a year, Circulation: 80,000 copies. This magazines is dedicated to ecology, health, personal, professional development in spiritual, health, religious, and creativity. Does business "in a spirit of unity, co-operation and understanding, while maintaining a high level of integrity, responsibility and service." Aims to inform, inspire readers in the areas of personal growth, ecology, healthy living. Pays 10 cents/word on publication for articles from 500 to 1,800 words. Query by phone or letter first before submitting an article.


COMMON GROUND Quarterly (Ont.)

356 Dupont St.

Toronto, ON M5R 1V9

Tel: (416) 964-0528

Contact: Julia Woodford, Editor.

Category: Health/Alternative Medicine/Natural Health.

Non-fiction: Yes. Fiction: No. Poetry: No. Graphics: Yes.

Notes: Published quarterly, circulation 52,000. *Common Ground Quarterly* is a guide to natural health and alternative medicine.


COMPANION MAGAZINE

600 - 695 Coxwell Avenue,

Toronto, ON M4C 5R6

Tel: (416) 690-5611. Fax: (416) 690-3320

E-mail: <FranCentre@aol.com>

Web page: <http://www.cmpa.ca>

Contact: Friar Richard Riccioli, Editor.

Category: News and Opinion / Religion.

Non-fiction: Yes. Fiction: Yes. Poetry: Yes. Graphics: Yes.

Notes: Published monthly, circulation 5,000. A Roman Catholic inspirational magazine with a down-to-earth, positive approach to living the faith. Also focuses on St. Francis of Assisi and related issues. Pays six cents/word on publication for 600 to 1,200 words. Guidelines available.

COMPASS: A JESUIT JOURNAL
50 Charles Street E.,
PO Box 400 Station F,
Toronto, ON M4Y 2L8
Tel: (416) 921-0653. Fax: (416) 921-1864
E-mail: <74163.2472@compuserve.com>
Contact: Robert Chodos, Editor.
Category: News & Opinion.
Non-fiction: Yes. Fiction: No. Poetry: No. Graphics: Yes.
Notes: Published six times a year. Circulation 3,200. *Compass* is a Roman Catholic review on contemporary social and religious issues with an ethical and ecumenical perspective. Publishes theme issues. Themes available in guidelines. Some non-theme articles accepted. Major features 1,500 to 2,500 words. Regular features, 750 words dealing with theology in daily life, a response to a previous article, a brief biographical sketch of a canonized saint or other holy person, related to the issue's theme. Both essay-length and brief book reviews. Pays $100 to $500 on publication. Send SASE for guidelines/themes.

COMPENIONS: Stratford Writer's Workshop
PO Box 2511
St. Marys, ON N4X 1A3
Tel: (519)284-1675. Fax;
Contact: Marco Balestrin, Editor.
Category: Literary.
Non-fiction: Yes. Fiction: Yes. Poetry: Yes. Graphics: Yes.
Notes: Published quarterly, circulation 25 to contributors and members. Invites submissions in every genre, 800 to 1,000 words preferred; 100 words min. 3,000 words max. Short-shorts 300-400 words. Charges $4.50 reading fee per manuscript. Send cover letter. Payment is two copies.

CONTACT
#400, 119-14 Street N.W.
Calgary, AB T2N 1Z6
Contact: The Editor.
Category: Arts.
Non-fiction: Yes. Fiction: No. Poetry: No. Graphics: Yes.
Notes: Published quarterly by the Alberta Potter's Association. *Contact* is a magazine about ceramic art, for professional ceramic and clay artists. Features cover Canadian and International ceramics, critical reviews of exhibitions, profiles of artists and institutions with ceramic departments. Pay varies for 750-1,500 words; photos, illustrations and short reviews of exhibitions sought. Query by letter with SASE. Back issues available for $8.

CONTEMPORARY VERSE 2
PO Box 3062
Winnipeg, MB R3C 4E5
Tel: (204) 949-1365
Contact: Janine Tschuncky or Clarise Foster.
Category: Literary.
Non-fiction: Yes. Fiction: Yes. Poetry: Yes. Graphics: Yes.
Notes: Quarterly literary journal, established in 1975 by Dorothy Livesay. *CV2* is a powerful, eclectic mix of literary essays, poetry, prose and reviews. Manuscripts from emerging and established writers are welcome. Focus on the experience of women. Please study several back issues (available for $5 each) prior to submitting a written query/proposal. Pays for published work. Guidelines available with SASE.

COTTAGE LIFE
111 Queen Street E, Suite 408
Toronto, ON M5C 1S2
Tel:(416) 360-6880. Fax:(416) 360-6814
E-mail: <cottage_life@magic.ca>
Contact: Ann Vanderhoof, Editor.
Category: Special Interest.
Non-fiction: Yes. Fiction: No. Poetry: No. Graphics: Yes.
Notes: Published bimonthly, circulation 1,200. *CL* magazine focuses on cottage lifestyle on Ontario's Lakes. Features about cottage history and practical advice on maintenance of docks, boats, roofs, winter closure preparations. Pays on acceptance for 150 to 3,500 words. Query by mail. Back issues and guidelines available with SASE.

COUNTRY CONNECTION, The
PO Box 100
Boulter, ON K0L 1G0
Tel: (613) 332-3651. Fax: (613) 332-5183
Web site: <http://www.cyberus.ca/~queenswood/pinecone/>
Contact: Gus Zylstra, Publisher.
Category: Special Interest/Lifestyle.
Non-fiction: Yes. Fiction: Yes. Poetry: Yes. Graphics: Yes.
Notes: *The Country Connection* is dedicated to the restoration of Canada's natural environment and ecosystems. Published twice a year, Summer/Autumn issue features summer touring routes and studio tours. Winter/Spring issue features culture, arts, history, gardening, country themes, human interest, lifestyle, nostalgia, events, how-to articles, fiction, leisure, environment. References to food and recipes must be vegetarian and contain natural wholesome ingredients. Articles 2,000 words max. Pays seven to 10 cents per word. Photography/graphics/maps $10 to $50. Send for writer's guidelines with SASE.

COUNTRY HEALTH

PO Box 80525

Burnaby BC V5H 3X9

Tel: (604) 438-4665. Fax: (604) 438-2029

Contact: Leo Albo, Publisher/Editor.

Category: Health.

Non-fiction: Yes. Fiction: No. Poetry: No. Graphics: Yes.

Notes: Published six times a year. Circulation 130,000.

Devoted to natural, organic foods, vitamins, herbs, natural healing, and health food stores products, therapies. In-depth articles 750 to 1,500 words. Query Editor re guidelines.

COUNTRY

RR#1

Holstein, ON N0G 2A0

Tel: (519) 334-3246 or 1-800-561-5522. Fax: (519) 334-3366

Contact: The Editor.

Category: Music.

Non-fiction: Yes. Fiction: No. Poetry: No. Graphics: Yes.

Notes: Published six times a year, *Country* covers country music news, reviews of the hottest country releases, and profiles of musicians. Submissions about all areas of country music welcome. Pay varies with length, 500 to 2,000 words, with or without photos. Query by phone. Send SASE for guidelines. Previous issues available for $4 each.

COUNTRY MUSIC NEWS

Box 7323, Vanier Terminal

Ottawa, ON K1L 8E4

Tel: (613) 745-6006. Fax: (613) 745-0576

Contact: Larry Delaney, Editor/Publisher.

Category: Music.

Non-fiction: Yes. Fiction: No. Poetry: No. Graphics: Yes.

Notes: Published monthly, circulation 12,000. *Country Music News* listens to the country music scene from coast to coast and reports from all major centres, including Nashville. Features 750 to 2,500 words, CD reviews 500 to 1000 words, reader contests, hit charts, and photos of country music favourites. Payment on publication. Send SASE for guidelines.

COUP DE POUCE
2001 University, Bureau 900
Montreal, QC H3A 2A6
Tel: (514) 499-0561. Fax: (514) 499-1844
E-mail: <entrenous@coupdepouce.com>
Contact: Michele Cyr, Publisher.
Category: People and Places.


CV PHOTO
4060 boulevard Saint-Laurent, espace 310
Montreal, QC H2W 1Y9
Tel: (514) 849-0508. Fax: (514) 284-6775
E-mail: <vpopuli@cam.org>
Web site: <http://www.cam.org/~vpopuli/>
Contact: Franck Michel, Publisher; Marcel Blouin Editor.
Category: Visual Arts.
Non-fiction: Yes. Fiction: No. Poetry: No. Graphics: Yes.
Notes: Published four times a year. Single copy $6.75 each. Contemporary photography welcome. Query first.


CYCLE CANADA
86 Parliament Street, Suite 3B
Toronto, M5A 2Y6
Tel: (416) 362-7966. Fax: (416) 362-3950
Contact: Bruce Reeve, Editor.
Category: Sports.
Non-fiction: Yes. Fiction: No. Poetry: No. Graphics: Yes.
Notes: *Cycle Canada* is published 10 times a year with a circulation of 31,000. Readers are motorcycle enthusiasts who are interested in technical information such as product testing, how-to maintenance, profiles of bikers, touring and personal stories. Pays $50 on acceptance for short 100-word news items, $500 for main features 4,000 words plus colour photos. Write for guidelines.

DALHOUSIE REVIEW, THE
Room 314, Dunn Building,
Dalhousie University,
Halifax NS B3H 3J5
Tel: (902) 494-2541. Fax: (902) 494-2319
E-mail: <dalrev@ac.dal.ca>
Contact: Dr. Alan Andrews, Editor.
Category: Literary.
Non-fiction: Yes. Fiction: Yes. Poetry: Yes. Graphics: Yes.
Notes: Published three times a year, circulation 700. Publishes articles, book reviews, short stories and poetry, essays on history, philosophy, 5,000 words max. Prefers submissions on disk (Word Perfect) occasionally reviews novels and short story collections. Does not pay. Guidelines available.

DANCE CONNECTION
815-1ST Street SW, #603
Calgary, AB T2P 1N3
Tel: (403) 263-3232. Fax: (403) 237-7327
Contact: Heather Elton, Editor.
Category: Performing Arts.
Non-fiction: Yes. Fiction: No. Poetry: No. Graphics: Yes.
Notes: Published five times a year, circulation 5,000. Encompasses the entire dance genre with articles, critical essays, profiles, and personal stories, memoirs, contemporary issues in politics and funding/theatre/venue related to dance. New products, changes, calendars and a forum for the dance community. Pays 10 cents/word on publication for 800-2500 word articles. Guidelines available.

DANCE INTERNATIONAL
Roedde House, 1415 Barclay Street
Vancouver, BC V6G 1J6
Tel: (604) 681-1525. Fax: (604) 681-7732
Contact: Maureen Riches, Editor.
Category: Dance.
Non-fiction: Yes. Fiction: No. Poetry: No. Graphics: Yes.
Notes: Published quarterly, circulation 3,000. *Dance International* (formerly *Vandance International*) covers world wide and Canadian dance through articles, features, reviews, reports, columns, new products, venues, calendars, profiles, history, memoirs, photo spreads on every aspect of dance. Pays $100 up for features, $75 and up for commentaries, $50 and up for reviews and notebook. Guidelines available.

DANDELION

9th Avenue S.E. #922

Calgary, AB T2G 0S4

Tel: (403) 265-0524

Contact: Bonnie Benoit, Editor.

Category: Literary.

Notes: *Dandelion* publishes twice a year an anthology of prose, fiction and poetry from new and established writers across Canada. It also has reviews, interviews, profiles about literature, writers, visual art and the literary scene. Articles are up to 5,000 words. Pay $125 per story on publication, $40 for reviews, $15 page for poetry. Guidelines are available.


DESCANT

PO Box 314, Station P,

Toronto, ON M5S 2S8

Tel: (416) 593-2557. Fax: (416) 593-2557

Contact: Karen Mulhallen, Editor.

Category: Literary.

Non-fiction: Yes. Fiction: Yes. Poetry: Yes. Graphics: Yes.

Notes: *Descant* is a literary journal published four times a year. Circulation, 1,200. This journal publishes poetry, prose, fiction, interviews, photographs, engravings, art, literary criticism, memoirs of travel, letters, and short-short fiction/prose. Publishes original unpublished work. Requires one-time rights. Pays an honorarium of $100 on publication to all contributors. Guidelines are available.


DISCOVER VANCOUVER AND WHISTLER

1001 Wharf Street, 3rd floor,

Victoria, BC V8W 1T6

Tel: (250) 388-4324. Fax: (250) 388-6166

Contact: Carolyn Camilleri, Editor.

Category: Travel and Tourism.

Non-fiction: Yes. Fiction: No. Poetry: No. Graphics: Yes.

Notes: Published annually, circulation 30,000. *Discover* is a tourist guide targeting Japanese visitors and features articles about vacation activities in Vancouver and Whistler. Published in Japanese, articles are written in English and translated. Prefer 2,500 words. Fees vary. Query first.

DIVA

364 Coxwell Avenue

Toronto, ON M4L 3B7

Tel: (416) 461-2744. Fax: (416) 461-3315

Contact: Fauzia Rafiq, Editor.

Category: Feminist/Special Interest.

Non-fiction: Yes. Fiction: Yes. Poetry: Yes. Graphics: Yes.

Notes: *Diva* is published quarterly, circulation 1,500. Publishes literary and visual arts by women with South Asian ancestry and women of colour. The purpose is to encourage and develop the arts of these authors and artists. Articles of 1,500 to 3,000 paid $50; poetry $25; fiction $75; art work $150 for colour, $30 B&W. Query first.

DOGS IN CANADA

89 Skymark Avenue, #200

Etobicoke, ON M9W 6R4

Tel: (416) 798-9778. Fax: (416) 798-9671

Contact: Allan Reznik, Editor.

Category: Special Interest.

Non-fiction: Yes. Fiction: No. Poetry: No. Graphics: Yes.

Notes: Published 12 times a year. Circulation 30,000. This is a specialized magazines for dog breeders and exhibitors or serious purebred dog enthusiasts. Articles cover all aspects of dog husbandry, disease, grooming tips, special diets, kennels, registrations, and provides a forum for subscribers. A special annual issue is directed to new and prospective dog owners with a manual in selecting, caring for and training a dog. Articles 1,000 to 3,000 pays $150 plus on acceptance. Photos, personal stories considered. Written queries with outline and tear-sheets of published work. Guidelines available.

DUGOUT

PO Box 265

Don Mills, ON M3C 2S2

Tel: (416) 515-0158. Fax: (416) 515-9072

Contact: The Editor.

Category: Sports.

Non-fiction: Yes. Fiction: No. Poetry: No. Graphics: Yes.

Notes: Published five times a year, Canada's baseball magazine features major leagues, past, present and future. It also travels the globe examining the game in Japan, Cuba, the Dominican Republic and compares the differences with North America. Baseball as a game, as a philosophy, as a social influence is dugout of the depths of the world's population. The discoveries are astounding, month after month. Articles range 500 to 2,500 words, fees vary, paid after publication. Study back issues, ($5 each) then query with ideas. Send a SASA for guidelines.

ECODECISION
276 St. Jacques West, Suite 924
Montreal, QC H2Y 1N3
Tel: (514) 284-3043. Fax: (514) 284-3045
Contact: The Editor.
Category: Environment.
Non-fiction: Yes. Fiction: No. Poetry: No. Graphics: Yes.
Notes: Published quarterly by the Policy Society (The Royal Society of Canada) *Ecodecision* takes a global perspective on the environment and the economy. Feature articles are scholarly researched scientific information and environmental policy. Send for guidelines and fee levels with SASE.

EDUCATION FORUM Magazine
60 Mobile Drive,
Toronto, ON M4A 2P3
Tel: (416) 751-8300. Fax: (416) 751-3394
Contact: Neil Walker, Editor.
Category: News & Opinion.
Non-fiction: Yes. Fiction: No. Poetry: No. Graphics: Yes.
Notes: Published three times a year by the Ontario Secondary School Teachers' Federation. 43,000 copies distributed to Ontario education workers. The magazine carries news, interviews, profiles, general issues of interest concerning secondary schooling, student programs, new and innovative teaching methods, policies at various school boards, funding, and reviews on new textbooks, computer programs, special needs programs, integrated education dealing with the disabled, sports competitions, music and bands information plus more. Buys articles 200 to 3,000 words. Fees vary. Queries welcome. Send SASE for guidelines.

EDUCATION TODAY
439 University Ave.
Toronto, ON M5G 1Y8
Tel: (416) 340-2540. Fax: (416) 340-7571
Contact: The Editor.
Category: News & Opinion.
Non-fiction: Yes. Fiction: No. Poetry: No. Graphics: Yes.
Notes: Published five times a year. Circulation 40,000. *Education Today* is a magazine for Ontario's educators. It covers contemporary issues and trends in elementary and secondary school systems. Students also contribute regularly, as well as supervisors, school boards, and legislators. Submissions about the latest news in education are invited. 2,000 to 3,000 words. Pays on publication. Fees vary. Send SASE for guidelines.

ELECTRONIC COMPOSITION AND IMAGING
2240 Midland Avenue. Suite 201
Scarborough, ON M1P 4R8
Tel: (416) 299-6007. Fax: (416) 299-6674
Contact: The Editor.
Category: Special Interest.
Non-fiction: Yes. Fiction: No. Poetry: No. Graphics: Yes.
Notes: Published six times a year. This is a How-To Guide for Desktop Technology with an outstanding reputation. Features cover industry, software, hardware reviews, columns by experts and caters to professionals in the desktop publishing fields. Query with SASE for guidelines.

ELLIPSE Journal
C.P. 10 F.L.S.H.
Université de Sherbrooke
Sherbrooke, QC J1K 2R1
Tel: (819) 821-3268. Fax: (819) 821-7285
Contact: The Editor.
Category: Literary.
Non-fiction: Yes. Fiction: Yes. Poetry: Yes. Graphics: Yes.
Notes: Published twice a year. *Ellipse*, means Oeuvres En Traduction/Writers In Translation. Every issue pairs two poets, one French, one English and offers selections of their work in translation thereby providing each cultural group access to the poetry of the other. Does not pay. Submit queries in writing. Guidelines available with SASE.

EN ROUTE
7 Chemin Bates,
Outremont, QC H2V 1A6
Tel: (514) 270-0688. Fax: (514) 270-4050
E-mail: <infor@enroute.publicor.com>
Contact: Lise Ravary, Editor.
Category: News & Opinion.
Non-fiction: Yes. Fiction: No. Poetry: No. Graphics: Yes.
Notes: Published monthly for Air Canada. Circulation 125,000. Contains all Canadian articles about business, tourism, travel, profiles, fashion, fine dining and special events in major cities along flight routes. Welcomes professional writers to submit queries with ideas first and enclose tear sheets. Fees are in competitive range. Send SASE for guidelines.

ENVIRONMENTS: A Journal of Interdisciplinary Studies
University of Waterloo, Faculty of Environmental Studies
Waterloo, ON N2L 3G1
Tel: (519) 855-1211 ext. 2072. Fax: (519) 746-2031
Contact: Gordon Nelson, Editor.
Category: Scholarly.
Non-fiction: Yes. Fiction: No. Poetry: No Graphics: Yes.
Notes: Published three times a year, circulation 500. *Environments* is a scholarly journal with deeply researched original and new information to benefit professionals in this area of expertise. Does not pay. To obtain information about submission guidelines check inside front cover.

EQUINOX
11450 boul. Albert-Hudon
Montreal North, QC H1G 3J9
Tel: (514) 327-4464. Fax: (514) 327 0514
Contact: Sylvia Barrett, Managing Editor or Alan Morantz, Editor.
Category: Discovery/science, wildlife, and human community.
Non-fiction: Yes. Fiction: No. Poetry: No. Graphics: Yes.
Notes: Published six times a year, circulation 120,000. *Equinox* is a magazine of discovery, dedicated to exploring the human community, the natural world, and the wonders of science and technology. It attempts to answer the five W's in a scholarly yet vibrant way. Pays $1,500 to $3,500 for 1,200 to 5,000 words on acceptance. With photos, extra. Nexus Pieces earn $250. Query in writing with SASE. Guidelines available.

ESPACE: Canada's Magazine of Sculpture
4888 Saint-Denis
Montreal, QC H2J 2L6
Tel: (514) 844-9858
Contact: Serge Fisette.
Category: Special Interest.
Non-fiction: Yes. Fiction: No. Poetry: No. Graphics: Yes.
Notes: Published quarterly since 1987, circulation 1,200. *Espace* covers multiple aspects of sculpture. Features are 500 to 2,500 words, about exhibitions, reviews, etc. *Espace* est une revue qui se consacre a la diffusion de la sculpture. *Espace* le multiples aspects de la sculpture contemporaine en utilisant dossiers, articles de fond, comptes rendus d'expostions, entrevues avec des artistes, etc. Send queries with SASE, guidelines available.

ESSAYS ON CANADIAN WRITING
2120 Queen St. E., Suite 200
Toronto, ON M4E 1E2
Tel: (416) 694-3348. Fax: (416) 698-9906
E-mail: <ecw@sympatico.ca>
Web site: <http://www.ecw.ca/press>
Contact: Jack David, Publisher.
Non-fiction: Yes. Fiction: No. Poetry: Yes. Graphics: No.
Notes: Published three time per year. Deals with Canadian biography and literary criticism.

ETC Montreal
1435 rue de Bleury
Montreal, QC H3A 2H7
Tel: (514) 848-1125. Fax: (514) 848-0071
Contact: The Editor.
Category: Visual Art.
Non-fiction: Yes. Fiction: No. Poetry: No. Graphics: Yes.
Notes: Published quarterly. Est. 1987. *ETC Montreal* covers original perspectives on contemporary visual art. Articles range 500 to 2,500 words about painting, sculpture, photography, video, performance and installations. The writing is scholarly and critical. Commentary on exhibitions, collections and cinema. Reviews debates and book launchings, profiles of artists and studios in institutions. Query before submitting. Send SASE for guidelines.

EVENT: The Douglas College Review
Douglas College, PO Box 2503
New Westminster, BC V3L 5B2
Tel: (604) 527-5293. Fax: (604) 527-5095
E-mail: <bonnie_bauder@douglas.bc.ca>
Contact: Calvin Wharton, Editor; Bonnie Bauder, Assistant Editor.
Category: Literary.
Non-fiction: Yes. Fiction: Yes. Poetry: Yes. Graphics: Yes.
Notes: Published three times a year, circulation 3,300. Devoted to publishing new and established Canadian/International writers. Invites submissions up to 5,000 words fiction and non-fiction or eight poems per submission. Pays $22 per page on publication. Hosts a yearly $500 Creative Non-Fiction Contest each spring. Guidelines available, SASE.

EXHUMED

PO Box 924

Kingston, ON K&L 4X8

Tel: (613) 544-5816. Fax: (613) 389-9264

Contact: The Editor.

Category: Literary.

Non-fiction: Yes. Fiction: Yes. Poetry: Yes. Graphics: Yes.

Notes: Published quarterly. *Exhumed* focuses on quality dark side fiction and poetry by developing writers. Major focus in on original and witty horror, science fiction and dark fantasy. Artwork by developing artists to illustrate the stories are commissioned. Submit photocopy samples of artwork. Study at least four back issues before submitting proposals. Send SASE for guidelines.

EXILE

PO Box 67, Station B,

Toronto, ON M5T 2C0

Tel: (416) 969-8877. Fax: (416) 966-9556

Contact: Barry Callaghan, Publisher.

Category: Literary.

Non-fiction: Yes. Fiction: Yes. Poetry: Yes. Graphics: Yes.

Notes: Published quarterly, circulation 1,200. Devoted to publishing Canadian drama on the edge, fine fiction, poetry, and submissions from all over the world. Pays on publication. Send written queries, study back issues first.

EXPLORE: Canada's Outdoor Adventure Magazine

# 420, 301-14th Street N.W.

Calgary, AB T2N 2A1

Tel: (403) 270-8890. Fax: (403) 270-7922

E-mail: <explore@cadvision.com>

Web site: <http://www.explore-mag.com>

Contact: Marion Harrison, Editor.

Category: Outdoors.

Non-fiction: Yes. Fiction: No. Poetry: No. Graphics: Yes.

Notes: Published bimonthly, circulation 30,000. This is an outdoor recreation magazine specializing in backpacking, cycling, paddling, kayaking, rock-climbing, and backcountry skiing and other self-propelled activities. Articles 1,500 to 2,500 words pay $450 to $800. Other topics about adventure, outdoor equipment, evaluations, new products, and environmental issues invited. Fee may vary. Photos, trails, illustrations invited. Submit on speculation with printouts and disk. Guidelines available. Study back issues.

FAITH TODAY
M.I.P. Box 3745
Markham, ON L3R 0Y4
Tel: (905) 479-5885. Fax: (905) 479-4742
E-mail: <ft@efc-canada.com>
Web site: <http://www.efc-canada.com>
Contact: Marianne Meed Ward, Editor.
Category: Special Interest/Religion.
Non-fiction: Yes. Fiction: No.
Poetry: No. Graphics: Yes.
Notes: Published six times a year. *FT* provides
evangelical perspective on the spiritual, political,
social and economic news of the day. Reporting
trends and events within the religious community.

Tip: take a current event and find the religious angle/involvement. Journalistic style.
Pays $25 per diem, photos negotiable, 30-50% kill fee, magazine 80% freelance
material. Prefers written inquiry.


FAMILY HEALTH
PO Box 2421
Edmonton, AB T5J 2S6
Tel: (403) 429-5189. Fax: (403) 498-5661
Contact: The Editor.
Category: Special Interest.
Non-fiction: Yes. Fiction: No. Poetry: No. Graphics: Yes.
Notes: Published quarterly, developed in association with the College of Family
Physicians of Canada. Articles give helpful advise about health care, fitness, infor-
mation about various disorders and practical care. Writers are medical doctors and
health professionals and reflect the type of advice a patient might receive during an
office visit. Query in writing for guidelines with SASE.


FIDDLEHEAD, The
Campus House, University of New Brunswick,
PO Box 4400
Fredericton, NB E3B 5A3
Tel: (506) 453-3501. Fax: (506) 453-4599
Contact: Sabine Campbell, Editor.
Category: Literary.
Non-fiction: Yes. Fiction: Yes. Poetry: Yes. Graphics: Yes.
Notes: Published quarterly, 900 circulation. A highly respected literary journal, pub-
lishing fine poetry, prose, book reviews and art work with a focus on freshness and
vitality. While retaining a special interest in writers of Atlantic Canada, it is open to
outstanding work from all over the country. Prose submissions may be 100 up to
4,000 words at $10 per page. Poetry submissions, three to 10 poems. Pays on publi-
cation. Guidelines available.

FIFTY-FIVE PLUS
PO Box 47, Battersea, ON K0H 1H0
Tel: (613) 353-2060. Fax: (613) 353-7681
Contact: Sharon Freeman, Editor.
Category: Lifestyles.
Non-fiction: Yes. Fiction: No. Poetry: No. Graphics: Yes.
Notes: Published six times a year, circulation 40,000. *FFP* is a magazine for active retirees in eastern Ontario. Many of the articles reflect successful retirement, options available to create a meaningful life, opportunities to travel and explore the world, hobbies, helping other seniors, volunteering in exciting and interesting fields previously not explored, and markets available to assist with the difficulties of mobility. Pays $60 to $350 for 800 to 2,500 words, on publication. Six-month reply time for queries. Send for guidelines with SASE.

FILLING STATION
PO Box 22135, Bankers Hall
Calgary, AB T2P 4J5
Tel: (403) 264-0573. Fax: (403) 256-1045
Contact: The Editorial Collective.
Category: Literary.
Non-fiction: Yes. Fiction: Yes. Poetry: Yes. Graphics: Yes.
Notes: Published quarterly, circulation 2,000. Established in 1995. *Filling Station* 's goal is to satisfy tastes for fine poetry, interesting fiction, plunging interviews, scandalous reviews and editorials by talented writers from around the world. Five Governor General Award winners have been published in *Filling Station*. Articles 500 to 1,500 words, fiction, 1,000 to 1,500 words, 25 lines of poetry, fee varies, on publication. Artistic photos and illustrations invited from graphic artists, for consideration send photocopies only. Submit biographies with submissions. Send SASE for replies.

FINANCIAL POST
333 King Street E, 3rd Floor,
Toronto, ONM5A 4N2
Tel: (416) 350-6172. Fax: (416) 350-6171
E-mail: <fpmag@fox.nstn.ca>
Contact: Wayne Gooding, Editor.
Category: Business.
Non-fiction: Yes. Fiction: No. Poetry: No. Graphics: Yes.
Notes: Published 11 times a year. Circulation 200,000. *The Financial Post* is a sophisticated lifestyle magazine for affluent Canadian society. Features about business, politics, the stock market, securities and holdings of investment companies, trends in the market, banking stories, and profiles successful executives. Seasoned freelance writers who specialize in financial markets, experts, seasoned journalists invited to submit. Pays $1 per word for articles 1,500 to 3,000 words, on acceptance. Prefer disk submissions. Query for details.

FIREWEED: A Feminist Quarterly
PO Box 279, Station B
Toronto, ON M5T 2W2
Tel: (416) 504-1339
Contact: Sandra Haar.
Category: Feminist.
Non-fiction: Yes. Fiction: Yes. Poetry: Yes. Graphics: Yes.
Notes: Published quarterly, Est. 1978, Circulation 2,000. *Fireweed* is a forum for creative arts, cultural expressions and cross-gender issues through fiction, poetry and graphic arts. Features tend to focus on profiles, interviews, political areas of feminism. Traditional and experimental poetry, photos and graphic arts all welcome. Length up to 5,000 words. Pays on publication, $30 first page, $10 thereafter. Send SASE for guidelines.

FLARE
777 Bay St., 7th Floor
Toronto, ON M5W 1A7
Tel: (416) 596-5461. Fax: (416) 596-5184
E-mail: <editors@flare.com>
Web site: <http://www.flare.com/>
Contact: David Hamilton, Publisher, Susanne Boyd, Editor.
Category: Special Interest.
Non-fiction: Yes. Fiction: Yes. Poetry: No. Graphics: Yes.
Notes: Pays $1 per word.

FOCUS
1025 Richmond Ave.
Ottawa, ON K2B 8G8
Tel: (613) 820-3272. Fax: (613) 820-3646
E-mail: <focus@governmentsource.com>
Contact: Ken Lagasse.
Category: Government Publication.

FOCUS ON WOMEN
1218 Langley Street, Suite 3A
Victoria, BC V8W 1W2
Tel: (250) 388-7231. Fax: (250) 383-1140
E-mail: <focus@octonet.com>
Contact: Leslie Campbell, Publisher or Kerry Slavens, Editor.
Category: People and Places.
Non-fiction: Yes. Fiction: Yes. Poetry: Yes. Graphics: Yes.
Notes: Published 12 times a year, circulation 30,000. *Focus on Women* is a magazine that celebrates the success of women on Vancouver Island and the West Coast. A

broad range of issues in politics, health, social, ethnic, arts, theatre, business, and relationships covered through well written articles, prose, poetry and photo spreads. The magazine is also a forum for readers opinions and views. Pays 10 cents a word, or $250 for 2,000 to 2,500-word articles on publication. All topics should reflect West Coast Women. No queries accepted—only articles on spec. Allow 30 days for response.

FRONT
Western Front Lodge
303 East 8th Ave.
Vancouver, BC V5T 1S1
Tel: (604) 876-9343. Fax: (604) 876-4099
E-mail: <front@smartt.com>
Web site: <http://www.eciad.bc.ca/~front/home.html>
Contact: Laiwan and Steve Chow, Editors.
Category: Visual Arts.
Non-fiction: Yes. Fiction: Yes. Poetry: Yes. Graphics: Yes.
Notes: Published five times a year. Established in 1973. *Front* focuses on the production and presentation of new art, exhibition, performance art, video production, computer graphics, telecommunications, poetry, dance, and music. Contains monthly calendars. Invites submissions in all genres. Query editors for guidelines and fees.

FULCRUM, THE
Student Federation of the University of Ottawa
07-85 University Pvt,
Ottawa, ON K1N 6N5
Tel: (613) 562-5260. Fax: (613) 562-5259
E-mail: <fulcrum@aix2.uotawa.ca>
Contact: Laurel Fortin, Non-Fiction Editor, Stephanie Power, Arts/Culture Editor.
Category: Literary.
Non-fiction: Yes. Fiction: Yes. Poetry: Yes. Graphics: Yes.
Notes: Published weekly during fall and winter university semesters. Circulation 10,000. *The Fulcrum* publishes various literary and cultural reviews in its arts and culture section. Once a year they publish an "Arts and Expressions" supplement to which students and university community members contribute. They do not pay contributors. Photos and graphics usually accompany articles. They do not publish unsolicited material. Query first. Get guidelines.

FUSE Magazine
401 Richmond Street West, Suite 454
Toronto, ON M5V 3A8
Tel: (416) 340-8026. Fax: (340) 340-0494
E-mail: <fuse@interlog.com>
Contact: Petra Chevrier, Production Coordinator.
Category: Visual Arts.
Non-fiction: Yes. Fiction: No.
Poetry: No. Graphics: Yes.

Notes: Published by ArtonUs Pub. Inc. *Fuse* examines artworks, cultural events in terms of political/contemporary culture provocatively with visionary suggestions towards transformation. Submissions for features should combine criticism, research and historical perspectives, 4,500 to 6,000 words. Reviews to be reflections on cultural events/practice comparing specifics to broader trends, debates, or controversies, 1,200 to 2,000 words. Graphics are invited about artist's projects. Upon acceptance by Editorial board, first NA serial rights. Pays 10 cents per word on publication plus three copies. Reviews, $100. Submit with SASE.


GEIST
103 - 1014 Homer St.
Vancouver, BC V6B 2W9
Tel: (604) 681-9161. Fax: (604) 664-8250
E-mail: <geist@geist.com>
Contact: Kevin Barefoot.
Category: Literary.
Non-fiction: Yes. Fiction: Yes. Poetry: Yes. Graphics: Yes.
Notes: Published quarterly. Seeks fiction and creative non-fiction. Publishes a limited amount of poetry. On the lookout for good visuals. Seldom publishes material written the passive voice. Query with SASE.


GLOBAL DIVERSITY Magazine
c/o Canadian Museum of Nature
PO Box 3443, Station D
Ottawa, ON K1P 6P4
Tel: (613) 993-5908. Fax: (613) 990-0318
E-mail: <darnold@mus-nature.ca>
Contact Person. D. Arnold, Editor.
Category: Environment.
Non-fiction: Yes. Fiction: No. Poetry: No. Graphics: Yes.
Notes: Published quarterly, *Global Diversity Magazine* is an international forum on the variety of life on earth. The magazine probes into the depths of many different life-forms and seeks to bring understanding into the connectedness with the environ-

ment. Explores the questions about a healthy planet through relationships with bugs, creatures, plants, weather, and endangered species. Writers with particular expertise in environmental issues and creatures/habitats are invited to submit written queries with SASE. Guidelines and back issue available for $7.50.

GOODTIMES
5148 St. Laurent Boulevard,
Montreal, QC H2T 1R8
Tel: (514) 273-9773. Fax: (514) 273-3408
Contact: Denise Crawford, Editor.
Category: Retirement.
Non-fiction: Yes. Fiction: No. Poetry: No. Graphics: Yes.
Notes: Published 10 times a year. *GoodTimes* focuses on retired Canadians and features of interest to that age group. Retirement financial planning, health, fitness, personal rights, interpersonal relationships, profiles of senior celebrities, leisure activities. Articles are assigned. Welcomes written queries only, with bios/tear sheets. Pays 40 cents per word on publication. Submissions on IBM-compatible disk. Send SASE for guidelines.

GRAFFITO: The Poetry Poster
Dept. of English, University of Ottawa
Ottawa, ON K1N 6N5
Tel: (613) 738-2366. Fax: (613) 738-1929
E-mail: <graffit@aix1.uottawa.ca>
Web site: <http://www.cyberperk.com/graffito>
Contact: B. Stephen Harding, Publisher/Editor.
Category: Literary.
Non-fiction: No. Fiction: No. Poetry: Yes. Graphics: No.
Notes: Published quarterly, Poetry.

GRAIL: An Ecumenical Journal
Novalis-Saint Paul University
223 Main Street
Ottawa, ON K1S 1C4
Tel: (613) 236-1393. Fax: (613) 782-3004
Contact: The Holy Grailer.
Category: Religion.
Non-fiction: Yes. Fiction: Yes. Poetry: Yes. Graphics: Yes.
Notes: Published quarterly, *The Grail* focuses on encouragement of ecumenical understanding. It invites submissions that promote dialogue, debate, and understanding among scholars and educated readers. Submit in writing, with SASA queries and requests for guidelines.

GRAIN

PO Box 1154 Regina SASK S4P 3B4

Tel: (306) 244-2828. Fax: (306) 565-8554

E-mail: <grain.mag@sk.sympatico.ca>

Web site: <http://www.sasknet.com/corporate/skwriter/GRAIN–Homepage.html>

Contact: J. Jill Robinson, Editor.

Category: Literary.

Non-fiction: Yes. Fiction: Yes. Poetry: Yes. Graphics: Yes.

Notes: Published quarterly, circulation 2,000. *Grain* is a literary journal published by the Saskatchewan Writer's Guild. High-quality literary and visual art, both traditional and experimental from national and international emerging and established writers. Invites original unpublished fiction, poetry, essays, creative non-fiction, excerpts from plays also considered. Pays $30 to $100 on publication. Guidelines, back issues available.

HARPWEAVER , The

Department of English Language and Literature

Brock University

St. Catharines, ON L2S 3A1.

Category: Literary.

Non-fiction: Yes. Fiction: Yes. Poetry: Yes. Graphics: Yes.

Notes: *Harpweaver* invites contributions in poetry, prose, short dramatic works, interviews, reviews, visual art, and photography. Please include a short biographical note and SASE. Issues cost $4.

HARROWSMITH COUNTRY LIFE

11450 boul. Albert-Hudon

Montreal North, QC H1G 3J9

Tel: (514) 327-4464. Fax: (514) 327 0514

Contact: Tom Cruickshank, Editor.

Category: People and Places.

Non-fiction: Yes. Fiction: No. Poetry: No. Graphics: Yes.

Notes: Published six times a year. Circulation 150,000. *Harrowsmith Country Life* is the essential guide to country living. It reflects family values associated with country lifestyle, gardens, renovating homes, cooking healthy meals, do-it-yourself projects, outdoor recreation and pets, children, relationships, fairs, family reunions. Length, 500 to 2,500 words. Fees vary, but pays on publication. Submit proposals in writing, with or without photos, biographical notes, tear-sheets, with SASE. Guidelines available.

HEALTH LIVING GUIDE
7436 Fraser Park Drive
Burnaby BC V5J 5B9
Tel: (604) 435-1919. Fax: (604) 435-4888
Contact: Lorna VanderHaeghe, Editor.
Category: Health/Special Interest.
Non-fiction: Yes. Fiction: No. Poetry: No. Graphics: Yes.
Notes: Published six times a year, circulation 100,000. *Healthy Living Guide* is a tabloid newspaper/magazine focusing on health of the body. Articles 1,000 to 2,500, in-depth by experts in health fields. Shorter pieces by freelance writers. Query Editor.

HECATE'S LOOM
PO Box 5206 Station B
Victoria, BC V8R 6N4
Tel: (250) 478-0401. Fax: (250) 478-9287
E-mail: <loom@islandnet.ca>
Web site: <http://www.hecate.com>
Contact: Yvonne Owens, Editor.
Category: News and Opinion/Special Interest.
Non-fiction: Yes. Fiction: Yes.
Poetry: Yes. Graphics: Yes.
Notes: Published quarterly, circulation: 2,000. Established in 1986. Publishes articles on the traditions of paganism, witchcraft and goddess-worship, past and present, Gaia consciousness, shamanism, history, culture, magic and herbology. Short fiction, poetry, reviews of pagan books, art and performance accepted, but does not pay. Queries welcome. Guidelines available.

HERITAGE CANADA
Heritage Canada Foundation
412 MacLaren Street
Ottawa, ON K2P 0M8
Tel: (613) 237-1066. Fax: (613) 237-5987
E-mail: <hercanot@sympatico.ca>
Contact: Veronica Vaillancourt.
Category: Special Interest/Heritage Preservation.
Non-fiction: Yes. Fiction: No.
Poetry: No. Graphics: Yes.

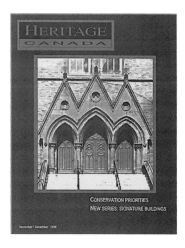

HERIZONS
PO Box 128
Winnipeg, MB R3C 2G1
Tel: (240) 744-6225. Fax: (240) 786-8038
Contact: Penni Mitchell, Editor.
Category: New and Opinion/Feminist.
Non-fiction: Yes. Fiction: No. Poetry: No. Graphics: Yes.
Notes: Published quarterly, circulation 5,000. Originally, *Herizons* began as a news-paper in 1979 and quickly grew into a national women's magazine, a hybrid of fem-inist politics and advocacy journalism. They invite in-depth articles on current issues, book and film reviews, profiles, business, that will foster awareness and debate within the feminist movement and broaden principles. Query in writing. Guidelines available.

HOMEMAKER'S/MADAME AU FOYER
25 Sheppard Avenue W., Suite 100
North York, ON M2N 6S7
Tel: (416) 733-7600 or 1-800-387-5800. Fax: (416) 733-8683
E-mail: <jelliott@telemedia.com>
Contact: Sally Armstrong, Editor-in-chief.
Category: People and Places.
Non-fiction: Yes. Fiction: Yes. Poetry: Yes. Graphics: Yes.
Notes: Published eight times a year by Telemedia Corp. Circulation 1.6 million. Specializes in information for women 25 to 54 with children at home. Articles of 1,200 to 2,500 words about issues women, their families, school, health, body and soul, religion, midwifery, fashion, decorating, menus, many food articles. Publishes in French as *Madame au Foyer*. Fees vary but pays on publication. Submit queries/proposals with/without photos, bios/tear-sheets, with SASE. Guidelines available.

HORSE SOURCE
Equicentre,
A2 - 2285 St. Laurent Blvd.,
Ottawa, ON K1G 4Z4
Tel: (613) 521-4392. Fax: (613)-521-5576
E-mail: <equicentre@cyberus.ca>
Web site: <http://www.cyberus.ca/~equicentre/>
Contact: Cindy Teevens, Editor; Mary MacMillan, Assistant Editor.
Category: Special Interest.
Non-fiction: Yes. Fiction: No. Poetry: No. Graphics: Yes.
Notes: *Horse Source* is an equestrian magazine. Regular features focus on practical advice, tips, training teaching and information that will interest to people in all areas of the horse industry. Guidelines available.

HORSE SPORT (The Corinthian)

225 Industrial Parkway, S.,

PO Box 670 Aurora, ON L4G 4J9

Tel:(905) 727-0107 or 1-800-505-7428. Fax:(905) 841-1530

E-mail: <74273.3167@compuserve.com>

Contact: Susan Stafford, Managing Editor.

Category: Sports/Outdoors.

Non-fiction: Yes. Fiction: No. Poetry: No. Graphics: Yes.

Notes: Published monthly, circulation 10,000. *Horse Sport* is Canada's authoritative news medium for equestrians. It features articles on horse care, riding and training techniques, breeding, animal health and provides coverage of sporting events. Prefers 1/2,000 words/ Pays 10-15 cents per word on publication. Contact editor before submitting. Guidelines available with SASE.


HORSEPOWER

225 Industrial Parkway,

PO Box 670 Aurora, ON L4G 4J9

Tel:(905) 727-0107 OR 1-800-505-7428. Fax:(905) 841-1530

E-mail: <74273.3167@compuserve.com>

Contact: Susan Stafford, Managing Editor.

Category: Children.

Non-fiction: Yes. Fiction: No. Poetry: No. Graphics: Yes.

Notes: Published six times a year, circulation 20,000. This magazine is for young horse lovers. It provides easily-understood information about riding (western, English), training, owning and caring for a horse (all breeds) or pony. Aimed at children aged six to 16, *Horsepower* is packed with games, puzzles and contests, that stress the focus of safety and having fun. Articles are 500 to 800 words/$50, 1,000 words/$75. Pays on publication. Contact editor before submitting. Guidelines available with SASE.


HUMANIST IN CANADA

PO Box 3769 Station C

Ottawa, ON J1Y 4J8

Tel: (613) 749-8929. Fax: same, phone first

E-mail: <jepiercy@cyberus.ca>

Contact: J.E. Piercy, President.

Category: Special Interest.

Non-fiction: Yes. Fiction: No.

 Poetry: Yes. Graphics: Yes.

Notes: Published quarterly, circulation 1,500. This magazine is a forum for non-believers with an interest in social issues. It aims to print literature with humanist content, reflecting the principle that human problems can best be solved by people relying on their own capabilities, without belief in the supernatural. Articles 1,000 to 2,500 words. They do not pay, but welcome submission inquiries. Guidelines available.

IMPACT

2007-2nd Street S.W.

Calgary, AB T2S 1S4

Tel: (403) 228-0605. Fax: (403) 228-0627

Contact: Heather Ellwood-Wright, Editor.

Category: Sports/Outdoors.

Non-fiction: Yes. Fiction: No. Poetry: No. Graphics: Yes.

Notes: Published six times a year, circulation 35,000. *Impact* features fitness and health, sports for Calgary residents and their surroundings. Articles 750 to 1,000 words. Query by phone or letter.

INSIGHT HEALTH

PO Box 8071

Victoria, BC V8W 3R7

Tel: (250) 479-2203. Fax: (250) 479-0363

Contact: Hannah Green, Publisher/Editor.

Category: Special Interest/Health.

Non-fiction: Yes. Fiction: No. Poetry: No. Graphics: Yes.

Notes: Published six times a year. Originated in 1996. *Insight Health* provides a forum for informative topics and views from health services. They welcome articles on health, spiritual and fitness issues by health professionals. Queries welcome. Guidelines available.

INTERFACE

3341 - 4252 Commerce Circle

Victoria, BC V8Z 4M2

Tel: (250) 953-2680. Fax: (250) 953-2659

E-mail: <interface@ifmagazine.com>

Web site: <http://www.ifmagazine.com/>

Contact: Robert K. McCourty, Publisher/Editor.

Category: E-zine.

Non-fiction: Yes. Fiction: Yes. Poetry: No. Graphics: Yes.

Notes: *InterFace* is only available via the Internet Web Site. They accept freelance materials. Query first. Writer's guidelines available online. Payment upon publication. Electronic submissions only. *InterFace* is constantly changing the face of the Internet. Topics should be timely to the electronic future. This international award winning publication expects submissions to reflect a high quality.

INUIT ART QUARTERLY
2081 Merivale Road,
Nepean, ON K2G 1G9
Tel: (613) 224-8189 or 1-800-830-3293. Fax: (613) 224-2907
Contact: Marybelle Mitchell, Editor.
Category: Visual Arts.
Non-fiction: Yes. Fiction: No. Poetry: No. Graphics: Yes.
Notes: Published quarterly, circulation 4,000. Carries stories exclusively on Inuit art. Explores Inuit traditions, lifestyles, history while reviewing an individual Inuit artist's life and/or work. Fees vary on publication. Query first before submitting. Guidelines available.

INUKTITUT
510 - 170 Laurier Ave. W.
Ottawa, ON K1P 5V5
Tel: (613) 238-8181. Fax: (613) 234-1991
E-mail: <itc@magi.com>
Contact: Ms. Looee Okalik, Editor-in-Chief.
Category: Cultural / Educational.
Non-fiction: Yes. Fiction: No. Poetry: Yes. Graphics: Yes.
Notes: Quarterly, trilingual, submitted articles—accompanied by photographs/artwork/ illustrations. Subscription free for Inuit, $29.96 (GST inclusive) for non-Inuit.

ISLAND PARENT
941 Kings Road
Victoria, BC V8T 1W7
Tel: (250) 388-6905. Fax: (250) 388-4391
Contact: Selinde Krayenhoff, Publisher/Editor.
Category: Special Interest.
Non-fiction: Yes. Fiction: No. Poetry: No. Graphics: Yes.
Notes: Published 12 times a year. Circulation, 25.000.
*Island Parents'* goal to raise the status and profile of parenting on Vancouver Island by providing information and support and encouragement, not advice or guilt trips. Average article 800 words and pays $25. Many new writers from Vancouver Island. Guidelines available.

ISSUES

254 Ellis Street

Penticton, BC V2A 4L6

Tel: (250) 979-0789. Fax: (250) 492-5328

Contact: Angele Rowe, Publisher.

Category; Health.

Non-fiction: Yes. Fiction: No. Poetry: No. Graphics: Yes.

Notes: Published 10 times a year, circulation 22,000. *Issues* is dedicated to natural health, alternative therapies, exercise, fitness, spiritual awareness and a holistic approach. Articles invited by BC writers 500-800 words. Query Publisher for guidelines and fee rates.

JOURNAL OF BAHÁ'Í STUDIES, THE

34 Copernicus St.

Ottawa, ON K1N 7K4

Tel: (613) 233-1903. Fax: (613) 233-3644

E-mail: <as929@freenet.carleton.ca>

Contact: Christine Zerbinis, Managing Editor.

Category: Scholarly, Interdisciplinary, Religion.

Non-fiction: Yes. Fiction: No. Poetry: No. Graphics: No.

JOURNAL OF CANADIAN ART HISTORY

ANNALES D'HISTOIRE DE L'ART CANADIEN

Concordia University

VA-432, 1455 boul. de Maisonneuve W.,

Montreal, QC H3G 1M8

Tel: (514) 848-4699. Fax: (514) 848-8627

E-mail: <JCAH@VAX2.concordia.ca>

Web site: <http://www.concordia.ca/arth/jcah>

Contact: Sandra Paikowsky, Editor.

Category: Scholarly.

Non-fiction: Yes. Fiction: No. Poetry: No. Graphics: Yes.

Notes: Publishes twice a year. The *Journal/Annales* is devoted to Canadian art, architecture, Inuit and Aboriginal art and decorative arts, art theory, criticism, feminist studies, museology, art institutions and education. Illustrated articles on these topics invited. Publishes English and French. Queries welcome. Guidelines available.

JOURNAL OF CANADIAN STUDIES
Trent University
PO Box 4800
Peterborough, ON K9J 7B8
Contact: Michele Lacombe, Editor.
Category: Scholarly.
Non-fiction: Yes. Fiction: No. Poetry: No. Graphics: Yes.
Notes: Published quarterly, circulation 1,300. Publishes a variety of scholarly articles, critical comment, and book reviews pertaining to Canadian history, politics, economy, education, literature, the arts, public policy, communications, anthropology and sociology. Accepts articles 3000 to 10,000 words. Does not pay but welcomes submission inquiries. Guidelines available.

JOURNEYWOMAN
50 Prince Arthur #1703
Toronto, ON M5R 1B5
Tel: (416) 929-7654. Fax: (416) 929-1433
E-mail: <editor@journeywoman.com>
Web site: <http://www.journeywoman.com>
Contact: Evelyn Hannon.
Category: Travel.
Non-fiction: Yes. Fiction: No. Poetry: No. Graphics: No.
Notes: Publishes four times per year. Interested in women's travel stories. No payment—honorarium is one year subscription ($24.00 value). Prefer articles of 750 or 1200 words in length. Sample copies available for $6. Guidelines available for SASE.

KIDS WORLD MAGAZINE
108-93 Lombard Ave.,
Winnipeg, MB R3B 3B1
Tel: (204) 942-2214. Fax: (204) 943-8991.
Web site: <http://www.kidsworld-online.com/>
Contact: Stuart Slayen, Editor.
Category: Children.
Non-fiction: Yes. Fiction: Yes. Poetry: No. Graphics: Yes.
Notes: Published five times a year. Circulation: 225,000, distributed to all Canadian schools. A general interest magazine for elementary students 9-12 years. Emphasis on entertainment and motivation. Articles 400 to 1,000 words paid 45 days after publication. Query editor. Short stories 750 words on various topics pays $100. Guidelines available.

KINDRED SPIRITS OF P.E.I.
PO Box 491
Kensington, PE C0B 1M0
Tel: (902) 436-7329. Fax: (902) 436-1787
Contact: George Campbell.
Notes: Publishes four times per year. Uses old photographs.

KINESIS
1720 Grant Street, #301
Vancouver, BC V5L 2Y6
Tel: (604) 255-5499. Fax: (604) 255-5511
Contact: Agnes Huang, Editor.
Category: News & Opinion.
Non-fiction: Yes. Fiction: No. Poetry: No. Graphics: Yes.
Notes: Published 10 times a year, circulation 3,000. A Canadian feminist newspaper for all women. Articles 800 to 1600 words invited about Canadian women activists and health, politics, poverty, violence against women, and aboriginal women's news, music, dance, literature, film, feminine perspective visual arts. Does not pay. Guidelines available.

LABOUR/LE TRAVAIL
Canadian Committee On Labour History
Department of History,
Memorial University of Newfoundland
St. Johns, NF A1C 5C7
Tel: (709) 737-2144. Fax: (709) 737-4342
E-mail: <cclh@morgan.ucs.mun.ca>
Web site: <http://www.mun.ca/cclh/>
Contact: Gregory S. Kealey, Editor.
Category: Literary/Scholarly.
Non-fiction: Yes. Fiction: No. Poetry: No. Graphics: Yes.
Notes: Published twice a year. Circulation 1,200. A bilingual, interdisciplinary, historical journal about the labour movement, workers and work. Articles 5,000 to 10,000 words, invited, but does not pay. Query and guidelines available. For further information contact <joanb@morgan.ucs.mun.ca>

LEAD

Equicentre

A2 - 2285 St. Laurent Blvd.,

Ottawa, ON K1G 4Z4

Tel: (613) 521-4392. Fax: (613) 521-5576

E-mail: <equicentre@cyberus.ca>

Web site: <http://www.cyberus.ca/~equicentre>

Contact: Cindy Teevens, Editor; Mary MacMillan, Assistant Editor

Category: Image and lifestyle

Non-fiction: Yes. Fiction: No. Poetry: No. Graphics: Yes.

Notes: *Lead* seeks interesting articles on fascinating people and places that relate to the mystery and beauty of the horse. *Lead* will celebrate and promote the sport, hobby and business of horses around the world. Guidelines are available.


LEGION

Canvet Publications Ltd.

359 Kent Street, Suite 407

Ottawa, ON K2P 0R6

Tel: (613) 235-8741. Fax: (613) 233-7159

Contact: Dan Black, Managing Editor.

Category: Consumer / Special Interest

Non-fiction: Yes. Fiction: No. Poetry: No. Graphics: Yes.

Notes: Published five times a year, circulation 475,000. Canada's war veterans, RCMP, Armed Forces, news, views, memoirs/nostalgia and information articles about defence, veterans affairs, health, base-living and pensions. Pays $150 to $1200 on acceptance for 600 to 2,200 words. Query for assignments. Guidelines and sample copies available.


LITERARY REVIEW OF CANADA, THE

3266 Yonge Street, PO Box 1830,

Toronto, ON M4N 3P6

Fax: (416) 322-4852

Contact: Pat Dutil, Editor.

Category: Literary/Scholarly.

Non-fiction: Yes. Fiction: No. Poetry: No. Graphics: No.

Notes: Published 11 times a year. Circulation, 2,000. Scholarly tabloid of Canadian non-fiction book reviews for highly educated readers. Accepts 3,000 to 5,000 word reviews, but does not pay. Fax or mail proposals and outlines. Guidelines available.

MACLEAN'S MAGAZINE
777 Bay Street
Toronto, ON M5W 1A7
Tel: (416) 596-5386. Fax: (416) 596-7730
Contact: Robert Lewis, Editor.
Category: News & Opinion.
Non-fiction: Yes. Fiction: No. Poetry: No. Graphics: Yes.
Notes: Published weekly, circulation 540,000 Canada's national news magazine that examines issues from a Canadian perspective. Has bureau network in five Canadian cities and 35 other countries. Freelancers contribute to weekly sections on politics, business, entertainment, sports, leisure, science, medicine and technology. Pays vary but excellent on acceptance. Query and guidelines available.

MALAHAT REVIEW, THE
University of Victoria
PO Box 1700, MS8524
Victoria, BC V8W 2Y2
Tel: (604) 721-8524. Fax: (604) 721-7212
E-mail: <dyand@uvic.ca>
Contact: Derk Wynand, Editor.
Category: Literary & Scholarly.
Non-fiction: Yes. Fiction: Yes. Poetry: Yes. Graphics: Yes.
Notes: Publishes quarterly, circulation 1,800. A literary journal publishing Canada's best poets and short story writers. Pays $25 per page on acceptance. No queries. Submit 6-10 pages of poetry and for fiction, send one complete story. (Replies six mos).

MATRIART
80 Spadina Ave Suite 506
Toronto, ON M5V 2J3
Tel: (416) 703-0074. Fax: (416) 703-0441
E-mail: <warc@intacc.web.net>
Contact: Linda Abrahams, Editor.
Category: Visual Arts.
Non-fiction: Yes. Fiction: Yes. Poetry: Yes. Graphics: Yes.
Notes: Published quarterly, circulation 2000. *Matriart* is a journal of contemporary women's art for readers in academic and feminist communities. Devoted to cultural diversity. Issues are thematic. Reviews 750 to 1,000 words; features 2,000 words. Pays five cents/word. Guidelines available.

MATRIX

1400 de Maisonneuve W., Suite 514-8

Montreal, QC H3G 1M8

Tel: (514) 848-2340. Fax: (514) 848-4501

Contact: Robert Allen, Editor.

Category: Literary & Scholarly.

Non-fiction: Yes. Fiction: Yes. Poetry: Yes. Graphics: Yes.

Notes: Published three times a year, circulation 1,800. *Matrix* is a literary/cultural magazine based in Quebec and open to all new and established Canadian writers for contemporary fiction, prose, poetry, articles and artwork. Accepted pieces 1,500 to 5,000 words pay $100 to $200, poetry $15 to $100 on publication. Guidelines available.

MATURITY

CYN Investments Ltd.

PO Box 397,

New Westminster BC, V3L 4Y7

Tel: (604) 540-7911. Fax: (604) 540-7912

E-mail: <cyn@mindlink.bc.ca>

Contact: Donald A. Causton, Publisher, Audrey Gill Editor.

Category: Special Interest/Seniors.

Non-fiction: Yes. Fiction: No. Poetry: No. Graphics: Yes.

Notes: Published six times a year. *Maturity* strives to provide its Canadian national audience with thoughtful, current articles and columns that will educate, inspire and entertain mature readers and to address the issues of particular concern in their lives. Articles and contributions welcome by mail with SASE.

MENNONITE BRETHREN HERALD

3-169 Riverton Ave.

Winnipeg MB R2L 2E5

Tel: (204) 669-6575. Fax: (204) 654-1865

Contact: Susan Brandt, Editor.

Category: Special Interest/Religion.

Non-fiction: Yes. Fiction: No. Poetry: Yes. Graphics: Yes.

Notes: Published 24 times a year for the Mennonite Brethren constituency in Canada. Buys 50% freelance material. Features 250 to 1500 words containing spiritual reflections, theology of Mennonite Brethren Church. Prefers one page 750 words. Reflections: a devotional meditation on a Bible passage 250 words. Columns expressing Christian opinion on a current topic in church society: 850 words. Crosscurrents: music, musician, CD, song books, TV programs, culture, art, computers. Internet: 500 words. 25 lines/maximum poetry, six to 12 selections a year. Pays on publication. Submit by e-mail, hard copy or disk on MS-DOS/Macintosh OS.

MESSENGER OF THE SACRED HEART, THE

661 Greenwood Ave.

Toronto, M4J 4B3

Tel: (416) 466-1195

Contact: Rev. F. J. Power, SJ.

Category: Special Interest/Religion.

Non-fiction: Yes, Fiction: Yes. Poetry: No. Graphics: Yes.

Notes: Published 11 times a year for adult Roman Catholics. General church issues, inspirational, personal experience with a spiritual theme, news and church politics. Pays four cents per word. Write for guidelines.


MONTREAL MIRROR

400 McGill St., 1st floor

Montreal, QC H2Y 2G1

Tel: (514) 393-1010. Fax: (514) 393-3173

E-mail: <mirror@babylon.montreal.qc.ca>

Contact: Annarosa Sabaddini, Editor.

Category: News & Opinion.

Non-fiction: Yes. Fiction: No. Poetry: No. Graphics: No.

Notes: Published by Eyal Kattan and Catherine Salisbury.

The *Montreal Mirror* is an independent news-weekly that covers culture, local area, people, places, profiles, columns, arts, business, politics, general interest. Query by e-mail for submission requirements.


MOSAIC

208 Tier Building,

University of Manitoba

Winnipeg, MB R3T 2N2

Tel: (204) 474-9763. Fax: (204) 261-9086

E-mail: <ejhinz@bildgarts.lanl.umanitoba.ca>

Contact: Dr. Evelyn J. Hinz, Editor.

Category: Literary.

Non-fiction: Yes. Fiction: No. Poetry: No. Graphics: No.

Notes: Published quarterly, circulation 900. *Mosaic* is a journal for the interdisciplinary study of literature for scholars, educators, students and sophisticated readers. Invites essays 5,000 to 6,000 words, but query first. Does not pay. Guidelines available.

MUSE JOURNAL, THE
226 Lisgar Street,
Toronto, ON M6J 3G7
Tel: (416) 539-9517. Fax: (416) 539-0047
E-mail: <egoncalves@ablelink.org>
Contact: Emanuel Goncalves, Editor.
Category: Scholarly.
Non-fiction: Yes. Fiction: Yes. Poetry: Yes. Graphics: Yes.
Notes: Published twice a year, circulation 1,000.
A journal for writers, poets and visual artists. Open to all topics, themes and genres, but emphasizing the metaphysical, philosophical and humorous. Prefers 800-1,600 words and pays only for solicited works. Guidelines available. Hosts a prose and poetry contest each year. Send SASE for details.

MUSIC MAGAZINE/CLASSICAL MUSIC MAGAZINE
PO Box 45045 - 81 Lakeshore Road East
Mississauga, ON L5G 4S7
Tel: (905) 271-0339. Fax: (905) 271-9748
E-mail: <classical_musica@inforamp.net>
Web site: <http://www.cmpa.ca/pa3.html>
Contact: Derek Deroy, Editor.
Category: Music.
Non-fiction: Yes. Fiction: No. Poetry: No. Graphics: Yes.
Notes: Published quarterly, circulation 7,000. Features classical music news, profiles of musicians, composers, orchestras, record cuts, performance reviews, history of music/instruments, photo features. Pays on publication 2,500 to 3,000 words/$300. Short articles, 100-200 words/$50. Send $5 for writers guidelines.

MUSICWORKS: THE JOURNAL OF SOUND EXPLORATION
179 Richmond Street W.
Toronto, ON M5V 1V3
Tel: (416) 977-3546. Fax: (406) 208-1084
Contact: Gayle Young, Editor.
Category: Performing Arts.
Non-fiction: Yes. Fiction: No. Poetry: songs. Graphics: Yes.
Notes: Published three times a year, circulation 2,500. Distributed with audio component-cassettes or CDs—to illustrate articles and interviews covering a broad range of contemporary classical and experimental music. Features 1,000 to 3,500 words. Fees negotiable. Pays on publication. Queries and guidelines available.

MYSTERY REVIEW, THE
PO Box 233
Colborne, ON K0K 1S0
Tel: (613) 475-4440. Fax: (613) 475-3400
E-mail: <71554.551@compuserv.com>
Contact: Barbara Davey, Editor.
Category: Literary.
Non-fiction: Yes. Fiction: Yes. Poetry: Yes. Graphics: Yes.
Notes: Published quarterly, 5,000 circulation. Specializes in mystery and suspense about new mystery titles, book reviews, interviews with authors, real-life unsolved mysteries, puzzles and word games relating to the genre. Pays honorarium on publication. Query first. Guidelines available.

NEW MARITIMES
PO Box 31269
Halifax, NS B3K 5Y5
Tel: (902) 425-6622
Contact: Scott Milsom, Editor.
Category: News & Opinion.
Non-fiction: Yes. Fiction: Yes. Poetry: Yes. Graphics: Yes.
Notes: Published six times a year, circulation 2,300. Essays and journalism highlighting themes in Maritimes, in politics, labour, culture, history, social justice, environment, feminism, book reviews, fiction and poetry. Does not pay. Guidelines available.

NEW QUARTERLY, THE
ELPP, PAS 2082,
Waterloo, ON N2J 2N5
Tel: (519) 888-4567 EXT 2837
E-mail: <mmerikle@watarts.uwaterloo.ca>
Web site: <http://watarts.uwaterloo.ca/~mmerikle/newquart.html>
Contact: Mary Merikle, Editor.
Category: Literary.
Non-fiction: Yes. Fiction: Yes.
Poetry: Yes. Graphics: No.

Notes: Published quarterly, January, April, July, October. Circulation 500. They have no preferences for various genres, "Just something that we feel is new and different". Query before submitting articles, interviews and essays. Fiction and poetry welcome on speculation. Pays $100 per story or novel, $25 for postcard fiction, $20 per poem. Guidelines available.

NeWEST REVIEW
PO Box 394, R.PO University,
Saskatoon, SK S7N 4J8
Tel: (306) 934-1444. Fax: (306) 242-5004
Contact: D. Larson, Manager.
Category: Literary.
Non-fiction: Yes. Fiction: Yes. Poetry: Yes. Graphics: Yes.
Notes: Published six times a year, circulation 1,000. Carries news and opinion on western Canadian cultural, social, and political issues. Reviews books and theatre, carries some fiction and poetry. Articles/stories 1,500 to 2,500 words. Pays $100 for 2,000 words; $25 for reviews; $60 for 800 word gazette items. Pays on publication. Query with proposals. Guidelines available.

NEWFOUNDLAND HERALD, The
PO Box 2015, Logy Bay Road,
St. John's, NF A1C 5R7
Tel: (709) 726-7060. Fax: (709) 726-8227
Contact: Greg Stirling, Editor.
Category: News and Opinion.
Non-fiction: Yes. Fiction: No. Poetry: No. Graphics: Yes.
Notes: Publishes weekly, circulation 50,000. This magazine focuses on people, news, opinion, and entertainment. Articles 1,000 to 5,000 words. Pays 10 cents a word on publication. Recommends reading three issues before you query the editor with proposals by phone or mail.

NORTHERN WOMAN JOURNAL
PO Box 144
Thunder Bay, ON P7C 4V5
Tel: (807) 346-8809
Contact: Jane Saunders, Editor.
Category: Feminist.
Non-fiction: Yes. Fiction: Yes. Poetry: Yes. Graphics: Yes.
Notes: Published quarterly, circulation 200. Feminist news and views, poetry and essays on issues affecting women with focus on northern women. Does not pay, but welcomes inquiries. Guidelines available.

ON SPEC: The Canadian Magazine of Speculative Writing
PO Box 4727
Edmonton, AB T6E 5G6
Tel: (403) 413-0215
Contact: Cath Jackel, Editor.
Category: Literary.
Non-fiction: Yes. Fiction: Yes. Poetry: Yes. Graphics: Yes.
Notes: Published quarterly, circulation 2,000. *On Spec* specializes in Canadian science fiction, fantasy, horror and magic realism in stories and poetry. Pays 2 1/2 cents per word up to 6,000 words. $25 for 1,000 words, $15 for 100 lines of poetry. Pays on acceptance. Send for copies ($6 each) and guidelines with format requirements—before submitting.

ONTARIO CRAFT
Chalmers Building,
35 McCaul Street
Toronto, ON M5T 1V7
Tel: (416) 977-3551. Fax: (416) 977-3552
Contact: Ann McPherson, Editor.
Category: Visual Arts.
Non-fiction: Yes. Fiction: No. Poetry: No. Graphics: Yes.
Notes: Published quarterly, circulation 4,500. Focus in on the contemporary craft movement in Canada. Profiles about craftspeople and their work, services, suppliers, craft shows calendars. Fees vary on articles 750 to 2,000 words, but pays on publication. Browse past issues. Guidelines available.

OTHER VOICES
Garneau PO Box 52059,
8210-109th Street
Edmonton, AB T6G 2T5
Contact: Editorial collective.
Category: Literary.
Non-fiction: Yes. Fiction: Yes. Poetry: Yes. Graphics: Yes.
Notes: Published twice a year. *Other Voices* is a small literary journal published in spring and fall, seeks submissions of fiction, poetry, black and white prints and artwork. Submission deadlines March 15 and Sept. 15. Payment by one-year subscription and small honorarium.

OUR FAMILY
PO Box 249,
Battleford, SK S0M 0E0
Tel: (306) 937-7771. Fax: (306) 937-7644
E-mail: <Gregmaryomi@sk.sympatico.ca>
Contact: Nestor Gregoire, Editor.
Category: Special Interest.
Non-fiction: Yes. Fiction: Yes. Poetry: Yes. Graphics: Yes.
Notes: Published 12 times a year. Circulation 10,000. A Christian general interest magazine. Buys photo stories on personalities, events and issues with religious themes. Pays 7 -11 cents/word on acceptance for pieces from 1,000 to 3,000 words. Enclose SASE or will not consider ms. Advise study of sample copies, $2.50 ea. Query in writing only. Guidelines available.

OUR TIMES
390 Dufferin Street,
Toronto, ON M6K 2A3
Tel: (416) 531-5762. Fax: (416) 533-2397
Contact: Lorraine Endicott, Editor.
Category: News and Opinion.
Non-fiction: Yes. Fiction: No. Poetry: No. Graphics: Yes.
Notes: Published six times a year, circulation 4,000. *Our Times* is unionized, worker-owned co-operative that focuses on current issues in the labour movement. Most articles written by labour activists to educate. Pays $25 for book reviews, $75 to $200 for features of 1,500 to 2,500 words on acceptance. Guidelines available.

OUTDOOR CANADA
703 Evans Avenue, Suite 202
Toronto, ON M9C 5E9
Tel: (416) 695-0311. Fax: (416) 695-0381.
Category: Outdoors.
Non-fiction: Yes. Fiction: No. Poetry: No. Graphics: Yes.
Notes: Published eight times a year, circulation 90,000. Carries articles on Canada's outdoors, fishing, boating, hunting, cross-country skiing, snowmobiling, canoeing, hiking, outdoor photography and camping. Features destination stories. Pays $200 to $450 on publication for pieces 800 to 2,500 words. Invites on-spec submissions. Guidelines available.

OWL Magazine
179 John Street, Suite 500
Toronto, ON M5T 3G5
Tel: (416) 971-5275. Fax: (416) 971-5294
E-Mail: <wiredowl@owl.on.ca>
Web site: <http://www.owl.on.ca/>
Contact: Catherine Jane Wren, Managing Editor.
Category: Children 8-12.
Non-fiction: Yes. Fiction: No. Poetry: No. Graphics: Yes.
Notes: Published nine times a year. Circulation 100,000. *OWL* is a discovery magazine for eight to 12-year-olds. Sparks children's curiosity about science, technology, animals, and the environment. Pays $200 for 500 to 800 words on acceptance. Study back issues for *OWL*'s approach. Query Editor. Guidelines available.

PACIFIC AFFAIRS Magazine
University of British Columbia,
2029 West Mall
Vancouver, BC V6T 1Z2
Tel: (604) 822-6504. Fax: (604) 822-9452
Contact: Bernie Shisholm, Editor.
Category: Scholarly.
Non-fiction: Yes. Fiction: No. Poetry: No. Graphics: Yes.
Notes: Published quarterly, circulation 2,800. Pacific region issues, people and places, news and opinion, politics and economic issues. Reviews 60 books each issue. Invites articles 6,000 to 6,500 words. Does not pay. See back cover for guidelines.

paperplates
19 Kenwood Ave.,
Toronto, ON M6C 2R8
Tel: (416) 651-2551. Fax: (416) 651-2910
E-mail: <paperplates@perkolator.com>
Web site: <http://www.perkolater.com>
Contact: Bernard Kelly, Publisher/Editor.
Category: Literary.
Non-fiction: Yes. Fiction: Yes. Poetry: Yes. Graphics: Yes.
Notes: Published quarterly, circulation 350. Publishes poetry, fiction, plays, travel pieces, essays, interviews, memoirs. Length 2,500 to 15,000. Does not pay but invites queries. Guidelines available.

PARACHUTE

4060 St. Laurent Boulevard, Suite 501

Montreal, QC H2W 1Y9

Tel: (514) 842-9805

Contact: Chantal Pontbriand, Editor.

Category: Visual Arts.

Non-fiction: Yes. Fiction: No. Poetry: No. Graphics: Yes.

Notes: Published quarterly, circulation 3,000. A bilingual review offering in-depth articles on theory and practise of art. Invites articles about music, cinema, photography, theatre, dance, video and interviews of artists. Pays $100 for 3,000 to 5,000 words on publication. Guidelines available.


PEACE

736 Bathurst Street,

Toronto. ON M5S 2R4

Tel: (416) 533-7581. Fax: (416) 531-6214

Contact: Metta Spencer, Editor.

Category: News and Opinion.

Non-fiction: Yes. Fiction: No. Poetry: No. Graphics: Yes.

Notes: Published six times a year, circulation 2,000. Devoted to multilateral disarmament and non-violent conflict resolution through interviews, commentary, features. Articles 1,000 to 3,000 words. Does not pay but welcomes submission inquiries.


PENTECOSTAL TESTIMONY, THE

6745 Century Ave.

Mississauga, ON L5N 6P7

Tel: (905) 542-7400. Fax: (905) 542-7313

E-mail: <testimony@paoc.org>

Contact: Rick Hiebert.

Category: Special Interest/Religion.

Non-fiction: Yes. Fiction: Yes. Poetry: Yes. Graphics: Yes.

Notes: Published monthly for members/adherents of churches in The Pentecostal Assemblies of Canada. Welcomes manuscripts from freelancers (15-20% of magazine) on news, opinion, spiritual/faith, inspirational in nature, well written. Pays $20-$50 per feature. Query in writing with SASE, guidelines available.

PERCEPTION
441 MacLaren, 4th Floor,
Ottawa, ON K2P 2H3
Tel: (613) 236-8977. Fax: (613) 236-2750
Contact: Nancy Perkins, Communications Coordinator.
Category: News and Opinion.
Non-fiction: Yes. Fiction: No. Poetry: No. Graphics: No.
Notes: Published quarterly, circulation 3,500. Social development issues, income security, employment, health, social services and aboriginal and women's issues are invited for submission, 700 to 1,500 words. Does not pay. Guidelines available.

PERFORMING ARTS & ENTERTAINMENT IN CANADA
104 Glenrose Ave.
Toronto, ON M4T 1K8
Tel: (416) 484-4534. Fax: (416) 484-6214
Contact: Karen Bell, Editor.
Category: Performing Arts.
Non-fiction: Yes. Fiction: No. Poetry: No. Graphics: Yes.
Notes: Published quarterly, circulation 44,000. Explores issues affecting performing arts in Canada, primarily theatre, dance, opera, ballet and film. Also profiles performers, companies and troupes. Invites articles 600 to 1,500 words and pays $95 to $180 on publication. Query first.

PHOTO LIFE
130 Spy Court,
Markham, ON L3R 0W5
Tel: (905) 475-8440. Fax: (905) 475-9560
Contact: Jerry Kobalenko, Editor.
Category: Visual Arts.
Non-fiction: Yes. Fiction: No. Poetry: No. Graphics: Yes.
Notes: Published eight times a year, circulation 40,000. Articles provide serious information to advanced photographers, 1,500 to 3,000 words, pays $500 on acceptance for feature articles, $75 for shorter items. Contributors are professional photographers who can write or writers familiar with photography. Guidelines available.

PLANT AND GARDEN
1 rue Pacifique,
Ste. Anne-de-Bellevue, QC H9X 1C5
Tel: (514) 457-2744. Fax: (514) 457-6255
Contact: Michael Spillane, Editor.
Category: Home & Garden.
Non-fiction: Yes. Fiction: No. Poetry: No. Graphics: Yes.
Notes: Published quarterly, circulation 35,000. A national magazine for Canadian gardeners. Articles 1,200 to 2,500 about gardening, horticulture, organic growing,

nature and environment, pays 17 cents word on publication. Department articles 500 to 750 words (Junior gardener, Step-by-Step, Down to Earth) Query with outline. Guidelines available.

POETRY CANADA
PO Box 1061
Kingston, ON K7L 4Y5
Tel: (613) 548-8429. Fax: (613) 548-1556
Contact: The Editor.
Category: Literary.
Non-fiction: Yes. Fiction: No. Poetry: Yes. Graphics: Yes.
Notes: Published quarterly, circulation 1,500. Canada's only magazine devoted entirely to publishing poetry, criticism of poetry and poetry news. Carries 30 poems each issue by Canada's best poets and new writers. Essays and in-depth interviews of 1,750 to 3,500 words, Pays $20/poem, $100/page, $50/review. Read back issues before submission.

POLICY OPTIONS
1470 rue Peel, Bureau 200,
Montreal, QC H3A 1T1
Tel: (514) 985-2461. Fax: (514) 985-2559
Contact: Alfred LeBlanc, Editor.
Category: News and Opinion.
Non-fiction: Yes. Fiction: No. Poetry: No. Graphics: Yes.
Notes: Circulation 3,000. Published 10 times a year by Institute for Research on Public Policy, a Canadian independent non-profit think-tank. Carries analysis of public policy to encourage debate of major issues. Articles 2,500 words. Does not pay. Qualified writers invited to query. Guidelines available.

POTTERSFIELD PORTFOLIO, THE
The Gatsby Press,
5280 Green Street
PO Box 27094
Halifax, NS B3H 4M8
Tel: (902) 443-9178. Fax: Same-phone ahead
E-mail: <icolford@is.dal.ca>
Contact: Ian Colford, Publisher; Karen Smythe, Editor.
Category: Literary.
Non-fiction: Yes. Fiction: Yes. Poetry: Yes. Graphics: Yes.
Notes: Published by The Gatsby Press three times a year. Circulation 500. Publishes excellent fiction and poetry in any theme or topic 500 to 5,000 words and short-shorts 100 to 500 words. Send manuscript with 50-word bio and cover letter with SASE. Sample copies $7. Pays in contributors copies.

PRAIRIE FIRE
100 Arthur Street, Suite 423
Winnipeg, MB R3B 1H3
Tel: (204) 943-9066. Fax: (204) 942-1555
Contact: Andris Taskans, Managing Editor.
Category: Literary.
Non-fiction: Yes. Fiction: Yes. Poetry: Yes. Graphics: Yes.
Notes: Published quarterly, circulation 1,500. Publishes poetry, fiction, essays, interviews, reviews, commentary, satire and literary arts criticism. Pays on publication, 150 to 5,000 words, fiction $40/first page, then $35/page; articles $35/$30; reviews $25/$20/$15. Guidelines available.

PRAIRIE JOURNAL OF CANADIAN LITERATURE, THE
Box 61203 Brentwood Postal Services
Calgary, AB T2L 2K6
Contact: A. E. Burke, Editor.
Category: Literary.
Non-fiction: Yes. Fiction: Yes. Poetry: Yes. Graphics: Yes.
Notes: Published twice a year. Prefers Canadian writers of creative writing and scholarly essays, reviews for literary audience. Needs contemporary literary prose, poetry, regional, excerpted novels and novellas. Submit minimum 100 to maximum 3,000 words, April 1 for spring/summer issue, October 1 for fall/winter issue. Study back issues, samples $6. Query with SASE. Pays in honoraria and contributor's copies.

PRESBYTERIAN RECORD
50 Wynford Drive
North York, ON M3C 1J7
Tel: (416) 441-1111. Fax: (416) 441-2825
E-mail: <pcrecord@web.net>
Contact: John Congram, Editor.
Category: Special Interest/Religion.
Non-fiction: Yes. Fiction: Yes.
Poetry: Yes. Graphics: Yes.
Notes: Published 11 times a year for Canadian Presbyterians. The magazine is responsible to the General Assembly and focuses on issues relative to Christian faith. Welcomes manuscripts from freelancers (20% of magazine) on current and timely news analysis and opinions of interest or importance to Presbyterians across Canada. Verbal inquiries accepted. Guidelines available.

PRISM International
Dept. of Creative Writing,
University of British Columbia
Buch E462 - 1866 Main Mall
Vancouver, BC V6T 2G9
Tel: (604) 822-2514. Fax: (604) 822-3616
E-mail: <prism@unixg.ubc.ca>
Web site: <http://www.arts.ubc.ca/crwr/prism/prism.htm>
Contact: Tim Mitchell, Executive Editor.
Category: Literary.
Non-fiction: Yes. Fiction: Yes. Poetry: Yes. Graphics: Yes.
Notes: Published quarterly, circulation 1,200. Features innovative new fiction, poetry, drama, creative non-fiction, and translation from Canada and world. Welcomes original work 500 to 5,000 words from established writers and new writers. Pays $20 per page plus $10 per page for selected authors whose work will appear on the WWW. Guidelines available.

PROFIT: The Magazine for Canadian Entrepreneurs
777 Bay Street, 5th floor
Toronto, ON M5W 1A7
Tel: (416) 596-5999. Fax: (416) 596-5111
E-mail: <profit@cbmedia.ca>
Contact: Rick Spence, Editor.
Category: Business.
Non-fiction: Yes. Fiction: No. Poetry: No. Graphics: No.
Notes: Published six times a year, circulation 100,000.Offers insights and practical advice on marketing, technology, finance, innovators and trends and personnel management. Pays 60 to 75 cents/word on acceptance for 1,500 to 2,500 words. Writers must be experienced in business. Guidelines available.

QUARRY
PO Box 1061
Kingston, ON K7L 4Y5
Tel: (613) 548-8429
Contact: Mary Cameron, Editor.
Category: Literary.
Non-fiction: Yes. Fiction: Yes. Poetry: Yes. Graphics: Yes.
Notes: Published quarterly, circulation 1,200. Committed to discovering talented new writers. Publishes new, innovative fiction, poetry, and essays by established writers, too. Pays $10 page fiction, $15 per poem after publication.

QUILL & QUIRE
70 The Esplanade, Ste 210
Toronto, ON M5E 1R2
Tel: (416) 360-0044. Fax: (416) 955-0794
E-mail: <quill@hookup.net>
Contact: Scott Anderson, Editor; Sharon McAuley, Publisher.
Category: Literary.
Non-fiction: Yes. Fiction: No. Poetry: No. Graphics: Yes.
Notes: Published 12 times a year, circulation 10,000. Tabloid newspaper about the book trade—for booksellers, librarians, educators, publishers and writers. Prints news, reviews, lists of recently published books, profiles of authors and publishing houses. Pays variable fee on acceptance.

RADDLE MOON
2239 Stephens Street
Vancouver, BC, V6K 3W5
Contact: Susan Clark, Catriona Strang, Lisa Robertson, Editors.
Category: Literary.
Non-fiction: Yes. Fiction: Yes. Poetry: Yes. Graphics: Yes.
Notes: Published twice a year. An international literary review featuring mostly Canadian and US poetry and criticism. Previously un-translated writing from many countries. Welcomes submission inquiries after you read several back issues.

RAMPARTS MAGAZINE CANADA
PO Box 401
Corydon, MB R3M 3V3
E-mail: <ramparts@tao.ca>
Web site: <http://www.tao.ca/sky/projects/0002.html>
Notes: "We strive to create a vehicle for the voice of all Anarchists and radicals across Canada. *Ramparts* is going to be nationally distributed, but will be divided into 'locals'. Each local issue will have features, columns and news included in all other local issues, but will also be customized to include stories and news of interest to the regional community."

RAW FICTION
Box 4065
Edmonton, AB T6E 4S8
Contact: Tim Campbell, Managing Editor.
Category: Literary.
Non-fiction: Yes. Fiction: Yes. Poetry: Yes. Graphics: Yes.
Notes: Published six times a year. *Raw Fiction* focuses exclusively on the short story. It's open to a wide range of content: sex, violence, despair, joy, love, intrigue, betrayal, addiction, insanity. Seeking stories 500-5,000 words with an edge, a narrative that keeps moving, characters that bend stereotypes; images that stick in the mind and themes relevant to everyday life.

RECREATION CANADA
306 - 1600 James Naismith Drive,
Gloucester, ON K1B 5N4
Tel: (613) 748-5651. Fax: (613) 748-5854
E-mail: <cpra@cdnsport.ca>
Contact: Heather Totten, Editor.
Category: Special Interest.
Non-fiction: Yes. Fiction: No. Poetry: No. Graphics: Yes.
Notes: Published five times a year, circulation 2,000. Focuses on issues relating to innovative leisure programs, facilities, environment, arts, culture, active living, healthy communities. Welcomes 1,500 to 2,500 word submissions. Does not pay volunteer writers in parks, leisure, recreation fields.

RESOURCES FOR FEMINIST RESEARCH
OISE, 252 Bloor Street W.
Toronto, ON M5S 1V6
Tel: (416) 923-6641. Fax: (416) 926-4725
Contact: Philinda Masters, Editor.
Category: Feminist.
Non-fiction: Yes. Fiction: No. Poetry: No. Graphics: Yes.
Notes: Published quarterly, circulation 2,000. A journal of feminist scholarship containing papers, abstracts, reviews, reports of work in progress, and bibliographies. Preferred length 3,000 to 5,000 words. Does not pay. Guidelines and back issues available.

ROOM OF ONE'S OWN
PO Box 46160, Station D
Vancouver, BC V6J 5G5
Contact: Growing Room Collective.
Category: Literary.
Non-fiction: Yes. Fiction: Yes. Poetry: Yes. Graphics: Yes.
Notes: Published quarterly, circulation 900. Solicits fine writing and editing from Canada's best women authors, well-known and unknown. Features original poetry, fiction, criticism and reviews. Articles 2,000 to 2,500 words, pays $25 honorarium plus two copies. Guidelines and back issues available.

ROTUNDA
Royal Ontario Museum, 100 Queen's Park
Toronto, ON M5S 2C6
Tel: (416) 586-5590. Fax: (416) 586-5827
Contact: Sandra Shaul, Editor.
Category: People and Places.
Non-fiction: Yes. Fiction: No. Poetry: No. Graphics: Yes.
Notes: Published quarterly, circulation, 20,000. A semi-scholarly magazine on art, archaeology, the earth, and life sciences, astronomy, and museology. Pays honoraria to academics and journalists for 2,000 to 2,500 words.

RURAL VOICE, THE
PO Box 429
Blyth, ON NOM 1H0
Tel: (519) 523-4311. Fax: (519) 523-9140
Contact: Keith Roulston, Publisher/Editor.
Category: Special Interest.
Non-fiction: Yes. Fiction: No. Poetry: No. Graphics: Yes.
Notes: Published monthly, circulation 16,000. A periodical featuring agricultural news for heartland of Ontario covering, politics, law, marketing, home and finances. Pays 12 cents per word for 1,000 to 2,000 words on publication. Guidelines and back issues available.

RV TIMES, THE: A Canadian Magazine
PO Box 160,
(129 West 2nd Ave)
Qualicum Beach, BC V9K 1S7
Tel: (250) 752-8266. Fax: (250) 752-8269
E-mail: <rvtimes@qb.island.net>
Contact: Sheila de Groen, Publisher/Editor.
Category: Outdoors.
Non-fiction: Yes. Fiction: Yes. Poetry: Yes. Graphics: Yes.
Notes: Published six times a year and focuses on recreational vehicle travel, camping, service/sales, clubs, meets, and provides a forum for readers. Does not pay but welcomes submissions, 50 word-tips, jokes, poems, to 2,500 articles, profiles and book reviews. Queries welcome.

SATURDAY NIGHT
184 Front Street, East, Suite 400
Toronto, ON M5A 4N3
Tel: (416) 368-7237. Fax: (416) 368-5112
Contact: Kenneth Whyte, Editor.
Category: People and Places.
Non-fiction: Yes. Fiction: Yes. Poetry No. Graphics: Yes.
Notes: Published 10 times a year, circulation 410,000. *Saturday Night* is a sophisticated magazine that features profiles of men, women and institutions prominent within Canadian society. In-depth discussions and research. High quality fiction. Contributing editors are well-established award-winning Canadian writers. Pays one dollar/word: $500 for one-page stories, $2,000 to $4,000 for features. Query with SASE for guidelines.

SCENES

PO Box 51531

2060 Queen St. E.

Toronto, ON M4E 3V7

Tel: (416) 690-0917

Contact: Ted Plantos.

Category: Literary.

Non-fiction: Yes. Fiction: Yes. Poetry: Yes. Graphics: Yes.

Notes: *Literary & Performance Scenes* is a free circulation literary magazine publishing four times per year. Publishes short fiction, poetry, book reviews, author profiles, interviews and articles on literary scenes.

SEASONS

355 Lesmill Road,

Don Mills, ON M3B 2W8

Tel: (416) 652-6556. Fax: (416) 444-9866

Contact: Gail Muir, Editor.

Category: Outdoors.

Non-fiction: Yes. Fiction: No. Poetry: No. Graphics: Yes.

Notes: Published quarterly, circulation 16,000. Published by the Federation of Ontario Naturalists as a nature and outdoor magazine with emphasis on natural history and environment. Features invited about Ontario's wildlife, wilderness, parks, and conservation issues. Prefers 1,500 to 3,000 words and pays $700 on publication. Study back issues. Guidelines are available. Queries by phone accepted.

SHARED VISION MAGAZINE

1625 W. 5th Ave.

Vancouver, BC V6J 1N5

Tel: (604) 733-5062 Toll Free: 1-800-929-0991 Fax: (604) 731-1050

E-mail: <Editorial@shared-vision.com>

Web site: <http://www.share-vision.com>

Contact: Samayan Ryane, Publisher, Olga Sheean, Editor.

Category: Special Interest/Creative Solutions.

Non-fiction: Yes. Fiction: No. Poetry: Yes. Graphics: Yes.

Notes: Published with great excitement and love 12 times a year. Circulation 50,000. *Shared Vision Magazine* is dedicated to positive living, mind, body and soul through meditation, alternative health therapies, natural foods, environmental stewardship, spiritual atunement and diversity. Features cover every area of mind, body and soul, new products, services and profiles of therapists, treatments, retreats, travels, and calendars of events. They ask that you contact their office before submitting any written material. They prefer submission on disks. Topics are assigned. Pays the standard rates. Photos extra.

SHARK QUARTERLY
129 Dunbarton Court,
Ottawa, ON K1K 4L6
Tel: (613) 741-7407. Fax: (613) 741-7407
E-mail: <waynellwood@amp1.CGGC.X-400.DFO-MPO.GC.CG>
Contact: Wayne Ellwood, Editor.
Category: Special Interest/Automotive.
Non-fiction: Yes. Fiction: No. Poetry: No. Graphics: Yes.
Notes: Published quarterly, 48 pages, B&W, $20 (US) / $24.95 (Cdn) by subscription only.

SHUNPIKING: A Discovery Magazine
6211 North Street
PO Box 31377,
Halifax NS B3K 5Z1
Tel: (902) 455-4922. Fax: (902) 455-7599
E-mail: <newmedia@ra.isisnet.com>
Web site: <http://www.shunpiking.com>
Contact: Tony Seed, Publisher/Editor.
Category: People and Places.
Non-fiction: Yes. Fiction: Yes. Poetry: Yes. Graphics: Yes.
Notes: Published 10 times a year with editions for Dec/Jan & Feb/Mar. Circulation 25,000. Est. Nov. 1995. *Shunpiking* was the recipient of 1996 Ambassador Award of Excellence, Tourism Industry Association of NS. Contents reflects the natural beauty and mysteries of the Maritimes in photo spreads of parks, wilderness, geography, ecology, culture and heritage. Submissions invited especially photography, illustrations, art work, fiction, poetry, and articles on Maritimes themes. Pays 15 cents/word on acceptance. Forward queries by e-mail or SASE for editorial guidelines. Deadlines 15th of preceding month. Samples $2.

SKI CANADA
117 Indian Road
Toronto, ON M6R 2V5
Tel: (416) 538-2293. Fax: (416) 538-2475
Contact: Iain MacMillan, Editor.
Category: Sports.
Non-fiction: Yes. Fiction: No. Poetry: No. Graphics: Yes.
Notes: Published seven times a year. Circulation 57,000. *Ski Canada* is published autumn, winter and one summer issue. Complimenting skiing are general articles about entertainment, how-to information about skiing, snowboarding, equipment, travel, instruction, competition, fashion, alpine-related news and stories. Editorial content selected six-months (February) for Autumn issue. Articles 400 to 2,500 words pays $100 for news, $500 to $800 for features, and varies, length, research and writer's experience. Query letters preferred—no phone calls. Back issues and guidelines available with SASE.

SOUTH AFRICAN REPORT
603-1/2 Parliament Street
Toronto, ON M4X 1P9
Tel:(416) 967-5562. Fax:(416) 978-1547 Attention: J. Vise
E-mail: <tclsac@web.net>
Web site: <http://www.web.net/~tlsac/>
Contact: Joe Vise, Editor.
Category: News & Opinion.
Non-fiction: Yes. Fiction: No.
Poetry: No. Graphics: Yes.

Notes: Published quarterly, by The Toronto Committee for Links Between Southern Africa & Canada. 36 pages, circulation 1,000. Contains news and analysis on South Africa with editorial viewpoint from the independent left. Articles 2,500 words paid 1yr sub. Graphics, good quality photographs on Southern Africa, and cartoons paid small honorarium. Send for back issues and guidelines with SASE.

STAGE Magazine
15 Curly Vineway,
North York, ON M2J 4JP
Tel: (416) 493-5740. Fax: (416) 493-5740
E-mail: <75709.3331@compuserve.com>
Contact: Katherine Goodes, Publisher.
Category: Performing Arts.
Non-fiction: Yes. Fiction: No. Poetry: No. Graphics: Yes.

Notes: Published five times a year, circulation 3,800. *Stage Magazine* (formerly *Theatrum*) provides a place for discussion and exposure for working professionals. Feature articles are about artists and every aspect of the business. Profiles, production, book reviews, festival reports, national calendar of events, fashion, techniques in stage makeup and news updates. Invites submissions and pays $50 to $300 after publication. Back issues and guidelines available.

STORYTELLER: Canada's Short Story Magazine
43 Lightfoot Place
Kanata, ON K2L 3M3
Tel: (613) 592-2776. Fax: (613) 592-2776
E-mail: <stories@direct-internet.net>
Web site: <http://www.direct-internet.net/StoryTeller_Magazine>
Contact: Terry Tyo.
Category: Literary.
Non-fiction: No. Fiction: Yes.
Poetry: No. Graphics: Yes.
Notes: Published quarterly. This magazine only pub-lishes short stories in humour, romance, drama, adventure, mystery, suspense, horror, science fiction, and speculative fiction, of literary merit and entertainment value. Submit 1,000 to 6,000 words with illustrations B&W, front cover colour. Guidelines available.

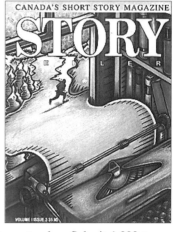

STUDIO MAGAZINE
124 Galaxy Boulevard,
Toronto, ON M9W 4Y6
Tel: (416) 675-1999. Fax: (416) 675-6093
Contact: Barbara Murray, Executive Editor.
Category: Visual Arts.
Non-fiction: Yes. Fiction: No. Poetry: No. Graphics: Yes.
Notes: Published seven times a year. Circulation 12,000. *Studio Magazine* appeals to professional designers, illustrators and photographers as professional development. This is a large format, full-colour design magazine and invites submissions from first-rate writers. Enclose cover letter, bio and tear-sheets with submission. Fee negotiated. Guidelines available.

SUB-TERRAIN
PO Box 1575, Bentall Centre
Vancouver, BC V6C 2P7
Tel: (604) 876-8710. Fax: (607) 879-2667
E-mail: <subter@pinc.com>
Contact: D. E. Bolen or Brian Kaufman, Co-Editors.
Non-fiction: Yes. Fiction: Yes. Poetry: Yes. Graphics: Yes.
Notes: Published quarterly, circulation 3,000. Primarily a literary magazine with lit-erary essays, criticism, poetry, short shorts, and themes about urban existence in Canada entering Year 2000. Accepts book reviews, prefers 200 to 3,000 words, Pays $25/page, $20/poem. Study back issues, Query, guidelines available with SASE.

SUCCESSFUL SENIOR
735 Market Street
Victoria, BC V8T 2E2
Tel: (250) 383-0882. Fax: (250) 384-1832
E-mail: <seniors@islandnet.com>
Web site: <http://www.islandnet.com/~seniors.html>
Contact: David Creed, Editor/Publisher.
Category: Special Interest/Seniors.
Non-fiction: Yes. Fiction: No. Poetry: Yes. Graphics: Yes.
Notes: Published eight times a year. This magazines is directed to successful seniors 55 years and older. Features include travel, memoirs, health, crafts, leisure activities, history, culture, gardening, finance, investment, and general life-style topics. Pays 10 cents a word. Articles 500 to 2,000 words, photos, maps, graphs extra. Queries welcome. Guidelines available.

SUSTAINABLE TIMES: The Newsmagazine About Solutions
1657 Barrington St, #508
Halifax, NS B3J 2A1
Tel: (902) 423-6709. Fax: (902) 423-9736
E-mail: <ip-cuso@chebucto.ns.ca>
Contact: Sean Kelly, Editor.
Category: News and Opinion.
Non-fiction: Yes. Fiction: No. Poetry: No. Graphics: Yes.
Notes: Published quarterly. The focus is news relevant to long-term issues around healthy community, environment, meaningful employment, feminist, aboriginal and minority races. Pays 10 cents/word for 1,000 to 1,500 words. Photos extra. Query Editor for guidelines.

TEAK ROUNDUP :The International Quarterly
West Coast Paradise Publishing
#5-9060 Tronson Rd,
Vernon, BC V1T 6L7
Tel: (250) 545-4186. Fax: (250) 545-4192
Contact: Yvonne and Robert Anstey, Publishers.
Category: Literary.
Non-fiction: Yes. Fiction: Yes. Poetry: Yes. Graphics: Yes.
Notes: Published quarterly, circulation 100. Established 1994. Invites adventure, children/juvenile, excerpted novel, ethnic/cultural, historical, humor/satire. literary, mainstream/contemporary, mystery/suspense (police procedural) regional, religious/inspirational, romance/contemporary/historical, sports, westerns, young adult/teen adventure. 1,000 words max. Fees negotiable. Guidelines and back copies available.

TESSERA

Dept. d'etudes anglaises

Université de Montreal

C.P.6128, Succ. A,

Montreal, QC H3C 3J7

Tel: (514) 343-7926. Fax: (514) 343-7926

Contact: Lianne Moyes and Jennifer Henderson, Editorial Collective.

Category: Literary.

Non-fiction: Yes. Fiction: Yes. Poetry: Yes. Graphics: Yes.

Notes: Published twice a year, circulation 250. *Tessera* is a bilingual journal of experimental writing, feminist theory and cultural critique. They encourage play along borders between creative and theoretical texts. Thematic issues. Pays $10/page on publication. Send submissions with cover letter, biographical note and printout plus diskette. Guidelines available.


TEXTSHOP: A Collaborative Journal of Writing

Dept. of English, University of Regina

Regina, SK S4S 0A2

Tel: (306) 585-4316

Contact: Andrew Stubbs, Editor.

Category: Literary.

Non-fiction: Yes. Fiction: Yes. Poetry: Yes. Graphics: Yes.

Notes: Published quarterly, circulation 200. Invites ethnic/multicultural, experimental, literary fiction, poetry and mixed genres, creative non-fiction, literary essays, and criticism. 500 to 1,000 words max. Pays contributor copy. Samples $2. Guidelines available.


THE MAGAZINE OF ARTIST–RUN CULTURE

401 Richmond Street W., Suite 446

Toronto, ON 5MV 3A8

Tel: (416) 506-1012. Fax: (416) 340-8458

Contact: Margaret Christakos or Amy Gotlieb, Co-Editors.

Category: Visual Arts.

Non-fiction: Yes. Fiction: No. Poetry: No. Graphics: Yes.

Notes: Published quarterly, circulation 4,000. A Canadian national magazine that reports developments in contemporary art, painting, sculpture, installations, video, new music, dance, and performance. Articles 2,000 to 2,500 words, negotiable rates. Query Editors for guidelines and submissions.

THE PRICECOSTCO CONNECTION

3550 Brighton Street

Burnaby, BC V5A 3H4

Tel.: (604) 421-8353. Fax: (604) 420-7005

E-mail: <prican@infobahnos.com>

Web site: <http://www.pricecostco.com>

Contact: Lorelle Gilpin

Category: Consumer.

Non-fiction: Yes. Fiction: No. Poetry: No. Graphics: Yes.

Notes: Published bimonthly for members. Contains increasing amount of general interest editorial.


THIS COUNTRY CANADA

PO Box 39, 1 Mill Street

Pakenham, ON K0A 2X0

Tel: (613) 624-5000. Fax: (613) 624-5952

Contact: Judith Haines, Editor.

Category: People & Places.

Non-fiction: Yes. Fiction: No. Poetry: No. Graphics: Yes.

Notes: Published quarterly, circulation 25,000. Celebrates the people and places in Canada in a large-format picturesque glossy. Invites modern/contemporary articles, historical features. Length 1,500 to 2,000 words, pay varies, on publication. Query with outline. Guidelines available.


THIS MAGAZINE

Red Maple Foundation

401 Richmond Ave. W. Suite 396

Toronto ON M5V 3A8

Tel: (416) 979-8400. Fax: (416) 979-1143

E-mail: <this-magazine@intacc.web.net>

Contact: Clive Thompson, Editor.

Category: Literary/New & Opinion.

Non-fiction: Yes. Fiction: Yes. Poetry: Yes. Graphics: Yes.

Notes: Published by Red Maple Foundation, eight times a year, circulation 7,000. This is an Alternative general interest magazine. Invites, ethnic, contemporary, experimental, fantasy, feminist, gay, lesbian, literary, mainstreams, prose, poem, regional. No commercial pulp fiction. Pays $200-$400 for 1,500 to 3,000 words/fiction, $250 to $500 cover story, $25/poem. Study back issues first, $4. Then query. Guidelines available.

TODAY'S PARENT
269 Richmond Street, West
Toronto, ON M5V 1X1
Tel: (416) 596-8680. Fax: (416) 596-1991
Contact: Fran Fearnley, Editor.
Category: Special Interest.
Non-fiction: Yes. Fiction: No. Poetry: No. Graphics: Yes.
Notes: Published nine times a year, circulation 160,000. *Today's Parent* appeals to parents with children under 13 years. Invites articles about child development, education, health and family life. 1,200 to 2,500 words/ $700 to $1,500 for features, $650 for departments, pays 30 days after acceptance. Query first with tear-sheets. Guidelines available.

TORONTO LIFE
59 Front Street East
Toronto, ON M5E 1B3
Tel:(416) 364-3333. Fax:(416) 861-1169
E-mail: <lifeline@tor-lifeline.com>
Web site: <http://www.tor-lifeline.com/new/tl/>
Contact: John Macfarlane, Editor.
Category: News & Opinion.
Non-fiction: Yes. Fiction: No. Poetry: No. Graphics: Yes.
Notes: Published monthly, circulation 100,000. Est. 1964. This high gloss magazine focuses on Toronto life, work, politics, real estate, business, sports, fashion, travel, and general interest subjects, people, arts, etc. Its style is a journalistic mixture of reporting and commentary. Has a stable of experienced writers and rarely accepts outside submissions. Pays on acceptance between $1,000 to $4,500 for 400 to 6,000 words. Guidelines available.

TORONTO REVIEW: Of Contemporary Writing Abroad
PO Box 6996, Station A,
Toronto ON M5W 1X7
Contact: Ms. Nurjehan Asis, Editorial Board.
Category: Literary.
Non-fiction: Yes. Fiction: Yes. Poetry: Yes. Graphics: Yes.
Notes: Published three times a year. Circulation: 2,000. *Toronto Review* formerly the *Toronto South Asian Review*, carries poetry, fiction, drama, criticism and book reviews and interviews pertaining to new Canadian and international writing. *The Globe and Mail* said *TR* is "The future...admire(d) for its iconoclasm and global perspective..." Submit queries in writing to the editor with SASE.

TRANSVERSIONS
1019 Colville Road,
Victoria, BC V9A 4P5
Tel: (250) 380-7150. Fax: (250) 383-4413
E-mail: <103124.356compuserve.com>
Web site: <http://www.astro.psu.edu/users/harlow/transversions>
Contact: Sally McBride & Dale Sproule, Publishers.
Category: Literary.
Non-fiction: No. Fiction: Yes. Poetry: Yes. Graphics: Yes.
Notes: Published three times a year by Island Specialty Reports, established in 1994. *Tranversions* is a journal of science fiction, fantasy, horror, magic realism, occult and speculative fiction. Sex OK, but must be an integral part of the story, but no explicit sex/violence. They pay one cent/word for stories 500 to 12,000 words, 25/cents/line for poetry, $50 for colour cover photo, $25 for B&W back cover photo, $5 for existing spot illustrations/artwork (not commissioned) Art reprints welcome. Pay on publication, back issues $5. Query/submit in writing. Guidelines available. (*Transversions* was preparing to relocate in May/97. Query for new address by E-mail.)

TREE HOUSE FAMILY
179 John Street, Suite 500
Toronto, ON M5T 3G5
Tel: (416) 971-5275. Fax: (416) 971-5294
Contact: Jane Weeks, Editor.
Category: Special Interest.
Non-fiction: Yes. Fiction: Yes. Poetry: Yes. Graphics: Yes.
Notes: Published quarterly, circulation 180,000. *Tree House Family* is sent to parents of *OWL* and *Chickadee* readers. Written primarily for busy mothers of 3-12 year-olds, short advice pieces, practical information, child development, and issues of interest. Length 500 to 1,500 words. Fees vary from $200 up, paid on acceptance. Guidelines available.

TRUCK NEWS: National Trucking and Equipment Buyer Guide
1450 Don Mills Road,
Don Mills, ON M3B 2X7
Fax: (416) 442-2092
E-mail: <jsmith@southam.ca>
Contact: John G. Smith, Editor,.
Category: Special Interest.
Non-fiction: Yes. Fiction: No. Poetry: No. Graphics: Yes.
Notes: National Trucking and Equipment Buyer Guide.

TV GUIDE
25 Sheppard Avenue West, Suite 100
North York, ON M2N 6S7
E-mail: <tvguide@telemedia.org>
Contact: Bill Anderson, Acting Editor.
Category: General Interest.
Non-fiction: Yes. Fiction: No. Poetry: No. Graphics: No.

UNITED CHURCH OBSERVER, THE
478 Huron Street
Toronto, ON M5R 2R3
Tel: (416) 960-8500. Fax: (416) 960-8477
E-mail: <observer@inforamp.net>
Contact: Fran Oliver, Editor.
Category: Special Interest/Religion.
Non-fiction: Yes. Fiction: Yes.
Poetry: No. Graphics: Yes.
Notes: Published 12 times a year. *TUCO* covers a
wide range of subjects, generally with a United
Church angle. Articles are invited about human
rights issues, social justice, Christian faith in action
and stories of personal courage or triumph. Fiction
suitable for children. Pays on publication. Pays $50
for photos, one-time use. Kill fee sometimes. Fifteen
per cent freelance material. Query submissions by letter or on speculation.
Guidelines available.

UNIVERSITY AFFAIRS
350 Albert St., #600
OTTAWA, ON K1R 1B1
Tel: (613) 563-1236. Fax: (613) 563-9745
E-mail: <ua@aucc.ca>
Web site: <http://www.aucc.ca/>
Contact: Christine Tausig Ford, Editor.
Category: News & Opinion/Post Secondary Education.
Non-fiction: Yes. Fiction: No. Poetry: No. Graphics: Yes.
Notes: *University Affairs* is Canada's newsmagazine on higher education. It is pub-
lished 10 times a year by the Association of Universities and Colleges of Canada. It
goes to more than 31,000 faculty administrators and staff at more than 88 Canadian
universities. They prefer story proposals by writers who have read the magazine and
their writer's guidelines. They also seek original art and cartoons.

UNIVERSITY OF TORONTO PRESS INC.
Journals Division
5201 Dufferin Street,
North York, ON M3H 5T8
Tel: (416) 667-7782. Fax: (416) 667-7881
E-mail: <fitzgera@gpu.utcc.utoronto.ca>
Contact: Theresa Fitzgerald, MA Coordinator.
Category: Scholarly.
Non-fiction: Yes. Fiction: Yes.
Poetry: Yes. Graphics: Yes.
Notes: several publications. Query for details.

UP HERE: LIFE IN CANADA'S NORTH
PO Box 1350,
Yellowknife, NT X1A 2N9
Tel: (403) 920-4652. Fax: (403) 873-2844
Contact: Rosemary Allerston, Editor.
Category: People and Places.
Non-fiction: Yes. Fiction: No. Poetry: No. Graphics; Yes.
Notes: Published bimonthly, circulation 40,000. A magazine about Northern travel, wildlife, arts, culture, lifestyles, and people who live with harsh winters. Articles 750 to 3,000 words. Pays 20 cents to 25 cents per word on publication. Other fees for columns, photos, news for first rate writing. Query first, study back issues, guidelines available.

VICTORIA BOULEVARD
PO Box 5667 Station B
Victoria, BC V8R 6S4
Tel: (250) 598-8111. Fax: (250) 598-3183
Contact: Evelyn Butler, Publisher, Vivian Sinclair, Editor.
Category: Visual Arts.
Non-fiction: Yes. Fiction: No. Poetry: No. Graphics: Yes.
Notes: Published six times a year by Bay Publishing Ltd. They also publish *Clipper* and *Japanese Visitor*. *Boulevard* is an arts and life-style magazine that includes interviews of prominent artists, actors, dancers, sculptors, artisans, photography/photographers, exotic food articles, and gallery calendar listings. Query first. Pay negotiable.

VICTORIA NATURALIST, The
2284 Cooperidge Ave.
Saanichton, BC V8M 1N2
Tel: (250) 370-3463. Fax: (250) 652-9619
E-mail: <wdrinnan@dataflux.bc.ca>
Contact: Warren Drinnan, Editor.
Category: Special Interest/Environment.
Non-fiction: Yes. Fiction: No. Poetry: Yes. Graphics: Yes.
Notes: Published every two months. *The Victoria Naturalist* promotes awareness about natural history, birding, botany, field trip reports, book reviews, photographs of birds and botany, maps, bogs, rivers, lakes, flower species and scenery. Does not pay. Queries welcome.

VOX
Room 127, MacEwan Hall
2500 University Drive,
Calgary, AB T2M 0X1
Tel: (403) 220-5156. Fax: (403) 289-8212
Contact: Ian Chiclo, Editor.
Category: Performing Arts.
Non-fiction: Yes. Fiction: No. Poetry: No. Graphics: Yes.
Notes: Published monthly, circulation 15,000. *VOX* is a forum for alternative arts magazine carrying articles on entertainment, actors, stage, local artists, and invites articles 1,500 to 2,000 words. Does not pay. Queries welcome.

WAVE~LENGTH
RR#1 Site 17
Gabriola Island, BC V0R 1X0
Tel: (250) 247-9789. Fax: (250) 247-9789
E-mail: <WaveNet@island.net>
Web site: <http://interchange.idc.uvic.ca/~wavenet>
Contact: Alan Wilson, Managing Editor.
Category: Outdoors.
Non-fiction: Yes. Fiction: No. Poetry: No. Graphics: Yes.
Notes: Published six times a year. *Wave~Length* is an independent magazine about paddling, boating, canoeing, sail-boating, kayaking, and areas of discovery around Vancouver Island. Calendar of Events, service listings, new equipment, and travel stories. Articles 500 to 2,500 words. Pays a small honorarium plus trades for advertising.

WEDDING BELLS
120 Front Street E., Suite 200
Toronto, ON M5A 4L9
Tel: (416) 862-8479. Fax: (416) 862-2184
Contact: Crys Stewart, Editor.
Category: Special Interest.
Non-fiction: Yes. Fiction: No. Poetry: No. Graphics: Yes.
Notes: Published twice a year, circulation 110,000. Glossy. *Wedding Bells* has a National edition, and other editions in Atlantic Canada, Saskatchewan, Calgary, Edmonton, Hamilton, London, Ottawa, Montreal, Toronto, Vancouver and Winnipeg. Informative and educational for brides, grooms, and their families about every aspect of wedding planning. Pays on acceptance for 1,000 to 2,000 words. Query by mail, but study back issues. Guidelines available.

WEDDINGS & HONEYMOONS
65 Helena Ave.,
Toronto, ON M6G 2H3
Tel: (416) 653-4986. Fax: (416) 653-2291
E-mail: <wed.hon@watch.tor250.org>
Contact: Joyce Barslow, Editor.
Category: Special Interest.
Non-fiction: Yes. Fiction: No. Poetry: No. Graphics: Yes.
Notes: Published twice a year, circulation 50,000. This is a glossy magazine, colour photos, informing brides-to-be on every aspect of weddings, tips, how-to pieces, second marriages, honeymoons and travel. Stories 50 to 1,250 words. Pays $50 to $150. Query. Guidelines available.

WEST COAST LINE
2027 East Annex,
Simon Fraser University,
Burnaby, BC V5A 1S6
Tel: (604) 291-4287. Fax: (604) 291-5737
Contact: Jacqueline Larson, Editor.
Category: Literary.
Non-fiction: Yes. Fiction: Yes. Poetry: Yes. Graphics: Yes.
Notes: Published three times a year, circulation 600. *West Coast Line* is devoted to contemporary writers who are experimenting or expanding boundaries of fiction, poetry and creative non-fiction. Invites submissions from western writers also in conventional poetry, essays, criticism, visual arts, photography, odd international features. Pays $8 page for up to 7,000 words after publication plus two copies. Study back issues $10, query first, guidelines available.

WESTCOAST REFLECTIONS
2604 Quadra Street
Victoria, BC V8T 4E/1
Tel: (250) 383-1149. Fax: (250) 388-4479
E-mail: <magazine@islandnet.com>
Web site: <http://www.islandnet.com/~magazine/>
Contact: Sharon Doherty, Publisher/Editor.
Category: People and Places.
Non-fiction: Yes. Fiction: No. Poetry: No. Graphics: Yes.
Notes: Published 12 times a year. Growing organic, environment, business, memoirs, comment, stage plays, entertainment, galleries, food, and events calendars. Pays 10 cents/word. Query editor. Guidelines available.

WESTERN LIVING
3rd Floor, East Tower
555 West 12th Street
Vancouver, BC V5S 4LC
Tel: (604) 877-7732. Fax: (604) 877-4849
E-mail: <western.living@cyberstore.ca>
Contact: Carolann Rule, Editor.
Category: Home and Garden.
Non-fiction: Yes. Fiction: No. Poetry: No. Graphics: Yes.
Notes: Published 10 times a year. Circulation 265,000. *Western Living* is Western Canada's home, leisure and social magazine. Regular features address social issues, trends, personalities, travel, fashion, recreation and cuisine. All stories should have a Western Canadian focus. Articles, 1,500 to 3,000 words, pays 50 cents per word on acceptance. Guidelines available with SASE.

WESTWORLD MAGAZINE
4180 Lougheed Highway, #401
Burnaby, BC V5C 6A7
Tel: (604) 299-7311. Fax: (604) 299-1899
Contact: Robin Roberts, Editor.
Category: Special Interest.
Non-fiction: Yes. Fiction: No. Poetry: No. Graphics: Yes.
Notes: Published quarterly, distributed to BCAA members. Features travel and automotive-related articles. Pays 50 cents/word for articles 800 to 1,200 words. Query, guidelines available.

WHERE
Capital Publishers.
400 Cumberland Street.
Ottawa, ON K1N 8X3
Tel: (613) 241-7888. Fax: (613) 241-3112
E-mail: <cappub@istar.ca>
Web site: <http://www.wheremags.com>
Contact: Stephen Ball, Publisher; Marlene Spatuk, Editor.
Category: Special Interest/Lifestyle.
Non-fiction: Yes. Fiction: No. Poetry: No. Graphics: Yes.
Notes: Published 12 times a year (Where Ottawa-Hull).

WHERE VICTORIA
1001 Wharf Street, 3rd Floor
Victoria, BC. V8W 1T6
Tel: (250) 388-4324. Fax: (250) 388-6166
Contact: Carolyn Camilleri, Editor.
Category: Special Interest.
Non-fiction: Yes. Fiction: No. Poetry: No. Graphics: Yes.
Notes: Published six times a year, circulation 30,000. A guide for visitors and residents featuring dining, shopping, entertainment, galleries and attractions. Articles 750 to 1,500 words. Pays a negotiated fee on publication.

WHETSTONE
English Dept.,
University of Lethbridge,
Lethbridge, AB T1K 3M4
Tel: (403) 329-2367. Fax:
Contact: Editorial Board.
Category: Literary.
Non-fiction: Yes. Fiction: Yes. Poetry: Yes. Graphics: Yes.
Notes: Published twice a year, circulation 500. Invites experimental, literary, mainstream, poetry, prose, drama, prints, photographs, music compositions, multimedia works and creative non-fiction, essays, criticism. Submit up to 10 pages, pays in contributors copies, back issues $7. Guidelines.

WHITE WALL REVIEW
63 Gould Street
Toronto, ON M5B 1E9
Tel: (416) 977-9924
Contact: Editors.
Category: Literary.
Non-fiction: Yes. Fiction; Yes. Poetry: Yes. Graphics: Some.
Notes: Published annually, circulation 500. Glossy cover, B&W photos/illustrations. Invites submissions Sept to Dec for next issue in any genre in good taste. Charges $5 reading fee and comments/criticism submissions rejected. 3,000 words max. Send cover letter with bio. Pays in contributors copies.

WINDSOR REVIEW
Dept. of English,
University of Windsor,
Windsor, ON N9B 3P4
Tel: (519) 973-7050
E-mail: <uwrevu@uwindsor.ca>
Contact: Alister MacLeod, Editor.
Category: Literary/Scholarly.
Non-fiction: Yes. Fiction: Yes. Poetry: Yes. Graphics: Yes.
Notes: Publishes twice a year, circulation 250. A Journal of the Arts, *Windsor Review*, invites submissions in fiction, poetry, creative non-fiction, art illustrations, photography, in every genre. Pays $50 and one copy on publication, sample copy $5. Free fiction guidelines.

WINDSPEAKER
15001-112th Ave.
Edmonton, AB, T5M 2V6
Tel: (403) 455-2700. Fax: (403) 455-7639
Contact: Linda Caldwell, Editor.
Category: Special Interest.
Non-fiction: Yes. Fiction: Yes. Poetry: Yes. Graphics: Yes.
Notes: Published monthly, circulation 15,000. This is a First Nations Magazine in newspaper format, that focuses on regional/local issues. Includes sports, entertainment, columns, features of 300 to 800 words. Invites stories, profiles on issues of concern to Aboriginal peoples and those who work with them. Pays $3 to $3.60 per column inch on publication for multi-source stories and profiles. Guidelines available.

WINETIDINGS

5165 Sherbrooke Street West, Suite 414

Montreal, QC H4A 1T6

Tel: (514) 481-5892. Fax: (514) 481-9699

Contact: Tony Aspler, Editor.

Category: Special Interest.

Non-fiction: Yes. Fiction: No. Poetry: No. Graphics: Yes.

Notes: Published eight times a year, circulation 16,000. *Winetidings* focuses on wines with reports about price trends, vintages, offers recipes and profiles of well-known wine cellars. Compares wines, grape types, reviews developments in the Canadian wine industry. Articles 500 to 1,500 words. Pays $200 on publication. Expert in wines prerequisite.


WOMEN AND ENVIRONMENTS

736 Bathurst Street,

Toronto, ON M5S 2R4

Tel: (416) 516-2600. Fax: (416) 531-6214

E-mail: <weed@web.net>

Web site: <http://www.web.net/~weed/>

Contact: Lisa Dale, Editor.

Category: Special Interest/Feminist.

Non-fiction: Yes. Fiction: No. Poetry: No. Graphics: Yes.

Notes: Published by Weed Foundation, quarterly. *W&E* is an international environmental feminist magazine, focusing on women's multiple relations to their many environments: natural, physical, built and social. For 20 years *W&E* has provided a forum for academic research and theory, professional practice and community networking and globally shared experience. Payments vary. Articles 1,500 to 2,500 words. Submit electronic query. Guidelines available.


WOMEN'S EDUCATION DES FEMMES

47 Main Street

Toronto ON M4E 2V6

Tel: (416) 699-1909. Fax: (416) 699-2145

E-mail: <cclow@web.net

Contact: Christina Starr, Editor.

Category: Feminist.

Non-fiction: Yes. Fiction: No. Poetry: Yes. Graphics: Yes.

Notes: Published quarterly, *Women's Education de Femmes* is a bilingual journal for professionals in the education field. Articles invited, 1,500 to 2,500 words on IBM-compatible disk, about informative research that emphasizes women in a positive perspective. Pays $25 honorarium for articles, poetry and graphics. Guidelines and back issues available. Queries welcome.

WORLD OF WHEELS
1200 Markham Road, Suite 220,
Scarborough, ON M1H 3C3
Tel: (416) 438-7777. Fax: (416) 438-5333
Contact: Joe Duarte, Editor.
Category: Special Interest.
Non-fiction: Yes. Fiction: No. Poetry: No. Graphics: Yes.
Notes: Published six times a year. Circulation 127,000. *World of Wheels* is for auto enthusiasts and for professionals interested in the auto industry. Articles evaluates and compares latest cars, light pickup trucks, vans, and sport-utility vehicles. Pays 30 cents per word on publication for articles 400 to 2,500 words. Query, guidelines available.

WRITER'S BLOCK MAGAZINE
Box 32, 9944-33 Avenue
Edmonton, AB T6N 1E8.
Category: Literary.
Non-fiction: Yes. Fiction: Yes. Poetry: Yes. Graphics: Yes.
Notes: Published twice a year, March and September. Spotlights exceptional stories in horror, mystery, science fiction/fantasy, romance, western, poetry, humour. Not longer than 5,000 words and pays five cents/word for fiction on publication and $25 for poems. Guidelines and back issues available.

WRITERS PUBLISHING, The
Box 55
Tofino, BC V0R 2Z0
Tel: (250) 725-2588 Toll Free: 1-800-655-0506
Fax: same as above. Call first.
Contact: Rebecca Tuck, Editor, Asst. Editor: Janice Lore.
Category: Literary.
Non-fiction: Yes. Fiction: Yes. Poetry: Yes. Graphics: Yes.
Notes: Published quarterly. Began November 1996. *Writers Publishing* is a magazine-style journal featuring selected poetry, short stories and memoirs. It prints the actual page that is submitted therefore must be camera ready. Pays $25 on publication.

XTRA WEST: Vancouver's Gay & Lesbian Biweekly
#501-1033 Davie Street
Mail: Box 93642, Nelson Park PO
Vancouver, BC V6E 4L7
Tel: (604) 684-9696. Fax: (604) 684-9697
E-mail: <xtrawest@descon.minet.com>
Contact: Cindy Filipenko, Editor.
Category: Special Interest.
Non-fiction: Yes. Fiction: Yes. Poetry: Yes. Graphics: Yes.
Notes: Published by Pink Triangle Press every two weeks. This tabloid magazine covers news, views, politics, culture of gay people, music, theatre, entertainment, and general interest topics. Query for guidelines and fee.

YOUTH FOCUS:
Publication of Canada Ltd.
945A Richmond Road
Ottawa, ON K2B 8B9
Tel: (613) 722-3781. Fax: (613) 722-1745
Contact: Blair Kirkpatrick.
Category: Special Interest.
Non-fiction: Yes. Fiction: No. Poetry: No. Graphics: Yes.
Notes: Published quarterly.

# Canadian Book Publishers

by Bryan Roscoe

The Internet is fast becoming the future of publishing. After all, where there is a page, there is a publisher trying to capitalise on it. The following publisher's listing is, for the most part, the result of hours of Cyber-surfing. Many publishers are posting their guidelines in full or in part. Equally useful information such as recent titles and contact names and addresses are also being listed. In some cases, chapters from recent titles are being published on the Net giving you the chance to read what the publisher considers publishable (one can hope that the writer is being paid for these electronic submissions). Having crowed enough about the Net, what follows in this brief introduction summarises some of what publishers are asking for.

In the main, publishers, big and small, continue to follow a system that has remained unchanged for many years. Publishers still require query letters before submissions, SASE—sent by snail-mail because though the Internet is the future, it is changing so quickly that publishers have yet to make room in their organisations for e-mail queries and e-mailed submissions. Many small publishers still accept unsolicited manuscripts, but appreciate query letters first. And it is the small publisher that is most likely to respond quickly to e-mail or snail-mail enquiries. They also have some of the best web sites. In comparison, larger publishers want more details than the standard query. Some ask that the writer describe the work and its importance—this is not the same as an advertisement for your prose, poetry, etc., but a balanced description of content and style. These publishers also ask for a CV highlighting your credentials as an author. Both large and small publishers suggest that when you have received your guidelines or read the guidelines published at their web site and are ready to submit something, submit three sample chapters with a cover letter that outlines in detail the theme, plot, structure and possible need for assistance on technical issues of graphics, pictures, and the like. As always send sufficient return postage, publishers big or small will not or cannot afford to pay for postage.

To conclude, publishers do not like amateurs in business, there is too much money at stake in a market that changes, quickly and radically— just consider the recent issues of split-run magazines, the continuing effect of the GST on books, the speed of change caused by the Internet and the issues it raises concerning electronic publishing rights, and the movement of large, multinational publishers in the global marketplace. Take the time to read the information in the following pages carefully and follow up by going on-line or writing to the publisher to gain as much information about the publisher, the types of books being published, etc., before you waste money on postage and handling. You may be a first time author, but you need not act like an amateur by sending out a query letter about your anthology of poetry to a publisher of Romance fiction or a technical manual to a publisher of children's literature. The information offered below along with your follow up should ease the search for a publisher for your book.

Best of luck!

**Editor's note:** We have included e-mail and web page addresses whenever they where available. However we would like to point out that the volatile nature of the Internet and the World Wide Web means that these could have changed by the time you read this publication. Be particularly careful with your address entry, but if you still fail to get through, use a Web search tool such as AltaVista <http://www.altavista.digital.com> to find the new address.

Bryan Roscoe's experience as an editor of a weekly newspaper and several years of working and travelling abroad, has given him a host of characters in search of themes and plots. He is now trying to gather these disparate characters and put them to work in short fiction. In the meantime, Bryan is still available as an editor / communications consultant.

49th Avenue Press
Langara College
100 West 49th Avenue
Vancouver, BC V5Y 2Z6
Web site: <http://www.islandnet.com/bendallbooks/>
Guidelines: 49th Avenue Press (formerly Vancouver Community College Press) is
operated by Langara College. For editorial matters, contact: Linda Holmes, President.

Addison-Wesley Publishers Ltd.
P.O. Box 580, 26 Prince Andrew Place
Don Mills, ON M3C 2T8
Phone: (416) 447-5101. Fax: (416) 443-0948
E-mail: <keithw@aw.com>
Web site: <http://www.aw.com>
Type of Books: Publishes in six specific areas: PC programming, graphics, database
programming, hardware, Macintosh programming, and on-line/Internet. Does not
publish textbooks or research/academic research (academic, corporate and profes-
sional division publishes for specialized readers in these areas).
Proposal Guidelines: Personal Information: why you are qualified to write this book,
résumé, professional/academic background, list of previous publications. Proposal:
description of book's contents and target audience, key features of book, Table of
Contents, sample chapter/writing sample, approximate length   and schedule, possible competition (if any).

Thomas Allen & Son Ltd.
390 Steelcase Road East
Markham, ON L3R 1G2
Phone: (905) 475-9126. Fax: (905) 475-6747

Alpel Publishing
CP 203
Chambly, QC J3L 4B3
Phone: (514) 658-6205
Types of books: Adult and young adult books.

Alta Press Inc.
10816-58 Avenue,
Edmonton, AB T6H 1C2
Phone: (403) 438 0754. Fax: (403) 430 1729
E-mail: <altapress@accessweb.com>
Web site: <http://www.altapress.com/>
Types of books: college books, isogrammie, parabasis, scholarly works.

Alter Ego Editions
3447 Hôtel-de-Ville Avenue
Montreal, QC H2X 3B5
Telephone and fax: (514) 849-9886
E-mail: <alterego@alterego.montreal.qc.ca>
Web site: <http://www.alterego.montreal.qc.ca/>
Types of books: "We plan to put out a small number of carefully selected titles a year in both fiction and non-fiction. A special focus will be translations of Quebec works."
Guidelines: Write for details.
Titles in print: *The Euguelion, The Wanderer.*

Annick Press
15 Patricia
Toronto, ON M2M 1H9
Phone: (416) 221-4802
Types of books: Children's and juvenile books.

Anvil Press
#204-A 175 East Broadway
Vancouver, BC V5T 1W2
Phone: (604) 876-8710. Fax: (604) 879-2667
E-mail: <subter@pinc.com>
Type of Books: Literary: fiction, poetry, drama.
Guidelines: send letter of enquiry and sample chapters. Does accept unsolicited manuscripts but only after enquiry. SASE an absolute must.
Titles in print: *Monday Night Man, Lonesome Monsters, A Circle of Birds, Fragments From the Big Piece.*

Arsenal Pulp Press
103-1014 Homer Street
Vancouver, BC V6B 2W9
Phone: (604) 687-4233. Fax: (604) 669-8250
E-mail: <arsenal@pinc.com>
Type of Books: Cultural Studies, pop culture, fiction, poetry, humour.
Guidelines: Outline and samples with unsolicited manuscripts. SASE for all returns.
Titles in print: *And Then I Wrote, Hard Core Logo, Eggplant Wife, Higher Grounds.*

B.R.M.N.A.
5124 - 33 Street N.W.,
Calgary, AB T2L 1V4
Phone: (403) 282-8456. Fax: (403) 289-3783
E-mail: <brmna@cadvision.com>
Web site: <http://www.cadvision.com/brmna/>
Types of books: "B.R.M.N.A. is a Calgary-based publishing company dedicated to

preparing low-cost, carefully researched and accurate pictorial reviews of Canadian transport subjects. At the moment, these cover mainly railway topics but we have published one work on Canadian Pacific Air Lines and another on Calgary Transit."

Guidelines: "We are always looking for new titles and are interested in hearing from anyone with suggestions for areas for us to cover. In addition, authors or would-be authors are welcome to contact us. All we ask is that authors provide the necessary photographs, an accurate sketch map of the area being covered and the captions. A standard book requires a minimum of 25 photographs and the captions should be 300 to 500 words long. The text should be submitted on a 3.5 floppy in PC format."

Titles in print: *Canadian Pacific Steam Power in British Columbia* and *Trainscape Two—Diesels in CN Lines Into Toronto.*

Bauhinea Press
109-3060 Norland Ave.
Burnaby, BC V5B 3A6
Phone: (604) 298-1391. Fax: (604) 298-7121
Types of books: ESL, Ethnic Publishing.
Guidelines: Accepts unsolicited manuscripts accompanied by SASE for returns.
Titles in print: *Survival English for New Canadians, Newcomers Map Book, B. C. Safe Driving Guide* (Chinese Version), *About Canada.*

Beach Holme Publishers
4252 Commerce Circle
Victoria, BC V8Z 4M2
Phone: (250) 727-6514. Fax: (250) 727-6418
E-mail: <editor@softwords.bc.ca>
Web site: <http://www.beachholme.bc.ca>
Types of books: We are interested in literary short fiction, novels, poetry and regional, historical young adult fiction (ages 8-12). To date, manuscripts have been selected for the 1997 season. Not interested in illustrated children's books, regional non-fiction or science fiction/fantasy. Also not considering any mystery, romance, detective, western, horror or action/adventure novels or biographies/autobiographies. Only considers submissions from Canadian authors.

Guidelines: Check the current publishing list. Please submit manuscripts with: cover letter (state if this is multiple submission), brief author biography (CV references, contacts), first 2 chapters (max. 50 pages), an approximate page count, the word processing package used (requires manuscripts on disc if accepted—Mac, DOS, Windows, or ASCII text), SASE. For young adult novel submissions: Target age group is 8-12. Particularly interested in works that have a historical basis and are set in the Pacific Northwest, or northern Canada. Include ideas for teachers and appropriate topics for the classroom. Proof-read very carefully. Send clear, double-spaced typed copy.

Bendall Books
P.O. Box 115
Mill Bay, BC V0R 2W0
Phone: (250) 743-2946. Fax: (250) 743-2910
E-mail: <bendallbooks@islandnet.com>
Web site: <http://www.islandnet.com/bendallbooks>
Types of books: Educational, Adult Basic Education, ESL.
Guidelines: Does not accept unsolicited manuscripts. Submit a proposal which includes: description of book and perceived need in the intended market, an outline, description of the market, your qualifications (CV), a description of the illustrative materials, sample chapter (if available). Titles are typically "on the small side (under 200 pages), and designed for a market which may be small but is identifiable. You are invited to contact the publisher for more details.
Titles in print: *Fiction Workshop Companion, College Style Sheet* (USA edition), *Chatting in Idiomatic English.*

Ben-Simon Publications
P.O. Box 318
Brentwood Bay, BC V8M 1C6
Phone: (250) 652-6332. Fax: (250) 652-6332
E-mail: <simon_sez@pinc.com>
Web site: <http://www.simon-sez.com/bensimon>
Types of books: Judaica, biography, history.
Guidelines: Does not accept unsolicited manuscripts, but accepts letters of enquiry, sample chapter, precise. SASE.
Titles in print: *The Old Brown Suitcase, Shared Fate, The Truth About Marvin Kalish, David Irving's Hitler.*

Big Bean Publishing
201-1508 Mariner's Walk
Vancouver, BC V6J 4X9
Phone: (604) 733-9355. Fax: (604) 736-7311
Types of books: Cooking.
Guidelines: Does not accept unsolicited manuscripts.
Titles in print: *Easy Beans.*

Black Rose Books
C.P. 1258 Succ. Place du Parc
Montreal, QC H2W 2R3
E-mail: <blakrose@web.net>
Web site: <http://www.web.net/blackrosebooks/>
Types of books: Black Rose Books publishes non-fiction books in the social sciences and the humanities—books that deal with gender equality, ecology, cities and neighbourhoods, and questions of peace, freedom and social justice.

Les Éditions du Blé
C.P. 31
St. Boniface, MB R2H 3B4
http://www.magic.mb.ca/~alexis/
alexis@magic.mb.ca
Les Éditions du Blé publient dans tous les genres, en français seulement, les textes d'auteurs du Manitoba ou des ouvrages qui, pour avoir une portée générale, touchent à l'Ouest canadien. Il est toujours préférable de soumettre le manuscit dactylographié avec un interligne double. Les manuscrits non-sollicités ne seront retournés que s'ils sont accompagnés des frais pour le retour du courrier.
Les Éditions du Blé publient un peu tous les genres, des recueils de poésie, des romans, des essais, des livres pour enfants, des cahiers de musique (piano, guitare, voix).

Blizzard Publishing
73 Furby Street
Winnipeg, MB R3C 2A2
Phone: (204) 775-2923. Fax: (204) 775-2947
E-mail: <atwood@blizzard.mb.ca>
Web site: <http://www.blizzard.mb.ca/catalog/>
Types of books: Publishes theatre plays and books.

Boston Mills Press
132 Main Street,
Erin, ON N0B 1T0
Phone: (800) 565-3111 or (519) 833-2407. Fax: (519) 833-2195
E-mail: <books@boston-mills.on.ca>
Web site: <http://www.boston-mills.on.ca>

Breakwater Books Ltd.
P.O. Box 2188
100 Water Street
St. John's, NF A1C 6E6
Phone: 1-800-563-3333 or (709) 722-6680. Fax: (709) 753-0708
E-mail: <breakwater@nfld.com>
Web site: <http://www.nfld.com/~krose/breakw.htm>

Broadview Press Ltd.
71 Princess
Peterborough, ON K9J 2A8
Phone: (705) 743-8990
Types of books: Educational textbooks.

Brucedale Press, The
Box 2259,
Port Elgin, ON N0H 2C0
Phone: (519) 832-6025. Fax: (519) 389-4962
Types of books: Non-fiction (mostly historical), fiction, poetry and children's books.
Guidelines: Seeks manuscripts with a regional (Bruce-Grey) focus. Holds workshops
for authors and works with literary community groups. Accepts unsolicited manu-
scripts or queries by mail only. Guidelines available for SASE. Contact Anne Duke
Judd, publisher.

Butterworths Canada Ltd.
75 Clegg Road,
Markham, ON L6G 1A1
Phone: 1-800-668-6481 or (905) 479-BOOK. FAX: (905) 479-2826
E-mail: Ruth Epstein <repstein@butterworths.ca>
Web site: <http://www.butterworths.ca:80/>
Types of books: "Butterworths is a pre-eminent publisher of legal materials with
offices around the world. Our authors include leading practitioners, academics and
prominent members of the judiciary."

Caitlin Press, The
P.O. Box 2387, Station B
Prince George, BC V2N 2S6
Phone: (250) 964-4953. Fax: (250) 964-4953
Types of books: Northern and Interior B.C.
Guidelines: Accepts unsolicited manuscripts with SASE.
Titles in print: *A Traveler's Guide to Northern British Columbia, Atlin's Gold,
Unfriendly Neighbours, High Heels 'n' Oil Rigs.*

Canada Communication Group Publishing
45 Blvd. Sacre-Coeur, Chambre A2403 E,
Hull, QC K1A 0S9
Phone: (819) 997-4962. Fax: (819) 997-8863
Web site: <http://www.ccg-gcc.ca/>
Types of books: Mostly professional publishing arm of the National Capital Region,
handling all publishing (including CD-ROM), printing, mailing and distribution, and
electronic document management services. Not a publisher, per se.

Canadian Almanac & Directory Publishing Co. Ltd.
55 St. Clair Ave. West, Suite 225
Toronto, ON M4V 2Y7
Phone: (416) 972-6645. Fax: (416) 972-6648
Web site: <http://www.canadainfo.com>
Types of books: Almanacs and various business directories.

Canadian Scholars' Press Inc.
180 Bloor W.
Toronto, ON M5S 2V6
Phone: (416) 929-2774
Types of books: Educational textbooks.

Carleton University Press
1125 Colonel By Dr.
Ottawa, ON K1S 5B6
Phone: (613) 520-3740
Types of books: Educational and scholarly books.
Carswell
One Corporate Plaza, 2075 Kennedy Road
Scarborough, ON M1T 3V4
Phone: (416) 609-8000. Fax: (416) 298-5094
Web site: <http://www.carswell.com>

CCH Canadian Limited
6 Garamond Court
North York, ON M3C 1Z5
Phone: (416) 441-0086. Fax: (416) 444-9011

Charlton Press
2040 Yonge St.
Toronto, ON M4S 1Z9
Phone: (416) 488-4653
Types of books: Hobby price guides.

Les Éditions de la Chenelière
215 Jean Talon Est
Montréal, QC H2R 1S9
Phone: (514) 273-1066. Fax: (514) 276-0324

Clare Educational Development Inc.
4188 Virginia Cres.
North Vancouver, BC V7R 3Z6
Phone: (604) 980-2598. Fax: (604) 988-7021

Coach House Books
401 Huron St. on bpNichol Lane
Toronto, ON M5S 2G5
Phone: (416)979-2217. Fax: (416)977-1158
E-mail: <chp@lglobal.com>
Web site: <http://www.chbooks.com/>

Commoners' Publishing Society Inc.
73 Eccles
Ottawa, ON K1R 6S5
Phone: (613) 238-3491
Types of books: Regional non-fiction.


Copp Clark Ltd.
2775 Matheson Blvd. East
Mississauga, ON L4W 4P7
Phone: (905) 238-6074. Fax: (905) 238-6075
Coteau Books
401 - 2206 Dewdney Ave.
Regina, SK S4R 1H3
Phone: (306) 777-0170. Fax: (306) 522-5152
E-mail: <coteau@coteau.unibase.com>
Web site: <http://coteau.unibase.com/welcome.html>
Types of books: "The literary press produces 12 books of fiction, poetry, drama and culturally related non-fiction each year."
Titles in print: Anne Szumigalski's *Voice*, Dianne Warren's *Bad Luck Dog*, Eugene Stickland's *Some Assembly Required*, Sharon Butala's *Queen of the Headaches*, Patrick Lane's *Winter* and Archie Crail's *The Bonus Deal*.


Doubleday Canada Limited
105 Bond Street
Toronto, ON M5B 1Y3
Phone: (416) 340-0777. Fax: (416) 340-9957
Web site: <http://www.bdd.com>
Prefers agented enquiries. There is one exception, however, Romance novels. In regard to Romance novels, the publisher states that "There are no guidelines for Women's Fiction—the stories and styles of our books cover the entire spectrum of the genre. If you wish to submit your work for consideration by Bantam and are unagented, send us a query letter. The query letter should be no more than three pages, covering the basics of who your characters are, what the conflict is that they face, and how your plot develops. It usually takes eight weeks to receive a response from us. Please don't submit sample chapters or a complete manuscript until we request them. Unfortunately, we cannot give comments on any submissions. Be sure to include a self-addressed, stamped envelope; we cannot respond to queries which are not accompanied by return postage." Submissions should be addressed to: Bantam Romance Editors, Bantam Books, 1540 Broadway, New York, NY 10036.


Douglas & McIntyre
1615 Venables Street
Vancouver, BC V5L 2H1
Phone: (604) 254-7191. Fax: (604) 254-9099
E-mail: <dm@douglas-mcintyre.com>
Types of books: General Non-fiction emphasising art, First Nations, natural history,

sports, regional history, and Greystone Imprints.
Guidelines: Does not accept unsolicited manuscripts.
Titles in print: *Bachelor Brothers' Bed and Breakfast Pillow Book, The Jade Peony, Fishing With My Old Guy, Barret.*

Dundurn Press Ltd.
2181 Queen E.
Toronto, ON M4E 1E5
Phone: (416) 698-0454
Types of books: Adult and educational non-fiction.
Durkin Hayes Publishing Ltd.
3375 North Service Rd, Units B7 & B8
Burlington, ON L7N 3G2
Phone: (905) 335-0393. Fax: (905) 332-3008
E-mail: <durhayes@netaccess.on.ca>

ECW PRESS
3483 rue Peel, suite 23
Montréal, QC H3A 1W8
Phone: (514) 398-8326. Fax: (514) 398-8220
E-mail: <rlecker@peterson.lan.mcgill.ca>
Web site: <http://www.ecw.ca/Press/>
Types of books: "We publish trade books of all kinds, including biographies of today's best-known rock stars, writers, artists, and television personalities, with an equal emphasis on sports and popular entertainment in Canada and the United States.
Contacts: Robert Lecker or Holly Potter.
Titles in print: *Hidden Montreal: The Unique Guidebook to Montreal's Secret Sites, Sounds, & Tastes, Melissa Etheridge: Our Little Secret.*

Ekstasis Editions
Box 8474, Main Postal Outlet
Victoria, BC V8W 3S1
Phone: (250) 385-3378. Fax: (250) 385-3378
Types of books: Poetry, fiction, criticism.
Guidelines: Accepts unsolicited manuscripts with SASE.
Titles in print: *The Ogre of Grand Remous, The Sun is Whatever You Say It Is, Locutions, Muskox andGoat Songs.*

Erin Publications
82 Edenstone View NW
Calgary, AB T3A 4T5
Phone: (403) 239-4318. Fax: (403) 239-0853
E-mail: <qnd@cadvision.com>
Web site: <http://www.islandnet.com/~qnd/customs/homepage.html>

H.B. Fenn and Company Ltd.
34 Nixon Road
Bolton, ON L7E 1W2
Phone: (905) 951-6600. Fax: (905) 951-6601
E-mail: <fenn@interhop.net>

Fitzhenry & Whiteside Limited
195 Allstate Parkway
Markham, ON L3R 4T8
Phone: (905) 477-9700. Fax: (905) 477-9179
E-mail: <godwit@fitzhenry.ca>
Web site: <http://www.fitzhenry.ca>
Types of books: Trade non-fiction, educational, history, geography, Native studies, social studies, natural sciences and architecture. Some picture books for children.
Guidelines: Canadian authors only. Publishes about 20 titles per year.

Formac Publishing Co Ltd.
5502 Atlantic St.
Halifax, NS B3H 1G4
Phone: (902) 421-7022
Types of books: Children's and juvenile fiction; adult guidebooks, biographies and histories.

Fraser Institute, The
626 Bute Street, 2nd Floor
Vancouver, BC V6E 3M1
Phone: (604) 688-0221. Fax: (604) 688-8531
E-mail: <info@fraserinstitute.ca>
Web site: <http://www.fraserinstitute.ca>
Send a letter of enquiry to the attention of: Kristin McCahon, Publications.

Gage Educational Publishing Co.
164 Commander Boulevard
Agincourt, ON M1S 3C7
Phone: (416) 293-8141. Fax: (416) 293-9009

Garamond Press
67 Mowat Avenue, Suite 144
Toronto, ON M6K 3E3
Phone: (416) 516-2709. Fax: (416) 516-0571
E-mail: Garamond@web.apc.org
Types of books: "The company's mandate is to provide an alternative to multinational textbook publishers and university presses, publishing critical works on such areas as political economy, popular culture and gender issues."
Guidelines: Style Guides are available for "preferred spelling, footnoting, indexing and bibliographic conventions."

Ginn Publishing Canada Inc.
3771 Victoria Park Ave.,
Toronto, ON M1W 2P9
Phone: (416) 497-4600
Types of books: Educational textbooks.

Grolier Limited
12 Banigan Dr.
Toronto, ON M4H 1E9
Phone: (416) 425-1924
Types of books: Children's and juvenile fiction.
Hancock House Publishers Ltd.
19313 Zero Ave.
Surrey, BC V3S 5J9
Phone: (604) 538-1114
Types of books: Nature, wildlife and regional biographies.

Harbour Publishing Co. Ltd.
P.O. Box 219
Madeira Park, BC V0N 2H0
Phone: (604) 883-2730. Fax: (604) 883-9451
E-mail: <harbour@sunshine.net>
Types of books: Non-fiction, literary, and children's books with a focus on BC
and BC authors.
Guidelines: Accepts unsolicited manuscripts with SASE.
Titles in print: *H. R.: A Biography of H. R. MacMillan, Starting from Ameliasburgh,
The Whole Fam Damily, Raincoast Chronicles, Eleven Up.*

Harcourt Brace & Company Canada Ltd.
55 Horner Avenue
Toronto, ON M8Z 4X6
Phone: (416) 255-4471. Fax: (416) 255-4046

Harlequin Enterprises Ltd.
255 Duncan Mill Road
Don Mills, ON M3B 3K9
Phone: (416) 445-5860. Fax: (416) 445-8655
Web site: <http://www.romance.net/>
Types of books: Romance fiction in a variety of genres and imprints.
Guidelines: Editorial guidelines are available by mail. Please send a self-addressed,
stamped envelope and your request to the attention of Maureen Stead.

HarperCollins Canada Ltd.
1995 Markham Road
Scarborough, ON M1B 5M8
Phone: (416) 975-9334. Fax: (416) 321-3033
E-mail: <hccanada@harpercollins.com>
Web site: <http://www.harpercollins.com/canada>
Types of books: Fiction: Adult, young adult; non-fiction: biography, social issue, women's, Canadian interest.
Guidelines: Agented submissions preferred. No unsolicited manuscripts. Query first.

Frederick Harris Music Co., Limited, The
Unit 1, 5865 McLaughlin Road
Mississauga, ON M5R 1B8
Phone: (905) 501-1595. Fax: (905) 501-0929
Hartley & Marks Publishers
3661 West Broadway
Vancouver, BC V6R 2B8
Phone: (604) 739-1771. Fax: (604) 738-1913
E-mail: <hartmark@direct.com>
Types of books: Family, health, environment, design.
Guidelines: Accepts unsolicited manuscripts with SASE. "When looking at a manuscript our first consideration is whether a good book on the subject already exists. If only a poor or limited one does, we may do a book that is more complete. If a good book does exist, we won't publish another." When submitting, include a brief description or outline of the book, approximately 100 words, chapter headings or brief chapter outline, 2-3 sample chapters, your CV. Address inquiries and submissions to: Susan Juby, Editorial Co-ordinator, Hartley & Marks Publishers, Box 147, Point Roberts, WA., 98281.
Titles in print: *A Child in Pain, Cohousing, LBS: A Doctor's Plan, Sold Partner.*

D.C. Heath Canada Ltd.
200 Adelaide Street West, 3rd Floor
Toronto, ON M5H 1W7
Phone: (416) 977-1345. Fax: (416) 977-3135
Now a part of Houghton Mifflin Web site: <http://www.hmco.com/>

Herald Press
490 Dutton Dr.
Kitchener, ON N2L 4C6
Phone: (519) 747-5722
Types of books: Christian children's, juvenile and adult fiction and non-fiction.

Heritage House Publishing Company Ltd.
310-3555 Outrigger Road
Nanoose, BC V0R 2R0
Phone: (250) 468-5328. Fax: (250) 468-5318

E-mail: <herhouse@island.net>

Web site: <http://www.islandnet.com/herhouse>

Types of books: Western Canadiana, recreational guides, biographies.

Guidelines: We recommend, for authors developing a non-fiction ms, that they provide   a book proposal which includes a subject overview, projected content summary, first   10-20 pages, description of proposed photo support (preferably with a sample) and a brief personal profile. If SASE is enclosed, we will offer a response within 45 days.

Titles in print: *Scarlet Tunic, Cariboo-Chilcotin Pioneer Memories, 101 Dives, The Valencia Tragedy*.

Horned Owl Publishing

3906 Cadboro Bay Road

Victoria, BC V8N 4G6

Phone: (250) 477-8488. Fax: (250) 721-1029

E-mail: <hornowl@islandnet.com>

Web site: <http://www.islandnet.com/~hornowl>

Types of books: Earth-centred spirituality, Aboriginal European religions, and the Western Mystery Tradition. "We are dedicated to publishing a variety of books: academic, children's, general, handbooks and chapbooks, books for families who are raising their children in these spiritual paths, and books which further understanding between members of different faiths.

Guidelines: Prefers titles that have strong educational or artistic merit. The publisher is NOT looking for trendy-sensationalism. The publisher is presently looking for the following: academic books: history, archaeology, classics, theology, sociology, linguistics, music; children's books: picture books, illustrated chapter books, fiction and non-fiction for pre-schoolers to young adults; and general books: handbooks, guidebooks, chapbooks, and books on Pagan parenting. Accepts unsolicited manuscripts but please include SASE or IRC. Accepts simultaneous submissions but please indicate in your letter of inquiry. You may also submit a number of chapters and a detailed outline. In the case of children's books, submit the entire manuscripts. Submissions can be by e-mail, on disk (DOS formatted), or traditional paper.

Royalties: 10% Canada, 8% USA, 5% of sales elsewhere.

Horsdal & Schubart Publishers Ltd.

623 - 425 Simcoe Street

Victoria, BC V8V 4T3

Phone: (250) 360-2031. Fax: (250) 360-0829

Types of books: Non-fiction on Western and Northern Canada.

Guidelines: Prefers a letter or phone call of enquiry before accepting unsolicited manuscripts.

Titles in print: *Sea-Silver: Inside BC's Salmon Farming Industry, John Tod: Rebel in the Ranks, Salt on the Wind, Silences of the Heart*.

House of Anansi Press Limited
1800 Steeles Avenue West
Concord, ON L4K 2P3
Phone: (905) 660-0611.
E-mail: <anansi@irwin-pub.com>
Web site: <http://www.the-wire.com/irwin/anansi/>
Types of books: publishes quality fiction, literary criticism, poetry and belles lettres by Canadian writers.

Hyperion Press Ltd.
300 Wales Ave.
Winnipeg, MB R2M 2S9
Phone: (204) 256-9204
Types of books: How-to, arts and crafts.

Inner City Books
Box 1271, Station Q
Toronto, ON M4T 2P4
Phone: (416) 927-0355. FAX (416) 924-1814
E-mail: <icb@inforamp.net>
Web sites: <http://www.inforamp.net/~icb> (text only)
or <http://www.bookworld.com/innercity> (text and graphics)
Types of books: "Inner City Books was started in 1980 to promote the understanding and practical application of the work of C.G. Jung. It is still the only publishing house in the world devoted exclusively to books written by Jungian analysts."

Irwin Publishing Inc.
1800 Steeles W
Thornhill, ON L4K 2P3
Phone: (905) 660-0611
Types of books: Educational textbooks.

James Lorimer And Company
35 Britain St.
Toronto, ON M5A 1R7
Phone: (416) 362-4762
Types of books: Children's books and trade books.

Jesperson Press Limited
39 James Lane
St John's, NF A1E 3H3
Phone: (709) 753-5700
Types of books: Non-fiction, fiction, drama and poetry.

John Wiley & Sons Canada Limited
22 Worcester Road
Etobicoke, ON M9W 1L1
Phone: (416) 236-4433. Fax: (416) 236-4446
Web site: <http://www.wiley.com>
"The focus of J. Wiley and Sons is on educational materials geared to the college, and professional academic/trade markets.
Guidelines: You are encouraged to submit a prospectus of 5 to 10 pages describing your purpose, scope, and features of your work. Also include sample chapters and a Table of Contents. All your materials will be sent to reviewers "so that you can get the most informed feedback possible." Further details: In a description and table of contents, explain why you are writing the book and how it will benefit the student. Identify the scope, target course(s), important features, level of presentation, major themes or approaches, prerequisites, and the scope of the illustration programme. Include in your table of contents subheadings which will give the editor a "feel for the depth of your work and its approach." About the competition: include information about which books are your chief competitors, and why. What specific advantages does your work have over your competitor's? About sample chapters: include three chapters, some traditional, but also one that is innovative and covers topics difficult to teach. Include a copy of your CV listing degrees, positions held, and publications.

Kalamalka Press
7000 College Way
Vernon, BC V1B 2N5
Phone: (250) 525-7291. Fax: (250) 545-3277
Types of books: Poetry.
Guidelines: Books are published as a result of the Kalamalka New Writers' Competition which is open to any Canadian citizen. The work submitted to this competition must not yet be published in book form. Does not accept unsolicited manuscripts.
Titles in print: *Valancy and the New World, Fat Moon, Worlda Mirth, Solstice on the Anacortes Ferry.*

Kitsch Publishing
Address not available; send query by e-mail
E-mail: <reignbo@geocities.com>
Types of books: Publishes both full-size collections as well as chapbooks. Kitsch intends to publish B.C. writers only, but will "consider writers from other regions in Canada." Publishes "poetry" and "plays that do not fit into any conventional categories." The publisher is not interested in poems about butterflies and "libido."
Guidelines: Does not accept unsolicited manuscripts. "Please send a query letter via e-mail first. We are not interested in nostalgic, rhyming greeting card poetry. We prefer eclectic work that is fresh and distinct! DO NOT send manuscripts via e-mail."

Knopf Canada
33 Yonge St.
Toronto, ON M5E 1G4
Phone: (416) 777-9477
Types of books: Trade fiction and non-fiction.

Little, Brown and Company (Canada) Limited
148 Yorkville Avenue
Toronto, ON M5R 1C2
Phone: (416) 967-3888. Fax: (416) 967-4591

Lone Pine Publishing
#206, 14426 81 Avenue
Edmonton, Alberta
Canada T6E 1X5
E-mail: <75667.2070@compuserve.com>
Web site: <http://ourworld.compuserve.com/homepages/LonePinePublishing/>
Lost Moose Publishing Ltd.
58 Kluane Crescent
Whitehorse, YK Y1A 3G7
Phone: (403) 668-3441. Fax: (403) 668-6223
E-mail: <plong@yknet.yk.ca>
Web site: <http://www.yukonweb.wis.net/business/lostmoose/>
Types of books: Northern/Yukon non-fiction. Lost Moose Publishing publishes
"books from the North about the North." Interested, primarily, in non-fiction dealing
with Yukon history, contemporary northern lifestyles, and the environment. Will consider "works of literature and fiction which have a purely northern or Yukon focus."
Guidelines: Does accept unsolicited, non-fiction manuscripts with SASE. First present, in writing, a brief summary of the book idea. If interested, Lost Moose will
request a package with the following: a copy of the manuscript or detailed outline
including introduction, table of contents, and three sample chapters; a summary of
content and explanation of scope and purpose; how does the book fit the publishing
mandate; marketing tips on audience for the book; list of competing titles and how
your text differs; samples of previously published work and your background. Send
copies of your work. The publisher is not responsible for lost manuscripts. Responds
within three months, ordinarily.
Titles in print: *Law of the Yukon, Yukon Colour of the Land, Another Lost Moose
Catalogue, Skookum's North: The Paws Collection.*

Macmillan Canada
29 Birch Ave.
Toronto, ON M4V 1E1
Phone: (416) 963-8830
Types of books: Canadian non-fiction trade books.

McClelland & Stewart
481 University Ave.
Toronto, ON M5G 2E9
Phone: (416) 598-1114
Web Main Page: <http://www.tceplus.com/mcclelland/mcclelland.htm>
Guidelines at: <http://www.tceplus.com/mcclelland/guidelin.htm>
Types of books: Publishes very few books for children; publishes only four books of poetry each year; publishes fiction, see guidelines on web pages: publishes non-fiction.
Guidelines: "McClelland & Stewart does not accept unsolicited manuscripts. Instead, send us a letter of inquiry of two or three pages telling us about the manuscript and about your writing or publishing experience, along with a stamped self-addressed envelope."

McGraw-Hill Ryerson Limited
300 Water Street
Whitby, ON L1N 9B6
Phone: (905) 430-5000. Fax: (905) 430-5020
Web site: <http://www.mcgrawhill.ca>
Types of books: College Division.
Guidelines: Extensive Prospectus Guidelines offered. "The ideal prospectus includes a convincing rational for the project, a strategic plan for its development, and a clear focus on its targeted market. A carefully prepared prospectus will explain why you want to undertake the project and will address ten questions." Briefly, the areas questioned are as follows (for full details check the McGraw-Hill web site): (1) The market, (2) The competition, (3) The content, (4) The format, (5) The pedagogy, (6) The Supplements, (7) The competitive edge and distinguishing features, (8) The schedule, (9) Special considerations: marketing strategy?, use of consultants?, (10) Annotated Table of Contents. Further, supply Sample Chapters and reviewer/consultant suggestions; and please enclose a CV describing credentials, education, etc.

Moonstone Press
167 Delaware St.
London ON N5Z 2N6
E-mail: <pbaltens@odyssey.on.ca>
Web site: <http://www.mirror.org/commerce/hmspress/moon.html>
Titles in print: James Deahl, *Even This Land Was Born of Light*, Janet Read, *Blue Mind's Flower*.

Mosaic Press
1252 Speers Rd.
Oakville, ON L6L 5N9
Phone: (905) 825-2130
Types of books: Trade fiction and non-fiction.

ITP Nelson Canada
1120 Birchmount Road
Scarborough, ON M1K 5G4
Phone: (416) 752-9100. Fax: (416) 752-9646
Web site: <http://www.thomson.com/nelson.html>

New Society Publishers
P.O. Box 189
Gabriola Island, BC V0R 1X0
Phone: (250) 247-9737. Fax: (250) 247-7471
E-mail: <nsp@island.net>
Web site: <http://www.swifty.com/nsp>
Types of books: Sustainability, nature writing, education.
Guidelines: Please write for submission guidelines. Does not accept unsolicited manuscripts.
Titles in print: *Our Ecological Footprint, Deschooling Our Lives, Transforming Abuse, Simplicity: Notes, Stories and Exercises for Creating Unimaginable Wealth.*

New Star Books
2504 York Avenue
Vancouver, BC V6K 1E3
Phone: (604) 738-9429. Fax: (604) 738-9332
E-mail: <newstar@pinc.com>
Types of books: Transmontanus series, social issues, politics, local history, literature.
Guidelines: Accepts unsolicited manuscripts with SASE. Editorial correspondence should be in writing, no faxes.
Titles in print: *Ghost in the Water, Highwire Act, Turning Lead Into Gold, All Possible Worlds.*

Nightwood Editions
R.R. #5, S26, C13
Gibsons, BC V0N 1V0
Phone: (604) 885-0212. Fax: (604) 885-0212
E-mail: <nightwood@sunshine.net>
Types of books: Children's, literary.
Guidelines: Accepts unsolicited manuscripts with SASE.
Titles in print: *Ferryboat Ride, Frogs in the Rain Barrel, Low Water Slack, Mayuk the Grizzly Bear.*

Nimbus Publishing Ltd.
3731 MacKintosh St.
Halifax, NS B3K 5A5
Phone:(902)455-4286. Fax:(902)455-3652
E-mail: <eiwaskow@hhmnewsgr.com>
Web site: <http://emporium.turnpike.net/A/AAllen/Nimbus/index.html>
Types of books: Social history, biographies, cookbooks, travel, nature, children's
and photographic books.

Northstone Publishing
330-1980 Cooper Road
Kelowna, BC V1Y 9G8
Phone: (250) 766-2926. Fax: (250) 766-1201
E-mail: <info@northstone.com>
Types of books: Not specified.
Guidelines: Welcomes outlines, sample chapters, table of contents and SASE. Does
not accept unsolicited manuscripts.
Titles in print: *The Alternative Wedding Book, God for Beginners, Minnow, The
Family Story Bible*.

Oolichan Books
P.O. Box 10
Lantzville, BC V0R 2H0
Phone: (250) 390-4839. Fax: (250) 390-4839
E-mail: <oolichan@mail.island.net>
Types of books: Fiction, poetry, regional history, outdoors, children's literature.
Guidelines: Accepts unsolicited manuscripts but prefers a letter of enquiry with
SASE. Submissions without SASE will not be returned. Enquiries or submissions
should be by mail. No phone calls or fax submissions.
Titles in print: *Visible Light, ed and mabel go to the moon, Historic Nelson,
Emily Carr's Woo*.

Orca Book Publishers
P.O. Box 5626, Station B
Victoria, BC V8R 6S4
Phone: (250) 380-1229. Fax: (250) 380-1892
E-mail: <orca@pinc.com>
Web site: <http://www.swifty.com/orca>
Types of books: Adult non-fiction with emphasis on West Coast material, children's
picture books, young adult fiction and non-fiction.
Guidelines, general: Query letter with outline, sample chapter and author biography
with SASE. Does not accept unsolicited manuscripts.
Brief Guidelines for Children's Literature: Certain areas are of prime interest: in pic-
ture books: stories derived from the author's own childhood experiences, historical
tales that are well researched, pioneer stories, and modern stories that may be located

anywhere in Canada but are "universal in theme." In older juvenile and young adult fiction: issue oriented, challenging language and themes, historical, (western) regional stories, "no high interest/low vocabulary, light mysteries or science fiction please. Picture book queries and submissions sent to the attention of Ann Featherstone, Children's Book Editor. Older juvenile and young adult to Robert Tyler, Publisher.

Oxford University Press
70 Wynford Dr.
North York, ON M3C 1J9
Phone: (416) 441-2941
Types of books: Educational textbooks plus trade fiction and non-fiction.

Pacific Edge Publishing Ltd.
R.R. 2, Site 21, C-50
Gabriola Island, BC V0R 1X0
Phone: (250) 247-8806. Fax: (250) 247-8299
E-mail: <pacedge@island.net>
Types of books: Educational, elementary activity books, teacher resources, textbooks.
Guidelines: Accepts unsolicited manuscripts for educational purposes only. No picture or story books.
Titles in print: *Beans and Their Buddies, Legends of the Chemainus Tribe, Soil Secrets, Alphabet Zoe, Spectacular Spiders.*
Pacific Educational Press
Faculty of Education, UBC
Vancouver, BC V6T 1Z4
Phone: (604) 822-5385. Fax: (604) 822-6603
E-mail: <cedwards@unixg.ubc.ca>
Types of books: Children's fiction and non-fiction, education books for teachers and teachers-in-training.
Guidelines: Accepts unsolicited manuscripts with SASE.
Titles in print: *In the Street of the Temple Cloth Printers, The Reluctant Deckhand, Windows on the World, A Sea Lion Called Salena.*

Pacific-Rim Publishers
R.R. 1, Site 28, C-7
Gabriola, BC V0R 1X0
Phone: (250) 247-0014. Fax: (250) 247-0015
Types of books: Educational.
Guidelines: Accepts unsolicited manuscripts, but no response without SASE. Please, no original artwork.
Titles in print: *Haiku: One Breath Poetry, Japanese: An Appetizer, Puzzling on the Rim, Telling Tales on the Rim.*

Peguis Publishers Ltd.
318 Mcdermot Ave.
Winnipeg, MB R3A 0A2
Phone: (204) 987-3500
Types of books: Educational resource books.

Pembroke Publishers
538 Hood Road
Markham, ON L3R 3K9
Phone: (905) 477-0650. Fax: (905) 477-3691

Pemmican Publications
1635 Burrows Ave.
Winnipeg, MB R2X 3B5
Phone: (204) 589-6346
Types of books: Children's fiction and non-fiction with Native or Metis slant.

Penguin Books Canada Limited
10 Alcorn Avenue, Suite 300
Toronto, ON M4V 3B2
Phone: (416) 925-2249. Fax: (416) 925-0068
Web site: <http://www.penguin.ca>

Playwrights Canada Press
54 Wolseley St., 2nd Floor
Toronto, ON M5T 1A5
Phone: (416) 703 0201. Fax: (416) 703 0059
E-mail: <cdplays@interlong.com>
Web site: <http://www.puc.ca/pcp/pcp.html>
Types of books: Playwrights Canada Press is the publishing imprint of the Playwrights Union of Canada.

Polestar Book Publishers
1011 Commercial Dr., 2nd Floor
Vancouver, BC V5L 3X1
Phone: (604) 251-9718. Fax: (604) 251-9738
E-mail: <mbenjami@direct.ca>
Types of books: Poetry, fiction, sports, young adult fiction.
Guidelines: Accepts unsolicited manuscripts with SASE. No children's picture books.
Titles in print: *The Garden Letters, Celebrating Excellence, Annie, Flapjacks & Photographs*.

Potlatch Publications
30 Berry Hill Ave.
Waterdown, ON L0R 2H4
Phone: (905) 689-1632
Types of books: General trade books.

Prairie Publishing Co., The
115 Garrioch Ave.
Winnipeg, MB R3J 2T2
Phone: (204) 885-6496
Types of books: General fiction and non-fiction with a prairie regional theme.

Prentice Hall Canada Inc.
1870 Birchmount Road
Scarborough, ON M1P 2J7
Phone: (416) 293-3621. Fax: (416) 293-0571
Web site: <http://www.prenhall.com>
Types of books: Academic, educational.
Guidelines: Detailed guidelines are available from the publisher's home page. Briefly, submit prospectus and outline. The book: brief description, outstanding features, pedagogical features, supplements, level, materials tested? Your background: description, CV, do you have other writing plans when this project is complete? The competition: top three books in the field and how does your book compare/contrast; compare topical coverage, be frank, are you aware of similar works in progress? The market: what is the primary course for which the book is intended? what other courses could it apply to? how large do you estimate the market to be?, send any market research you may have done. The outline: overview the entire work, chapter heads followed by sub-heads that offer some explanation, use paragraphs to clarify the outline, always provide a revised outline. Sample chapters: should illustrate the strongest and most distinctive aspects, submit three chapters. Additional information: schedule of completion? approximate length, what art is required? Is the material being word processed? Please list names of qualified reviewers and their qualifications.

Press Gang Publishers
#101, 225 East 17th Ave.
Vancouver, BC V5V 1A6
Phone: (604) 876-7787. Fax: (604) 876-7892
E-mail: <pgangpub@portal.ca>
Types of books: Women's fiction and non-fiction, lesbian and gay material.
Guidelines: Not accepting unsolicited poetry or children's material. Accepts letter of enquiry and sample chapters with SASE.
Titles in print: *When Fox is a Thousand, Restricted Entry: Censorship on Trial, Her Tongue on My Theory, Bending at the Bow.*

Quarry Press Inc.
240 King St. E.
Kingston, ON K7L 3A6
Phone: (613) 548-8429
Types of books: Educational texts, non-fiction, fiction and poetry.

Ragweed Press
222 Grafton St.
Charlottetown, PE C1A 1L4
Phone: (902) 566-5750
Types of books: Atlantic regional fiction and non-fiction.

Raincoast Books
8680 Cambie Street
Vancouver, BC V6P 6M9
Phone: (604) 323-7100. Fax: (604) 323-7109
E-mail: <info@raincoast.com>
Types of books: Canadiana, nature, children's illustrated, travel, food.
Guidelines: Does not accept unsolicited manuscripts.
Titles in print: *Hiking on the Edge, Diane Clement at the Tomato, Guide to the Queen Charlotte Islands, Fragments of Paradise.*

Random House of Canada Ltd.
(Editorial, Publicity, and Production Offices)
33 Yonge Street, Suite 210
Toronto, ON M5E 1G4
Phone: (416) 777-9477. Fax: (416) 777-9470
Web site: <http://www.randomhouse.com>
Types of books: Trade non-fiction and fiction.

Riverwood Publishers Ltd.
471 Eagle St.
Newmarket, ON L3Y 1K7
Phone: (905) 853-8887
Types of books: Juvenile fiction.

Riverwood Publishers Ltd.
6 Donlands Avenue, P.O. Box 70
Sharon, ON L0G 1V0
Phone: (905) 478-8396. Fax: (905) 478-8380

Rocky Mountain Books
4 Spruce Centre S.W.,
Calgary, AB T3C 3B3
Phone: (403) 249-9490. Fax: (403) 249-2968
E-mail: Tony Daffern <tonyd@cadvision.com>

Web site: <http://www.ffa.ucalgary.ca/rmb/index.html>
Types of books: Climbing, hiking, biking, skiing, paddling sports, wilderness travel
Titles in print: *Planning a Wilderness Trip In Canada and Alaska,*
*My Valley: The Kananaskis.*

Ronsdale Press
3350 West 21st Avenue
Vancouver, BC V6S 1G7
Phone: (604) 738-1195. Fax: (604) 731-4548
E-mail: <ronhatch@pinc.com>
Types of books: Literature, regional, history, children's.
Guidelines: Send opening chapters with letter of enquiry, SASE and brief author's
biography and publishing credentials, if any.
Titles in print: *Blackouts to Bright Lights, Living Rivers of BC, Edge of Time,*
*Frankie Zapper and the Disappearing Teacher.*

Royal British Columbia Museum
675 Belleville Street
Victoria, BC V8V 1X4
Phone: (250) 387-2478. Fax: (250) 387-5360
E-mail: <gtruscott@RBML.01.rbcm.gov.bc.ca>
Web site: <http://www.rbcm/.rbcm.gov.bc.ca>
Types of books: Natural history, anthropology, history, museum studies.
Guidelines: Does not accept unsolicited manuscripts.
Titles in print: *Food Plants of Coastal First Peoples, Indian History of BC, Plant*
*Collecting for the Amateur, Bats of BC.*

Rubicon Publishing Inc.
1134 Morrison Heights Dr.
Oakville, ON L6J 4J1
Phone: (905) 849-8777
Types of books: Emphasizes titles which reflect the multicultural nature of Canadian
society, and which avoid stereotyping of people by sex, race, age, and physical/men-
tal ability. Rubicon publishes both fiction and non-fiction, as well as educational
material for use in schools and colleges.

Sandhill Publishing
99-1270 Ellis Street (Rear)
Kelowna, BC V1Y 1Z4
Phone: (250) 763-1406. Fax: (250) 763-4051
Types of books: Non-fiction, local interest.
Guidelines: Does not accept unsolicited manuscripts. Long distance calls will be
returned collect.
Titles in print: *How to Self-Publish and Make Money, Ogopogo, Valley of the*
*Ghosts.*

Scholastic Canada Ltd.
123 Newkirk Road
Richmond Hill, ON L4C 3G5
Phone: (905) 883-5300. Fax: (905) 883-4113
Web site: <http://www.scholastic.ca/>
Types of books: Non-fiction and fiction, including picture books, for pre-school to young adults.

Second Story Press
720 Bathurst St., #301,
Toronto, ON M5S 2R4
Phone: (416) 537-7850. Fax: (416) 537-0588
E-mail: <secstory@fox.nstn.ca>
Web site: <http://www.coolbooks.com/~outpost/pubs/second/index.html>
Types of books: Second Story Press is a women's press specializing in quality fiction & non-fiction, children's picture books and juvenile novels.
Titles in print: *Power Surge: Sex, Violence and Pornography (non-fiction); The Best Laid Plans* (fiction).

Self-Counsel Press
1481 Charlotte Road
North Vancouver, BC V7J 1H1
Phone: (604) 986-3366. Fax: (604) 986-3947
E-mail: <selfcoun@pinc.com>
Web site: <http://www.swifty.com/scp>
Types of books: Business, legal for lay person, reference.
Guidelines: Accepts unsolicited manuscripts. with SASE.
Titles in print: *Start and Run a Profitable Student-Run Business, Kick Start Guide to Coast Rica, Importing, Write On!*
Les éditions du Septentrion
Web site: <http://www.cam.org/~ybern/septentrionE.html>
Types of books: Septentrion is primarily a publisher of history books, but it also covers a range of general social sciences, including titles on archaeology, political science, ethnology, and other subjects, as well as fiction, primarily historical novels.

Somerville House Books Limited
Aquisitions Department, Children's Division
3080 Yonge Street
Suite 5000
Toronto, ON M4N 3N1
Web site: <http://www.sombooks.com/>
Types of books: publishes children and adult books, focusing on imaginative books-plus (books packaged with some form of manipulative) in a broad range of categories including natural science kits, craft kits and activity kits in all age groups. We also accept submissions for fiction series and picture books.

Guidelines: "Our acquisitions team evaluates new submissions based on the following criteria: originality, market potential, educational content, quality of writing and/or illustrations, and kid-appeal. Somerville House does accept unsolicited manuscripts and proposals. Please send to the attention of Children's Acquisitions along with a self-addressed-stamped envelope."

Sono Nis Press
1745 Blanshard Street
Victoria, BC V8W 2J8
Phone: (250) 382-1024. Fax: (250) 382-1575
E-mail: <sono.nis@islandnet.com>
Web site: <http://www.islandnet.com/~sononis/>
Types of books: History, poetry, historical biography, art.
Guidelines: Send a letter of enquiry, publication history, and SASE. Does not accept unsolicited manuscripts.
Titles in print: *Shadow Weather, BC Place Names, Steam on the Kettle, Born To Be Hung.*

Gordon Soules Book Publishers Ltd.
1352-B Marine Drive
West Vancouver, BC V7T 1B5
Phone: (604) 688-5466. Fax: (604) 688-5442
E-mail: <books@gordon.soules.com>
Types of books: Canadiana, gardening, guidebooks, health, social issues, environment.
Guidelines: Will accept unsolicited manuscripts, but prefers that a letter of enquiry, sample chapter and SASE be sent first.
Titles in print: *Arctic Adventures, The Vancouver Area Diving Guide, Why Vegetarian, Exploring the Seashore.*

Stage Hand Publishers
RR #1
La Have, NS B0R 1C0
Phone: (902) 688-1103
E-mail: <editor@stagehand.ca>
Web site: <http://www.stagehand.ca/publish/>
Types of books: Drama.
Titles in print: *TWO, BY GEORGE!* by George Elroy Boyd, *Gideon's Blues* and *Consecrated Ground*; two plays that touch on the life of the black communities in Halifax.

Stoddart Publishing Co Ltd.
34 Lesmill Rd.
North York, ON M3B 2T5
Phone: (416) 445-3333
Web site: <http://www.genpub.com:80/stoddart/>

Talon Books Ltd.
104-3100 Production Way
Burnaby, BC V5A 4R4
Phone: (604) 444-4889. Fax: (604) 444-4119
E-mail: <talon@pinc.com>
Web site: <http://www.swifty.com/talon/>
Types of books: Poetry, fiction, drama, social issues/ethnography.
Guidelines: Only accepts letter of enquiry with SASE. Does not accept unsolicited manuscripts.
Titles in print: *There'll Be Another, The First Quarter of the Moon, The Weekend Healer, Too Good To Be True.*

Tecumseh Press
8 Mohawk CR
Ottawa, ON K2H 7G6
Phone: (613) 829-0150
Types of books: Poetry, fiction and non-fiction.

Theytus Books Ltd.
P.O. Box 20040
Penticton, BC V2A 8K3
Phone: (250) 493-7181. Fax: (250) 493-5302
E-mail: <gyoungin@awinc.com>
Types of books: Fiction/non-fiction, Native studies, children's art, poetry, science fiction, anthologies, history, literary journals.
Guidelines: Accepts unsolicited manuscripts with SASE from Aboriginal writers only.
Titles in print: *In Honour of Our Grandmothers, Just Talking About Ourselves, A Tortured People, Stories of the Road Allowance People.*

Trifolium Books Inc.
Suite 28, 238 Davenport Road
Toronto, ON M5R 1J6
Phone: (416) 925-0765. Fax: (416) 485-5563
Web site: <http://www.pubcouncil.ca/trifolium/>
Types of books: Resources for educators and students in science, technology and career development.
Guidelines: Trifolium authors are educators, professionals who write on a royalty basis. "If you have a science, technology, or career development project under consideration for educators, students, professionals, or the interested layperson, consider Trifolium Books Inc. as a potential publisher." Contact the publisher directly.
Titles in print or in development: *Take a TechnoWalk* and *Linking Classroom Skills to the Future.* For students: *How To Analyze Issues in Science & Technology*, for professionals: *Scientific Presentation Skills: A Guide for Scientists, Medical Researchers, and Health Care Professionals*; for the layperson, *Biotechnology Today* and *The Rats in the Velcro Suits.*

Turnstone Press
#607 - 100 Arthur St.
Winnipeg, MB R3B 1H3
Phone: (204) 947-1555
Types of books: Adult non-fiction, fiction, poetry and literary criticism.

University of Alberta Press
141 Athabasca Hall
Edmonton, AB T6G 2E8
Phone (403) 492-3662. Fax (403) 492- 0719
E-mail: <u.a.p@ualberta.ca>
Web site: <http://www.quasar.ualberta.ca/press>
Types of books: The University of Alberta Press is looking for original works of significant scholarship which complement the existing list and are written for a reasonably wide readership.
Guidelines: Manuscripts of 500 pages or fewer will have a greater chance of acceptance than longer works because of escalating production costs. Book proposals should be sent to the attention of the Press Director.

University of British Columbia Press
6344 Memorial Road
Vancouver, BC V6T 1Z2
Phone: (604) 822-3259. Fax: (604) 822-6083
Web site: <http://www.ubcpress.ubc.ca>
Types of books: Canadian history and political science, regional history, Native and Asian studies, geography, environment, sociology, women's studies.
Guidelines: Accepts unsolicited manuscripts but prefers a letter of enquiry, outline, sample chapter, and SASE first.

University of Calgary Press
2500 University Drive N.W.
Calgary, AB T2N 1N4
Phone: (403) 220-7578. Fax: (403) 282-0085
Fax: (403) 282-0085
E-mail: <75001@ucdasvm1.admin.ucalgary.ca>
Web site: <http://www.ucalgary.ca/UofC/departments/UP>
Types of books: The University of Calgary Press is committed to the advancement of scholarship through the publication of first-rate monographs and academic journals. We publish scholarly books in a wide range of fields. Occasionally, we will also publish conference proceedings, *Festschriften*, and other similar collections; however, such works are considered for publication only if they have been substantially edited prior to submission and display an identifiable thematic unity.

University of Toronto Press Inc.
10 St. Mary Street, Suite 700
Toronto, ON M4Y 2W8
Phone: (416) 978-5171. Fax: (416) 978-4738
E-mail: <stmary@gpu.utcc.utoronto.ca>
Web site: <http://library.utoronto.ca/www/utpress/publish/publish.htm>
Types of books: UTP's Scholarly Publishing division focuses on Canadian studies, particularly history, political science, and literature. Other strengths include classical studies, medieval and Renaissance studies, modern languages and literature, philosophy, Erasmian studies, law and criminology, Slavic studies, religion and theology, and sociology.

Vanmarkin Publications
PO Box 315
Dominion, NS B0A 1E0
Phone: (902) 425-7616. Fax: (902) 425-2075
E-mail: <vanmarkin@monarchy.com>
Web site: <http://www.chatsubo.com/vanpub/>
Types of books: Interested in short stories, novels, articles, poems, and music. Also biography, fiction, children's, political, mystery, or books of any other genre.
Guidelines: "There are no fees. We take the risk, you get the recognition and the royalties."

Vanwell Publishing Limited
1 Northrup Cres.
St. Catharines, ON L2M 7M3
Phone: (905) 937-3100
Types of books: Regional and historical non-fiction and fiction.

Véhicule Press
P.O.B. 125, Place du Parc Station
Montreal, QC H2W 2M9
Phone: (514) 844-6073. Fax: (514) 844-7543
Email: <vpress@cam.org>
Web site: <http://www.cam.org/~vpress/>
Types of books: Specializes in fiction, poetry, politics, jazz, Quebec studies, Jewish studies, and books in translation. At present we are not looking at fiction or poetry manuscripts.
Guidelines: Please query first by letter.

Weigl Educational Publishers Limited
1902 - 11Street SE
Calgary, AB T2G 3G2
Phone: (403) 233-7747. Fax: (403) 233-7769
E-mail: <weigl@agt.net>
Web site: <http://www.weigl.com/>
Types of books: Publishes educational library resources and textbooks for the
K-12 market.

Whitecap Books
351 Lynn Avenue
North Vancouver, BC V7J 2C4
Phone: (604) 980-9852. Fax: (604) 980-8197
E-mail: <whitecap@pinc.com>
Types of books: Natural history, gardening, cooking, general trade and juvenile
non -fiction.
Guidelines: No full manuscripts, but will accept annotated outline with SASE.
Titles in print: *Double Exposure, Paces of BC, Pacific Passions Cookbook, Buffalo
Sunrise.*

Wilfrid Laurier University Press
Waterloo, ON N2L 3C5
Phone: (519) 884-0710. Fax: (519) 725-1399
E-mail: <press@mach1.wlu.ca>
Web site: <http://info.wlu.ca/~wwwpress/home.html>
Types of books: Wilfrid Laurier University Press was established in 1974 to publish
scholarly books and journals in the humanities and social sciences.
Guidelines: Submissions and inquiries should be made in writing to
Sandra Woolfrey, Director.

Wuerz Publishing Ltd.
895 McMillan Avenue
Winnipeg, MB R3M 0T2
Phone: (204) 453-7429. Fax: (204) 453-6598
Yinka Dene Language Institute
P.O. Box 7000
Vanderhoof, BC V0J 3A0
Phone: (250) 567-9263. Fax: (250) 567-3851
Types of books: Carrier legends and stories.
Guidelines: We publish native legends, stories and songs about the Carrier-Sekani
People. We do not accept unsolicited manuscripts.

# Contributors Notes

Audrey W. Babb is a Victoria, BC writer with several books and numerous periodical credits. Her work has been published in *Western People, Modern Romance, Monday Magazine, Canadian Writer's Journal* and, of course, *Canadian Author & Bookman* (now *Canadian Author*) magazine.

G. Perry Bauchman's business career was occupied with writing and decoding legal documents. Since retirement his writing has been devoted to articles and short stories followed by his recent successful book, *Spitfire Pilot*.

Rosemary Bauchman joined C.A.A. in 1963, branching out with short stories and poems, progressing to articles, book reviews and radio talks. Her first book, *Evelyn's Guiding Stars*, was published in 1981 and was followed by five others. Recently she has taken up editorial work, which she greatly enjoys.

Catherine Lazers Bauer taught art and English before she began writing in 1970. She has sold over 500 essays, articles, and short stories to such markets as *The Christian Science Monitor, Spiritual Life, Catholic Digest, Bloomsbury Review, Modern Maturity, The Lion, The Rotarian,* and *Creation Spirituality*. Several of her essays have been reprinted in anthologies.

Bruce O. Boston is a columnist, book author and editorial consultant. He operates Wordsmith Inc., from a base in Reston, Virginia. He is a former editor of *The Editorial Eye* newsletter and author of *Language on a Leash*.

Karleen Bradford is the award-winning author of 13 books for children and young adults, including *WRITE NOW! How to turn your ideas into great stories.* (Scholastic Canada, 1996.) When we went to press, Karleen was Vice-Chair of the Public Lending Right Commission

Arthur Bray lives in Ottawa and is the author of four non-fiction books, two on Unidentified Flying Objects and two on financial planning. He is currently working on another non-fiction book on an unrelated topic.

Joan Eyolfson Cadham, a past CAA regional vice-president is now a Saskatchewan Writers Guild board member. She counts two top Saskatchewan weekly newspaper editorials and two winning Canadian church press columns among her 4,000 plus writing credits. She is an occasional contributor to CBC radio, is in two editions of *Morningside Papers* and is a storyteller of Icelandic fables.

Robert Collins has been a staff writer with *Maclean's* and *Readers Digest* and editor of *Toronto Life*. The latest of his 13 books is *Who He?: Reflections on a Writing Life*.

R. G. Condie is a published author whose non-fiction, fiction and poetry has appeared in a wide variety of magazines and newspapers. He is also the CAA's Metro Toronto Branch writer-in-residence.

J. A. Davidson, a retired minister of The United Church of Canada, lives in Victoria, B.C.

Ann Douglas is the President of Page One Productions Inc., an award-winning communications company based in Peterborough, Ontario. She is also an accomplished journalist whose work has appeared in *The Chicago Tribune*, *The Globe and Mail*, *Cottage Life*, *Canadian Living*, and numerous other publications. She can be contacted via e-mail at <pageone@oncomdis.on.ca>.

Betty Dyck is the Winnipeg-based author of three non-fiction books, editor of two church histories, and freelance writer who conducts workshops for the CAA Manitoba Branch.

Heather Ebbs, a book, periodical and database indexer, has indexed 100s of items in a broad range of subjects and genres. Her clients include trade publishers, national associations, high tech firms and individual authors. She is a past president of the (Freelance) Editors' Association of Canada and the winner of the 1986 Tom Fairley Award for Editorial Excellence for a book she both edited and indexed.

Margaret Bunel Edwards is the author of two picture books and teaches a writing course in this field. Her young adult historical novel, *The Ocean Between*, was short-listed for the Geoffrey Bilson Award.

Anne Rockwell Fairley is a Winnipeg-based writer who uses travel and research experiences to publish articles in periodicals across Canada. She teaches writing and has edited four books. With a collection of 5,000 herbal and oldtime cure-alls in her database, she also entices editors to accept manuscripts on such eclectic topics as contraception, whooping cough and warts!

Beatrice Fines has taught creative writing in adult continuing education classes and has participated in Manitoba's Artists in the Schools Program. Beatrice's sixty short stories and over two-hundred articles have been published in Canada, the United States and Great Britain.

Katharine Fletcher has over 23 years experience in writing, editing and publishing. She thrives on diversification: she gives seminars (e.g. *Publish Yourself!*), leads hikes of Gatineau Park—and telecommutes from her electronic cottage in West Quebec. Since 1970, Eric Fletcher has assisted clients with their computer, software training and electronic publishing needs. He leads seminars, such as *The Electronic Cottage*. Eric and Katharine can be reached via e-mail at: <fletcher@hookup.net>.

Peggy Fletcher, former editor of *Canadian Poetry* and *Mamashee*, has had four poetry books and a short story collection published. Her work has appeared internationally. She has won awards for her poetry and playwriting. Also a visual artist, she lives in Sarnia, Ontario.

Gill Foss is an award-winning writer/editor with *Reader's Digest* among her clients. She chairs the National Awards Committee of the

Canadian Authors Association, has been a CAA Regional V.P., and Ottawa Branch President. Gill has programmed two national writers' conferences and teaches as a subject specialist for a consulting company.

Gwen Foss is an experienced freelance editor with a B.A. in Professional Writing and an M.A. in Linguistics. Her clients include Simon & Pierre Publishing Co., Nortel, Xerox, the Ontario Ministry of Transportation, the University of Toronto and the University of Ottawa. In 1992 she was a speaker at the Plain Language Conference in Toronto.

Albert Fowler is the author of *Peacetime Padres: a history of Canadian military chaplains*, and has written a wide variety of magazine articles.

Brian M. Fraser teaches the art of science fiction to university students.

Renato M. Gasparotto is a lawyer in London, Ontario, whose practice includes advising several newspapers and radio stations on libel issues. He has lectured occasionally in media law at the School of Journalism, Ryerson Polytechnic University, Toronto, Ontario.

Donna Gephart is a freelance writer who has worked as a greeting card editor, has sold gift books and written humor for national magazines. She continues to write for the greeting card market from a base in Jupiter, Florida.

Brenda Gibson is a freelance write and photographer who teaches adult literacy.

L. B. Greenwood is the author of four published novels and several novellas, short stories and articles. Holding a BA and MA, she has taught English at universities and has given workshops in creative writing from coast to coast.

London-born Harold Griffin has been an editor, journalist and author since the 1920s. He has edited a BC weekly labor newspaper and *The Fisherman, organ of the United Fishermen and Allied Workers* Union. He is now retired and living in Vancouver, BC.

Gail Hamilton has taught high school, written advertising and camped across the Sahara to Timbuktu. To date, she has produced nine romance novels and adapted the immensely popular *Road to Avonlea* TV series, published a reference book for charitable organizations and is still going strong.

W.G. Hardy, scholar, sportsman and author, was professor of classics at the University of Alberta from 1920 to 1964. He won the Governor General's Medal at the University of Toronto and in 1974 became a member of the Order of Canada. He served as president of the Canadian Amateur Hockey Association and the Canadian Authors Association. But he was best known as a writer; the author of five historical novels, one modern novel, four histories, two textbooks and numerous articles and short stories.

Lyn Harrington was an active member of the Canadian Authors Association, and the author of numerous articles and books, including her 1981 CAA history, *Syllables of Recorded Time.*

Lesley Ellen Harris is a Copyright & New Media lawyer and the author of *Canadian Copyright Law* (second edition, 1995, McGraw-Hill Ryerson). She can be reached at (416) 226-6768 or at <Copyrtlaw@aol.com> or <http://www.mcgrawhill.ca/copyrightlaw>.

Jeff Herman is a respected and well-known New York agent and author of *Insider's Guide To Book Editors, Publishers And Literary Agents*. Contact him at (212) 941-0540 or look for more information at AUTHORLINK!, an on-line information service for editors, agents and writers, located at <http://www.authorlink.com>.

Deidre A. Hill, a member of the Canadian Authors Association Victoria & Islands Branch, has been published in local and national publications regularly since Spring 1996. She is the founding editor of a storytellers' newsletter, *Word Weavers*. She planned to continue her study of literature and storytelling by entering university in the fall of 1997.

Raymond Hull was the author of over a dozen books. One of his best-known works was *The Peter Principle: Why Things Go Wrong*, (New York: Morrow, 1969) co-authored with Laurence J. Peter. To quote The Peter Principle, "In a hierarchy every employee tends to rise to his level of incompetence."

Linda Jeays often uses her experience as a high school teacher, workshop leader, post graduate student and adult educator in her freelance articles. She is also a poet with almost 100 published poems. She writes regularly for a wide variety of magazines and newspapers from her home in Nepean, Ontario.

Robert H. (Bob) Jones is the author of *Tangled Lines and Patched Waders* (1995), winner of the 1996 Outdoor Writers of Canada Communications Award, and *Dull Hooks and Squeaky Reels* (1997), both published by Horsdal & Schubart. In addition, he has won 10 awards for excellence in craft for magazine writing. He is a past president and life member of the Outdoor Writers of Canada, and an active member of the Outdoor Writers Association of America. He resides in Courtenay, B.C., with Vera, his wife of 40 years, who is also a writer.

Bess Kaplan, a Winnipeg-based freelance writer, has edited a weekly newspaper . She has also written numerous short stories, magazine articles and a radio play. Her novels include *Corner Store* and *Malke Malke*. She is currently working on a non-fiction book.

Mark Kearney has been a journalist for 20 years and has published hundreds of articles in some 40 magazines and newspapers in North America. His latest book, *The Great Canadian Trivia Book*, was published in 1996. He lives in London, Ontario.

Fred Kerner is an author, journalist, editor and publisher who retired from the business world and keeps busy as a consultant to publishers.

Crawford Kilian has published almost 20 books since 1968, including 11 science-fiction and fantasy novels, and over 500 articles in newspapers and magazines. His most recent titles include *2020 Visions: The Futures of Canadian Education* (Arsenal Pulp Press, 1995) and *The Communications Book: Writing for the Workplace* (Allyn & Bacon Canada, 1997). He teaches at Capilano College in North Vancouver, BC.

Bryan M. Knight, MSW. PhD., is the author of several books, including *Love, Sex & Hypnosis: Secrets of Psychotherapy* and *Health and Happiness with Hypnosis*. His article "Hypnosis for Writers" can be read on his web site at <http://www.odyssee.net/~drknight/>.

Michael Lasser is the theatre reviewer for the *Rochester Democrat & Chronicle*. His nationally-syndicated public radio program, *Fascinatin' Rhythm*, won a 1994 George Foster Peabody Award. He writes about the performing and visual arts for a wide range of national and regional magazines.

Ruth Latta is the author of three books, most recently *A Wild Streak* (General Store, 1995). Her fiction, poetry and articles appear in US and Canadian publications. She lives in Ottawa with her husband and her cats.

Mark Leiren-Young is a screenwriter, playwright, journalist and performer. In addition to extensive TV and stage credits, his humorous commentaries have been featured in such publications as *The Hollywood Reporter, The Toronto Star* and *The Vancouver Sun* and are frequently heard on CBC radio. Mark is the writer for the new CBC TV variety series *Terminal City*.

Bernice Lever, a CAA member for more than 25 years, has been leading creative writing workshops and clubs for 30 years. She teaches English at Seneca College in the Toronto area. Editor of *Waves* (1972-1987), her sixth book of poems is *Things Unsaid*, Black Moss, 1996.

Paul Lima is a working freelance writer and the former editor of *Maple Syrup Simmering*, a now discontinued electronic magazine. He also teaches Creative Writing and Freelance Writing courses by e-mail. Contact him at <tiko@idirect.com>.

Kevin Longfield has a long list of publishing credits in poetry, fiction, non-fiction and drama. He was the Winnipeg correspondent for *Theatrum* magazine for five years. His play, *Going Down the River*, has won three awards and was published in the anthology, *Canadian Mosaic*.

Rowland Lorimer is the director of Simon Fraser University's Master of Publishing program and Canadian Centre for Studies in Publishing. He conducts research on a wide variety of publishing and communication issues. Study co-author, Roger Barnes, is a marketing planning consultant and bookstore co-owner.

Bruce Madole is President of Bruce Madole & Associates Inc., a communications consulting firm.

Alex Mair has written, spoken , and taught at the University and College level on a variety of topics, always introducing an element of humour into his presentations. He is the author of *How To Speak In Public*, as well as *How To Be A Great M.C.*, and a wide variety of historical works. His item on CBC radio was a light look at the world through his eyes, and ran twice daily for over eleven years. Following that, he wrote a daily humour column for the *Edmonton Journal* for five years. He continues to be in demand as a speaker at a variety of events, workshops and seminars.

John Melady is the author of seven books and numerous magazine and newspaper articles. Among his books are: *Korea: Canada's Forgotten War* and Pilots, *Canadian Stories from the Cockpit*. He was a secondary school vice-principal for many years, but now writes full time.

Allen Melton has written gags for a number of professional cartoonists.

Betty Millway is a west-coast short-story and article writer. She enjoys helping other writers on the local and national level.

Ishbel Moore is the author of *The Summer of the Hand, The Medal, Branch of the Talking Teeth*, and *Dolina May*, all novels for young adults. Ishbel has also won awards for her short stories. In the non-fiction field, she researched and wrote the text for the Winnipeg Philharmonic Choir's 75th anniversary publication. An active member of the Canadian Authors Association, she facilitates writing-related workshops throughout Manitoba.

F.C. Larry Muller has been active on the Canadian children's writing scene for more than 30 years as a writer, editor and publisher. He is currently president of Scholastic Canada Ltd., a leading publisher and distributor of children's books. He was the 1996 winner of the Canadian Authors Association's Allan Sangster Award.

Sheldon Oberman is a writer, film maker and storyteller. Among his ten books are *The Always Prayer Shawl*, an award winning children's book and *This Business With Elijah*, set in Winnipeg's North End. He travels extensively, speaking and giving workshops on writing out of personal and family experiences.

Anne Osborne has contributed to magazines from time to time and edited *Canadian Author & Bookman* magazine (when it still had that name) for five years. She is a teacher/librarian and most recently has acted as online teacher/moderator for the Writers In Electronic Residence (WIER) programme.

Gerald Walton Paul is a United Church minister who, while serving urban congregations and university campuses, managed to write occasional articles and columns for periodicals and newspapers. Since 1983, he has been a full-time freelancer. An amateur naturalist, he also contributes articles on the natural world to magazines and newspapers.

Adrian Peetoom authored and co-authored over 15 books during his career in educational publishing. He also translated a book of Dutch poetry and an account of persecuted Christians in Siberia. In addition, he has written numerous articles for a variety of journals, most notably the *Christian Courier* (formerly *Calvinist Contact*).

Lois J. Peterson teaches students to write from life through Continuing Education classes in Surrey, British Columbia, and to inmates at the Corrections Canada Matsqui Institute. She also uses the methods described above in her own fiction, poetry and nonfiction. She has developed an on-line writing workshop page on the World Wide Web at <http://mindlink.net/summit/welcome.htm>.

Teresa Pitman has published more than 400 magazine and newspaper articles; her work is seen most frequently in *Today's Parent*, *Great Expectations* and other parenting publications. Her first book, *All Shapes and Sizes*, was published by Harper Collins in 1994 and her next will be published in early 1998. Teresa has also won awards for her short fiction and has had several stories for children published.

Dorothy M. Powell has sold short stories to many major magazines, has written a children's book, and has taught creative writing at the college level.

Roma Quapp is an award-winning author whose numerous stories and articles have appeared in magazines and newspapers as diverse as *The New Quarterly*, *Peace and Environment News* and *The Globe and Mail*. She was employed as a federal government translator for six years and edited a monthly magazine for the Conference of Mennonites in Canada for three.

Ron Reichart is a freelance writer who understands the secrets of how to sell successfully.

Susan Romvary is a published writer of humourous stories about being an immigrant in Canada. *Zsusa Not sa Zsa, Balance With a Smile* was translated into French.

Bryan Roscoe's experience as an editor of a weekly newspaper and several years of working and travelling abroad, has given him a host of characters in search of themes and plots. He is now trying to gather these disparate characters and put them to work in short fiction. In the meantime, Bryan is available for work as an editor / communications consultant.

Elma Schemenauer, a former teacher, has written over 50 books, many for young people. Titles include *A New True Book: Canada, Yesterstories, Hello Montreal, Hello Edmonton*, and *Jacob Jacobs Gets Up Early*.

Lynne Schuyler is a British Columbia Interior writer who loves to discover exciting human interest stories. She is a frequent contributor to *Reader's Digest* and, at last count, has had 16 original articles published in various international editions of the *Digest*.

Murphy Shewchuk is a BC freelance writer/photographer with nine illustrated books, hundreds of newspaper and magazine articles and over 1,000 photographs published. His articles, photographs and maps appear regularly in *BC Outdoors* magazine. He also offers a stock photo service and can be reached via e-mail at <mshewchu@vbcs.awinc.com>.

Robert Shipley has published several books on Canadian history. He returned to university in 1990 to study and teach urban issues. His is also active in the local community in the Waterloo Region of Ontario.

Nancy Smith's poetry has appeared in various literary magazines. A radio play was short-listed for the CBC's literary competition. She is currently completing a graduate degree in English and American Literature at Harvard University Extension School.

Lola Sneyd is a poet, short story writer, journalist and teacher of creative writing and writing for children, (adult and children students). She has written five books for children, writes for and about all ages, and is published in Canada, U.S., England and Australia. Her first book of poetry for children, *The Asphalt Octopus*, has been reprinted three times.

Margaret Springer is an award-winning author of dozens of published stories, articles and poems for children. Her book credits include *A Royal Ball* (Boyds Mills Press) and *Move Over, Einstein* (Penguin UK, 1997). She also teaches writing and gives workshops.

Elizabeth St. Jacques, author of eight books, has been a published writer for thirty years, her work published in ten countries. Currently, she is Associate Editor of *SIJO WEST*, Poetry Editor of *Canadian Writer's Journal*, contributing editor with *Small Press Review* and a book review editor with *Albatross* (Romania). Her profiles have appeared in *Canadian Living, Our Family, Sunday Digest, Purpose* and others.

A. C. Stone is a freelance writer from Windsor, Ontario whose work has appeared in more than 70 US, Canadian and UK publications.

Gordon E. Symons, a former business executive, retired to write fiction and non-fiction from his home in Ailsa Craig, Ontario.

Gary Thomson is the author of one book, *Village Life in Upper Canada*, and numerous travel and feature pieces for Canadian, U.S. and British magazines. He teaches senior secondary school English in Belleville, Ontario.

W. D. Valgardson is the author of numerous books and plays. He has recently written two children's picture books: *Thor* (Mr. Christie Award Winner) and *Sarah and the People of Sand River*. He is a member of the Department of Writing at the University of Victoria.

Dr. Frederick Walker holds the Ph.D. in English Literature from Queen's University. He has taught at Ottawa U. and Heritage College. He is a published playwright, poet, fantasy and science fiction short story writer and author of true crime articles, including the award-winning *Jack the Ripper: The Key to the Mystery*. He is currently writing sketch comedy for television.

Douglas Waugh had a checkered career that took him from railway labourer to army medical officer to Dean of the Medical Faculty at Queen's University. From the time of his professional retirement in 1983 until his death in April, 1997, he had been a columnist, book author and speech writer. Several of his essays have been reprinted in *Reader's Digest*.

Sandra E. Weatherby has been an award winning journalist/photographer for the last seventeen years. She has sold freelance stories and photos to many Canadian magazines, journals, and daily newspapers.

Florence M. Weekes has worked as newspaper reporter and columnist, television news writer and producer, public relations writer, editor, and freelancer in non-fiction, poetry and fiction. Her work has appeared in many newspapers and magazines in Canada and the United States.

Don Wetmore (1907-01-23 to 1992-09-07) was a Nova Scotia playwright, actor, director, musician and educator. He was founder of the Nova Scotia Drama League, founding member of the Writer's Federation of Nova Scotia, and served as National President of the Canadian Authors Association. All of Don Wetmore's 26 plays were produced, and several chronicled Nova Scotia history.

Bert Williams is the author of several novels for young readers, as well as a contributor to historical journals.

Gregson Winkfield is a director and playwright. He has written two plays for radio and seven plays for stage, four of which have won awards. He has also published essays on theatre, and poetry. He is currently artistic director of Upper Canada Playhouse in Morrisburg, Ontario.

Sarah Yates, a member of the Periodical Writers Association of Canada, has been a professional freelance writer, editor and researcher for more than 20 years, publishing across Canada, in the US, England, France and Hong Kong. Her children's books include *Can't You be Still?* (1992), *Nobody Knows!*(1994) and *Here's What I Mean to Say...*(1997). She has also written two textbooks for Lerner Publications in Minneapolis.

Shulamis Yelin is a Montreal-born poet and writer. Some of her books of poetry include: *Seeded In Sinai; Au Soleil de Ma Nuit*; and *Many Mirrors Many Faces*. She was the recipient of the Canadian 125 Anniversary of Confederation Medal and a winner in the 1996 Greater Montreal Prix des Aìnés Contest. Shulamis has also appeared regularly on CBC TV.

Mark Zuehlke has been writing full-time since 1981. His books include the Book-of-the-Month Club selections *The Gallant Cause: Canadians in the Spanish Civil War, 1936-1939* and *Scoundrels, Dreamers, & Second Sons: British Remittance Men in the Canadian West*. He is also co-author of *Magazine Writing From The Boonies*, which *Quill & Quire* declared a book of exceptional merit that "should be on every writer's shelf." During 1996-1997, he served as National President of the Periodical Writers Association of Canada.